LIBRARY OF NEW TESTAMENT STUDIES

283

Formerly Journal for the Study of the New Testament Supplement Series

Editor
Mark Goodacre

THE WAR BETWEEN THE TWO BEASTS AND THE TWO WITNESSES

A Chiastic Reading of Revelation 11.1–14.5

ANTONINUS KING WAI SIEW

t & t clark

Published by T&T Clark
The Tower Building,   15 East 26th Street,
11 York Road,   Suite 1703,
London SE1 7NX   New York, NY 10010

www.tandtclark.com

British Library Cataloguing-in-Publication Data
A catalogue record for this book is available from the British Library

Library of Congress Cataloging-in-Publication Data
Siew, Antoninus King Wai
   The war between the two beasts and the two witnesses : a chiastic reading of
Revelation 11:1-14:5 / Antoninus King Wai Siew.
      p. cm. - - (Journal for the study of the New Testament. Supplement series ; 283)
   Includes bibliographical references (p.) and index.
   ISBN 0-567-03021-0
      1. Bible. N.T. Revelation 11:1-14:5--Criticism, interpretation, etc. I. Title. II. Series

   BS2825.52.S54 2005
   228'.066- -dc22

                                                                      2005048631

ISBN 0567030210 (hardback)

Typeset by Tradespools, Frome, Somerset
Printed on acid-free paper in Great Britain by Antony Rowe, Chippenham, Wiltshire

TABLE OF CONTENTS

Preface   ix
List of Abbreviations   xi

Chapter 1
INTRODUCTION   1
  1. The Purpose of This Study   1
  2. The Limitation of This Study   4
  3. The Method of This Study   4
  4. A Literary Analysis: A Methodological Approach   7
  5. The Macro-Chiasm   37
  6. The Criteria for Evaluating a Macro-Chiasm   47
  7. Other Features of Hebraic Rhetoric: Parataxis and
     Structural Parallelism   53
  8. The Plan of this Study   64
  9. Summary   65

Chapter 2
THE LITERARY UNITY OF REVELATION 11.1–14.5   67
  1. Introduction   67
  2. The Unity of Revelation 11.1–14.5   67
  3. The *Leitwörter* and Key Motifs in Revelation 11.1–14.5   70
  4. The Macro-Chiasm of Revelation 11.1–14.5   75
  5. The Frame Passages of Revelation 11.1–14.5: 10.11 and
     14.6–7   80
  6. Conclusion   83

Chapter 3
A LITERARY-STRUCTURAL ANALYSIS OF REVELATION 11.1–19   84
  1. Introduction   84
  2. The Genre of Revelation 11.1–13   84
  3. The Temple and the City in Revelation 11.1–13:
     The Spatial Indicator   85

4. The three-and-a-half in Revelation 11.1–13: The Temporal
Indicator   88
5. The Measuring of the Temple, Altar, and the
Worshippers (Revelation 11.1–2)   89
6. The Parallelism of Revelation 11.2–3   103
7. The Ministry of the Two Witnesses (Revelation 11.3–6)   107
8. The Death and the Vindication of the Two Witnesses
(Revelation 11.7–13)   110
9. 'The Second Woe has passed; Behold, the Third Woe
comes quickly' (Revelation 11.14, 15–19)   113
10. Conclusion   122

Chapter 4
A LITERARY-STRUCTURAL ANALYSIS OF REVELATION 12.1–14.5   123
1. Introduction   123
2. The Signs of Revelation 12.1–17   123
3. The Chiasm of Revelation 12.1–17   124
4. The Meaning and Significance of the Signs   149
5. The Career of the First Beast (Revelation 13.1–10)   168
6. The Career of the Second Beast (Revelation 13.11–18)   175
7. The Concluding Unit (Revelation 14.1–5)   180
8. Summary   181

Chapter 5
THE ABCDD'C'B'A' PARALLELS: TESTING THE MACRO-CHIASM   182
1. Introduction   182
2. The AA' Parallels (11.1–2 = 14.1–5): The Inclusio of
Revelation 11.1–14.5   182
3. The BB' Pair (11.3–6; 13.11–18): The Two Prophets vs.
The False Prophet   198
4. The CC' Pair (11.7–13; 13.7–10): The Making of
War and Conquering of the Two Witnesses and the Saints   201
5. The DD' Pair (11.15–19; 13.1–6): The Kingdom of the Lord
and his Christ and the Throne and Power of the Dragon
and the Beast   205
6. Testing the Macro-Chiasm of Revelation 11.1–14.5
(ABCDEFGF'E'D'C'B'A')   209
7. Conclusion   212

Chapter 6
THE IDENTITY OF THE TWO WITNESSES AND THE TWO BEASTS   214
1. Introduction   214
2. The Two Witnesses as Prophets   215
3. The Two Olive Trees and the Two Lampstands   219

4. The Signs of the Two Witnesses — 233
5. Summary — 249
6. The Identity of the (First) Beast — 250
7. The Identity of the Second Beast — 266
8. The War Waged by the Two Witnesses against the Two Beasts — 272
9. Conclusion — 277

Chapter 7
SUMMARY AND CONCLUSIONS — 279
1. Summary and Findings — 279
2. Suggestions for Further Study — 284
3. Final Conclusion — 284

Bibliography — 286

Index of References — 315

Index of Authors — 327

PREFACE

This book is a slightly revised version of my dissertation submitted for the degree of Doctor of Philosophy at the University of Otago, New Zealand in 2003. My study of the book of Revelation is the climax of a long theological journey. It has been a personal goal to seek to understand the last book of the Bible. I want to first of all thank the University of Otago for granting me a scholarship for doctoral study over three years.

Research inevitably involves the use of libraries and the assistance of librarians. First and foremost, I want to thank the librarians of Otago University Central Library and Hewitson Library, Knox College in Dunedin for their assistance and kindness. Many thanks also to the Registrar of Duta Wacana Christian University (Universitas Kristian Duta Wacana) and the librarian of St Paul's Seminary, Yogjakarta, Indonesia for their hospitality and assistance during my study trip to Indonesia in April–May 2001. Last but not least I enjoyed the most fruitful time over nearly three months (March–May 2002) at Kinder Library, St John's College, Auckland and the libraries of Auckland Consortium of Theological Education (ACTE) where most of my research was completed. Living in a flat just a couple of minutes from the library was closest to what I imagine to be heaven on earth!

I want to thank Professor Paul Trebilco of Otago University and Revd Dr Tim Meadowcroft of the Bible College of New Zealand for their expertise in the supervision of my study. I am grateful to Paul for his unfailing kindness and for gently nudging me to publish my work. Special thanks to Dr David Burfield for his encouragement and friendship. I want also to thank my friend Mr Leng Chun Koh for helping me with formatting. I want to thank my publishers T & T Clark International for their willingness to publish my work in the Library of New Testament Studies.

Finally, I want to thank my wife Paulin for making it possible for me to concentrate all my time and energy on this book; and our son Cyrus and daughter Angel who give me great joy and love. This book is dedicated to my daughter Angel who is very very precious to her mummy and daddy though she is still too young to understand. May the truth of God's Word contained in the book of Revelation be a beacon for years to come in all the churches of our Lord Jesus Christ to the glory of God the Father. When I was about to send my manuscript to my publishers, the Tsunami struck the coast of Penang on the 26th December 2004 as a result of a massive earthquake north of Sumatra. The disaster happened close to home and it reminded me that the book of Revelation speaks much of earthquakes. The places most severely affected by the tidal waves – Aceh and Sri Lanka were facing civil wars and southern Thailand were torn by civil unrest for over a year. My prayer is that out of this catastrophe, nations, tribes, and kings will lay down their weapons of war and make peace and give glory to the God of heaven and earth.

Tony Siew

cyrus55@pd.jaring.my

ABBREVIATIONS

2 Bar.	Syriac *Apocalypse of Baruch* (in *OTP*)
1 En.	Ethiopic *Book of Enoch* (in *OTP*)
1QH	*Thanksgiving Hymns* (Qumran Cave 1)
1QM	*War Scroll* (Qumran Cave 1)
1QpHab	*Pesher on Habakkuk* (Qumran Cave 1)
1QS	*Rule of the Community* (Qumran Cave 1)
4QFlor	4QFlorilegium
AB	Anchor Bible Commentary
ANET	James B. Pritchard (ed.), *Ancient Near Eastern Texts Relating to the Old Testament* (Princeton: Princeton University Press, 1950)
ANTC	Abingdon New Testament Commentaries
ANF	Ante-Nicene Fathers
Ant.	Josephus, *The Antiquities of the Jews*
AJT	*Asia Journal of Theology*
AUSS	*Andrews University Seminary Studies*
BDAG	Bauer, W., F.W. Danker, W.F. Arndt, F.W. Gingrich., *Greek-English Lexicon of the New Testament and Other Early Christian Literature* (Chicago: Chicago University Press, 3rd edn, 2000).
Bib	*Biblica*
BA	*Biblical Archaeologist*
BARev	*Biblical Archaeology Review*
BBR	*Bulletin for Biblical Research*
BDB	Francis Brown, S.R. Driver and Charles A. Briggs, *A Hebrew and English Lexicon of the Old Testament* (Oxford: Clarendon Press, 1907)
BDF	Friedrich Blass, A. Debrunner and Robert W. Funk, *A Greek Grammar of the New Testament and Other Early Christian Literature* (Cambridge: Cambridge University Press, 1961)
BETL	Bibliotheca ephemeridum theologicarum lovaniensium

BibInt	*Biblical Interpretation: A Journal of Contemporary Approaches*
BJRL	*Bulletin of the John Rylands University Library of Manchester*
BR	*Biblical Research*
BSac	*Bibliotheca sacra*
BT	*The Bible Translator*
BTB	*Biblical Theology Bulletin*
BZNW	Beihefte zur *ZNW*
CBQ	*Catholic Biblical Quarterly*
CD	Cairo Genizah copy of the *Damascus Document*
CH	*Church History*
Cont	*Continuum*
CTJ	*Calvin Theological Journal*
CTR	*Criswell Theological Review*
CurBS	*Currents in Research: Biblical Studies*
CurTM	*Currents in Theology and Mission*
DSD	*Dead Sea Discoveries*
DJG	*Dictionary of Jesus and the Gospels.* Edited by J. B. Green and S. McKnight (Downers Grove, 1992).
ET	English Translation
DBI	*Dictionary of Biblical Interpretation* Leland Ryken et al. (eds.) (Downers Grove: Inter-Varsity Press, 1998).
EvQ	*Evangelical Quarterly*
ExpTim	*Expository Times*
HAR	*Hebrew Annual Review*
HBT	*Horizons in Biblical Theology*
HDR	Harvard Dissertations in Religion
HeyJ	*Heythrop Journal*
HSM	Harvard Semitic Monographs
HTR	*Harvard Theological Review*
HUCA	*Hebrew Union College Annual*
IB	*Interpreter's Bible*
IBC	Interpretation: A Bible Commentary for Teaching and Preaching
ICC	International Critical Commentary
Int	*Interpretation*
Ign. *Eph.*	Ignatius, *Letter to the Ephesians*
Ign. *Magn.*	Ignatius, *Letter to the Magnesians*
Ign. *Trall.*	Ignatius, *Letter to the Trallians*
JBL	*Journal of Biblical Literature*
JECS	*Journal of Early Christian Studies*
JETS	*Journal of the Evangelical Theological Society*

JPS	JPS Hebrew-English Tanakh (Philadelphia: The Jewish Publication Society, 2nd edn, 2003)
JR	*Journal of Religion*
JSJ	*Journal for the Study of Judaism in the Persian, Hellenistic and Roman Period*
JSNT	*Journal for the Study of the New Testament*
JSNTSup	Journal for the Study of the New Testament, Supplement Series
JSOT	*Journal for the Study of the Old Testament*
JSOTSup	Journal for the Study of the Old Testament, Supplement Series
JSP	*Journal for the Study of Pseudepigrapha*
JSPSup	Journal for the Study of the Pseudepigrapha, Supplement Series
JTS	*Journal of Theological Studies*
J.W.	Josephus, *The Jewish War*
Jub	*Jubilees* (in *OTP*)
LXX	Septuagint
LAI	Lembaga Alkitab Indonesia (Indonesia Bible Society)
MT	Massoretic Text
Mart Isa.	*Martyrdom of Isaiah* (in *OTP*)
NA27	B. Aland, K. Aland, J. Karavidopoulos, C.M.Martini, and B.M.Metzger (eds.), *Novum Testamentum Graece (Nestle-Aland)* (Stuttgart: Deutsche Bibelgesellschaft, 27th edn, 1993)
NAC	New American Commentary
NASB	New American Standard Bible
NCB	New Century Bible
Neot	*Neotestamentica*
NIB	*The New Interpreter's Bible*
NICNT	New International Commentary on the New Testament
NICOT	New International Commentary on the Old Testament
NIGTC	New International Greek Testament Commentary
NIV	New International Version
NRSV	New Revised Standard Version
NTS	*New Testament Studies*
NovT	*Novum Testamentum*
NovTSup	Novum Testamentum, Supplements
Numen	*Numen: International Review for the History of Religion*
OBT	Overtures to Biblical Theology
OTL	Old Testament Library
OTP	J.H. Charlesworth (ed.), *The Old Testament Pseudepigrapha* (London: Darton, Longman and Todd, 1983)
PSB	*Princeton Seminary Bulletin*

Pss. Sol.	*Psalms of Solomon*
RB	*Revue biblique*
ResQ	*Restoration Quarterly*
RSV	Revised Standard Version
Sib. Or.	*Sibylline Oracles* (in *OTP*)
SBL	Society of Biblical Literature
SBLDS	SBL Dissertation Series
SBLSP	SBL Seminar Papers
SNTSMS	Society for New Testament Studies Monograph Series
SJT	*Scottish Journal of Theology*
TDNT	Gerhard Kittel and Gerhard Friedrich (eds.), *Theological Dictionary of the New Testament* (trans. Geoffrey W. Bromiley; 10 vols.; Grand Rapids: Eerdmans, 1964–)
TDOT	G. J. Botterweck and H. Ringgren (eds.), *Theological Dictionary of the Old Testament* (trans. D. E. Green; 10 vols.; Grand Rapids: Eerdmans, 1974–1998)
Tg. Isa.	*Targum of Isaiah*
Theod.	Theodotion's Greek translation of the Hebrew Bible
TorJT	*Toronto Journal of Theology*
TrinJ	*Trinity Journal*
TynBul	*Tyndale Bulletin*
TNTC	Tyndale New Testament Commentaries
VT	*Vetus Testamentum*
VTSup	*Vetus Testamentum*, Supplements
WBC	Word Biblical Commentary
WTJ	*Westminster Theological Journal*
ZAW	*Zeitschrift für die alttestamentliche Wissenschaft*
ZNW	*Zeitschrift für die neutestamentliche Wissenschaft*
ZTK	*Zeitschrift für Theologie und Kirche*

Chapter 1

INTRODUCTION

1. *The Purpose of This Study*

The book of Revelation is a complex book. The author, John, claims to write concerning the things that must come to pass quickly (Rev. 1.1). We would expect that he would set the events in some linear chronological order so as to assist his audience in discerning the pattern of events soon to be unfolded. Nevertheless the book of Revelation, or the Apocalypse of John as it is sometimes called, does not appear to present a consistent chronological or linear development. At a casual glance, most of the book consists of a collection of visions on the face of it unrelated to one another. Modern readers will agree with G. Biguzzi's assessment that: 'John's Apocalypse puzzles and troubles at every page.'[1]

Is it because of the very nature of the book as an apocalypse[2] that John purposefully teases his audience with a 'reveal yet conceal' dialectic

---

1. G. Biguzzi, 'A Figurative and Narrative Language Grammar of Revelation', *NovT* 45 (2003), pp. 382–402 (400).
2. David E. Aune defines 'apocalyptic' in terms of four different but related aspects: '(1) "Apocalyptic eschatology", a *world of beliefs and symbols* based on a cosmic dualism of good and evil centering on the expectation of the imminent end of the world. (2) "Apocalyptic movement", a *form of collective behavior* based on those beliefs and symbols. (3) "Apocalypse," a *type of literature* which consists of a pseudonymous autobiographical report of a supernatural revelation mediated by an angel or other heavenly being concerning the end of the world (in some apocalypses the visionary ascends to heaven, while in others the heavenly revealer comes to earth). (4) "Apocalyptic imagery," the *language of apocalyptic eschatology*, i.e. themes and motifs found in a variety of literary settings but no longer used in the context of a coherent apocalyptic world view.' D. E. Aune, 'Qumran and the Book of Revelation', in Peter W. Flint and James C. VanderKam (eds.), *The Dead Sea Scrolls* Vol. 2: *A Comprehensive Assessment after Fifty Years* (Leiden: Brill, 1999), pp. 622–48 (624). See also Richard Sturm, 'Defining the Word "Apocalyptic": A Problem in Biblical Criticism', in Joel Marcus and Marion L. Soards (eds.), *Apocalyptic and the New Testament: Essays in honour of J. Louis Martyn* (Sheffield: Sheffield Academic Press, 1989), pp. 17–48. We will discuss the genre of Revelation in a later section.

approach?[3] While a certain linear progression can be seen in the narration of the three series of sevens (the seven seals, the seven trumpets and the seven bowls) yet the series of the seals and trumpets are interrupted by apparent lengthy asides or interludes. Between the sixth seal and the seventh seal, ch. 7 of Revelation intervenes and after the sixth trumpet at the end of Rev. 9, a much larger 'interruption' occurs from 10.1 to 11.14 before the seventh trumpet is sounded in 11.15. This lengthy interlude begins with the narration of the descent of an angel who swears: 'There will be no more delay! In the days when the seventh angel is about to sound his trumpet, the mystery of God will be accomplished, just as he announced it to his servants the prophets' (10.7).[4] More perplexing still is that when the seventh trumpet finally sounds in 11.15 the end is still not in sight. Three chapters and a bit (Rev. 11.16–19 to Rev. 12–14) intrude before the final series of sevens (bowls) commence in 15.1.

'The *days* of the seventh trumpet' (10.7) seems to suggest that the end will not come immediately but will begin another series of events drawn out over a number of days leading to the end. To confound further the attempt to discern a chronological pattern there is another puzzling editorial remark by John before the sounding of the seventh trumpet that: 'The second woe has passed. Behold the third woe is coming very soon' (11.14). But the third woe is left undefined and left to the readers' imagination. The first woe is said to be ended at the conclusion of the events brought about by the fifth trumpet (9.12) and the second woe is completed at the end of the narration of the two witnesses (11.3–13). The third woe is then left mysteriously unspecified in the rest of Revelation. It is not surprising then that any attempt to understand John's composition as portraying a chronological or a linear progression in the description of visions and events of the book faces enormous difficulties. However, in Rev. 11–13, the repeated mention of the temporal period of three and a half years (11.2–3; 12.6, 14; 13.5) in different computations (42 months [11.2; 13.5], 1260 days [11.3; 12.6], and 'a time, times, and half a time' [12.14]) may be a clue to John's readers that the events depicted in Rev. 11–13 are to be understood as unfolding at the same temporal time-span.

As our study is limited to Rev. 11.1–14.5, we will seek to clarify the nature of events set within a specific temporal time-span of three-and-a-half years by way of analyzing the literary-structural form of said literary unit. We will argue that this block of text is an integral whole clearly delimited by literary and narrative markers at the beginning and the end of

---

3.   See D. E. Aune, 'The Apocalypse of John and the Problem of Genre', *Semeia* 36 (1986) pp. 65–96 (84–86).

4.   All biblical quotations are taken from the New Revised Standard Version (NRSV) unless otherwise stated.

the literary unit patterned in a macro-chiasm. Specifically, we will look at how the three and a half year period binds 11.1–14.5 as a literary unit. It is our contention that this chronological marker is the interpretative key to this middle section of Revelation. We will argue that understanding how this 42 months/1260 days/'a time, times and half a time' period is used by John to bind together the events found in Rev. 11–13 will be vital to understanding John's essential message.

We will contend that the message of Rev. 11.1–14.5 concerns the church's conflict with society in the last days preceding the parousia of Christ. Revelation 11.1–14.5 tells of the source of the conflict as a war in heaven (Rev. 12) and how the heavenly warfare results in an earthly conflict between two groups on earth: the church on one hand and the rest of the inhabitants of the earth on the other hand. John portrays this conflict between church and society through apocalyptic imagery, beginning in heaven as a war between Michael and his angels against the dragon and his angels, and continued on earth as a war between the two witnesses of Rev. 11 and the two beasts of Rev. 13. The war in *heaven* between the Lord/Michael[5] and Satan is played out on *earth* by their respective agents: the two witnesses on the side of God and the two beasts as Satan's henchmen.

This study will pay special attention to John's principle of *duality* in framing his literary creation in the said textual unit of 11.1–14.5. The figure *two* as a pairing as well as denoting comparison, contrast, antithesis and conflict will be crucial in determining the thematic and theological intent of the textual unit. This duality or binary opposition carries over into the *dualism* of opposing spheres and forces: heaven and earth, light and darkness, good and evil, prophets and beasts, death and resurrection, torment and celebration, dragon and woman, city and wilderness and the like.[6]

John provides interpretive keys throughout. For example, 'the lamp-stands', are explicitly identified as 'churches' (1.20). Yet on occasions, John can identify a character or characters with metaphorical language: the two witnesses are said to be 'the two olives trees and the two lampstands' (11.4), which demands greater processing or interpretive effort on the part of the readers. In our view, the two olive trees refer to two individuals while the two lampstands point to the corporate dimension of the two witnesses as the churches. Hence, it is my contention that the two witnesses are not only two individuals but they are also the corporate church in its

---

5. Why Michael and not the Lord is the dragon's protagonist will be answered in a later section.

6. For a discussion of this principle, see L. Thompson, 'The Literary Unity of the Book of Revelation', in Vincent L. Tollers and John Maier (eds.), *Mappings of the Biblical Terrain: The Bible as Text* (Lewisburg, Penn.: Bucknell University Press, 1990), pp. 347–63.

role as witness to the world. Similarly, the two beasts are individuals but they also personify the society at large in their opposition to God/Christ and the church.[7]

2. *The Limitation of This Study*

As the title of this book suggests, the focus of this study is the war between the two witnesses and the two beasts of Rev. 11–13. We will concentrate especially on our task of examining how, by way of a chiastic reading of the middle chapters of Revelation, the contents of Rev. 11.1–14.5 are to be understood as a cohesive literary unit. While we will look at the wider implications of such a reading on the theology of Revelation as a whole, our aim is primarily limited to the textual unit of 11.1–14.5. It is not our purpose to provide a comprehensive exegetical study of *every* verse in 11.1–14.5, but significant interpretive-exegetical study of units and sub-units will be carried out as far as it will advance our main thesis. It is also beyond the scope of this study to deal with the history of interpretation of the main units found in 11.1–14.5.

It will be self evident as this study progresses that John's use of the Old Testament and parallels with extra-biblical literature especially the Dead Sea Scrolls will be vital in illuminating the form and meaning of the literary unit under discussion. While not arguing for literary dependence of Revelation on any of these texts, we will probe how these parallels help us to interpret 11.1–14.5. It is commonly noted that John is so saturated with the Old Testament that it is near impossible to prove whether John has *consciously* depended on an Old Testament text or texts in composing the book of Revelation. This book contends that 11.1–14.5 is best understood by way of a concentric chiastic reading. This chiastic analysis yields John's purpose in depicting a heavenly war with resultant effect on earth. The war in heaven results in a deadly conflict between the two witnesses and the two beasts in the last eschatological period of three and a half years before the coming again of Jesus Christ.

3. *The Method of This Study*

In narrative terms, the main units within Rev. 11.1–14.5 present an integral story within itself as a coherent unit. Chapter 11 of Revelation is a literary unit in itself which presents the ministry of the two witnesses in its entirety. Revelation 12 is also a unified unit in that the two main characters, the

---

7.   The identity and function of the two witnesses and the two beasts will be discussed in detail in a later chapter.

woman and the dragon are the two signs through which the whole narrative is understood and interpreted. Similarly, Rev. 13 too can stand on its own in that the chapter depicts the nature and activities of the two beasts. Yet, the last verse of Rev. 13 (13.18) does not provide the conclusion to ch. 13 for the climactic end of the whole literary unit from 11.1 is found, as we will argue, in the unit of 14.1–5. It is perhaps because of the self-contained nature of chs 11–13 of Revelation that most commentaries and monographs have treated them separately without seriously considering the connections that bind these chapters.

Most commentators note the links between Rev. 12–13 where the dragon's role vis-à-vis the two beasts (12.18; 13.1) are apparent and therefore are not in dispute. What becomes the bone of contention here is that Rev. 11 is often thought of as totally separate from Rev. 12 and the chapters that follow. My book argues that Rev. 11 must be seen as an integral part of Rev. 11.1–14.5. Any attempt to treat Rev. 11 separately from 12.1–14.5 will inevitably lead to missing the vital links which John makes in composing the literary unit of 11.1–14.5.

As noted earlier, the three chapters have the same chronological setting for the stories they depict, namely, the three and a half years, variously expressed as the forty-two months (11.2; 13.5), 1260 days (11.3; 12.6) or 'a time, times and half a time' (12.14). The period of forty-two months during which the nations are allowed to trample on the holy city is the same period during which the two witnesses are to prophesy for 1260 days (11.2–3). Likewise in Rev. 12, the woman is said to be nourished for a time, times, and half a time (12.14) or that they will nourish her (the woman) for 1260 days (12.6). The beast of Rev. 13 is given the authority to act for a period of forty-two months (13.5). Clearly, this particular chronological period repeated five times in three different ways binds the chapters together and as such we must ask what *significance* this time-frame has in the interpretation of the events portrayed therein. We submit that it is only reasonable to assume the narrative contained within each chapter must be interpreted in the light of the other episode explicitly stated by the author to unfold within the same temporal period. Biguzzi is right when he claims that the events in Rev. 11–13 are not extraneous to each other because 'the time lapse in which they take place is one and the same'.[8] To gain an

8. Biguzzi, 'Figurative and Narrative Language', p. 392. Almost all commentators take the three-and-a-half years periods in Rev. 11–13 as coinciding with one another and are therefore contemporaneous. Gregory K. Beale is representative as he writes: '[these three-and-a-half year periods] do not follow one another chronologically but refer to the same events'. G. K. Beale, *The Book of Revelation* (NIGNT; Grand Rapids: Eerdmans, 1999), p. 132. Speaking of the forty-two months of Rev. 13.5, David E. Aune comments: 'A period of forty-two months was referred to earlier in Rev 11.2 as the period of time when the nations would hold the holy city under subjection. The two witnesses are also said to be granted 1,260 days

understanding of John's literary aims here, an attempt must be made to see how each component part contributes to the whole, or the whole impacts on various constituent parts in the total scenario depicted within these three and a half years. Apart from this common denominator of three-and-a-half years, is there also a structural pattern on the face of the text, which demands that these episodes and scenes in different chapters be linked together? We suggest that the answer is in the affirmative as this phenomenon can be explained on the grounds that the events of Rev. 11 and Rev. 13 are best seen as *parallel* accounts with Rev. 12 as the apex centre of a formal structure called a *concentric chiasm*.[9]

Rev. 12
(war in *heaven*)

Rev. 11 – (war on *earth*) – Rev. 13

In between the pair of paralleled chapters (11 and 13) stands a pivotal statement about heavenly reality unseen by human eyes. It is the war in heaven resulting in the casting out of Satan from heaven to earth, which is the real cause of the horrendous suffering of the church on earth. Yet the church is called not to silence but to active witness (Rev. 11). Revelation 12 clearly spells out that Satan's time is short (12.12) and the kingdom of God and the authority of Christ will eventually replace all rule and authority on earth (12.10). In chs 2–5 of this book, we will seek to establish that the unit of text in 11.1–14.5 is structured as follows:

---

to prophesy, i.e., 42 months of 30 days each (11.3). The woman in 12.6 was protected in the wilderness for 1,260 days, referred to in 12.14 as "a time, times, and half a time" (an allusion to Dan. 7.25; 12.7). It is clear that the author intends the reader to understand that the period during which the first beast is active coincides with the period during which the two witnesses will prophesy. Their death must therefore coincide with the end of this predestined period of time.' D. E. Aune, *Revelation 6–16* (Nashville: Thomas Nelson, 1998), p. 743. Also L. J. L. Peerbolte writes: 'This repeated mention of the period suggests that the description of the Beast from the sea refers to the same period as the visions of chapters 11 and 12. Just like the visions of those chapters, the vision of chapter 13 describes the final period preceding the end.' L. J. L. Peerbolte, *The Antecedents of Antichrist: A Traditio-Historical Study of the Earliest Christian Views on Eschatological Opponents* (Leiden: Brill, 1995), p. 143.

9.   Towards the completion of my dissertation, I came across Michael J. Svigel's statement as to how Rev. 12 is structured within the text of Revelation. Svigel writes: 'Within the larger unit, it appears that Revelation 12 lies in the center of chiastic structure in which the two witnesses' triumphant authority for 1260 days in chap. 11 mirrors the two beasts' totalitarian authority for forty-months in chap. 13.... Whether this chiastic structure extends outwards towards both ends of the Revelation is debatable, but it does appear that the centrality of the twelfth chapter within the unit of Rev 11–13 is a safe assertion.' M. J. Svigel, 'The Apocalypse of John and the Rapture of the Church: A Reevaluation', *TrinJ* 22 (2001), pp. 23–74 (55–56). Svigel, however, does not discuss his proposed chiastic pattern in any detail.

A – 11.1–2

  B – 11.3–6

    C – 11.7–13

      D – 11.15–19

        E – 12.1–4

          F – 12.5–6

            G – 12.7–12

          F' – 12.13–14

        E' – 12.15–17

      D' – 13.1–6

    C' – 13.7–10

  B' – 13.11–18

A' – 14.1–5

4. *A Literary Analysis: A Methodological Approach*

Richard Bauckham's seminal study on Revelation, *The Climax of Prophecy* began with this observation: 'The book of Revelation is an extraordinarily complex literary composition.... This complexity has rarely been fully appreciated. The major literary study of Revelation which will do justice to it has yet to be written.'[10] Bauckham's observation is still valid despite a host of recent commentaries including those by C. Keener, B. Malina, M. Barker, P. Prigent, M. G. Reddish, C. Koester, G. R. Osborne, B. Witherington III, and the two monumental commentaries by D. E. Aune (3 volumes) and Beale, which in my opinion, failed to produce a convincing literary study of the text.[11] This book will follow

10. R. Bauckham, *The Climax of Prophecy* (Edinburgh: T & T Clark, 1993), p. 1.

11. C. Keener, *Revelation* (The NIV Application Commentary; Grand Rapids: Zondervan, 2000); B. Malina, *Social-Science Commentary on the Book of Revelation* (Minneapolis: Fortress Press, 2000); M. Barker, *The Revelation of Jesus Christ* (Edinburgh: T & T Clark, 2000); P. Prigent, *Commentary on the Apocalypse of St. John* (trans. Wendy Pradels; Tübingen: Mohr, 2001); M. G. Reddish, *Revelation* (Macon, GA; Smith and Helwys, 2001); C. Koester, *Revelation and the End of All Things* (Grand Rapids: Eerdmans, 2001); G. R. Osborne, *Revelation* (Baker Exegetical Commentary on the New Testament; Grand Rapids: Baker Academic, 2002); B. Witherington III, *Revelation* (Cambridge: Cambridge University Press, 2003); D. E. Aune, *Revelation 1–5* (Dallas: Word, 1997); *idem, Revelation 6–16*; *idem, Revelation 17–22* (Nashville: Thomas Nelson, 1998); Beale, *Revelation* (1999).

Bauckham's lead and focus on the literary features of Revelation albeit on a modest scale, as our study is limited to Rev. 11.1–14.5.

We agree with E. Schüssler Fiorenza that Revelation's theology is embodied 'in a unique fusion of content and form'.[12] Commentators of other biblical books have also noted the importance of structure in understanding the content of a particular book. As William Holladay contends: 'Structure and content always interact'.[13] Jacob Milgrom's comment is stark: 'structure is theology'.[14] We are not interested in analyzing the form and structure for their own sake, aesthetically pleasing as they may be, but more importantly to see the way structural patterns inform the *theology* of the materials they contain. Unless we are sensitive to the artistry of John's composition and his creative use of many literary devices and techniques, it is unlikely that we can fully mine the depths of meanings contained in the text.

a. *The Literary Unity of Revelation*
Bauckham is not alone in acknowledging the literary unity of Revelation. David L. Barr observes that, 'whereas our concern is to divide the book, John's concern is to bind it together'.[15] It is thus important to note how John binds not only smaller units but also larger divisions or blocks of materials together. Even in major divisions of the book, linkage to what precedes and what follows are readily apparent. An *inclusio* employed to frame a unit of text often functions to end a section as well as to begin a new unit. S. Bar-Erfat writes:

> In the field of biblical narrative particularly it seems to be impossible to define the boundaries of the literary units rigidly. In the Bible narratives which are more or less complete in themselves link up with one another so as to create larger literary units. In other words, narratives which on the one hand can be considered as self-contained units may be regarded on the other hand as parts of larger wholes.[16]

Aune's commentary is monumental in many other ways though it fails sufficiently to undertake a thorough literary analysis of the text. The section on the 'literary analysis' of each unit under consideration is not the most impressive part of his commentary.

12. E. Schüssler Fiorenza, *The Book of Revelation: Justice and Judgment* (Philadelphia: Fortress Press, 2nd edn, 1998), p. 159.

13. W. Holladay, *The Architecture of Jeremiah 1–20* (Lewisburg, Penn.; Bucknell University Press, 1976), p. 22.

14. J. Milgrom, *Numbers*, (JPS Torah Commentary; Philadelphia: Jewish Publication Society, 1990), p. xxii.

15. D. L. Barr, 'The Apocalypse as a Symbolic Transformation of the World: A Literary Analysis', *Int* 38 (1984), pp. 39–50 (43). Other scholars who acknowledge the literary unity of the Book include G. B. Caird, R. Mounce, E. Schüssler Fiorenza, C. Talbert, C. H. Giblin, G. E. Ladd, M. E. Boring, and others cited throughout this book. For a recent hypothesis that the book of Revelation was written in two editions, see Aune, *Revelation 1–5*, cxx–cxxxiv.

16. S. Bar-Erfat, 'Some Observations on the Analysis of Structure in Biblical Narrative', *VT* 30 (1980), pp. 154–73 (156).

From a micro-unit level to a macro-unit level, John weaves the parts into one connected whole making the book of Revelation 'one of the most unified works of the New Testament'.[17]

The book of Revelation is meant for oral enactment and delivery (1.3) and though this fact must be acknowledged, we cannot assume that the hearers of Revelation will understand the book on the first hearing.[18] It is safe to postulate that those designated as 'readers' (1.3) would re-read and study the text and explain it to less literate members of the church over time.[19] The length of the Book may indicate that the whole Book might not have been read in its entirety in one sitting, though even this cannot be ascertained conclusively, since at least on one occasion early Christians met for a long session.[20] For our purposes, it suffices to bear in

17. Bauckham, *Climax of Prophecy*, p. 1 n. 1.

18. See D. L. Barr, 'The Apocalypse of John as Oral Enactment', *Int* 40 (1986), pp. 243–56. For a general discussion on the subject of orality and its significance on the interpretation of biblical texts, see John D. Harvey, 'Orality and Its Implications for Biblical Studies: Recapturing an Ancient Paradigm', *JETS* 45 (March 2002), pp. 99–110.

19. R. E. Clements argued cogently that Jewish apocalyptic was 'a scribal activity, developed with the aid of written texts and dependent upon the ability of the interpreter to recognize specific allusions and to make certain verbal connections that would not be obvious to the non-literate person.... The skilled literate person, well-versed in the art of picking up this complex range of contextual images and ideas, would be expected to explain and assist the less skilled in appreciating their value.' R. E. Clements, 'Apocalyptic, Literary and Canonical Tradition', in W. Hulitt Gloer (ed.), *Eschatology and the New Testament: Essays in Honor of George Raymond Beasley-Murray* (Peabody, MA: Hendrikson, 1988), pp. 15–27 (19). Also Bauckham remarks that: 'Revelation was evidently designed to convey its message to some significant degree on first hearing (cf. 1.3), but also progressively to yield fuller meaning to closer acquaintance and assiduous study.' Bauckham, *Climax of Prophecy*, p. 1. John Sweet states that, 'even if the book was in the first instance read aloud as a whole, we can be sure that like Paul's letters it was subsequently pored over in detail'. J. Sweet, *Revelation* (London: SCM, 1979), p. 13. J. Webb Mealy comments thus: 'That its author intended it to be studied carefully and in detail is beyond doubt.' J. W. Mealy, *After the Thousand Years: Resurrection and Judgement in Revelation 20* (JSNTSup, 70; Sheffield: JSOT Press, 1992), p. 60 n. 1. D. E. Aune argues that the book is first communicated to John's fellow prophets (cf. Rev. 22.16) and then read and interpreted by the prophets to the seven churches. See D. E. Aune, 'The Prophetic Circle of John of Patmos and the Exegesis of Revelation 22:16', *JSNT* 37 (1989), pp. 103–16. This is not unlike the taking of the book of the law by Ezra and reading and explaining the law to the congregation as seen in Nehemiah 8. Ezra was helped by Levites who 'read from the book, from the law of God, explaining to give sense so that they understood the reading' (Neh. 8.8). See also G. K. Beale, *John's Use of the Old Testament in Revelation* (Sheffield: Sheffield Academic Press, 1998), p. 70.

20. The book of Revelation can be read in full in about an hour and a half. So Sweet, *Revelation*, p. 13 and Hans-Ruedi Weber, *The Way of the Lamb: Christ in the Apocalypse* (Geneva: WCC Publications, 1988), p. viii. In Acts, Paul spoke past midnight until someone fell asleep and fell from the window (Acts 20.9). It must be said that evidence in the New Testament as to how the early churches conducted their meetings is scarce. In the Old Testament, during times of major festivals, it is not unknown for the Law to be read for three

mind the oral setting within a liturgical context[21] in which the text of Revelation was first read when we come to exegete the passages concerned. Any message that is intended for oral communication is likely to be composed with literary devices and techniques that seek to maximize and heighten the rhetorical effectiveness demanded of such delivery. Hence, it will be our task to investigate closely these 'distinctive literary techniques by which Revelation conveys meaning'.[22] To do that, it is paramount that we appreciate how ancient Hebrew minds worked, and the conventional compositional techniques and repertoire of linguistic devices, which were ordinarily employed as part of their literary arsenal.

b. *The Language and Style of Revelation*
We have noted that the book of Revelation is saturated with the Old Testament. It is our contention that the language and style of the Old Testament in general and the prophetic literature in particular has influenced significantly the language and style of Revelation. Specifically, we submit that the literary unit of Rev. 11.1–14.5 can be best analyzed using Hebraic literary conventions and compositional techniques such as chiasm, parallelism, and parataxis.

Scholars agree that Revelation is the most Semitic of all New Testament books.[23] The Greek of Revelation contains many peculiarities not found in other New Testament books. 'The Greek of Revelation is not only difficult and awkward, but it also contains many lexical and syntactical features that no native speaker of Greek would have written.'[24] R. H. Charles claimed that Revelation contained more grammatical irregularities than any other Greek document of the ancient world.[25] Charles accounted for this grammatical phenomenon on the ground that, 'while he [John] writes in Greek, he thinks in Hebrew, and the thought has naturally *affected the*

---

hours per session as the Ezra/Nehemiah text shows (Neh. 9.3). We are, therefore, not convinced by A. Garrow's proposal that the book of Revelation is read over six separate instalments. See A. Garrow, *Revelation* (London: Routledge, 1997), pp. 14–65.

21.　See U. Vanni, 'Liturgical Dialogue as a Literary Form in the Book of Revelation', *NTS* 37 (1991), pp. 348–72.

22.　Bauckham, *Climax of Prophecy*, p. x.

23.　So Daniel B. Wallace, *Greek Grammar Beyond the Basics: An Exegetical Syntax of the New Testament* (Grand Rapids: Zondervan, 1996), p. 32.

24.　Aune, *Revelation 1–5*, p. cxcix.

25.　R. H. Charles, *A Critical and Exegetical Commentary on the Revelation of St. John* Vol. 1 (Edinburgh: T & T Clark, 1920), p. cxliii. See Charles' discussion of the grammatical features of Revelation at pp. cxvii–cxlii.

vehicle of expression.[26] Beale and most recent scholars concur with Charles.[27] Steven Thompson's monograph, *The Apocalypse and Semitic Syntax* goes further than Charles' position and argues that the Semitic syntax of Biblical Hebrew provides the basis for understanding the Greek of Revelation.[28] Thompson comments on 'the Seer's indebtedness to the OT not only for symbols and metaphors but for his very language'.[29] But we would not go as far as to posit as Thompson appears to do, that Revelation's Greek is almost a kind of Jewish or Semitic Greek. Despite numerous solecisms and grammatical peculiarities, Porter argues that Revelation's Greek falls within 'the range of possible registers of Greek usage of the 1st century'.[30] While Turner acknowledges the Semitic quality of Revelation's Greek, he concludes that it is 'only a matter of degree, not kind, in its difference from other Biblical Greek authors'.[31] Beale, however, doubts Porter's assertion says much about the language and style of Revelation. Beale states the issue thus:

> It is true that one could say that such Septuagintalisms 'fall within the range of possible registers' of first-century Greek usage. The question, however, is not about a mere few grammatical irregularities but the great number of the difficulties, and the frequency of the phenomena in comparison with other works. Furthermore, why does John use such peculiar language on occasion and yet keep the rules of standard Hellenistic Greek most of the time?[32]

26.   Charles, *Revelation* Vol. 1, p. cxliii (my emphasis). A. Feuillet agrees with Charles and remarks that the Greek of Revelation is based on Hebrew thought and can be understood only by those who know Hebrew. See A. Feuillet, *The Apocalypse* (trans. Thomas Crane; New York: Alba House, 1964), p. 99.

27.   Beale, *John's Use of the Old Testament*, p. 125. Also Sweet, *Revelation*, p. 16; A. Yarbro Collins, *Crisis and Catharsis: The Power of the Apocalypse* (Philadelphia: Westminster Press, 1984), p. 46; G. Mussies, *The Morphology of Koine Greek as Used in the Apocalypse of John: A Study in Bilingualism* (NovTSup, 27; Leiden: E. J. Brill, 1971) and *idem*, 'The Greek of the Book of Revelation', in D. Hellholm (ed.), *Apocalypticism in the Mediterranean World and the Near East* (Tübingen: Mohr, 1989), pp. 167–77; N. Turner, 'The Style of the Book of Revelation', in *A Grammar of New Testament Greek by J. H. Moulton*, Vol. 4 *"Style"* (Edinburgh: T & T Clark, 1976), pp. 145–59. For a contrary view, see Stanley E. Porter, 'The Language of the Apocalypse in Recent Discussion', *NTS* 35 (1989), pp. 582–603.

28.   S. Thompson, *The Apocalypse and Semitic Syntax* (SNTSMS, 52; Cambridge: Cambridge University Press, 1985). Thompson (p. 104) concludes that: 'One cannot escape the impression that the biblical Hebrew (and Aramaic) tense system, profoundly different from Greek, is to be seen nearly everywhere in the language of the Apc.'

29.   Thompson, *Semitic Syntax*, p. 105.

30.   Porter, 'The Language of the Apocalypse in Recent Discussion', p. 603.

31.   Turner, 'Style', p. 149.

32.   G. K. Beale, 'Solecisms in the Apocalypse as Signals for the Presence of OT Allusions', in C. A. Evans & J. A. Sanders (eds.), *Early Christian Interpretation of the*

Beale's answer is worth quoting in full:

> The explanation is that these peculiarities at just these points are not
> mere reflections of unusual though possible registers of Greek usage, but
> are stylistic Septuagintalisms; such semi-irregular Hellenistic expressions
> may occur more frequently in Revelation because they would have felt
> natural for the author as a result of his Hebrew and especially Old
> Testament Greek background. Other cases of John's solecisms are even
> to be more specifically explained as grammatically awkward because
> they are parts of actual Old Testament verbal allusions carried over in
> their original syntactical form as they stood in the Old Testament
> passage. The overall purpose of these Septuagintalisms, stylistic
> Semitisms, and awkward Old Testament allusions was probably to
> create a 'biblical' effect in the hearer and, hence, to show the solidarity
> of his writing with that of the Old Testament.[33]

We accept Beale's explanation and also Charles' conclusion that John
wrote in Greek but thought in Hebrew as the basis for handling the
language and style of the book. As it is not within the purview of this book
to debate the nature of Revelation's Greek, we will adopt the observations
made by Charles and Beale in our literary analysis of Rev. 11.1–14.5.

First, the Hebraic flavoured Greek style of Revelation is largely due to
John's dependence on the Old Testament languages (Hebrew and
Aramaic) and imagery as a 'vehicle of expression' (Charles' phrase), to
convey his vision reports and prophetic narratives to his readers. Although
Revelation never cites or quotes an Old Testament text or texts, Revelation
alludes to the Old Testament more often than all the other New Testament
books put together. Jörg Frey writes: 'Die wichtigste Quelle der
Bildersprache der Apokalypse ist das Alte Testament. Obwohl es an
keiner einzigen Stelle ausdrücklich zitiert wird, finden sich hier mehr
Anklänge an alttestamentliche Texte als in jeder anderen Schrift des Neuen
Testamentes.'[34] I. Suharyo states that, 'Dari 404 ayat yang terdapat dalam

---

Scriptures of Israel (Sheffield: Sheffield Academic Press, 1997), pp. 421–43 (425). Beale's essay
(pp. 421–25) provides an excellent summary of the scholarly debate regarding Revelation's
Greek.

33. Beale, 'Solecisms in the Apocalypse', pp. 425–26.

34. J. Frey, 'Die Bildersprache der Johannesapokaypse', *ZThK* 98 (2001), pp. 161–85
(170). Scholars have long recognised that the book of Revelation is heavily influenced by Old
Testament language and imagery. For recent discussion on John's use of the Old Testament,
see S. Moyise, 'The Language of the Old Testament in the Apocalypse', *JSNT* 76 (1999), pp.
97–113, *idem*, *The Old Testament in the Book of Revelation* (JSNTSup, 115; Sheffield: Sheffield
Academic Press, 1995) and Beale, *John's Use of the Old Testament*. For a general study on the
relevance and significance of the Old Testament in the New Testament, see S. Moyise (ed.),
The Old Testament in the New Testament. Essays in honour of J. L. North (Sheffield: Sheffield
Academic Press, 2000).

Kitab Wahyu, 278 memuat sekurang-kurangnya satu gagasan Perjanjian Lama.' (ET: Out of 404 verses in the book of Revelation, 278 verses have at least one allusion to the Old Testament).[35] J. Fekkes lists various scholars' proposals of between 250 and 700 Old Testament allusions in Revelation.[36] Peter Wongso suggests that there are 447 Old Testament allusions from 32 different Old Testament books.[37] Jon Paulien concludes that: 'A careful collation of the evidence in the ten major works yielded proposed allusions to 288 different OT passages.'[38] We will see that of the 60 verses within Rev. 11.1–14.5, allusions to the Old Testament are found in almost every verse. Often the conflation of two or three Old Testament sources is alluded to in one sentence or verse.[39] Despite divergence on the exact number of Old Testament allusions, scholars agree that Revelation is

35. I. Suharyo, *Kitab Wahyu: Paham dan Maknanya bagi Hidup Kristen* [ET: *The Book of Revelation: Its Understanding and Purpose for Christian Life*] (Lembaga Biblika Indonesia; Yogjakarta, Indonesia: Kanisius, 1993), p. 19. For all Indonesian/Malay texts quoted in this thesis, we will first cite the text in the original language followed by a translation into English.
36. J. Fekkes, *Isaiah and the Prophetic Traditions in the Book of Revelation: Visionary Antecedents and Their Development* (Sheffield: JSOT Press, 1994), p. 62.
37. P. Wongso, *Kitab Wahyu* (Malang, Indonesia: Seminari Alkitab Asia Tenggara, 1996), p. 183. Wongso (pp. 167–82) lists all the verses of Revelation which in his opinion, contain one or more Old Testament references. Dr. Peter Wongso has written the most comprehensive commentary on Revelation in Indonesian totaling 805 pages.
38. J. Paulien, 'Elusive Allusions: The Problematic Use of the Old Testament in Revelation', *BR* 33 (1988), pp. 37–53 (37). Paulien's list of ten major works is cited in p. 49 n. 1. For a discussion on how OT allusions in Revelation can be verified, see J. Paulien, *Decoding Revelation's Trumpets* (Andrews University Seminary Doctoral Dissertation Series, 21; Berrien Springs: America University Press, 1988), pp. 159–94. Paulien (p. 179 n. 3) defines allusion in this manner: 'An allusion consists of one or more words which by their peculiar character and general content are traceable to a known body of text, but which do not constitute a complete reproduction of any part of it.' Apart from a number of monographs already cited, Beale has also written a series of essays and articles on the use of OT in Revelation. See Beale, 'Solecisms in the Apocalypse', pp. 421–43; 'The Use of Daniel in the Synoptic Eschatological Discourse and the Book of Revelation', in David Wenham (ed.), *Gospel Perspectives: Jesus Tradition Outside the Gospels* Vol. 5 (Sheffield: JSOT Press, 1985), pp. 129–54; 'The Danielic Background for Revelation 13.18 and 17.9', *TynBul* 31 (1980), pp. 163–70; 'The Use of the Old Testament in Revelation', in D. A. Carson and H. G. M. Williamson (eds.), *It is Written: Scripture Citing Scripture* (Festschrift B. Lindars; Cambridge: Cambridge University Press, 1988), pp. 318–52.
39. In the first half of the twentieth century commentators debated whether John utilized the Masoretic Text (MT) or the Septuagint (LXX) as his main source of OT allusions with Charles (*Revelation Vol. 1*, p. lxvi) arguing that John preferred Semitic sources and H. B. Swete arguing for John's preference for LXX. See H. B. Swete, *The Apocalypse of John* (London: Macmillan, 3rd edn, 1908), pp. cxl–clviii. Recent scholars have concluded, in our view rightly, that John was adept in using both MT and LXX as his sources whenever the occasion suited him. Moyise concludes that, 'John knew and used both Greek and Semitic sources and that the consensus view, that John *preferred* Semitic texts, remains unproven.' Moyise, 'The Language of the Old Testament in the Apocalypse', p. 113 (his emphasis).

saturated with the Old Testament. Steve Moyise notes that: 'Even a conservative estimate works out at about one allusion for every verse.'[40] P. Prigent comments thus: 'L'Apocalypse est littéralement saturée d'AT, personne n'en doute.'[41] With such rich and dense use of Old Testament (both MT and LXX) in the text of Revelation, it is understandable that Revelation's Greek contains many Semitic idioms and Septuagintalisms. Though the Old Testament is never explicitly quoted, Turner observes that, 'much material derives from there [OT] and from later Jewish tradition, and this is bound to account in part for the Semitic quality of the language'.[42]

Secondly, Mussies has shown that Semitisms are found throughout Revelation and are not restricted to particular sections of the book.[43] Thompson further notes that, with the exception of the seven letters to the seven churches which are nearly free from Semitisms, Semitic constructions abound in all portions of Revelation, and are especially concentrated in chs 11 and 12 of Revelation, a major part of the textual unit under discussion in this book.[44] Why is there such concentration of Hebraisms or Semitisms in the Greek text of Revelation? Beale answers in this vein:

> Perhaps one of the reasons for the high degree of Old Testament influence in the Apocalypse is that the author could think of no better way to describe some of his visions, which were difficult to explain, than with *the language already used by the Old Testament prophets* to describe similar visions.[45]

Beale's conclusion leads us to our third point, that among the books of the Old Testament, the prophetic books provide the major source of John's language and imagery. Since the prophetic books in the Old Testament are mainly composed in poetic form, it is not surprising then to find that a large part of Revelation follows a poetic style akin to the prophetic literature.[46] Wongso comments that, 'Kitab Wahyu ditulis dalam bentuk syair orang Ibrani . . . ' (ET: The book of Revelation was written according

---

40. S. Moyise, *The Old Testament in the New* (Continuum: London and New York, 2001), p. 117.

41. P. Prigent, *L'Apocalpyse de Saint Jean* (Lausanne: Delachaux et Niestlé, 1981), p. 367.

42. Turner, 'Style', p. 145.

43. Mussies, *Morphology*, pp. 350–51.

44. Thompson, *Semitic Syntax*, p. 107.

45. Beale, *John's Use of the Old Testament*, p. 126 (my emphasis).

46. For a discussion on the practice of rhetorical analysis on the prophetic books, see David L. Jeffrey, 'How to Read the Hebrew Prophets', in Vincent L. Tollers and John Maier (eds.), *Mappings of the Biblical Terrain: The Bible as Text* (Lewisburg, PA: Bucknell University Press, 1990), pp. 282–98. Jeffrey's essay (pp. 284–88) contains an excellent discussion on the nature of Hebrew prophecy and the role of the prophet as author.

to the Hebrew poetic form...).[47] R. H. Charles noted that 'poetical parallelism' pervaded the way in which Revelation was composed and he commented thus:

> The next feature[48] that characterizes John's style is his frequent use of the poetical parallelism we find in Hebrew poetry. Though he has for his theme the inevitable conflicts and antagonisms of good and evil, of God and the powers of darkness, yet his Book is emphatically a Book of Songs.... Nearly always when dealing with his greatest themes the Seer's words assume consciously or unconsciously a poetic form. To print such passages as prose is to rob them of half their force. And it is not only form that is thereby lost, but also much of the thought that in a variety of ways is reinforced by the parallelism.[49]

Not only do the Old Testament prophets provide a fertile ground for John's message but more so John portrays himself as continuing the tradition of Old Testament prophecy. Heinrich Kraft states thus: 'Johannes fühlt sich als Fortsetzer und abschließender Ausleger der alttestamentlichen Prophetie. Da es derselbe Geist ist, der die alten Propheten inspirierte und der ihn inspiriert, sieht er sich auch der Sprache der alttestamentlichen Prophetie verpflichtet.'[50] John's re-commission narrated in Rev. 10 (esp. vv. 8–11) is constructed after the manner of Ezekiel's call to prophesy (cf. Ezek. 2.8–3.4) and Daniel's encounter with an angel in Daniel 10.[51] The patterning of John's commission after the call narratives of Ezekiel and Daniel functions rhetorically to convey to John's

---

47. Wongso, *Kitab Wahyu*, p. 190. See Wongso's discussion how Hebrew parallelism works in Revelation at pp. 50–55. See also Isabelle Donegani's discussion on Hebrew parallelism affects the interpretation of Revelation in I. Donegani, *"A cause de la parole de Dieu et du témoignage de Jésus...": Le témoignage selon l'apocalypse de Jean: Son enracinement extra-biblique et biblique: Sa force comme parole de sens* (Ebib n.s. 36; Paris: Gabalda, 1997), pp. 370–80.

48. The first feature of Revelation is John's 'abounding Hebraisms and unique Greek Grammar.' R. H. Charles, *Lectures on the Apocalypse: The Schweich Lectures 1919* (London: Oxford University Press, 1922), p. 40.

49. Charles, *Lectures on the Apocalypse*, p. 41. Charles' primary emphasis here is that the text of Revelation is mostly poetic [Book of Songs], not only in those places where hymns or songs are found.

50. H. Kraft, *Die Offenbarung des Johannes* (Tübingen: Mohr, 1974), p. 16.

51. John Kaltner argues convincingly that the narrative of Daniel's encounter with an angel in Dan 10 consists of a prophetic call narrative in which Daniel's experience is presented 'in a way that echoes the prophets' calls'. J. Kaltner, 'Is Daniel Also among the Prophets?: The Rhetoric of Daniel 10–12', in Gregory Bloomquist and Greg Carey (eds.), *Vision and Persuasion: Rhetorical Dimensions of Apocalyptic Discourse* (St Loius, MO: Chalice Press, 1999), pp. 41–59 (52). John's call in Rev. 10 adopts a conflation of both Ezekiel's and Daniel's call narratives where John's encounter with the strong angel and subsequent revelation is patterned after Daniel's encounter, while the eating of the book and subsequent commission

readers the author's unmistakable identity and calling as a prophet in the manner of Old Testament prophets. 'He writes "words of the prophecy" (1.3) so we may conclude that he is a Christian prophet, though he never refers to himself as such.'[52] That John thought of himself as a prophet is hardly surprising given that John claimed that what he saw and testified to was 'the word of God and the testimony of Jesus Christ' (1.2) making up the contents of his vision, which he labeled as 'the words of the prophecy' (1.3). The *inclusio* at the end of Revelation reiterates John's view that the whole content of his book, 'the words of this book' (22.9) are heard and read as *prophecy*,[53] hence John's repeated affirmations of the prophetic nature of his book and the insistence that his audience truly heeds the warning of 'the words of the prophecy of this book' (22.18) and keep intact 'the words of the book of this prophecy' (22.19) without adding or subtracting from it. By referring to his composition as 'the word of this prophecy', 'the author was undoubtedly encouraging the reader to associate this work with earlier prophetic books in the Israelite and early Jewish tradition'.[54]

The strong claim by John himself that his book belongs to the *prophetic genre*, in our view, is often not given due consideration despite E. Schüssler Fiorenza's plea that: 'The claim of Rev. to be early Christian

to prophesy follow Ezekiel's account. For a discussion on the differences between John's call and Ezekiel's account, see David E. Holwerda, 'The Church and the Little Scroll (Revelation 10–11)', *CTJ* 34 (1999), pp. 148–61 (153–55).

52. L. Thompson, *Revelation* (ANTC; Nashville: Abingdon Press, 1998), p. 22. John's description of his call to prophesy in Rev. 10 is a clear indication of his self-consciousness as a prophet though he never calls himself a prophet in Revelation. For a discussion on what constitutes Christian prophecy, see D. Hill, *New Testament Prophecy* (London: Marshall, Morgan & Scott, 1979); D. E. Aune, *Prophecy in Early Christianity and in the Ancient Mediterranean World* (Grand Rapids: Eerdmans, 1983) and *idem*, 'The Prophetic Circle', pp. 103–16; G. Houston, *Prophecy Now* (with a foreword by I. Howard Marshall; Leicester: Inter-Varsity Press, 1989). Gerald F. Hawthorne defines a Christian prophet as 'a powerful authority-figure in the early church who was inspired by the Holy Spirit and impelled by the Spirit to speak his message to individuals and to the church with authority and power. He was a person who received and proclaimed divine revelations, not merely a person who preached "good news" in a traditional way.' G. Hawthorne, 'The Role of the Christian Prophets in the Gospel Tradition', in Gerald F. Hawthorne with Otto Betz (eds.), *Tradition & Interpretation in the New Testament: Essays in Honor of E. Earle Ellis for his 60th birthday* (Grand Rapids: Eerdmans, 1987), pp. 119–33 (119).

53. For a discussion on how the literary device *inclusio* functions in Revelation, see Bruce Longenecker, 'Linked Like a Chain: Rev 22.6–9 in Light of an Ancient Transition Technique', *NTS* 47 (2001), pp. 105–17.

54. D. E. Aune, 'Intertexuality and the Genre of the Apocalypse', in *SBL Seminar Papers* (Atlanta: Scholars Press, 1991), pp.142–60 (146). Aune (p. 146) adds that: 'The concluding emphasis on obeying the message of the book (1.3) emphasizes the paraenetic function of the work which is certainly more characteristic of prophecy than of apocalyptic.'

prophecy…be taken seriously.'[55] Revelation is often categorized as belonging to the literary genre of apocalypse partly due to the fact that the word ἀποκάλυψις appears at the head of the first verse of the book, introducing John's book as 'The revelation (or apocalypse) of Jesus Christ which God gave to him' (1.1). However, the term 'apocalypse' in 1.1 does not indicate the genre of John's book but is used functionally to designate that what John saw was revealed to him by Jesus, a revelation which was first given to Jesus by God. Aune states that: 'John is not describing his composition as belonging to a literary type called "apocalypse", since he characterizes his work as a "prophecy" (1.3) or "prophetic book" (22.7, 10, 18–19).'[56] George Linton observes that, 'the most popular generic

55. E. Schüssler Fiorenza, 'Apocalypsis and Propheteia: Revelation in the Context of the Early Christian Prophecy', in J. Lambrecht (ed.), *L'Apocalypse johannique et l'Apocalyptique dans le Nouveau Testament* (BETL, 53; Leuven: Leuven University Press, 1980), pp. 105–28 (113).

56. Aune, *Revelation 1–5*, p. 12. Aune (p. 12) further notes that the book of Revelation comes to be viewed as a literary type of 'apocalypse' in the second century. George Linton comments thus: 'It was later that *apocalypsis* became a genre-designation for a certain group of works among which interpreters saw significant similarities. At the earliest, the word was used in this way by the patristic writers of the second century.' G. Linton, 'Reading the Apocalypse as an Apocalypse', in *SBL Seminar Papers* (Atlanta: Scholars Press, 1991), pp. 161–86 (175). It is doubtful that John's first century audience would have recognized the genre of the book of Revelation as 'apocalyptic' given that the apocalyptic genre is not fully established until the late second century. Even the book of Daniel, the most apocalyptic book of the Old Testament is understood by the ancient readers as prophecy. Daniel is seen as a prophet and explicitly called thus by Jesus in Mt. 24.15. Josephus also called Daniel a prophet (*Ant.* 10.267–68). The earliest reference to the 'prophet Daniel' is from Qumran, 4QFlor, where it is said, 'as it is written in the book of Daniel the prophet', followed by quotations from Dan. 12.10 and 11.32. See John C. Trever, 'The Qumran Teacher – Another Candidate?', in Craig A. Evans & William F. Stinespring (eds.), *Early Jewish and Christian Exegesis: Studies in Memory of William Hugh Brownlee* (Atlanta: Scholars Press, 1987), pp. 101–22 (106 n. 14). Lester L. Grabbe remarks: 'Scholars of our times see the book of Daniel as an apocalypse, but for centuries Daniel was the prophet *par excellence*.' L. Grabbe, 'Dan(iel) for All Seasons: For Whom was Daniel Important?', in John J. Collins and Peter W. Flint (eds.), *The Book of Daniel: Composition and Reception* Vol. 1 (Leiden: Brill, 2001), pp. 229–46 (244). David Russell considers the book of Daniel an apocalypse but acknowledges that the book of Daniel appears 'in all first-century sources and in Greek, Latin, and succeeding translations as one of the four major prophets within the prophetic corpus' whereas it appears in the section known as 'the Writings' of the Hebrew-Aramaic Bible only between the fifth and eighth centuries. D. Russell, *Prophecy and the Apocalyptic Dream: Protest and Promise* (Peabody, MA: Hendrickson, 1994), pp. 4–5. Per Bilde remarks that: 'Jewish apocalypticism is a modern, scholarly construct.' P. Bilde, 'Josephus and Jewish Apocalypticism', in Steven Mason (ed.), *Understanding Josephus: Seven Perspectives* (Sheffield: Sheffield Academic Press, 1998), pp. 35–61 (40). Schüssler Fiorenza states that: 'We know that contemporary Jewish apocalyptic writers understood themselves and their works in terms of prophecy…. Because OT classical prophecy was known as "literary prophecy", the writers could understand their

category in which the Apocalypse is placed at the present time is that of apocalypse. Yet ... apocalypse is a genre that did not exist at the time John wrote since its conventions had not yet been explicated.'[57] Schüssler Fiorenza comments as follows:

> Exegetes still question whether the author intended his work to be a prophecy or an apocalypse. He understands himself as a Christian prophet and intends his work to be a 'word of prophecy'. Moreover, he employs most of the traditional prophetic forms. Rev. contains prophetic vision reports and messenger speeches, prophetic oracles and symbolic actions, announcements of judgment and proclamations of salvation. Prophetic summonses, warnings, threats and exhortations, technical legal language as well as hymns of praise, woe oracles, and laments or dirges are found in the book. The author not only uses prophetic forms but also patterns whole sections after OT prophetic books.[58]

The term 'apocalypse' in Rev. 1.1 'describes the process of unveiling and the truth unveiled concerning the issues of history'.[59] It points to a literary

---

activity and authority as a continuation of that of the classical prophets. Literary activity constitutes only a difference in degree but does not destroy the prophetic character of apocalyptic works.' Schüssler Fiorenza, 'Apocalypsis and Propheteia', p. 113.

57.   Linton, 'Reading the Apocalypse as an Apocalypse', p. 178. Linton (p. 173) argues that Revelation comes under multiple genres in what he calls 'hybrid genre'. Some scholars are now apt to classify the book of Revelation within a triple-genre of apocalyptic, prophetic and epistolary. See Barbara W. Snyder, 'Triple-Form and Space/Time Transition: Literary Structuring Devices in the Apocalypse', in *SBL Seminar Papers* (Atlanta: Scholars Press, 1991), pp. 440–50. John J. Collins acknowledges that: 'The designation [of Revelation] as Christian prophecy is not wrong. Revelation is presented not only as *apokalypsis*, but also as a prophecy (1.3; 22.6–7), and its author is properly regarded as an early Christian prophet. Prophecy was a broad category in the Hellenistic and Roman worlds; it could encompass various kinds of revelation including what we call apocalyptic.' J. J. Collins, *The Apocalyptic Imagination: An Introduction to the Jewish Matrix of Christianity* (Grand Rapids: Eerdmans, 2nd edn, 1998), p. 269. Collins (pp. 269–73) argues that Revelation is best seen as an apocalypse and a prophecy. The oft-quoted and most influential definition of the apocalypse genre is that proposed by Collins: ' "Apocalypse" is a genre of revelatory literature with a narrative framework, in which a revelation is mediated by an otherworldly being to a human recipient, disclosing a transcendent reality which is both temporal, insofar as it envisages eschatological salvation, and spatial, insofar as it involves another, supernatural world.' J. J. Collins, 'Introduction: Toward the Morphology of a Genre', *Semeia* 14 (1979), pp. 1–20 (9). For an excellent summary of John J. Collins' writings on apocalypticism, see Jarot Hadianto, 'Apokaliptisme Menurut Uraian John J. Collins [ET: Apocalypticism according to the Writings of John J. Collins]', *Forum Biblika* 12 (2000), pp. 10–16.

58.   Schüssler Fiorenza, *The Book of Revelation*, p. 168.

59.   G. R. Beasley-Murray, *The Book of Revelation* (NCB; Grand Rapids: Eerdmans, 1974), p. 50. George E. Ladd notes that: 'In Theodotion's Greek version of Daniel the word [apocalypse or its verbal form] is used several times of the divine disclosure through the

work 'which mediates divine revelation'.[60] The pervasive apocalyptic imagery in Revelation does not take the book out of the prophetic ambit as many prophetic writings incorporate strong apocalyptic elements in their books. Allan McNicol remarks: 'What is often labeled as apocalyptic imagery and symbolism in Revelation is present essentially in the Old Testament books.'[61] For example, Isaiah 24–27 and 56–66, Ezekiel 38–39, Daniel 7–12, Joel 3–4, Habakkuk 3, Zechariah 1–6 and 9–14 are 'apocalyptic' and have been rightly recognized as such within the prophetic corpus.[62] We will see that these 'apocalyptic' sections within the said prophetic books are major sources of John's work.[63] So it is not unusual that prophecy employs apocalyptic imagery as a vehicle of expressing its prophetic message.[64] That Revelation employs it so pervasively throughout the book is no reason to disassociate it from being seen as primarily a prophetic work as the author himself explicitly claims.[65]

prophet to the king of events which, in the providence of God, were destined to take place in the future.' (cf. Dan. 2.10, 19, 22–23, 28–29, 47). G. E. Ladd, *A Commentary on the Revelation of John* (Grand Rapids: Eerdmans, 1972), p. 19.

60. Aune, 'Intertexuality and the Genre of the Apocalypse', p. 145.

61. A. McNicol, 'Revelation 11.1–14 and the Structure of the Apocalypse', *ResQ* 22 (1979), pp. 193–202 (194).

62. For a discussion on how prophecy and apocalypticism interrelate, see Stephen L. Cook, *Prophecy and Apocalypticism: The Postexilic Social Setting* (Minneapolis: Fortress Press, 1995); P. D. Hanson, *The Dawn of the Apocalyptic* (Philadelphia: Fortress Press, 2nd edn, 1979), pp. 1–31; Michael Knibb, 'Prophecy and the Emergence of the Jewish Apocalypses', in R. J. Coggins *et al.* (eds.), *Israel's Prophetic Traditions* (Cambridge: Cambridge University Press, 1982), pp. 155–80; J. J. Collins, 'From Prophecy to Apocalypticism: The Expectation of the End', in John J. Collins (ed.), *The Encyclopedia of Apocalypticism* Vol. 1: *The Origins of Apocalypticism in Judaism and Christianity* (New York: Continuum, 1998), pp. 129–61. Aune rightly notes that: 'In some respects, the dichotomy between prophecy and apocalyptic is a false one, since neither "prophecy" nor "apocalypse" designates a static type of literature; rather each represents a spectrum of texts composed over centuries.' Aune, *Revelation 1–5*, p. lxxv.

63. For example, see Fekkes, *Isaiah and the Prophetic Traditions in the Book of Revelation*; G. K. Beale, *The Use of Daniel in Jewish and Apocalyptic Literature and in the Revelation of St. John* (Lanham: University Press of America, 1984); J.-P. Ruiz, *Ezekiel in the Apocalypse: The Transformation of Prophetic Language in Revelation 16,17–19,10* (Frankfurt am Main: Peter Lang, 1993). And more recently Steve Moyise notes that Revelation alludes to Ezekiel, Daniel, and Isaiah extensively. S. Moyise, 'Does the Author of Revelation Misappropriate the Scriptures?', *AUSS* 40 (2002), pp. 3–21. We will see that the book of Zechariah and the Psalms are also major sources for John in the book of Revelation.

64. E. Schüssler Fiorenza writes: 'The apocalyptic language and imagery of the book serve prophetic interpretation.' E. Schüssler Fiorenza, 'Composition and Structure of the Book of Revelation', *CBQ* 39 (1977), pp. 344–66 (358).

65. Suharyo notes as follows: 'Menarik untuk diperhatikan, Yohanes yang sangat kenal dengan arus pemikiran apokaliptik tidak mengutip satu pun tulisan apokaliptik yang dikenalnya.' (ET: It is of interest to note that John who is so familiar with apocalyptic thought does not once quote from the apocalyptic writings known to him). Suharyo, *Kitab Wahyu*,

Recently, F. Mazzaferri has argued that Revelation falls within the category of classical prophecy.[66] Revelation's prophetic character explains John's heavy dependence on the prophetic books by way of frequent allusion to them.[67] More specifically, parts of Revelation often follow the structural patterns found in prophetic books. Beale states that:

> There is general acknowledgement that the OT books to which Apocalypse is most indebted are the Psalms, Isaiah, Ezekiel, and Daniel.... It is likely no coincidence that *the structure* of Isaiah, Daniel, and Ezekiel is primarily characterized by recapitulation, sometimes in *chiastic* form. Zechariah is also significantly used (about fifteen times) and it likewise exhibits a *chiastically parallel structure*.... Daniel's structure of five synonymous parallel visions (chs. 2, 7, 8, 9, 10–12) may be the most influential on the structure of Revelation.[68]

p. 19. Robert A. Briggs makes similar comments when he concludes that John is not influenced by 'non-scriptural Jewish literature'. R. A. Briggs, *Jewish Temple Imagery in the Book of Revelation* (Frankfurt am Main: Peter Lang, 1999), p. 217. I would agree with Suharyo that John did not 'quote' from other apocalyptic literature but disagree with Briggs that John was not 'influenced' by non-scriptural writings as we will see that the Dead Sea Scrolls could be seen as an influence in John's composition of Rev. 12.

66.   F. Mazzaferri, *The Genre of the Book of Revelation from a Source-Critical Perspective* (Berlin: de Gruyter, 1989). Also David Hill, 'Prophecy and Prophets in the Revelation of St. John', *NTS* 18 (1971–1972), pp. 410–18. See especially Mazzaferri's analysis of generic features of 'classical prophecy' (pp. 85–156) as distinguished from 'classical apocalyptic' (pp. 157–84). The main weakness of Mazzaferri's thesis appears to be the use of the term, 'classical' to qualify both prophecy and apocalyptic, which seems to downplay that these literary categories are fluid concepts and that their so-called generic features often overlap. While Aune (*Revelation 1–5*, p. lxxvi) affirms the merits of Mazzaferri's thesis that Revelation's composition shares conscious continuity with Old Testament prophecy, he nonetheless thinks that Mazzaferri's descriptions of 'classical apocalyptic' are a caricature of those apocalyptic texts. Also R. Bauckham, *The Fate of the Dead: Studies on Jewish and Christian Apocalypses* (Leiden: Brill, 1998), p. 269 n. 2. Bauckham in the same footnote agrees with Schüssler Fiorenza (*The Book of Revelation*, p. 165) that it is right to refuse the alternative of prophecy or apocalyptic. See also Bauckham's discussion on the differences between Revelation and the major Jewish apocalypses in Bauckham, *Climax of Prophecy*, pp. 174–77.

67.   See Aune, *Revelation 1–5*, p. lxxvi. In an earlier article, Aune claimed that: 'From the perspective of the original reader, it has become obvious that the sequence of literary forms in the Apocalypse conforms to no known ancient literary conventions.' Aune, 'Intertextuality and the Genre of the Apocalypse', p. 159. However, Aune (p. 159 n. 26) acknowledges that his statement 'must be qualified by the admission that the problem of the literary patterns evident in the sequence of constituent literary forms in apocalypses is a subject which has not been investigated'. It is our aim in this thesis to examine the literary patterns of Revelation according to Hebraic literary conventions.

68.   Beale, *Revelation*, p. 135 (emphasis mine). Beale's notion of recapitulation is not entirely clear but he seems to mean that some of the visions in Daniel for example, are parallel visions.

The Psalter and the books of Daniel and Zechariah are among the most influential, as we will see in the literary unit of Rev. 11.1–14.5.[69] It is likely no coincidence that large textual units of Isaiah, Daniel and Zechariah are structured chiastically as are many textual units in Revelation, in particular the unit of Rev. 11.1–14.5.[70] The Psalms which are entirely in poetry exhibit parallelism in nearly every instance. Chiastic patterns are found regularly among the Psalms.[71] The structure of Psalm 2 which is the most influential Psalm in our literary unit of Rev. 11.1–14.5 is also seen to be chiastic.[72] Outside the biblical Psalms, the Qumran hymns are also relevant to our study. The hymn found in 1QH 11.3–18 which will be critical to our analysis of Rev. 11.1–14.5, is also structured in a chiastic pattern.[73]

69.   Most of the Psalms alluded to by John in Rev. 11.1–14.5 are what scholars label as 'prophetic' or 'eschatological' psalms such as Pss. 2 and 149. The strong prophetic flavour of the Psalms has been recognized by various Christian writings and traditions like the Gospels and the Dead Sea Scrolls. Susan Gillingham notes that, 'in some traditions the psalms were seen as a continuation of the prophetic books, forming, as it were, a fifth "prophetic" scroll after Isaiah, Jeremiah, Ezekiel, and the Book of the Twelve'. S. Gillingham, 'From Liturgy to Prophecy: The Use of Psalmody in the Second Temple Judaism', *CBQ* 64 (2002), pp. 470–89 (479). One important motif in the Psalms which is repeatedly mentioned in Rev. 11.1–14.5 (cf. 12.10; 11.15) is the coming reign of God. For a discussion of this motif in the Psalms, see D. C. Mitchell, *The Message of the Psalter: An Eschatological Programme in the Book of Psalms* (JSOTSup, 252; Sheffield: Sheffield Academic Press, 1997), pp. 78–89.

70.   The visions of Zech. 1–6 are said to be structured chiastically. See Joyce G. Baldwin, *Haggai, Zechariah, Malachi*, (Leicester: Inter-Varsity Press, 1972), pp. 74–81. Also Eric Meyers and Carol Meyers, *Haggai, Zechariah 1–8* (AB; New York: Doubleday, 1987), pp. liii–lx; Bart B. Bruehler, 'Seeing through the עינים of Zechariah: Understanding Zechariah 4', *CBQ* 63 (2001), pp. 430–43 (432); M. Butterworth, *Structure and Zechariah* (JSOTSup, 130; Sheffield: JSOT Press, 1992), p. 299; Al Wolters, 'Confessional Criticism and the Night Visions of Zechariah', in Craig Bartholomew *et al.* (eds.), *Renewing Biblical Interpretation* (Grand Rapids: Paternoster Press, 2000), pp. 90–117 (98). The arrangement of the narrative in Dan. 2–7 is also seen as chiastic. See A. Lenglet, 'La Structure Littéraire de Daniel 2–7', *Bib* 53 (1972), pp. 169–90; J. Goldingay, *Daniel* (WBC 30; Waco: Word, 1989), p. 158. Most of the apocalyptic themes in the prophetic books are also found in the Psalms. See S. Gillingham, 'Psalmody and Apocalyptic in the Hebrew Bible: Common Vision, Shared Experience?', in John Barton & David J. Reimer (eds.), *After the Exile: Essays in Honour of Rex Mason* (Macon, GA: Mercer University Press, 1996), pp. 147–69. Lawrence Boadt thinks that, 'Chiasms are common in Second Isaiah even in units larger than a line'. L. Boadt, 'Isaiah 41.8–13: Notes on Poetic Structure and Style', *CBQ* 35 (1973), pp. 20–34 (29 n. 28).

71.   James Crenshaw states that apart from parallelism, chiasm and *inclusio* are the most common poetic devices in the Psalter. See J. Crenshaw, *The Psalms: An Introduction* (Grand Rapids: Eerdmans, 2001), pp. 96–97.

72.   Peter Craigie remarks that: 'Parallelism and chiasmus are both commonly used poetic devices throughout the Psalm [Ps 2],…which contribute to its literary quality.' P. Craigie, *Psalms 1–50* (WBC; Waco: Word, 1983), p. 65.

73.   See Christopher G. Frechette, 'Chiasm, Reversal and Biblical Reference in 1QH 11.3–18 (=Sukenik Column 3): A Structural Proposal', *JSP* 21 (2000), pp. 71–102 (73).

Iain Provan laments the fact that, 'the tendency has been vastly to under-estimate the influence on Revelation of every part of the Hebrew canon, whether in content, language, structure or style'.[74] This study will seek to rectify such deficiency. It is submitted, therefore, that the language and style of Revelation in general and Rev. 11.1–14.5 in particular, are best analyzed under the rubric of the Old Testament prophets' literary conventions, rhetorical devices and compositional techniques. Among the most common, are parallelism, chiasm, parataxis and parallel structuring.[75] John's artistry in employing parallelism, chiastic arrangement, parataxis and parallel structures shows his use of Hebraic literary techniques as his preferred style. The literary analysis which we propose for Rev. 11.1–14.5 will focus on these Hebraic rhetorical devices employed by John.

c. *The Literal and the Symbolic in Revelation*
We have examined the nature of Revelation's language and style and we may note that the language of Revelation is essentially symbolic as John utilizes images and symbols primarily from the Old Testament stock of imagery.[76] While we agree with Beale that 'the majority of the material in it [the book of Revelation] is revelatory symbolism', one cannot discount the

74. I. Provan, 'Foul Spirits, Fornication and Finance: Revelation 18 from an Old Testament Perspective', *JSNT* 64 (1996), pp. 81–100 (85). Provan is an Old Testament scholar who has written an incisive article on Rev. 18 due to his extensive knowledge of the language and style of the Old Testament from which Rev. 18 draws upon heavily. To the best of my knowledge, no Old Testament scholar has attempted to write a commentary or monograph on any major textual unit of Revelation.

75. J. J. de Heer agrees that Revelation is best viewed as a prophetic work. He writes: 'Jadi Kitab Wahyu adalah sejalan sama sekali dengan para nabi PL, yang mengucapkan Firman Allah, dengan penerapannya kepada zaman mereka sendiri. Berhubung dengan itu, menurut hemat kami, *metode yang paling tepat untuk penafsiran Kitab Wahyu ialah: menafsirkan Kitab Wahyu dengan cara yang sama seperti kita menafsirkan kitab-kitab para nabi dalam PL*.' (ET: So the book of Revelation is similar to the Old Testament prophets who spoke the Word of God with its message to their own generations. In this connection, in our view, *the most correct method for the interpretation of the book of Revelation is: to interpret the book of Revelation in the same way we interpret the prophetic books in the Old Testament*). J. J. de Heer, *Kitab Wahyu* (Jakarta: BPK Gunung Mulia, 2000), p. 11 (his emphasis). Dr. de Heer is a Dutch scholar who has taught in Indonesia since 1966. His recent commentary published in the Indonesian language is the most useful of all Indonesian commentaries surveyed in this thesis. One outstanding feature is that de Heer interacts critically with English and North American as well as European scholarship throughout his commentary. On almost every important topic, he gives a wide range of scholarly opinions before presenting his own views on the issue under discussion. One drawback is that often de Heer does not give the full references for his citations.

76. Given the importance of symbolism in Revelation, it is surprising that not many commentaries deal specifically with this question in any substantial way. For a study of symbolism in the book of Revelation, see N. Lund, *Studies in the Book of Revelation* (Chicago:

fact that John on occasions, as determined from the context, intends his narration of events or characters be understood literally.[77] A vital interpretive issue is how one distinguishes the obviously symbolic language on one hand, and the literal components of Revelation's language, on the other hand. Dale C. Allison Jr rightly notes that, 'it is often no easy task to determine when [in ancient Jewish texts] we are dealing with metaphor or with something literal'.[78] The challenge in hermeneutics is to avoid interpreting an obviously symbolic text literally and conversely the literal symbolically. Even if a textual unit has much symbolism, this does not mean it must be wholly symbolic if the text demands careful distinction between what is literal on one hand, and what is symbolic on the other hand. Allison rightly notes that, 'one can hardly infer from the appearance of parabolic language in one part of the book that it contains nothing else besides parables'.[79] Allison argues that: 'Most eschatological language functions as both sign and symbol; that is, it has a literal referent – it denotes – and a symbolic dimension – it connotes.'[80] The author gives the examples of the beliefs that the Son of Man will come on the clouds and the general resurrection. According to Allison, these events must be viewed literally without denying 'that these events represent: the vindication of Jesus, the triumph of the believers, the judgment of the wicked, the fulfilment of prophecy, etc. The literal and the symbolic need not be sundered.'[81]

A variety of symbols or images are employed in John's literary arsenal to weave the tapestry of the text of Revelation. Thompson writes,

> 'Image' is, I think, the best term to use in describing John's visionary words. A word-image is material and concrete, but at the same time it creates a surplus of meaning, a 'more' that transcends its concrete-

Covenant Press, 1955), esp. ch. 3 'A Study in Symbolism', pp. 28–33; Beale, *John's Use of the Old Testament*, esp. ch. 4 'The Influence of the Old Testament upon the Symbolism of Revelation', pp. 295–317.

77. Beale, *John's Use of the Old Testament*, p. 298.

78. Dale C. Allison Jr., 'Jesus & the Victory of the Apocalyptic', in Carey C. Newman (ed.), *Jesus and the Restoration of Israel: A Critical Assessment of N.T. Wright's Jesus and the Victory of God* (Downers Grove: Inter-Varsity Press, 1999), pp. 126–41 (128). For a study of the language and imagery of the Bible in general, see G. B. Caird, *The Language and Imagery of the Bible* (Philadelphia: Westminster Press, 1980); J. C. L. Gibson, *Language and Imagery in the Old Testament* (London: SPCK, 1998).

79. Dale C. Allison Jr., *Jesus of Nazareth: Millenarian Prophet* (Minneapolis: Fortress Press, 1998), p. 164.

80. Allison, *Jesus of Nazareth*, p. 164.

81. Allison, *Jesus of Nazareth*, p. 164. Allison (pp. 152–71) argues against Caird's and N. T. Wright's views that much of Jesus' eschatological language is metaphorical. See Caird, *Language and Imagery*, pp. 243–71 and N. T. Wright, *The New Testament and the People of God* (Minneapolis: Fortress Press, 1992), pp. 280–338.

ness.... The images should be taken literally. However, they also point
to something more.... By being both concrete and metaphorical
(pointing to something more), John's images should be understood
literally (descriptively) and figuratively (metaphorically). That is, an
image refers to the material object that the word names, and it also
opens an empty space to be filled by the disciplined imagination.[82]

Thompson cites the example of 'clothing' as an image in the book of
Revelation.[83] Various characters are said to be dressed with something or
to wear coloured clothes. For example, the martyred souls under the altar
are dressed in white (Rev. 6.11). Likewise the great multitude that stands
before the throne in the vision of Rev. 7.9–17 are said to be robed in white
and that they have washed their robes and made them white in the blood of
the Lamb (vv. 9, 13–14). When the images are taken literally, Thompson
suggests that they are indeed robed in white according to John's vision but
the image of white robes transcend its concreteness and points to
something more, namely 'white' represents 'pure, godly, victorious,
heavenly, immortal, transfigured, [and] enlightened'.[84] The editors of
Dictionary of Biblical Imagery write:

> An image is any word that names a concrete thing... or action. Any
> object or action that we can picture is an image. Images require two
> activities from us as readers of the Bible. The first is to experience the
> image as literally and in as fully a sensory way as possible. The second is
> to be sensitive to the connotations or overtones of the image.[85]

A symbol is defined as 'an image that stands for something in addition to
its literal meaning'.[86] Thus when we find that John is using symbols in his
communication, the primary meaning of the images lies not in their
literalness or concreteness but in their symbolism or what the images
symbolize. For example, in Rev. 12, it is obvious that John is using the
images of the woman and the dragon as symbols, not to be understood
literally but denoting what the woman and the dragon represent. Lund
comments: 'The correct understanding of a symbol requires that the
distinction between the symbol and the thing symbolized should be drawn
clearly and always maintained in interpretation. Endless confusion results
from disregarding this simple rule.'[87] Further, the editors of *DBI* explain
the meanings of metaphor and simile as follows:

82. Thompson, *Revelation*, p. 36.
83. Thompson, *Revelation*, pp. 35–6.
84. Thompson, *Revelation*, p. 36.
85. Leland Ryken *et al.* (eds.), *Dictionary of Biblical Imagery* (Downers Grove: Inter-
Varsity Press, 1998), p. xiv. Henceforth referred to as *DBI*.
86. *DBI*, p. xiv.
87. Lund, *Studies in the Book of Revelation*, p. 32.

Metaphor and *simile* function much like symbol, and nothing much is lost if these items are used interchangeably. A *metaphor* is an implied comparison. For example, when Paul writes that 'I planted, Apollos watered' (1 Cor. 3.6), he is not speaking of a literal plant. He refers to a figurative planting and watering in the form of proclaiming the Gospel to produce conversion and the teaching of the truth to produce Christian nurture. A *simile* also compares one thing to another, but it makes the comparison explicit using the formula *like* or *as*.[88]

Janet Soskice defines a metaphor as 'that figure of speech whereby we speak about one thing in terms which are seen to be suggestive of another'.[89] P. M. Macky defines a metaphor as 'that figurative way of speaking (and meaning) in which one reality, the Subject, is depicted in terms that are more commonly associated with a different reality, the Symbol, which is related to it by Analogy'.[90] As Lund has observed: 'We should not expect *all* details in a symbol to be meaningful, for some symbols have only a general meaning.'[91] There is ever a danger of over interpretation of symbols when every minute detail of the symbol is taken to refer to something of significance. Throughout this book, we will pay special attention to how symbolism is understood in Rev. 11.1–14.5.

Revelation 11.1–14.5 contains some of the most vivid and striking imagery found in the book of Revelation. The two witnesses are identified as the two olive trees and the two lampstands (11.4). Fire is said to come out of the two witnesses' mouths (11.5). Revelation 12 begins with two signs in heaven – a pregnant woman clothed with the sun with a crown of twelve stars on her head who meets a seven-headed dragon that waits to devour the child soon to be born. Not only is the woman taken to the wilderness by a two-winged eagle (12.14), she is also saved from being swept away by the waters spewed out from the serpent's mouth when the earth comes to her aid and opens its mouth to swallow the waters (12.15–16). Revelation 13 presents two beasts – a beast with seven heads and ten horns rising from the sea and another beast with two horns which looks like a lamb but speaks like a dragon rising from the earth. It is not

---

88. *DBI*, p. xiv.

89. J. Soskice, *Metaphor and Religious Language* (Oxford: Clarendon Press, 1985), p. 15. For a general study on the metaphorical language of the Bible, see J. Soskice, *Speaking in Parables* (repr., London: SCM, 2002).

90. P. M. Macky, *The Centrality of Metaphors to Biblical Thought: A Method for Interpreting the Bible* (Studies in the Bible and Early Christianity; Lewiston: Edwin Mellen Press, 1990), p. 49. See also P. M. Macky, 'More about Metaphors', in A. Orden (ed.), *Metaphor and Thought* (Cambridge: Cambridge University Press, 1979), pp. 19–43.

91. Lund, *Studies in the Book of Revelation*, p. 31.

surprising that it is not easy at times to decipher what the highly symbolic imagery means. More difficult still is to tell when John is speaking literally and when he is making a purely symbolic reference. To further add to the interpretive quagmire, John is quite capable, as we will argue, of speaking literally and symbolically at the same time. To put it simply, John's language can be elusive and contains multi-layered meanings.

As an example we will look briefly at two symbols in the first chapter of Revelation. The seven stars in Jesus' right hand and the seven lampstands in John's inaugural vision are symbols (1.12, 16). They are interpreted as the seven angels and the seven churches respectively (1.20). In this instance John interprets the symbols explicitly. But generally, John does not interpret the symbols or give explanation to a variety of images which he uses. For example, most of the images or symbols in 11.1–14.5 are not further elaborated upon and John appears to assume that his readers who are familiar with the Old Testament should be able to make sense of his symbolic word-images. As the seven lampstands have been interpreted in 1.20 as referring to the seven churches, it seems clear that a lampstand is a symbolic reference for the church. As such, when John speaks of the two witnesses as the two lampstands in 11.4, it is apparent that the two witnesses are churches or representatives of the church. But the identification of the two witnesses is not so clear cut since John identifies them first as the two olive trees and also as the two lampstands. As the two olive trees are not interpreted within Rev. 11 or anywhere else in Revelation, we must turn to the Old Testament reference alluded to by John. We will see that in most instances throughout 11.1–14.5, detecting the clear and also the more subtle and nuanced allusions to the Old Testament, is vital to understanding the rich symbolic and pictorial language of the said literary unit.

In addition, nearly all commentators have noted John's use of numbers in a symbolic way apart from its function as a structural device to mark large units throughout Revelation.[92] We will see that from Rev. 6–16 the vision of the seven seals, the seven trumpets, and the seven bowls make up the largest block of text in the book of Revelation. The number seven is thus a structuring device in John's composition.[93]

The number seven is the most important number in the book of Revelation. It is rich in symbolism. It is a number for completeness,

---

92. See Aune, *Revelation 1–5*, p. xciii–xcv; J. Lambrecht, 'A Structuration of Revelation 4,1–22,5', in J. Lambrecht (ed.), *L'Apocalypse johannique et l'Apocalyptique dans le Nouveau Testament* (BETL, 53; Leuven: Leuven University Press, 1980), pp. 77–104; *idem*, 'The Opening of the Seals (Rev 6,1–8,6)', *Bib* 79 (1998), pp. 198–221.

93. See the discussion on the use of the number seven as a structural marker in our chapter on 'The Literary-Structural Analysis of Rev. 11.1–19'.

perfection, and universality.[94] But the number seven is used literally when John wrote seven messages to the seven churches in Asia Minor. No scholar or serious reader will doubt that the seven letters were intended for the seven local churches or congregations situated in the seven cities of western Asia Minor (modern Turkey) named by John in 1.12 (cf. 1.4, 20; 2–3). Yet almost all scholars think that these seven literal churches stand for the universal church or the whole church.[95] So John's Revelation is not only intended for the seven churches named in Rev. 1–3 but also to the other churches whether they are in Asia Minor or outside of the Asian province. In this instance the use of the number seven can be seen as incorporating both the literal and symbolic meanings. Speaking generally of the relationship between the literal and the symbolic reading of a text, Allison comments: 'A literal reading need not be flat or unimaginative reading. Put otherwise, the literal can be symbolic.'[96] At a theoretical level, it is not easy to describe how a symbol or metaphor works. We will discuss in detail how John intends the images used in Rev. 11.1–14.5 to be understood when we come to the exegesis proper of the textual unit.

It is important to point out that the immediate context within which an image or a symbol is found is likely to determine whether the image or symbol is to be understood literally or symbolically or perhaps even literally *and* symbolically. The immediate context of a passage may demand that an object or image be understood literally and thus should not be spiritualized or interpreted symbolically in the first instance. For example, we will argue that it is best to view the temple, the altar, the worshippers, and the holy city as literal images or objects (Rev. 11.1–2). Likewise the nations that will trample over the holy city and the two witnesses who are to prophesy are events that should be understood literally (11.2–3). By literal we mean that the temple mentioned in Rev. 11.1 is the physical temple in Jerusalem and that the nations are really nations of the world that will conquer the holy city,

94. See A. Yarbro Collins, 'Number Symbolism in Jewish and Early Christian Apocalyptic Literature', in A. Yarbro Collins, *Cosmology and Eschatology in Jewish and Christian Apocalypticism* (Leiden: E. J. Brill, 1996), pp. 55–138; François Bovon, 'Names and Numbers in Early Christianity', *NTS* 47 (2001), pp. 267–88.

95. For example, James Resseguie comments that: 'John opens Revelation with a reference to seven churches (1.4) which represents the complete church'. J. Resseguie, *Revelation Unsealed* (Leiden: E. J. Brill, 1998), p. 58. Also Vanni comments that, 'the symbolic number seven [the seven churches] confers a character of totality and universality'. Vanni, 'The Liturgical Dialogue', p. 355. Allison A. Trites writes: 'The number seven is used symbolically to indicate the church at large…. John used the number seven to point to the fact that his message is addressed to the whole church.' A. A. Trites, *The New Testament Concept of Witness* (SNTSMS, 31; Cambridge: Cambridge University Press, 1977), p. 165.

96. Allison, 'Jesus and the Victory of the Apocalyptic', p. 132.

Jerusalem.[97] Further, we will argue that the term 'Mount Zion' in 14.1 literally denotes the temple mount of the city of Jerusalem but it has a much wider symbolic connotation. Mount Zion represents the dwelling place of God, the place where God reigns and defeats his enemies and the place for the eschatological gathering of God's people in the new age.[98] So before one decides how to interpret a passage or textual unit (whether it is literal or symbolic or both literal and symbolic) which contains various images or symbols, it is essential to first determine the setting, genre, and the immediate context of the passage in question.

d. *E. Schüssler Fiorenza, James Muilenburg and Rhetorical Criticism*[99]

In the revised edition of her seminal study on the book of Revelation, Schüssler Fiorenza argued that she had advocated a 'rhetorical approach to Revelation'[100] since the publication of her book in 1985. Specifically, she calls for a 'concentric, conic-spiraling' approach to the book of Revelation.[101] But our discussion of rhetorical analysis must begin with James Muilenburg's method of rhetorical criticism.[102] Muilenburg in his Presidential address to the Society of Biblical Literature entitled 'Form Criticism and Beyond' argued for the importance of studying the text as it stands from a literary-structural (rhetorical) perspective. Muilenburg propounded thus:

> What I am interested in, above all, is in understanding the nature of Hebrew literary composition, in exhibiting the structural patterns that are employed for the fashioning of a literary unit, whether in poetry or in prose, and in discerning the many and various devices by which the predications are formulated and ordered into a unified whole. Such an enterprise I should describe as rhetoric and the methodology as rhetorical criticism.[103]

97. We will discuss this point in detail in our chapter 3 'A Literary-Structural Analysis of Rev. 11.1–19'.

98. This point will be argued in detail in chapter 5 of this thesis.

99. For the purposes of this thesis, the term 'rhetorical criticism' or 'rhetorical analysis' is subsumed under our wider discussion on 'literary analysis'.

100. Schüssler Fiorenza, *The Book of Revelation*, p. 211. See the 'Epilogue: The Rhetoricality of Apocalpyse and the Politics of Interpretation', pp. 205–36.

101. Schüssler Fiorenza, *The Book of Revelation*, p. 207.

102. An excellent summary of the impact of James Muilenburg on rhetorical criticism from 1968–1997 is found in J. Lundbom, *Jeremiah: A Study in Ancient Hebrew Rhetoric* (Winona Lake: Eisenbrauns, 2nd edn, 1997), pp. xix–xliii, esp. xxvi–xxxiii.

103. J. Muilenburg, 'Form Criticism and Beyond', *JBL* 88 (1969), pp. 1–18 (8). As the title of his address suggests, Muilenburg stressed the need to move beyond Form Criticism and take the final text as it stands as a worthy subject of inquiry by way of investigating all the rhetorical devices employed to produce the final text. He writes (p. 6): 'Perhaps more serious is the skepticism of all attempts to read a pericope in its historical context. The truth is that in a

We prefer to call our study a literary analysis as our main emphasis will be on discerning firstly the literary structure of the text and how this structure, fashioned by various literary features and devices (the chief of which are *inclusio*, parallelism and chiasm), convey meaning. Kennedy puts it thus:

> If rhetorical criticism is to be valid, it must be practiced with some awareness of the traditions of Jewish speech, of which chiasmus is one, and if it is to be useful it must embrace more than style. If fundamental and universal features of rhetoric are kept in mind and if we seek to use them in describing the logical and structural features of the text before us, rather than simply quarrying a text for examples of classical figures, we can significantly enhance our appreciation of its meaning without violence to the author's intent. The ultimate goal of rhetorical analysis, briefly put, is the discovery of the author's intent and of how that is transmitted through a text to an audience.[104]

Rhetorical criticism, according to I. Kikawada, is the study of the Hebrew Bible 'from a synchronistic perspective, in an effort to appreciate the received text and to describe not only what the text says but also how it conveys the message'.[105] Our literary analysis is not interested only in

---

vast number of instances we are indeed left completely in the dark as to the occasion in which the words were spoken, and it is reasonable to assume that it was not the primary interest to the compilers of traditions.' Since 1969, Muilenburg's proposed method of rhetorical criticism has influenced numerous studies of the Hebrew Bible utilising rhetorical criticism. See the collection of essays and articles following Muilenburg's footsteps in Paul R. House (ed.), *Form Criticism and Beyond* (Winona Lake: Eisenbrauns, 1992). Some biblical scholars who are influenced by Muilenburg's proposals, nevertheless, prefer to call the method literary criticism. So Cheryl J. Exum, 'Promise and Fulfilment: Narrative Art in Judges 13', *JBL* 99 (1980), pp. 43–59 (44 n. 5). But George Kennedy prefers to distinguish between rhetorical criticism proper and literary criticism. G. Kennedy, *New Testament Interpretation Through Rhetorical Criticism* (Chapel Hill, NC: University of North Carolina Press, 1984), pp. 4–5. Literary criticism can be confused with the study of literary sources. Also Holladay writes as follows: 'rhetorical criticism analyses what is unique and distinctive about a given unit of material, and therefore a description of its rhetorical forms must proceed inductively, on the basis of the specificities before us. So, most simply, I can say: we shall be looking for repetition, parallels, and contrasts in words, phrases, syntax, and other structures, to see what they can teach us.' Holladay, *The Architecture of Jeremiah 1–20*, p. 21.

104. Kennedy, *New Testament Interpretation*, p. 12. We would qualify Kennedy's apparent optimism in discovering the 'author's intent' despite the best endeavours at close reading and detecting rhetorical features of the text. Yarbro Collins states: 'I would agree that full explanatory power should not be given to the author's intention. What the author *intended to say* and what he or she actually *said* may not always fully coincide. I would also agree that a text has its own symbolic coherence, that it proposes a way of looking at things. By being committed to writing and being preserved and circulated beyond its original situation, a text is, in a sense, cut loose from the existential, historical situation in which it emerged.' Yarbro Collins, *Crisis & Catharsis*, p. 19 (her emphasis).

105. I. Kikawada, 'Some Proposals for the Definition of Rhetorical Criticism', *Semitics* 5 (1977), pp. 67–91 (67).

ascertaining the literary features of the text but also in how the text seeks to persuade the audience. For the purposes of this book, literary analysis as practised here includes an examination of the *rhetoric* of the text by which it functions to persuade the readers.[106]

As we have shown that Revelation's text follows the style of Old Testament in general and the prophetic books in particular, Muilenburg's rhetorical method is a useful starting point in our study. Hence, it is necessary to quote him at some length. After noting the significance of 'structural patterns' and setting out the methodology as rhetorical criticism, he goes on to state that the first concern of a rhetorical critic is to:

> Define the limits or scope of the literary unit, to recognize precisely where and how it begins, and where and how it ends. He will be quick to observe the formal rhetorical devices that are employed, but more important, the substance or content of these most strategic loci.... The delimitation of the passage is essential if we are to learn how its major motif, usually stated at the beginning, is resolved. The latter point is of special importance because no rhetorical feature is more conspicuous and frequent among poets and narrators of ancient Israel than the proclivity to bring the successive predications to their culmination. One must admit that the problem is not always simple because within a single literary unit we may have and often do have several points of climax. But to construe each of these as a conclusion to the poem is to disregard its structure, to resolve it into fragments, and to obscure the relation of the successive strophes to each other. This mistaken procedure has been followed by many scholars, and with unfortunate consequences.[107]

The major motif of Rev. 11.1–14.5 focuses on the temple mentioned in the beginning of the unit and culminates in the restoration of the Temple, which we will argue is described in the scene atop Mount Zion in 14.1. It is precisely this failure to recognize where a literary unit begins and ends that has led scholars to divide up ch. 11 of Revelation into various fragments. Failure to note successive links from one chapter to another (from Rev.

---

106. For a discussion of the recent development in rhetorical criticism, see Anders Eriksson, Thomas H. Olbright and Walter Übelacker (eds.), *Rhetorical Argumentation in Biblical Texts. Essays from the Lund 2000 Conference* (Emory Studies in Early Christianity; Trinity Press Interntional, 2002). See also Martin Kessler, 'A Methodological Setting for Rhetorical Criticism', in David J. A. Clines *et al.* (eds.), *Art and Meaning: Rhetoric in Biblical Literature* (JSOTSup, 19; Sheffield: JSOT Press, 1982), pp. 1–19, and Wilhelm Wueller, 'Where is Rhetorical Criticism Taking Us?', *CBQ* 49 (1987), pp. 448–63. See also Vernon K. Robbins, 'The Present and Future of Rhetorical Analysis', in Stanley E. Porter and Thomas H. Olbricht (eds.), *The Rhetorical Analysis of Scripture: Essays from the London Conference* (Sheffield: Sheffield Academic Press, 1997), pp. 24–52.

107. Muilenburg, 'Form Criticism and Beyond', p. 9.

10–14) with clear structural devices at the beginning and end of each chapter (esp. Rev. 11–12) has also led many scholars totally to disassociate Rev. 11 from Rev. 12. Muilenburg enunciates a number of ways to define the limits or scope of the literary unit. First, he proposes that often there is

> the presence of climactic or ballast lines, which may indeed appear at several junctures within a pericope, but at the close have an emphasis which bears the burden of the entire unit…. The second clue for determining the scope of a pericope is to discern the relation of beginning and end, where the opening words are repeated or paraphrased at the close, what is known as ring composition, or … the *inclusio*.[108]

It is important to note with Kennedy that we cannot rely on chapter divisions or the paragraphing of modern translations to delineate a literary unit. Kennedy writes,

> [Here] we must experiment by seeking the signs of opening and closure (for which the term *inclusio* is sometimes used), of proem and epilogue. Of course we must not rely on chapter divisions, since they are work of later editors and not a part of the original text. Often the paragraphing of modern editions and translations will be found rhetorically faulty.[109]

---

108. Muilenburg, 'Form Criticism and Beyond', p. 9.

109. Kennedy, *New Testament Interpretation*, p. 34. While Kennedy attempts to utilize rhetorical criticism to understand New Testament texts, we are not wholly convinced that the Graeco-Roman rhetorical categories listed by Kennedy (judicial, deliberative, and epideictic [p. 19]) are applicable to the study of the book of Revelation, which aligns itself closer to the prophetic works of the Old Testament. Note that in Kennedy's work no examples are given from the book of Revelation. It appears that the rhetorical criticism proposed by Kennedy is more suited to the study of the gospels and the (esp. Pauline) Epistles. For an attempt at using rhetorical criticism to analyse a prophetic-apocalyptic text in the New Testament, see C. Clifton Black, 'An Oration at Olivet: Some Rhetorical Dimensions of Mark 13', in Duane F. Watson (ed.), *Persuasive Artistry: Studies in the New Testament Rhetoric in Honor of George A. Kennedy* (Sheffield: Sheffield Academic Press, 1991), pp. 66–92, and Gregory L. Bloomquist, 'Rhetorical Argumentation and the Culture of Apocalyptic: A Socio-Rhetorical Analysis of Luke 21', in Stanley E. Porter and Dennis L. Stamps (eds.), *The Rhetorical Interpretation of Scripture* (JSNTSup, 180; Sheffield: Sheffield Academic Press, 1999), pp. 173–209. Note again that no essay there focuses on the book of Revelation. Most essays concentrate on Pauline epistles. Stanley E. Porter argues that, 'it is difficult to establish what and how much Paul could have known [of the rhetorical categories] on a conscious or formal basis'. Stanley E. Porter, 'Theoretical Justification for the Application of Rhetorical Categories to Pauline Epistolary Literature', in Stanley E. Porter and Thomas H. Olbricht (eds.), *Rhetoric and the New Testament: Essays from the 1992 Heidelberg Conference* (JSNTSup, 90; Sheffield: JSOT Press, 1993), pp. 100–22 (105). Porter criticizes Kennedy's assertion that the Graeco-Roman rhetorical categories are applicable to all discourse. Porter (p. 106) writes: 'This is the extent of Kennedy's "argument": the simple assertion that the categories of classical oratory are applicable to all discourse, with no reference to any ancient sources or precedents for their analytical use.'

It is pertinent to bear Kennedy's observations in mind as we will show that the chapter divisions and various paragraphings over these middle chapters of Revelation in most Greek and English texts are rhetorically faulty.

Applying Muilenburg's and Kennedy's proposals, the *inclusio* of the said unit is the Temple/Mount Zion word-pair found in the opening words of the unit and repeated at the close in Rev. 14.1–5. Within this larger chiasm, the mention of the temple of God in Rev. 11.1 and the end of the chapter (11.19) is probably also intended by John to serve as an *inclusio*, a literary device (Muilenburg calls it a rhetorical device) framing the whole of Rev. 11 as a literary unit. In fact, it is our contention that the temple in 11.1 is repeated at 14.1 not by the same word but a conventional word-pair, a word which would have been immediately recognizable to a Hebrew/ Christian audience as paralleled to the temple, namely the term 'Mount Zion'. John Breck writes:

> as with all forms of parallelism, the tendency is not merely to repeat or reflect in A' what was already stated in A. Rather, inclusion incorporates an element of *intensification* from A to A', such that the conclusion is 'more than' the beginning: it rounds out or fulfills the major theme(s) of the passage as a whole.... Inclusion, then, is not merely a practical device used to facilitate the telling or reading of an element of tradition. It serves to *complete* that tradition as well as to frame it. Accordingly, analysis of the movement from the first to the second element of an inclusion (from A to A') is essential for discerning the meaning of the entire passage.[110]

Thus we submit that the word-pair, the temple of God (A) /Mt. Zion (A') frames the textual unit of Rev. 11.1–14.5 as a distinct and unified literary whole. We will argue that the temple of God under attack by hostile nations at the beginning of the three-and-a-half years (A) [Rev. 11.1–2] will be liberated by the Lamb and his 144,000 companions on Mount Zion at the end of the three-and-a-half year period (A') [Rev. 14.1–5].

After citing various examples in which this literary phenomenon of *inclusio* is readily seen in the Bible, Muilenburg states as follows:

> The second major concern of the rhetorical critic is to recognize the structure of a composition and to discern the configuration of its component parts, to delineate the warp and woof out of which the literary fabric is woven, and to note the various rhetorical devices that are employed for marking, on the one hand, the sequence and

---

110. J. Breck, *The Shape of Biblical Language: Chiasmus in the Scriptures and Beyond* (Crestwood, New York: St. Vladimir's Seminary Press, 1994), p. 33 (his emphasis).

movement of the pericope, and on the other, the shifts or breaks in the development of the writer's thought.[111]

We see it as our task to discern the configuration of the component parts in Rev. 11.1–14.5, the literary fabric in which 11.1–14.5 is woven and to note various literary (rhetorical) devices employed for marking the sequence and movement of the pericope as well as the shifts or breaks in the development of this unit of text under consideration. Among a number of rhetorical devices discussed by Muilenburg, the notion of *repetition* deserves special mention. Muilenburg expresses it thus:

> Repetition serves many and diverse functions in the literary composition of ancient Israel....The repeated words or lines do not appear haphazardly or fortuitously, but rather in rhetorically significant collocations. This phenomenon is to be explained perhaps in many instances by the originally spoken provenance of the passage, or by its employment in cultic celebrations, or, indeed, by the speaking mentality of the ancient Israelite. It served as an effective mnemonic device. It is the key word which may often guide us in our isolation of a literary unit, which gives to it its unity and focus, which helps us to articulate the structure of the composition, and to discern the pattern or texture into which the words are woven. It is noteworthy that repetitions are most abundant in crucial contexts.[112]

The use of repetition of the key word 'city' is vital in Rev. 11 as this key word delineates 11.1–13 as a major literary sub-unit focusing on the ministry of the two witnesses. The key word appears in crucial contexts. First, the statement that the nations trample upon the holy *city* (11.1–2) provides the context and setting for the introduction of the two witnesses (11.3). Secondly, at the end of their testimony, the two witnesses meet their deaths in the great *city* (11.8). Finally in another crucial context, the resurrection and ascension of the two witnesses are followed immediately by an earthquake that destroys a tenth of the *city* (11.13) at which point in time, the two witnesses vanish out of sight and make their exit from the text. Robert Alter comments thus:

> One of the most imposing barriers that stands between the modern reader and the imaginative subtlety of biblical narrative is the extraordinary prominence of verbatim repetition in the Bible.... Repetition is, I would guess, the feature of biblical narrative that looks most 'primitive' to the casual modern eye, reflecting, we may imagine, a

---

111. Muilenburg, 'Form Criticism and Beyond', p. 10.
112. Muilenburg, 'Form Criticism and Beyond', p. 17. For another incisive article on repetition, see J. Muilenburg, 'Hebrew Rhetoric: Repetition and Style', in G. W. Anderson *et al.* (eds.), *Congress Volume* (Leiden: E. J. Brill, 1953), pp. 97–111.

mentality alien to our own and a radically different approach to ordering experience from ones familiar to us.[113]

He goes on to state that: 'The repetition of single words or brief phrases often exhibits a frequency, a saliency, and a thematic significance quite unlike what we are accustomed to from other narrative traditions.'[114] Mary Douglas observes that: 'By disregarding deliberate repetitions, signals for reading the conventional structures are missed.'[115] For example, the announcement that the kingdom of this world has become the possession of the Lord and of his Christ in Rev. 11.15 is affirmed in similar terms in 12.10: 'Now the salvation and power and the kingdom of our God and the authority of his Christ have come.' The theme of God's rule coming on earth links chs. 11 and 12 of Revelation unmistakably.[116] Failure to perceive these clear linkages, besides other lexical and thematic parallels in Rev. 11–12 has led most scholars into 'unfortunate consequences' of separating Rev. 11 and Rev. 12. We will say more about the function of repetition when we come to the exegesis proper in a later chapter.

Apart from Muilenburg, Kennedy and Alter, Meir Sternberg's influential *The Poetics of Biblical Narrative* requires some discussion. Sternberg, in line with what we have discussed above, argues that for any interpretation of a text, certain literary components must be evaluated and recognized for their rhetorical functions. He lists the following as the most important:

1. Temporal ordering, especially where the actual sequence diverges from the chronological.
2. Analogical design: parallelism, contrast, variation, recurrence, symmetry, chiasm.
3. Point of view, e.g., the teller's powers and manipulation, shifts in perspective from external to internal rendering or from narration to monologue and dialogue.
4. Representational proportions: scene, summary, repetition.
5. Informational gapping and ambiguity.
6. Strategies of characterization and judgement.
7. Modes of coherence, in units ranging from a verse to a book.

---

113.   R. Alter, *The Art of Biblical Narrative* (New York: Basic Books, 1981), p. 88.

114.   Alter, *The Art of Biblical Narrative*, p. 179.

115.   M. Douglas, 'The Poetic Structure in Leviticus', in David P. Wright, David Noel Freedman and Avi Hurvitz (eds.), *Pomegranates & Golden Bells: Studies in Biblical, Jewish, and Near Eastern Ritual, Law, and Literature in Honor of Jacob Milgrom* (Winona Lake: Eisenbrauns, 1995), pp. 239–56 (245).

116.   Other mentions of 'kingdom' in Revelation do not deal with the fact of the kingdom *coming* or *having come* (cf. 1.9; 5.10).

8. The interplay of verbal and compositional patterns.[117]

Sternberg's list of eight literary components is important for our study as the temporal ordering of most of Rev. 11.1–14.5 diverges from the chronological as we will argue that most events described therein are contemporaneous with one another set within time references of three-and-a-half years or three-and-a-half days or after three-and-a-half days. It can be said that the blocks of texts in question are designed analogically with heavy use of parallelism, contrast, symmetry, and chiasm throughout. The shift from dialogue to monologue separates Rev. 10.11–11.3 and 11.4ff. There is informational gapping and some ambiguity as the location of the two witnesses' appearance is not made explicit.[118] Strategies of characterization feature large in the portrayal of the main protagonists, the two witnesses and the two beasts, the woman and the dragon and finally the use of the formula 'I saw' to introduce three animals – two *Beasts* (cf. 13.1, 11) and a *Lamb* (14.1). We will see that John creatively and artistically uses many literary and rhetorical devices as modes of coherence from verse or sentence level to a passage or pericope and larger units of texts.

We have noted earlier that among the chief literary structural devices employed in Rev. 11.1–14.5 are *inclusio*, parallelism and chiasm. As we have already discussed how *inclusio* works, now we will briefly examine the compositional technique called parallelism.

What is 'parallelism'? It is not our purpose to give a detailed summary of the nature and function of parallelism except to highlight some general principles and features that will serve as guidelines to our study of Rev. 11.1–14.5. According to Edward Greenstein, parallelism 'describes a very particular structural relationship between two lines...the repetition of a syntactic pattern'.[119] William Holladay describes a typical parallelism as one 'in which a second line renews or reinforces the first line by a synonymous or supplementing image'.[120] Parallelism is commonly under-

---

117. M. Sternberg, *The Poetics of Biblical Narrative: Ideological Literature and the Drama of Reading* (Bloomington: Indiana University Press, 1985), p. 39.

118. Informational gapping occurs where the author purposefully leaves out a detail which is intended to be filled in by the readers. This literary technique encourages the readers' response and participation in the interpretation of the text. Although it is not explicitly stated where the two witnesses will appear, the text encourages the readers to connect the episode of the nations' trampling on the holy city (Rev. 11.2) with the appearance of the two witnesses (11.3) in the same place, namely Jerusalem, the holy city. This point will be argued in detail in our literary analysis of 11.2–3.

119. Edward L. Greenstein, 'How Does Parallelism Mean?', in *A Sense of Text: The Art of Language in the Study of Biblical Literature* (Philadelphia: The Dropsie College, 1982), pp. 41–70 (44).

120. W. Holladay, *Jeremiah: Spokesman Out of Time* (Philadelphia: United Church Press, 1975), p. 31.

stood as consisting of two lines (A and B), where A makes a statement or begins a clause or sentence which is 'completed' by B. B acts far more than just a 'seconding element' to A. William Brownlee, another eminent Hebrew scholar who writes, 'I believe that the love of parallelism to be characteristic of Hebrew literature, not merely in poetic verse structure but also in larger units'.[121]

James Kugel defines the concept of parallelism as follows: 'A is so, and *what's more* B.'[122] Kugel argues that: 'B was connected to A, had something in common with it, but was not expected to be (nor regarded as) mere restatement... B will have an *emphatic* character... its very reassertion is a kind of strengthening and reinforcing.'[123] A and B are rarely identical, and B functions to add, expand and complete what is said in A either affirming the same idea or as a way of contrast and antithesis. Kugel cites many examples to show that, 'the ways of parallelism are numerous and varied, and the intensity of the semantic parallelism established between clauses might be said to range from "zero perceivable correspondence" to "near-zero perceivable differentiation" (i.e. just short of word-for-word repetition)'.[124]

It suffices to note with Kugel that, 'biblical lines are parallelistic not because B is meant to be a parallel of A, but because B typically *supports* A, carries it further, backs it up, completes it, goes beyond it'.[125] To R. Alter, in parallelism, the line B serves to *intensify* line A. Often there is a *heightening* effect from A to B. Alter uses terms like specification, focusing, heightening, and emphatic repetition to describe the relationship between A and B.[126] There is nearly always 'dynamic movement within the line' where the second verset 'becomes a focusing, a heightening, a concretization of the original material'.[127] Such a structural relationship creates a *correspondence* between A and B, a feature that is rightly seen as

---

121. W. Brownlee, *The Meaning of Qumran Scrolls for the Bible with Special Attention to the Book of Isaiah* (New York: Oxford University Press, 1964), p. 257. See also Elmer A. Martens, 'Narrative Parallelism and Message in Jeremiah 34–38', in Craig A. Evans & William F. Stinespring (eds.), *Early Jewish and Christian Exegesis: Studies in Memory of William Hugh Brownlee* (Atlanta: Scholars Press, 1987), pp. 33–49 (34).

122. J. Kugel, *The Idea of Biblical Poetry: Parallelism and Its History* (New Haven: Yale University Press, 1981), p. 1.

123. Kugel, *The Idea of Biblical Poetry*, p. 8 (his emphasis).

124. Kugel, *The Idea of Biblical Poetry*, p. 7. See the list of examples cited by Kugel (pp. 3–7).

125. Kugel, *The Idea of Biblical Poetry*, p. 52.

126. R. Alter, *The Art of Biblical Poetry* (New York: Basic Books, 1985), pp. 62–64.

127. R. Alter, 'The Characteristics of Ancient Hebrew Poetry', in Robert Alter and Frank Kermode (eds.), *Literary Guide to the Bible* (Cambridge, Mass.; Harvard University Press, 1987), pp. 611–24 (616).

foundational in any parallelism. 'They [the workings of parallelism] strongly establish the feeling of correspondence between A and B.'[128]

Finally, parallelism (particularly so within a chiasm) is a useful device to delimit small and large units. Kugel writes that, 'B [i.e. the line/verset B after A] has a closural quality that allows it to break discourse into fairly short units, organizing the flow of clauses into twos and threes'.[129]

It is not within the purview of this thesis to discuss the full range of ways in which parallelism works.[130] How parallelism functions for the text of Rev. 11.1–14.5 will be amply shown throughout our subsequent exegesis. For our purposes, Kugel's and Alter's understandings of the basic idea of parallelism are adopted as giving the general guideline as to the workings of parallelism.

5. *The Macro-Chiasm*

We have already noted that Revelation is unique among New Testament books in that 'poetical parallelism' pervades the texture of the book.[131] Other scholars have long noted that the literary device of the *chiasm* or *chiasmus*[132] is a compositional technique favoured by John. Chiasm is a literary device where the basic concept is 'that of a symmetrical structure involving an inverted order of corresponding lines'.[133] As such, a chiasm is a specific and unique form of parallelism where corresponding parallel elements are structured in reverse order.[134] If a simple parallel line has A and then, B, a chiasm is structured in a shape resembling the Greek letter χ

---

128.   Kugel, *The Idea of Biblical Poetry*, p. 29.

129.   Kugel, *The Idea of Biblical Poetry*, p. 55.

130.   See also A. Berlin, *The Dynamics of Biblical Parallelism* (Bloomington: University of Indiana Press, 1985); *idem*, 'Motif and Creativity in Biblical Poetry', *Prooftexts* 3 (1983), pp. 231–41; Wilfred G. E. Watson, *Classical Hebrew Poetry: A Guide to its Techniques* (JSOTSup, 26; Sheffield JSOT Press, 1984), and *idem*, 'Problems and Solutions in Hebrew Verse: A Survey of Recent Work', *VT* 93 (1993), pp. 372–84.

131.   See Charles, *Lectures on the Apocalypse*, p. 41. See also Alter, 'The Characteristics of Ancient Hebrew Poetry', p. 611.

132.   For the purposes of this book, chiasm or chiasmus will be used interchangeably.

133.   John D. Harvey, *Listening to the Text* (Grand Rapids: Baker Book House, 1998), p. 99.

134.   Kugel writes: '[But] chiasmus in Hebrew...ought rightly not to be separated from the context of parallelism itself...it is truly a concomitant of the binary structure of parallelistic sentences, and it therefore represents a decision *not to parallel* the word order of A.' Kugel, *The Idea of Biblical Poetry*, p. 19 (his emphasis).

(chi) from which the figure derives its name:[135]

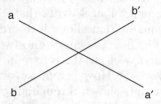

Although, chiasms will be noted throughout our study, Rev. 11.1–14.5 is structured not by a simple chiasm as shown above but by an 'extended chiasm' or 'macro-chiasm'.[136] Within this proposed extended chiasm, we will also show that there are many smaller chiasms.[137] Of the many literary devices and structural patterns employed by biblical writers, perhaps the most challenging pattern is the one called 'concentric symmetry'. Harvey describes this pattern, also called 'extended chiasm', as involving *'multiple, inverse correspondences that extend over a considerable expanse of material and having a single element at the center'*.[138] Milgrom argues that while simple chiasm may be a purely aesthetic device, the extended chiasm, which Milgrom calls 'introversion' can have didactic implications.[139]

Nils Lund is the most influential author of the modern era who has argued for the prevalence of chiasm as a compositional technique among New Testament authors.[140] Lund argued the book of Revelation was structured chiastically. He also demonstrated that chiasm or chiastic patterns were found regularly in several levels of the text: from the level of a micro-unit of a sentence or a passage to the macro-unit of a large block

135.   Harvey, *Listening to the Text*, p. 99.

136.   This term 'macro-chiasm' is used by Wayne Brouwer in his book on *The Literary Development of John 13–17: A Chiastic Reading* (SBLDS, 182; Atlanta: Society Biblical Literature, 2000). For the purposes of this book, macro-chiasm or extended chiasm is used interchangeably. Macro-chiasm or extended chiasm can be seen as a form of distant parallelism between corresponding pairs.

137.   John Welch notes that often smaller chiasms are to be found within an extended chiasm. See J. Welch, (ed.), *Chiasmus in Antiquity: Structure, Analyses, Exegesis* (Hildesheim: Gerstenberg Verlag, 1981), p. 13.

138.   Harvey, *Listening to the Text*, p. 104. Kennedy comments thus: 'In the Old Testament passages are often composed chiastically, with the parts arranged in a sequence of A, B, C, . . . C', B', A'. This elaborated chiasmus is also found as a compositional technique in Greek as early as Homer and is again very common in Latin poetry of the Augustan period, but it is ignored by classical rhetoricians and literary critics alike.' Kennedy, *New Testament Interpretation*, pp. 27–28.

139.   Milgrom, *Numbers*, p. xxii.

140.   See N. Lund, *Chiasmus in the New Testament: A Study in Formgeschichte* (repr., Peabody, MA: Hendrickson, 1992).

of text that may extend over several chapters.[141] It is unfortunate that Lund's analysis of Revelation has not received the attention that it deserved from commentators on the book.[142] It is perhaps the perceived subjectivity involved in identifying intricate structures over large blocks of materials, let alone the whole book, which has led to scepticism among scholars. In this section, we will firstly discuss the nature and function of chiasm and then propose a rigorous and exacting standard as to how a macro-chiasm can be discerned. We intend to apply this standard rigorously to test our proposed concentric chiasm in Rev. 11.1–14.5.

Lund propounded seven laws of chiastic structures, which have been taken up, critiqued and refined by later scholars. Lund summarized the seven 'laws' as follows:[143]

1. *The centre is always the turning point.* The centre may consist of one, two, three or even four lines.

2. At the centre there is often a change in the trend of thought, and an antithetic idea is introduced. This is called the *law of the shift at the centre.*

3. Identical ideas are often distributed in such a fashion that *they occur in the extremes and at the centre* of their respective system, and nowhere else in the system.

4. There are also many instances of ideas, occurring at the centre of one system and recurring in the extremes of a corresponding system, the second system evidently having been constructed to match the first. We shall call this feature *the law of the shift from the centre to the extremes.*

5. There is a definite tendency of certain terms to gravitate toward certain positions within a given system.

6. Larger units are frequently introduced and concluded by *frame-passages.*[144]

7. There is frequently a mixture of chiastic and alternating lines within one and the same unit.

---

141. Lund, *Studies in the Book of Revelation.*

142. Aune's recent 3 volume commentary did not even mention Lund's work once! Beale is more generous in the space afforded to Lund as Lund's work is cited in a few footnotes. Beale writes of Lund's chiastic interpretation: 'Some of Lund's analyses of various segments are illuminating' but he does not specify which ones. Beale, *Revelation*, pp. 111–12 n. 28. Kennedy, an eminent literary critic describes Lund's book, *Chiasmus in the New Testament* as an 'important work' in the field of rhetorical criticism in the New Testament. See Kennedy, *New Testament Interpretation*, p. 11.

143. Lund, *Chiasmus in the New Testament*, pp. 40–41 (his emphasis).

144. As we will see, Rev. 10.11 and Rev. 14.6–7 frame Rev. 11.1–14.5.

A number of scholars have followed Lund's lead in seeing chiasm as a vital compositional technique in the New Testament.[145] The most significant monograph for our purposes is written by John Breck entitled *The Shape of Biblical Language: Chiasmus in the Scriptures and Beyond* in which he argues cogently for the necessity and importance of identifying the literary structure of a unit for a proper interpretation of a biblical text. Breck in particular extends and builds on the work of Lund and previous scholars in this area and argues that chiasm is a persistent compositional device employed by virtually all biblical authors. It is so pervasive throughout the Bible that Scripture, so argues Breck, must be read chiastically.[146] 'Read "chiastically", the Scriptures reveal a beauty and vitality that is otherwise lost.'[147] Nevertheless, Douglas notes that, '[the] modern convention of reading requires a strong linear connection'.[148] If a chiastic pattern is glossed over in favour of our modern [Western] linear reading to the neglect of an intended structural pattern, then our reading of the text as a whole will be much poorer. Douglas proposes that, 'we [should] consciously subdue our own interest in strict linear sequence in favor of a cultivated interest in the links of each part with the whole'.[149]

Breck reduces Lund's seven 'laws' into four principles:[150]

1.   *Chiastic units are framed by inclusion.*[151]

This is nearly equivalent to Lund's sixth 'law' but subtle differences in theory and application must be noted. Lund notes that larger units are normally introduced and concluded by *frame-passages*.[152] By *frame-passages*, Lund appears to mean that an extended chiasm (a large unit) is normally preceded by a passage which introduces the unit and another

145.   For example, see I. Thomson, *Chiasmus in the Pauline Letters* (JSNTSup, 111; Sheffield: Sheffield Academic Press, 1995); Harvey, *Listening to the Text*; Welch (ed.), *Chiasmus in Antiquity*.

146.   Breck writes: 'Hardly a commentary appears today that does not at least note the presence of isolated chiastic micro-units, since they occur in virtually every book of the canon.' Breck, *The Shape of Biblical Language*, p. 334. One cannot fail to be impressed by the multiple examples set forth by Breck in his book to prove his case. It is unfortunate that Breck does not delve much into the book of Revelation.

147.   Breck, *The Shape of Biblical Language*, p. iv.

148.   Douglas, 'The Poetic Structure in Leviticus', p. 243. Douglas commented positively on Milgrom's identification of chiasm and parallelism as the two most influential literary devices to unravel the structure and theology of the book of Numbers.

149.   Douglas, 'Poetic Structure in Leviticus', p. 244. Though Douglas' proposal deals with her reading of the book of Leviticus, it is equally valid, in our view, for our reading of Revelation.

150.   Breck, *The Shape of Biblical Language*, pp. 335–39 (Breck's four principles are given in italics).

151.   Breck, *The Shape of Biblical Language*, p. 335.

152.   Lund, *Chiasmus in the New Testament*, p. 41.

passage following the unit and functioning to conclude it. These frame passages may not be a component part of the larger unit (an extended chiasm) but they are related to the larger unit in that they provide the rhetorical context and an envelope-like closure to the said unit. These frame-passages together form the larger framework within which the unit is interpreted. On other occasions, the extreme lines of an extended chiasmus serve as an *inclusio* and therefore function to frame the unit concerned. In these instances, the *inclusio* is part and parcel of the larger unit and is an intricate component of the unit as a whole.[153]

2. *The central element* (or pair of elements) *serves as the pivot and/or thematic focus of the entire unit.*[154]
3. *A heightening effect occurs from the first parallel line or strophe to its prime complement.*[155]
4. *The resultant concentric or spiral parallelism, with progressive intensification from the extremities inward, produces a helical movement that draws the reader/hearer toward the thematic center.*[156]

While the first three principles are commonly noted with minor variations, the fourth principle proposed by Breck is probably his most significant contribution to the discussion of chiastic structure as a literary device thus far. We will see how Breck's fourth principle helps to advance our exegesis of Rev. 11.1–14.5. More significantly, Breck concludes that certain 'hermeneutic principles or insights can be derived from the study of chiasmus that directly serve the task of exegesis'.[157] Concerning the effect of chiastic patterns on exegesis, Breck lists seven principles, of which the first five are stated as follows:[158]

1. Most importantly, recognition of chiastic structures permits the interpreter to locate the *conceptual center* of the unit and thereby determine the primary point the author sought to convey.... Not only does it pinpoint the author's central theme; it also signals a turning point in the flow of thought.... Yet as the illustration of the conical helix demonstrates..., that central focus provides the

---

153. It is important to note that while every chiasmus is necessarily an example of *inclusio*, not every example of *inclusio* is chiastic. See Thomson, *Chiasmus in Pauline Letters*, p. 15. A good example is the structure of the book of Revelation, which is evidently framed by an *inclusio* (1.1–8; 22.6–21) but the book's structure as a whole may or may not be chiastic.

154. Breck, *The Shape of Biblical Language*, p. 336.

155. Breck, *The Shape of Biblical Language*, p. 338.

156. Breck, *The Shape of Biblical Language*, p. 339.

157. Breck, *The Shape of Biblical Language*, p. 341.

158. The list of 1 to 5 cited above are directly quoted from Breck's *The Shape of Biblical Language* at pp. 341–44 (his emphasis).

meaning to each of the several parallel elements that surround it. Whereas the parallels elucidate the center, the center lends content and form to the entire passage. Detection of that center is impossible with a purely narrative reading of the text. It can only be discerned by 'reading chiastically'.[159]

2. The *helical flow* through progressive intensification or heightening draws the reader/hearer into the movement of the passage as into a vortex.[160]

3. Biblical language that assumes a chiastic shape is in essence *poetry....* Poetic language expresses meaning in its own way and on its own terms... the theologian must to some degree be a poet, to hear and assimilate the rhythms and nuances of the Scriptures he or she is called to interpret.[161]

4. The study of chiastic forms also demonstrates the importance of *the entire semantic context.*[162]

5. The study of chiastic forms frequently obliges the exegete to reopen questions concerning the *unity of composition* of an individual passage or an entire writing.[163]

Breck concludes his summary of the functions of chiastic structures by stating that:

> The final aim of chiastic analysis should be for us to acquire an intuitive sense for the actual shape of biblical language and the flow of meaning that issues from it. This means that we need to grasp and appreciate the helical movement of a chiastically structured passage as the biblical author himself did, and thereby learn to read and to hear the text in the same accents in which it was composed.[164]

---

159. Breck, *The Shape of Biblical Language*, pp. 341–42. On a sentence level, F. I. Andersen has shown that a chiastic 'construction must be viewed as a whole, as *one sentence*, with complex integrating *grammatical* relationships between them'. F. I. Anderson, *The Sentence in Biblical Hebrew* (The Hague: Mouton, 1974), p. 123 (his emphasis). Cited approvingly by Raymond C. van Leeuwen, 'What Comes out of God's Mouth: Theological Wordplay in Deuteronomy 8', *CBQ* 47 (1985), pp. 55–57 (56 n. 5). R. van Leeuwen (p. 56 n. 5) writes: 'Similarly, larger chiastic constructions also define the boundaries of a complex literary whole. The parts of a chiasmus which correspond to one another are mutually significative.'

160. Breck, *The Shape of Biblical Language*, p. 342.

161. Breck, *The Shape of Biblical Language*, pp. 342–43.

162. Breck, *The Shape of Biblical Language*, p. 343.

163. Breck, *The Shape of Biblical Language*, p. 344. However, we agree with van Leeuwen that for a study based on the final form of a text, 'it matters little... whether the chiasmus is seen as proof of unitary authorship... or as a creation of later redaction'. van Leeuwen, 'What Comes out of God's Mouth', p. 56 n. 4.

164. Breck, *The Shape of Biblical Language*, p. 348.

As Breck's helical model will be influential in our own approach to Rev. 11.1–14.5, it is important to set out how this rhetorical helix works. Breck describes this concentric aspect of chiastic parallelism as, 'a *spiraling*, or more precisely, a *helical* effect that on the one hand produces the forward or focusing movement from line to line and strophe to strophe, and on the other provides *meaning* to the passage by focusing upon 0, its thematic center.'[165] Breck illustrates his concept with a diagram as follows:[166]

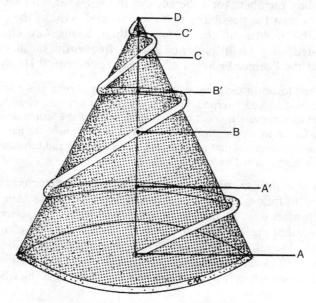

Illustration taken from Breck, *The Shape of Biblical Language*. Reproduced by permission of St. Vladimir's Seminary Press, 575 Scarsdale Rd, Crestwood, NY 10707, USA.

What Breck means by 'the helical movement' is that of a forward, narrative development within the concentric flow producing a double movement either from the extremities toward the centre, or moving from the centre outward. In short, from extreme of '2' to '1' to '0' or from the centre '0' to '1' to '2' and so forth.[167] As we will demonstrate, this double helical movement from the centre outward or from the extremities inward best explains the constant flux of movement between heaven and earth and between earth and heaven in Rev. 11.1–14.5.

165. Breck, *The Shape of Biblical Language*, p. 42. Breck prefers to use numbers, 0, 1, 2, 3 and so forth while we prefer the letters A, B, C, D and so forth in describing a chiastic pattern.
166. Breck, *The Shape of Biblical Language*, p. 57.
167. Breck, *The Shape of Biblical Language*, pp. 43–45.

Roland Meynet's *Rhetorical Analysis: An Introduction to Biblical Rhetoric* is another recent study that focuses on the rhetorical approach to biblical studies.[168] Meynet's research affirms Breck's study on chiasm. Meynet finds resonance with Breck's rhetorical helix where the apex at the centre of a concentric pattern is the pivot of the whole poem.[169] Korpel and de Moor confirm that the more extensive the poem, the more likely it tends to grow in 'concentric circles' and depends upon parallelism between its corresponding members for coherence.[170] If the text is read linearly, the readers may miss the possibility that the crux and pivot of the poem may lodge in the middle of the poem. Nathan Klaus has convincingly demonstrated that pivot patterns appear frequently in literary units throughout the Former Prophets of the Old Testament.[171] He writes,

> First and foremost the pivot pattern enables us to arrive at a complete understanding and interpretation of a particular episode, because the central idea appears in most cases at the climax of the structure, at its pivot. That is to say that the literary form of any section of the pattern is not merely structural, but is connected to the content and serves as full partner in the moulding of meaning.[172]

Read in a straightforward linear manner, the scenes depicted in Rev. 12 may appear to follow after Rev. 11 and likewise Rev. 13 is seen to follow sequentially after Rev. 11 and Rev. 12. Read chiastically or concentrically, we will show that the 'heart of the matter'[173] lies in the middle chapter, Rev. 12 with Rev. 11 and Rev. 13 as parallel episodes finding cohesion from the pivot of Rev. 12. A close reading of Rev. 12 will reveal that the literary unit of 12.7–12 serves not only as the pivot of Rev. 12 but also the whole of the

---

168.   R. Meynet, *Rhetorical Analysis: An Introduction to Biblical Rhetoric* (JSOTSup, 256; Sheffield: Sheffield Academic Press, 1998).

169.   Meynet, *Rhetorical Analysis*, pp. 176–77.

170.   M. C. A. Korpel and J. C. de Moor, 'Fundamentals of Ugaritic and Hebrew Poetry', in W. van der Meer and J. C. de Moor (eds.), *The Structural Analysis of Biblical and Canaanite Poetry* (JSOTSup, 74; Sheffield: JSOT Press, 1988), pp. 1–61 (60).

171.   N. Klaus, *Pivot Patterns in the Former Prophets* (JSOTSup, 247; Sheffield: Sheffield Academic Press, 1999). Thus we are not convinced by the argument put forward by M. J. Boda who disputes that the central idea of a poem lies in its pivot. See M. J. Boda, 'Chiasmus in Ubiquity: Symmetrical Mirages in Nehemiah 9', *JSOT* 71 (1996), pp. 55–70 (58). Boda (p. 59) does not argue his case but cites David J. A. Clines' comment that 'it would be unwise in our present state of knowledge about Hebrew poetry to conclude that the centre of the strophic structure is also centre of the thought of the poem'. David J. A. Clines, *Ezra, Nehemiah, Esther* (NCB; Grand Rapids: Eerdmans, 1984), p. 192. Recent studies cited throughout this book support the notion argued by Breck and Meynet that the central idea of a poem lies in its pivot.

172.   Klaus, *Pivot Patterns*, p. 26.

173.   Klaus, *Pivot Patterns*, p. 54.

textual unit from 11.1–14.5. Such a reading will be crucial to our analysis of our text in 11.1–14.5.

A number of scholars since Lund have taken a chiastic approach to the book of Revelation.[174] Thompson remarks that: 'The seer tends to develop his material concentrically into ever-widening rings'.[175] Apart from what Schüssler Fiorenza calls a 'concentric, conic-spiraling' approach to the book of Revelation,[176] she argues that 'the technique of intercalation of texts' is very important for the composition and structure of Revelation.[177] What Schüssler Fiorenza labels as intercalation is somewhat similar to what we have discussed above. Intercalation can be viewed as a form of chiasm. Schüssler Fiorenza explains thus:

> The author employs the method of intercalation in the following way:
> He narrates two formal units or episodes (A and A') that essentially belong together. Between these two formal units or episodes he intercalates another form or scene (B) and thus requires the reader to see the combined text as a whole.[178]

Schüssler Fiorenza finds the method of intercalation utilized in Rev. 10–14 patterned as A (10.1–11.14) – B (11.15–19) – A' (chs. 12–14).[179] As noted above, we believe that Rev. 12 (B) is intercalated between Rev. 11 (A) and Rev 13.1–14.5 (A'). Though we disagree with Schüssler Fiorenza's patterning in this instance, it is our view that this chiastic or intercalation method is crucial to understanding the middle chapters of Revelation. While chiasm focuses the readers to look for correspondence between the chiastic pairs through lexical, structural and thematic similarities or dissimilarities, intercalation is a literary technique in which one story is begun but is then interrupted by another story after which the initial story is rejoined and completed.

---

174. See Lund, *Studies in the Book of Revelation*; C. H. Giblin, 'Recapitulation and the Literary Coherence of John's Apocalypse', *CBQ* 56 (1994), pp. 81–95 (95); *idem*, 'Structural and Thematic Correlations in the Theology of Revelation 16–22', *Bib* 55 (1974), pp. 487–504; C. Talbert, *The Apocalypse* (Louisville: Westminster/John Knox Press, 1994); Michelle V. Lee, 'A Call to Martyrdom: Function as Method and Message in Revelation', *NovT* 40 (1998), pp. 164–94; Barbara W. Snyder, 'Combat Myth in the Apocalypse: The Liturgy of the Day of the Lord and the Dedication of the Heavenly Temple' (Unpublished PhD dissertation; Graduate Theological Union and University of California, Berkeley, 1991), pp. 84–99, 106, 320; William Shea, 'Chiasm in Theme and by Form in Revelation 18', *AUSS* 20 (1982), pp. 249–56; Kenneth A. Strand, 'Chiastic Structure and Some Motifs in the Book of Revelation', *AUSS* 16 (1978), pp. 401–08; J. H. Sims, *A Comparative Literary Study of Daniel and Revelation* (Lewiston: Edwin Mellen Press, 1994), pp. 118–19.
175. Thompson, 'The Literary Unity in the Book of Revelation', p. 354.
176. Schüssler Fiorenza, *The Book of Revelation*, p. 207.
177. Schüssler Fiorenza, *The Book of Revelation*, p. 172.
178. Schüssler Fiorenza, *The Book of Revelation*, p. 172.
179. Schüssler Fiorenza, *The Book of Revelation*, p. 172.

Although we will argue that Rev. 11.1–14.5 is best seen structurally as a macro-chiasm, the method of intercalation as noted by Schüssler Fiorenza is also useful for our purpose. Schüssler Fiorenza does not distinguish sharply between the method of intercalation and the chiastic-concentric approach she outlines for the structure of Revelation.[180] The story about the two witnesses commenced in Rev. 11 and interrupted by John's vision of the two signs in heaven (Rev. 12) and then rejoined in the story of the two beasts in Rev. 13.1–14.5 supports the overall chiastic reading that we have envisaged for Rev. 11.1–14.5.

This method of intercalation is not unique in Revelation among New Testament texts as it is also evident in Mark's Gospel.[181] While it is not our purpose to discuss the use of intercalation as a structuring device in Mark, it is significant that Revelation and the Gospel of Mark being the most Semitic books in the New Testament corpus use this literary technique to structure large units or to combine different episodes.[182] Martin Hengel remarks thus: 'I do not know of any other work in Greek which has as many Aramaic or Hebrew words and formulae in so narrow a space as does the second Gospel.'[183] We have already noted that Charles and others said similar things regarding the book of Revelation. Aune states that: 'It appears that Revelation and Mark have a distinctive paratactic style that makes exceptionally frequent use of καὶ as a discourse marker to begin new sentences, similar to the Greek style that characterizes the LXX.'[184] What Revelation and the Gospel of Mark have in common, *inter alia*, is the use of certain Hebraic literary techniques (parataxis and intercalation) to compose and structure large blocks of texts into literary wholes.[185]

---

180. Schüssler Fiorenza proposes that the book of Revelation is structured chiastically in an ABCDC'B'A' pattern after the shape of the seven-branched menorah. Schüssler Fiorenza, *The Book of Revelation*, p. 175.

181. See Tom Shepherd, 'The Narrative Function of Markan Intercalation', *NTS* 41 (1995), pp. 522–40 (522). Shepherd (p. 522) lists six units in Mark's Gospel which he thinks fall under this method of intercalation (3.20–35; 5.21–43; 6.7–32; 11.12–25; 14.1–11; 14.53–72). See also James Edwards, 'Markan Sandwiches: The Significance of Interpolations in Markan Narratives', *NovT* 31 (1989), pp. 193–216 and Geert van Oyen, 'Intercalation and Irony in the Gospel of Mark', in F. Van Segbroeck *et al.* (eds.), *The Four Gospels 1992* (Festschrift Frans Neirynck; Leuven: Leuven University Press, 1992), pp. 949–74.

182. Wallace lists Mark's Gospel as the second most Semitic New Testament book after Revelation. See Wallace, *Greek Grammar*, p. 32.

183. M. Hengel, *Studies in the Gospel of Mark* (trans. J. Bowden; Philadelphia: Fortress Press, 1985), p. 46.

184. Aune, *Revelation 1–5*, p. cxxxiii. According to Aune (p. cxci), 73.79 per cent of the 337 sentences (following the punctuation in NA27) in Revelation begin with καὶ while the percentage in Mark is 62.64 per cent.

185. The literary phenomenon called parataxis will be discussed further in a later section.

6. *The Criteria for Evaluating a Macro-Chiasm*

In this section, we will set out a workable model by which the structure of Rev. 11.1–14.5 as a macro-chiasm can be rigorously tested. Thomson remarks thus: 'The fact that an adequate methodology for identifying, verifying and using chiasmus as an exegetical tool has yet to emerge is at the root of many unresolved problems.'[186] This is true even if one considers Breck's contribution, as *The Shape of Biblical Language* focuses more on the *function* of a chiasm and less on the criteria or methodology whereby the existence or otherwise of a chiasm can be rigorously tested. Though Thomson's study is limited to chiasm of intermediate length involving '10–20 elements that may encompass perhaps 7–15 verses', his more rigorous assessment of an alleged chiasm is welcome and can be applied to the testing of a macro-chiasm.[187] Thomson acknowledges Lund's contribution and expands on Lund's principles on a number of points.[188] He elaborates on Lund's principle of 'frame passages' which function to introduce and conclude a chiasm by stating that, 'a "frame passage" is a spring-board from which to launch into a chiasmus, or a section which acts as a tail piece to a chiasmus without being part of the chiastic pattern'.[189] Thomson's definition of 'frame passages' is useful for our purpose. We shall see that two visionary reports of *another angel* in Rev. 10.1–11 (esp. v. 11) and Rev. 14.6–7 serve as frame passages to the macro-chiasm of 11.1–14.5.

Thomson also insists that 'balancing elements are normally of approximately the same length' but adds that 'on the few occasions when this is not the case, some explanation seems to be called for'.[190] This criterion should be applied with caution as there is no reason why the corresponding element in the second half must be the same length as its member in the first half. In Hebrew parallelism as Kugel and Alter have noted, the second line seldom repeats what is spoken in the first line but functions to complement, expand and intensify the first line. This means ordinarily, the second line is longer in length than the first line as it normally contains more information as it seeks to expand on what is stated in the first line. For example, Rev. 11.1–2 contains two verses but its corresponding member in 14.1–5 consists of five verses. We shall see that the often neglected phrase 'those who worship in it' in 11.1 is identified as the 144,000 in 14.1 whose identification and role are expanded upon in

186. Thomson, *Chiasmus in Pauline Letters*, p. 22.
187. Thomson, *Chiasmus in Pauline Letters*, p. 23.
188. Thomson, *Chiasmus in Pauline Letters*, p. 27. We will discuss only those points made by Thomson which are substantially different from those proposed by Lund.
189. Thomson, *Chiasmus in Pauline Letters*, p. 27.
190. Thomson, *Chiasmus in Pauline Letters*, p. 27.

14.2–5. All the other balancing elements in the macro-chiasm of 11.1–14.5 are of approximately the same length.

What may be Thomson's contribution to the discussion on chiasm is his section on 'Procedures for Identifying Chiasmus'.[191] He admits that the process for identifying chiasm is inevitably complex and also unavoidably circular. First, Thomson suggests that proper interpretation of each part or element depends on proper appreciation of the whole. However, appreciation of the whole can only be built upon interpretation of the parts. This requires the exegete to have a feel for the whole while at the same time probing how each part or element contributes to the understanding of the whole. Thomson agreeing with Kennedy thinks that this process involves a certain amount of 'experiment', specifically looking for signs of opening and closure.[192]

Thomson then suggests a 'two-step methodology' where the first stage is to give careful and detailed attention to the text in terms of vocabulary and syntax, and then in terms of content. 'As a general rule, the greater the number of objective balances of vocabulary and syntax in potentially corresponding elements, the more likely there is to be an authentic chiasmus present.'[193] Thomson adds that an *inclusio* may indicate that further analysis will reveal greater symmetry. This is true of Rev. 11.1–14.5 where if the *inclusio* (the temple of God/holy city in 11.1 and Mount Zion in 14.1) is recognized, further analysis will reveal greater symmetry throughout chs 11 to 13 of Revelation. Likewise, argues Thomson, 'a sudden change in a unit of text may turn out to be the shift and reversion at the centre of a chiasmus'.[194] When we reach Rev. 12.7–9 there is a sudden change in the unit of text as the 'war in heaven' motif is introduced with repercussions in heaven and on earth set out in 12.10–12 which turns out to be the shift and reversal at the centre of a chiasm.

The second step proposed by Thomson is 'to test the suggested pattern at the conceptual level by exegesis in order to validate the hypothesis'.[195] This step unfortunately is not elaborated upon by Thomson but may mean that not only verbal and syntactical parallels are to be present but also on a conceptual level the chiastic halves should point to a common theme or theology. For a chiasm to be valid, Thomson suggests that three criteria must be met:[196]

---

191. Thomson, *Chiasmus in Pauline Letters*, pp. 33–34.
192. Thomson citing Kennedy's *New Testament Interpretation*, pp. 33–34.
193. Thomson, *Chiasmus in Pauline Letters*, p. 33.
194. Thomson, *Chiasmus in Pauline Letters*, p. 33.
195. Thomson, *Chiasmus in Pauline Letters*, p. 34.
196. Thomson, *Chiasmus in Pauline Letters*, pp. 28–29.

1. The chiasmus will be present in the text as it stands, and will not require unsupported textual emendation in order to 'recover' it.
2. The symmetrical elements will be present in precisely inverted order.
3. The chiasmus will begin and end at a reasonable point.

Thomson admits that the third requirement is somewhat vague. He writes,

> It is difficult to define what a 'reasonable point' would be in many instances because of the variety of possible situations that might be encountered. Sometimes a chiasmus will equate with a 'rhetorical unit' (corresponding to the *pericope* in form criticism), although a complicating factor is the possible presence of a frame passage which, while not strictly part of the chiastic pattern, might be said to belong to the same 'rhetorical unit'.[197]

We have already noted that the frame passages of Rev. 11.1–14.5 are 10.11 and 14.6–7, but they are not part of the chiastic pattern we envisage for 11.1–14.5. Further, we have seen that a large block of text extending to several chapters or even the whole book can be structured as a chiasm. So Thomson's third criterion is not helpful as the range of what constitutes a reasonable unit of text is hard to determine rigidly. Thomson acknowledges that 'the validity of a chiasmus depends on the *cumulative impact* of a number of criteria'[198] and not on fulfilment or non-fulfilment of any single criterion. Thomson concludes by stating that, 'no matter how careful the inquiry, it is unlikely that absolute certainty will be reached, and most cases will result in a balance of probability'.[199]

John Welch also argues that chiastic analysis must produce rigorous and verifiable results. He writes,

> If any aspect of the chiastic analysis is to produce rigorous and verifiable results, the inverted parallel orders, which create the chiasms upon which that analysis is based must be evidenced in the text itself and not imposed upon the text by Procrustean design or artifice of the reader. Therefore, one's predominant concern is over objectivity. In striving for objectivity, it is reasonable to require significant repetitions to be readily apparent, and the overall system to be well balanced. The second half of the system should tend to repeat the first half of the system in a recognizably inverted order, and the juxtapositon of the central sections should be marked and highly accentuated.... Key words, echoes, and balancing should be distinct and should serve defined purposes within the structure.[200]

---

197. Thomson, *Chiasmus in Pauline Letters*, p. 29.
198. Thomson, *Chiasmus in Pauline Letters*, p. 32.
199. Thomson, *Chiasmus in Pauline Letters*, p. 34.
200. Welch (ed.), *Chiasmus*, p. 13.

However, Welch is quick to admit that a level of subjectivity cannot be avoided in determining whether a literary unit is structured chiastically. He remarks,

> Nevertheless the objective criteria alone do not alone tell the whole story. Evidence of chiasmus is not entirely objective and quantifiable. For example, chiasmus operates by definition within literary units. Yet defining what constitutes such a literary unit and determining where it begins and ends is often a predominantly subjective matter especially if multiple structures operate simultaneously.... Furthermore, wherever synonyms, cognates, antitheticals or logically proximate terms appear in a chiastic system, substantial subjective judgment is again involved in the process of deciding which terms in the first portion of the system match (if at all) with particular terms in the second portion of the system.[201]

Welch's observations should caution us that the case for testing and evaluating macro-chiasm can never be totally objective or scientific.

Wayne Brouwer in his monograph *The Literary Development of John 13–17: A Chiastic Reading* joins the growing number of New Testament scholars who specialize in utilizing chiasm as a tool for interpreting New Testament texts. He has comprehensively summarized the state of research into the use of chiasm as a literary device in the Bible with particular focus on the New Testament.[202] Brouwer argues convincingly that extended chiasm, or what he calls 'macro-chiasm', is a common literary device or compositional technique used by many New Testament authors. He rightly criticizes Ian Thomson for only allowing possible chiastic structures over small units of texts either at the level of sentence or of short passage made up of several sentences.[203] Brouwer prefers Lund's and Breck's approaches which suggest that a large unit of text from the level of a section in a chapter to texts over several chapters or even the whole book can be structured by way of a macro-chiasm. Brouwer spends nearly half his thesis in first, setting out the prevalence of chiasm and its characteristics in the Bible and also other literature of antiquity and secondly, and more significantly for our purposes, contending that proposing a macro-chiasm that covers texts over several chapters constitutes a legitimate exercise. Whereas Thomson discusses in general how a chiasm can be detected and identified with a degree of certainty, Brouwer's approach is considerably

---

201. Welch (ed.), *Chiasmus*, p. 13.

202. Brouwer, *John 13–17: A Chiastic Reading*, pp. 1–85.

203. As discussed above, Ian Thomsom has otherwise provided an incisive discussion on the background and methodological matters concerning chiasm and its function as a whole especially in regard to micro-chiasm as a tool for the study of the New Testament with special focus on the Pauline epistles. See Thomson, *Chiasmus in Pauline Letters*, pp. 13–45.

more rigorous in that the *testing* of his proposed macro-chiasm takes up most of the second part of his monograph. Brouwer's proposed criteria for evaluating the existence of a macro-chiasm follows the list of nine tests propounded by Craig Blomberg. Blomberg lists the nine criteria in his seminal article as follows:[204]

1. There must be a problem in perceiving the structure of the text in question, which more conventional outlines fail to resolve.... If a more conventional and straightforward structure can adequately account for the textual data, recourse to less obvious arrangements of the material would seem, at the very least, to risk obscuring what was already clear.

2. There must be clear examples of parallelism between the two 'halves' of the hypothesized chiasmus, to which commentators call attention even when they propose quite different outlines for the text overall. In other words, the chiasmus must be based on actual verbal repetitions or clear thematic parallels in the text which most readers note, irrespective of their overall synthesis. Otherwise it is too simple to see what one wants to see and to impose on the text an alien structural grid.

3. Verbal (or grammatical) parallelism as well as conceptual (or structural) parallelism should characterize most if not all of the corresponding pairs of subdivisions. The repetitive nature of much biblical writing makes it very easy for general themes to recur in a variety of patterns.

4. The verbal parallelism should involve central or dominant imagery or terminology, not peripheral or trivial language. Ancient writers often employed key terms as catchwords to link passages together, although the material they considered central does not always match modern preconceptions of what is important.

5. Both the verbal and conceptual parallelisms should use words and ideas not regularly found elsewhere within the proposed chiasmus. Most unpersuasive proposals fail to meet this criterion; while the pairings suggested may be plausible, a little ingenuity can demonstrate equally close parallelism between numerous other pairs of passages which do not support a chiastic whole.

6. Multiple sets of correspondences between passages opposite each other in the chiasmus as well as multiple members of the chiasmus itself are desirable. A simple ABA' or ABB'A' pattern is so common to so many different forms of rhetoric that it usually yields few startlingly profound insights. Three or four members repeated in

---

204. C. Blomberg, 'The Structure of 2 Corinthians 1–7', *CTR* 4 (1989), pp. 3–20 (5–7).

      inverse sequence may be more significant. Five or more elements paired in sequence usually resist explanations which invoke subconscious or accidental processes.

7.   The outline should divide the text at natural breaks which would be agreed upon even by those proposing very different structures to account for the whole. If a proposed chiasmus frequently violates the natural 'paragraphing' of the text which would otherwise emerge, then the proposal becomes less probable.

8.   The center of the chiasm, which forms its climax, should be a passage worthy of that position in light of its theological or ethical significance. If its theme were in some way repeated in the first and last passages of the text, as is typical in chiasmus, the proposal would become that much more plausible.

9.   Finally, ruptures in the outline should be avoided if at all possible. Having to argue that one or more of the members of the reverse part of the structure have been shifted from their corresponding locations in the forward sequence substantially weakens the hypothesis; in postulating chiasmus, exceptions disprove the rule!

Brouwer accepts Blomberg's criteria wholesale and proceeds to test his reading of John 13–17 accordingly. Brouwer notes that Porter and Reed dispute, *inter alia*, Blomberg's seventh criterion that the outline should divide the text at natural breaks.[205] Porter and Reed argue that if the breaks in the text are natural then a chiastic reading is not necessary.[206] Despite Brouwer's protestations, Porter and Reed, in our view, have made a valid point. A chiastic interpretation over a large unit of texts especially one which extends over several chapters is unlikely to be apparent at first or second reading. David J. Clark observes that chiasms should be evaluated based on cumulative collection of evidence that may be less than fully apparent at the first reading.[207] The breaks in the text are unlikely to be natural; in fact Blomberg's first criterion, which insists that 'there must be a problem in perceiving the structure of the text in question', appears to contradict his seventh principle. We have already cited Muilenburg's proposal that the critic's task is 'to note various rhetorical devices that are employed for marking, on one hand, the sequence and movement of the pericope, and on the other, the shifts or breaks in the development of the

---

205.   Stanley E. Porter and Jeffrey T. Reed, 'Philippians As a Macro-Chiasm and Its Exegetical Significance', *NTS* 44 (1998), pp. 213–31 (220).

206.   Porter and Reed appear to conceive 'natural' breaks as those breaks that are easily detected by a casual reading of the text.

207.   David J. Clark, 'Criteria for Identifying Chiasm', *Linguistica Biblica* 5 (1975), pp. 63–72 (66).

writer's thought'.[208] Thus breaks or shifts that are not so 'natural' on surface reading might turn out to be natural when a chiastic structure is evident on close reading. Hence, Blomberg's phrase of 'natural paragraphing of the text' is unhelpful and seems self-contradictory as to the need of identifying chiasm before one can determine breaks or paragraphing of the text. Barring this observation, we agree with Brouwer that 'Blomberg's criteria for macro-chiasm show great care and insight'[209] and that it 'appears to provide a reasonable and thorough measure by which to determine the possible existence and scope of chiastic paralleling in biblical and other texts'.[210]

Brouwer has shown that macro-chiasm is a common literary device utilized by various New Testament authors in their compositions. Lund's initial principles of the essentials of chiasm have now been improved by Breck and Thomson. Brouwer's extensive interaction with the works of these recent authors and his synthesis of the form and function of a macro-chiasm is especially illuminating. Further, Brouwer following Blomberg's lead is careful to set out the criteria by which one may vigorously test the existence and usefulness of an alleged macro-chiasm. Brower's thesis goes a long way towards answering the objections of some scholars who are still wary of the level of subjectivity involved in detecting chiasm in a text in general and macro-chiasm in particular.

7. *Other Features of Hebraic Rhetoric:* *Parataxis and Structural Parallelism*

We have noted earlier that parataxis and structural parallelism feature large in the literary unit of Rev. 11.1–14.5. Parataxis and structural parallelism are best viewed as Hebraic rhetorical conventions and are used throughout the Bible. Meynet argues for the application of Hebraic rhetoric as distinct from Greek rhetoric in the study of biblical texts including the New Testament.[211] He states thus:

> I would not want to avoid the question of the relationship between classical and Hebrew rhetoric. This question is particularly relevant for

---

208. Muilenburg, 'Form Criticism and Beyond', p. 10.
209. Brouwer, *John 13–17: A Chiastic Reading*, p. 42.
210. Brouwer, *John 13–17: A Chiastic Reading*, p. 44.
211. We do not think it wise to lump all the New Testament books into one category as Meynet appears to do. The genre of the gospels differs from that of Paul's letters. And the book of Revelation stands apart on its own. While Meynet's observations may be applicable to the interpretation of Revelation given its Old Testament influence, it is not within the purview of this book to critically examine Meynet's contention that Hebraic rhetoric is applicable across the whole spectrum of New Testament literature.

the texts of the New Testament, written in Greek, and not in Hebrew, in a middle-eastern world which was influenced, at least in certain sections of its population, by Greek civilisation and learning. It is therefore perfectly legitimate to look for what would denote this influence in the New Testament. Rhetorical analysis, however, poses – 'presuppo- ses'... that the authors of the New Testament, being impregnated to the bone with the literature of the Jewish Scriptures, have followed – consciously or unconsciously – the laws of composition of Hebrew rhetoric. Consequently, we are perfectly in our rights to speak of Hebraic rhetoric, but more broadly of a biblical rhetoric.[212]

Meynet thus argues strongly for the application of certain laws of composition of Hebrew rhetoric or what he calls 'Hebraic or biblical rhetoric' in contrast to Greek rhetoric in the study of New Testament texts. Stanley E. Porter in two recent essays likewise questions the validity of using classical Graeco-Roman rhetoric to interpret the New Testament.[213] He argues against the growing number of scholars following Kennedy's footsteps in employing classical rhetorical categories (judicial, deliberative, epideictic) to analyse the New Testament in general and the Pauline epistles in particular.[214] Porter's arguments are best quoted in full:

> Although some New Testament exegetes talk about rhetoric as being universal, most who examine the New Testament apply the categories of ancient rhetoric, especially found in the rhetorical handbooks.... In the end, their analyses do such things as identify the species (or genres) of rhetoric, and analyse the disposition or arrangement, invention, proofs and style (and occasionally even the delivery) – all of this implicitly or explicitly as if this is what the ancients would have done or would have expected to do when reading or hearing a letter. The reasons marshalled

212. Meynet, *Rhetorical Analysis*, p. 176. Kenneth Bailey also prefers to study the phenomena of chiasm in the New Testament (esp. of Luke's Gospel) through the categories of Hebrew parallelism. See Kenneth Bailey, *Poet and Peasant and Through Peasant Eyes* (Grand Rapids: Eerdmans, 1983) and more recently, 'Inverted Parallelism and Encased Parables in Isaiah and Their Significance for Old and New Testament Translation and Interpretation', in L. J. de Regt *et al.* (eds.), *Literary Structures and Rhetorical Strategies in the Hebrew Bible* (Assen: Van Grocum, 1996), pp. 14–30.

213. Stanley E. Porter, 'Ancient Rhetorical Analysis and Discourse Analysis of the Pauline Epistles', in Stanley E. Porter and Thomas H. Olbricht (eds.), *The Rhetorical Analysis of Scripture: Essays from the London Conference* (Sheffield: Sheffield Academic Press, 1997), pp. 249–74, and 'Theoretical Justification for the Application of Rhetorical Categories to Pauline Epistolary Literature', pp. 100–22.

214. See especially the essays in Duane F. Watson (ed.), *Persuasive Artistry: Studies in the New Testament Rhetoric in Honor of George A. Kennedy* (Sheffield: Sheffield Academic Press, 1991). For a summary of Kennedy's methods, see C. Clifton Black, 'Rhetorical Criticism', in Joel Green (ed.), *Hearing the New Testament* (Grand Rapids: Eerdmans, 1995), pp. 256–77.

for this (if they are given) are that Paul himself may have been trained in or had some contact with rhetorical schools of the time (cf. Acts 17.15–32), a *doubtful proposition*, or simply that classical rhetoric pervaded the ancient world (a view often attributed to G. A. Kennedy), *an assumption that still must be proved* regarding its specific influence on Paul. Since this is fairly slender evidence on which to establish such a far-reaching theory, some scholars have attempted to bolster it by making more systematic statements regarding the pervasive character of rhetoric. However, analysis of the rhetorical handbooks and other ancient sources regarding rhetoric and epistolography, most of which are in fact much later than the New Testament, provides little or no proof that letters were considered a part of rhetoric in terms of production or analysis of them, apart possibly from the matter of style . . . . If all of this is true, the first major problem with utilizing rhetorical and discourse analyses of the Pauline letters is that, apart from the matter of style . . . the methodological approach is already theoretically suspect.[215]

Porter's caution should be acknowledged and for the purposes of this book, we will proceed with our own methodological approach which leans more on 'the distinctive rhetoric of Hebrew Scriptures'[216] of the kind proposed by James Muilenburg, John Breck, Roland Meynet, and more recently by Wayne Brouwer.[217]

215. Porter, 'Ancient Rhetorical Analysis and Discourse Analysis of the Pauline Epistles', pp. 251–52 (my emphasis).

216. Thomas Olbricht writes: 'Muilenburg was aware of classical rhetoric, but was more interested in what he perceived to be the distinctive rhetoric of the Hebrew Scriptures.' 'The Flowering of Rhetorical Criticism in America', in Stanley E. Porter and Thomas H. Olbricht (eds.), *The Rhetorical Analysis of Scripture: Essays from the London Conference* (Sheffield: Sheffield Academic Press, 1997), pp. 79–102 (91).

217. Apart from Lund's *Chiasmus in the New Testament* and *Studies in the Book of Revelation*, of the books and articles surveyed and cited here, there are very few attempts to study the text of Revelation by way of rhetorical analysis. See Talbert, *The Apocalypse*, and C. H. Giblin, *The Book of Revelation* (Good News Studies, 34; Collegeville: The Liturgical Press, 1991). Both commentaries give some attention to literary features of Revelation but because of the nature of a commentary, it is not surprising to find that insufficient space is given to the analysis of literary features and how they function rhetorically within the text. While my survey is in no way exhaustive, it is fair to say that there is little work done on Revelation through *Hebraic* rhetorical analysis. Witherington in his commentary published in 2003 remarks that: 'The study of the rhetoric of Revelation is still in its nascent stages, and different studies offer different levels of sophistication.' Witherington, *Revelation*, p. 53. For studies of Revelation that utilize rhetorical analysis, see Edith M. Humphrey, 'In Search of a Voice: Rhetoric through Sight and Sound in Revelation 11.15–12.17', in Gregory Bloomquist and Greg Carey (eds.), *Vision and Persuasion: Rhetorical Dimensions of Apocalyptic Discourse* (St Louis: Chalice Press, 1999), pp. 141–60; J. T. Kirby, 'The Rhetorical Situations of Revelation 1–3', *NTS* 34 (1988), pp. 197–207; R. M. Royalty Jr., 'The Rhetoric of Revelation', in *SBL Seminar Papers* (Atlanta: Scholars Press, 1997), pp. 596–617; *idem, The Streets of Heaven: The Ideology of Wealth in the Apocalyse of John* (Macon, GA; Mercer University Press, 1998);

a. *Parataxis*

Meynet's observations that Hebraic rhetoric is distinguishable from Greek rhetoric are worth noting. He writes:

> I would identify three characteristics of Hebrew rhetoric that distinguishes it from classical rhetoric: *it is more concrete than abstract, it uses parataxis more than syntax, it is more involutive than linear*. First of all, Hebrew literature is essentially *concrete*. When Greek rhetoric looks to illustrate or prove abstract ideas, through examples, Hebrew rhetoric tends to follow the opposite path: it describes reality, leaving the reader to conclude. The Jew shows, the Greek wants to demonstrate.... The second characteristic of Hebrew rhetoric is that it is *paratactic*. That is to say that it juxtaposes or coordinates more than it subordinates.... The third characteristic of Hebrew rhetoric is the specific manner in which it composes parallel dispositions and most of all concentric arrangements. Instead of developing its argumentation in a linear way, in the Graeco-Roman fashion, to a conclusion which is the point of the resolution of the discourse, it is organized most of the time

Loren Johns, 'The Lamb in the Rhetorical Program of the Apocalypse of John', in *SBL Seminar Papers* (Atlanta: Scholars Press, 1998), pp. 762–84; David A. deSilva, 'The Persuasive Strategy of the Apocalypse: A Socio-Rhetorical Investigation of Revelation 14.6–13', in *SBL Seminar Papers* (Atlanta: Scholars Press, 1998), pp. 785–806. These studies except Humphrey's article utilize Graeco-Roman rhetorical categories in the study of Revelation. See the review and summary by Ian Smith, 'A Rational Choice Model of the Book of Revelation', *JSNT* 85 (2002), pp. 97–116 (102–03). After reviewing the application of Graeco-Roman rhetoric in the study of Revelation, Smith (p. 103) writes: 'The absence of consensus regarding the species of classical rhetoric to which Revelation is most closely related is not surprising. As is well recognized by these scholars [Kirby, Royalty, and Johns], the book is not a classical oration restricted to delivery in the standard venues of a law court, a political assembly or a ceremonial occasion.' Hence, we disagree with Royalty's assertion that Revelation's 'audience would have been more knowledgeable about Greco-Roman culture, in which they lived, than the Hebrew prophets, whom they may have never read'. Royalty, *Streets of Heaven*, pp. 18–19. Richard Hays has shown that the Corinthian church (a mostly Gentile one) was expected to understand Paul's use of Scripture in making his arguments about a host of issues raised in the Corinthian correspondence. R. Hays, 'Conversion of Imagination', *NTS* 45.3 (1999), pp. 392–412. See also R. Hays, *Echoes of Scriptures in the Letters of Paul* (New Haven: Yale University Press, 1989). The addressees of Revelation consist of a significant Jewish audience (Rev. 2–3) and it is not unreasonable to assume that even Gentiles who had become believers were taught the Hebrew Scriptures from their conversion as demonstrated by Hays in the article cited. On rhetorical studies on the apocalyptic texts in the Gospels of Mark and Luke, see Vernon K. Robbins, 'Rhetorical Ritual: Apocalyptic Discourse in Mark 13', in Gregory Bloomquist and Greg Carey (eds.), *Vision and Persuasion: Rhetorical Dimensions of Apocalyptic Discourse* (St Louis, MO: Chalice Press, 1999), pp. 95–121; Black, 'An Oration at Olivet: Some Rhetorical Dimensions of Mark 13' and Bloomquist, 'Rhetorical Argumentation and the Culture of Apocalyptic: A Socio-Rhetorical Analysis of Luke 21'.

in an involutive manner around a centre which is the focal point, the keystone, through which the rest finds cohesion.[218]

The second characteristic listed by Meynet requires further elaboration. Meynet rightly recognizes that one of the characteristics of Hebrew narrative is parataxis. Juxtaposition and coordination of seemingly unrelated characters, events and episodes are often the literary style preferred by biblical authors.[219] Robert Alter observes that the design of biblical structure resists the classic categories of 'episodic' or 'unitary' but must instead be perceived as one of 'artful juxtaposition of seemingly disparate episodes'.[220] As noted by Aune, nearly 74 per cent of all sentences in Revelation (following the punctuation in NA27) start with καὶ giving Revelation a distinctive paratactic style.[221] Thompson recognizes the paratactic style of Revelation and he remarks that,

> Critics may refer to [the Book of Revelation] as 'visionary' literature which has no coherence: one vision is connected to another vision with

---

218. Meynet, *Rhetorical Analysis*, pp. 173–77. Meynet (pp. 21–22) writes: 'Rhetorical analysis asserts that these compositions do not obey the rules of Graeco-Roman rhetoric, but the specific laws of Hebraic rhetoric, of which the authors of the New Testament are the direct inheritors.' For another discussion on the difference of Greek and biblical style, see Erich Auerbach, *Mimesis* (trans. W.R. Trask; Princeton: Princeton University Press, 1974), pp. 3–23.

219. Theophile Meeks remarks that: 'Hebrew and Aramaic are languages in which the co-ordination of clauses is the rule and the subordination the exception. In contrast, English is quite the opposite, with subordination rather more frequent than co-ordination.' T. Meeks, 'Old Testament Translation Principles', *JBL* 81 (1962), pp. 143–54 (145).

220. R. Alter, 'Sodom as Nexus: The Web of Design in Biblical Narrative', in Regina M. Schwartz (ed.), *The Book and the Text: The Bible and Literary Theory* (Oxford: Basil Blackwell, 1990), pp. 146–60 (146–47). Alter's observation is also noted approvingly by Marie Sabin, 'Reading Mark 4 as Midrash', *JSNT* 45 (1992), pp. 3–26 (8 n. 5). Meir Sternberg says, '*juxtaposition* arranges two or more contemporaneous events (acts, episodes, arenas, plots) in narrative sequence, often relating them through a formula like "at that time". The "time" invoked as a common framework is extremely flexible in reference, and with it in juxtapositional range.' M. Sternberg, 'Time and Space in Biblical (Hi)story Telling: The Grand Chronology', in Regina M. Schwartz (ed.), *The Book and the Text: The Bible and Literary Theory* (Oxford: Basil Blackwell, 1990), pp. 81–145 (106) [his emphasis]. For a recent discussion on how parataxis operates within biblical narrative, see Jack R. Lundbom, 'Parataxis, Rhetorical Structure, and the Dialogue over Sodom in Genesis 18', in Philip R. Davies and David J. A. Clines (eds.), *The World of Genesis: Persons, Places, Perspectives* (JSOTSup, 257; Sheffield: Sheffield Academic Press, 1998), pp. 136–45. Lundbom (p. 140) discusses the incident of the two messengers sent to Sodom (Gen. 18–19) and he writes: 'The story in its final form provides clear evidence of parataxis, for example, the shifts between "men", "messengers" and "Yahweh". These strike the modern reader as poor editing, resulting in a narrative that is inconsistent and possibly incoherent. But from another point of view more background is created.' Similarly, we see in Rev. 11, the shifts between 'two witnesses' (11.3), 'two prophets' (11.10) and 'the Lord' (11.4, 8).

221. So Aune, *Revelation 1–5*, p. cxxxiii.

little attempt to provide a literary or linguistic unity.... More recent critics have discovered that the paratactic style of the Book of Revelation can be given a structuralist interpretation with the various unconnected units becoming mythemes forming binary oppositions which reflect fundamental conflicts in life and society, especially conflicts between harsh social, political realities and the claims of Christian faith.[222]

This book seeks to establish these binary oppositions (the war between the two witnesses and the two beasts) within a chiastic reading of Rev. 11.1–14.5.

A. Hauser defines parataxis in this vein:

Parataxis refers to the placing side by side of words, images, clauses, or scenes without connectives that directly and immediately coordinate the parts with one another.... Parataxis does not present a complete picture, but normally selects only certain elements which often at the first glance do not appear to correlate well with one another. This does not mean that the adjacent parts lack a common unity or exist in a vacuum separate from one another. The unity that is present is subtle, implicit, indirect, and below the surface. It comes to expression not so much in the words of the writer as in the thoughts the writer creates in the mind of the audience.[223]

The understanding of the use of the paratactic 'and' according to Hebraic rhetoric goes a long way to resolving some of the oft-disputed passages such as the relationship between verses 2 and 3 of Rev. 11.[224]

b. *Structural Parallelism*

While we have shown how parataxis works within smaller units of a sentence or paragraph level, paratactic constructions also embrace larger units of texts, a phenomenon which we will call structural parallelism. Structural parallelism differs from the method of intercalation in that structural parallelism places two or more episodes side by side without being interrupted by another story as happens with intercalation. While chiastic patterns always exhibit structural parallelism (correspondence between chiastic pairs is a form of structural parallelism), parallel episodes are not necessarily chiastic. The author uses structural parallelism to place episodes and characters in panels or matching sequences which may be narrated over an extended unit of text. We have stated that Rev. 11 and Rev. 13.1–14.5 stand as parallel episodes which must be read together with

---

222. Thompson, 'The Literary Unity of the Book of Revelation', p. 347. See also Smith, 'A Rational Choice Model', pp. 102–3.

223. A. Hauser, 'Judges 5: Parataxis in Hebrew Poetry', *JBL* 99 (1980), pp. 23–41 (26).

224. This question will be discussed in a later chapter.

Rev. 12. In addition, we will see that the careers of the two beasts are structured as parallel episodes within Rev. 13. By structural parallelism, we will argue that John links Rev. 11 and Rev. 12 through lexical and thematic parallels. In structural parallelism, the concern is not merely with parallelism of sentences or short passages but the paralleling of large units across several chapters.

Robert Cohn in two articles illustrates the importance of recognizing the paratactic nature of Hebrew narrative and the narrative parallelism in seeming disparate passages or chapters.[225] He argues convincingly that the narrative of the Elijah cycle in 1 Kgs. 17–19 is an integral unit which has as 'its central theme the battle for the establishment of the exclusive worship of Yahweh in Israel against the forces of Baal'.[226] Cohn believes that thematically the said narrative 'operates on two levels' whereby on the first level it presents the sacred biography of the prophet Elijah from his first appearance in Israel until the appointment of his successor. The narrative, seen by Cohn as divided into three parts, 'charts the coming of age of Elijah, his public life, and his resignation from office' and he goes on to say that on another level, 'the life of Elijah serves as a context for the struggle between Yahweh and the forces of Baal in Israel'.[227] Cohn's comment with regard to how the narrative functions structurally is worth quoting in full:[228]

> Structurally, the artistry of the narrative may be seen from two perspectives. On the one hand, the episodes are arranged in a logical linear progression. Although they may originally have functioned in other contexts, they have been creatively integrated into this narrative and subordinated to its theme and purpose. Through the repetition of key-words and motifs, the discrete episodes become scenes in an ordered drama. On the other hand, each of the three chapters displays the same sequence of elements. This parallel development creates a set of correspondences cutting across the three chapters and reinforcing the unity of the whole. Parallel episodes build upon each other and thus generate a cumulative logic subliminally undergirding the narrative.

Cohn goes on to show how 1 Kgs. 17–19 falls into the pattern which he has proposed. We will see how parallel development in Rev. 11.1–14.5 creates a set of correspondences cutting across more than three chapters of Revelation and reinforcing the unity of the whole. The parallel episodes of the two witnesses in Rev. 11 and the two beasts in Rev. 13 build on each

---

225. R. Cohn, 'The Literary Logic of 1 Kings 17–19', *JBL* 101 (1982), pp. 333–50 and *idem*, 'Literary Technique in the Jeroboam Narrative', *ZAW* 97 (1985), pp. 23–35.
226. Cohn, 'The Literary Logic of 1 Kings 17–19', p. 334.
227. Cohn, 'The Literary Logic of 1 Kings 17–19', p. 334.
228. Cohn, 'The Literary Logic of 1 Kings 17–19', p. 334.

other and will be shown to generate a cumulative logic subliminally undergirding the whole narrative.

Martens further demonstrates how this parallel patterning works in the book of Jeremiah.[229] Martens argues that parallel patterning of larger blocks of material occurs frequently in Jeremiah. He proposes that chs 34–38 of Jeremiah are an integral unit based on 'similar themes and the parallel structuring... but also an *inclusio* feature'.[230] Martens argues that Jer. 34.1–7 and the closing section (38.14–23) are linked by the technique of *inclusio*, and goes on to demonstrate how chs 34 and 35 conform to a stylistic parallel structure and also parallelism of theme.[231] The lack of integrity shown by Zedekiah in breaking the covenant of the Lord (34.15) is contrasted with the commitment of the Rechabites in keeping their forefathers' stipulation not to drink wine in ch. 35. Martens concludes that:

> The accounts are essentially built upon this contrast... the juxtaposition and the parallelism of these two stories suggest that chaps. 34–35 should be considered a unit for investigation at least at some stage in the interpretative process. Each narrative, though treated separately initially, must be exegeted in relation to its complement.[232]

Further Martens adds that: 'The interpretation of two passages, when seen as a whole, in two parallel halves, brings about a different cast, a different flavour than when each is interpreted singly.'[233] Martens concludes that when two accounts are intentionally stylistically structured and compositionally arranged so as to correspond to/complement one another, such an arrangement invites comparisons of the two narratives. More importantly, it invites close attention to the theology embedded in the conjunction of the narratives.[234]

---

229. Martens, 'Narrative Parallelism', pp. 33–49. Martens (pp. 34–35) provides an excellent summary of the phenomena of parallelism in narrative. Martens cites with approval Thomas Overholt's observation that Jer. 27–29 is an integral unit structured in parallelism where chs 27–28 deal with the problem of false prophecy in Israel while ch. 29 deals with false prophecy in Babylon. See Thomas W. Overholt, *The Threat of Falsehood: A Study in the Theology of the Book of Jeremiah* (Naperville: Allenson, 1970), pp. 29–30. Overholt's book which focuses on Jeremiah's conflict with false prophets is important to our thesis, as in Rev. 11 and Rev. 13 we also have a contest between true and false prophecy.

230. Martens, 'Narrative Parallelism', p. 38.

231. See Martens, 'Narrative Parallelism', p. 40.

232. Martens, 'Narrative Parallelism', p. 42.

233. Martens, 'Narrative Parallelism', p. 43.

234. Martens, 'Narrative Parallelism', p. 46.

Richard J. Clifford finds pervasive use of structural parallelism as a literary device in Deutero-Isaiah.[235] Clifford states:

> Structural parallelism is but one instance of a larger phenomenon which pervades biblical thought and expression.... In a manner different from an English poet who often aims at a single statement memorable by its compression, the Hebrew poet generally aims at dramatic interplay, the reverberation, between two (sometimes three) similar statements....
> What is true for parallelism of verses holds true also for larger assemblages: parallelism between scenes and parallelism between actors.[236]

It is important to note with Clifford that this parallelism does not only operate at verse level but also over larger segments. Clifford laments the fact that 'this aspect of biblical style is sometimes overlooked'.[237] He cites an example in Exodus 1–15 where parallel actors in a narrative are juxtaposed and contrasted: 'Pharaoh with his magicians, and Yahweh with Moses and Aaron, are portrayed in parallel, locked in combat for possession of the Hebrews. The plagues are assaults in the holy war. Yahweh wins and brings his people to serve him in his land.'[238] Similarly, we will see that the dragon with his two beasts (Rev. 13) and God/Jesus with his two witnesses (Rev. 11) are portrayed in parallel, locked in combat for the allegiance of the people in the world. The two witnesses are locked in mortal combat with their opponents (cf. 11.5). And in the manner of Moses and Aaron, the two witnesses cast plagues on God's behalf as assaults in the holy war (11.5–6). God triumphs at the resurrection of the two witnesses and brings his people, the church safely into his kingdom (cf. 11.11, 15).

The technique of structural parallelism is evident in the book of Revelation. Revelation 4–5, for example, is an integral literary unit divided into two parallel scenes; Rev. 4 introduces a scene in heaven – 'the One seated on the throne' is surrounded by his divine entourage in attendance, while in Rev. 5, the Lamb becomes the focus of attention. It appears that the Lamb becomes the 'mirror image' of 'the One seated on the throne' depicted in ch. 4. The correspondences between the parallels are remarkable through use of repetition with narrative development from

---

235. Richard J. Clifford, *Fair Spoken and Persuading: An Interpretation of Second Isaiah* (New York: Paulist Press, 1984), pp. 38–43.

236. Clifford, *Fair Spoken and Persuading*, p. 41.

237. Clifford, *Fair Spoken and Persuading*, p. 41.

238. Clifford, *Fair Spoken and Persuading*, p. 42. Clifford (pp. 56–58) also makes an insightful study of the polarity between the servant and the people in Deutero-Isaiah which will be useful in our analysis of the two witnesses as individuals as well as representatives of the corporate people of God.

Rev. 4 to Rev. 5. First, the One *sitting* on the throne surrounded by the twenty-four elders and four living beasts (4.3–6) is mirrored by the Lamb *standing* in the midst of the throne and of four living beasts and in the midst of twenty-four elders (5.6a). Secondly, the seven lamps of fire burning brightly before the throne identified as the seven spirits of God (4.5) are now depicted as the Lamb's seven horns and eyes sent out into all the earth (5.6b). Thirdly, the One seated on the throne is seen to hold a book at his right hand (5.1) while the movement in the narrative shows the Lamb approaching the throne and taking the book from his hand (5.7). Lastly, when the Lamb took the book from the One seated on the throne, the divine attendants worshipped the Lamb (5.8–10) in the manner in which they had worshipped the One seated on the throne (4.8–11). The climactic conclusion to the whole vision report of Rev. 4–5 brings together the One seated upon the throne and the Lamb as the centre of worship by all in heaven and on earth:

> [v. 13] Then I heard every creature in heaven and on earth and under the earth and in the sea, and all that is in them, singing, 'To **the one seated on the throne and to the Lamb** be blessing and honor and glory and might forever and ever!' [v. 14] And the four living creatures said, 'Amen!' And the elders fell down and worshiped. (Rev. 5.13–14).

This parallel structure can be tabulated as follows:

The One Sitting on the Throne	*The Lamb that was Slain*
1. And the one seated there looks like jasper and carnelian, and around the **throne** is a rainbow that looks like an emerald. Around the throne are twenty-four thrones, and seated on the thrones are twenty-four **elders**, dressed in white robes, with golden crowns on their heads... **four living creatures**... (Rev. 4.3–6)	1. Then I saw between the **throne** and the **four living creatures** and among the **elders** a Lamb standing as if it had been slaughtered, (Rev. 5.6a)
2. From the throne issue flashes of lightning, and voices and peals of thunder, and before the throne burn seven torches of fire, which are **the seven spirits of God**; (Rev. 4.5)	2. having seven horns and seven eyes, which are **the seven spirits of God** sent out into all the earth. (Rev. 5.6b)

3. 'You are **worthy**, our Lord and God, to **receive glory and honor and power**, for you created all things, and by your will they existed and were created.'
(Rev. 4.11)

3. '**Worthy** is the Lamb that was slaughtered to **receive power** and wealth and wisdom and might and **honor and glory** and blessing!'
(Rev. 5.12)

4. Then I saw in the right hand of the one seated on the throne **a scroll** written on the inside and on the back, sealed with seven seals.
(Rev. 5.1)

4. He went and took **the scroll** from the right hand of the one who was seated on the throne.
(Rev. 5.7)

By carefully structuring the portrayal of the Lamb in parallel to 'the One who sits on the throne', John depicts the Lamb as sharing the characteristics of 'the One who sits on the throne'. M. Eugene Boring rightly sees that the Lamb in Rev. 5 defines 'the One sitting on the throne' in Rev. 4. He states: 'John intentionally withholds any description of the central figure on the throne, leaving a blank center in the picture to be filled in by the figure of the Lamb – yet another means of affirming that God is the one who defines himself by Christ.'[239] More significantly the Lamb is seen as the authorized agent and executor of God's purposes for the earth since the Lamb alone is deemed worthy to take and open the book with seven seals (5.7). We will see that the literary technique of structural parallelism is employed with great effect in our literary analysis of Rev. 11.1–14.5.

Finally in this section, we will briefly discuss Paul Barnett's article entitled 'Polemical Parallelism: Some Further Reflections on the Apocalypse'.[240] Barnett comes closest to setting forth the biblical style of structural and narrative parallelism which we envisage for the interpretation of Rev. 11.1–14.5. However, Barnett focuses more on thematic parallelism which he finds in Revelation: worship, Roman ritual and true prophecy. According to Barnett, John's work is fundamentally a polemical tract. Does one worship the Dragon and the Beast or God and the Lamb? Does one belong to the community of Christ, the bride of the Lamb, characterized by chastity, truthfulness and endurance (14.4–5) or the community of the beast, the great harlot, characterized by murder, fornication, sorcery and falsehood (21.8)?[241] Yet even in his discussion on

---

239. M. E. Boring, *Revelation* (Louisville: John Knox Press, 1989), p. 103.
240. P. Barnett, 'Polemical Parallelism: Some Further Reflections on the Apocalypse', *JSNT* 35 (1989), pp. 111–20.
241. Barnett, 'Polemical Parallelism', pp. 112–13.

'Who is the True Prophet?', he fails to link the two witnesses-prophets as an intended parallel to the second beast, the false prophet (13.11–18; cf. 16.13; 19.20; 20.10).[242] Nevertheless, Barnett's thesis that John composes his book by way of polemical parallelism goes some way towards understanding what we argue is one of the main characteristics of John's literary style.

Likewise, we will see that Rev. 11 and Rev. 13 present two stories about the two witnesses and two beasts but these stories are juxtaposed and set in contrast within a larger concentric pattern. Neither Rev. 11 nor Rev. 13.1–14.5 can be exegeted fully on its own without reference to its complement. We will argue that Rev. 11 and Rev. 13.1–14.5 are also intentionally stylistically structured and compositionally arranged so as to correspond or complement one another and as such invite comparisons of the two narratives. It follows that the full theological impact of Rev. 11 and Rev. 13.1–14.5 can only be comprehended when the narratives are interpreted jointly. Unless they are read together, the activities of the two witnesses and two beasts are seen to be unrelated and disjointed from one another. Our contention is that Rev. 11 and Rev. 13.1–14.5 must not only be read as an integral whole with Rev. 12 as the pivot but that the careers of the two witnesses and the two beasts are arranged in a purposive manner whereby contrasting images of the dual protagonists are juxtaposed to great effect to highlight the dramatic conflict on earth which has its source and cause in heaven. The war between God and Satan in heaven is played out by their respective agents on earth. The two witnesses are God's witnesses, the dragon gives the first beast his authority; the two witnesses prophesy the word of God, the beast blasphemes God; the two witnesses are killed by the beast but resurrected by God; the beast suffers a plague of death but is healed (by Satan?); the two witnesses kill their enemies with fire, the second beast calls fire from heaven; the two witnesses can turn water into blood and call down plagues, the second beast performs great signs to deceive; the two witnesses' resurrection and ascension result in the people giving glory to God, the second beast causes the peoples to worship the first beast.[243]

8. *The Plan of this Study*

In the introduction (Chapter 1), we have set out the thesis of this study and propose that the textual unit in question is best analyzed utilizing Hebraic literary conventions and compositional techniques. In Chapter 2 we will identify the key words and key themes found throughout Rev. 11.1–14.5

---

242. Barnett, 'Polemical Parallelism', pp. 116–20.
243. These contrasts will be examined in detail in a later chapter.

and seek to show that these key words and themes unify the literary unit of 11.1–14.5 as a coherent whole. In Chapter 3, we will begin with a literary-structural analysis of Rev. 11. We will show that Rev. 11 is divided into four sub-units of vv. 1–2, vv. 3–6, vv. 7–13, and vv. 15–19 (ABCD). In Chapter 4 we will demonstrate that 12.1–17 is structured as a chiasm (EFGF'E') and in the same chapter we will also show that the unit of 13.1–14.5 is made up of four sub-units of 13.1–6, 13.7–10, 13.11–18, and 14.1–5 (D'C'B'A'). We will also discuss the meaning and significance of the major symbols in Rev. 12. In Chapter 5 we will seek to establish that Rev. 11 corresponds to Rev. 13.1–14.5 and together with Rev. 12 make up the extended chiastic pattern or macro-chiasm as we have proposed. In the same chapter, we will also test the proposed macro-chiasm. As our thesis argues that the war in heaven is reflected on earth in the war between the two witnesses of Rev. 11 and the two beasts of Rev. 13 we will discuss in detail the identity of the two witnesses and the two beasts and explore the nature of the warfare between these main antagonists (Chapter 6). The final chapter provides a brief conclusion summing up the main results of this study.

9. *Summary*

We have set out above the methodological approach that we will take in interpreting Rev. 11.1–14.5. Our *literary* and *rhetorical* analysis will utilize several approaches. Muilenburg's rhetorical criticism will be especially apposite in our quest for structure and in noting rhetorical or literary devices employed to delimit one passage from another. Delimiting component parts is an essential exercise in constructing the larger whole. We will adopt Schüssler Fiorenza's 'concentric, conic-spiraling approach' as a way forward in our analysis of 11.1–14.5.[244] Meynet's thesis that biblical narrative evidences a Hebraic rhetoric is preferred to Kennedy's usage of Greek rhetorical categories to understand our text in question. Breck's three dimensional helical concentric model is particularly illuminating as it helps to concretize in structural terms how the war in heaven (Rev. 12.7–12) has a cascading and downwards effect on the events on earth (Rev. 11 and Rev. 13). If there is any lingering doubt as to the validity of Lund's initial work on macro-chiasm as a possible structuring pattern in the New Testament, Breck, Meynet and more recently Brouwer

---

244. Recent articles that touch on Revelation's structure and figurative language have not persuaded me from departing from a chiastic reading of Rev. 11.1–14.5. See José Adriano Filho, 'The Apocalypse of John as an Account of a Visionary Experience: Notes on the Book's Structure', *JSNT* 25 (2002), pp. 213–34 and Biguzzi, 'A Figurative and Narrative Language', pp. 382–402.

have confirmed Lund's thesis and in our view, convincingly demonstrated that macro-chiasm is a common literary device or compositional technique employed not only in the Hebrew Bible but also in the New Testament. Blomberg's nine criteria provide a basis upon which a proposed macro-chiasm can be rigorously tested.

Alter's, Sternberg's and Meynet's works discussed above set out how biblical narrative and poetry have their unique literary qualities which invite literary reading or analysis. Finally Cohn, Clifford and Martens have highlighted for us the need to be sensitive to parallel patterns with special regards to the paratactic nature of Hebrew narrative. In structural parallelism, episodes and characters across several passages or even chapters are purposefully juxtaposed and contrasted for particular effect to yield a cumulative reading of the narrative as a whole.[245] Our analysis of Rev. 11.1–14.5 will attempt to follow the methodology set out above. Although we aim in this book to demonstrate that Rev. 11.1–14.5 is structured in a macro-chiasm, we acknowledge that as much as anything it is the cumulative impact of all the arguments put forth which will validate the proposed analysis. Not all the suggested chiastic patterns or parallelisms proposed will be equally convincing but *cumulatively* we believe that a chiastic reading of 11.1–14.5 is a viable approach to the interpretation of the text in question.[246] More significantly a chiastic analysis contributes to the understanding of the whole as well as the parts of this major textual unit of Revelation.

---

245.   For an excellent analysis of how characters in the book of Genesis are paralleled and juxtaposed across an extended unit of text, see Gary R. Rendsburg, 'Redactional Structuring in the Joseph Story: Genesis 37–50', in Vincent L. Tollers and John Maier (eds.), *Mappings of the Biblical Terrain: The Bible as Text* (Lewisburg, PA: Bucknell University Press, 1990), pp. 215–32.

246.   We agree with Schüssler Fiorenza that, 'in a rhetorical paradigm of interpretation, one does not need to claim that only one structuration is correct and all others are wrong'. Schüssler Fiorenza, *The Book of Revelation*, p. 207.

Chapter 2

THE LITERARY UNITY OF REVELATION 11.1–14.5

1. *Introduction*

In the next four chapters of this book, we will seek to demonstrate that the literary unit of Rev. 11.1–14.5 is structured as a macro-chiasm in the form of an ABCDEFGF'E'D'C'B'A' pattern. In this chapter we will examine the key words and key motifs found in 11.1–14.5 that function to unite the said textual unit into a coherent literary whole. We will also set out to describe in general the main chiastic pairs making up the macro-chiastic pattern we envisage for 11.1–14.5.

2. *The Unity of Revelation 11.1–14.5*

From a narrative standpoint, the unit of Rev. 10.1–11.13 is found after the commencement of the sixth Trumpet/second Woe at 9.13, which is said to conclude at 11.14 with the statement: 'The second woe has passed. The third woe is coming quickly.' This narrative and temporal marker gives the appearance that v. 14 of ch. 11 signals a major division between what has gone before and what comes after.[1] Furthermore, John appears to begin a new series of visions in Rev. 12 by stating that: 'a great sign was seen in heaven' (12.1). The spatial setting has shifted from earth (most of Rev. 11) to heaven (cf. 12.1, 7–12). The historical-prophetic narrative that characterizes Rev. 11 takes a dramatic turn in ch. 12 where the language returns to the more common form of a visionary report with the exception that its apocalyptic mythical imagery is greatly heightened. It is thus not surprising to find that most scholars conclude that Rev. 12 begins a distinct block of vision reports lasting to the end of Rev. 14. For example, Bauckham goes so far as to say that Rev. 12 intrudes on the readers like 'a characteristically abrupt start, devoid of literary links with anything that

---

1. For example, Peter Wongso divides chs 10–14 of the book of Revelation into two major literary units consisting 10.1–11.14 and 11.15–14.20. See Wongso, *Kitab Wahyu*, pp. 536, 556.

precedes'.[2] Agreeing with Bauckham, Leo Percer, in a recent thesis, remarks that: 'Revelation 12 interferes with the flow of an otherwise clean story and introduces new characters and new ideas into a story which for all practical purposes had ended!'[3]

It is the purpose of my book to challenge the view of the majority of the scholars who see Rev. 12–14 as unrelated to Rev. 11. Against the majority view, Sweet argues that, 'there is no structural break at the end of ch. 11 . . . the references to 'three and a half' bind 11–13 together (11.2f, 9, 11; 12.6, 14; 13.5)'.[4] Mazzaferri likewise contends that, '[Chapters] 11 and 12f. are strongly linked by the time period and the beast'.[5] However, Sweet and Mazzaferri do not go on to elaborate how Rev. 11–12 or Rev. 11–13 are bound together, a task we will attempt in this thesis by means of a detailed literary-structural analysis of the said textual unit.

---

2. Bauckham, *Climax of Prophecy*, p. 15. Also Boring, *Revelation*, p. 150. Yarbro Collins argues that Revelation 12 introduces the second great cycle of vision accounts (12.1–22.5). She comments that, '4.1–11.19 is a tightly integrated unit with its focus on the scroll with seven seals. The second signal is the new commission vision of ch. 10, which points ahead, not to ch. 11, but to ch. 12 and what follows.' A. Yarbro Collins, *The Combat Myth in the Book of Revelation* (HDR, 9; Missoula: Scholars Press, 1976), p. 157. It is difficult to see how ch. 10 points ahead to ch. 12 and not ch. 11 as Yarbro Collins alleges. 'Revelation 12 formally begins a new major text-sequence, covering the second half of the book.' Stephen W. Pattemore, 'The People of God in the Apocalypse: A Relevance-Theoretic Study' (Unpublished PhD dissertation; University of Otago, Dunedin, New Zealand, 2000), p. 283. Also Feuillet, *The Apocalypse*, pp. 54–62. Feuillet (p. 55) argues that Rev. 12.1 to Rev. 21.8 makes up the second half of the book on the ground that 'the historical background of this section [Rev. 12ff] is the persecution of which the Roman emperors have unleashed against the Church'. Even if the beast of Rev. 13 is seen as Rome or a Roman emperor (see our discussion on the beast in a later chapter), the persecution of the church begins not in Rev. 12 but is already evident in Rev. 11.7–10 where the beast that ascends from the abyss makes war and kills the two witnesses.

3. L. Percer, 'The War in Heaven: Messiah and Michael in Revelation 12' (Unpublished PhD dissertation; Texas: Baylor University, 1999), p. 3. J. Ramsey Michaels notes that, 'Almost all outlines of the Book of Revelation recognize a clear break between chapters 11 and 12.' J. R. Michaels, *Interpreting the Book of Revelation* (Grand Rapids: Baker Book House, 1992), p. 62. Beasley-Murray thinks that Rev. 12.1–14.2 'constitutes the most substantial parenthesis in the Revelation'. Beasley-Murray, *Revelation*, p. 191. Beale writes: 'The chapter [12] begins a new series of visions which end in 15.4.' Beale, *Revelation*, p. 621. So Frederick Murphy states: 'Chapter 12 begins the second half of Revelation.' F. Murphy, *Fallen is Babylon: the Revelation to John* (Harrisburg, PA: Trinity Press International, 1998), p. 275. M. de Jonge writes: 'In chapter 12 clearly a new section of the Apocalypse begins.' M. de Jonge, 'The use of the expression ὁ χριστὸς in the Apocalypse of St. John', in J. Lambrecht (ed.), *L'Apocalypse johannique et l'Apocalyptique dans le Nouveau Testament* (BETL, 53; Leuven: Leuven University Press, 1980), pp. 267–81 (268). Aune, however, notes the link between the last verse of ch. 11 (11.19) with the first verse of ch. 12 by the use of the clause, 'was seen in heaven'. See Aune, *Revelation 6–16*, p. 661.

4. Sweet, *Revelation*, p. 46.

5. Mazzaferri, *Genre*, p. 360.

The main contentious issue is whether Rev. 11 is in any way connected to Rev. 12 and if so, how? In his recent commentary on Revelation published in 2001, Prigent argues that the vision of Rev. 12 is a continuation of Rev. 11. He writes: 'The vision of chapt. 12 does not include the customary brief narrative introduction that offers a rough framework for the principal scenes of the book of Revelation (cf. 1.10; 4.1; 6.1; 7.1; 8.1–2; 10.1)…this new vision [Rev. 12] is in fact merely a continuation of the preceding one [Rev. 11].'[6] We cannot agree more.

Chapters 12 and 13 of Revelation are seen to belong together, and within the chapters themselves the division of units making up these two chapters is fairly ascertainable without much dispute. The divisions within Rev. 11 are more contentious as to how the units within the chapter are organized internally. For example, scholars have debated how sections or smaller units in Rev. 11 are structured. Some writers see 11.1–2 as independent from 11.3–13[7] while other scholars have viewed 11.1–13 or 11.1–14 as a continuous narrative.[8]

Of special importance in refuting the argument that Rev. 12 begins a major section which is unrelated to Rev. 11 is our attempt to link Rev. 11–12 through lexical and thematic parallels within the concentric pattern proposed for 11.1–14.5. We will attempt to show how the larger textual units are linked and delimit the structural divisions of smaller units within each chapter. We do well to note with Kennedy that, 'the rhetoric of large units often has to be built up from an understanding of the rhetoric of smaller units'.[9]

---

6. Prigent, *Commentary on the Apocalypse*, p. 367.

7. These writers posit two separate sources for 11.1–2 and 11.3–13. See Charles, *Revelation* Vol. 1, p. 274; M. Black, 'The "Two Witnesses" of Rev. 11.3f. in Jewish and Apocalyptic Tradition', in E. Bammel, C. K. Barrett, and W. D. Davies (eds.), *Donum Gentilicium: New Testament Studies in Honour of David Daube* (Oxford: Clarendon Press, 1978), pp. 225–37; Yarbro Collins, *Combat Myth*, p. 95 n. 60; C. H. Giblin, 'Revelation 11.1–13: Its Form, Function, and Contextual Integration', *NTS* 30 (1984), pp. 433–59 (454 n. 4); Helmut Seng, 'Apk 11,1–14 im Zusammenhang der Johannesapokalypse. Aufschluss aus Lactantius und Hippolytos', *Vetera Christianorum* 27 (1990), pp. 111–21 (114–15).

8. Joseph S. Considene, 'The Two Witnesses: Apoc. 11.3–13', *CBQ* 4 (1946), pp. 377–92 (382). Allan McNicol argues that the literary unit beginning at Rev. 11.1 ends at v. 14 and as such, Rev. 11.1–14 is coherent literary unit. McNicol, 'Revelation 11:1–14 and the Structure of the Apocalypse'. E. Lohmeyer argued that Rev. 11.1–14 should be divided between vv. 1–6 and vv. 7–14. See E. Lohmeyer, *Die Offenbarung des Johannes* (Tübingen: Mohr, 2nd edn, 1953), p. 87. Kraft distinguishes between Rev. 10.8–11.2 and 11.3–14. See Kraft, *Offenbarung*, pp. 150–55.

9. Kennedy, *New Testament Interpretation*, p. 33.

3. *The* Leitwörter *and Key Motifs in Revelation 11.1–14.5*

Lexical and thematic parallels are clearly evident across Rev. 11.1–14.5. The beast that ascends from the abyss makes a brief appearance in 11.7 and becomes the central character in Rev. 13. Likewise the persecution of the two witnesses and their martyrdom at the hands of the beast of ch. 11 is not only mirrored in 13.7 but also serves as the *leitmotiv* in the whole of Rev. 12, albeit in a different form and imagery. The woman and her son and her other offspring of Rev. 12 become the target of the dragon's anger and persecution.

a. *The War Motif*

War and images of warfare pervade the literary unit of Rev. 11.1–14.5. The word 'war' (πόλεμος, 12.7) and its cognates, 'warring' (πολεμῆσαι, 12.7 [x2]; 13.4) and 'to make war' (πόλεμον, 11.7; 12.17; 13.7) and other lexemes denoting warfare dominate the unit.[10] Significantly, the beginning (11.1–2) and the end (14.1–5) of the textual unit depict warfare. The statement that the nations will trample (πατήσουσιν) the holy city describes warfare in the holy city, which we will argue ends in the re-conquest of the city by warfare (14.1–5). Although there is no explicit mention of war in 14.1–5, recent scholars have now, following the lead of G. B. Caird and Bauckham, concluded that the Lamb and his 144,000 associates are 'holy warriors' waging war on or on behalf of Mount Zion.[11]

Closely related to the war motif is the νικάω word-group, which appears once in each chapter (11.7; 12.11; 13.7), as we will argue, at crucial junctures.[12] It is especially significant that the word 'conquer' is found once in each of the narratives under discussion, namely in the careers of the two

10. The noun, 'war' appears elsewhere in 9.7, 9; 16.14; 19.19; 20.8. The verb πολεμέω appears once before 11.1–14.5 in 2.16 and after 14.5 in 17.14 and 19.11. This means outside of 11.1–14.5 the word 'war' (noun and verbal forms) appears in total 8 times compared to 7 times within 11.1–14.5.

11. G. B. Caird, *A Commentary on the Revelation of St. John the Divine* (New York: Harper and Row, 1966), pp. 178–79, and R. Bauckham, 'The Apocalypse as a Christian War Scroll', in *idem, Climax of Prophecy*, pp. 210–37, esp. pp. 229–32. For example, Jonathan M. Knight remarks that: 'These 144,000 of Revelation 14 are on active service.... They are about to undertake the eschatological battle.' J. M. Knight, *Revelation* (Sheffield: Sheffield Academic Press, 1999), p. 103. Also David L. Barr comments that, 'this band [the 144,000] is pictured as gathered for battle against the beasts'. D. L. Barr, *Tales of the End: a narrative commentary on the book of Revelation* (Santa Rosa, CA: Polebridge Press, 1998), p. 114. Keener writes: 'The 144,000 portray the woman's seed not as persecuted saints but as a conquering army.' Keener, *Revelation*, p. 369.

12. The word νικάω and its forms appears 17 times in Revelation (8 times in Rev. 2–3 and elsewhere in 5.5; 6.2 [x2]; 15.2; 17.14; 21.7) but is found only once in each of chs 11, 12 and 13 respectively as shown above. See R. Leivestad, *Christ the Conqueror: The Idea of Conflict and Victory in the New Testament* (London: SPCK, 1954), p. 212.

witnesses and two beasts respectively (11.7; 13.7) and in the pivotal section of the war in heaven of 12.7–12. The beast who *conquers* (νικήσει) the two witnesses in ch. 11 (11.7) is also the one who *conquers* (νικῆσαι) the saints in ch. 13 (13.7), but in ch. 12 the fortunes are reversed, the saints conquer Satan/the beast: 'they *conquered* (ἐνίκησαν) him [Satan/the beast] by the blood of the Lamb and the word of their testimony' (12.11). A helical three-dimensional flow can be shown as follows:

Rev. 12.11 (***declaration from heaven***)

(They *conquered* him by the blood of the Lamb and the word of their testimony)

Rev. 11.7 (***on earth***)
(When they finished their testimony, the beast that comes up from the bottomless pit will make war and *conquer* them and kill them)

Rev. 13.7 (***on earth***)
(Also it was allowed to make war on the saints and *conquer* them)

Although the war motif appears elsewhere in Revelation, it is by far the most concentrated and sustained in 11.1–14.5. Alter cites Martin Buber's definition of the *Leitwort* as follows:

> A *Leitwort* is a word or word-root that recurs significantly in a text, in a continuum of texts, or in a configuration of texts: by following these repetitions, one is able to decipher or grasp a meaning of the text, or at any rate, the meaning will be revealed more strikingly. The repetition, as we have said, need not merely be of the word itself but also of the root word; in fact, the very difference of words can often intensify the dynamic action of the repetition. I call it 'dynamic' because between combinations of sounds related to one another in this manner a kind of movement takes place: if one imagines the entire text deployed before him, one can sense waves moving back and forth between the words. The measured repetition that matches the inner rhythm of the text, or rather, wells up from it, is one of the most powerful means for conveying meaning without expressing it.[13]

---

13. Alter, *The Art of Biblical Narrative*, p. 93. Alter cites Martin Buber, *Werke*. II, *Schriften zur Bibel* (Munich: Kösel, 1964), p. 1131 (Alter's translation). Alter (p. 93) laments the fact that most English translations constantly translate the same word with different English equivalents for the sake of fluency and supposed precision. This so-called dynamic equivalence translation method is applied in the latest edition of the Malay Bible, *Alkitab*

The word 'war' is the *Leitwort* in this segment of text.[14] Forms of this term 'war' (πόλεμος) and the war-motif recur in the rest of the narrative of 11.1–14.5, unifying the textual unit as an integral whole. Altogether it occurs seven times in crucial contexts (11.7; 12.7 [x3], 17; 13.4, 7). Other lexemes apart from πολεμέω and νικάω are also used by John to convey this war motif as the major theme in the textual unit. The war between the dragon and Michael in 12.7–12 extends also to the conflict between the dragon and the woman. The image of a woman crying out in birthpangs (12.2) could be seen as a metaphor for a city under siege by a military power (cf. Jer. 4.31; Mic. 4.9–11 and 1QH 11.3–18). Lexemes such as ἔστηκεν and καταφάγῃ in 12.4 denote the dragon's warfare against the woman and her child.[15] Further, it is said that the dragon ἐδίωξεν the woman (12.13), which speaks of violent persecution. The imagery of the dragon's mouth spewing out water like a river to sweep away its opponent is also a metaphor of warfare (12.15).[16]

b. *The Worship Motif*

The worship motif is another significant theme in the parallel accounts in Rev. 11 and Rev. 13.1–14.5. In Rev. 11, two scenes depict worship proffered to God. First, there are those who worship (προσκυνοῦντας) in the temple on earth (11.2) and the twenty-four elders who worship (προσεκύνησαν) God in heaven (11.16).[17] In contrast, Rev. 13 depicts the worship of Satan and the beast. The inhabitants of the world who rejoice at the slaying of the two witnesses (11.9–10) worship the dragon and the

(Bahasa Melayu; Bible Society of Malaysia, 1996). For example, the word μαρτυρέω in John's gospel, a key word in John 1–4 is translated by using three different Malay words (mengkhabarkan [1.8], memberitahukan [1.7; 3.11, 32], berkata [4.39]) supposedly for fluency and precision allegedly on the ground of semantic equivalence instead of the Malay word 'saksi', which is the closest word to μαρτυρέω in the Greek. Phyllis Trible also notes that rhetorical features in the Hebrew text stand out clearly if translators 'use the same English word for the equivalent Hebrew word' and 'do not translate a single Hebrew word by a variety of English words'. P. Trible, *Rhetorical Criticism: Context, Method and the Book of Jonah* (Minneapolis: Fortress Press, 1995), p. 105.

14. Alter notes that, 'word-motif. . . is one of the most common features of the narrative art of the Bible'. Alter, *The Art of Biblical Narrative*, p. 92.

15. The word καταφάγῃ (to devour) is a metaphor for military action to devastate a land or a city. See LXX Jer. 28.34 (MT – Jer. 51.34) which reads: 'κατέφαγέν με ἐμερίσατό με κατέλαβέν με σκεῦος λεπτὸν Ναβουχοδονοσορ βασιλεὺς Βαβυλῶνος κατέπιέν με ὡς δράκων ἔπλησεν τὴν κοιλίαν αὐτοῦ ἀπὸ τῆς τρυφῆς μου ἐξῶσέν με.' King Nebuchadnezzar of Babylon is depicted as a dragon, which has devoured Zion by warfare.

16. See for example, Isa. 8.8 where the imagery of mighty flood waters of the River is a metaphor for the King of Assyria sweeping across the land of Judah with its military might. We will examine these images in detail when we come to exegete the passages in question.

17. The scene described in Rev. 11.13 could also be seen as 'worship' as the rest of the inhabitants 'gave glory to the God of heaven'.

beast (13.4). Conversely, those who refuse to worship the beast are put to death (13.15). The second beast makes it his policy to enforce the worship of the (first) beast on the pain of death (13.15).[18] The word προσκυνέω and its verbal forms runs through 13.1–18 as a thread making it the *Leitwort* of Rev. 13 (13.4 [x2], 8, 12, 15):

1. προσεκύνησαν τῷ δράκοντι (13.4)
2. προσεκύνησαν τῷ θηρίῳ (13.4)
3. προσκυνήσουσιν αὐτὸν πάντες οἱ κατοικοῦντες ἐπὶ τῆς γῆς (13.8)
4. τὴν γῆν καὶ τοὺς ἐν αὐτῇ κατοικοῦντας ἵνα προσκυνήσουσιν τὸ θηρίον τὸ πρῶτον (13.12)
5. προσκυνήσωσιν τῇ εἰκόνι τοῦ θηρίου (13.15)

The literary unit of Rev. 11.1–14.5 ends with a worship scene depicting the company of 144,000 participating in the singing a new song before the throne of God (14.2–5).[19] What is of significance is that both the beginning and the end of the literary unit in question juxtapose the scenes of worship with warfare. Thus, we may conclude that the dual themes of worship and warfare ring the unit of 11.1–14.5 in an *inclusio*.[20]

In ch. 12 of Revelation, two key words provide the clue to the unity of this segment of text. The word 'dragon' appears eight times in Rev. 12 and thrice in Rev. 13.[21] The other key word is the verb ἔβαλεν (from the verb βάλλω) which in its active and passive forms appears eight times in Rev. 12. This word is used to describe the deeds carried out by the dragon and actions done to the dragon:

1. καὶ ἡ οὐρὰ αὐτοῦ σύρει τὸ τρίτον τῶν ἀστέρων τοῦ οὐρανοῦ καὶ ἔβαλεν αὐτοὺς εἰς τὴν γῆν (12.4).
2. καὶ ἐβλήθη ὁ δράκων ὁ μέγας, ὁ ὄφις ὁ ἀρχαῖος, ὁ καλούμενος Διάβολος καὶ ὁ Σατανᾶς, ὁ πλανῶν τὴν οἰκουμένην ὅλην, ἐβλήθη εἰς τὴν γῆν, καὶ οἱ ἄγγελοι αὐτοῦ μετ' αὐτοῦ ἐβλήθησαν (12.9 [x3]).
3. ἐβλήθη ὁ κατήγωρ τῶν ἀδελφῶν ἡμῶν (12.10).
4. Καὶ ὅτε εἶδεν ὁ δράκων ὅτι ἐβλήθη εἰς τὴν γῆν (12.13).
5. καὶ ἔβαλεν ὁ ὄφις ἐκ τοῦ στόματος αὐτοῦ ὀπίσω τῆς γυναικὸς ὕδωρ ὡς ποταμόν (12.15).

18. Unless specified, the designation 'the beast' refers to the first beast described in Rev. 13.1–10.

19. 'Whom do you worship?' becomes the key question in Rev. 11 and 13.1–14.5, a point which we will return in our detail discussion of the lexical, structural, and thematic parallels between Rev. 11 and 13.1–14.5.

20. We will discuss the *inclusio* of Rev. 11.1–14.5 in detail in a later section.

21. Rev. 12.3, 4, 7 [x2], 9, 13, 16, 17; 13.2, 4, 11; elsewhere in Rev. 16.13 and 20.2. The word 'dragon' does not appear elsewhere in the New Testament. See Wongso, *Kitab Wahyu*, p. 573.

6. καὶ κατέπιεν τὸν ποταμὸν ὃν ἔβαλεν ὁ δράκων ἐκ τοῦ στόματος αὐτοῦ (12.16).

The dual themes of war and worship are the central motifs unifying 11.1–14.5. While the theme of worship is important elsewhere in Revelation (cf. Rev. 4–5; 15.2–4; 19.1–10; 21.22–22.6), it is only in 11.1–14.5 that the worship motif is placed side by side with the war motif. We have already noted that 11.1–2 and 14.1–5 combine warfare and worship motifs. Further, we see that as a result of a great earthquake, a sign of divine warfare, the rest of the city's population give glory to God (11.13). The defeat of the dragon in the heavenly war initiates a summons to heavens and those who dwell there to rejoice, perhaps an occasion for heavenly worship (12.12). The worship of the dragon and the beast is linked to the fact that in the eyes of the earth dwellers, no one can war (πολεμῆσαι) against the beast (13.4).[22]

On the face of it, war and worship seem to be poles apart in terms of ideology, theology, content and meaning. As we shall see it is through worship that the church wars against the beasts. Conversely, it could be argued that the 144,000's war against its enemies on Mount Zion is itself an act of worship as depicted in 14.1–5. J. Tremper Longman III and Daniel G. Reid are right when they comment that: 'As odd as it may seem to modern sensibilities, battle is portrayed as an act of worship in the Hebrew Bible.'[23] Thus it is not surprising that various passages in 11.1–14.5 merge these seemingly contradictory themes side by side. It appears that even in the times of great distress for the people of God, they are exhorted to worship God. As we will see, the insistence of the saints on worshipping God is the reason why the dragon and the beast war against the people of God. Paradoxically, it is in and through worship the church wages war against the beast. The juxtaposition of these two themes undergirds the whole narrative as a unified literary unit. Thus we have *two* overarching themes in this middle section of Revelation: warfare and worship.

22.   Steven J. Friesen comments: 'In this vision of the imperial Beast [Rev. 13], the themes of worship and warfare are intertwined in different ways around the character of the Beast and the Lamb. The demonic pretender to world dominion is worshipped for his ability to defeat all opponents. The figure who is truly worthy of receiving worship and dominion, on the other hand, is described precisely as the one who was victimized and defeated.' S. J. Friesen, *The Imperial Cults and the Apocalypse of John: Reading Revelation in the Ruins* (Oxford: Oxford University Press, 2001), p. 176.

23.   J. T. Longman III and D. G. Reid, *God is a Warrior* (Studies in Old Testament Biblical Theology; Grand Rapids: Zondervan, 1995), p. 34.

4. *The Macro-Chiasm of Revelation 11.1–14.5*

This eschatological warfare has been variously labelled as 'Holy War',[24] the 'Divine Warrior motif'[25] or the 'Combat Myth'.[26] I prefer to call it the 'War-in-Heaven' motif borrowing directly from 12.7a, Καὶ ἐγένετο πόλεμος ἐν τῷ οὐρανῷ.[27] This passage (12.7–12), which describes the war in heaven and its resultant effects in heaven and on earth, becomes the central focus of the literary unit 11.1–14.5. Verses 7–12 of Rev. 12 make up not only the pivotal unit of Rev. 12 but of the whole unit of 11.1–14.5. Peter A. Abir's thesis that '12.7–12 is at the centre not only of ch. 12 but also of the whole

24. Bauckham states that: 'In Jewish eschatological expectation the theme of holy war plays a prominent role.' Bauckham, *Climax of Prophecy*, p. 210. Aune states thus: 'A final eschatological holy war is a frequent motif in prophetic and apocalyptic scenarios of the series of events which bring the present age to a decisive end (Ezek. 38.7–16; 39.2; Joel 3.2; Zech. 12.1–9; 14.1; *I En.* 56.5–7; 90.13–19; 99.4; *Jub.* 23.23; 4 Ezra 13.33–34; *Sib. Or.* 3.663–68).' Aune, 'Qumran and the Book of Revelation', p. 641. Giblin argues that the thematic pattern in Rev. 4–22 is 'God's holy war, by which "kingdom come".' Giblin, 'Recapitulation and the Literary Coherence of John's Apocalypse', p. 84. Also Jan A. du Rand writes: 'The image of the messianic war describes the whole process of establishing the kingdom of God on earth.' J. du Rand, '"Your Kingdom Come on Earth as it is in Heaven": The Theological motif of the Apocalypse of John', *Neot* 31 (1997), pp. 59–75 (67).

25. See Patrick D. Miller Jr., *The Divine Warrior in Early Israel* (Cambridge, MA: Harvard University Press, 1973); J. T. Longman III, 'The Divine Warrior: The New Testament Use of an Old Testament Motif', *WTJ* 44 (1982), pp. 290–307; Longman and Reid, *God is a Warrior*, esp. ch. 11 'Revelation: Visions of Divine Warfare', pp. 180–92. Also Frank M. Cross., 'The Divine Warrior in Israel's Early Cult', in Cyrus Gordon (ed.), *Biblical Motifs* (Cambridge, MA: Harvard University Press, 1966), pp. 12–30. For other general studies on God as Divine warrior, see Gregory Boyd, *God at War: The Bible and the Spiritual Conflict* (Downers Grove: Inter-Varsity Press, 1997); S.-M. Kang, *Divine War in the Old Testament and the Ancient Near East* (BZAW, 177; Berlin: de Gruyter, 1989); C. Kloos, *Yhwh's Combat with the Sea: A Canaanite Tradition in the Religion of Ancient Israel* (Leiden: Brill, 1986); Tom Yoder Neufeld, *Put on the Armour of God: The Divine Warrior from Isaiah to Ephesians* (JSNTSup, 140; Sheffield: Sheffield Academic Press, 1997); Mary Wakeman, 'The Biblical Earth Monster in the Cosmogonic Combat Myth', *JBL* 88 (1969), pp. 313–20; *idem, God's Battle with the Monster: A Study in Biblical Imagery* (Leiden: E.J. Brill, 1973); John Day, *God's Conflict with the Dragon and the Sea: Echoes of a Canaanite Myth in the Old Testament* (Cambridge: Cambridge University Press, 1985).

26. See Yarbro Collins, *Combat Myth*; Snyder, 'Combat Myth in the Apocalypse'; N. Forsyth, *The Old Enemy: Satan and the Combat Myth* (Princeton, N.J.: Princeton University Press, 1987).

27. After coining this phrase 'war-in-heaven' motif, I came across similar phraseology by William J. Dumbrell in describing the vision of Dan. 7.1–8 as follows: 'Once this "war-in-heaven" motif of the vision has been disposed, the judgement scene which provides the core of the chapter [7] follows in verses 9–14.' W. Dumbrell, *The End of the Beginning: Revelation 21–22 and the Old Testament* (NSW, Australia: Lancer Books, 1985), p. 186. However, one is hard pressed to find in Dan. 7.1–8 the notion of a war in heaven. The 'war-in-heaven' motif is much more evident in Dan. 10 where the angels Gabriel and Michael fought with the princes of Greece and Persia.

book' is persuasively argued in his monograph *The Cosmic Conflict of the Church: An Exegetico-Theological Study of Revelation 12.7–12.*[28] The centrality of Rev. 12.7–12 is shown in the proposed macro-chiasm as follows:

A – 11.1–2 (Temple Measured/Holy City Trampled)

  B – 11.3–6 (The Signs of the 2 Witnesses)

    C – 11.7–13 (The death, resurrection, and ascension of the 2 Witnesses)

      D – 11.15–19 (God's Kingdom comes)

        E – 12.1–4 (The Dragon's Conflict with the Woman)

          F – 12.5–6 (The Woman's Escape & Refuge)

            G – 12.7–12 (The War in Heaven)

          F' – 12.13–14 (The Woman's Escape & Refuge)

        E' – 12.15–17 (The Dragon's Conflict with the Woman)

      D' – 13.1–6 (The Kingdom of the Beast/Dragon)

    C' – 13.7–10 (The death of the Saints)

  B' – 13.11–18 (The Signs of the 2nd Beast)

A' – 14.1–5 (The Temple/Holy City Restored)

The pattern we propose for Rev. 11.1–14.5 is a clear example of what Schüssler Fiorenza terms the 'concentric, conic-spiraling' approach to a main section of Revelation. This helical concentric pattern creates 'a sense of ascent and descent, linking the elements of the narrative into a single architecture marked off from what precedes and follows it'.[29] From heaven (G) to earth (FF', EE', DD', and so on), this pattern creates, in Viviano's words, an 'image of the cascade or descent into increasing degrees of

---

28. P. A. Abir, *The Cosmic Conflict of the Church: An Exegetico-Theological Study of Revelation 12.7–12* (Frankfurt am Main: Peter Lang, 1995), p. 29. Speaking generally of chiasmus in Revelation, Mark Wilson is correct to note that Rev. 12 is uniformly placed at the climax or crossing point in all proposed structural models of Revelation. See M. Wilson, 'Revelation', in Clinton E. Arnold (ed.), *Zondervan Illustrated Bible Backgrounds Commentary* Vol. 4 (Grand Rapids: Zondervan, 2002), pp. 244–383 (317).

29. Cohn, 'Literary Technique in the Jeroboam Narrative', p. 25. Cohn's comments quoted above are on the Jeroboam narrative in 1 Kings 11.26–14.20.

concreteness'.[30] Once the chiastic pattern is grasped by the readers, as Breck has demonstrated, the reading of the unit within the macro-chiasm can either begin from the extremities (11.1–2; 14.1–5) towards the pivot (12.7–12) or from the pivot towards the extremities.[31] If it is read from the latter perspective, then from a mythical battle in heaven between extra-terrestrial beings (G), the pattern descends into the concreteness of events on earth: The woman's escape to the wilderness (FF'), the dragon's conflict with the woman (EE'), the kingdom of the beast and the kingdom of God (DD'), the prophetic testimony of the two witnesses and the church in the context of the persecution of the beasts (CC', BB'), the desecration of the Temple-Holy City and the Lamb's victory on Mount Zion (AA').

The vision report contained in Rev. 12 appears to show a heaven/earth dichotomy or above/below perspective or a two-layered reality. While the war between the dragon and Michael are fought in heaven (G), the events represented by the other chiastic pairs appear to take place on earth.[32] Abir notes thus:

> The scene is set, first of all, in heaven. Both the *great signs* appear first only in heaven. But there is a spatial transition on the part of the Woman and the Dragon, from heaven to the earth. The Woman escapes to the desert from the Dragon (εἰς τὴν ἔρημον), while the Dragon, whose tail extends from the heaven to the earth (v. 4), is thrown down to the earth (ἐβλήθη εἰς τὴν γῆν: v. 9).[33]

We surmise that Rev. 12 on its own is structured in a concentric pattern of EFGF'E' as shown above. We suggest it is closely linked to Rev. 11 and 13.1–14.5 making a larger concentric pattern of ABCDEFGF'E'D'C'B'A. This larger concentric pattern with the pivotal pattern focusing on the war in heaven functions rhetorically to inform John's readers that whatever happens on earth corresponds to, and in a large degree is determined by, what happens in heaven. According to John's apocalyptic worldview, though heavenly events are invisible to the naked eye on earth, their reality and impact on earth are undeniable. John the Seer through revelation 'saw' the war in heaven between the angelic host led by Michael and Satan and his angels. Satan's defeat in the heavenly war and his casting down from heaven to earth is the cause of *the conflict between society and the church on earth. This conflict is portrayed by John as a war between the two*

---

30. Benedict T. Viviano, 'The Structure of the Prologue of John (1.1–18): A Note', *RB* 105 (1998), pp. 176–84 (181). Viviano's comments quoted above are on the structure of Jn 1.1–18.

31. See Breck, *The Shape of Biblical Language*, pp. 43–45, and our discussion on Breck's helical model in chapter 1 of this book.

32. For a discussion on John's literary technique of the 'above/below' point of view, see Resseguie, *Revelation Unsealed*, p. 43.

33. Abir, *Cosmic Conflict*, p. 67.

witnesses and the two beasts. This earthly conflict is a result of the war in heaven. According to Mary E. Mills, the inter-penetration between heaven and earth finds expression and meaning 'within a society which believed in a parallelism between heaven and earth so close that it allowed for the immanence of heavenly powers in earthly forms and the transcendence of earthly affairs to find their true meaning in the heavenly sphere'.[34]

We will argue that the outcome of the war-in-heaven in Rev. 12.7–12 determines what transpires on earth in Rev. 11 and Rev. 13. Michael defeats Satan in heaven (12.7–8) and casts Satan out of heaven down to earth (12.9, 12). This momentous event in heaven has unimaginable earthly repercussions. It results in the most severe conflict for the church, a period called 'the great tribulation' (7.14) which is narrated in Rev. 13 (cf. 11.7).[35]

34.   M. E. Mills, *Human Agents of Cosmic Power* (Sheffield: JSOT Press, 1990), p. 69. We will argue that the heavenly war in Rev. 12.7–12 alludes to the war in heaven between the angel Gabriel and the princes of Persia and Greece in Dan. 10. John J. Collins thinks that the wars between the king of the north and the king of the south in Dan. 11 are the outworkings of the war between the divinities in heaven of Dan. 10. He writes: 'The wars on earth were conceived merely as reflections, or at least the working out of the war between the divinities in heaven.' J. J. Collins, 'The Mythology of Holy War in Daniel and the Qumran War Scroll: A Point of Transition in Jewish Apocalyptic', *VT* 25 (1975), pp. 596–612 (598). Tim Meadowcroft argues that the princes of Persia and Greece of Dan. 10 are not angelic beings but political leaders on earth and that the celestial beings like Gabriel and Michael are directly engaged in warfare with them on an earthly plane. T. Meadowcroft, 'Who are the Princes of Persia and Greece (Daniel 10)? Pointers Towards the Danielic Vision of Earth and Heaven', *JSOT* 29 (2004), pp. 99–113. While there is an interaction between earthly and heavenly forces that defies precise categorization and clear boundaries in Dan. 10–12, as Meadowcroft points out, I remain unconvinced that the princes of Persia and Greece of Dan. 10 could be anything apart from angelic beings that operate in the heavens. That is, as traditionally understood, angelic beings of the unseen world engage in warfare against God's angel, to prevent Gabriel from reaching Daniel on earth with a heavenly message (Dan. 10.12–14). The Danielic scenario in Dan. 10 is clearly alluded to in the war in *heaven* between the angel Michael and the dragon (Rev. 12.7–12).

35.   A feature of John's literary style is introducing a character, theme, or concept in one text only to expand or elaborate on it in a later text. Here, the notion of 'the great tribulation' is introduced without further explanation but will be filled in by the elaboration of events said to unfold within the last three-and-a-half years narrated in Rev. 11–13. Giblin thinks of the great tribulation in 7.14 as 'comprising all three woes' which, in his opinion are narrated from 9.1–15.8. See Giblin, 'Recapitulation and the Literary Coherence of John's Apocalypse', pp. 88 n. 30, 95. Michael Goulder comments that the great tribulation in Revelation covers the events under the Trumpet series from Rev. 8 to Rev. 14. See M. Goulder, 'The Apocalypse as an Annual Cycle of Prophecies', *NTS* 27 (1981), pp. 322–41 (322). See also C. Rowland, 'Excursus: The Tribulations of the Messianic Age', in 'The Book of Revelation', *The New Interpreter's Bible* (12 Vols; Nashville: Abingdon Press, 1998), pp. 501–743 (635–36). Other examples of this literary style include the introduction of the Beast in 11.7 (expanded in Rev. 13 and Rev. 17) and the announcement of Babylon's fall in 14.8 (expanded in Rev. 18).

In the midst of this great suffering, God's gospel or mystery is proclaimed with even greater intensity (cf. 11.3–7; 10.7, 11; 14.6–7).[36]

It is important to emphasize at this point that the little scroll of Rev. 10 becomes the subject of John's commission to prophesy again (10.11) and chs 11–13 bound by the temporal period of three-and-a-half years coming immediately after John's re-commissioning present a strong *prima facie* case that these middle chapters of Revelation are part and parcel of that prophecy contained in the little scroll.[37] Edith Humphrey comments thus:

> His [John's] prophecy, the little scroll, includes the vision of the two witnesses, the Woman and the Dragon, the two beasts, the Lamb with the 144,000 and the final judgment. Some symmetry is to be seen in these events. *The two witnesses are foiled, for example, by the two beasts.* This is underscored by the time-period used in both chapters (1260 days = 42 months at 11.2, 3 and 13.5), and by the early reference to the beast in 11.7. It is also highlighted by references to the miracles performed by each couple, by the resurrection of the witnesses and the false resurrection of the beast, and by contrasting reactions to these wonders; ἔδωκαν δόξαν τῷ θεῷ τοῦ οὐρανοῦ (11.13) over against καὶ προσεκύνησαν τῷ δράκοντι (13.4). Again, just as all peoples, tribes, languages and nations refuse the two witnesses burial (11.9), so all the peoples, tribes, languages and nations follow the beast (13.7).[38]

The symmetry of correspondences and contrasts noted in passing by Humphrey falls neatly into the chiastic parallel pairs in the structure of Rev. 11.1–14.5 which we have proposed above.

We will seek to demonstrate that the concentric pattern proposed above is a valid and viable structure envisaged by John himself. We will show that the episodes surrounding the Temple/Mount Zion in the extremities AA' are intimately linked with the heavenly war in the pivot. We are well aware of scholars' caution in detecting concentric or chiastic patterns in biblical texts as a feature perhaps subjectively determined by the beholder or the

36. Leonard Thompson remarks that: 'For John "suffering" is probably the most essential ingredient in the Christian proclamation.' L. Thompson, 'A Sociological Analysis of Tribulation in the Apocalypse of John', *Semeia* 36 (1986), pp. 147–74 (150). We will discuss this theme of suffering and witness in a later chapter.

37. Bauckham understands that John in Rev. 11.2 'begins to divulge the contents of the scroll as prophecy'. Bauckham, *Climax of Prophecy*, p. 267.

38. E. Humphrey, *The Ladies and the Cities: Transformation and Apocalyptic Identity in Joseph and Aseneth, 4 Ezra, the Apocalypse and the Shepherd of Hermas* (JSPSup, 17; Sheffield: Sheffield Academic Press, 1995), p. 100 (emphasis mine). A. Garrow, however, argues that the little scroll foreshadows the events in Rev. 11.1–14.5. 'The foreshadowing function of the little scroll is supported by the strong correlation between the events described in 11.1–13 and those recorded in greater detail in 12.1–14.5; 16:19.' A. Garrow, 'Revelation's Assembly Instructions', in Kent E. Brower and Mark W. Elliot (eds.), *Eschatology in Bible and Theology* (Downers Grove: Inter-Varsity Press, 1999), pp. 187–98 (194).

writer who proposes the existence of such structure. While such caution is noted, Douglas has pointed out in her study on the book of Leviticus that, 'the discipline of looking for structure is not one that may be shirked. Assuming that a text is written with no structure is imposing the linear sequential structure of our own conventions.'[39] Thus we suggest that the literary forms of chiasm and parallelism (whether in clearly poetic texts or prose) pervade the way Rev. 11.1–14.5 is composed.[40] We cannot concur more with John Heil's statement that: 'To be truly convincing a chiastic structure must adhere to rigorous criteria and methodology. It must be evident that the chiasm has not been *imposed upon* the text but actually subsists and operates *within* the text.'[41] We seek to establish this concentric pattern by analysing the text of Rev. 11.1–14.5 in detail with close attention to its form (literary-structural analysis) and content (thematic and theological analysis).

5. *The Frame Passages of Revelation 11.1–14.5: 10.11 and 14.6–7*

As Lund has pointed out, often an extended chiasm is enveloped by frame passages which immediately precede and follow the unit in question. In our case, the literary unit that precedes 11.1 is 10.1–11 in general and 10.11 in particular. The passage that follows 14.1–5 consists of the three messages announced by three angels. The text of 14.6 reads thus: 'Then I saw another angel flying in midheaven...', which is followed by '...another angel, a second...' (14.8) and '...another angel, a third...' (14.9). It is clear that v. 6 of Rev. 14 begins a new literary unit consisting of a vision report of another three angels and their pronouncements that are distinct from the sub-unit in 14.1–5.[42] Robert L. Thomas remarks that: '"Another

---

39.   Douglas, 'Poetic Structure in Leviticus', p. 245.

40.   See previous discussions in chapter 1 on works by Lund, Welch, Breck, Thomson, Meynet and Brouwer for the preponderance of chiasm in the NT. Such stylistic and compositional techniques and conventions are mostly concentrated in the literary Prophets (esp. Isaiah) and Wisdom writings of the Old Testament (esp. Psalms) from which Revelation draws much for inspiration and thought. See especially Dale A. Brueggemann, 'The Use of the Psalter in John's Apocalypse' (Unpublished PhD dissertation; Westminster Theological Seminary, 1995), and Gillingham, 'Psalmody and Apocalyptic in the Hebrew Bible', pp. 147–69. According to Moyise, the book of Isaiah and the Psalms provide the greatest number of allusions in Revelation. See Moyise, *The Old Testament in the Book of Revelation*, p. 16. Wongso concurs with Moyise's estimation and suggests that there are 84 allusions to Isaiah and 59 allusions to the Psalms in the book of Revelation. See Wongso, *Kitab Wahyu*, p. 183.

41.   J. Heil, 'The Chiastic Structure and Meaning of Paul's Letter to Philemon', *Bib* 82 (2001), pp. 178–206 (179) [his emphasis].

42.   Aune remarks that Rev. 14.6–12 'despite the diversity of their content, form a literary unit.' *Revelation 6–16*, p. 796. Also de Silva, 'The Persuasive Strategy of the Apocalypse', pp. 785–806.

angel" [14.6] marks a new turn in the drama as "another angel" did at 7.2; 8.3; 10.1.'[43] If *another* angel of 10.1 introduces the literary unit of 11.1–14.5, then *another* angel in 14.6 signals the beginning of a new section. Both Rev. 10 and 14.6 are introduced by John seeing *another* angel, passages which we will argue function as frame passages for the macro-chiasm under discussion:

Καὶ εἶδον ἄλλον ἄγγελον ἰσχυρὸν . . . (10.1)
Καὶ εἶδον ἄλλον ἄγγελον . . . (14.6)

John's vision of another angel is narrated over two verses in 14.6–7:

[v. 6] Καὶ εἶδον ἄλλον ἄγγελον πετόμενον ἐν μεσουρανήματι, ἔχοντα εὐαγγέλιον αἰώνιον εὐαγγελίσαι ἐπὶ τοὺς καθημένους ἐπὶ τῆς γῆς καὶ ἐπὶ πᾶν ἔθνος καὶ φυλὴν καὶ γλῶσσαν καὶ λαόν, [v. 7] λέγων ἐν φωνῇ μεγάλῃ, Φοβήθητε τὸν θεὸν καὶ δότε αὐτῷ δόξαν, ὅτι ἦλθεν ἡ ὥρα τῆς κρίσεως αὐτοῦ, καὶ προσκυνήσατε τῷ ποιήσαντι τὸν οὐρανὸν καὶ τὴν γῆν καὶ θάλασσαν καὶ πηγὰς ὑδάτων.

It is significant to note that the correspondences between the message of another angel in Rev. 10 and the one in 14.6–7 extend beyond what we have discussed above. Both angels preach the good news/gospel. The verb εὐηγγέλισεν in 10.7 corresponds to the verb εὐαγγελίσαι in 14.6. These are the only two occasions where the verbal form of εὐαγγελίζω are found in the book of Revelation. The noun εὐαγγέλιον, good news or gospel also appears here in 14.6 and nowhere else in Revelation. In 10.7, the object of the good news preached (εὐηγγέλισεν) to God's servants the prophets is the mystery of God (τὸ μυστήριον τοῦ θεοῦ). In 14.6, the angel preaches the eternal gospel (εὐαγγέλιον αἰώνιον). If parallelism is at work here, a case can be made that the mystery of God contained in the little opened scroll preached to the prophets appears to be related to the eternal gospel preached by the angel in 14.6–7.[44] The unit of 14.6–7 functions thus to sum up the message of the strong angel of Rev. 10 as the eternal gospel preached to the world. We will see this correlation between the mystery of God (10.7) and eternal gospel (14.6) has significant bearing on the question

---

43. Robert L. Thomas, *Revelation 8–22* (An Exegetical Commentary; Chicago: Moody Press, 1995), p. 201. A. P. van Schaik likewise separates Rev. 14.1–5 from 14.6–20. He writes: 'Dann ist das Fragment V. 6–20 [Rev. 14] wahrscheinlich eine literarische Einheit, möglicherweise kommt es aus derselben Tradition.' A. P. van Schaik, "Ἄλλος ἄγγελος in Apk 14', in D. Hellholm (ed.), *Apocalypticism in the Mediterranean World and the Near East* (Tübingen: Mohr, 1989), pp. 217–28 (217).

44. Beasley-Murray says that: 'It need not to be doubted that John intended the loud voice of the angel [14.6] to represent the tongues of Christ's witnesses in the time of tribulation. In their distress they have the obligation of bearing witness to the gospel (so 11.3ff.).' Beasley-Murray, *Revelation*, p. 224. See also A. P. van Schaik, "Ἄλλος ἄγγελος in Apk 14', pp. 218–22.

of the function of the two witnesses, a topic which we will discuss in detail in a later chapter. Presently, we will focus on the remarkable lexical and structural similarities between Rev. 10 and 14.6–7. The angel's main task in Rev. 10 is to impart the contents of the little opened book to John as is apparent in the angelic command to John to take and eat the book from the angel's hand (10.8–10). After John has eaten the book, he is re-commissioned to prophesy again (10.11):

καὶ λέγουσίν μοι, Δεῖ σε πάλιν προφητεῦσαι ἐπὶ λαοῖς καὶ ἔθνεσιν καὶ γλώσσαις καὶ βασιλεῦσιν πολλοῖς.

Again, we see John's commission parallels that of the other angel's in 14.6. The angel's task is to: εὐαγγελίσαι ἐπὶ τοὺς καθημένους ἐπὶ τῆς γῆς καὶ ἐπὶ πᾶν ἔθνος καὶ φυλὴν καὶ γλῶσσαν καὶ λαόν (14.6b). John's call to προφητεῦσαι parallels the angel's task to εὐαγγελίσαι where both verbs are in the aorist infinitive active form followed by the preposition ἐπὶ. The target audience of both John's and the angel's intended message is the world population worded in the familiar four-grouping formula used elsewhere in Revelation.[45] Thus we see that these striking lexical and structural parallels between specific passages in Rev. 10 (esp. 10.7, 11) and 14.6–7 frame the larger textual unit of 11.1–14.5 and provide the wider context within which the extended chiasm is interpreted.

On the other hand, Rev. 14.1–5 is intimately connected with the concluding passage of Rev. 13. Those who follow the beast are marked with the mark or number of the beast on their foreheads or on their right hands (13.16–18) and are contrasted with those who follow the Lamb on whose foreheads are written the names of the Father and the Lamb (14.1). Beale comments thus: 'The immediate juxtaposition of the Lamb in 14.1 to the beasts of ch. 13 serves the contrast between the two sides.'[46] Keener links the unit of 14.1–5 to the preceding chapters and remarks: 'Now the narration returns to the woman's offspring, who preferred bearing the Lamb's name to the beast's (13.7–14.1) and who preferred obeying God's commands (12.17) to the fake phylacteries of the worshippers of the beast.'[47] Thus we conclude that the passage of 14.1–5 is at least not related immediately to what follows but arguably functions as the concluding sub-unit in the large block of texts from Rev. 11 to Rev. 13.[48]

45.   The other five formulas appear in 5.9, 7.9, 11.9, 13.7, and 17.15. For a discussion on this fourfold formula for the nations, see Bauckham, *Climax of Prophecy*, pp. 326–37.

46.   Beale, *Revelation*, p. 731.

47.   Keener, *Revelation*, p. 369.

48.   E. Schüssler Fiorenza thinks that Rev. 12.18–14.5 forms a literary unit where the two beasts and the Lamb make up 'three *visionary figures*'. E. Schüssler Fiorenza, *Revelation: Vision of a Just World* (Minneapolis: Fortress Press, 1991), p. 82.

6. *Conclusion*

We have examined a number of key words and key motifs which function to unite the textual unit of Rev. 11.1–14.5 into a coherent and integral whole. We found that the images of warfare dominate the whole literary unit of 11.1–14.5. We have seen that Rev. 12.7–12 is the pivot of the macro-chiasm. In the said pivot, the defeat and fall of the dragon is emphasized. In sum, the war in heaven between Michael and the dragon and the latter's fall to earth (12.7–12) results in the war on earth between the two witnesses of Rev. 11 and the two beasts of Rev. 13. We have laid out the said textual unit in the chiastic pattern of ABCDEFG-F'E'D'C'B'A' which we hope to demonstrate in the next three chapters of this book. We have also shown that the frame passages for the said macro-chiasm are found in the passages in 10.11 and 14.6–7. Before we attempt to demonstrate the correspondence between the chiastic pairs as set out in our proposed macro-chiasm, we will need to establish the division of textual units by way of a literary-structural analysis of 11.1–14.5. We will begin with an analysis of ch. 11 of Revelation in the next chapter.

Chapter 3

A LITERARY-STRUCTURAL ANALYSIS OF REVELATION 11.1–19

1. *Introduction*

In discussing how Rev. 11 fits into the larger concentric structure set out earlier, we have begun to elucidate numerous links which, in our view, integrate ch. 11 within the literary unit from 11.1 to 14.5. Revelation 11 is often thought to be made up of two distinct units of 11.1–13 and 11.15–19 separated by the editorial remark: 'The second woe has passed. The third woe is coming very soon' (11.14). As noted earlier, some scholars divide 11.1–13 into two further units, 11.1–2 and 11.3–13, but it is our contention that 11.1–2 is best seen as an integral part of 11.1–13. We will also show that 11.1–13 is integrally related to the rest of Rev. 11. The literary unit in 11.15–19 begins with a statement that the seventh trumpet has sounded (11.15a) and a declaration from heaven that the kingdom of God has come (11.15b). A thanksgiving hymn follows (11.16–18) and ch. 11 is concluded with the remark that the temple of God is opened in heaven (11.19). While this brief outline is well accepted by most scholars, the integrity of Rev. 11 as a whole has been disputed strongly.

2. *The Genre of Revelation 11.1–13*

Before we proceed to analyse Rev. 11, it is important to note that 11.1–13 or at least 11.3–13 is distinctive in form from the preceding unit in Rev. 10 and the subsequent vision of the two signs in heaven of Rev. 12. Bauckham remarks that the passage in 11.3–13 'is not a vision or even interpretation of a vision (as in 17.7–18), but a narrative prophecy (comparable in form with, e.g., Daniel 11)'.[1] Aune states that: 'It is important to observe that the narrative about the two witnesses in vv 4–13 is *not* a vision report' and

---

1. Bauckham, *Climax of Prophecy*, p. 267.

he classifies the unit of 11.3–13 as 'a prophetic narrative'.[2] Bauckham and Aune seem to suggest that while the literary form of the book of Revelation mainly consists of visionary reports, the passage in 11.3–13 narrates future historical events unfolding on earth in a matter-of-fact manner.

What we will propose is that the narrative prophecy seen to be evident in 11.3–13 extends beyond Rev. 11 to include 11.14–14.5. We will argue that despite the use of καὶ εἶδον in 13.1, 11 and 14.1, the unit from 13.1–14.5 is not dissimilar in form to Rev. 11. The careers of the two beasts in Rev. 13 are purposefully conceived and composed as a contrast to the prophetic testimony of the two witnesses in Rev. 11. After the brief introduction of the beast in 13.1–2, the textual unit, 13.3–18 takes on a similar literary form to the passage in 11.3–13. The beast's appearance from the sea and his dominion over the whole earth within the time-period of three-and-a-half years (13.5) can be classified as a prophetic narrative similar to the passage in 11.1–13, not dissimilar to the narrative in Dan. 11. The unfolding of the careers of the first and second beasts is narrated as future historical events not unlike the ministry of the two witnesses in Rev. 11.1–13 and thus arguably fit into the literary form of narrative prophecy.

On the other hand, the visionary form of Rev. 12 with its apocalyptic imagery is often taken by commentators as reason to disassociate Rev. 12 from Rev. 11. It is submitted that such a proposition is misconceived as Rev. 12 provides a mythical framework to explain that the events that unfold on the earth (Rev. 11 and Rev. 13) are the results of the cosmic struggle between the dragon and the woman and the heavenly war between the dragon and Michael.[3] This will be fully demonstrated in a later chapter.

3. *The Temple and the City in Revelation 11.1–13: The Spatial Indicator*

The first main segment of Rev. 11.1–13 is bound together tightly by the observation that the events unfold in a particular location, the spatial and geographical setting of the temple and the city. We do well to note with Resseguie that: 'In Revelation, it is essential to identify the spatial, temporal, psychological, phraseological, and ideological point of view of

---

2. Aune, *Revelation 6–16*, pp. 585–86 (his emphasis). It seems arbitrary to suggest the prophetic narrative begins only at 11.3 or 11.4 as 11.1–2 is an integral part of Rev. 11 as a whole.

3. Martin McNamara writes: 'It is difficult for us in the twenty-first century to appreciate how real the mythological symbolic world was for the writers and readers of Old and even New Testament books. Because this symbolic world was real these writers could use it to convey political, religious and other messages.' M. McNamara, 'Symbolic Animals', *The Way* 41 (2001), pp. 211–23 (212–13).

the author or narrator to avoid misreadings.'[4] In the case of Rev. 11.1–13, spatial and temporal indicators are pivotal in the construction of the whole narrative. Kenneth Strand notes that 'the imagery of a temple setting' dominates Rev. 11.[5] He cites the explicit mention of the temple in 11.1–2 'followed by the pericope concerning the prophetic two witnesses (vv. 3–13) who are introduced in terms of the temple imagery of two olive trees that are also two lampstands (vv. 3–4)' as undergirding the narrative of ch. 11 within a temple setting.[6] McNicol comments:

> In the structure of Revelation 11.1–14, two basic themes emerge. Whereas in 11.1, 2 the theme is of the measurement and the fate of the temple, in 11.3–14 the essential theme is the fortune and destiny of the two witnesses in Jerusalem (esp. v. 8). The common factor in this section is the connection between Jerusalem and the temple and the occurrence of key events in this place.[7]

Further, the temple setting is augmented by the reference to the temple of God in 11.19, a fact which we have already noted. The temple which is built on Mount Zion is often mentioned together with the holy city, Jerusalem as is the case here in 11.1–2. The city is further mentioned on two other occasions in Rev. 11, first in v. 8 (the great city) and finally in v. 13 (the city).

In Rev. 11.1–14.5, John appears to have divided the world into three spheres: the city, the wilderness and the sea. While the action in Rev. 11 appears to centre on the city, the conflict between the woman and the dragon in Rev. 12 extends to the wilderness (cf. 12.6, 14–17). In Rev. 13, we have two beasts – the first ascends from the sea (13.1) and the latter rises from the earth (13.11). The city and the wilderness make up the land or earth as opposed to the sea. The earth and the sea make up the whole created world. The strong angel of Rev. 10 is explicitly described as planting his right foot on the sea and his left foot on the earth (10.2b),

---

4.   Resseguie, *Revelation Unsealed*, p. 7.

5.   K. Strand, 'The "Spotlight-on-Last-Events" Sections in the Book of Revelation', *AUSS* 27 (1989), pp. 201–21 (208). Also James C. VanderKam writes: 'The language of measuring the sanctuary and its appurtenances reminds one of Ezekiel 40.3–42.20; but the writer also predicts that the nations 'will trample over the holy city for forty-two months' – a clear citation of Daniel's frequent appeal to days and months totaling three and one-half years (e.g., 7.25; 8.13–14 [where the trampling theme also figures; cf. Lk. 21.24]; 9.26–27 [where destruction of the temple and city appears]; 12.7, 11, 12). That is, the seer is addressed in words that recall two eschatological works of the Hebrew Bible in which temple and city play a role. Within this setting he introduces the two witnesses.' J. VanderKam, '1 Enoch, Enochic Motifs, and Enoch', in James C. VanderKam and William Adler (eds.), *The Jewish Apocalyptic Heritage in Early Christianity* (Assen: Van Gorcum, 1996), pp. 33–101 (89–90).

6.   Strand, 'The "Spotlight-on-Last-Events"', p. 208.

7.   McNicol, 'Revelation 11.1–14', p. 199.

signalling God's sovereignty over the sea and the earth, the two spheres from which the two beasts ascend to rule the world. The mention of the sea before the earth in 10.2 corresponds to the order in which the two beasts are said to ascend, the first from the sea and the second from the earth.[8]

In all the three places where the term 'city' is found (11.2, 8, 13), it is articular, which suggests that the same city is referred to. Twice, 'the city' is qualified adjectivally, first as *the holy city* in 11.2 and secondly, *the great city* in 11.8 and finally simply as *the city* in 11.13. While we have noted that the whole of ch. 11 is ringed by the lexical unit, 'the temple of God', the segment of 11.1–13 is enveloped by the specification of a geographical location, 'the city'. This key term appears at critical junctures as seen in the narrative of 11.1–13 as follows:

1. The nations trample on **the holy city** for *42 months* (11.1–2).
2. The two witnesses prophesy in **the city** [implied] for *1260 days* (11.3–6).
3. The two witnesses lay dead in **the great city** for *three-and-a-half days* (11.7–10).
4. The two witnesses are resurrected in **the city** [implied] and ascend to heaven *after three-and-a-half days* (11.11–12).
5. *At that hour* (i.e. at the ascension of the two witnesses) a tenth of **the city** fell by a great earthquake (11.13).

The spatial and geographical settings of the temple and the city frame the ministry of the two witnesses. At the moment of the holy city's desolation by the nations, the two witnesses make their entrance in the narrative story-line. The parallelism between v. 2 and v. 3 of Rev. 11, which we will demonstrate in a later section, shows that the two witnesses appear in the

---

8. Wayne A. Meeks points out that Paul in 2 Cor. 11.26 'separates the world' into three areas: 'city, wilderness and sea'. This may well accord with John's demarcation in Rev. 11.1–14.5. See W. A. Meeks, *The First Urban Christians: The Social World of the Apostle Paul* (New Haven: Yale University Press, 1983), p. 9. Like Paul, John was also a person of the city. The underlying theme in Revelation is the contrast between two cities, the great city Babylon and the heavenly Jerusalem. For a detailed study of this theme, see Barbara Rossing, *The Choice Between Two Cities: Whore, Bride, and Empire in the Apocalypse* (Harrisburg, PA: Trinity Press International, 1999); Bruce Malina, *The New Jerusalem in the Revelation of John: The City as Symbol of Life with God* (Collegeville: The Liturgical Press, 2000); Klaus Wengst, 'Babylon the Great and the New Jerusalem: The Visionary View of Political Reality in the Revelation of John', in Henning Graf Reventlow, Yair Hoffman and Benjamin Uffenheimer (eds.), *Politics and Theopolitics in the Bible and Postbiblical Literature* (JSOTSup, 171; Sheffield: Sheffield Academic Press, 1994), pp. 189–202. Also William P. Brown and John T. Carroll, 'The Garden and the Plaza: Biblical Images of the City', *Int* 54 (2000), pp. 3–12, and Eleanor Scott Meyers, 'The Church in the City: Past, Present and Future', *Int* 54 (2000), pp. 23–35.

holy city.⁹ While their ministry is not limited to the city as we will argue, it is significant that the two witnesses' prophetic testimony which begins in the holy city ends in the great city when they are killed by the beast (vv. 7–8). The focus returns once more to the city where their corpses lie unburied in the street of the great city for three-and-a-half days as the inhabitants of the city gaze on the dead bodies and celebrate the prophets' demise (vv. 9–10). After the three-and-a-half days comes the two witnesses' vindication when they are resurrected and ascend into heaven in full view of their enemies (vv. 11–12). At that very hour (ἐν ἐκείνῃ τῇ ὥρᾳ) a great earthquake strikes the city and kills seven thousand persons and dramatically concludes the narrative of the two witnesses with a scene depicting the rest of the city's populace giving glory to God (11.13). So ends the second woe with the third woe to follow speedily (11.4). Thus John rhetorically narrates the appearance, death and disappearance of the two witnesses as happening in the city.

4. *The three-and-a-half in Revelation 11.1–13: The Temporal Indicator*

The time references in Rev. 11 serve critical structural functions in the literary unit of 11.3–13. In speaking about time in general in narratives, Shimon Bar-Erfat notes that: 'The shaping of time within the narrative is functional and not random or arbitrary, making a genuine contribution, in coordination and cooperation with the other elements, to the character, meaning and values of the entire narrative.'¹⁰ The appearance of the two witnesses is mentioned within a temporal framework in that they will prophesy for *1260 days* (11.3) coinciding with the *forty-two months* of the nations' trampling over the holy city (11.2). Of this period of 1260 days as Lund correctly observes, 'there is another echo in 11.6, "during the *days* of their prophecy"'.¹¹ Another temporal clause – '*when* (ὅταν) they finish their testimony' marks the end of their prophetic work, at which point in time the beast that ascends from the abyss will kill the two witnesses (11.7). Their corpses are said to lie on the streets of the great city for *three and a half days* (11.9). Just as their testimony and signs confront and torment

9. Malina notes that the section in Rev. 11.3–14a 'offers a new scenario featuring God's two witnesses who are coming to Jerusalem, undoubtedly soon'. Malina, *Revelation*, p. 146. Malina, however, fails to relate the two witnesses' appearance with the preceding passage in 11.1–2.

10. S. Bar-Erfat, *Narrative Art in the Bible* (Sheffield: Sheffield Academic Press, 2000), p. 142.

11. Lund, *Studies in the Book of Revelation*, p. 143 (his emphasis).

society for three-and-a-half years, their dead bodies likewise remain in public gaze for three-and-a-half days.[12]

Chronology continues to dominate the fast-moving narrative from the appearance of the two witnesses to their deaths in some five short verses (11.3–7), and subsequent resolution of the witnesses' tale. After the three and a half days (11.11), the two witnesses are said to be resurrected and ascend to heaven in full view of the gazing populace, vanishing out of sight of the public as suddenly and dramatically as they first appeared. Temporal reference is once again emphasized for, at the ascension of the two witnesses, a great earthquake hits the city *at that hour*. At the end of the two witnesses' narrative, John concludes with another chronological reference: 'The second woe has passed. Behold, the third woe comes quickly' (11.14).[13] If chronological details mark the structure and flow of the narrative at every turn, one must ask the question of its significance in understanding the unit of 11.1–14 (and also Rev. 12.1–14.5). Whether we understand the three and a half years and the three and a half days to denote literal time-spans or purely symbolic time-spans is not especially important. What is significant is that during these time periods, events will happen in Jerusalem and more significantly, at the end of the time-periods, the kingdom of God and his Christ will dawn on earth (11.15; 12.10).

5. *The Measuring of the Temple, Altar, and the Worshippers (Revelation 11.1–2)*

Next to the pivot, the extremities of a large concentric pattern are often the most significant as they also function to provide the setting for the rest of the narrative which they envelope. L. Hartman observes that 'episode-demarcators, i.e, information concerning time and place' are usually found 'at the beginning of the narrative' or 'at a borderline' as is the case with

---

12.   Aune comments: 'The statement that the two prophets were lying dead in the public square for *three and half* days suggests a partial parallel to the three-day period between the death and the resurrection of Jesus.' Aune, *Revelation 6–16*, p. 587 (his emphasis).

13.   We disagree with Beale that Rev. 11.14 only gives the order of visions seen by John. 'As in 9.12, the chronological language does not concern the order of the history represented in the three woe visions but refers only to the order of visions.' Beale, *Revelation*, p. 609. It is apparent that just as in 9.12 the chronological references in 9.12 and 11.14 are intended to convey that the events of each woe will unfold after the preceding woe has passed. Osborne is correct to note that the woes are separate events that will unfold sequentially as John's language makes clear: 'The first woe has passed. There are still two woes to come' (9.12) and imminent arrival of the third woe after the second has passed (11.14). See Osborne, *Revelation*, p. 337.

Rev. 11.1–2.[14] The place is centred in the temple and the holy city and the time-frame given is the Danielic temporal period of forty-two months or 1260 days which is the equivalent of three-and-a-half years. Although the first two verses of Rev. 11 are connected to 10.11, it is clear that 11.1 begins a new literary unit. Revelation 10 concludes with the angelic command to John to prophesy again (10.11). Revelation 11.1 shifts in focus, as now John begins to fulfil his prophetic commissioning. The setting is concretized as John is given a reed and commanded to measure the temple, the altar and the worshippers. 'This shows that John's fulfilment of his prophetic commission, given in 10.11, now begins.'[15] Further, the time-period of three-and-a-half years (i.e. 42 months) is first introduced in 11.2 indicating the start of a literary unit different from the preceding one; the first mention of the three-and-a-half years in v. 2, which is repeated in v. 3, strongly points to the beginning of a major literary unit covering the events to unfold within the three-and-a-half years stretching from Rev. 11 to Rev. 13 (cf. 12.6, 14; 13.5).[16] The textual unit of 11.1–2 reads as follows:

---

14.   L. Hartman, 'Form and Message: A Preliminary Discussion of "Partial Texts" in Rev. 1–3 and 22. 6ff.', in David Hellholm (ed.), *Apocalypticism in the Mediterranean World and the Near East* (Tübingen: Mohr, 1989), pp. 129–49 (141).

15.   Bauckham, *Climax of Prophecy*, p. 266.

16.   For a recent thesis that Rev. 11.1 begins a new cycle or section of the book, see Mark Seaborn Hall, 'The Hook Interlocking Structure of Revelation: The Most Important Verses in the Book and How They May Unify Its Structure', *NovT* 44 (2002), pp. 278–96. Hall argues that Rev. 10.11–11.1 functions as the hook interlocking a two-cycle division of the book. According to Hall (p. 278), 10.11 is the end of the first cycle where the writer is told to prophesy again and the second cycle begins in 11.1 where 'a prophetic measurement of three elements that fit "back" into a part of the first cycle (the 6th trumpet/2nd woe)'. Hall (p. 278) argues that: 'These three elements are the temple (11.19–15.4), the altar (15.5–16.21), and the worshippers (17.1–22.7).' While Hall (pp. 284–87) argues convincingly that a major division occurs in 11.1, we are not persuaded that 10.11–11.1 divides the book of Revelation into two halves or two cycles. First, Hall fails to take into account the significance of the three-and-a-half figure as a structural indicator in Rev. 11–13. Second, Hall's proposal that the second cycle is divided into three sections according to the prophetic measurement of the temple, the altar, and the worshippers in 11.1 appears altogether arbitrary. Hall reads too much into the phrase ἐν αὐτῷ in 11.1. Hall (p. 291) comments: 'At the beginning of 11.1, the writer "was given a reed like a staff". If ἐν αὐτῷ is instrumental then this implies that the command to measure is three distinct elements that encompass the remainder of the book.' Although it is true that the measurement covers three distinct elements of the temple, the altar, and the worshippers, there is no indication in the text of 11.1 or elsewhere that these three elements encompass the remainder of the book of Revelation. There is no indication in the text that 'the temple' dominates 11.19–15.4, 'the altar' (15.5–16.21), and the 'the worshippers' (17.1–22.7) as Hall alleges. 'The temple' continues to be mentioned in 16.1, 17 where it is used as an *inclusio* to ring the action of the seven angels given the authority to pour out the seven bowls of plagues. In fact, 15.5 which Hall takes as the beginning of 'the altar' section mentions 'the temple of the tent of witness' and not the altar. Further, the final section under 'the worshippers' (17.1–22.7) deals with the rise and fall of Babylon (Rev. 17–18), the coming of

[v. 1] Καὶ ἐδόθη μοι κάλαμος ὅμοιος ῥάβδῳ, λέγων, Ἔγειρε καὶ μέτρησον τὸν ναὸν τοῦ θεοῦ καὶ τὸ θυσιαστήριον καὶ τοὺς προσκυνοῦντας ἐν αὐτῷ. [v. 2] καὶ τὴν αὐλὴν τὴν ἔξωθεν τοῦ ναοῦ ἔκβαλε ἔξωθεν καὶ μὴ αὐτὴν μετρήσῃς, ὅτι ἐδόθη τοῖς ἔθνεσιν, καὶ τὴν πόλιν τὴν ἁγίαν πατήσουσιν μῆνας τεσσεράκοντα [καὶ] δύο.

John's symbolic action is twofold. The command to measure the temple, the altar and those who worship in it, is contrasted with the command to cast out (ἔκβαλε ἔξωθεν) and not to measure the court which is outside the temple. The ὅτι clause which follows, states the rationale for the casting out of the court outside the temple for it is given over to the nations, 'who also trample on the whole city of Jerusalem'.[17]

The Temple of God and the Holy City (Revelation 11.1–2): Literal or Symbolic?

In recent years, much has been written about the temple of God in Revelation. Three monographs attest to the continuing interest and debate about the temple motif and its significance in Revelation. Andrea Spatafora's monograph, *From the 'Temple of God' to God as the Temple: A Biblical Theological Study of the Temple in the Book of Revelation* (1997) is followed by Briggs' *Jewish Temple Imagery in the Book of Revelation* (1999) and Gregory Stevenson's *Power and Place: Temple and Identity in the Book of Revelation* (2001).[18] Space will not permit us to summarize

Christ (Rev. 19), the millennial kingdom (20.1–6), and the New Jerusalem (Rev. 21). The theme of worship or worshippers in 17.1–22.7 is at best incidental and appears in isolated texts (cf. 22.3, 9). Surprisingly, Rev. 22.9, which has the explicit command to worship God, lies outside of Hall's final section under 'the worshippers' (17.1–22.7).

17. Bauckham, *Climax of Prophecy*, p. 269.

18. A. Spatafora, *From the 'Temple of God' to God as the Temple: A Biblical Theological Study of the Temple in the Book of Revelation* (Tesi Gregoriana Serie Teologia, 27; Rome: Gregorian University Press, 1997); Briggs, *Jewish Temple Imagery*; G. Stevenson, *Power and Place: Temple and Identity in the Book of Revelation* (Berlin: de Gruyter, 2001). Many general studies have been written about the temple and its symbolism. See Menahem Haran, *Temples and Temple Service in Ancient Israel* (Winona Lake: Eisenbrauns, 1985); R. E. Clements, *God and Temple* (Oxford: Basil Blackwell, 1965); Richard Clifford, *The Cosmic Mountain in Canaan and the Old Testament* (Cambridge, MA: Harvard University Press, 1972); R. J. McKelvey, *The New Temple* (Oxford: Oxford University Press, 1969); George A. Barrios, *Jesus Christ and the Temple* (Crestwood, New York: St. Vladimir's Seminary Press, 1980); Carol L. Meyers, 'Realms of Sanctity: The Case of "Misplaced" Incense Altar in the Tabernacle Texts of Exodus', in Michael Fox *et al.* (eds.), *Texts, Temples and Tradition: A Tribute to Menahem Haran* (Winona Lake: Eisenbrauns, 1996), pp. 33–46; B. Gärtner, *The Temple and Community in Qumran and the New Testament. A Comparative Study in the Temple Symbolism of the Qumran Texts and the New Testament* (SNTSMS, 1; Cambridge: Cambridge University Press, 1965); Mark S. Smith, (with contributions by Elizabeth M. Bloch-Smith), *The Pilgrimage Pattern in Exodus* (JSOTSup, 239; Sheffield: Sheffield Academic Press, 1997), esp. ch. 2 'The Temple and its Symbolism', pp. 81–117; Elizabeth Bloch-Smith, '"Who is the

these writers' works but we will critically evaluate their discussion on the temple where it is relevant to our task of interpreting Rev. 11.1–2.

We submit that the temple of God and the holy city must be understood as the literal and physical temple of God in Jerusalem the holy city.[19] Commentators who reject a literal understanding of the temple and city fall into two main groups. Some scholars argue that the temple is the heavenly temple[20] while others argue that the references to the temple and city (even if understood literally) are purely symbols for the people of God, and so John evinces no interest in the physical temple or the earthly city of Jerusalem.[21] A third group of commentators interpret the temple as the Jerusalem temple and argue that since no physical temple is standing in 95 C.E., the book of Revelation must be written before 70 C.E.[22]

We have noted that Rev. 11 is a narrative prophecy of events that will unfold on earth in a particular place and time. The setting is the temple of God in the holy city (11.1–2) within the time-frame of three-and-a-half years (11.2–3). Court comments thus: 'The references to the "temple of God" (11.1) and "the court outside" (11.2), coupled with the place reference, "where the Lord was crucified" in 11.8, are indicative of the Jerusalem temple.'[23] To say that the temple of God in 11.1 is the heavenly

King of Glory?" Solomon's Temple and Its Symbolism', in M. D. Coogan, J. C. Exum and L. E. Stager (eds.), *Scripture and Other Artifacts: Essays on the Bible and Archaeology in Honor of Philip J. King* (Louisville: Westminster/John Knox Press, 1994), pp. 18–31; C. T. R. Hayward, *The Jewish Temple: A Non-Biblical Sourcebook* (London: Routledge, 1996).

19. Frederick Danker, the famous lexicographer lists the temple of Rev. 11.1 as the physical temple in Jerusalem. See F. Danker (ed.), *A Greek-English Lexicon of the New Testament and Other Christian Literature* (Chicago: Chicago University Press, 3rd edn, 2000), p. 666. Henceforth cited as BDAG.

20. Giblin, *Revelation*, p. 112 and M. Bachmann, 'Himmlisch: der "Tempel Gottes" von Apk 11.1', *NTS* 40 (1994), pp. 474–80.

21. Caird, *Revelation*, p. 130; Bauckham, *Climax of Prophecy*, p. 272; Sweet, *Revelation*, p. 182; P. Walker, *Jesus and the Holy City: New Testament Perspectives on Jerusalem* (Grand Rapids: Eerdmans, 1996), pp. 246–48; Spatafora, *The Temple*, pp. 168–70; Charles, *Revelation* Vol. 1, p. 274; Simon J. Kistemaker, 'The Temple in the Apocalypse', *JETS* 43 (2000), pp. 433–41; Garrow, *Revelation*, pp. 73–75; A. Feuillet, *Johannine Studies* (trans. Thomas Crane; New York: Alba House, 1964), p. 235.

22. John Robinson, *Redating the New Testament* (Philadelphia: The Westminster Press, 1976), p. 13; John W. Marshall, *Parables of War: Reading John's Jewish Apocalypse* (Ontario: Wilfrid Laurier University Press, 2001), pp. 1–2. Also Briggs, *Jewish Temple Imagery*, pp. 23–39. Though we agree with Marshall and Briggs that the temple of God in 11.1 must be the physical temple, we reject their arguments that Revelation must be written prior to 70 C.E. In our view, John is writing concerning events to unfold in the last three and a half years before the coming of God's kingdom and hence we propose that the temple spoken of in 11.1 is the future Jerusalem temple that will be standing in those last days before Christ's coming to inaugurate his kingdom on earth.

23. J. Court, *Myth and History in the Book of Revelation* (Atlanta: John Knox Press, 1979), p. 83.

temple is inconsistent with John's presentation in 11.1–2. It is evident that the court outside the temple is a literal space or area as it is given over and occupied by the nations for three-and-a-half years. It is impossible by any stretch of imagination that the nations on earth can occupy the heavenly temple, which is the absolute domain of the God of heaven, who sits on his throne in the heavenly temple.[24] If the court outside the temple is a literal and physical court then the temple as part of the larger structure must also be the literal and physical Jerusalem temple. Aune states thus:

> The temple described here is certainly the earthly temple in Jerusalem, for the distinction between the temple proper (ναὸς) and the forecourt holds for both the temple of Solomon and the Herodian temple, though the real or imagined architecture is somewhat more complex.[25]

Similarly, the holy city which is said to be trampled by the nations for three-and-a-half years must be a physical city for it to be subjugated by the nations. The holy city where the temple stands must then be Jerusalem and not the heavenly or new Jerusalem. It is impossible for the nations to trample on the heavenly Jerusalem. It follows that the 'great city' in 11.8 must also be Jerusalem, as John explicitly states that it is the place where the Lord was crucified. J. Massyngberde Ford is succinct: 'The great city in vs. 8 cannot be other than Jerusalem.'[26] We have noted already that Aune also takes the temple and the holy city as the literal and physical temple of God in the city of Jerusalem. Aune observes that 'the phrase τὸν ναὸν τοῦ θεοῦ, "temple of God" is used elsewhere in Revelation only in 11.19, where it is qualified with the phrase ὁ ἐν τῷ οὐρανῷ, "which is in heaven", to distinguish it from the earthly temple of God in Jerusalem referred to here [11.1].'[27]

---

24. Giblin argues that the temple of God in 11.1–2 is the heavenly temple and that measuring is taken to mean 'the immune sanctuary of heaven' and that the forecourt which is excluded stands for 'the profaned earth, the forecourt of heaven, the world at large'. Giblin, *Revelation*, p. 112. If John is speaking of the heavenly temple in 11.1, there will be no need to measure it as nothing in the text of Revelation suggests that the heavenly temple is in danger from any attack by external forces. Hence, we agree with de Heer who writes: 'Mustahil itu bait suci di sorga, sebab sebagian dari bait suci yang diukur Yohanes, diserahkan kepada orang-orang kafir.' (ET: It is impossible to say that this is the holy temple in heaven because a part of the temple that is measured by John is given over to the Gentiles). de Heer, *Kitab Wahyu*, p. 141.

25. Aune, *Revelation 6–16*, p. 605.

26. J. M. Ford, *Revelation*, (AB; New York: Doubleday, 1975), p. 180.

27. Aune, *Revelation 6–16*, p. 605. We may add that the abrupt introduction of 'signs' in Rev. 12.1–3 in the following chapter contrasts with the events in Rev. 11, which are not spoken of in the context of 'signs' and thus cannot be of a purely symbolic nature. Michael Bachmann argues that the temple in 11.1 is the temple in heaven based on the fact, among others, that the surrounding context of Rev. 10 and Rev. 12 is situated in heaven and thus it is more probable that the context of Rev. 11 is also located in heaven. See Bachmann,

A New Testament parallel found in the Gospel of Luke may buttress our case. The Lukan description of Jerusalem being trampled by the nations until the times of the nations are fulfilled (Lk. 21.24), or the tradition behind this Lukan eschatological scenario, may also be behind John's description in Rev. 11.2.[28] If this is so, it goes further towards showing that the holy city is to be understood as the literal city of Jerusalem as is the case in Lk. 21.20, 24. The times of the nations/Gentiles (καιροὶ ἐθνῶν, Lk. 21.24) are interpreted in Rev. 11.2 as 42 months or καιρὸν καὶ καιροὺς καὶ ἥμισυ καιροῦ (cf. Rev. 12.14), the Danielic three-and-a-half years.[29] Jerusalem will not be trodden down forever, but when these 'times' expire, Jerusalem will again be restored.[30]

'Himmlisch: der "Tempel Gottes" von Apk 11.1', p. 479. We demur as we will show that events in Rev. 11 and Rev. 13 take place on earth as a result of the war in heaven (12.7–12). Further, the strong angel of Rev. 10 descends from heaven to earth and that John is located on earth when he receives the command to eat the book and the commission to prophesy again (10.8–11). As there is nothing to suggest that the setting has changed in 11.1–2, which follows immediately from 10.11, it is more probable that the setting of 11.1–2 is still located on earth. See also Briggs, *Jewish Temple Imagery*, p. 25 n. 78.

28.　So Aune, *Revelation 6–16*, p. 608. Also L. A. Vos, *The Synoptic Tradition* (Kampen: Kok, 1965), pp. 120–25. Vos (p. 125) writes: 'The significant element for the present is that Rev. 11.2b clearly alludes to this prediction of Jesus in its historically orientated form which is found only in the Gospel of Luke. Thus it would seem that John was either acquainted with the Gospel of Luke, which would have to be the case had Luke rewritten and interpreted the Marcan form of the prediction of Jesus, or both Luke and the Apocalyptist were acquainted with a separate tradition in which this specific prediction of Jesus was found with its explicit historical orientation.' A. J. Beagley writes: 'We believe that John, in the same way as Luke, is referring to the trampling down of the literal city of Jerusalem by the Gentiles (Romans) in A.D. 70.' A. J. Beagley, *The 'Sitz im Leben' of the Apocalypse with Particular Reference to the Role of the Church's Enemies* (BZNW, 50; Berlin: de Gruyter, 1987), p. 62. While we agree with Beagley that the literal city of Jerusalem is meant in Rev. 11.2, it is not necessary to conclude that the trampling mentioned in Rev. 11.2 refers to the Roman conquest in 70 C.E. We will argue that it is a future event that will unfold in the final three-and-a-half years before the dawn of the kingdom of God (cf. Rev. 11.2–3, 15).

29.　Vos comments: 'Although the Apocalyptist substitutes "forty and two months" for Luke's "times of the Gentiles", it is evident that in both passages the same period is stipulated. Luke's "time of the Gentiles" extended likewise until the consummation.' Vos, *The Synoptic Tradition*, p. 123.

30.　We should note that Luke's Gospel evinces an interest in Jerusalem and the Temple. Luke narrates the accounts of Simeon who looked forward to the consolation of Israel (Lk. 2.25) and Anna and others who looked for the redemption of Jerusalem (Lk. 2.38). Even after Jesus' resurrection, the disciples asked: 'Lord, is this the time when you will restore the kingdom to Israel?' (Acts 1.6). Jesus did not deny the validity of his disciples' question, only that they were not privileged to know the times and periods that the Father had set by his own authority (1.7). Jesus' answer certainly implies that there will be a time or season when the kingdom will be restored to Israel. I. Howard Marshall suggests that the disciples' question in Acts 1.6 could be due to the possibility that 'Luke's readers might think that the "times of the

T. W. Mackay argues strongly against an allegorical approach to the interpretation of the temple in Rev. 11.1.[31] Mackay observes that the notion of the restoration of the temple is a severe embarrassment to some Christian writers. Mackay writes: 'This conviction of the uniqueness of the Temple has produced a persistent fear or hope that the Temple might be restored.... Consequently, commentators regularly equate the Church and the Temple, and thus they dismiss summarily a restoration of the Temple.'[32] Mackay argues that 'John's description of the Temple in Apocalypse 11, can only be of a literal Temple at Jerusalem' and asks 'Is this, in fact, the Temple which was destroyed in A.D. 70, or some other Temple?'[33] Mackay answers thus:

> Inasmuch as this is placed at the *eschaton*, the literal interpretation would take this to be the prophetic vision of a Temple which was not yet constructed when John had his vision. Needless to say, such a position was not popular in normative Christian exegesis.[34]

Nevertheless, Aune's statement that: 'Most interpreters understand the primary reference in vv. 1–2 to be the literal temple in Jerusalem' is challenged by a number of commentators.[35] Thus Walker states the contrary view: 'The majority of commentators conclude that John is speaking of a different temple [11.1], namely, the Christian community.'[36]

It is clear that any resolution of this issue will only come with a close reading of the text in its immediate context of Rev. 11 and its surrounding context of 11.1–14.5. We are not suggesting that by understanding the temple as the earthly Jerusalem temple, we are rejecting the possibility of any further symbolic meaning in the text. It is important to interpret the

---

Gentiles", during which Jerusalem was to be desolate, ought now to be coming to an end and giving place to the coming of the kingdom (Lk. 21.24, 31)'. I. H. Marshall, *Acts* (TNTC; Leicester: Inter-Varsity Press, 1980), p. 60.

31. T. W. Mackay, 'Early Christian Exegesis of the Apocalypse', in E. A. Livingstone (ed.), *Studia Biblica 1978* (JSNTSup, 3; Sheffield: JSOT Press, 1980), pp. 257–63 (258).

32. Mackay, 'Early Christian Exegesis of the Apocalypse', p. 258.

33. Mackay, 'Early Christian Exegesis of the Apocalypse', p. 259.

34. Mackay, 'Early Christian Exegesis of the Apocalypse', p. 259.

35. Aune, *Revelation 6–16*, p. 596.

36. Walker, *Jesus and the Holy City*, p. 247. Walker (p. 246) acknowledges that 11.1–13 speaks of 'earthly realities' and only in 11.19 does the scene revert to heaven as God's temple *in heaven* in 11.19 makes clear. Nevertheless, Walker ultimately rejects a literal interpretation of the temple and the holy city based on the supposedly symbolic nature of John's references throughout Revelation. Walker (p. 247 n. 40) follows Caird (*Revelation*, p. 131) who says, 'it is hardly too much to say that in a book in which all things are expressed in symbols, the very last things the "Temple" and "holy city" could mean would be the physical Temple and the earthly Jerusalem'. It is our view that Walker and Caird are wrong to assume that a general rule that John uses mostly symbolic language must in *all* instances preclude references to literal objects or events as the immediate context dictates.

sentence or passage in question in relation to the syntactical arrangement of its constituent parts. As Nigel Turner states: 'The paragraph determines the gist of the individual words within it.'[37] The phrases 'the temple of God' and 'the holy city' cannot be interpreted on their own without examining the context of the sentence or passage where they are found. We dissent, therefore, from the interpreters who are too quick to jump into symbolic or figurative readings without first, in our view, sufficiently understanding the immediate context within which a text is found. We will deal briefly with some of the main objections raised against understanding 11.1 as a reference to a literal and physical temple.

We can rule out immediately the argument put forward that John speaks of the heavenly temple throughout Revelation and therefore he must be speaking of the same in 11.1. Bachmann uses this argument as one of his reasons for arguing that the temple in 11.1 is the heavenly temple. Bachmann says: 'Wollte man (ὁ) ναὸς (τοῦ) θεοῦ und (τὸ) θυσιαστήριον in 11.1–2 nicht vom himmlischen Heiligtum verstehen, müsste man also eine innerhalb der Johannesoffenbarung singuläre Verwendung der Begriffe annehmen.'[38] The argument fails because hermeneutically it is not sound to interpret a passage by reference to other passages without first considering the immediate context of the said passage under discussion. Second, John's general use of symbolic language in Revelation cannot be taken as a sweeping and all encompassing rule that 'all things are expressed in symbols' in the book of Revelation.[39] Third, we reject Spatafora's assertion that: 'In the book of Revelation, there are no references to the historical Israel, either to its temple or to its people.'[40] Revelation 11.1 could be just

---

37. N. Turner, *Christian Words* (Edinburgh: T & T Clark, 1980), p. viii.

38. Bachmann, 'Himmlisch: der "Tempel Gottes" von Apk 11.1', p. 478. Also Beale, *Revelation*, p. 562. Beale (p. 562) says, 'the people of God, the members of God's temple in heaven, are referred to in their existence on earth as "the temple of God"'. We reject Beale's assertion that the people of God on earth are members of the heavenly temple, neither is there any text to support Beale's contention that the people of God on earth exist as 'the temple of God'. Revelation 15.6 explicitly states that, 'no one could enter the temple [in heaven] until the seven plagues of the seven angels were ended'. This is plainly an exercise in spiritualizing by Beale without regard to the immediate context. Beale (p. 562) also says that, 'Rev. 11:1–2 depicts the temple of the age to come as having broken into the present age'. How can one imagine the nations to trample on the outer court of the temple of the new age? Further, Rev. 11.1–2 explicitly states that the period of trampling on the temple's court occurs in the time-period of three-and-a-half years *before* the new age breaks in at the coming of God's kingdom in 11.15.

39. So Caird, *Revelation*, p. 130. Briggs rightly asks that, 'how many times must a motif be used before it can have any literal nuances?' Briggs, *Jewish Temple Imagery*, p. 29 n. 86.

40. Spatafora, *The Temple*, p. 165. Also Bauckham says: 'It is highly unlikely that in Rev. 11.1–2 John intends to speak literally of the temple which had been destroyed in A.D. 70 and the earthly Jerusalem, in which he nowhere else shows any interest. He understands the temple and the city as symbols of the people of God.' Bauckham, *Climax of Prophecy*, p. 272.

such a statement showing that John is interested in the physical temple in Jerusalem and the city's inhabitants in 11.13 where, at the ascension of the two witnesses and a great earthquake, the rest of the people in the city give glory to God.[41] While it is true that, 'every time the name Jerusalem is used in the book it always refers to the eschatological city and never to the terrestrial city',[42] it does not follow that other references to 'the city' must not be the earthly Jerusalem. In fact, the articular phrase '*the* holy city' in 11.2 is peculiar as a holy city is here mentioned for the first time in Revelation. Normally in John's usage, the first mention of an object is stated without the article except when the item named is already well known to John's readers as it is here in 11.1–2.[43] It is likely, therefore, *the* holy city and the court outside the temple given over to be trampled by the nations for 42 months appear to be objects and events that are easily recognized by John's readers.[44]

We will look at the command to measure the temple of God, the altar and those who worship in it, and the command to cast out and not measure the court outside the temple, which is the gist of 11.1–2.[45] It is not stated whether John carried out the command. This may not be important in the narrative, for the execution of the command (if carried out) can only take place in the visionary realm as it is physically impossible to measure the whole temple with a reed, let alone measure all the worshippers that are

41. The text in Rev. 11.9–10 makes clear that there are representatives from all nations gathered in the great city, thus it seems clear that not only Jews but the rest of the nations make up the inhabitants of the city who are said to witness all the events narrated by John in 11.7ff.

42. Spatafora, *The Temple*, p. 165.

43. Rev. 11 consists of a number of exceptions to the rule as the two witnesses are also articular though they are mentioned for the first time in Revelation in 11.3. Also the beast is articular in 11.7. It appears that John assumed that his readers were familiar with most of the things in Rev. 11 and understood what he meant by the holy city, the two witnesses and the beast when he penned Rev. 11.

44. The first mention of 'the holy city' in the Gospel of Matthew is also articular (Mt. 4.5). As is the case in Rev. 11.1–2, the holy city is mentioned together with the temple in Mt. 4.5. It appears that Matthew assumed that his readers would have understood his reference to the holy city in Mt. 4.5 and also in Mt. 27.53 as the city of Jerusalem. The latter reference in Matthew's Gospel is especially significant in that even though Jerusalem and its leaders have rejected Jesus and put him to death, after Jesus' resurrection, the bodies that rose from the graves are said to enter the *holy* city. Another parallel in the Qumran writings may help to illuminate our text in Rev. 11.1–2. Although the sanctuary is pronounced unclean in CD 20. 22b-23, Jerusalem is still called in the same passage 'the holy city'. See K. H. Tan, *The Zion Traditions and the Aims of Jesus* (Cambridge: Cambridge University Press, 1997), p. 38.

45. We agree with Bauckham that the temple (ναὸς) is the temple proper which contains the holy place and the holy of holies. See Bauckham, *Climax of Prophecy*, p. 268. The court outside the temple is not the court of the Gentiles but the court where the altar of burnt offering and the molten sea are located.

found in it. As a prophetic-symbolic action in the manner of Old Testament prophetic acts, it is not the literal action that is important but what the symbolic act represents to the prophet's intended audience.

While an angel is said to measure the New Jerusalem with a golden measuring rod/reed (μέτρον κάλαμον χρυσοῦν) in Rev. 21.15, here John is given a reed like a staff (κάλαμος ὅμοιος ῥάβδῳ).[46] It is often thought that Ezek. 40.2–42.20 provides the background for Rev. 11.1–2.[47] However, it is our contention that the text in Ezekiel is more relevant to the measuring of the New Jerusalem in Rev. 21.15ff where the angel measures the city's structure in like manner to the measuring of the temple's structure in Ezek. 40 onwards.[48]

Aune rightly notes that the passage in Zech. 2.1–5 is 'much closer to Rev. 11.1 [than Ezek. 40] because of the absence of the actual act of measuring and the focus on the theme of divine protection'.[49] In the Zecharianic passage, the angel does not do the measuring but commands a man to measure Jerusalem (Zech. 2.4). Similarly, in Rev. 11.1, the angel commands John to perform the measuring. Second, as noted by Aune, it is not stated whether the man in Zech. 4.2 actually measures Jerusalem as is the case for John in Rev. 11.1. Third, the casting out and not measuring the court outside the temple lead to the desecration by the nations of the temple's outer court, which in turn suggests that the measuring of the temple of God, the altar and the worshippers symbolizes protection or

---

46.   There is a significant difference between the reed in 11.1 and the one in 21.15. The reed in 11.1 is not called a measuring reed or measuring rod as it is in 21.15. It has often been assumed that 11.1 is a measuring reed/rod because of the command to measure next to it. However, we will argue that the 'reed like a staff' (κάλαμος ὅμοιος ῥάβδῳ) is more than just a measuring rod or staff. The reed symbolizes the prophetic ministry of the two witnesses and their authority to perform miracles in the manner of Moses where the rod of Moses played a critical role in most miracles. McNicol comments: 'In Ezekiel 29.6 (LXX) the prophet is told he was a *rabdos kalaminos* (a rod made of reed) to the house of Israel for their protection against the Egyptians. In Revelation 11.1 the prophet was given a *kalamos* similar to a *rabdos*. Whereas in Ezekiel 29.6 the function of the rod was a symbol of Yahweh's protective presence and his ability to destroy the Egyptians, in Revelation 11.1, 2 the function of the rod was the measurement of the temple.' McNicol, 'Revelation 11.1–14', p. 198. McNicol is correct to note the Ezek. 29.6 (LXX) background to Rev. 11.1 but fails to note that the reed is more than a measuring rod in Rev. 11.1ff. For a study on the symbolism of the staff of God or Moses' staff, see Johnson T. K. Lim, *The Sin of Moses and the Staff of God* (Assen: Van Gorcum, 1997), esp. ch. 8 'The staff of God', pp. 156–66.

47.   Beale is representative and says: 'The measuring is best understood against the background of the temple prophecy in Ezekiel 40–48.' Beale, *Revelation*, p. 559.

48.   We agree with Kraft who says: 'Bei Hesekiel geschieht das, um die Masse des himmlische Tempels festzustellen. Das ist hier nicht gemeint; es kann schon darum nicht der himmlische Tempel sein, weil ein Teil des Bezirks nicht vermessen, sondern den Heiden überlassen werden soll.' Kraft, *Offenbarung*, p. 152.

49.   Aune, *Revelation 6–16*, p. 604.

preservation for the objects measured. This protection theme accords well with the measuring in Zech. 2.1–5 (MT – Zech. 2.5–9) as measuring there symbolizes Jerusalem's protection as it is written: 'For I [God] will be a wall of fire all around it, says the LORD, and I will be the glory within it' (Zech. 2.5). Fourth, the immediate context of measuring in Zech. 2 is due to the need to protect Jerusalem from those nations that come against Jerusalem:

> [1.18 (MT 2.1)] And I looked up and saw four horns. I asked the angel who talked with me, 'What are these?' And he answered me, 'These are the horns that have scattered Judah, Israel, and Jerusalem.' ... [v. 21 (MT 2.4)] And I asked, 'What are they coming to do?' He answered, 'These are the horns that scattered Judah, so that no head could be raised; but these have come to terrify them, to strike down the horns of the nations that lifted up their horns against the land of Judah to scatter its people.'
> (Zech. 1.18, 21; MT – Zech. 2.1, 4).[50]

Likewise, we see that the need for measuring is also due to the nations' subjugation of Jerusalem in Rev. 11.1–2. In contrast to Zech. 2.1–5, the holy city is not measured in Rev. 11.1–2 and hence together with the court outside the temple is given over to the nations. Apart from the vision of the four horns symbolizing invading nations, Bauckham observes that the LXX of Zech. 12.3 provides the background for the nations' trampling over Jerusalem.[51] The LXX of Zech. 12.3 reads as follows:

καὶ ἔσται ἐν τῇ ἡμέρᾳ ἐκείνῃ θήσομαι τὴν Ιερουσαλημ λίθον καταπατούμενον πᾶσιν τοῖς ἔθνεσιν πᾶς ὁ καταπατῶν αὐτὴν ἐμπαίζων ἐμπαίξεται καὶ ἐπισυναχθήσονται ἐπ' αὐτὴν πάντα τὰ ἔθνη τῆς γῆς.

The clause θήσομαι τὴν Ιερουσαλημ λίθον καταπατούμενον πᾶσιν τοῖς ἔθνεσιν is indeed close to the our text in Rev. 11.2: ἐδόθη τοῖς ἔθνεσιν, καὶ τὴν πόλιν τὴν ἁγίαν πατήσουσιν. We agree with Bauckham and Aune who suggest that John is dependent on the LXX rather than the MT in this instance.[52] John's allusion to Zech. 12.3, which speaks of the nations gathering for war against Jerusalem supports our view that the holy city in Rev 11.2 is the earthly Jerusalem which will also be subject to the nations' military

---

50. The MT versification makes it clear that the preceding vision about the four horns (MT 2.1–4) provides the context for the measuring of Jerusalem in MT 2.5–9.

51. Bauckham, *Climax of Prophecy*, pp. 270–271. The MT reads: 'I will make Jerusalem as a stone of burden for all the peoples (אָשִׂים אֶת־יְרוּשָׁלַ͏ִם אֶבֶן מַעֲמָסָה לְכָל־הָעַמִּים).'

52. Aune, *Revelation 6–16*, p. 608.

conquest.[53] The verb πατέω in 11.2 is a military term meaning subjugation and control of the city by the nations.[54] In its religious and cultic context, trampling signals defilement or desolation.[55] The court outside the temple and the holy city are thus desecrated. The impossibility of the nations trampling on the court of the heavenly temple or the heavenly city rules out the argument that John is speaking of the heavenly temple or the heavenly city in 11.1–2. Fifth, Zechariah's visions of Joshua and Zerubbabel in Zech. 3–4 provide the model for John's depiction of the two witnesses as 'the two olive trees' in Rev. 11.4 (cf. Zech. 4.14).

It is clear that John has made extensive use of Zecharianic allusions in the first four verses of Rev. 11. What is seldom noticed is that the passage on measuring in Zech. 2.1–5 is also significant in determining whether the holy city (and also the temple) are earthly objects or otherwise. The symbolic measuring of Jerusalem in Zech. 2 does not mean Jerusalem itself exists only in the realm of the angelic vision. Jerusalem in Zech. 2.1–5 is the earthly city of Jerusalem, the object of measurement which points to its protection and future restoration.[56] The *visionary* element here in Zech. 2 as it is in Rev. 11.1–2 is the act of *measuring* (and not measuring as is the case in Rev. 11.2), an act which, whether executed in the visionary realm or not, has symbolic significance. Just as the city of Jerusalem is protected by the divine command to measure, the command to measure has the same effect in Rev. 11.1 in that the temple of God, the altar, and the worshippers are also protected while the symbolism of casting out and not measuring means the court outside the temple and the holy city are handed over to the nations who will trample on it for 42 months.

---

53.   That Zechariah and Revelation could use the same imagery but interpret it differently is of course a possibility, but it is our contention that Rev. 11.1–2 depicts a literal invasion of Jerusalem by the nations, very much like the scenes described in LXX Zech. 12.3 and Zech. 2.2ff.

54.   Aune, *Revelation 6–16*, pp. 607–08.

55.   'The verb *trample* implies that the Gentiles will walk all over Jerusalem (the holy city) as haughty conquerors of a defeated city.' Robert G. Bratcher, *A Translator's Guide to the Revelation to John* (New York: United Bible Societies, 1984), p. 87. BDAG (p. 786) defines the meaning of πατέω as 'to tread heavily with feet, with implication of destructive intent' and adds that the word is normally used to describe 'the undisciplined swarming of a victorious army through a conquered city'.

56.   John W. Marshall likewise sees Zech. 2.2ff as decisive for the proper interpretation of Rev. 11.1–2. Marshall writes: 'The clearest pretext for Rev. 11.1–2 is Zech. 2.2ff.... What follows in Zechariah's third vision [2.6–13; MT – 2.10–17] is the restoration of Jerusalem under God's protection, with predictions of God's vengeance on the oppressor nations, typified by Babylon. This is the same perspective that John conveys in his vision.' Marshall, *Parables of War*, p. 168. In our literary unit of Rev. 11.1–14.5, God's vengeance on the oppressive nations is described in 11.18 and 14.1–5.

One final remark on the symbolism of Rev. 11.1–2 is the use of phrase ἔκβαλε ἔξωθεν in conjunction with the command not to measure the court outside the temple. The text of 11.2 reads:

καὶ τὴν αὐλὴν τὴν ἔξωθεν τοῦ ναοῦ ἔκβαλε ἔξωθεν καὶ μὴ αὐτὴν μετρήσῃς, ὅτι ἐδόθη τοῖς ἔθνεσιν, καὶ τὴν πόλιν τὴν ἁγίαν πατήσουσιν μῆνας τεσσεράκοντα [καὶ] δύο.

The phrase ἔκβαλε ἔξωθεν cannot mean simply 'exclude' or 'leave out',[57] otherwise μὴ μετρήσῃς would have sufficed to convey the sense of excluding what is not measured. It seems that John wishes to convey a much stronger sense of repulsion of the space designated as the court *outside* the temple (τὴν αὐλὴν τὴν ἔξωθεν τοῦ ναοῦ). It is this court outside the temple (mentioned first before the verb) that is to be cast out to the outside (note the use of ἔξωθεν in conjunction with ἔκβαλε) which constitutes the object left unmeasured by John and given over to the nations. The occasion for such repulsion which elicits the prophetic-symbolic act of casting out to the outside is not stated in the text and it is here that 'gaps' must be filled in by correctly identifying the Old Testament allusions that John makes so extensively in Rev. 11 as a whole and 11.1–2 in particular. Bauckham's carefully reasoned comments on the allusions in Rev. 11.2 are worth quoting at some length:

> This curious use of ἔκβαλε has never been explained, because its source in Daniel has not been recognized. The whole phrase is John's translation of the last three words of Daniel 8.11: וְהֻשְׁלַךְ מְכוֹן מִקְדָּשׁוֹ (literally: 'and the place of his sanctuary was cast down / out'). John has taken the unique phrase מְכוֹן מִקְדָּשׁוֹ, which uses the rare (מְכוֹן), to mean the court belonging to (i.e. outside) the temple building. שׁלך would mean 'to cast down, to overthrow' if it referred to the temple itself, but can hardly mean this if, as John supposes, it refers to the court of the temple. However, 'to cast out' (ἐκβάλλω) is an appropriate translation, because John assumes that the reason it has been 'cast out' is that the pagan nations have defiled it. They have removed the burnt offering (Daniel 8.11; 11.31; 12.11) and erected the idolatrous 'transgression that makes desolate' (11.31; 12.11), presumably in place of the altar of burnt-offering.[58]

---

57. So Aune, *Revelation 6–16*, p. 607.

58. Bauckham, *Climax of Prophecy*, p. 270. One other possible background to Rev. 11.1–2 is the desecration of the temple mentioned in Ezek. 8–10 where the presence of God is said to leave the temple on account of the defilement by idolatry. Commenting on Ezek. 8–10, Jeffrey J. Niehaus remarks: 'God's abandonment of his temple, his "house," is a sign that he has forsaken his people because of their sin.' J. J. Niehaus, *God at Sinai: Covenant & Theophany in the Bible and Ancient Near East* (Grand Rapids: Zondervan, 1995), p. 136. The sins of Jerusalem were the main cause why the holy city was given over to the Babylonians. It is said that, 'Jerusalem and Judah were a cause of anger for the LORD, so that He cast them out of

If Bauckham's arguments are sound, then it is understandable that strong language in the form of ἔκβαλε ἔξωθεν is used to express the divine revulsion at the desecration of the altar of the burnt offering that will occur for 42 months. It is pertinent to note the beginning and the end of the passage in Dan. 8.9–14. The casting out of the place of the sanctuary is told within the context of the little horn from the midst of the four prominent horns growing exceedingly great reaching even to 'the beautiful land' (הַצְּבִי), which is interpreted as referring to Jerusalem where he will defy the prince of the host and take away the regular burnt offering (Dan. 8.9).[59] If this Danielic passage as a whole is relevant to Rev. 11.1–2, then it is understandable that John depicts the desolation taking place within the holy city, Jerusalem. Perhaps it is not so abrupt and sudden that the beast is introduced as appearing in the city where he kills the two witnesses (Rev. 11.7), if this Danielic background is kept in mind in reading not just Rev. 11.1–2 but the whole of Rev. 11 as well as Rev. 12 and Rev. 13.[60]

His presence' (2 Kings 24.20 [JPS]). Marko Jauhiainen in a recent article argues that Ezek. 8–10 provides the background to Rev. 11.1–2. Jauhiainen offers a novel reading of Rev. 11.1 where he translates as follows: 'Get up and measure the temple of God *but* the altar *and* those worshipping near it, *that is* the court outside the temple, cast out outside and do not measure it.' M. Jauhiainen, 'The Measuring of the Temple Reconsidered', *Bib* 83 (2002), pp. 507–26 (519–20) [italics mine]. It is unlikely that John would use the three 'καὶ' in Rev. 11.1 in three different ways as Jauhiainen alleges since no other example in the book of Revelation is given by Jauhiainen that John would use the connective 'καὶ' in such a way. Whether the temple of God as a whole and the altar in particular are desecrated in fact by the nations alongside the court outside the temple is not overly important because the symbolism of 'measuring' points to their future restoration and reconsecration. Similarly, the worshippers who are measured may suffer persecution and even death, but the promise is that since they are 'measured', they will eventually be vindicated as their counterparts, the 144,000 in Rev. 14.1–5 shows. Thus although Jauhiainen's argument that Ezek. 8–10 does provide some background to the casting out of the outer court has merits, it is not necessary to interpret the Greek of Rev. 11.1–2 to read that 'the altar and the worshippers' are also cast out.

59.   Commenting on Dan. 8.9, Collins says: 'From the visionary's viewpoint, the goal of the little horn's action was the Jerusalem temple, and the following verses are largely concerned with the attack on the Jerusalem cult.' Collins, *Daniel*, p. 331. See also Goldingay, *Daniel*, p. 209. For a study on the displacement of the daily burnt offering by the abomination of desolation in Daniel, see J. Lust, 'Cult and Sacrifice in Daniel: The Tamid and the Abomination of Desolation', in J. Quaegebeur (ed.), *Ritual and Sacrifice in the Ancient Near East* (Leuven: Peeters, 1993), pp. 285–99. Jonathan Klawans writes: 'The purpose of the daily burnt offering – and perhaps some other sacrifices as well – is to provide constant pleasing odour for the Lord, so that the divine presence will continually remain in the sanctuary.' J. Klawans, 'Pure Violence: Sacrifice and Defilement in Ancient Israel', *HTR* 94:2 (2001), pp. 133–55 (154). Therefore, if the daily burnt offering is taken away and is replaced by some foreign object or sacrifice, then the presence of God in the temple can no longer be maintained. As such the casting out of the temple's outer court in Rev. 11.2 is a sign of divine displeasure when the nations trample on the holy city and defile the temple of God.

60.   Note also that the city of Jerusalem is described as the perfection of beauty and the joy of all the earth (Lam. 2.15). Lamentation 2.1 speaks of the casting down of the daughter of

The end of the passage of Dan. 8.9–14 records an angelic conversation: 'For how long is this vision concerning the regular burnt offering, the transgression that makes desolate, and the giving over of the sanctuary and host to be trampled?' (Dan. 8.13b). The answer given was two thousand three hundred evenings and mornings; then the sanctuary shall be restored to its rightful state (Dan. 8.14). In other places in Daniel, it is 'a time, times, and half a time', namely three-and-a-half years (cf. Dan. 7.25; 12.7) or 1290 days (Dan 12.11) or even 1335 days (Dan. 12.12). John in Revelation chooses to round off the numbers. John is consistent in using the time-period of three-and-a-half years: 42 months (Rev. 11.2; 13.5) which is equivalent to 1260 days (Rev. 11.3; 12.6) and the more enigmatic Danielic period of 'a time, times, and half a time' is used only once in Rev. 12.14. Bauckham's view that: 'Revelation 11.1–2 results from a quite precise interpretation of Daniel 8.11–14, in connexion with Zechariah 12.3',[61] only explains in part the conflation of a number of texts from Daniel and Zechariah that have influenced John in composing the first two verses of Rev. 11. If these texts from Daniel and Zechariah are taken seriously, then understanding the temple of God as the physical temple in Jerusalem and the holy city as earthly Jerusalem are not far-fetched but are reasonable and plausible according to the immediate context of Rev. 11.

6. *The Parallelism of Revelation 11.2–3*

The major objection to the integrity of ch. 11 of Revelation is that numerous scholars have argued that 11.1–2 is a separate tradition about the temple before the temple of Jerusalem was razed by the Romans in 70 C.E. and somewhat disjunctively incorporated here at Rev. 11.[62] Charles summed up this position as follows:

Zion from heaven to earth. While in Lam. 2.1 the action of throwing down is ascribed to the Lord's anger, in Daniel 8.10 the earthly ruler Antiochus Epiphanes is the subject of the action. Likewise, in Rev. 12.4 the dragon is said to cast down a third of the stars from heaven to earth. Daniel 8.10 speaks of the little horn casting down some of the host to the earth and trampling on them, a text which is alluded to in Rev. 12.4. The little horn of Daniel provides the background for the activities of the dragon and the beast in Rev. 12 and Rev. 13 respectively as we will see in a later chapter.

61. Bauckham, *Climax of Prophecy*, p. 271.
62. Charles, *Revelation* Vol. 1, p. 274. Also I. T. Beckwith, *The Apocalypse of John* (New York: Macmillan, 1919), pp. 586–87; Beasley-Murray, *Revelation*, pp. 176–77; Boring, *Revelation*, p. 143; Walker, *Jesus and the Holy City*, p. 250; U. B. Müller, *Die Offenbarung des Johannes* (Gütersloh: Gütersloher Verlagshaus Mohn, 1984), p. 207; David Flusser, *Judaism and the Origins of Christianity* (Jerusalem: The Magnes Press, 1988), p. 391; E. Lohse, *Die Offenbarung des Johannes* (Göttingen: Vandenhoeck & Ruprecht, 1976), p. 65.

These two verses, xi. 1–2, are a fragment...an oracle written before 70 C.E. by one of the prophets of the Zealot party in Jerusalem, who predicted that, though the outer court of the Temple and the city would fall, the Temple and the Zealots who had taken up their abode within it would be preserved from destruction.[63]

Charles argued that since the temple was destroyed in 70 C.E. and John wrote the book of Revelation during the reign of Domitian (95 C.E.), verses 1–2 of Rev. 11 must be interpreted symbolically or eschatologically.[64] This Zealot tradition which allegedly lies behind the passage in 11.1–2 must be rejected. Heinz Giesen states that: 'Diese Annahme ist allein schon deshalb unwahrscheinlich, weil kaum verständlich zu machen ist, warum der Seher eine historisch nicht eingetroffene zelotische Weissagung christlich rezipieren könnte.'[65] Further, we must be cautious about seeing historical reference in John's mention of the temple here. Thompson reminds us that references to the temple in Rev. 11 do not require 'a date prior to the destruction of the temple in 70 CE, for John sees many things in his visions that did not "exist" when he wrote'.[66] Leivestad regards Rev. 11 as 'one of the most mysterious sections, which resists all attempts at an explanation from contemporary events'.[67] We must be cautious about equating any part of John's prophetic narrative with any contemporary event unless strong evidence suggests otherwise. If John's claim is to be believed that 'the things that must come to pass' (1.1; cf. 4.1) are indeed *prophetic words* (1.3; 22.9, 18–19), then from John's perspective, events contained in the little scroll (the subject of John's commission to prophesy again, 10.11), lie in the future. We agree with G. Quispel who says, 'John lived round the year 90, so he was well aware of

63.   Charles, *Revelation* Vol. 1, p. 274.

64.   'Hence no literal interpretation is possible. The verses must be taken wholly eschatologically, and several phrases symbolically.' Charles, *Revelation* Vol. 1, p. 274. de Heer put forward an ingenuous suggestion that while John wrote Revelation in 95 C.E., however, in this particular passage in 11.1–2, he was taken back to the past, i.e., before the destruction of the temple in 70 C.E. See de Heer, *Kitab Wahyu*, p. 141.

65.   H. Giesen, *Die Offenbarung des Johanes* (Regensburg: Friedrich Pustet, 1997), p. 240. Caird speaks of the Zealot tradition as, 'improbable, useless, and absurd: improbable, because, once the outer court had fallen to the army of Titus, not even the most rabid fanatic could have supposed that he would be content to occupy it for three and a half years and leave the sanctuary itself inviolate; useless, because, whatever these words might have meant to a hypothetical Zealot, they certainly meant something quite different to John twenty-five years after the siege; and absurd, because of the underlying assumption that John could not have intended these words to be taken figuratively unless someone else had previously used them in their literal sense.' Caird, *Revelation*, p. 131.

66.   Thompson, *Revelation*, p. 23.

67.   Leivestad, *Christ the Conqueror*, p. 228.

the fact that the temple has been destroyed. Here, however, he is looking into the future and he sees the temple built up again.'[68]

Recent scholars have argued for the integrity of Rev. 11.1–2 with the following narrative of the two witnesses at least to 11.13. Thus Aune remarks that, 'Rev. 11.1–13 is a coherent literary unit consisting of two major subunits, vv 1–2 and vv 3–13'.[69] Aune bases his arguments on the grounds that 11.1–2 is clearly linked to 11.3–13:

> by the temporal reference to forty-two months specified for the subjugation of the outer court and the holy city to the Gentiles (v 2), which is equivalent to the 1,260 days of the ministry of the two witnesses (v 3), and by reference to 'the holy city' in v 2, which is matched by the reference to 'the great city' in v 8 (both presumably referring to Jerusalem)... the occurrence of the verb προφητεύιεν, 'prophesy,' in 10.11 and 11.3 (and the noun προφήτης, 'prophet,' in 11.10).[70]

While we agree with Aune concerning the connection between the v. 2 and v. 3 by reference to the three-and-a-half years period, Sweet notes, correctly in our view, that the link between the two verses is made virtually certain by a formal parallelism between v. 2 and v. 3. Sweet writes: 'The parallelism is intentional: the being trampled which is allowed by God, and the witnessing commissioned by God are two sides of the coin.'[71] Likewise Court comments thus: 'And I will grant my two witnesses to prophesy' (11.3). In Greek the construction is Hebraic and the wording, if not the idiom, is parallel to the preceding sentence in 11.2.'[72] Nevertheless, neither Sweet nor Court goes on to set out how the parallelism is formally structured in respect of 11.2–3, a task which we will presently attempt.

The Greek text of 11.2–3 reads as follows:

[v. 2] καὶ τὴν αὐλὴν τὴν ἔξωθεν τοῦ ναοῦ ἔκβαλε ἔξωθεν καὶ μὴ αὐτὴν μετρήσῃς, ὅτι ἐδόθη τοῖς ἔθνεσιν, καὶ τὴν πόλιν τὴν ἁγίαν πατήσουσιν μῆνας τεσσεράκοντα [καὶ] δύο. [v. 3] Καὶ δώσω τοῖς δυσὶν μάρτυσίν μου καὶ προφητεύσουσιν ἡμέρας χιλίας διακοσίας ἑξήκοντα περιβεβλημένοι σάκκους.

The casting out of the temple's outer court to the outside and its handing over to the nations which will trample the holy city for 42 months (v. 2) at

---

68. G. Quispel, *The Secret Book of Revelation* (New York: McGraw-Hill, 1979), p. 73. While we agree that John's Revelation speaks much to John's world in the first century C.E., hence the seven letters to the seven churches indicate present concerns, it goes a bit too far to say as Reddish does, that John's Revelation was not intended to 'provide details about the future'. Reddish, *Revelation*, p. 26.

69. Aune, *Revelation 6–16*, p. 585.

70. Aune, *Revelation 6–16*, p. 594.

71. Sweet, *Revelation*, p. 184.

72. Court, *Myth and History*, p. 87. Thompson also thinks that: 'No sharp break should be made between 10.11 and 11.3.' Thompson, *Revelation*, p. 125.

first glance do not appear to correlate well with the giving of the two witnesses to prophesy for 1260 days (v. 3). However, the connective 'and' at the beginning of verse 3 coordinates the two episodes and if this paratactic construction is recognized, then it is not necessary to separate 11.1–2 from 11.3–14 as deriving from different sources.[73] By the use of parataxis, John binds the episode of the nations' trampling over the holy city with the appearance of God's two witnesses. This purposeful paratactic construction is made more evident as the parallelism between vv. 2 and 3 shows. The giving over of the temple's outer court and the trampling of the nations over the holy city for forty-two months parallel the giving of God's two witnesses to prophesy for 1260 days. The parallelism is structured as follows:

Verse 2	Verse 3
A – Given (ἐδόθη) the outer court	**A'** – I will give (δώσω)
B – To the nations (τοῖς ἔθνεσιν)	**B'** – To my two witnesses (τοῖς δυσὶν μάρτυσίν μου)
C – They will trample the holy city	**C'** – They will prophesy [to and in Jerusalem]
(τὴν πόλιν τὴν ἁγίαν πατήσουσιν)	(προφητεύσουσιν)
D – 42 months	**D'** – 1,260 days

Structurally, this parallelism in the form of ABCDA'B'C'D' is impressive.[74] The giving of the temple's outer court to the nations is contrasted to

---

73. de Heer writes: 'Kita mendapat kesan, bahwa pekerjaan mereka di *Yerusalem*, oleh kerana ayat 3 (di mana pekerjaan mereka diberitahu) dihubungkan dengan kata 'dan' dengan ayat 2 yang mendahului; dan dalam ayat dua itu dibicarakan tentang *Yerusalem*. Dan kesan ini bahwa mereka bekerja di Yerusalem, sangat diperkuatkan oleh ayat 8, di mana dikatakan bahwa kedua saksi ini dibunuh 'di kota besar, di mana juga Tuhan mereka disalibkan.' [ET: We note that their ministry is in Jerusalem, because verse 3 (where their ministry is made known) is connected with the preceding verse 2 by the word 'and'; and verse 2 speaks of Jerusalem. That they minister in Jerusalem is greatly strengthened by verse 8, where it is said the two witnesses are killed 'in the great city where their Lord was crucified'.]. de Heer, *Kitab Wahyu*, p. 145.

74. We disagree with Giesen who says: 'Der Subjektwechsel in v. 3 markiert deutlich einen Neubeginn.' Giesen, *Offenbarung*, p. 241. Bauckham remarks that: 'The two passages (11.2–3 and 11.3–13) are linked purely by the time-period, given in different forms in 11.2 and 11.3.' Bauckham, *Climax of Prophecy*, p. 267. Bauckham (p. 267 n. 39), however, acknowledges that 'it is correct to treat 11.1–2 as providing the setting for 11.3–13'. Spatafora fails to detect the paratactic καί and says: 'The καί at the beginning of verse 3 introduces a new subject that is loosely connected with the preceding.' Spatafora, *The Temple*, p. 160. So Spatafora (p. 160) thinks, in our view wrongly, that 11.1–2 is unrelated to and a distinct unit from 11.3–14.

God's act of giving of the two witnesses. The nations will trample (future tense) on the holy city just as the two witnesses will prophesy (future tense) in or against the city. Both lexical terms 'the nations' and 'the two witnesses' in the dative further enhance the formal and structural coherence of vv. 2–3 of Rev. 11. The addition of μου qualifying 'the two witnesses' yields the emphatic statement that the two witnesses belonging to God/Christ are to be seen as a contrast to the nations which oppose God by desecrating his holy temple and city. Finally, the parallelism is made complete by the temporal reference to the three-and-a-half years period in D as forty-two months and 1,260 days in D'. 'The relationship between the two episodes is expressed with precision by juxtaposing of the two equivalent time references in vv. 2 and 3.'[75]

Further, the clause at the end of v. 3 that the two witnesses are 'clothed in sackcloth' thematically links v. 3 with v. 2 in that the two witnesses mourn (represented by the sackcloth) the desecration carried out by the nations in God's holy place and city. Further, 11.1–3 is composed in first person direct speech from 11.1 up to v. 3 as God or Christ is still seen to be speaking thus: '*I* will give my two witnesses'. Revelation 11.4, on the other hand, is narrated in the third person: 'These are the two olive trees and the two lampstands standing before the Lord of the earth.... They have authority'.[76] Since verse 3 of Rev. 11 is narrated in the first person, a strong case can be made that v. 3 is connected to vv. 1–2, and thus must be regarded as integral to the discourse of vv. 1–3.

7. *The Ministry of the Two Witnesses (Revelation 11.3–6)*

We have shown that the episode of the nations' trampling on the holy city (11.2) and the appearance of the two witnesses to prophesy (11.3) are related by the literary technique of parallelism and parataxis. So 'A' is linked with 'B' in our macro-chiasm. The two witnesses who will prophesy are then identified as 'the two olive trees and the two lampstands who stand before the Lord of the earth' (11.4). This is not so much identification as an explicit reference to ch. 4 of the book of Zechariah, specifically to Zech. 4.14.[77] These two witnesses who are primarily prophets (for they prophesy, cf. 11.3, 10) are characterized as having the powers described in 11.5–6. Again we see John structures the sentences with the verb θέλω functioning as an *inclusio*: 'καὶ εἴ τις αὐτοὺς θέλει ἀδικῆσαι' (and if

---

75. Court, *Myth and History*, p. 87.

76. So Giblin, 'Revelation 11.1–13', p. 440.

77. Aune notes as follows: 'That τοῖς δυσὶν μάρτυσίν is articular indicates that it refers to figures well known to the readers. In this case it is likely that the author assumes the readers' familiarity with Zech. 4.2–14.' Aune, *Revelation 6–16*, p. 579.

anyone *wishes* to harm them) in the beginning of v. 5 which is concluded by a reference to the two witnesses' power to πατάξαι τὴν γῆν ἐν πάσῃ πληγῇ ὁσάκις ἐὰν θελήσωσιν (to strike the earth with all manner of plagues as often as they *wish*). By the use of the word θέλω here in vv. 5–6, John delimits the passage which contains the gist of the two witnesses' ministry apart from the initial mention that they will prophesy in v. 3. Verse 5 is structured in a parallelism:

A – καὶ εἴ τις αὐτοὺς θέλει ἀδικῆσαι
B – πῦρ ἐκπορεύεται ἐκ τοῦ στόματος αὐτῶν καὶ κατεσθίει τοὺς ἐχθροὺς αὐτῶν·
A' – καὶ εἴ τις θελήσῃ αὐτοὺς ἀδικῆσαι,
B' – οὕτως δεῖ αὐτὸν ἀποκτανθῆναι.

The AA' is explicitly synonymous except the word order αὐτοὺς θέλει in A is reversed in A'. The pair of BB' explains the manner in which the enemies of the two witnesses must be (δεῖ) killed, that is by fire which comes out of the mouth of the two witnesses.[78] This is followed by verse 6 which describes their authority to perform signs, two of which are explicitly identified as 'shutting the heavens that it will not rain in the days of their prophecy' and 'turning water into blood' and another general but more encompassing sign that they can strike the earth with every plague as often as they wish. Again, this sentence in v. 6 is structured in a parallelism as follows:

A – οὗτοι ἔχουσιν τὴν ἐξουσίαν κλεῖσαι τὸν οὐρανόν, ἵνα μὴ ὑετὸς βρέχῃ τὰς ἡμέρας τῆς προφητείας αὐτῶν,
A' – καὶ ἐξουσίαν ἔχουσιν ἐπὶ τῶν ὑδάτων στρέφειν αὐτὰ εἰς αἷμα καὶ πατάξαι τὴν γῆν ἐν πάσῃ πληγῇ ὁσάκις ἐὰν θελήσωσιν.

The main clause 'they have authority' (οὗτοι ἔχουσιν τὴν ἐξουσίαν) is repeated in the next line though as in verse 5, the word order ἔχουσιν τὴν ἐξουσίαν in A is reversed in A' as ἐξουσίαν ἔχουσιν which gives the sentence a chiastic effect.[79] The lack of the article before ἐξουσίαν in A' links it to the authority in A, which authority empowers the two witnesses to execute the signs as described in vv. 5 and 6. Arranged in a parallel pair (AA') as shown above, the authority of the two witnesses is impressive indeed. They

78.   The singular form of στόματος (their mouth) is likely to be due to John's portrayal of the two witnesses as acting jointly or in unison. Likewise, the singular corpse in 11.8a (τὸ πτῶ μα αὐτῶν [their corpse]) may be John's attempt to convey that in life and in death, the two witnesses are one.

79.   Charles noted that the word order ἐξουσίαν ἔχουσιν appeared here only in Revelation. Charles, *Revelation* Vol. 1, p. 285. Aune states that: 'The ministry of the two witnesses is described succinctly in negative terms in two synonymous couplets in vv 5–6.' Aune, *Revelation 6–16*, p. 586. Aune fails to notice the chiastic effect produced by the inversion of word order in vv. 5–6.

have the authority over the sky (τὸν οὐρανόν) and also authority over the waters and the earth. If the phrase 'the waters' (τῶν ὑδάτων) here encompasses the seas and the rivers, the authority of the two witnesses is almost absolute; covering all spheres of God's creation: heaven, seas, rivers and earth.

The first four trumpets are seen to unleash judgments on the earth, the seas, the rivers and the sky respectively (8.7–12). The fifth trumpet (first woe) depicts a demonic-locust plague tormenting the earth's inhabitants (9.1–11) but not killing them, while the sixth trumpet (second woe) kills a third of humankind (9.13–21). The two witnesses, whose ministry takes place within the sixth trumpet (cf. 11.14) appear to unleash judgment in the manner similar to those under all the six trumpets. They not only have power over the sky, the waters and the earth but they also torment the inhabitants of the earth (cf. 11.10) as the fifth trumpet's blast. They are also empowered to kill if they are attacked by their enemies (11.5). John appears to sum up the acts of the two witnesses as similar to those judgments unleashed under all the six trumpets making the career of the two witnesses a microcosm of what will happen to God's created order under the six trumpets in totality.[80]

Obviously, given the clear allusion to Zech. 4.14 in Rev. 11.4, we will have to ask what John wants his readers to infer about the two witnesses apart from the material given in vv. 3–6. This Zecharianic text may give us a clue as to the link between the temple in Rev. 11.1–2 and the two witnesses who in Rev. 11.4 are modeled after Zerubbabel and Joshua, the two olive trees of Zech. 4.14, better known as the temple builders in the book of Zechariah. Further, the content of the two witnesses' testimony is left unstated in Rev. 11.3–6. As our focus in this chapter is on the literary structure of Rev. 11, these questions will be answered in a later chapter in this book.

Hence, we conclude that structurally Rev. 11.1–2 is linked strongly to 11.3–14 as shown by the parallelism in vv. 2–3. Further, the passage concerning the two witnesses in 11.3–6 can be further divided into two sub-units: vv. 3–4 and vv. 5–6. The sub-unit of 11.3–4 formally sets out the primary role of the two witnesses as prophetic messengers of God and v. 4 serves further to clarify their identities and functions with reference to an allusion to Zech. 4.14. Verses 5 and 6 of Rev. 11, on the other hand, describe their ministry as executors of judgment, namely killing those who would harm them and performing signs in the manner of Elijah and Moses as a torment to the inhabitants of the earth (cf. 11.10).

---

80. Beale under the heading 'The Relationship of the Two Witnesses' Ministry to the Trumpet Plagues' enumerates a list of lexical and conceptual parallels linking the trumpet plagues with those performed by the two witnesses. See Beale, *Revelation*, pp. 585–86.

8. The Death and the Vindication of the Two Witnesses
(Revelation 11.7–13)

The next literary unit in Rev. 11.7–13 describes the events which occur after the completion of the two witnesses' prophetic testimony. Müller notes that: 'Der ganze Abschnitt Vers 3–13 unterteilt sich in die Einheiten Vers 3–6 und 7–13.'[81] The ministry of the two witnesses with powerful signs and plagues is summed up as τὴν μαρτυρίαν αὐτῶν (11.7), a phrase which sums up the nature of their activity as τοῖς δυσὶν μάρτυσίν (11.3) sent by God. The use of the noun form μαρτυρία in 11.7 which begins the unit of 11.7–13 links the said unit with the preceding unit of 11.3–6 which commenced by the description of God's two agents as μάρτυς. The sudden appearance of the beast and its role in killing the two witnesses in 11.7 will be discussed in our analysis of the chiastic pair of 11.7–13 and 13.7–10 (CC') in a later chapter.

Although this proposed unit is often divided into two sub-units, vv. 7–10 and vv. 11–13, vv. 7–13 are best seen as a literary unit with the literary device, an *inclusio*, enclosing the said unit beginning at vv. 7–8 and ending at vv. 12–13 in an ABB'A' pattern:[82]

> **A** – The Beast ascends (ἀναβαῖνον) from the sea . . . kills (ἀποκτενεῖ) the two Witnesses . . . corpse lie on the street of the great city (τῆς πόλεως τῆς μεγάλης) [vv. 7–8].
>
> **B** – The nations gaze (βλέπουσιν) at the corpses for *three-and-a-half days* and rejoice (χαίρουσιν) over their deaths [vv. 9–10].
>
> **B'** – After *the three-and-a-half days*, the spirit of life from God enters the two Witnesses and they stand on their feet . . . great fear (φόβος μέγας) falls on those who look on (θεωροῦντας) [vv. 11].
>
> **A'** – The two Witnesses ascend (ἀνέβησαν) to heaven . . . a great earthquake strikes a tenth of the city (τῆς πόλεως) and kills (ἀπεκτάνθησαν) seven thousand persons [vv. 12–13].

The chiastic pattern unites the narrative from the death of the two witnesses (vv. 7–8) to their vindication (vv. 12–13). A number of repeated key words and concepts at the beginning and the end of the textual unit give rise to the *inclusio*. The beast that ascends from the sea onto the earth (11.7) is contrasted with the ascent of the two witnesses from the earth to

---

81. Müller, *Offenbarung*, p. 208.

82. For example, Giblin divides Rev. 11.1–13 into four sub-sections consisting of vv. 1–2, vv. 3–6, vv. 7–10, and vv. 11–13. Giblin, 'Revelation 11.1–13', pp. 436–37. Aune notes the anomaly that the passage in 11.3–10 is dominated by verbs in the future tense and then by verbs in the past tense (vv. 11–13). Aune, *Revelation 6–16*, p. 586. The grammatical division accords well with the two halves of the chiastic pattern, vv. 7–10 and vv. 11–13.

heaven (11.12). The killing of the two witnesses by the beast is avenged by God in the killing of seven thousand persons through the great earthquake. The parallelism between vv. 7–8 and vv. 12–13 is further strengthened by setting the events in the geographical location of the city. Just as the corpses of the two prophets lie unburied on the street of the great city and become the object of rejoicing by the inhabitants of the city, the righteous judgment of God falls on the city's populace as the great earthquake strikes a tenth of the city.

The movement of the narrative from A to B, i.e., from the murder by the beast to the gazing of the nations' representatives on the dead bodies of the two prophets and their rejoicing, links the beast with those nations' representatives that are present in the great city. Peoples out of every nation (ἐκ τῶν λαῶν καὶ φυλῶν καὶ γλωσσῶν καὶ ἐθνῶν) approve of the beast's murderous act for the two prophets have tormented them with plagues (v. 10). The reversal comes in B' as the nations' celebration is short-lived for after the three and a half days, the dead prophets become alive again through divine intervention. BB' parallels are indeed pivotal as the reversal of fortune is told dramatically here.

The phrases τὸ πτῶμα αὐτῶν (x 2) and τὰ πτώματα αὐτῶν are mentioned thrice in two brief verses (vv. 8–9), a repetition which functions to highlight the plight of the dead bodies of the two witnesses who are not only refused burial but become the trophies of their conqueror, the beast and his cohorts, the nations who gaze in delight at the corpses and exchange gifts with one another in celebration. Just as their corpses become public spectacles, so too is their vindication by God's direct intervention from heaven when they stand on their feet very much alive again and ascend to heaven in a cloud in full public view. The earthquake that follows immediately killing seven thousand persons in the city completes their vindication with the concluding remark that the rest of the inhabitants (of the city) give glory to the God of heaven. Significantly, the nations' repentance,[83] which the two witnesses cannot accomplish in life, is secured through their death, resurrection and ascension.

---

83. The majority of commentators rightly see that the clause 'the rest of the inhabitants gave glory to the God of heaven' indicate that the people repent and turn to God. In Rev. 16.9, repentance and giving glory to God are linked: 'and they refused to repent and give him glory'. Beasley-Murray notes that in Josh. 7.19 and Jer. 13.16, 'to give glory to God means to confess sin and repent of it'. Beasley-Murray, *Revelation*, p. 187. For other biblical references which link repentance with giving glory to God, see Thomas, *Revelation 8–22*, p. 99. Caird observes that the angel's commission: 'Fear God and give him glory' in Rev. 14.7 and the linkage between repentance and giving glory to God in 16.9 provide the decisive answer to Johannine usage in 11.13 that 'giving glory to God' denotes repentance. Caird concludes: 'In John's vocabulary "fear", "do homage", and "repent" are almost synonymous terms.' Caird, *Revelation*, p. 140. So Schüssler Fiorenza, *Revelation: Vision of a Just World*, p. 79; Murphy,

While it is not our purpose to analyze in detail every verse in this passage (vv. 7–13), a number of verses demonstrate John's literary style in utilizing parallelism and chiasm in constructing sentences and short paragraphs. For example, the sentence in 11.10 is composed in the form of a chiasm:

A – καὶ οἱ κατοικοῦντες ἐπὶ τῆς γῆς
   B – χαίρουσιν ἐπ'αὐτοῖς καὶ εὐφραίνονται καὶ δῶρα πέμψουσιν ἀλλήλοις,
   B' – ὅτι οὗτοι οἱ δύο προφῆται ἐβασάνισαν
A' –τοὺς κατοικοῦντας ἐπὶ τῆς γῆς.

The chiasm is enclosed by the repeated and synonymous phrase 'the ones dwelling on the earth' in the beginning and the end of the sentence. The inhabitants of the earth are said to rejoice and make merry and send presents to one another at the deaths of the two witnesses because (ὅτι) the two prophets are said to have tormented the inhabitants during the days when they were alive (cf. 11.6). The three verbs in the present tense in B depicting a celebratory and congratulatory mood on the part of the earth dwellers are contrasted with just one verb in aorist tense 'tormented' in B'. In B, the people rejoice over them (ἐπ' αὐτοῖς), the identities of whom are disclosed in B' with the emphatic '*these* (οὗτοι) two prophets' – these ones who have tormented them but now have met their deaths, thus giving the inhabitants of the earth the reason and cause (hence the use of ὅτι) for rejoicing, making merry and sending gifts to one another.

The narrative continues to move forward swiftly to the next phase marked by another temporal indicator: 'And after the three and a half days.' The sub-unit of 11.11–12 is likewise structured as a parallelism thus:

[v. 11] Καὶ μετὰ τὰς τρεῖς ἡμέρας καὶ ἥμισυ
A – πνεῦμα ζωῆς ἐκ τοῦ θεοῦ εἰσῆλθεν ἐν αὐτοῖς,
   καὶ ἔστησαν ἐπὶ τοὺς πόδας αὐτῶν,
   B – καὶ φόβος μέγας ἐπέπεσεν ἐπὶ τοὺς θεωροῦντας αὐτούς.
A' – [v.12] καὶ ἤκουσαν φωνῆς μεγάλης ἐκ τοῦ οὐρανοῦ λεγούσης αὐτοῖς·
   Ἀνάβατε ὧδε. καὶ ἀνέβησαν εἰς τὸν οὐρανὸν ἐν τῇ νεφέλῃ,
   B' – καὶ ἐθεώρησαν αὐτοὺς οἱ ἐχθροὶ αὐτῶν.

The articular temporal phrase 'and after *the* three and a half days' in 11.11 serves two structural and chronological purposes. First, it links the resurrection narrative with the non-burial of the two witnesses for three-and-a-half days in the preceding sub-unit of vv. 9–10. Second, the temporal indicator provides a temporal and chronological framework within which the events are said to unfold after the three-and-a-half days following the deaths of the two prophets. The first clause 'a spirit from God entered into

Fallen is Babylon, p. 268; Thompson, *Revelation*, p. 128; Charles, *Revelation Vol. 1*, pp. 291–92; Sweet, *Revelation*, p. 189; Keener, *Revelation*, pp. 296–97; Aune, *Revelation 6–16*, pp. 628–29.

them' in A mirrors 'a loud voice from heaven saying to them: "Come up
here"' in A' in a remarkable degree of correspondence:

πνεῦμα ζωῆς   =   φωνῆς μεγάλης
ἐκ τοῦ θεοῦ   =   ἐκ τοῦ οὐρανου
εἰσῆλθεν ἐν αὐτοῖς   =   λεγούσης αὐτοῖς

The second clause 'and they *stood* on their feet' in A corresponds to the
clause in A' 'they *ascended* into heaven'. The degree of correspondence is
enhanced by the aorist verbs in each clause. The parallels are made more
effective as the members in each AA' do not only correspond but also A'
brings the narrative forward sequentially and chronologically from
resurrection in A to ascension in A' in one swift and terse narrative.

BB' completes the parallel structure by each describing the resurrection and ascension as being watched by the crowd in B made up
apparently of those from every people, tribe, tongue, and nation (cf.
11.9) who are then identified as the enemies of the two prophets in B'.
The parallelism here in BB' is made clear by the repeated key concept
'watch':

θεωροῦντας αὐτούς (B)   =   ἐθεώρησαν αὐτοὺς (B')

It is unlikely that John mixes his tenses haphazardly but that in verse 11
the present participle θεωροῦντας functions to link it with a previous
verb βλέπουσιν in the present indicative active tense in verse 9. The
present tense of θεωροῦντας and βλέπουσιν impresses John's readers as to
the vividness of the scenes which John is describing. Just as the people
gaze at the corpses for three and a half days, they also witness the
moment when the dead corpses come back to life and stand on their
feet whole. Thus it is not surprising that a *great* fear falls on those who
are watching the semi-decomposed bodies suddenly becoming whole and
being resurrected to life. Their gaze of glee and triumph turns into
shock and horror as they watch the resurrected prophets taken up by a
cloud and ascend into heaven. All these chain of events or objects –
corpses, the dead coming back to life and the ascension – are narrated
as unfolding in the sight of a large section of the world-populace. The
vividness of these scenes demonstrates John's creativity and artistry in
composing this climactic segment of the saga in the life of the two
witnesses.

9. 'The Second Woe has passed; Behold, the Third Woe comes quickly' (Revelation 11.14, 15–19)

Verse 14 of Rev. 11 is often seen as concluding the narrative of the two
witnesses and appears to serve as the transition to the next literary unit of

11.15–19. We must ask why John's remark that 'the second woe has passed and the third woe comes quickly' is placed at this juncture in ch. 11 which at first appearance seems to intrude into an otherwise smooth narrative. Does verse 14 of Rev. 11 function to separate the story of the two witnesses from what follows next in the narrative story-line? The answer must be given in the negative. We venture to suggest two important reasons for the placement of the temporal marker at 11.14. First, 11.14 functions to connect the episode of the nations' trampling on the holy city and the ministry of the two witnesses (11.1–13) as events which take place under the sixth trumpet or the second woe which commenced in 9.13 (cf. 8.13).[84] With this narrative indicator within the series of the seven trumpets, John ensures that his readers are made aware that the events narrated from 11.1–13, which are the sixth trumpet's events, take place at the very end of history, since when the last and seventh trumpet sounds, 'all God's mysteries will be fulfilled and there will be no more time' (10.6–7). Following John's narrative story-line and the schema of the series of the seven trumpets, the episode of the two witnesses makes up God's *penultimate* mystery before the End.[85] This is evident as the seventh angel sounds his trumpet at 11.15 immediately following the end of the narrative about the two witnesses in 11.13.

It is often thought 11.14 divides the ascension of the two witnesses and the accompanying earthquake in 11.12–13 from the seventh trumpet's sounding in time and space (11.15). But on closer reading, these two events are linked together as formal and literary markers in 11.15 indicate. Chronologically, the series of events seen to unfold *after* the three and a half days in 11.11 are contemporaneous or nearly contemporaneous with each other. It is at the hour of the two witnesses' ascension that the great earthquake (ἐν ἐκείνῃ τῇ ὥρᾳ ἐγένετο σεισμὸς μέγας) strikes the city (11.13). In other words, the resurrection and the ascension of the two witnesses

---

84.   Thus, it is a mistake to view Rev. 10.1–11.13 as an interlude or parenthesis. So Beale, *Revelation*, p. 609. For a list of scholars of the same persuasion as Beale on this point, see Andrew E. Steinmann, 'The Tripartite Structure of the Sixth Seal, the Sixth Trumpet, and the Sixth Bowl of John's Apocalypse (Rev. 6.12–7.17; 9.13–11.14; 16,12–16)', *JETS* 35 (1992), pp. 69–79 (69 n. 1). However, Lambrecht's view is to be preferred as he remarks that: 'With regard to the structure, the fact that it is explicitly stated in 11, 14 that the second Woe has passed proves that for John this woe as well as the sixth trumpet contains, in a certain sense, not only 9, 13–21 (the sixth trumpet proper) but also ch. 10 and 11, 1–13.' Lambrecht, 'A Structuration of Revelation 4,1–22,5', p. 93. We will even go further than Lambrecht to state that 10.1–11.13 unfolds within the 'the sixth trumpet proper' as 8.13 explicitly identifies the last three trumpets with the three woes, namely the sixth trumpet *is* the second woe that is said to be concluded in 11.14. Sweet says, 'v. 14 (*the second woe has passed*) binds in 10 and 11.1–13 with the sixth trumpet blast and second woe'. Sweet, *Revelation*, p. 181.

85.   The last mystery is the blowing of the seventh trumpet (11.15) which is the pouring out of the seven bowls of plagues described in Rev. 15–16.

coincide with the great earthquake and conclude the second woe (11.14a). The third woe follows immediately (11.14b) with the sounding of the seventh trumpet (11.15a).

Furthermore, the narrative indicator in 11.14 prepares the readers for the unfolding of the third woe: '*Behold* (ἰδου), the third woe is coming quickly' (11.14b).[86] The third woe is never mentioned again or explicitly described anywhere in the book of Revelation. To unravel what is intended by John as the contents of the third woe or seventh trumpet, one has to appreciate John's literary schema of the series of seven seals, the seven trumpets and the seven bowls. Each of the first six seals is opened with attendant events in Rev. 6. The first six seals make up a closed unit and are distinct from the seventh seal.[87] When the seventh seal is opened, there is only silence (8.1). Nothing unfolds under the seventh seal in contrast to the preceding six seals. J. Lambrecht argues convincingly that, 'the seventh seal encompasses the seven trumpets' (8.1–5), and that the seventh trumpet or the third woe has no content in itself but consists of the seven last bowls of judgment.[88] Aune, following Lambrecht, summarizes John's schema as follows:

---

86. The vocative ἰδου more than the simple 'I saw' (εἶδον) stresses John's vision and elicits a heightened response or insight on the part of the readers to understand the accompanied statement or narrative. Ἰδου occurs 26 times in the book of Revelation. In the literary schema of the seven seals, seven trumpets and seven bowls, the word ἰδου is used to introduce the first three seals (6.2, 5, 8) and to announce the final two woes (9.12). It may be that the fourth seal has no introductory ἰδου as the fourth seal functions to summarize the contents of the first three seals.

87. Thompson notes that: 'The opening of the sixth seal discloses divine judgment. Introduced by the same formula as the opening first seal (And I saw when he opened . . .), that formula rings the first six seals.' Thompson, *Revelation*, p. 105.

88. J. Lambrecht, 'The Opening of the Seals (Rev. 6,1–8,6)', *Bib* 78 (1998), pp. 198–221 (216). Lambrecht (p. 216 n. 38) states: 'One is probably also justified to expect that John will use the same encompassing technique for the seventh trumpet as well.' Likewise, Thomas comments thus: 'Just as the seventh seal included all the seven trumpets, the seventh trumpet includes all seven bowls described in 16.1 ff.' Thomas, *Revelation 8–22*, p. 104. Dave Hagelberg also thinks that, 'sangkakala yang terakhir ini mengandungi ketujuh cawan. . . . Sama seperti segel yang ketujuh yang mengandung ketujuh sangkakala, demikian juga sangkakala ketujuh mengandung ketujuh cawan.' (ET: The last trumpet contains the seven bowls. . . . Just as the seventh seal contains the seven trumpets, so also the seventh trumpet contains the seven bowls). D. Hagelberg, *Tafsiran Kitab Wahyu: Dari Bahasa Yunani* (Yogjakarta, Indonesia: Yayasan ANDI, 1997) [ET: *A Commentary on the book of Revelation: From the Greek Text*], pp. 228–29. Beasley-Murray rightly concludes that, 'The third woe coincides with the events of the seventh trumpet' but wrongly cautions against identifying 'the third woe with the seven bowls or the like'. Beasley-Murray, *Revelation*, p. 187. Beale also rightly identifies the third woe with the seventh trumpet but errs in concluding that the events of the third woe are described by John in 11.15–19. Beale remarks that: 'If 11.15–19 is the seventh trumpet, then it must also be the third woe.' Beale, *Revelation*, p. 610. It is submitted that the seventh angel *trumpeted* in 11.15a and although related to 11.15b-19, the events of

The seventh seal (8.1), which is separated from the sixth seal by an excursus on the protection of the 144,000 in 7.1–17, contains within itself all the plagues of the seven trumpets and seven bowls that follow. Further, the seventh trumpet, again separated from the sixth trumpet by 10.1–11.13, contains within itself the plagues of the following seven bowls. The seventh bowl is not separated from the sixth bowl; it, with the series of divinely caused plagues inflicted on the people of the world, ends with the decisive announcement 'It is done!' (16.17).[89]

The blowing of the seventh trumpet *is* the unfolding of the third woe (just as the fifth and sixth trumpets are the first and second woes respectively, cf. 8.13) which immediately follows the declaration that the second woe has passed (11.14–15).[90] The seventh trumpet or third woe following John's literary schema in itself has no separate content but it consists of and encompasses the seven last bowls of God's wrath which are only narrated fully in chs 15 and 16 of Revelation. This disruption of several chapters between the announcement of the seventh trumpet/third woe in 11.15 and the actual outpouring of the seven last plagues in Rev. 15–16 should not come as a surprise as John in Rev. 11–13 is still focusing on the events that come under the three and a half years period before the End. This apparent literary arrangement is made more plausible by our proposed concentric chiasm which strongly supports the coherence and unity of 11.1–14.5, bound tightly by the temporal figure of three and a half.[91]

11.15b-19 are separate and distinct from 11.15a. The events of 11.16–18 are indeed the final climactic judgment *after* the seven bowls of judgments are poured out in the days of the seventh trumpet's blast and hence should not be equated with the seventh trumpet as Beale has done.

89.   Aune, *Revelation 1–5*, p. xcv.

90.   This is another reason why the narrative indicator in 11.14 should be seen as integral to what precedes and what follows since 11.15 goes on to announce the blowing of the seventh trumpet which is the third woe. Aune thinks that 11.14 is out of place here. 'This sentence [11.14] would appear more appropriate if it were placed after 9.21, and it is also difficult to reconcile with the result of the sounding of the seventh trumpet in 11.15–18, which can hardly be described as a "woe."' Aune, *Revelation 6–16*, p. 630. Aune is mistaken in three instances. First, he fails to connect the episode of the two witnesses (11.1–13) with the second woe or sixth trumpet (9.13–21) which the narrative indicator of 11.14 seeks to do. So Swete, *Apocalypse*, p. 141. Secondly, the seventh trumpet is not expanded further in 11.15b-18 but that it 'sounded' in 11.15a. Thirdly, the seventh trumpet is indeed a woe, a greater woe than the preceding two for as the last and final woe it consists of the seven last bowls of judgment that will exhaust God's wrath poured out to the world. It is thus difficult to concur with Thomas that, '9.20–21 clearly marks the end of the sixth trumpet, which is the second woe' when the narrative marker that concludes the sixth trumpet/second woe occurs in 11.14. Thomas, *Revelation 8–22*, p. 99.

91.   Hence, we have to disagree with Aune's remark that, 'Rev. 11.15–18 is a short isolated textual unit that forms an apparently anticlimactic continuation of 8.1–9.21, interrupted by 10.1–11.14 and is immediately followed by 11.19–12.17 and two other sections (12.18–13.18

The outpouring of the seven last plagues thus occurs with the sounding of the seventh trumpet in 11.15a, even though the full narration of the plagues occurs only in chs 15 and 16. The seventh trumpet's sounding is anticipated earlier in 10.7 where it is said that, 'but in the days when the seventh angel is to blow his trumpet, the mystery of God will be fulfilled (ἐτελέσθη), as he announced to his servants the prophets'.[92] It appears that the seven last plagues will be executed in the *days* of the seventh trumpet's blast, the expiry of which will bring to an end God's mystery. This accords well with the description of the seven plagues as the seven *last* plagues (πληγὰς ἑπτὰ τὰς ἐσχάτας) the execution of which coincides with the end to God's wrath (ἐτελέσθη ὁ θυμὸς τοῦ θεοῦ) (15.1). God's mystery contained in the little book is destined to be fulfilled when the seven last plagues are poured out immediately following the ascension of the two witnesses.[93] Thus, it is not surprising when the mystery of God is fulfilled in the seventh trumpet's blast in 11.15a, no mystery or event remains other than the arrival of God's kingdom on earth in 11.15b. The key text of 11.15 can now be better understood in its literary context:

Καὶ ὁ ἕβδομος ἄγγελος ἐσάλπισεν·
καὶ ἐγένοντο φωναὶ μεγάλαι ἐν τῷ οὐρανῷ λέγοντες·
ἐγένετο ἡ βασιλεία τοῦ κόσμου τοῦ κυρίου ἡμῶν καὶ τοῦ Χριστοῦ αὐτοῦ,
καὶ βασιλεύσει εἰς τοὺς αἰῶνας τῶν αἰώνων.

Here is a clear instance where verse division as set out in NA27 and most English translations is a stumbling block to exegesis.[94] We propose that

and 14.1–20), none of which is very carefully integrated into an overarching compositional plan'. Aune, *Revelation 6–16*, p. 635. We venture to suggest that unless one discerns the large concentric pattern over these chapters by paying close attention to the literary and narrative markers throughout the text, then one will come to a conclusion (wrongly) as Aune has, that John's arrangement of this major block of text lacks an 'overarching compositional plan'.

92. 'The days of the seventh trumpet' (10.7) are narrated and expanded fully in chs 15 and 16 of Revelation.

93. This probably explains why the seven last plagues are narrated under 'another great sign' (15.1) with reference to the two signs in 12.1, 3. The events under the first two signs unfold within the three and a half years followed by the seven last plagues, all of which constitute the mystery of God (10.7) before time is no more (χρόνος οὐκέτι ἔσται) and the kingdom of God comes.

94. Alexander Rofé states that: 'The first step to be taken toward the understanding of the text is to identify the textual unit and establish its exact extent in order to pinpoint its start and end.... An obstacle of consequence is the division of the Scriptures into chapters, carried out in the thirteenth century by Bishop Stephen Langton, who was working on the Latin version (Vulgate)... the division into chapters is often a stumbling block in biblical studies.' A. Rofé, *Introduction to the Prophetic Literature* (Sheffield: Sheffield Academic Press, 1997), p. 45. For a discussion on the origins of chapter and verse divisions, see Joseph Hong, 'Chapter and Verse Divisions in the Bible: Their Origins, and Their Use in Today's Common Language Translations', *BT* 48 (1997), pp. 401–10.

there should be a full stop indicating a break after ἐσάλπισεν in 11.15a. The text which reads Καὶ ὁ ἕβδομος ἄγγελος ἐσάλπισεν of 11.15a follows immediately the declaration that the second woe has passed and the third woe comes quickly. It has often been thought puzzling that John does not go on to specify the execution or the completion of the third woe. We venture to suggest that 11.15a does just that! We submit that John's readers, after re-reading his book and becoming familiar with his literary schema, would connect the seventh trumpet with the seven plagues of Rev. 15–16. The ending of the first woe and announcement of the two other woes to come follow exactly the same pattern:

[v. 12] Ἡ οὐαὶ ἡ μία ἀπῆλθεν· ἰδοὺ ἔρχεται ἔτι δύο οὐαὶ μετὰ ταῦτα.
[v. 13a] Καὶ ὁ ἕκτος ἄγγελος ἐσάλπισεν·
(9.12–13a).

Again we see that most English Bible translators and editors have separated the narrative and temporal indicator in 9.12 from the sounding of the sixth trumpet which is put in the following verse of 9.13a. In this instance, the sixth trumpet's events are narrated immediately from 9.13b onwards to v. 21. This has led most scholars to read the seventh trumpet's blast in 11.15 in similar vein thinking that the contents of the seventh trumpet are set out in 11.15b-19 after the seventh trumpet's blast in 11.15a. What has not been fully recognized is that just as the seventh seal has no separate contents but consists of the seven trumpets, the seventh trumpet encompasses the seven last plagues of Rev. 15–16. Thus the loud voices announcing the arrival of God's kingdom in 11.15b and the hymnic response by the twenty-four elders in 11.16–18 cannot be the contents of the seventh trumpet. All the preceding six trumpets narrate actual judgments being executed upon the elements of the universe and there is no reason to think that the seventh trumpet will be any different in kind but consists only of a heavenly declaration and a doxology.

Structurally, the loud voices in 11.15b belong to the unit of 11.15b-18:

A – [v. 15b] καὶ ἐγένοντο φωναὶ μεγάλαι ἐν τῷ οὐρανῷ λέγοντες·

B – ἐγένετο ἡ βασιλεία τοῦ κόσμου τοῦ κυρίου ἡμῶν καὶ τοῦ Χριστοῦ αὐτοῦ, καὶ βασιλεύσει εἰς τοὺς αἰῶνας τῶν αἰώνων.

A' – [v. 16] Καὶ οἱ εἴκοσι τέσσαρες πρεσβύτεροι [οἱ] ἐνώπιον τοῦ θεοῦ καθήμενοι ἐπὶ τοὺς θρόνους αὐτῶν ἔπεσαν ἐπὶ τὰ πρόσωπα αὐτῶν καὶ προσεκύνησαν τῷ θεῷ [v. 17] λέγοντες·[95]

B' – Εὐχαριστοῦμέν σοι, κύριε ὁ θεὸς ὁ παντοκράτωρ, ὁ ὢν καὶ ὁ ἦν, ὅτι εἴληφας τὴν δύναμίν σου τὴν μεγάλην καὶ ἐβασίλευσας.

---

95. That verse 17 is located here before λέγοντες is an example of the arbitrariness of verse division in modern Bibles.

[v. 18] καὶ τὰ ἔθνη ὠργίσθησαν,
    καὶ ἦλθεν ἡ ὀργή σου

καὶ ὁ καιρὸς τῶν νεκρῶν κριθῆναι
καὶ δοῦναι τὸν μισθὸν τοῖς δούλοις σου τοῖς προφήταις
καὶ τοῖς ἁγίοις καὶ τοῖς φοβουμένοις τὸ ὄνομά σου,
τοὺς μικροὺς καὶ τοὺς μεγάλους,
καὶ διαφθεῖραι τοὺς διαφθείροντας τὴν γῆν.

As already noted, the plural ἐγένοντο and the singular ἐγένετο in 11.15 set
the scene for the arrival of God's kingdom. The clause, 'The loud voices
(plural) in heaven are *saying* (λέγοντες)' in A parallels the *saying* (λέγοντες)
of twenty-four elders in A'.[96] The saying of A introduces another ἐγένετο in
B that the kingdom of the world now belongs to the Lord and his Christ.
The force of the ἐγένετο here must be given its due as something that has
come or happened.[97] The kingdom of God has come in fact and in reality
on earth according to John's narrative story-line in 11.15b. It is not a
proleptic announcement of the coming kingdom but according to the
narrative story-line of ch. 11, 11.15b is said to take place *after* the three-
and-a-half years period has lapsed (11.7ff), *after* the three and a half days
(11.11), and more significantly *after* the seventh angel has trumpeted, i.e.,
after the seven last bowls of judgments have been poured out (11.15a; cf

96.   Aune remarks that 'it is not at all clear why the plural is used of loud voices in 11.15
instead of the singular "loud voice" elsewhere in Revelation'. Aune, *Revelation 6–16*, p. 638.
Aune fails to notice that the plural 'loud *voices*' is probably intended to parallel the *voices* of
the twenty four elders as shown in our proposed parallelism.

97.   We disagree with Rowland that the ἐγένετο in 11.15 is best translated as 'is' or 'was'
and not 'become' or 'became'. Rowland argues that 'the kingdom of this world has never
belonged to anyone other than God' and 11.15 does not indicate that the kingdom of the
world *has become* the kingdom of the Lord and his Christ. Rowland, 'The Book of
Revelation', p. 643. While it is to be acknowledged that γίνομαι is widely used in Revelation
and is usually translated 'is' or 'was', it is equally important to note that on occasions, the
translation of ἐγένετο is best translated 'happened' or 'has become'. However, Rowland (p.
643) acknowledges that such is the case in 12.10 which is basically a repetition of 11.15.
Rowland argues that the first ἐγένετο in 11.15 concerning the loud voices and the second
ἐγένετο associated with the kingdom of God must be given the same meaning and thus
translated as 'was' or 'were'. What Rowland fails to notice is that the first ἐγένετο is preceded
by καὶ, which is likely to be a Hebraism from the Hebrew phrase ויהי translated 'And it came
to pass' or simply 'Now it happened'. J. Weingreen suggests that the Waw Consecutive ויהי
'rather than implying a continuation with what has preceded, has little more force than "Now
it happened".' J. Weingreen, *A Practical Grammar for Classical Hebrew* (Oxford: Clarendon
Press, 2nd edn, 1959), p. 92. BDAG (p. 198) lists the phrase καὶ ἐγένετο as equivalent to the
Hebrew ויהי and functions 'to indicate the progress of the narrative'. BDAG (p. 198) translates
ἐγένετο ἡ βασιλεία τοῦ κόσμου τοῦ κυρίου ἡμῶν in Rev. 11.15 as 'the kingdom of the world has
come into the possession of the our Lord'.

Rev. 15–16).[98] After all these things mentioned have unfolded historically in the world as foreseen by John in 11.1–15a, the kingdom of the world *became* (ἐγένετο) the kingdom of the Lord and his Christ (11.5b). The emphatic ἐγένετο in the beginning of the statement heightens the fact that the transference of the kingdom ruled by the dragon and beast to the Lord and his Christ is now a *fait accompli*.

The parallel pair AA' is now made clear. The loud voices *in heaven* proclaiming the arrival of the kingdom in the third person is greeted by the elders on the thrones *before God* with a thanksgiving in a direct speech addressed to God (B') supplementing, expanding and focusing on what is said in B. The announcement that the kingdom of the *Lord* and his Christ has come corresponds to the statement that the *Lord* God Almighty who was and who is, has taken great power. The missing attribute – 'who is to come' in the title of God of 'who was and who is and who is to come' in 11.17 confirms that to John, at this point in time, historically according to the narrative story-line, God has come in fact and in reality on earth. The second line in B, 'he will reign (βασιλεύσει) forever and ever' is mirrored by the second line in B' that 'you reigned (ἐβασίλευσας)' in the aorist tense indicating that his reign has in fact begun in the world. Aune notes that the term ἐβασίλευσας may be construed as an ingressive aorist 'emphasizing the beginning of a state, i.e., have/has begun to reign as king'.[99] B' further

---

98. It is not necessary to see that the word ἐγένετο introducing the kingdom as proleptic or used as a 'prophetic perfect' as Aune does, for in John's chronological schema in Rev. 11, the kingdom of God comes in fact historically *after* all the events spoken therein have transpired (11.1–15a). See Aune, *Revelation 6–16*, p. 638. Revelation 11 thus functions to summarize the events in chronological order in the last three and a half years until the establishment of the kingdom of God on earth. The numerous units in Rev. 12.1–19.21 expand and reiterate the various details spoken of in Rev. 11. For example, Rev. 12 functions to explain why the temple's outer court and the holy city are trampled upon (11.1–2) and the reason for church's suffering in the last three-and-a-half years. Rev. 13 expands on the role of the Beast in 11.7. The unit of Rev. 15–16 narrates the outpouring of the seven last plagues which is the seventh angel's trumpet-blast (11.15a). Rev. 17–18 expands on the role of the Beast vis-à-vis the Woman-Harlot who is drunk with the blood of the saints and the witnesses of Jesus (17.6; cf. 11.7, 13.7). Revelation 19 describes the manner in which heaven is opened for the Rider on the white horse to descend to earth who judges and makes war against the Beast and his cohorts (cf. 11.15b-19). John's literary style is akin to Daniel in Dan. 7–12. The vision in Dan. 7 is repeated and expanded in the remainder of the book from Dan. 8–12. Speaking of the variations and repetitions in Daniel's visions recorded in Dan. 2 and 7, H. H. Rowley says: 'It is unreasonable to demand that an author must say everything he has to say on a subject every time he deals with it.' H. H. Rowley, *The Servant of the Lord* (Oxford: Basil Blackwell, rev. 2nd edn, 1964), p. 264. Likewise, John rarely writes on a topic which does not need filling in at a later text or texts.

99. Aune, *Revelation 6–16*, p. 642. Aune (p. 643) goes on to say that 'construing ἐβασίλευσας as an ingressive aorist need not mean that God did not reign as king previously; rather it could mean that his kingship has only now become effective over the world'.

expands on what the coming of God's reign and his taking of great power means by the hymnic expansion in v. 18.[100] In brief, God is coming to judge in wrath the rebellious nations who rise up in anger against God and his people. Second, God's coming entails rewards for his servants and all who fear him. Third, he will put away evil by destroying those who destroy the earth.

The coming of God's kingdom from heaven to earth entails the temple of God in heaven being opened as the Lord enthroned in his heavenly temple makes his entry into the world and this is exactly what John goes on to narrate in 11.19.[101] Verse 19 can be divided into two parts. The term 'the temple' is used to ring the first part of v. 19, which appears to be better served by ending the sentence with a full stop after τῷ ναῷ αὐτου. The text of 11.19 is set out below:

Καὶ ἠνοίγη ὁ ναὸς τοῦ θεοῦ ὁ ἐν τῷ οὐρανῷ καὶ ὤφθη ἡ κιβωτὸς τῆς διαθήκης αὐτοῦ ἐν τῷ ναῷ αὐτοῦ, καὶ ἐγένοντο ἀστραπαὶ καὶ φωναὶ καὶ βρονταὶ καὶ σεισμὸς καὶ χάλαζα μεγάλη.

We propose that Καὶ ἠνοίγη ὁ ναὸς τοῦ θεοῦ ὁ ἐν τῷ οὐρανῷ καὶ ὤφθη ἡ κιβωτὸς τῆς διαθήκης αὐτοῦ ἐν τῷ ναῷ αὐτοῦ should be a complete sentence in itself as John's style of utilizing repeated words or phrase to close a unit or sentence is again evident here. Further, we have seen earlier that the phrase καὶ ἐγένοντο is used to introduce events which are to be distinguished from what has gone before (cf. 11.15b; 12.10). Verse 19 is best translated as follows:

And the temple of God in heaven was opened and the ark of his covenant was seen within his temple. And there were lightning and voices and thunders and an earthquake and great hail.

The signs of the theophany introduced by the final ἐγένοντο in 11.19 herald 'the coming of God in judgment'.[102] With this theophany formula repeated in 16.18–21 at the conclusion of the seven last plagues, Bauckham is correct to conclude that: 'Just as the theophany formula in 8.15 encompasses the whole series of trumpet judgments up to its recurrence in 11.19, so a comparison of 15.5 and 16.17–21 with 11.19 suggests that the

---

100. The hymn in 11.16–18 will be looked at in detail when we come to examine the chiastic pair of 11.15–19 and 13.1–6.

101. The scene in 11.19 will be expanded in 19.11–21, again in accordance with John's literary style of stating an event in passing only to be filled in at a later text.

102. Bauckham, *Climax of Prophecy*, p. 204. Bauckham (pp. 199–209) discusses the function of the theophany formula in four different texts, namely 4.5, 8.5, 11.19, and 16.18–21. It is interesting to note that only the formulas in 11.19 and 16.18–21 include 'great hail' as the sign indicating the end has come.

whole series of the seven last plagues is summed up in 11.19.'[103] As we have shown that the seventh trumpet's blast which begins the passage in 11.15–19 consists of the outpouring of the seven last plagues, then the theophany formula in 11.19 which sums up the series of the seven last plagues functions to ring the unit of 11.15–19 in an *inclusio*.

The sub-unit of 11.15–19 is an integral part of Rev. 11. As we have shown, it is the purpose of 11.14 to link what precedes with what follows. The earthquake in 11.13 with the first ἐγένετο of Rev. 11 links the unit of 11.1–13 with 11.15–19 which is concluded by the mention of another earthquake with other theophanic signs introduced by the fourth and final ἐγένοντο (11.19). It appears that John intends to depict a series of happenings represented by the four occurrences of ἐγένετο from v. 13 onwards as the events that will finally usher in the kingdom of God immediately following the two witnesses' ascension to heaven. This unit of 11.15–19 is thus the climax to a chain of events foretold by John to happen after the chronological period of three-and-a-half years has expired.

10. *Conclusion*

We have attempted to delimit the boundaries of the units that make up ch. 11 of Revelation. We have found that Rev. 11 is divided into four main sub-units of vv. 1–2, vv. 3–6, vv. 7–13, and vv. 15–19 (ABCD). Revelation 11.14 is especially significant as the temporal and chronological marker indicates to John's readers that the nations' trampling over the holy city and the ministry of the two witnesses (11.1–13) take place within the sixth trumpet/second woe. As 11.14 announces that the second woe has passed and that the third woe is coming quickly, the verse functions to introduce the last sub-unit of Rev. 11, namely the trumpet-blast of the seventh angel (= the third woe) and the coming of God's kingdom. We have demonstrated that the sounding of the seventh angel's trumpet (11.15a) consists of the seven last bowls of plagues described in Rev. 15–16 and as such is not to be equated with the kingdom announcement in 11.15b-18. In summary, Rev. 11 depicts the events that will unfold within the last three and a half years (11.1–13) leading to the establishment of God's kingdom on earth (11.15–19).

---

103. Bauckham, *Climax of Prophecy*, p. 204.

Chapter 4

A LITERARY-STRUCTURAL ANALYSIS OF REVELATION 12.1–14.5

1. *Introduction*

It is the purpose of this chapter to analyse the literary unit of Rev. 12.1–14.5 and demonstrate that the macro-chiasm envisaged for 11.1–14.5 continues in Rev. 12 (EFGF'E'). In fact, we submit that the chiastic pattern for 11.1–14.5 only emerges clearly in Rev. 12. Before we set out what we believe to be the divisions of the smaller units within ch. 12 of Revelation, a casual reader will pick up some distinctive features in the texts (especially in comparison to the previous chapter, Rev. 11).

Revelation 12 begins with John speaking of a great sign (a woman) in heaven, thus locating the scene in heaven. In 12.3, another sign (a great dragon) was also seen in heaven. Thus the two signs introduced in the beginning of the chapter provide the two main characters and the major motif of conflict that will dominate the remainder of the chapter. It is noteworthy, however, that at the end of ch. 12, the conflict of the dragon and woman is not resolved in that the dragon continues to pursue the rest of the woman's seed after the woman is safely taken into refuge in the wilderness (12.14–18). The end of ch. 12 does not bring a conclusion to the drama which commenced in 12.1 but carries it further to ch. 13, in fact to 14.1–5 making the latter passage the climax of the literary unit begun at 11.1–2.

2. *The Signs of Revelation 12.1–17*

The woman and the great dragon are depicted under the term σημεῖον (12.1, 3) and it is reasonable to assume that all other characters associated with the woman and the dragon are subsumed under these signs reportedly seen by John. The readers should immediately ask, 'What do these signs signify?' We have noted in Rev. 1.1 that Jesus' task through the angel was to show or make known (ἐσήμανεν) what must soon come to pass. Aune's remark is of note:

The verb σημαίνειν, meaning 'to indicate clearly' (Louw-Nida, 33.153; see Acts 25.27), occurs only here in Revelation and appears to be in tension with the symbolic and enigmatic character of much of what follows.... In Rev. 1.1, σημαίνειν cannot mean 'to indicate clearly'. But using the term σημαίνειν, the author expresses difficulty in understanding the revelation narrated in the text that follows, and perhaps even emphasizes the necessity of informed interpretation.[1]

Given the significance of σημαίνειν to the text of Revelation as a whole, the two signs in Rev. 12 take on added prominence, as apart from 15.1, 12.1–3 provide the only places where the term σημεῖον is found. These signs, in our view, are integral to the main contents of Jesus' revelation shown (ἐσήμανεν) to the churches, thus making the signs of Rev. 12 pivotal in understanding John's Revelation as a whole. Only in one other place is the term σημεῖον mentioned in Revelation, namely, the seven angels with the seven last bowls of plagues introduced in 15.1. We have already noted earlier that these signs are part and parcel of God's mystery to be revealed before time in this present age is no more and the kingdom of God is fully established on earth (cf. 10.7, 11.15). These signs are encoded mysteries, which John sets out in order to reveal (and conceal) the nature of these events that must soon take place. The call to wisdom and understanding (cf. 13.18) and paying heed closely to what the Spirit is saying to the churches (cf. Rev. 2–3) are part of John's rhetoric in eliciting the required response. John does not provide a comprehensive blueprint as to how these signs must be interpreted though sufficient clues and indicators are given to those with the requisite knowledge to decipher what is seemingly hidden but ready to be disclosed to those with true perception and insight.

3. *The Chiasm of Revelation 12.1–17*

It is often noted that Rev. 12 is divided into three main units: 12.1–6, vv. 7–12, and vv. 13–17. Schüssler Fiorenza writes:

> Chapter 12 takes the form of an inclusion. Between the great portent of the glorious woman and the powerful dragon (12.1–6) on the one hand and the vision of the dragon's persecution of the woman (12.13–17) on the other, John inserts the vision about the war in heaven waged by the dragon (12.7–12).[2]

Humphrey proposes an outline for Rev. 12 in an ABCA'B' pattern:

---

1. Aune, *Revelation 1–5*, p. 15.
2. Schüssler Fiorenza, *Revelation: Vision of a Just World*, p. 80. Also Talbert, *The Apocalypse*, p. 48.

Intro	Two portents	vss. 1–3
A	Woman persecuted and flight	vss. 4–6
B	War in heaven	vss. 7–9
C	Declaration	vss. 10–12
A'	Woman persecuted and flight	vss. 14–16
B'	War on earth	vs. 17[3]

Humphrey admits that for a structure to be chiastic it should be ABCB'A' instead of ABCA'B' as proposed. We cannot agree with Humphrey's analysis as 12.1–4 already anticipates the conflict of the woman and the dragon, which is later elaborated in the rest of the vision report in 12.13–17. Abir remarks that: 'The phrase καὶ ὁ δράκων ἕστηκεν ἐνώπιον τῆς γυναικὸς τῆς μελλούσης τεκεῖν (v. 4b) introduces the conflict that is about to start between the Woman and the Dragon.'[4] Humphrey entitles v. 17 'war on earth', which appears arbitrary as the war on earth is already apparent in v. 13 when the dragon having been cast down to earth forthwith persecutes the woman. Further the pivot of Rev. 12 begins in v. 7 and goes to v. 12 and neatly divides ch. 12 into two halves as noted by Schüssler Fiorenza. Thematically, the war in heaven is pivotal as it gives the heavenly perspective of earthly events, highlighting that the warfare between the dragon and the woman and her seed comes about as a result of another earlier battle in heaven between the dragon and Michael and their angelic allies. Abir proposes another chiastic pattern for Rev. 12 as follows:

A: Introduction (1–6)

  B: War in heaven (7)

    C: Defeat of the dragon and his allies (8–9)

      D: **Conquest of the Lamb & martyrs (10–11b)**

    C': Call to rejoice (12a)

  B': War continues (12b)

A': Conclusion (13–18)[5]

---

3. Humphrey, *Ladies and the Cities*, p. 101. See also Humphrey, 'In Search of a Voice: Rhetoric through Sight and Sound in Revelation 11.15–12.17', p. 149. Humphrey (p. 149) adds v. 18 to B' under the title 'war on earth'. In both proposals, Humphrey fails to account for v. 13, a verse which we believe is crucial to the flow of the plot where the dragon is cast out from heaven and finds himself on earth.

4. Abir, *Cosmic Conflict*, p. 63.

5. Abir, *Cosmic Conflict*, p. 63.

We submit that Abir's proposal cannot stand up to the criteria which we have set out for the testing of a chiasm. First, the A element which is simply entitled 'Introduction' covers a host of critical events including the casting down of a third of the stars in v. 4a, the catching up of the male son to heaven (v. 5) and the escape of the woman to the wilderness (v. 6), which is repeated in v. 14. Second, it is difficult to see how B and B' are parallel, as B' (v. 12b) consists only of an announcement of woe to the earth. The war continues in v. 13 when the dragon having been cast down to earth persecutes the woman. Third, Abir's CC' parallels are also arbitrary as the defeat of the dragon and the call to rejoice may have some thematic correspondence but the two lengthy verses of vv. 8–9 hardly can be said to balance the half verse of 12a. In his discussion of the internal structure of Rev. 12.7–12, Abir does not appear to follow his proposed structure as he states that: 'Rev. 12.7–12 is composed of two parts: i. the narrative part (vv. 7–9) and ii. The proclamative or the celebrative part (vv. 10–12).'[6] We propose that Rev. 12 exhibits a chiastic pattern in the form of ABCB'A' (or EFGF'E') as set out in our larger concentric pattern for 11.1–14.5 as follows:

A	(E)	The War between the Woman and the Dragon	vv. 1–4
B	(F)	The Escape of the Son and the Mother	vv. 5–6
C	(G)	The War in Heaven	vv. 7–12
B'	(F')	The Escape of the Woman who bore the Son	vv. 13–14
A'	(E')	The War between the Dragon and the Woman/Seed	vv. 15–17

Revelation 12.1–6 narrates the vision of the conflict between the dragon and the woman whereby the dragon stood before the woman about to give birth in order to devour her child. The child and the woman, however, make their escape. In the second main unit of 12.7–12, the scene shifts dramatically as now the dragon and his angels are depicted as engaging in warfare with Michael and his angels (12.7–9) followed by a hymn celebrating the victory over the dragon (vv. 10–12). The final main unit again (vv. 13–17) focuses on the dragon's persecution of the woman who 'again' makes her escape (v. 14). The dragon's wrath is now aimed at the rest of the woman's seed.

On closer examination, a concentric pattern is discernible where the first main section (12.1–6) corresponds to the final main unit making up 12.13–17. Both units tell of the dragon's malicious intention to do harm to the woman and her man-child on one hand and the rest of her seed on the other. Words connoting the dragon's antagonism towards the woman and

---

6. Abir, *Cosmic Conflict*, p. 65.

others include: 'cast out' (ἔβαλεν), (12.3, 15), 'stood' (ἔστηκεν) (12.4), 'devour' (καταφάγῃ) (12.4), 'war' (πολεμῆσαι, πόλεμον) (12.7, 17), 'accuse' (κατηγορῶν) (12.10), and 'persecute' (ἐδίωξεν) (12.13). This series of related words all pointing to different aspects of the dragon's evil intention and deeds against the woman and her seed (and their angels-protectors) give ch. 12 of Revelation remarkable cohesion and unity of theme.

A concentric pattern emerges as we note that 12.6 is nearly identical to 12.14.[7] The text of vv. 6 and 14 are set out as follows:

καὶ ἡ γυνὴ ἔφυγεν εἰς τὴν ἔρημον, ὅπου ἔχει ἐκεῖ τόπον ἡτοιμασμένον ἀπὸ τοῦ θεοῦ, ἵνα ἐκεῖ τρέφωσιν αὐτὴν ἡμέρας χιλίας διακοσίας ἑξήκοντα. (12.6).

καὶ ἐδόθησαν τῇ γυναικὶ αἱ δύο πτέρυγες τοῦ ἀετοῦ τοῦ μεγάλου, ἵνα πέτηται εἰς τὴν ἔρημον εἰς τὸν τόπον αὐτῆς, ὅπου τρέφεται ἐκεῖ καιρὸν καὶ καιροὺς καὶ ἥμισυ καιροῦ ἀπὸ προσώπου τοῦ ὄφεως. (12.14).

John, in our view, is not aimlessly being repetitious nor is he saying that the woman is caused to flee to the wilderness twice. If we read the text linearly, we will inevitably think of John as being repetitive or worse illogical. But read chiastically, repetition is a literary device that functions to highlight a theme, which in this instance shows God's protection in the midst of persecution.[8] Thus, 12.14 recapitulates what occurs in 12.6;

---

7. Yarbro Collins notes the verbal similarity between v. 6 and v. 14 and says: 'Such repetition is a common redactional device for returning to the major source after making an insertion.' Yarbro Collins, *Combat Myth*, p. 102. Aune also fails to detect the chiastic pattern and argues that the repetition of v. 6 and v. 14 as a literary phenomenon known as '*resumption* technique used in a variety of ways by Greek writers'. Aune, *Revelation 6–16*, p. 666 (his emphasis). We submit that the literary phenomenon at work is more likely to be the Hebraic literary device, chiasm. Kelvin G. Friebel remarks that: 'Resumptive statements can be part of the original so as to refer the auditor/reader back to previous concept.' K. G. Friebel, *Jeremiah's and Ezekiel's Sign-Acts: Rhetorical Nonverbal Communication* (JSOTSup, 283; Sheffield: Sheffield Academic Press, 1999), p. 83 n. 13.

8. A good example in the NT is found in the prologue of John where the witness of John the Baptist mentioned in Jn 1.6 is repeated in 1.15 as parallel elements in a chiastic structure proposed for the prologue of John's Gospel from 1.1–18. See Viviano, 'The Structure of the Prologue of John (1:1–18)', pp. 176–84. Also Wes Howard-Brook, 'John's Gospel's Call to Be Reborn of God', in Wes Howard-Brook and Sharon H. Ringe (eds.), *The New Testament – Introducing the Way of Discipleship* (Maryknoll, New York: Orbis Books, 2002), pp. 80–102. W. Howard-Brook (p. 82) proposes that the chiasm that makes up the prologue of John's Gospel is structured thus:

A Vv. 1–5: Relationship of *logos* to God, creation, humanity
  B Vv. 6–8: Witness of John (the Baptist) (negative)
    C Vv. 9–11: Journey of light/*logos* (negative)
      D Vv. 12–13: Gift of authority to become children of God
    C' V. 14: Journey of *logos* (positive)
  B' V. 15: Witness of John (the Baptist) (positive)
A' Vv. 16–18: Relationship of *logos* to humanity, 're-creation,' God

likewise the devouring intent of the dragon against the woman's child in 12.4 is mirrored by the former warring against the rest of the latter's children in 12.17. We will discuss the lexical and thematic parallels between 12.6 and 12.14 in a later section.

a. *The Woman and the Dragon and the Impending Conflict (Revelation 12.1–4)*

The analysis of smaller units and their forms will confirm the larger concentric chiasm proposed above. Any close reading of a text must come to terms with how the text is structured and composed. John's employment of distinctive stylistic and compositional techniques should assist the readers to delineate where a unit of text begins and ends. In the analysis of the larger unit of Rev. 12, we have so far discussed what appears on the face of the text. Now we will engage in close reading paying attention to all literary features that might help us not only to mark divisions of sub-units but also the narrative flow of one sub-unit to the next (plot development). This process of careful investigation will also help to elucidate the meaning of the texts examined in their respective parts and how they combine to make up the whole. We will now proceed to analyse ch. 12 in detail. The text of 12.1 reads as follows:

> Καὶ σημεῖον μέγα ὤφθη ἐν τῷ οὐρανῷ, γυνὴ περιβεβλημένη τὸν ἥλιον, καὶ ἡ σελήνη ὑποκάτω τῶν ποδῶν αὐτῆς καὶ ἐπὶ τῆς κεφαλῆς αὐτῆς στέφανος ἀστέρων δώδεκα,

The NRSV translates the word ὤφθη as 'appeared'. This seemingly unimportant grammatical detail is in fact significant to link 12.1 with the last verse of ch. 11. Thus the passage of 11.19–12.1 reads as follows:

> Καὶ ἠνοίγη ὁ ναὸς τοῦ θεοῦ ὁ <u>ἐν τῷ οὐρανῷ καὶ ὤφθη</u> ἡ κιβωτὸς τῆς διαθήκης αὐτοῦ ἐν τῷ ναῷ αὐτοῦ, καὶ ἐγένοντο ἀστραπαὶ καὶ φωναὶ καὶ βρονταὶ καὶ σεισμὸς καὶ χάλαζα μεγάλη. Καὶ σημεῖον μέγα <u>ὤφθη ἐν τῷ οὐρανῷ</u>, γυνὴ περιβεβλημένη τὸν ἥλιον, καὶ ἡ σελήνη ὑποκάτω τῶν ποδῶν αὐτῆς καὶ ἐπὶ τῆς κεφαλῆς αὐτῆς στέφανος ἀστέρων δώδεκα.[9]

Aune notes the link between 11.19 and ch. 12 and writes: 'The term ὤφθη, "appeared," is an aorist passive verb that occurs in this form just three times in Revelation (11.19; 12.1, 3). The close proximity of these occurrences of ὤφθη provides another formal indication that 11.19 is intended to introduce 12.1–17.'[10] This observation alone should lead us

---

9. Note the order of words 'in heaven and was seen' in 11.19 is reversed in 12.1 as 'was seen in heaven.' This inverse order may be due to John's penchant for inversion of the order of words or his chiastic way of writing.

10. Aune, *Revelation 6–16*, p. 679.

to be cautious in proposing that ch. 12 begins a totally new section unrelated to Rev. 11 as a whole. First we must examine how the small units of ch. 12 are structured. The first two signs are presented in an ABCA'B'C' structure as follows:

A – [v. 1]   Καὶ σημεῖον μέγα ὤφθη ἐν τῷ οὐρανῷ,

B –   γυνὴ περιβεβλημένη τὸν ἥλιον,
                 καὶ ἡ σελήνη ὑποκάτω τῶν ποδῶν αὐτῆς
                 καὶ ἐπὶ τῆς κεφαλῆς αὐτῆς στέφανος ἀστέρων δώδεκα,

C – [v. 2]   καὶ ἐν γαστρὶ ἔχουσα,
                 καὶ κράζει ὠδίνουσα
                 καὶ βασανιζομένη τεκεῖν.

A' – [v. 3] καὶ ὤφθη ἄλλο σημεῖον ἐν τῷ οὐρανῷ,

B' –   καὶ ἰδοὺ δράκων μέγας πυρρὸς
                 ἔχων κεφαλὰς ἑπτὰ καὶ κέρατα δέκα
                 καὶ ἐπὶ τὰς κεφαλὰς αὐτοῦ ἑπτὰ διαδήματα,

C' – [v. 4a] καὶ ἡ οὐρὰ αὐτοῦ σύρει τὸ τρίτον τῶν ἀστέρων τοῦ οὐρανοῦ
                 καὶ ἔβαλεν αὐτοὺς εἰς τὴν γῆν.

The two signs 'woman' and 'dragon' are juxtaposed in the following sequence:

1. *Introduction* of the sign in heaven (12.1a, 3a) [**AA'**].
2. *Description* of the woman and the dragon (12.1b, 3b) [**BB'**].
3. The *state/activity* of the woman and the dragon (12.2, 4a) [**CC'**].

It is important to note the juxtaposition of the two main characters in Rev. 12 as John intends to set them up for contrast and comparison.[11] It is also intended to serve as the introduction to the plot in the rest of the chapter as Humphrey has noted. The glorious beauty and majesty of the woman is contrasted with the freakish and monstrous appearance of the seven-headed dragon. It is like the reverse of the 'Beauty and the Beast' theme that most modern readers are familiar with, for there is no love lost between the beautiful woman and the beastly dragon.

---

11. So William K Hedrick, 'The Sources and Use of the Imagery in Apocalypse 12' (Unpublished Th.D. dissertation; Berkeley, California: Graduate Theological Union, 1971), p. 8.

The pair of AA' is parallel as the introductory formulas are nearly identical. Both signs in heaven are introduced in identical fashion except for the variation of word order, which is typical of John's style. The pair of BB' likewise corresponds in a remarkable degree by way of juxtaposition. The woman clothed with the *sun* meets a great *red/fiery* dragon.[12] The woman radiates brightness and light while the dragon is red with fury and lust for blood.[13] Both characters stake claims to royal authority; the woman with a crown of twelve stars and the dragon with seven diadems on its seven heads.[14] In CC', the woman is said to be crying out in birthpangs and in torment while the dragon's malicious nature is shown forth for the first time by dragging with its tail a third of the stars from heaven to earth. A grammatical parallelism helps to link both CC' together. The woman's crying out, κράζει (present indicative active) is contrasted with the dragon's dragging, σύρει (present indicative active) of a third of the stars.[15] The woman's act of giving birth (τεκεῖν – aorist active

12.   Instead of 'red' some manuscripts (C 046 1611 1854 2329 2344 *pm*) read πυρος, 'fire', in place of πυρρος, 'red' or 'fiery red' (so BDAG, p. 900). Aune observes that the change from -ρρ- to -ρ- occurred relatively late. Aune, *Revelation 6–16*, p. 652.

13.   Mounce suggests that the colour red of the dragon symbolizes the murderous character of Satan. He cites Homer (*Iliad* 2.308) where the ancient author speaks of a δράκων δαφοινός (blood red). Mounce, *Revelation*, p. 233 n. 9. Beasley-Murray cites an Egyptian myth which speaks of a dragon Typhon as a red dragon who pursues Hathor who is about to give birth. Beasley-Murray, *Revelation*, p. 12. We will return to the background and imagery of Rev. 12 in a later section.

14.   Thompson writes: 'Each head [of the dragon] supports a diadem, indicating royal power…, just as the celestial goddess's "crown of twelve stars" symbolizes royal power.' Thompson, *Revelation*, p. 133. The woman's twelve stars is probably an allusion to the twelve sons of Jacob/Israel (cf. Gen. 37.9). The number twelve is used constantly by John to symbolize the people of God. There are twelve tribes of the sons of Israel and twelve thousand out of each tribe are said to be sealed (Rev. 7.2–8). There are also twelve tribes of the sons of Israel inscribed on the gates of the New Jerusalem (21.12) and the twelve names of twelve apostles written on the twelve foundations of the city (21.14). The diadems on the seven heads of the dragon speak of the dragon's total sovereignty over the kingdoms of the world (cf. 13.1–4). For a discussion of numerical symbolism of the numbers seven and twelve in Revelation, see Yarbro Collins, *Cosmology and Eschatology*, pp. 122–34. Also Resseguie, *Revelation Unsealed*, pp. 58–67. Resseguie (p. 64) states: 'Twelve occurs 23 times in Revelation out of 75 times in the New Testament. Like the number seven, it is a number of completeness; but unlike seven, which is used for both divine and the demonic, twelve is reserved exclusively for the people of God.' For a general discussion of the symbolism of the number twelve in biblical and Qumranic literature, see Scott McKnight, 'Jesus and the Twelve', *BBR* 11 (2001), pp. 203–31 (212–18).

15.   Aune says: 'In the first subunit of text, 12.1–4a, two main verbs in the present tense are used to describe the two central *dramatis personae*, κράζει (the groaning of the woman in v 2) and σύρει (sweeping down of the stars by the dragon in v 4a), both historical presents that function to highlight this part of the narrative by making it more vivid.' Aune, *Revelation 6–16*, p. 665.

infinitive) is contrasted with the dragon's act of casting down (ἔβαλεν – aorist indicative active) the stars. The danger faced by the woman is made clear in 12.4b:

A – Καὶ ὁ δράκων ἕστηκεν ἐνώπιον τῆς γυναικὸς

  B – τῆς μελλούσης τεκεῖν,

  B' – ἵνα ὅταν τέκῃ

A' – τὸ τέκνον αὐτῆς καταφάγῃ.

For the first time in ch. 12, the two characters are said to 'meet' with the dragon standing in front of or before the woman. The chiastic structure as shown above captures the scene well.[16] BB' has the woman *about* (μελλούσης) to give birth and at the moment of birth (ὅταν), the dragon waits to devour the child. In BB' also, the two temporal conjunctions ('about' and 'when') and the word, 'giving birth' appear to be chiastically balanced (μελλούσης, ὅταν and τεκεῖν, τέκῃ) – the couplet in parallelism highlighting that the child's birth is about to take place.

AA' is also well balanced in that the focus on the woman in A is now shifted to her child in A' enveloped by the two verbs ('stood' in A, 'devour' in A') depicting the malicious intent of the dragon. 'Stood' in A may be a neutral word on its own but seen in the light of its corresponding term 'devour' in A', the second parallel line A' explicates the nature of the dragon's standing in front of the woman so as to position himself to devour the child at the moment of birth.[17] What is stated in A in broad generalisation is thus specified, completed or brought into a climax in A'.

b. *Escape of the Male Child and the Woman (Revelation 12.5–6)*
The drama thickens in suspense as a fiery-red seven-headed dragon waiting to pounce on the child watches the woman in the final throes of giving birth. The drama climaxes in the birth of the child who is described as to its sex and its (future) destiny. The child is a son, a male (υἱὸν ἄρσεν) who is destined (μέλλει) to rule the nations with an iron rod/staff. With the repetition of the word τεκεῖν in 12.4, the readers are led to focus on the

---

16. We are not saying that every chiasm proposed here is intended by John. It is more of John's style of writing chiastically.

17. Mounce notes that the word ἕστηκεν is in the perfect tense, giving it the sense that the dragon was positioning himself to devour the child. See Mounce, *Revelation*, p. 233 n. 13. The word 'stand' from the Hebrew עמד is often used to speak of warfare or opposition. In Dan. 10.13, the prince of Persia is said to stand (MT – עמד; Theod. – εἱστήκει) against Gabriel, i.e., to engage in warfare against Gabriel. Michael, Israel's prince is called 'the standing one' in Dan. 12.1 (MT – הָעֹמֵד; LXX and Theod. – ὁ ἑστηκὼς) apparently referring to Michael's role as the angelic warrior for Israel. See David E. Stevens, 'Daniel 10 and the Notion of Territorial Spirits', *BSac* 157 (2000), pp. 410–31 (418–19).

event of the birth of the child against the background of a man-eating dragon ready to devour its prey. The resolution of this high drama beckons. The child (and mother?) seems destined to die at birth in the hands (mouth) of the dragon but in the nick of time at birth, the child is snatched away to God and to his throne. The child's mother also makes her escape as she is said to flee to the wilderness to a place God has prepared. Verses 5 and 6 are set out as follows:

A – [v. 5] καὶ ἔτεκεν υἱὸν ἄρσεν, ὃς μέλλει ποιμαίνειν πάντα τὰ ἔθνη ἐν ῥάβδῳ σιδηρᾷ. καὶ ἡρπάσθη τὸ τέκνον αὐτῆς πρὸς τὸν θεὸν καὶ πρὸς τὸν θρόνον αὐτοῦ.

A' – [v. 6] καὶ ἡ γυνὴ ἔφυγεν εἰς τὴν ἔρημον, ὅπου ἔχει ἐκεῖ τόπον ἡτοιμασμένον ἀπὸ τοῦ θεοῦ, ἵνα ἐκεῖ τρέφωσιν αὐτὴν ἡμέρας χιλίας διακοσίας ἑξήκοντα.

It is important to read verses 5 and 6 together. Reading v. 5 alone apart from v. 6 misses the clearly intended depiction of the *dual* escape: the child to the throne of *God* and the woman to a place prepared by *God*.[18] The aorist indicative passive of ἡρπάσθη (snatched) in 12.5 is parallel to the aorist indicative active of ἔφυγεν (fled) in 12.6. Even the prepositions are well constructed to show balance and contrast in the two lines: the dual πρός to God and πρός to his throne in v. 5 are parallel to the double preposition of εἰς to the wilderness... a place prepared ἀπο by God in v. 6.

Thus we can surmise that 12.1–6 as a literary unit is divided into two segments consisting of vv. 1–4 and vv. 5–6. Verses 1–4 introduce the two main characters of Rev. 12 and set up their impending conflict. The second segment (vv. 5–6) depicts the resolution of the encounter as the man-child and woman escape from the clutches of the dragon. While these smaller units are thus arranged as proposed, there is no doubt as to their interconnectedness as an integral unit giving the first six verses of Rev. 12 cohesion and integrity as a literary whole. Under the rubric of the two signs, a woman in the pains of child-birth is met with a fiery dragon ready to consume her soon-to-be delivered child, while at the moment of birth both child and mother escape and are taken away to safety by God.

c. *The War in Heaven (Revelation 12.7–12)*
Revelation 12.7 begins a new unit of text as follows: Καὶ ἐγένετο πόλεμος ἐν τῷ οὐρανῷ. The continuity with the preceding pericope is not entirely absent as the phrase ἐν τῷ οὐρανῷ shows. Just as the signs are said to be seen ἐν τῷ οὐρανῷ (12.1, 3), now another event is narrated by John as

18.   Aune is right to observe that: '[Yet] the statement that the child will be caught up to heaven (v 5) indicates that the confrontation between the dragon and the woman takes place on earth. When the dragon is cast down to the earth (v 13), he pursues the woman, so her location on the earth in v 4b must be presumed.' Aune, *Revelation 6–16*, p. 686.

happening in heaven.[19] The use of the phrase Καὶ ἐγένετο seems to contrast the events of vv. 1–6 and suggest what is happening in heaven in v. 7 is no longer a 'sign' but a simple statement of fact that an event did take place: 'There was a war in heaven' or 'Now a war in heaven happened'. The chiastic pattern of v. 7 is set out as follows:

Καὶ ἐγένετο πόλεμος ἐν τῷ οὐρανῷ,

    A – ὁ Μιχαὴλ καὶ οἱ ἄγγελοι αὐτοῦ

      B – τοῦ πολεμῆσαι μετὰ

        C – τοῦ δράκοντος.

        C' – καὶ ὁ δράκων

      B' – ἐπολέμησεν

    A' – καὶ οἱ ἄγγελοι αὐτοῦ,

Verse 7 is structured in a balanced concentric chiastic pattern of ABCC'B'A'. The angel Michael and his fellow angels are said to war with the dragon and his fellow angels. This sentence is a prime example of how chiasm is used as an aesthetics device as well as functioning to emphasize certain elements within the statement. The chiasm in this instance is of the essence of poetry.[20] Form and substance interact; beauty in structure is not antithetical to the solemnity of the message, which John seeks to convey. Theology is embodied in a fusion of form and content.

There are a number of syntactical features in the sentence that need explanation. Beale observes that: 'There is a grammatical difficulty in the phrase ὁ Μιχαὴλ καὶ οἱ ἄγγελοι αὐτοῦ τοῦ πολεμῆσαι, since the nominative (ὁ Μιχαὴλ καὶ οἱ ἄγγελοι αὐτοῦ) serves as the subject of the infinitive, instead of the normal accusative.'[21] Following Charles, Beale suggests that a plausible solution is to view the construction as reflective of a Hebrew idiom where the subject preceding the *lamedh* prefix (*le*) + infinitive

---

19.   Yarbro Collins' failure to discern an overall pattern in Rev. 12 has caused her to argue for the use of various sources for vv. 1–6, vv. 7–9, and vv. 10–12. She says: 'The abruptness of the transition from vs. 6 to 7, the formal distinctiveness of the hymnic passage (vss. 10–12), the repetition in vss. 6 and 14, and the unclarity about the movement from heaven to earth might be taken as signs of the use of sources.' Yarbro Collins, *Combat Myth*, p. 103. Failing to discern the function of repetition of vv. 6 and 14 within the chiastic pattern in Rev. 12, Ford comments: 'It is logical to omit vs. 6 and proceed directly from vs. 5 to vs. 14; vss. 7–13 should also be omitted as coming from a different source.' Ford, *Revelation*, p. 201.

20.   See Breck, *The Shape of Biblical Language*, p. 342. The pivot which centres on the dragon accords well with the *leitmotiv* of Rev 12 which focuses on the deeds of the dragon and the fall of the dragon.

21.   Beale, 'Solecisms in the Apocalypse', p. 430.

occurs.[22] Charles argued that this kind of construction (subject in the nominative followed by the articular genitival infinitive) reflects a 'literal reproduction of a pure Hebraism' which is often found in the LXX.[23] As such Charles concludes that τοῦ πολεμῆσαι is a Hebraism from לְהִלָּחֵם meaning 'to fight'. Beale, however, argues that such a Hebraism or Semitism 'is not likely due to a general Semitic influence upon John, but is accounted for more precisely on the basis of the specific allusion to Dan. 10.20 (from either the Hebrew or Greek Old Testament text), which is present in Rev. 12.7'.[24] The text Dan. 10.20 (Theod.) reads as follows:

καὶ εἶπεν Εἰ οἶδας ἵνα τί ἦλθον πρὸς σέ καὶ νῦν ἐπιστρέψω τοῦ πολεμῆσαι μετὰ
ἄρχοντος Περσῶν καὶ ἐγὼ ἐξεπορευόμην καὶ ὁ ἄρχων τῶν Ἑλλήνων ἤρχετο

The verb ἐπιστρέψω 'I will return' refers to Gabriel but is associated with Michael (cf. Dan. 10.21) who in unison must fight with the prince of Persia and also the prince of Greece. According to Beale, this may account for the fact that Michael and his angels are used in the nominative in allusion to the same Danielic text.[25]

Thus Rev. 12.7 suggests that Michael and his entourage of warrior angels must fight the war with the dragon and his angels.[26] Nevertheless, the point is not who started the war but the *fact* of a war as the term ἐγένετο makes clear. There is no hint here as suggested by Percer that Michael had to fight the war against the dragon as a rearguard action in defending the child.[27] A more likely explanation is found in v. 3 where the dragon is said to drag and cast down one third of the stars from heaven to earth. This action appears to be the probable cause of war between Michael and the dragon. Michael has to fight with the dragon as the dragon is causing havoc in heaven by casting down a third of the stars. The stars in v. 3 are cast down to earth (ἔβαλεν αὐτοὺς [the stars] εἰς τὴν γῆν) by the tail of the dragon;[28] this mirrors the outcome of the war in heaven resulting in the dragon and his entourage being cast down from heaven to

22. Beale, 'Solecisms in the Apocalypse', p. 432.
23. Charles, *Revelation* Vol. 1, p. 322. Charles lists Hos. 9.13, Ps. 25.14, 1 Chron. 9.25, and Eccl. 3.15 as examples.
24. Beale, 'Solecisms in the Apocalypse', p. 432.
25. Beale, 'Solecisms in the Apocalypse', p. 433.
26. We disagree with Mounce who suggests that Michael initiated the war. Mounce, *Revelation*, p. 241. Hagelberg remarks that, 'Mikhael mengambil inisiatif menyerang Iblis, dan bukan sebaliknya. (ET: Michael took the initiative to attack the devil and not the reverse). Hagelberg, *Tafsiran Kitab Wahyu*, p. 239 n. 1.
27. Percer writes: 'the reason they [Michael and the angels] had to fight could be that they were attacked by the dragon for defending the child'. Percer, 'The War in Heaven', p. 175.
28. This point will be taken up further when we discuss in a later section how the stars (v. 4) are related to the woman crowned with twelve stars on her head (v. 1).

earth (ἐβλήθη εἰς τὴν γῆν). Thus we disagree with Yarbro Collins who comments: 'The remark that the dragon sweeps down one-third of the stars of the heaven and casts them on the earth is not an integral part of the narrative of Revelation 12 as it stands.'[29]

It is our contention that v. 4a is integral to Rev. 12 as it stands. The fate of the third of the stars as a result of the dragon's violence in v. 4a becomes the fate of the dragon and his angels in vv. 9 and 13. Punishment meted out befits the crime.[30] One interesting fact we learn from v. 7 is that the dragon is seen as an angelic being similar to Michael. Just as Michael the angel has his army of other angels, the dragon is said to be in like company with his angelic army. The notion of good and bad angels is not stated explicitly but can be reasonably deduced from the characterisation made by John. The outcome of the war is stated as follows (12.8–11):

A – [v. 8] καὶ <u>οὐκ ἴσχυσεν</u> οὐδὲ τόπος εὑρέθη αὐτῶν ἔτι ἐν τῷ οὐρανῷ.

B – [v. 9] καὶ <u>ἐβλήθη</u> ὁ δράκων ὁ μέγας,
ὁ ὄφις ὁ ἀρχαῖος,
ὁ καλούμενος Διάβολος καὶ ὁ Σατανᾶς,
ὁ πλανῶν τὴν οἰκουμένην ὅλην,
<u>ἐβλήθη</u> εἰς τὴν γῆν,
καὶ οἱ ἄγγελοι αὐτοῦ μετ' αὐτοῦ
<u>ἐβλήθησαν</u>.

C – [v. 10] καὶ ἤκουσα φωνὴν μεγάλην ἐν τῷ οὐρανῷ λέγουσαν·
Ἄρτι ἐγένετο ἡ σωτηρία καὶ ἡ δύναμις
καὶ ἡ βασιλεία τοῦ θεοῦ ἡμῶν καὶ ἡ ἐξουσία τοῦ
Χριστοῦ αὐτοῦ,

B' ὅτι <u>ἐβλήθη</u>
ὁ κατήγωρ τῶν ἀδελφῶν ἡμῶν,
ὁ κατηγορῶν αὐτοὺς ἐνώπιον τοῦ θεοῦ ἡμῶν ἡμέρας καὶ
νυκτός.

A' – [v. 11] καὶ αὐτοὶ <u>ἐνίκησαν</u> αὐτὸν
διὰ τὸ αἷμα τοῦ ἀρνίου
καὶ διὰ τὸν λόγον τῆς μαρτυρίας αὐτῶν
καὶ οὐκ ἠγάπησαν τὴν ψυχὴν αὐτῶν ἄχρι θανάτου.

---

29. Yarbro Collins, *Combat Myth*, p. 76. Yarbro Collins correctly notes the Danielic allusion in Rev. 12.3, a text which is most influential in Rev. 11.1–2. This is another indicator that Rev. 12 is integrally linked with Rev. 11. We will say more on the Danielic allusion in a later section.

30. Court remarks that: 'in the setting of the chapter the dragon anticipates, by his activity, his own defeat.' Court, *Myth and History*, p. 114.

A – The Defeat of the Dragon by Michael (12.8).

   B – The Casting down of the Dragon from heaven to earth (12.9).

      C – The Coming of Salvation and God's Kingdom (12.10a).

   B' – The Casting down of the Accuser (12.10b).

A' – The Defeat of the Dragon by the Saints (12.11).

This central section of 12.7–12 is divided into three smaller units of v. 7, vv. 8–11 and v. 12. After a brief statement as to the war in heaven, vv. 8–11 expands on the outcome of the war with a closing command in v. 12. Often translators and scholars alike have regarded the hymn of vv. 10–12 as marking out a new unit or section of text.[31] However, we will contend that such is not the case, as the declaration of the coming of salvation and of God's kingdom in v. 10 is the pivot of an elaborate chiasm which

---

31. For example, Aune says: 'This section [12.7–12] consists of two subsections: (a) the narrative of the heavenly battle... (vv 7–9), and (b) the hymnic commentary on the mythic narrative in vv 7–9... which was sandwiched between vv 1–6 and vv 13–17.... This section is framed by the mention of Satan's having been cast down to earth in v 9..., which is repeated in v 13...thereby framing the insertion in vv 10–12.' Aune, *Revelation 6–16*, p. 663. In our view, it is arbitrary to say that v. 9 and v. 13 frame vv. 10–12 since the fact of the dragon being cast down is not only mentioned in vv. 9 and 12 but also found in vv. 10 and 12. For a study of hymns in Revelation, see Michael A. Harris, 'The Literary Functions of Hymns in the Apocalypse of John' (Unpublished PhD dissertation; Louisville, Kentucky: Southern Baptist Theological Seminary, 1988); John J. O'Rourke, 'The Hymns of the Apocalypse', *CBQ* 30 (1968), pp. 399–409; David Carnegie, 'Worthy is the Lamb: The Hymns in Revelation', in Harold Rowdon (ed.), *Christ the Lord. Studies in Christology Presented to Donald Guthrie* (Leicester: Inter-Varsity Press, 1982), pp. 243–56; Robert H. Smith, '"Worthy is the Lamb" and Other Songs of Revelation', *Current Theology of Mission* 25 (1998), pp. 500–6; Edouard Cothenet, 'Earthly Liturgy and Heavenly Liturgy according to the Book of Revelation', in *Roles in the Liturgical Assembly: the Twenty-Third Liturgical Conference Saint Serge* (trans. M. J. O'Donnell; New York: Pueblo, 1981), pp. 115–35; Joseph A. Grassi, 'The Liturgy of Revelation', *The Bible Today* (1986), pp. 30–37; J. M. Ford, 'Christological Function of the Hymns in the Apocalypse of John', *AUSS* 36 (1998), pp. 207–29. That verses 10–12 are considered hymnic in form does not invalidate our proposed structure. Harris observes that there is 'no discernible difference in grammatical style between hymns and other aspects of the Apocalypse'. See Harris, 'The Literary Functions of Hymns', p. 15. Among the criteria for identifying hymns in Revelation, Harris (p. 12) lists 'the use of careful structuration, especially *parallelismus membrorum*, with it...inclusio or ring composition, chiasmus,...and antithesis.' The stylistic features listed by Harris as characteristic of hymns are present in not only vv. 10–12 but also vv. 7–9. Our proposed structure of vv. 8–11 as a chiasmus helps to link the defeat of the dragon in v. 8 and the casting down of the dragon to earth in v. 9 with the dawn of the kingdom of God and his Christ announced in v. 10 and the defeat of the dragon by the saints in v. 11. The hymnic nature of vv. 10–12 is probably due to the narrative context of worship where John's readers are invited to participate and experience through worship, the coming eschatological salvation and the victory already now exists in heaven.

commenced in v. 8 as shown above. In v. 8, it is said that the dragon was not strong enough, which implies defeat in battle.

The phrase οὐκ ἴσχυσεν appears only here (12.8) in the book of Revelation. It seems a surprising choice of words to denote defeat for the dragon but read in conjunction with the strong angel (ἄγγελον ἰσχυρὸν) of Rev. 10 it is possible to postulate that Michael the angel of Rev. 12 is another strong angel, in fact stronger than the angelic being, the dragon. It is not necessary here to establish that the angel of Rev. 10 is Michael, which in all probability he is not, if the background of Dan. 10–12 is intended throughout Rev. 10–13. The angel Gabriel told Daniel what was inscribed in the book of truth (Dan. 10.21; cf. the angel of Rev. 10 brought an open book to John). Gabriel also informed Daniel that only Michael the archangel was fighting alongside him [Gabriel] against the prince of Persia and the prince of Greece (Dan. 10.13, 21; 12.1). If this scenario is intended as background to Rev. 10–13, then the strong angel of Rev. 10 is likely to be Gabriel followed by Michael in Rev. 12 as another *strong* angel enabled to out-muscle the dragon. Michael is thus portrayed as stronger than the dragon.[32] Given the unusual phrase ἴσχυσεν in v. 8, the above interpretation is not implausible.

Further, the verb ἴσχυσεν meaning conquered or prevailed in warfare is found in Dan 7.21 (Theod.) where the beast's horn is said to make war with the saints and prevail against (ἴσχυσεν) them:

ἐθεώρουν καὶ τὸ κέρας ἐκεῖνο ἐποίει πόλεμον μετὰ τῶν ἁγίων καὶ ἴσχυσεν πρὸς αὐτούς

This Danielic text is also clearly alluded to in Rev. 13.7a where the beast is said to make war and conquer the saints:

καὶ ἐδόθη αὐτῷ ποιῆσαι πόλεμον μετὰ τῶν ἁγίων καὶ νικῆσαι αὐτούς

---

32. A parallel in Lk. 11.20–22 may illuminate the concept of a stronger one conquering a strong one. The Greek of Lk. 11.20–22 reads: 'v. 20 εἰ δὲ ἐν δακτύλῳ θεοῦ [ἐγὼ] ἐκβάλλω τὰ δαιμόνια, ἄρα ἔφθασεν ἐφ' ὑμᾶς ἡ βασιλεία τοῦ θεοῦ. v. 21 ὅταν ὁ ἰσχυρὸς καθωπλισμένος φυλάσσῃ τὴν ἑαυτοῦ αὐλήν, ἐν εἰρήνῃ ἐστὶν τὰ ὑπάρχοντα αὐτοῦ· v. 22 ἐπὰν δὲ ἰσχυρότερος αὐτοῦ ἐπελθὼν νικήσῃ αὐτόν, τὴν πανοπλίαν αὐτοῦ αἴρει ἐφ' ᾗ ἐπεποίθει καὶ τὰ σκῦλα αὐτοῦ διαδίδωσιν.' Here in Lk. 11.20–22, the driving out of demons is a sign of the kingdom of God, a concept which is akin to the idea of Rev. 12 where the dragon having been defeated and driven out from heaven leads to the announcement of the kingdom of God (Rev. 12.8–10). The term ἐκβάλλω used in Lk. 11.20 is found in Rev. 11.2 (cast out the court outside the temple) and is semantically related to the term βάλλω used to describe the casting out of the dragon from heaven. The stronger one in Lk. 11.20–22 refers to Christ while in Rev. 12.7–9, it is Michael who defeats the dragon. We should note that the one stronger than Satan comes and νικήσῃ αὐτόν (Lk. 11.22) is similar to the clause in Rev. 12.11: αὐτοὶ ἐνίκησαν αὐτὸν. It is of interest to note that the strong one (ὁ ἰσχυρὸς) in Lk. 11.21 is the enemy (Satan) whereas in Rev. 12.8, the dragon presumably is also a strong one but is not strong enough to prevail against Michael, hence the use of the phrase οὐκ ἴσχυσεν to depict the defeat of the dragon.

In Rev. 13.7a, it is clear that John is dependent on Dan. 7.21 (Theod.) except that he uses the word νικῆσαι instead of ἴσχυσεν of Dan. 7.21.[33] Instead John's use of οὐκ ἴσχυσεν in Rev. 12.8 to describe the dragon's defeat by Michael is also an allusion to Dan. 7.21,[34] which in our view is intended to correspond to the statement that the saints conquered (ἐνίκησαν) the dragon in 12.11. In heaven, Michael conquered the dragon, while the saints conquered the dragon on earth. Thus it is arguable that John uses the words ἴσχυσεν and ἐνίκησαν to frame the passage of 12.8–11 in a chiastic pattern.

The defeat of the dragon and his allies sees them being cast down from heaven to earth. An action done to others (a third of the stars) in v. 3 is now done to the instigator and the dragon and his angels are in a free fall as the thrice repeated ἐβλήθη in v. 9 shows. There is no more emphatic statement in the rest of Revelation than the fall, fall and *fall* of the dragon from heaven to earth. The readers are caught up in envisioning the downfall of the dragon with the emphatic and repeated use of ἐβλήθη.

Verse 9 is again structured in a chiasm:

A – καὶ ἐβλήθη ὁ δράκων ὁ μέγας,

   B – ὁ ὄφις ὁ ἀρχαῖος,

      C – ὁ καλούμενος Διάβολος καὶ ὁ Σατανᾶς,

   B' – ὁ πλανῶν τὴν οἰκουμένην ὅλην,

A' – ἐβλήθη εἰς τὴν γῆν,

      καὶ οἱ ἄγγελοι αὐτοῦ μετ' αὐτοῦ ἐβλήθησαν.

The casting down of the dragon from heaven to earth (AA') frames the *naming* of the dragon, as 'the devil' and 'Satan' (C). The dragon is finally unmasked. The *sign* is now shown to be what it *is*. The ancient serpent is also called the deceiver of the whole world (BB'), a description that the ancient readers will invariably link with the account of the serpent's deception of Eve in Gen. 3.

The story of the first woman Eve's encounter with the serpent ends with the claim by Eve that, 'The serpent *deceived* me, and I ate' (Gen. 3.13b, NIV) and with Adam and Eve being cast out (ἐξέβαλεν – LXX) from the

---

33. Prigent comments that the phrase in Rev. 13.7a 'is copied almost literally from Dan. 7.21'. Prigent, *Commentary on the Apocalypse*, p. 409.

34. Beale likewise thinks that Rev. 12.8 alludes to Dan. 7.21 in view of the verbal similarity. Together with the allusion to Dan. 10.20 in Rev. 12.7, Beale concludes that: 'In both instances of Rev. 12.7–8 the same wording of the Old Testament text is preserved, despite reflecting somewhat awkward (in the case of 12.8) or unusual Greek syntax (in the case of 12.7), in order to highlight for the reader the Daniel background.' Beale, 'Solecisms in the Apocalypse', p. 433.

Garden of Eden (Gen. 3.24).[35] The reversal is complete. The deceiver is now cast out while the woman is taken to safety. The significance of the Genesis account will be discussed further later on. The pivot of the chiasm serves to focus on the identity of the dragon as the Devil and Satan. Satan has already been mentioned twice in the letters to the seven churches (2.13; 3.9). John makes the connection here that the originator of evil for humankind in the Garden of Eden is now the source of tribulation in the churches of Asia Minor and will again be the cause of trouble for the whole world in the last eschatological period. No wonder he is called the *ancient* serpent! Court states thus: 'Just as Satan was at work throughout the Old Testament, from the activity of the serpent in the garden of Eden (Gen. 3), so he is now very much at work in the current, or anticipated, hostilities to the Christian Church.'[36]

The pivot of the chiasm of vv. 8–11 consists of the declaration from heaven that the salvation and the power have come (ἄρτι ἐγένετο) which is explained as the in-breaking of the kingdom of our God and the authority of his Christ in v. 10a. The announcement of the kingdom introduced by the abrupt use of the verb ἤκουσα (I heard) is rightly recognized by Aune as a distinctive feature of this section.[37] This audition marks a shift from the preceding passage and signals a climactic event, which is the arrival of the kingdom of God as the central idea or pivot in vv. 7–12. In addition, the use of ἐγένετο v. 10a indicates progression from what has preceded in vv. 7–9. The phrase ἄρτι ἐγένετο creates a sense of immediacy that salvation, power, God's kingdom and the authority of his Christ have finally arrived. Yet the kingdom does not arrive immediately as the dragon is given a

---

35. The verb πλανάω (to deceive) is used in Rev. 12.9, while the verb ἀπατάω is used in LXX Gen. 3.13. Court suggests that the use of πλανάω 'introduces a special significance to this expression, because of its later-Jewish and in particular its apocalyptic background. Deception – the leading astray of those buoyed up with eager expectations – is a characteristic feature of the Last Days (cf. Mark 13.6//s; 2 Thess. 2.11)'. Court, *Myth and History*, p. 112. For a discussion of how this term πλανάω links Satan with Jezebel and the beast from the earth of Rev. 13.11–18, see Paul B. Duff, *Who Rides the Beast? Prophetic Rivalry and the Rhetoric of Crisis in the Churches of the Apocalypse* (Oxford: Oxford University Press, 2001), pp. 115–25.

36. Court, *Myth and History*, p. 111. For a study on how the serpent is seen intertextually throughout the Bible, see Elaine A. Phillips, 'Serpent Intertexts: Tantalizing Twists in the Tales', *BBR* 10.2 (2000), pp. 233–45. In speaking of Satan's hostility against the church in Revelation, Phillips (p. 243) writes: 'The community for which Revelation was written was facing what appeared to be the ultimate force of evil.'

37. Aune writes: 'One of the distinctive features of this section [12.7–12] is the abrupt use of the verb, "I heard", in a text unit in which there are otherwise no first-person verbs, nor is the narrative in 11.19–12.17 presented as a vision in the author's usual vision-report style.' Aune, *Revelation 6–16*, p. 663.

'short time' on earth (12:12b).[38] This pivotal statement of v. 10a is made up of two couplets of balanced statements as follows:

Now have come,

> **A** – the *salvation* and the *power*
> **A'** – the *kingdom* of our God and the *authority* of his Christ.

The salvation and the power are parallel to the kingdom of God and the authority of Christ. Read as two parallel lines, line A' completes line A in defining the nature of salvation and power to come as the establishment of God's kingdom and the authority of his Christ. The pivot is extremely significant as far as the central message of Rev. 12 and the literary unit of 11.1–14.5 is concerned. Out of the midst of the war in heaven and the attack of the dragon on the woman and her seed, the readers are not led into thinking all is woe and tribulation. The good news is that the outcome of the war and the coming down to earth of the dragon, frightful as it is, is not the whole story. It is only a prelude to salvation and power! The throne of the dragon and the beast will yield to the kingdom of God and the authority of his Christ (cf. 13.4).[39] The pivot thus serves to focus the hearts and minds of the readers on the coming kingdom as they brace themselves for suffering and persecution in the assurance that victory is assured if only they will persevere.[40]

The shift from third person pronouns to first person plural in v. 10a 'the kingdom of *our* God' involves the author and readers in the litany of the heavenly chorus and makes the hymn of victory a participatory event like the other doxologies in Revelation (1.5–6; 5.10; 11.15; 19.1, 5–7). Through worship, those on earth unite with those who dwell in heaven in declaring the salvation of God and the imminent arrival of his kingdom and affirm its *future reality as present experience* in anticipation of the fullness that is to come.[41] Commenting on worship in Revelation, Prigent writes: 'Only

---

38.   This is in contrast to the declaration in 11.15 where the kingdom of God has indeed come after the three-and-a-half years and three-and-a-half days have lapsed and after the seventh trumpet has sounded.

39.   We will see this reversal brought out clearly in our chiastic pair of 11.15–19 and 13.1–6.

40.   See Y. Bambang Mulyono's excellent monograph, *Teologi Ketabahan: Ulasan Atas Kitab Wahyu Yohanes* ([*The Theology of Endurance: A Commentary on the Book of the Revelation of John*] Jakarta: BPK Gunung Mulia, 1996) for an excellent discussion on the theme of endurance as a key theme to understanding the book of Revelation.

41.   Speaking of worship in the early church in general, Larry Hurtado writes: 'Collective worship was also experienced as having strong eschatological significance. In fact, for religious groups with a strong sense of heavenly realities and eschatological hopes, worship is logically seen as the occasion when the heavenly realities come to expression on earth and when the foretastes of eschatological hopes are experienced in the present.' L. Hurtado, *On the*

worship can allow one to celebrate eschatological realities as being present by affirming the presence on earth of heavenly realities that point to the *eschaton*.'[42] Prigent's comment applies well to the context of worship in Rev. 12.10–12. Thus in 12.10–12 the future (salvation and power) is brought to bear on the present (woe on earth); in fact transforming the present in the light of the future in order that sufferings and martyrdom are not only endured in the hope of the coming salvation and kingdom (12.10) but also in the realization that it is in and through the very sufferings and martyrdom that the dragon is conquered (12.11).

BB' of the extended chiasm in vs. 8–12 concentrates on the fall of the dragon from heaven to earth. In B' (v. 10b), the casting down of the dragon is repeated and expanded to include further characterization of the dragon. The dragon is now named as the accuser of our brethren who has been previously called the ancient serpent, the devil, Satan and the deceiver of the whole world in v. 9. Thus the second corresponding element B', adds and further explicates what is described in B. The ὅτι of v. 10b links the announcement that God's kingdom has come to the casting down of the dragon. Percer mistakenly, in our view, suggests that the kingdom of God's coming coincides temporally with the casting down of the dragon.[43] The announcement of the coming of the kingdom in 12.10 is proleptic despite the emphatic use of ἄρτι ἐγένετο as the subsequent narrative in 12.12 states that the dragon having gone to earth is given a short time, i.e., three-and-a-half years (a time, times, and half a time) before the kingdom of God finally arrives.

The word ἐβλήθη is the *Leitwort* of ch. 12 highlighting the casting down of the dragon from heaven to earth as the *leitmotiv* of the plot as a whole. In heaven, the dragon is the troublemaker casting down a third of the stars. Michael engages him in a war and as a result the dragon himself together with his angels are cast out from heaven to earth. The casting down of the dragon brings an announcement of the kingdom's coming because from thence, the dragon's time on earth will be short as predetermined by God, before the authority of Christ is fully established on earth at the coming of the kingdom of God.

Origins of Christian Worship (London: The Paternoster Press, 1999), p. 51. On the question of how the future eschatological salvation is experienced in the present especially through worship of the community, see L. Thompson, 'Cult and Eschatology in the Apocalypse of John', *JR* 49 (1969), pp. 330–50; D. E. Aune, *The Cultic Setting of Realized Eschatology in Early Christianity* (Leiden: E.J. Brill, 1972).

42. Prigent, *Commentary on the Apocalypse*, p. 48.

43. Percer writes: 'The two events [casting out of the dragon and the coming of the kingdom of God] coincide. The dragon's expulsion from heaven is not merely the result of the war, it results in the authority of Christ being established.' Percer, 'The War in Heaven', p. 177.

AA' (vs. 8, 11) are the extremities of the extended chiasm of 12.8–11. A'
complements A in enclosing the chiasm with the theme of the dragon's
defeat. The defeat of the dragon by Michael the angel in *heaven* (v. 8) is
now mirrored by the defeat of the dragon by the 'saints' (αὐτοι) on *earth* (v.
11). It reads:

καὶ αὐτοὶ ἐνίκησαν αὐτὸν
διὰ τὸ αἷμα τοῦ ἀρνίου
καὶ διὰ τὸν λόγον τῆς μαρτυρίας αὐτῶν καὶ οὐκ ἠγάπησαν τὴν ψυχὴν αὐτῶν
ἄχρι θανάτου.

Grammatical parallelism is again evident here as ἴσχυσεν in v. 8 and
ἐνίκησαν in v. 11 are both aorist indicative active verbs. Both these verbs
speak of warfare. The pronoun αὐτοὶ here is emphatic as it is placed before
the verb 'conquered'. It is *they* who conquered *him*. Michael defeats the
dragon in v. 8 while the saints or the brothers (cf. v. 10) conquer the
dragon in v. 11. The saints' conquest of the dragon is accomplished
through (διὰ) the blood of the Lamb and through (διὰ) the word of their
testimony, for they love not their lives unto death.[44] The passage on the
war in heaven is closed off by v. 12:

διὰ τοῦτο

A – εὐφραίνεσθε,

B – [οἱ] οὐρανοὶ καὶ οἱ ἐν αὐτοῖς σκηνοῦντες.

A' – οὐαὶ

B' – τὴν γῆν καὶ τὴν θάλασσαν,

ὅτι κατέβη ὁ διάβολος πρὸς ὑμᾶς ἔχων θυμὸν μέγαν,
εἰδὼς ὅτι ὀλίγον καιρὸν ἔχει.

By the use of διὰ τοῦτο, 12.12 marks a shift and transition from the
preceding pericope and emphatically points to the dragon's expulsion from
heaven as the cause of the twin command. The command to rejoice is
directed to heaven itself and those who dwell in heaven. In contrast, woe is
pronounced on the earth and the sea. The poetic flourish heightened by
this parallelism is hard to escape as the doublets in juxtaposition show. The
heavens *and* those who dwell in them are juxtaposed with the earth *and* the
sea making up a perfect balance to the dual objects of the heavenly
command. The ground for rejoicing for the heavens and heaven dwellers is
that the dragon no longer has a place in heaven. Presumably peace now
reigns in heaven for the war in heaven has ended. The heavens' joy is woe

---

44. We will discuss the nature of warfare waged by the saints against the dragon and the
beasts in a later chapter.

instead for the earth and the sea. There is now woe on the earth and the sea *for* (ὅτι) the dragon has come down to *you* having great wrath. The dragon is angry because he has been defeated and cast out from heaven and having been thrown to earth, his wrath is directed to his new home, namely the earth and the sea.

d. *The Woman's Escape (12.13–14) = The Woman's Escape (vv. 5–6)* [FF']

Verse 13 reads as follows:

Καὶ ὅτε εἶδεν ὁ δράκων ὅτι ἐβλήθη εἰς τὴν γῆν,
ἐδίωξεν τὴν γυναῖκα ἥτις ἔτεκεν τὸν ἄρσενα.

The defeat of the dragon (12.7–8) and his casting down from heaven to earth (12.9) is rounded off in 12.13, which also functions to redirect the reader's attention back to the first main section of the chapter (12.1–6) where the woman is one of the central characters. It is here at 12.13–14 that the concentric pattern proposed for the whole of Rev. 12 becomes most evident. Not only is the attention refocused on the woman but it is explicitly repeated that the woman is the one who has given birth to the man-child (12.13 = 12.5):

καὶ ἔτεκεν υἱὸν ἄρσεν (12.5a) = τὴν γυναῖκα ἥτις ἔτεκεν τὸν ἄρσενα (12.13b)

The readers are left in no doubt that the same woman of 12.1–4 is being referred to in 12.13, as 12.14 goes on to make it abundantly clear. In another repetition, the woman now is said to be given wings to fly to the wilderness to be nourished for a time, times, and half a time (12.14 = 12.6).[45] There are at least four similarities between v. 6 and v. 14:

---

45.   Aune says: 'V 14 is essentially a doublet of v 6.... Further, v 14 seems out of place, at least chronologically, for in the third subsection (c) [vv. 15–16], the serpent (= dragon) attacks the woman by trying to wash her away with a river of water.... This brief episode would be appropriate before the woman reached her sanctuary in the wilderness mentioned in v 14. Otherwise (to keep a generally chronological order), one must suppose that the period of her protection ended in v 14 and that she was again vulnerable to the renewed attack of the serpent (= dragon).' Aune, *Revelation 6–16*, p. 646. Aune is mistaken on a number of points. First, while he acknowledges that v. 14 is a doublet for v. 6, he thinks that it is out of place since he does not discern the chiastic pattern as we have proposed. Second, the events or episodes found in Rev. 12 do not unfold chronologically since only the timeframe within which the events are said to unfold is given, namely the three-and-a-half years period in vv. 6 and 14. John has employed chiasm as the key structuring principle of Rev. 12 and as such events are arranged *thematically* and chiastically in a succession of skilfully paralleled accounts. Verses 13–14 are intended to mirror vv. 5–6, which passages speak of the refuge for both the woman and the man child. The dragon's war against the woman and the woman's seed in vv. 15–17 expands and completes the account concerning the conflict between the

1. The woman goes to the wilderness.
2. The woman goes to a particular place prepared for her.[46]
3. The woman is nourished in that place.[47]
4. The woman is in the place for three-and-a-half years.[48]

The verbal parallels are tabulated as follows:

Rev. 12.6		Rev. 12.14
ἡ γυνὴ	=	τῇ γυναικὶ
εἰς τὴν ἔρημον	=	εἰς τὴν ἔρημον
τὸν τόπον αὐτῆς	=	ἐκεῖ τόπον
ἐκεῖ τρέφωσιν αὐτὴν	=	τρέφεται ἐκεῖ
ἡμέρας χιλίας διακοσίας ἑξήκοντα	=	καιρὸν καὶ καιροὺς καὶ ἥμισυ καιροῦ

The conceptual parallels and contrasts are listed as follows:

ἔφυγεν	=	πέτηται
ἀπὸ τοῦ θεοῦ	=	ἀπὸ προσώπου τοῦ ὄφεως

A concentric pattern is clearly evident in this instance. Verses 6 and 14 of Rev. 12 share many identical lexemes as shown above. Conceptually, the flight of the woman carried by the wings of the eagle in 12.14 (B') explains the means of escape by the woman in 12.6 (B). Thus B' supplements and completes B. In addition, the place prepared especially for the woman *from God* (12.6) is the place where she is hidden *from the face of the serpent* (12.14). Revelation 12.6 focuses on God as the source of refuge and protection for the woman while 12.14 highlights the woman's protection from the persecution of the serpent. Thus we conclude that the unit of 12.5–6 corresponds to 12.13–14 within the chiastic structure of Rev. 12.[49]

woman and the dragon introduced in vv. 1–4. Bauckham writes: 'As always, the evidence which the source critics took to indicate a variety of sources turn out to be evidence of John's meticulous and subtle use of language.' Bauckham, *Climax of Prophecy*, p. 240.

46. Court writes: 'The woman's destination ("the place" – 12.14) seems surprisingly precise; the definite article serves to refer the reader back to the place mentioned in 12.6 – this is "a" place, but it is a place prepared by God, and therefore a precise reference.' Court, *Myth and History*, p. 116.

47. The present active τρέφωσιν is used in v. 6 while the present passive τρέφεται is found in v. 14.

48. In v. 6, the period is 1260 days while in v. 14, it is 'a time, times, and half a time'.

49. Svigel states that: '12.13–18 [sic] recapitulates the events after the catching up of the male child, filling in details regarding the pursuit of the woman and the preservation initially described in 12.6.' Svigel, 'The Apocalypse of John', p. 56.

e. *The Dragon's War with the Woman's Seed (12.15–17) = (vv. 1–4) [EE']*
The last sub-unit of ch. 12 (12.15–17) continues to focus on the dragon's anger towards the woman and is a parallel to the earlier encounter in 12.1–4. The Greek text of 12.15 reads as follows:

καὶ ἔβαλεν ὁ ὄφις ἐκ τοῦ στόματος αὐτοῦ ὀπίσω τῆς γυναικὸς ὕδωρ ὡς ποταμόν,
ἵνα αὐτὴν ποταμοφόρητον ποιήσῃ.

The use of ἔβαλεν here to describe the dragon's action is significant. In 12.4, the same word ἔβαλεν is used of the dragon whose tail casts down (ἔβαλεν) a third of the stars to the earth. Only in 12.4 and 12.15 is the lexeme ἔβαλεν used to denote the acts done *by* the dragon. The other usage of the word as we have seen, describes action done *to* the dragon, namely, the fall or casting out of the dragon from heaven to earth. In v. 4, it is the dragon's *tail* that cast down a third of the stars. Here in 12.15, it is his *mouth* that casts out rivers of water in an attempt to sweep away the woman. The power of the tail and the mouth has been used by John elsewhere to describe the harm done by the horses under the sixth trumpet (9.13–21) and hence, another indication that 12.15 is intended to parallel 12.4.[50] Further, a contrast is set up between vv. 1–4 where a red/fiery dragon wants to consume the male son with *fire* and vv. 15–17 where the serpent attempts to drown the mother with *water*.[51]

---

50. The power of the dragon is in his tail and his mouth just like the horses under the sixth trumpet: 'For the power of the horses is in their mouths and their tails' (9.19a). The horses' mouths kill a third of humankind and their tails inflict harm (9.18–19). The correlation between the power of the dragon in Rev. 12 and the horses in Rev. 9.13–21 is further established when we understand that in John's schema, the events of 11.1–13.18 are said to happen under the sixth trumpet as we have shown earlier. The woe in 12.12 which is announced in *heaven* but directed at *the earth* and the sea is likely to parallel the eagle's cry in *midheaven*: 'Woe, woe, woe to the inhabitants of *the earth*' (8.13a). The dragon's fall from heaven to earth mirrors the fall of a star from heaven to earth under the fifth trumpet/first woe in 9.1. Further, the king of the locust hordes is called 'the angel of the bottomless pit named Abaddon in Hebrew and Apollyon in Greek' (9.11). While we are not proposing that the dragon is to be identified with the angel of the bottomless pit of the fifth trumpet/first woe, it is interesting to note the similarity, in that the dragon is also an angelic being (12.7) and that the dragon calls forth the beast that will ascend from the sea (12.18–13.1) or from the bottomless pit (11.7). It is evident that the angel of the bottomless pit called Abaddon/Apollyon is at least a satanic messenger if not Satan himself. What is apparent is that the series of three woes or the last three trumpets depict events that suggest satanic influence and involvement. The appearance of the angel of the bottomless pit as Satan's emissary under the fifth trumpet/first woe lasting five months prepares the way for the appearance of Satan in the person of his representatives, the two beasts of Rev. 13 under the sixth trumpet/second woe. This is John's way of telling his audience that in the last days, the battle between good and evil will intensify and with increasing satanic involvement climaxing in the coming of Satan to earth in the last three and a half years.

51. While fire is not explicitly stated as coming out of the mouth of the dragon, it is arguably implied in the description of the dragon as a *fiery* dragon waiting to devour the

The parallel metaphors of the devouring by wild beast (the dragon) and the sweeping away by floods of water are found in Ps. 124 in the same order.[52] The Psalm reads as follows:

> [v. 1] If it had not been the LORD who was on our side – let Israel now say –

> [v. 2] if it had not been the LORD who was on our side, when our enemies attacked us,

> [v. 3] then they would have swallowed us up alive, when their anger was kindled against us;

> [v. 4] then the flood would have swept us away, the torrent would have gone over us;

> [v. 5] then over us would have gone the raging waters.

> [v. 6] Blessed be the LORD, who has not given us as prey to their teeth.

> [v. 7] We have escaped like a bird from the snare of the fowlers; the snare is broken, and we have escaped.

> [v. 8] Our help is in the name of the LORD, who made heaven and earth.

In this Psalm, the community of Israel is under attack by their enemies (v. 1–2). The psalmist uses two metaphors to describe the violence planned against the nation. Cuthbert C. Keet comments as follows: 'The enemies of Israel are represented as ravening monsters . . . the simile of beasts devouring their prey frequently occurs in Hebrew literature . . . . The metaphor is changed [in v. 4]; the enemies of Israel are compared with a surging and swollen stream.'[53] Wild beasts and the waters represent hostile nations ready to wage war on Israel. Structurally, we see that the juxtaposition of two metaphors of the devouring beasts and torrents of waters in Ps. 124 is reflected in our proposed parallel between Rev. 12.1–4

woman's child with his mouth. Further, if there is an intended correspondence between the dragon and the horses of the first woe, the horses' mouths are said to pour *fire*, smoke, and sulphur (9.18). Yarbro Collins writes: 'In Revelation 12 the dragon is associated with both fire (he is fire-colored or red – vs. 3) and water (vs. 15). The same combination is found in Job 41 with regard to Leviathan.' Yarbro Collins, *Combat Myth*, p. 76. Fire and water are a word-pair in the Psalms (cf. Ps. 66.12) and also in the book of Isaiah (cf. Isa. 43.1–2). For a discussion of the fire/water word-pair in Isaiah, see Peter D. Miscall, 'Isaiah: The Labyrinth of Images', *Semeia* 54 (1991), pp. 103–21 (109–11).

52.   We are not suggesting that John had this particular Psalm in mind when he wrote Rev. 12.15–17, but it is illuminating to note the striking and remarkable verbal and conceptual parallels between these two texts.

53.   C. C. Keet, *A Study of the Psalms of Ascents: A Critical and Exegetical Commentary upon Psalms CXX – CXXXIV* (London: The Mitre Press, 1969), p. 42. Keet (p. 42) lists Pss. 7.2; 22.13; 35.25; 54.2; 57.4; Jer. 51.34; Isa. 9.11; Dan. 7.7 as examples where the metaphor of devouring beasts is found.

(devouring dragon) and 12.15–17 (raging waters from the serpent). Furthermore, Ps. 124.7 speaks of the escape of the community from the clutches of the enemy like a bird: 'We have escaped like a bird from the snare of the fowlers; the snare is broken, and we have escaped.' This imagery is also echoed in Rev. 12 since the picture of the devouring dragon (v. 4) is immediately followed by the escape of the male child and the woman from the clutches of the enemy (vv. 5–6). Even the imagery of a bird making its escape in Ps. 124 is similar to the picture of the woman given the wings of an eagle (a kind of transformation to a bird) with which she flees to the wilderness for refuge (Rev. 12.14 = 12.6). The repetition of the woman's escape in vv. 6 and 14 as we find in Rev. 12 is likely due to John's preference for chiasm as the key structuring device.[54]

In Rev. 12.16, the earth comes to aid the woman by opening its mouth and swallowing the water:[55]

---

54. The imagery of the woman taken by the two wings of the eagle in 12.14 followed by the casting out of water by the serpent's mouth (12.15) may allude to the passage in Isa. 8.7–8: '[v. 7] Therefore, the Lord is bringing up against it the mighty flood waters of the River, the king of Assyria and all his glory; it will rise above all its channels and overflow all its banks; [v. 8] it will sweep on into Judah as a flood, and, pouring over, it will reach up to the neck; and its outspread wings will fill the breadth of your land, O Immanuel.' As we have noted earlier, the Assyrian invasion is pictured under the metaphorical image of a rampaging river. The mention of the outstretched wings in Isa. 8.8b appears strange as a river does not have wings. Hence, J. J. M. Roberts argues that Isa. 8.8b should be understood as conveying the idea of protection or refuge under the wings of Yahweh. Roberts thus interprets Isa. 8.8b as 'Yahweh's wings stretched over the whole land to protect it'. J. J. M. Roberts, 'Isaiah and his Children', in Ann Kort and Scott Morschauser (eds.), *Biblical and Related Studies Presented to Samuel Iwry* (Winona Lake: Eisenbraun, 1985), pp. 193–203 (199). If Roberts is correct, then we have in the passage of Isa. 8.7–8 a juxtaposition of the images. At the time of the Assyrian invasion pictured liked a rampaging river to sweep Judah as a flood, Yahweh will outstretch his wings to protect the land. The term 'Immanuel' (God with us) at the end of verse 8 appears to support that Yahweh's presence is there to protect the people of Judah. This juxtaposition is similar to what we find in Rev. 12.13–17. In Rev. 12.14 the image of the eagles' wings is mentioned first before the image of the rampaging river in v. 15 in reverse to the images we have in Isa. 8.7–8. Again, we postulate that the order of ideas in Rev. 12.14–17 in contrast to the one found Isa. 8.7–8 is due to the chiastic patterning in Rev. 12 where the idea of the woman's protection in 12.14 parallels that of 12.6 and the warfare imagery of 12.15–17 is intended to correspond to 12.1–4. For a study on the metaphor of God's wings, see Silvia Schroer, ' "Under the Shadow of Your Wings": The Metaphor of God's Wings in the Psalms, Exodus 19.4, Deuteronomy 32.11 and Malachi 3.20, as Seen through the Perspectives of Feminism and History of Religion', in Athalya Brenner & Carole R. Fontaine (eds.), *Wisdom and Psalms* (The Feminist Companion to the Bible [Second Series]; Sheffield: Sheffield Academic Press, 1998), pp. 264–82.

55. Revelation 12.16 probably alludes to the episode where the earth opened its mouth and swallowed Korah, Dathan, Abiram, and those who rebelled against Moses' leadership (Num. 16.32). The LXX of Num. 16.2 reads: καὶ ἠνοίχθη ἡ γῆ καὶ κατέπιεν αὐτοὺς καὶ τοὺς οἴκους αὐτῶν καὶ πάντας τοὺς ἀνθρώπους τοὺς ὄντας μετὰ Κορε καὶ τὰ κτήνη αὐτῶν.

καὶ ἐβοήθησεν ἡ γῆ τῇ γυναικὶ καὶ ἤνοιξεν ἡ γῆ τὸ στόμα αὐτῆς καὶ κατέπιεν τὸν ποταμὸν ὃν ἔβαλεν ὁ δράκων ἐκ τοῦ στόματος αὐτοῦ.

It appears that the woman is once again safe. But the dragon's anger rages on as he goes away and makes war against the rest of the woman's offspring. Verse 17 of ch. 12 gives additional information on the woman's family. The woman not only has a male son but also 'other offspring' (τῶν λοιπῶν τοῦ σπέρματος αὐτῆς). Now its parallel element tells of the rest of the male son's siblings, which also become the target of the dragon's warfare.

The phrase ποιῆσαι πόλεμον (to make war) that characterizes the dragon's action in A' states the true import of the dragon's colour, 'red' in A.[56] This also explains the nature of persecution (ἐδίωξεν) of the dragon in 12.13 as warfare. Revelation 12.17 brings into climactic conclusion the theme of persecution against the woman and her offspring. John's audience is told in no uncertain terms that they will face persecution in this three-and-a-half years period called the great tribulation because the devil has come down to the earth and his remaining days are spent in making war against the saints.

Finally, ch. 12 of Revelation closes with the dragon standing on the seashore: καὶ ἐστάθη ἐπὶ τὴν ἄμμον τῆς θαλάσσης (12.18). It is important to note here, as Beale does, that: 'The καὶ introduces, not a narration of events taking place after the events of 12.13–17, but a vision occurring after the vision in ch. 12. The analysis of ch. 13 will reveal that the historical time period is parallel with ch. 12, especially 12.6, 13–17.'[57] This verse is often thought as an introduction to the careers of the two beasts and as such its place belongs to Rev. 13 and not Rev. 12. In our view, it is not necessary to decide whether 12.18 belongs more properly to Rev. 12 or Rev. 13 because it is more likely that literarily 12.18 functions to conclude 12.1–17 *and* also to introduce the appearance of the beast from the sea in 13.1. John is adept in using link verses that function to conclude a preceding passage and also to introduce the next episode. We have seen that 11.19 functions as a link verse whereby it concludes Rev. 11 but also links ch. 11 unmistakably with ch. 12.

Revelation 12.18 is a fitting conclusion to 12.13–17 as Satan is situated on earth, standing on the sand of the sea menacingly as if ready to strike, namely to call forth the beasts from the sea and the earth. The word ἐστάθη (stood) in v. 18 may be significant as a parallel to the dragon's standing (ἕστηκεν) before the woman in v. 4, thus framing the activity of the dragon in ch. 12 in an *inclusio*. But 12.18 also links with 13.1 as the location τῆς θαλάσσης in both verses indicates. Just as the dragon is seen standing on the sand of the sea, the beast is seen to ascend from the sea: Καὶ εἶδον ἐκ τῆς

---

56. The red horse of the second seal unleashes warfare on earth (Rev. 6.3–4).

57. Beale, *Revelation*, p. 681.

θαλάσσης θηρίον ἀναβαῖνον (13.1a). Jan Willem van Henten writes: 'The final location of the dragon near the sea in 12.18 and the rising of the first beast out of the sea in 13.1 show that the vision of the two beasts can be considered as a continuation of the vision of ch. 12.'[58]

In summary, we have seen how the macro-chiastic pattern we propose for Rev. 11.1–14.5 takes shape in Rev. 12 (EFGF'E') with the introduction of two protagonists, the woman and the dragon and their conflict in vv. 1–4, which is then elaborated and expanded in vv. 15–17 (EE'). The tale of the woman's escape and refuge in the wilderness for three-and-a-half years in v. 6 is retold in v. 14, making such repetition a clear sign of the existence of a concentric structure (FF'). The centrality of the 'war-in-heaven' motif in vv. 7–12 makes up the pivot of this textual unit (G). The war between Michael and the dragon in heaven and the dragon's expulsion from heaven explain why the dragon makes war against the woman and her offspring on earth (vv. 4, 15–17). Yet in the midst of warfare, God is able to protect the woman and her children (vv. 5–6, 13–14).

4. *The Meaning and Significance of the Signs*

The highly complex symbolic language of Rev. 12 demands greater interpretative effort than any other chapter of Revelation. The characters and events of ch. 12 come under the rubric of the two signs in heaven, namely the woman and the dragon. A sign is not to be taken literally. The sign 'dragon' needs no further decoding as John himself identifies the dragon as 'the devil and Satan' in 12.9. But we are not told what the sign 'woman' stands for. Feuillet says: 'The Woman whom John contemplates is first and foremost the ideal Sion of the prophets, who, by bearing (metaphorically) the Messiah, becomes the Church.'[59] We

---

58. J. W. van Henten, 'Dragon Myth and Imperial Ideology in Revelation 12–13', in *SBL Seminar Papers* (Atlanta: Scholars Press, 1994), pp. 496–515 (502). Similarly, de Heer states: 'Sebenarnya tidak baik untuk memisahkan pasal 12 dari pasal 13. Ayat penghabisan dari pasal 12 dan ayat pertama dari pasal 13 merupakan suatu kesatuan. Sang naga, yakni Iblis, berdiri di pantai laut, dan memanggil seekor binatang liar keluar dari dalam laut.' (ET: There is no need to separate ch. 12 from ch. 13. The last verse of ch. 12 and the first verse of ch. 13 form a unity. The dragon, namely Satan, stands at the seashore, and calls a beast out of the sea). de Heer, *Kitab Wahyu*, p. 179. Schüssler Fiorenza says: 'The statement of 12.18 forms a bridge that links the conclusion of 12.17 with the new image of the wild beast from the sea (13.1). It therefore functions as an introduction to the whole section, which begins with the image of the dragon standing at the shore of the sea and concludes with the Lamb standing on Mount Zion.' Schüssler Fiorenza, *Revelation: Vision of a Just World*, p. 82.

59. Feuillet, *Apocalypse*, p. 115. Elsewhere Feuillet writes: 'We agree, therefore, with those commentators who see the woman of Apocalypse XII *first and foremost a personification of the people of God.*' Feuillet, *Johannine Studies*, p. 276 (his emphasis). A. Yarbro Collins writes: 'The woman clothed with the sun is best understood as the Heavenly Israel; she is portrayed as

submit that the woman symbolizes the church which consists of the persecuted people of God living in the last days of three-and-a-half years. Roger D. Aus states: 'It is a suffering, persecuted church which the author of Revelation addresses.'[60]

The woman pictured as clothed with the sun with twelve stars on her head and the moon under her feet clearly alludes to Joseph's dream recorded in Gen. 37.9.[61] The eleven stars which bowed down to Joseph were the eleven sons of Jacob or Israel, who together with Joseph became the twelve patriarchs of the twelve tribes of Israel. The twelve tribes constitute the people of God, Israel or Zion in the Old Testament. John in Rev. 12.1–2 has conflated a number of Old Testament texts. Apart from Gen. 37.9, the figure of a 'woman' as personifying the people of God is taken mainly from the prophets. Zion or Jerusalem is often personified as a woman, the wife of Yahweh and on occasions pictured as giving birth to her children (cf. Isa. 66.7–14; Jer. 4.31; Mic. 4.9–10; Ps. 87).[62] As Zion is equated with Jerusalem, it is significant that Mother Zion is often seen as

God's spouse, whom he protects, as mother of the messiah, and of all believers (v. 17).' A. Yarbro Collins, 'Feminine Symbolism in the Book of Revelation', *BibInt* 1 (1993), pp. 20–33 (24). The question whether the male son refers to the Messiah will be answered in a later section. Ford states: 'In the OT the image of a woman is a classical symbol for Zion, Jerusalem and Israel, e.g. Zion whose husband is Yahweh (Isa. 54.1, 5, Jer. 3.20, Ezek. 16.8–14, Hosea 2.19–20), who is a mother (Isa. 49.21, 50.1, 66.7–11, Hosea 4.5, Bar. 4.8–23), and who is in the throes of birth (Micah 4.9–10, cf. Isa. 26.16–18, Jer. 4.31, 13.21, Sir. 48.19[21]).' Ford, *Revelation*, p. 195. For general studies on Yahweh as the husband of Israel, see Nelly Stienstra, *Yahweh is the Husband of his People* (Kampen: Kok Pharos, 1993) and Julie Galambush, *Jerusalem in the Book of Ezekiel: The City as Yahweh's Wife* (SBLDS, 130; Atlanta: Scholars Press, 1992).

    60.   R. D. Aus, 'The Relevance of Isaiah 66.7 to Revelation 12 and 2 Thessalonians 1', *ZNW* 67 (1976), pp. 252–68 (256). Yarbro Collins disputes the identification of the woman with the church as she could not accept that the church could give birth to Christ in 12.5. If the male son does not refer to Christ in 12.5 (see later), then Yarbro Collins' objection against the woman being the church is not sustainable. Apart from her mistaken understanding of 12.5, Yarbro Collins acknowledges that: 'The ecclesiological interpretation [woman as the church] fits vss. 6 and 14–17 quite well. The woman would then be a symbolic representation of the Church undergoing persecution instigated by Satan, and guaranteed safety by God.' Yarbro Collins, *Combat Myth*, p. 106.

    61.   So Court, *Myth and History*, p. 108; Sweet, *Revelation*, p. 195; Keener, *Revelation*, p. 314; Thomas, *Revelation 8–22*, pp. 118–19; Hagelberg, *Tafsiran Kitab Wahyu*, p. 235.

    62.   Tan states that: ' "Jerusalem" and "Zion" are used synonymically in the OT (see especially Zech. 8.2–3; Micah 3.12–4.2 among others.' Tan, *Zion traditions*, p. 24. This Jerusalem as mother motif is not limited to the Old Testament but is also found in the New Testament. In the Gospels of Matthew and Luke, Jerusalem is seen as a mother with her children (Mt. 23.37; Lk. 13.34). We should note that both Mt. 23.37 and Lk. 13.34 associate Jerusalem and her children closely with the temple.

the holy city Jerusalem. John J. Schmitt remarks that 'the wife of God in the Hebrew Bible is always a city'.[63]

The woman in Rev. 12.1 is Zion, the city of Jerusalem personified as a woman giving birth to her children. The children within the city are the city's dwellers. Often the name of a city is a synonym for the city's inhabitants.[64] For example, 'Jerusalem' stands for the inhabitants of Jerusalem and is often mentioned alongside her people (cf. Jer. 4.3, 5, 11; Dan. 9.16, 19, 24). This means the woman-city of Rev. 12.1 is a symbol for the people of God, the *church* as the woman's children are 'those who keep the commandments of God and hold to the testimony of Jesus' (12.17).[65] The concept of a woman as a symbol for a city is utilized by John in two other places in the book of Revelation. The woman-harlot of 17.1–7 is

63. J. J. Schmitt, 'The Motherhood of God and Zion as Mother', *RB* 92 (1985), pp. 557–69 (561). Conversely, if the city sins against God, then it is abandoned by God, often to invading armies. The desolate Jerusalem is a figure of a city that is emptied of its inhabitants either taken away as captives or who perish in war (cf. Jer. 4.27). Kamila Blessing states that: 'The desolate Jerusalem is always a figure for the people collectively.' K. Blessing, 'Desolate Jerusalem and Barren Matriarch: The Distinct Figures in the Pseudepigrapha', *JSP* 18 (1998), pp. 47–69 (53).

64. F. I. Andersen and D. N. Freedman write: 'When prophets address Daughter-Zion, they are talking to the residents of the city.' F. I. Andersen and D. N. Freedman, *Micah* (AB; New York: Doubleday, 2000), p. 446.

65. It is not necessary to decide whether the woman symbolizes Israel of old or the new Israel as some scholars have done. For example, Court thinks that the woman represents 'the ideal remnant of Israel, the chosen people of God.... The ideal figure of Israel...has a worthy place in the divine plan. In this respect, then, the author of Revelation agrees with Paul that God has by no means rejected his original chosen people; rather "all Israel will be saved", when the full number of the Gentiles has been gathered in (Rom. 11.1, 25–26).' Court, *Myth and History*, p. 121. Svigel argues that the woman of Rev. 12 'primarily represents Israel of the OT in travail'. Svigel, 'The Apocalypse of John', p. 59. James Davila states that the woman should be 'interpreted as Israel, the figurative mother of a Jewish messiah'. J. Davila, 'Melchizedek, Michael and War in Heaven', in *SBL Seminar Papers* (Atlanta: Scholars Press, 1996), pp. 259–73 (265). It appears that Court, Svigel and Davila fail to recognize that for John, the OT image of Zion or Israel is adapted in Revelation to represent the people of God of both Jews and Gentiles, which John calls the church elsewhere (Rev. 1.19–3.22). According to Beale: 'The apocalyptist has a tendency to apply to the world what in the Old Testament was limited to Israel or other entities.... The title which Yahweh gave Israel in Exod. 19.6 ("kingdom and priests") is applied in Rev. 1.6 and 5.10 to the *church*.' Beale, *John's Use of the Old Testament*, p. 100 (emphasis mine). Elsewhere, Beale writes: 'The "ten days of tribulation" experienced by Daniel and his friends (Dan. 1.12) and the three-and-a-half years of Israel's tribulation (Dan. 7.25; 12.7) are both extended to the tribulation of the church – the eschatological, true Israel – throughout the world.' Beale, 'The Use of the Old Testament in Revelation', pp. 327–28. Similarly, M. Rissi has also shown that the descriptions of 'my people' in Rev. 18.4 and 21.3 that are used to refer to Israel in the OT are applied to the church in book of Revelation. See M. Rissi, *Time and History: A Study on the Revelation* (Virginia: John Knox Press, 1965), p. 89. Also McNicol, 'Revelation 11:1–14', p. 200 n. 15. David de Silva notes that Fifth Ezra (= 2 Esdras 1–2), thought to be written in the wake of the

identified as 'the great city that rules over the kings of the earth' (17.18). More significantly, the bride of the Lamb is shown to be 'the holy city Jerusalem coming down out of heaven from God' (21.9–10).[66] The bride of the Lamb in 19.7–8a has been identified with the saints (19.8b). It appears that the heavenly city is primarily a metaphor for the people of God, the saints.[67] Donal A. McIlraith writes: 'The wife is identified with the "saints," all who respond to Christ and continue "overcoming".... It implies that the wife is the entirety of all the redeemed.'[68]

Most scholars agree that the passage in Isa. 66.6–8 is the most likely background to Rev. 12.1–5.[69] The text of Isaiah reads thus:

> [v. 6] Listen, an uproar from the city! A voice from the temple! The voice of the LORD, dealing retribution to his enemies! [v. 7] Before she was in labor she gave birth; before her pain came upon her she delivered a son. [v. 8] Who has heard of such a thing? Who has seen such things? Shall a land be born in one day? Shall a nation be delivered in one moment? Yet as soon as Zion was in labor she delivered her children.

Aune notes that the temple motif in Isa. 66.6 is very similar to the context of Rev. 11.19–12.5.[70] In Rev. 11.19, it is said that, 'the temple of God in

---

Second Jewish Revolt (132–135 C.E.), 'affirms the church as the successor to a faithless and disobedient Israel in God's plan'. D. de Silva, *Introducing the Apocrypha: Message, Context, and Significance* (Grand Rapids: Baker Academic, 2002), p. 324.

66.   A striking parallel to the notion of a woman who is subsequently portrayed as a city is found in 2 Esdras 9.38–10.59. Ezra saw a woman weeping and mourning for her only son who died on his wedding day. Ezra was angry that the woman wept for her son when 'Zion, the mother of us all is in deep grief and great distress' (10.7). While Ezra was talking to the woman, the woman suddenly changed into a city: 'When I looked up, the woman was no longer visible to me, but a city was being built, and a place of huge foundations showed itself' (10.27). Then Uriel the angel interpreted Ezra's vision as follows: 'The woman whom you saw is Zion, which you now behold as a city being built' (10.44). The woman's son who died represented the destruction that befell the city of Jerusalem (10.48). Ezra was found worthy to be shown 'the brilliance of her glory and the loveliness of her beauty' (10.50), which can be seen as a parallel to the glorious beauty of the woman of Rev. 12.1. In 2 Esdras 9–10, both woman and son are symbols for the corporate people of God personified as Zion and Jerusalem respectively.

67.   Yarbro Collins writes: 'The Bride, the new Jerusalem, in Revelation symbolizes the community of the faithful at the time of their uniting with God and the Lamb in the new age.' Yarbro Collins, 'Female Symbolism', p. 25.

68.   D. A. McIlraith, ' "For the Fine Linen is the Righteous Deeds of the Saints": Works and Wife in Revelation 19:8', *CBQ* 61 (1999), pp. 513–29 (526).

69.   So Aune, *Revelation 6–16*, pp. 662, 687; Aus, 'The Relevance of Isaiah 66.7', pp. 252–68; Beale, *John's Use of the Old Testament*, pp. 341–43; Svigel, 'The Apocalypse of John', p. 58.

70.   Aune, *Revelation*, p. 662. Though the city motif is absent in Rev. 11.19, the city and the temple combination is found in 11.1–2 where both the temple's court and the city are said to be trampled by the nations. Rev. 11.19 may be seen as God coming out from his heavenly

heaven was opened' with attendant 'noises' as God acts to deal retribution to his enemies.[71] Then it is followed by John's vision of the woman in labour-pains and a male son was born forthwith as is also the case in Isa. 66.7. The woman in Isa. 66.7-8 is identified as Zion. As soon as Zion was in labour she delivered a son (v. 7) or her children (v. 8b). It is best to put vv. 7 and 8 of Isa. 66 in its formal structure as follows:

A – [v. 7] Before *she* was in labor she gave birth; before her pain came upon her she delivered a *son* (MT – זָכָר; LXX – ἄρσεν).

B – [v. 8] Who has heard of such a thing?
Who has seen such things?

B' – Shall a land (MT – אֶרֶץ; LXX – γῆ) be born in one day?
Shall a nation (MT – גּוֹי; LXX – ἔθνος) be delivered in one moment?

A' – Yet as soon as *Zion* was in labor she delivered *her children* [בָּנֶיהָ].

The feminine figure in A is identified as Zion in A'. Worthy of note is the parallelism between the woman giving birth to a 'male' [זָכָר] in A to 'her sons' [בָּנֶיהָ] in A'.[72] Isaiah's lady-Zion does not only give birth to a son but also to many sons. Beale comments thus:

The combination of 'son' and 'male' in Rev. 12.5 is based, at least in part, on the close parallelism of Isa. 66.7 with 66.8 in the MT.... In addition to the verbal parallelism, the singular 'male' of 66.7 is replaced in 66.8 with the plural 'sons', both apparently referring to Israel.[73]

---

temple to deal retribution to those who trample on his earthly temple and city. In Isa. 66.6, the city and the temple refer to the earthly temple and the city of Jerusalem. Targum Isa. 66.6 identifies the city as 'the city of Jerusalem'. See Chilton, *Isaiah Targum*, p. 127.

71. R. H. Whybray remarks that in Isa. 66.6, 'the prophet in imagination hears the sound of the battle proceeding from the city and the Temple. This probably refers to Yahweh's going out from the city and the Temple to wreak vengeance on external enemies'. R. H. Whybray, *Isaiah 40–66* (Grand Rapids: Eerdmans, 1981), p. 283.

72. The LXX of Isa. 66.7 translates זָכָר as ἄρσεν, which is alluded to in Rev. 12.5. We should note the irregularity of ἔτεκεν υἱὸν ἄρσεν of Rev. 12.5. Beale writes: 'The masculine υἱὸν followed by the neuter pronominal adjective ἄρσεν ('male son') appears to be irregular, since adjectives should be in the same gender as nouns which they modify.' Beale suggests that the solecism here is intended by John to point to the OT allusion in Isa. 66.7. Beale, *John's Use of the Old Testament*, p. 341.

73. Beale, *John's Use of the Old Testament*, pp. 341–42. We should note that the woman and the rest of her children in 12.17 are both images for the church. The woman represents the church is her heavenly existence (12.1) and protection by God (12.6, 14) while the rest of her children stands for the members of the church that will be persecuted by the dragon and the beasts of Rev. 13.

In BB', the identity of Zion's son or children is made known. Zion's son (or her children) is a metaphor for a land or a nation. The land or nation to be born is the land or nation of Israel.

The imagery of a woman in birthpangs is also found in Isa. 26.16–18. In this passage the people of Judah or Israel is likened to a woman with child, who writhes and cries out in her pangs (26.17).[74] What is of interest in this verse is that we have in the LXX Isa. 26.17, the word ἐκέκραξεν (cried out) that is not found in Isa. 66.7–8 but is mentioned by John in the description of the woman in birthpangs who κράζει (cries out) in torment to give birth: κράζει ὠδίνουσα καὶ βασανιζομένη τεκεῖν (Rev. 12.2).[75] We have already noted that the woman's crying out in 12.2 is parallel to the dragon's dragging (σύρει) a third of the stars down from heaven to earth in 12.4. We have cited Dan. 8.9–14 as the most probable background for the casting out of the court outside the temple in Rev. 11.1–2. It is said in Dan. 8.10 that the little horn 'threw down some of the host and some of the stars and trampled on them'. Beale argues that the stars in Dan. 8.10 represent the oppressed of Israel. Beale writes: 'The interpretation of the vision in Dan. 8.1–12 in Dan. 8.22–25 demonstrates that Israelites living on earth are the primary objects of the persecution... "stars" are clearly metaphors of true saints in Dan. 12.3.'[76]

Is there a link between the throwing down of a third of the stars by the dragon in Rev. 12.4 with the crown of twelve stars on the woman's head in 12.1? Beale rightly sees the connection between the stars of Rev. 12.4 and the twelve stars on the woman's head in 12.1. He comments thus: 'The portrayal of the stars in v 4 must have a close relationship with the "twelve stars" only three verses earlier. The falling stars must symbolize an attack on Israel, since the twelve stars in v 1 represent the heavenly identification of the true Israel.'[77] The third of the stars that are cast down by the dragon's tail represents the saints that suffer martyrdom as a result of the dragon's persecution and fury. Thus we conclude that the woman's pains and torment are due to her children (symbolized by the stars) being attacked by the dragon in 12.1–4, a scenario which further confirms our contention that vv. 1–4 are intended to parallel vv. 15–17, where the dragon wages war against the woman's other offspring.

---

74.   Court says: 'Rev. 12.2–5 contains allusions to Isa. 66.7 and 26.17f.' Court, *Myth and History*, p. 107.

75.   Feuillet remarks that the present tense of the verbs κράζει and βασανιζομένη indicate 'prolonged suffering'. Feuillet, *Johannine Studies*, p. 262.

76.   Beale, *Revelation*, p. 636.

77.   Beale, *Revelation*, p. 637. Willem F. Smilek observes that: 'The association of the righteous with angels, stars and light became well attested and widespread.' W. F. Smilek, 'On Mystical Transformation of the Righteous into Light in Judaism', *JSJ* 26 (1995), pp. 122–44 (125). See the references listed by Smilek at p. 125 n. 15.

Furthermore, the passage in Isa. 26.16–18 clearly speaks of *the people* of Judah in distress compared to a woman in birthpangs:[78]

> [v. 16] O LORD, in distress they sought you, they poured out a prayer when your chastening was on them. [v. 17] Like a woman with child, who writhes and cries out in her pangs when she is near her time, so were we because of you, O LORD; [v. 18] we were with child, we writhed, but we gave birth only to wind. We have won no victories on earth, and no one is born to inhabit the world.

Images of the woman in birthpangs in both Isa. 26.16–18 and 66.7–8 speak of the people of Israel collectively. In addition, the male child in Isa. 66.7 is a collective figure for the land and nation of Israel and in Isa. 26.16–18 the woman with child stands for Israel. We may conclude that Isa. 66.7–8 and Isa. 26.16–18 are both probably influential in John's depiction of the woman in birthpangs in Rev. 12.1–5. It is not unreasonable, therefore, to conclude that both the woman and her male son in Rev. 12.1–5 are symbols for the corporate people of God.[79]

One other significant point about the imagery of a woman in birthpangs needs be made. As it is in Isa. 26.16–18, many other Old Testament passages (cf. Jer. 4.19, 31; Mic. 4.9–10) also speak of a woman in birthpangs as a metaphor for the city of Jerusalem or Zion under attack from military forces. Barbara B. Kaiser states that: 'In the poetry of the Hebrew Bible the image of a woman experiencing the pangs of childbirth occurs so frequently as a metaphor for the terror of an impending invasion...that it seems to be a hackneyed image.'[80] John could have adopted this stock imagery of Jerusalem under siege as the symbol for the church under attack from enemy forces. The hostility of the dragon against the woman and her children is one of the major motifs of Rev. 12. If we are correct in seeing a connection between birthpangs and attack by enemies,

---

78.   B. R. Gaventa remarks that the term *ōdinein* (birthpangs) 'usually appears in contexts having to do with the situation of the people collectively, rather than with the situation of an individual'. B. R. Gaventa, 'The Maternity of Paul: An Exegetical Study of Galatians 4:19', in R. T. Fortna and B. R. Gaventa (eds.), *The Conversation Continues: Studies in Paul and John in honor of J. Louis Martyn* (Nashville: Abingdon Press, 1990), pp. 189–201 (193).

79.   Court observes that the larger context of chs 26 and 27 provides a parallel account to the arrangement of ideas in Rev. 12.1–6. Court notes that the section following the image of the childbirth in Isa. 26.17 refers to 'the idea of hiding for a little while, until the wrath is past (like the woman who is carried away by the eagle to safety in the wilderness)' (Isa. 26.20) followed by the statement that the Lord will slay the dragon in the sea (Isa. 27.1). Court, *Myth and History*, p. 112. Also Day, *God's Conflict with the Dragon*, p. 145. Although the slaying of the dragon is not found in Rev. 12, the idea is already present there that the dragon is defeated in heaven and has only a short time on earth (12.8, 12).

80.   B. B. Kaiser, 'Poet as "Female Impersonator": The Image of Daughter Zion as Speaker in Biblical Poems of Suffering', *JR* 67 (1987), pp. 164–82 (166).

then we can suggest Rev. 12.1–4 also reflects a city (= the church) under military siege. This imagery of a city under military siege in Rev. 12.1–4 may be intended to parallel the actual trampling of the nations on the holy city, Jerusalem, in 11.1–2. We have seen that the two units in Rev. 11.1–2 and 12.1–4 relied closely on the passage in Dan. 8.9–14. While the armies of the nations besiege Jerusalem for 42 months, the church is also under attack from the beast for the same period (cf. 11.7; 12.6, 14–17; 13.5, 7). The imagery of the dragon (Satan) standing and ready to devour the male child (the church) is a military metaphor. Satan is said to stand (עמד) against Israel in 1 Chron. 21.1, implying malice and opposition towards Israel. In this regard the representation of king Nebuchadnezzar as a dragon ready to devour Israel in LXX Jer. 28.34 (MT – 51.34) is a most pertinent text for Rev. 12.4. The LXX of Jer. 28.34 is set out as follows:

κατέφαγέν με ἐμερίσατό με κατέλαβέν με σκεῦος λεπτὸν Ναβουχοδονοσορ βασιλεὺς Βαβυλῶνος κατέπιέν με ὡς δράκων ἔπλησεν τὴν κοιλίαν αὐτοῦ ἀπὸ τῆ ς τρυφῆς μου ἐξῶσέν με

Verbal similarities between Rev. 12.4 and LXX Jer. 28.34 are striking. First, the word καταφάγη in Rev. 12.4 is identical to the term κατέφαγέν in LXX Jer. 28.34. Second, the king of Babylon is likened to a dragon. Third, the idea that king Nebuchadnezzar has cast out (ἐξῶσέν) Israel may be echoed in the casting out of water in Rev. 12.15. The imagery in Jer. 28.34 (LXX) clearly speaks of the king of Babylon devouring Israel like a dragon as a metaphor for waging war and destroying Israel. It seems clear that John has alluded to Jer. 28.34 (LXX) in Rev. 12.4 and this supports our contention that the imagery of Rev. 12.1–4 speaks of warfare between the dragon and the woman.[81]

---

81.   Hence, it is not true as alleged by van Henten that the imagery of a woman and her infant persecuted by a dragon is 'absent in the Hebrew bible and in Jewish traditions'. van Henten, 'Dragon Myth and Imperial Ideology in Rev 12–13', pp. 503–4. In Rev. 12.1–6, we have seen that John has conflated a number of passages from OT texts including Gen. 37, Dan. 8, Isa. 26 and 66, and LXX Jer. 28. On the conflation of OT texts in Rev. 12, see Koester, *Revelation*, pp. 124–25. Koester (p. 124) also lists Jer. 51.34 (LXX – 28.34) as a possible background for Rev. 12.4. In the light of our discussion of the OT background for Rev. 12.1–6, the contention that John used pagan traditions in Rev. 12 like the Seth and Typhon traditions is not entirely proven despite strong arguments presented by Yarbro Collins in favour of the Graeco-Roman myth as the background to Rev. 12. See Yarbro Collins, *Combat Myth*, pp. 73–85. Also Frey, 'Die Bildersprache der Johannesapokalypse', p. 179. Paul Minear argues that the conflict between the serpent and the woman and the woman's seed in Gen. 3 provides the background for much of the conflict between the dragon and the woman and the serpent and the woman's seed in Rev. 12. See P. Minear, 'Far as the Curse is Found: The Point of Rev. 12.15–16', *NovT* 33 (1991), pp. 71–77. Minear (p. 75 n. 8) lists no fewer than ten motifs in Genesis that may be found in the book of Revelation. They include: 'the role of the ancient serpent; the conflict of the serpent and the woman; the association of the serpent with the beasts of the earth; the conflict between the seed of the woman and the seed of the serpent;

a. *Is Christ's birth referred to in Revelation 12.5?*

Following our discussion of the woman and her male son, it appears clear that the male son is a symbolic reference for the corporate people of God. Nevertheless, the majority of scholars have argued or assumed that the male son of Rev. 12.5 refers to the historical birth of Christ.[82] We will see that lately, the scholarly opinion may have shifted as for example, Aune and Resseguie in more recent times have argued that Rev. 12.5 primarily cannot refer to the birth of Christ. Resseguie comments thus:

> First, there is no mention of Jesus as the male child in 12.1–7. Moreover, all interpretations that see the phrase – 'was snatched away and was taken to God and his throne' – as a reference to the resurrection and ascension of Jesus seem forced. Second, the faithful remnant – not Jesus – is 'to rule all the nations with a rod of iron [12.5]'. In 2.26–27, Jesus

the injury done to the head of the serpent; the accent upon the act of giving birth and its painful character; the strategic use of the terms brother and blood, with implicit contrasts between two brothers and their two deaths; the prominent, multiple, contrasted roles assigned to the mouth of the earth'. Another possible allusion in the OT is found in Pharaoh's attempted murder of the infant Moses where the infant Moses was hidden and was taken to safety. A number of parallels between Rev. 12.1–5 and the Mosaic infancy narrative can be observed. Pharaoh, the king of Egypt is traditionally known as 'a dragon' (Ezek. 29.3; 32.2). First, every Hebrew *male* child is to be killed by Pharaoh's midwives at the moment of birth (Exod. 1.16). Second, Moses is hidden (Exod. 2.2) and later placed among the reeds on the bank of the river (Exod. 2.3). In Moses' case, the river proves to be the place of deliverance, but in Rev. 12.15–16, the water like a river becomes the source of danger for the woman. Moses' name, meaning 'saved from water', echoes the situation of the woman who is 'saved from the water' when the earth opens its mouth and swallows the water (Rev. 12.16). On the meaning of Moses' name, see Josephus, *Ant.* 2.9.6. See also Paul E. Hughes, 'Moses' Birth Story: A Biblical Matrix for Prophetic Messianism', in Craig A. Evans and Peter W. Flint (eds.), *Eschatology, Messianism, and the Dead Sea Scrolls* (Grand Rapids: Eerdmans, 1997), pp. 10–22 (15). Hughes (p. 16) recognizes 'the *leitmotif* of birth in the introductory chapters of Exodus, noting that each subsection contains a form of the root ילד, which can be used verbally as "to bear, give birth," or a noun meaning "son." ' Also in Rev. 12.1–5, we have the stress on the woman about to give birth where the verbal form τίκτω (give birth) is mentioned three times in v. 4 alone and once in v. 5 and v. 13. Also Rev. 12.2 is verbally close to LXX Exod. 2.2: καὶ ἐν γαστρὶ ἔλαβεν καὶ ἔτεκεν ἄρσεν ἰδόντες δὲ αὐτὸ ἀστεῖον ἐσκέπασαν αὐτὸ μῆνας τρεῖς. In Rev. 12.2, 5a we also have a pregnant woman giving birth to a male son: καὶ ἐν γαστρὶ ἔχουσα, καὶ κράζει ὠδίνουσα καὶ βασανιζομένη τεκεῖν (12.2),...καὶ ἔτεκεν υἱὸν ἄρσεν...(12.5a). In Exodus, the infant was hidden for three months but the woman of Revelation (by implication, the male son as well) is taken to safety for three-and-a-half years (12.6). For a comparison of the Moses' infant narrative and Jesus' birth narrative and his descent into Egypt, see Hughes, 'Moses' Birth Story', p. 13.

82. The list of writers who hold that the male child is Jesus Christ is too long to mention here. It is perhaps ironic to note that the events and objects of Rev. 11.1–2 have been given a symbolic interpretation by commentators when it seems clear that the passage there consists of a prophetic narrative which tells of actual events happening literally within the setting of the temple and the city while the heavily symbolic language of a 'male son' in Rev. 12.5 is interpreted literally to mean the birth of a son, namely Jesus Christ!

promises to those who conquer and continue to do his works to the end to 'give authority over the nations; *to rule them with an iron rod*, as when clay pots are shattered'. The male child represents those who remain faithful, the true messianic community, in 12.1–7.[83]

We will show that Resseguie's position is to be preferred as far as the identity of the male child is concerned in 12.5. Whether this text speaks of Christ's birth is crucial to the interpretation of the three-and-a-half years' period in Rev. 11–13. If indeed Rev. 12.5 speaks of the birth of the Messiah, then Rissi could be right in that the three-and-a-half years in Revelation may be taken as an 'intermediary time' between Christ's first coming and his parousia at the end of the age.[84] If the said text does not primarily refer to Christ's birth, then a case can be made that the three-and-a-half years' period (whether literal or symbolic of a short period) arguably is the last duration of time before the parousia of Christ.

We have noted earlier that the characters and events of ch. 12 come under the concept of the two signs, namely the woman and the dragon. The woman giving birth to a male child is a sign. A sign in Rev. 12 is not to be taken literally. All commentators agree that the woman is not to be taken literally. Neither is there a dragon literally speaking in the sky but the sign of a dragon is a figure or symbol for the devil or Satan, explicitly named in Rev. 12.9. In fact the two signs of ch. 12 are symbols or picture-images seen by John in a vision to depict heavenly (and earthly) realities beyond the literalness of signs. Hence, it is surprising that the male child of Rev. 12 is given a most literalistic meaning, in that it is interpreted literally to mean Christ's birth. If the woman does not mean literally a woman, then it is unlikely that we should interpret the male child in a literal manner. As the woman–sign is symbolic of some deeper meaning or signification, then the male child born by the woman must also be symbolic of some meaning other than a literal male child. Paul Tan's series of rhetorical questions best capture the inconsistency in the interpretations

83.   Resseguie, *Revelation Unsealed*, p. 144 (his emphasis). Anna Maria Schwemer writes: '[Aber] die Frau symbolisiert hier die Kirche, nicht die Messiasmutter; sie hat Kinder, die das Zeugnis Jesu haben und weiter vom Drachen verfolgt werden, sie hat aber auch ein zu Gott entrücktes Kind, das sind die zu Gott entrückten Märtyrer.' A. M. Schwemer, 'Prophet, Zeuge und Märtyrer: Zur Entstehung des Märtyrerbegriffs im frühesten Christentum', *ZThK* 96 (1999), pp. 320–50 (341). Aune, on the other hand, is more cautious in departing from the majority opinion as he does not state his opinion clearly. While Aune comments that: 'In its present context this statement probably refers to the ascension of Jesus, and that is clearly how Christian interpreters have traditionally understood the passage . . . .There are convincing reasons, however, for maintaining that this is a secondary application'. *Revelation 6–16*, p. 689. Yet, in later comments, Aune (p. 691) does not follow through his caution in identifying the male child as the Messiah as he reverts to the majority opinion that Rev. 12.5 speaks of 'the birth and ascension of the Messiah'.

84.   Rissi, *Time and History*, p. 40.

that take the male child literally. He forcefully argues thus: 'We need to be consistent in our interpretation. Is the woman literal? Is the sun literal? Is the moon literal? Are the stars literal? Is the dragon literal? The answer to these questions is a definite NO!!! Is the man–child literal then? Of course not!'[85]

The text of Rev. 12 gives scant evidence that it is speaking of some historical happening in the past. Ford correctly notes that, 'in our present text [Rev. 12.5] there seems to be no Christological reference'.[86] The man-child is born and straight away caught up to God and to his throne. Nothing of that sort fits the circumstances surrounding the birth of Christ in Bethlehem, a century before John penned Rev. 12. The symbolic language must be given its proper interpretation as figurative depiction of the safety accorded to the woman's son at birth. As the snatching of the male child to heaven coincides with the mother's escape to the wilderness for a period of 1,260 days, it is apparent that the son's escape to heaven takes place at the commencement of this three-and-a-half years' period.[87] To say that the birth of the male son is the birth of Christ and the catching up of the male son to God and to his throne is the ascension of Christ are plainly an interpretation which, in our view, finds no support from the text of Rev. 12 or elsewhere in Revelation.

85. P. Tan, *In Power and Glory* (Singapore, 1987), p. 116.
86. Ford, *Revelation*, p. 201.
87. The wilderness spoken of in 12.6, 14 is unlikely to be literally a wilderness but a symbol of refuge from spiritual dangers posed by the enemies of the church. D. Scheunemann says, 'Gereja itu dilindungi Tuhan di tempat padang gurun. Dunia bagi Gereja sebagai padang gurun. Di situ gereja itu terlindung.' (ET: The church is protected by God in the wilderness. To the church the world is a wilderness. The church is protected there [in the world]. D. Scheunemann, *Berita Kitab Wahyu* (Malang, Indonesia: Yayasan Penerbit Gandum Mas, 1997), p. 124. See also Shermaryahu Talmon, 'The "Desert Motif" in the Bible and in Qumran Literature', in A. Altmann (ed.), *Biblical Motifs* (Cambridge, Mass.: Harvard University Press, 1966), pp. 32–63. Mark McVann comments, 'the wilderness is a place where loyalty to God and transformation of status are tested'. M. McVann, 'Rituals of Status Transformation in Luke-Acts', in Jerome H. Neyrey (ed.), *The Social World of Luke-Acts* (Peabody, MA: Hendrickson, 1991), pp. 333–60 (349). It appears that the wilderness of Rev. 12.6, 14 is not only a symbol of refuge and nourishment but also of testing and trial as the serpent continues to persecute the woman in the wilderness (12.14). If the church is successful in overcoming the onslaught of the serpent in the wilderness for three-and-a-half years, the church is promised the kingdom of God (12.10; 11.15). For a study of the wilderness motif as a state of liminality, see B. J. Oropeza, Apostasy in the Wilderness: The Eschatological Warning of Paul to the Corinthian Congregation (Unpublished Ph.D. dissertation; University of Durham, 1998); *idem*, 'Apostasy in the Wilderness: Paul's Message to the Corinthians in a State of Eschatological Liminality', *JSNT* 75 (1999), pp. 49–68.

b. *Who rules with a rod of iron in Revelation 12.5?*

It is alleged that this male's destiny to rule the nations with a rod of iron must refer to the Messiah (cf. 19.15). If there is a future reference in Rev. 19.15 with regard to the Messiah, it must be secondary, as John's hearers have been told earlier (before Rev. 12) that it is the overcomer, the church who is given authority over the nations and to rule them with a rod of iron (2.26b–27a). Thus, to rule the nations with a rod of iron is firstly ascribed to the church as the community of overcomers. It is then plausible to view the male son of 12.5 as a symbol of the overcoming church now in the throes of tribulation (in the three-and-a-half years' period) but destined to rule the nations with a rod of iron. The mention of 'the rest of the woman's seed' (12.17) parallels the male son in 12.5 and further supports the corporate symbolism of the male son. As the male child and the woman's seed are symbols, they can both be seen to symbolize the church. The two contrasting fates of the woman's children in 12.5 and 12.17 represent the heavenly and earthly existence of the church: The catching up of the male son to God and his throne symbolizes the church protected and secure in its heavenly existence while the church on earth (symbolized by the woman's other offspring in 12.17) suffers from the wrath of the dragon's fury.[88]

The symbolism of the woman taken to refuge in the wilderness to be nourished and hidden from the face of the serpent tells of God's provision in the midst of famine and persecution, even if the economic system of the world is opened only to those marked with the mark or number of the beast (Rev. 13.17). Again, the paradox of suffering on earth is juxtaposed with the assurance of God's provision and protection depicted through the imagery of the woman being nourished in the wilderness and the male son being caught up to God and his throne. The theme of Rev. 12 (esp. 12.5–6, 13–14) is God's protection and provision for his people in conflict with God's arch foe, the devil throughout the three-and-a-half years' period of the great tribulation.[89]

Svigel discusses the identity of the male child of Rev. 12.5 at some length and his conclusions support our contention that the male child is a

---

88.   Yarbro Collins describes the woman of Rev. 12.5 as 'characterized both by power and by weakness.... Like her, they [John's audience] have a heavenly identity: they are God's kingdom in the world, God's priests (1.6); their names are written in the book of life (3.5). But they are also vulnerable: some have been arrested, some killed; their legal status in Roman empire is precarious. The rescue of the woman and her being nourished in the wilderness suggests that God will deliver them as God delivered the people of Israel from Egypt.' Yarbro Collins, 'Female Symbolism', p. 24.

89.   Svigel states thus: 'The vision of Revelation 12 focuses primarily on those who will be miraculously delivered from the wrath of the dragon, both the male child and the woman.' Svigel, 'The Apocalypse of John', p. 55.

symbolic reference for the corporate people of God.[90] He proposes five reasons why in his view the male child should be identified with 'the corporate body, the Church'.[91] First, Svigel notes that, 'Revelation 12 is a chapter of symbolic representations of reality, not a picture of the reality itself.... To take the male child, then, as only an individual man, Jesus of Nazareth, would be to break consistency within the symbols of Rev. 12.1–7.'[92] Second, Svigel argues that identifying the male son with the body of Christ best explains the allusion to Isa. 66.7.[93] Third, the corporate figure of the male son takes seriously the language of Rev. 12.5. Svigel argues that the language of 12.5 can hardly refer to the ascension of Christ. The verb ἁρπάζω (the passive ἡρπάσθη is used in 12.5) is never used of the ascension of Christ but according to Svigel, correctly in our view, is used here in 12.5 in the positive sense of rescue from attack.[94] Svigel writes thus:

> The vision clearly portrays imminent danger toward the male child from an intended attack by the dragon. Thus, the term ἁρπάζω here seems to be used in a rescue context, a context that is appropriate for the term.... Such a rescue nuance is utterly incompatible with the NT portrayal of the ascension of Christ. Jesus Christ was not snatched away to God to escape any threat, either real or imagined, either from Satan or from any other.[95]

Fourth, Svigel believes that identifying the male child as the body of Christ best harmonizes with Ps. 2.9. Svigel objects to commentators identifying the male child as Jesus Christ on the basis of Ps. 2.9 because like Resseguie, whom we have already quoted, Svigel notes that in Rev. 2.26–27, Ps. 2.9 is alluded to in reference not to Christ but to the overcomers (i.e. members of the church). The overcomers are promised authority over the nations and the right to rule them with a rod of iron (2.26–28).[96] Finally, Svigel

---

90. Svigel, 'The Apocalypse of John', pp. 59–73.

91. Svigel, 'The Apocalypse of John', p. 61.

92. Svigel, 'The Apocalypse of John', p. 60. Svigel (pp. 60–61) does not discount the fact that Jesus Christ may be included as part of the vision, only that he is not the primary identification. Svigel goes on to state that the body of Christ in union with Christ as the head of the body may be represented as the male child in Rev. 12.5.

93. Svigel, 'The Apocalypse of John', pp. 61–62.

94. Svigel, 'The Apocalypse of John', p. 63. Svigel lists the negative use of the verb ἁρπάζω to denote seizing or snatching the persons or property of others or robbery with violence. See the list of references in support of Svigel's view at p. 62 n. 117.

95. Svigel, 'The Apocalypse of John', p. 64.

96. Svigel, 'The Apocalypse of John', p. 65. Svigel (p. 66) reads Rev. 19.14–15 together with Rev. 2.26–28 and Rev. 12.5 which allude to Ps. 2.9 and argues that Rev. 12.5 'does not deny that something of Christ is in view, but contends that it is Christ in union with his spiritual body, the Church, that is being symbolized'. I am not convinced with Svigel's argument here that one can clearly say the male-child symbolism combines the representations of Christ's body with Christ in a way proposed by Svigel. By arguing that the male child may

observes that Rev. 12.5 contains no reference to the death and resurrection of the Messiah.[97] He refutes the idea of foreshortening or telescoping raised by some scholars[98] or interpreting the passage in a non-temporal and transcendental sense.[99] The notion of telescoping contends that the death and resurrection of Christ are implied in the snatching away of the male child, which we refute as baseless when the ascension of Christ allegedly symbolized by the catching up of the male child is in itself unproven. We should not ignore the fact that the snatching away of the male child coincides with the woman's escape to the wilderness for 1260 days (12.6). Svigel argues that any interpretation that ignores clear temporal indicators falls into the trap of 'spiritualizing out of time and space'.[100] Svigel notes that:

> The chronological indicators in Rev. 12.6 ('one thousand two hundred and sixty days') and 12.14 ('time, times, and half a time'), which are allusions to the same time elements in Dan. 12.7 and likely 9.27, . . . serve to anchor the vision to time-space events of the future.[101]

We agree with Svigel that the male son symbolizes the corporate body of Christ, the church. Further, we do not think that the text in Rev. 12.5 and its immediate context contains any reference to Christ. But Svigel fails to note a significant parallel in the Qumran hymns which would have strengthened his arguments further. We now turn to this.

c. *The Qumran Hymn (1QH 11.3–18)*

The imagery found in a Qumran hymn (1QH 11.3–18) is akin to that of Rev. 12.1–5. The said Qumran hymn supports the view that the woman who gives birth to a male son signifies the birth of the messianic community and not the Messiah. The community is rescued through the messianic woes or great tribulation as if having come to 'death's crashing waves' (1QH 11.8) but then is freed (1QH11.10). 1QH11.6–9 reads as follows:

> [line 6] . . . they regard me and set my life like a ship in the depths [of the sea]
> [line 7] And like a fortified city (besieged) [by the enemy].
> I am in distress like a woman in labor giving birth to her first child:

contain some reference to Christ, this line of reasoning appears to weaken Svigel's otherwise well-argued reasons why the male child should be identified with the corporate body of Christ, the Church.

97.   Svigel, 'The Apocalypse of John', p. 66.
98.   For example, Beale, *Revelation*, p. 639.
99.   Svigel (p. 66 n. 130) cites Beckwith, *Apocalypse*, pp. 616–17 as taking this view.
100. Svigel, 'The Apocalypse of John', p. 67.
101. Svigel, 'The Apocalypse of John', p. 68.

When her pangs have surged [line 8] and her birth canal has suffered torturous pain making a pregnant woman's first-born writhe, when children have come (to the brink of) death's crashing waves [line 9] and she who is pregnant with a man has pressed hard in her pain, (and) when amid death's crashing waves she delivers a male.[102]

Frechette has demonstrated, convincingly in our view, that lines 3 to 18 of 1QH 11 are structured in a chiasm.[103] It is interesting to note that 1QH 11.3–18 is similar in form and style (poetic) and also in structure (chiasm or concentric structure) to Rev. 12 as a whole. Revelation 12 and 1QH 11 both use symbolic language and imagery to depict the experiences of a community. Frechette states thus: 'The theological aim here [1QH 11] seems clear: to express in striking imagery the significance of the speaker's present trials. They are but precursors to God's great deliverance, which is imminent.'[104] In the said Qumran hymn, the images of a ship tossed in the sea, a city besieged and a woman with severe birthpangs function to depict the Qumran community under duress and facing great hostility from her enemies.[105]

We agree with Holm-Nielsen that the male child in the Qumran hymn (line 9) refers to the corporate Qumran community and not an individual.[106] Matthew Black comments thus: 'A closer study of this

---

102. This translation follows the one proposed by Frechette, 'Chiasm in 1QH 11.3–18', p. 73. For alternative translations, see G. Vermes, *An Introduction to the Complete Dead Sea Scrolls* (London: SCM, 1999), pp. 239–40; F. Garcia Martinez, *The Dead Sea Scrolls Translated: The Qumran Texts in English* (trans. Wilfred G. E. Watson; Leiden: E. J. Brill, 1994), pp. 331–32; W. Brownlee, *The Meaning of Qumran Scrolls for the Bible with Special Attention to the Book of Isaiah* (New York: Oxford University Press, 1964), p. 274; Svend Holm-Neilsen, *Hodayot: Psalms from Qumran* (Aarhus: Universitetsforlaget, 1960), p. 51. Holm-Neilsen discusses the Hebrew text of the said Hymn at pp. 52–60. Minor differences in translations do not affect our interpretation of the passage in relation to Rev. 12.1–5.

103. Frechette, 'Chiasm in 1QH 11.3–18', pp. 71–102. The chiastic pattern proposed by Frechette is set out at p. 73.

104. Frechette, 'Chiasm in 1QH 11.3–18', p. 79.

105. The speaker of the Hymn here is likely to be the Teacher of Righteousness, the leader of the Qumran community, speaking in a representative capacity of the community sufferings. This is not unlike some of the prophetic laments in the OT. According to Barbara B. Kaiser, the prophets on occasions 'become women when expressing the full intensity of the community's suffering'. Kaiser cites the example of Jeremiah in Jer. 4.19–26, whom she thinks, 'adopts the persona of a woman in childbirth to impel his audience to experience the intensity of the community's agony'. B. B. Kaiser, 'Poet as "Female Impersonator" ', pp. 166–67. Beverley Roberts Gaventa argues that Paul in Gal. 4.19 takes on a mother persona in relation to the Galatian Christians. Gaventa says, 'Paul is the mother. Here [Gal. 4.19] he is in the process of giving birth *again*'. B. R. Gaventa, 'Our Mother St. Paul: Toward the Recovery of a Neglected Theme', *PSB* 17 (1996), pp. 29–44 (33) [her emphasis]. See also *idem*, 'The Maternity of Paul: An Exegetical Study of Galatians 4:19', pp. 189–201.

106. Holm-Neilsen, *Hodayot*, pp. 55–56.

remarkable hymn, however, has yielded the quite certain result that it is not of the birth of any particular individual of which the author is speaking, but the birth of a whole community of people.'[107] Further, the imagery of a woman with birthpangs about to give birth to her male child speaks of the corporate sufferings of the people of God as part of 'the Messianic woes, i.e., signs and warnings of the dawn of the Messianic era'.[108] This is what we find in Rev. 12.1–17 where we have argued that the imagery of a woman in birthpangs and in torment to give birth to a male son in 12.1–5 points to the sufferings of the church and the conflict between the followers of the Messiah and the dragon (12.17) in the three-and-a-half years (12.6, 14) leading to the dawn of the kingdom of God and the authority of his Messiah (12.10; cf. 11.15).

In conclusion, we have shown that both the pictures of the woman and her male son are symbols for the corporate people of God, the church, depicting the church's existence on earth in different aspects. The woman clothed with the sun with twelve stars on her head and the moon at her feet speaks of the church's heavenly status as majestic and glorious but on earth, the church suffers persecution and tribulation in the last days as part of the messianic woes (symbolized by the birthpangs) leading to the dawn of the messianic era in the form of the kingdom of the Lord and his Messiah on earth. The male son being caught up to God and his throne symbolizes the security and ultimate salvation afforded to the church while the church (symbolized by the woman's other offspring) suffers persecution and martyrdom on earth on account of the warfare waged against it by the dragon.

d. *Why Michael and Not Christ in Revelation 12.7?*

The introduction of Michael the angel as the main protagonist against the dragon in the heavenly war in the pivotal section of Rev. 12.7–9 needs further explication. Davila considers that the passage in 12.7–9 originates from a Jewish source or a Jewish author. He writes: 'the war in heaven features Michael as the divine hero..., although we would expect Jesus to take on this role (as in Revelation 19) if the narrative were composed by a Christian'.[109] Davila's reasoning fails to convince us regarding the authorship of this passage as John the author of Revelation as a Christian prophet utilizes the Old Testament to present his essentially Christian message.[110] As a Jewish Christian, John sees the Old Testament as

---

107. M. Black, *The Scrolls and Christian Origins: Studies in the Jewish Background of the New Testament* (California: Scholars Press, 1961), p. 150.

108. Black, *The Scrolls and Christian Origins*, p. 61.

109. Davila, 'Melchizedek, Michael and War in Heaven', p. 265.

110. See our discussion on John's use of the Old Testament in Revelation in our introductory chapter.

belonging to the Christian community called the church, only that now the Old Testament is read in the light of the Christ event. It is hardly persuasive to argue that John could not have written a particular message just because we think that it is not sufficiently 'Christian'.[111] For example, we find Jude as a Christian writes about Michael striving with Satan concerning the body of Moses (Jude 9).

It is significant that the angel Michael is only found in Revelation in this passage in Rev. 12.7–12 as we have seen how influential the book of Daniel has been in Rev. 11–12 and also throughout Rev. 13.1–14.5 as we will demonstrate.[112] We have already indicated that Michael who fought alongside Gabriel against the princes of Persia and Greece (Dan. 10.13–21) provides a readily recognized background for the heavenly war between Michael and the dragon in Rev. 12.7.[113] More significantly, Michael appears for the last time in the book of Daniel as Israel's prince and protector during the onset of the most terrible tribulation to come upon the people of Israel:

> At that time Michael, the great prince, the protector of your people, shall arise. There shall be a time of anguish, such as has never occurred since nations first came into existence. But at that time your people shall be delivered, everyone who is found written in the book.
> (Dan. 12.1).

Likewise Michael appears as the victor over the dragon at the critical juncture of the life of the church signalling that the great tribulation is about to unfold (symbolized by the woman's birthpangs in 12.2) in the final eschatological period of three-and-a-half years (12.6, 14; cf. Dan. 12.7, 11–12).[114] In Rev. 12, Michael's conquest of Satan in heaven is

---

111.   David Frankfurter points out the difficulty in labelling John as a Christian as opposed to a Jew. He writes: '"Christian" would imply that his [John's] Jesus devotion somewhat displaces or preempts his Jewishness, a thesis derived not from the text but from prior theological assumptions.' D. Frankfurter, 'Jews or Not? Reconstructing the "Other" in Rev. 2.9 and 3.9', *HTR* 94 (2001), pp. 403–25 (408). See also Marshall, *Parables of War*, pp. 45–54.

112.   For a discussion on the different streams of traditions in biblical and extra-biblical materials on Michael the angel, see Percer, 'The War in Heaven', pp. 101–40.

113.   Phillips says: 'Perhaps the cosmic conflict of Revelation highlights the personalities alluded to in Daniel 10'. Phillips, 'Serpent Intertexts', p. 243.

114.   It is possible that John follows the order of events recorded in the Markan and Matthean 'Little Apocalypses' where the birthpangs or the beginning of sorrows are followed by the great tribulation (cf. Mt. 24.8, 15–21; Mk. 13.8, 14–19). An interesting parallel from 2 Esdras 16.37–39 (a much later text than Revelation) may illustrate the symbolism of a woman with birthpangs as signifying sufferings or beginning of sorrows that lead to greater calamities or tribulation: 'The calamities draw near, and are not delayed. Just as a pregnant woman, in the ninth month when her time of her delivery draws near, has great pains around her womb for two or three hours beforehand, but when the child comes forth from the womb, there will

reflected by the saints' victory over the enemy on earth (12.8, 11). This heaven/earth inter-penetration is not unlike the war fought by Joshua with the aid of the commander of Yahweh's armies in Josh. 10.10–12.[115] Thus with the assurance that Michael wages war on behalf of the saints in heaven, the saints on earth make war against the beasts (cf. Rev. 11.3–7; 13.7–10).

Apart from the influence of the book of Daniel (and possibly the book of Joshua), we suggest that the immediate context of Rev. 12.7–12 informs us why Michael is portrayed as the one engaged in warfare with the dragon and not Christ. First, it is a battle between angels: Michael with his angels and the dragon with his angels (v. 7). The dragon, as powerful as he is depicted in Rev. 12–13, is only an angel. He meets his match in his encounter with Michael an angel. Christ, on the other hand, is never portrayed as an angel.[116] Jesus Christ is seen as divine and worthy of worship alongside God.[117] Multitudes of angels with the throng of humanity worship God and the Lamb (5.11–14). On the other hand, the attempt by John to worship an angel is rebuffed (19.10). Jesus sends his angel to John and holds the seven angels in his right hand (symbolized by the seven stars) in 1.20–2.1 (cf. 3.1). Christ alone is deemed worthy to open the book with seven seals (5.5). Angels are agents of Christ or God who execute his commands in the unfolding of the seven seals, the seven trumpets and the seven bowls (8.2; 15.1). All these passages suggest that Jesus does not only possess a higher rank than angels, but also he is depicted as the object of worship by the angels. Wongso writes:

> Setan adalah makluk ciptaan, yang berada di bawah kekuasaan Kristus, maka setan dan para pengikutnya tidak layak untuk melawan Kristus; Kristus juga tidak mengizinkan setan untuk menentang Dia. Karena itu ia mengutus Mikhael dengan para pengikutnya melawan setan serta pengikutnya.[118]

---

not be a moment's delay, so the calamities will not delay in coming upon the earth, and the world will groan, and pains will seize it on every side.' See de Silva, *Introducing the Apocrypha*, pp. 349–51.

115. P. Miller writes: 'The general of Yahweh's heavenly armies had come to the general of Yahweh's earthly armies to indicate that the holy war against Canaan had begun and that the armies of heaven were joined with those of earth in the enterprise (cf. Josh. 10.10–12).' P. Miller, 'Cosmology and World Order in the Old Testament: The Divine Council as Cosmic-Political Symbol', *HBT* 9.2 (1987) 53–78 (58).

116. On Jesus Christ's relationship with the angels in the book of Revelation, see Peter R. Carrell, *Jesus and the Angels: Angelology and the Christology of the Apocalypse of John* (Cambridge: Cambridge University Press, 1997), pp. 119–28, 130–39.

117. See Bauckham, 'The Worship of Jesus', in *Climax of Prophecy*, pp. 118–49. Also Carrell, *Jesus and the Angels*, pp. 113–18, 222–23.

118. Wongso, *Kitab Wahyu*, p. 591.

(ET: Satan is a creature who is under the authority of Christ, so Satan and his followers are not worthy to fight Christ; Christ also will not permit Satan to contend with him. On this account, he sends Michael and his followers to fight Satan and his followers).

We agree with Wongso since John places Christ on the level of God. This is made evident as after the dragon's fall from heaven in 12.9, the declaration that the kingdom of God and the authority of his Christ has come (12.10; cf. 11.15) immediately follows. The dragon that is not strong enough for Michael, an angelic being, is surely beneath the power and authority of Christ. At no point in Revelation, does Christ deal directly with the dragon or Satan. Even the capture of the dragon before the commencement of the thousand-year reign of Christ is ascribed to an angel coming down from heaven (20.1–3).

Thus we conclude that the introduction of Michael at 12.7 is not out of place with what precedes and what follows in Rev. 12. The war that Michael undertakes against the dragon and the dragon's defeat is found in the pivotal section of Rev. 12. If the pivot is perceived as central to the plot of Rev. 12 as a whole, then the war in heaven and its aftermath determines how we interpret the other parallel textual units (vv. 1–4, 15–17 [EE'] and vv. 5–6, 13–14 [FF']) in the chapter. The defeat of the dragon by Michael in heaven which leads to the dragon's fall from heaven to earth (G) explains why the woman and her offspring suffer the dragon's fury on earth (EE'). Yet in between the narratives concerning the wars in heaven and on earth, the protection given to the woman and her male child is highlighted (FF').

If the chiastic pattern is recognized, then it is not necessary to posit either that the narrative in Rev. 12 derives from different sources or that the author is inept in inserting passages that appear to be disjointed or out of place. The plot of Rev. 12 read chiastically can now be summarized. The beginning of ch. 12 sets the scene for the impending conflict between the woman and the dragon. The metaphor of the birthpangs points to the time of messianic woes leading to the great tribulation before the new age breaks in. This eschatological period of three-and-a-half years of the great tribulation from the book of Daniel is alluded to in 12.6 (cf. v. 14). Not surprisingly Michael is immediately mentioned in the next verse (Rev. 12.7) alluding to Danielic time of anguish for the people of God when Michael stands up for God's people (Dan. 12.1). As in Daniel, John's readers are comforted to know that Michael stands up for them in this critical period.[119] Michael defeats the dragon, and the time the dragon has left on earth is the short time predetermined by God before the arrival of the kingdom of God and the authority of Christ (Rev. 12. 7–12). The escape of

---

119. In Dan. 12.1 (Theod.), it is explicitly stated that Michael will stand in the time of tribulation (καιρὸς θλίψεως).

the male child and the woman's refuge in the desert (vv. 5–6 and vv. 13–14) stated at the intersection of the conflict between the woman and the dragon on earth (vv. 1–4 and vv. 15–17), and the conflict between the dragon and Michael in heaven (vv. 7–12) highlights the protection afforded to the church in this time of great distress. Whatever happens in heaven or on earth, God is in control. He is able to protect his people. He sets the agenda and the timetable of how the events will unfold in historical place and time. When the time is up, God will intervene decisively and overturn the kingdom of the world and establish his kingdom that will last forever (12.10; cf. 11.15).[120]

We submit that any reader who is familiar with the book of Daniel and other relevant passages in the prophets alluded to by John in Rev. 12 can make sense of the flow and movement in the narrative of Rev. 12.1–17. As such, if the chiastic pattern is a plausible explanation for the structural arrangement of the literary units in Rev. 12, then it is not unreasonable to view ch. 12 as a literary unity composed by John with remarkable skill and creativity.

5. *The Career of the First Beast (Revelation 13.1–10)*

We have shown earlier that Rev. 12.18 functions as a transitional verse at the end of Rev. 12 and introduces Rev. 13 where the dragon now having come down to earth stands on the seashore calling first a beast from the sea (13.1) and another beast from the earth (13.11). By using the narrative marker 'I saw' at 13.1 and 13.11, John divides ch. 13 into two halves, the first half tells of the career of the first beast (vv. 1–10) and the second half of the chapter from vv. 11–18 depicts the deeds of the second beast. The two units of text are evidently parallel to one another:[121]

---

120. Frances Flannery Dailey says: 'God is the master of time, who has preordained the times, or periods, since God has preordained their content: "for he has weighed the age in the balance, and measured the times by measure, and numbered the times by number; and he will not move or arouse them until that measure is fulfilled" (4 Ezra 4.36–37). God is distinguished from humans in having control over time, as well as by possessing all knowledge of time: "You alone know the end of times before it has arrived" (*2 Bar.* 21.8; cf. 48.2; *1 En* 46.1ff; 1 QH 9.24).' F. F. Dailey, 'Non-Linear Time in Apocalyptic Texts: The Spiral Model', in *SBL Seminar Papers* (Atlanta: Scholars Press, 1999), pp. 231–45 (240).

121. Wongso states: 'Jikalau kita menyadari bahwa bagian ini ditulis dalam bentuk syair Ibrani, maka binatang yang keluar dari laut dalam Pasal 13 merupakan kalimat paralel dengan binatang yang keluar dari bumi'. (ET: If we realize that this section is written in Hebrew poetic style, then the beast that ascends from the sea in ch. 13 is parallel to the account of the beast that ascends from the earth). Wongso, *Kitab Wahyu*, p. 604. Lund remarks: 'Again the reader's attention is called to the literary structure of the chapter. The two halves of the chapter (vvs. 1–10 and vss. 11–18) match each other as two *medallions*.' Lund, *Studies in the Book of Revelation*, p. 148 (his emphasis).

A – The First Beast (13.1–10)
A' – The Second Beast (13.11–18)

We have also argued that 13.18, which purports to bring the narrative of the two beasts to a closure, does not provide the climax of the narrative bound together by the figure of three-and-a-half throughout Rev. 11–13 (cf. 11.2, 3, 9, 11; 12.6, 14; 13.5). Those that receive the mark of the beast on their right hands or on their foreheads (13.16–18) are contrasted with another group who have the name of the Lamb and the name of the Lamb's Father written on their foreheads (14.1–5).

The dragon that stands on the seashore in 12.18 is contrasted with John's vision of the Lamb standing on Mount Zion in 14.1. This, we propose, is John's way of framing the whole of ch. 13 with the vision of the dragon and the Lamb *standing* – the former on shifting sand of the sea and the latter on solid rock of God's holy mountain.[122] The animal imagery used for both protagonists enhances the contrast.[123] The ferocious dragon and the slaughtered Lamb engage in deadly conflict on earth through their emissaries – the two beasts of the dragon (Rev. 13) and the two witnesses of the Lamb (Rev. 11; cf. 11.4, 8). The beasts empowered by the dragon kill the witnesses and the saints (cf. 11.7; 13.7, 15), but in reality from a heavenly perspective the saints and the witnesses have conquered the

---

122. The seashore may be a metaphor for the instability and impermanence of the dragon's reign while the symbol of Mount Zion speaks of the permanence and stability of the Lamb's reign (cf. 11.15; 12.10). Sweet comments thus: 'Satan *stood* on the *sand*: up came a beast with *slaughtered* head, and another that looked *like a lamb*. But the Lamb is *standing* (as at 5.6) on the rock and, over against the multitude who take the *name* and *number* of the beast (13.16f), the army of twelve tribes of Israel stands foursquare with the *name* on their foreheads.' Sweet, *Revelation*, p. 221 (his emphasis). Likewise, Swete remarked, 'the Beast [the dragon] is on the sand, the Lamb on the rock'. Swete, *Apocalypse*, p. 177. Also Osborne notes that 'the idea of "standing" is a military metaphor and pictures the Lamb as a divine warrior ready to annihilate his enemy'. Osborne, *Revelation*, p. 525. This further strengthens our argument that the Lamb standing on Mount Zion in 14.1 depicts war.

123. For a study of the symbolism of animals, see McNamara, 'Symbolic Animals', pp. 211–23. McNamara (pp. 211–12) writes: 'The primordial force of evil (for instance the Dragon) could manifest itself in earthly rulers. In fact when prophets or sacred writers wrote to encourage their people in the face of foreign rulers or potentates, they could compare these with one or other of the primordial monsters.... In the biblical mindset it was commonly believed that the End-time would be similar to the beginning – the *Endzeit* to the *Urzeit*. As God was believed to have overcome or even destroyed his enemies, in particular his archenemy the Dragon, at the beginning, so too will he do in the new creation, when he makes all things new, when all things are made subject to Christ and God's kingdom has really come.' The contrast in Revelation between a murderous fiery dragon and a Lamb that was slaughtered could not be starker.

dragon and his cohorts through the blood of the Lamb and the word of their testimony (12.11).

a. *The Beast's Blasphemy against God (Revelation 13.1–6)*

On closer examination of the textual unit (13.1–10), it is submitted that it can be further divided into two sub-units of 13.1–6 and 13.7–10. These two subunits are composed with care using *inclusios* to frame the beginning and the end of the units respectively. The notion of 'blasphemy' in v. 1 (βλασφημίας) and v. 6 (βλασφημίας and βλασφημῆσαι) frames the first sub-unit, while the key phrase τῶν ἁγίων (the saints) mentioned in v. 7 and v. 10 frames the second sub-unit. It appears that the key activity of the beast in vv. 1–6 is directed against *heaven* and those who dwell in heaven while his activity in vv. 7–10 is directed against those who dwell on *earth* and the saints in particular. The structure of vv. 1–6 is chiastic in form:

A – [v. 1–2a] The Beast's head has blasphemous names (ἐπὶ τὰς κεφαλὰς αὐτοῦ ὀνόμα[τα] βλασφημίας). The Beast has a mouth like lion (τὸ στόμα αὐτοῦ ὡς στόμα λέοντος).

B – [v. 2b] The Dragon gave (ἔδωκεν) the Beast great authority (ἐξουσίαν μεγάλην).

C – [v. 3] The Beast has a death wound but is healed.

C' – [v. 3b] The world is amazed and follows after the Beast.

B' – [v. 4] The world worships the Dragon who has given (ἔδωκεν) the authority (τὴν ἐξουσίαν) to the Beast and the world worships the Beast.

A' – [vv. 5–6] The Beast is given a mouth saying great things and blasphemies (στόμα λαλοῦν μεγάλα καὶ βλασφημίας) and he opens his mouth to blaspheme God, blaspheming his name and his dwelling and those who dwell in heaven (καὶ ἤνοιξεν τὸ στόμα αὐτοῦ εἰς βλασφημίας πρὸς τὸν θεὸν βλασφημῆσαι τὸ ὄνομα αὐτοῦ καὶ τὴν σκηνὴν αὐτοῦ, τοὺς ἐν τῷ οὐρανῷ σκηνοῦντας).

The characteristics of the beast are described in 13.1–2. Verse 1 tells of John's vision of a beast rising from the sea which has ten horns and seven heads with the further description of ten crowns on the ten horns and blasphemous names on the heads:

κέρατα δέκα = ἐπὶ τῶν κεράτων αὐτοῦ δέκα διαδήματα
κεφαλὰς ἑπτὰ = ἐπὶ τὰς κεφαλὰς αὐτοῦ ὀνόμα[τα] βλασφημίας

It is interesting to note that in 13.1 the blasphemous names are mentioned last in the sentence. Similarly, the mouth of the beast which is said to be like a lion's is also mentioned last in v. 2 after the beast is depicted to be like a leopard and his feet like a bear's.[124] The blasphemy–mouth word order in A (vv. 1–2) is reversed in A' (vv. 5–6), where the beast's mouth is mentioned first as speaking great things which are blasphemies and specified as blaspheming against God, his dwelling and those who dwell in heaven. His goal is to blaspheme God, 'that is, to blaspheme his name and dwelling'.[125] The beast's nature as having blasphemous names and a lion's mouth in A (vv. 1–2) is reflected in A' (vv. 5–6) which depicts the beast being true to his nature – speaking blasphemous things against God and all that belongs to God.

Verse 2b should begin a new verse or sentence as the figure of the dragon is reintroduced since it last appears in 12.17–18 and here as one who gives the beast his power, his throne and great authority.[126] Verses 2b and 4 read as follows:

καὶ ἔδωκεν αὐτῷ ὁ δράκων τὴν δύναμιν αὐτοῦ καὶ τὸν θρόνον αὐτοῦ καὶ ἐξουσίαν μεγάλην (13.2b).
καὶ προσεκύνησαν τῷ δράκοντι, ὅτι ἔδωκεν τὴν ἐξουσίαν τῷ θηρίῳ, καὶ προσεκύνησαν τῷ θηρίῳ λέγοντες, Τίς ὅμοιος τῷ θηρίῳ καὶ τίς δύναται πολεμῆσαι μετ' αὐτοῦ; (13.4).

The mention of 'the authority' with the article in v. 4 refers to the indefinite 'great authority' in v. 2b. The giving of great authority by the dragon to

---

124. The order of the beasts that appear in Dan. 7.1–6 is first the lion, then the bear and third the leopard. In Rev. 13.1–2, John's stylistic preference to vary the order is again evident. He lists the beast as having the features of the first three beasts of Dan 7 but in a different order: leopard, bear, and lion.

125. Following Aune who remarks that, 'the infinitive βλασφημῆσαι is used epexegetically in order to specify precisely how the beast blasphemed God: "that is, to blaspheme his name and his dwelling."' Aune, *Revelation 6–16*, p. 717.

126. It is the dragon's action that is emphasized – giving the beast his power, his throne and great authority, in order that the dragon and his authorized representative the beast are both worshipped. It is thus difficult to agree with Aune's comments that: 'The dragon, while he played a central role in 12.1–17, is essentially extraneous to the narratives in 13.1–18 and is mentioned only in redactional additions (12.18; 13.2d, 4a).' Aune, *Revelation 6–16*, p. 735. From 12.18–13.4, the dragon plays a significant role as the persona that acts while the Beast remains in the background. Hence it is not correct as supposed by Aune that these dragon's activities or portrayal are merely 'redactional additions'. We have noted earlier that the dragon's standing in 12.18 is pivotal as it frames the whole literary unit from 12.18–14.5 climaxing in the Lamb standing on Mount Zion in 14.1. Even though the role of the dragon is not mentioned after v. 4, the whole of ch. 13 is coloured by the fact that it is the dragon standing on the seashore calling forth the beast from the sea and giving him all the authority necessary to enforce his will on an unwitting world. Moreover, it is implied that the second beast is also called forth from the earth (13.11) by the dragon and that the second beast's power to give spirit or breath to the image of the beast is Satanic as the clause 'it is given (ἐδόθη) to him to give life to the image of the beast' suggests (13.15a).

the beast in v. 2 is now seen as the reason why the world population worships the dragon and also the beast (v. 4).

Aune alleges that these verses (13.2b, 4a) which state that the dragon gives authority to the beast are 'redactional' and 'out of place'.[127] If the chiastic pattern of 13.1–6 is recognized as we propose, then it is clear that the verses as they stand in the text are not out of place but are composed according to a concentric and symmetrical pattern. Thus we conclude that verse 4a, 'They worshipped the dragon because he gave the authority to the beast' is a repetition of v. 2b, which together with other parallel pairs of AA' and CC' form a chiastic pattern.

The pivot of the chiasm (CC') now introduces a new but significant fact about the beast. One of his heads has been slaughtered to death (μίαν ἐκ τῶν κεφαλῶν αὐτοῦ ὡς ἐσφαγμένην εἰς θάνατον), but the blow of his death is miraculously healed, which occasions the world's amazement and allegiance to him.[128] 'The sea beast's recovery causes people to worship both the dragon and the beast, rather than God.'[129] That the world willingly follows and subjects itself to the beast is explained by John as due to the beast's remarkable recovery from a death wound. The pivot CC' focuses on the characterization of the beast as dying and living again. This characteristic of the beast constitutes the key identification for the beast as he is so described again in vv. 12 and 14.[130] The beast's death and resurrection is the reason for the world's marvel (13.3) which leads to the worship of the beast, a key motif in Rev. 13 (13.4, 8, 12).

b. *The Beast's War against the Saints (Revelation 13.7–10)*
The sub-unit of vv. 7–10 introduces a new phase in the beast's activity in that the beast makes war with the saints and conquers them (v. 7):

καὶ ἐδόθη αὐτῷ ποιῆσαι πόλεμον μετὰ <u>τῶν ἁγίων</u> καὶ νικῆσαι αὐτούς, καὶ ἐδόθη αὐτῷ ἐξουσία ἐπὶ πᾶσαν φυλὴν καὶ λαὸν καὶ γλῶσσαν καὶ ἔθνος.

The *inclusio* to this literary unit is seen at the end of v. 10 where John writes as follows:

127.   Aune, *Revelation 6–16*, p. 725.
128.   We agree with Beale that the translation of ὡς ἐσφαγμένην εἰς θάνατον must reflect the intent of the passage, namely that the beast in fact suffers death. Translations which have 'seemed to have a mortal wound' (RSV) or 'as if it had been slain' (NASB) or 'seemed to have received a death-blow' (NRSV) according to Beale, are 'misleading and makes it appear as if the beast only looked slain but was not'. Beale, *Revelation*, p. 689. Whether the head that was slaughtered referred to Nero the Roman Emperor will be discussed in detail in a later chapter.
129.   Thompson, *Revelation*, p. 139.
130.   We should note with Court that: 'The wound, although at first in 13.3 it is assigned to one of the heads of the beast, is later, in vv. 12 and 14, assigned to the beast itself.' Court, *Myth and History*, pp. 127–28.

Ὧδέ ἐστιν ἡ πομονὴ καὶ ἡ πίστις <u>τῶν ἁγίων</u>.

The sentence in v. 7 juxtaposes the beast's war against the saints with his authority over every tribe, people, tongue, and nation of the world. The division between these two groups of peoples is based on one fact – the worship of the beast by all the inhabitants of the earth: καὶ προσκυνήσουσιν αὐτὸν πάντες οἱ κατοικοῦντες ἐπὶ τῆς γῆς (v. 8a). Aune observes that the sudden switch from the aorist in the previous verse (ἐδόθη) to the future indicative (προσκυνήσουσιν) here, 'suggests that this part of the vision, the adoration of the beast by all the inhabitants of the earth, lies in the future.... This cannot then refer to any situation in the past or present but must refer to the eschatological future when the rule of the beast will include the entire known world.'[131]

The world population who worship the beast are said to be those whose names are not written in the book of life of the Lamb who was slain before the foundation of the world (v. 8b). Conversely, this implies that the saints are not part of the idolatrous world community for the saints have their names written in the slain Lamb's book of life. Contrast, antithesis and irony undergird this segment of text. The beast wars *with* the saints and vice versa. The saints wage war with the beast by refusing to worship him. Because of that, the beast makes war and conquers them. The saints 'lose' this battle with the beast and it seems that most of the saints suffer martyrdom following the example of the Lamb that was slain for his faithful witness. The irony is that those who appear to lose their lives (the saints) are those whose names are written in the book of life while those who hang on to their lives on earth are those who are not found in the book of life.[132]

The order of the blasphemy motif (vv. 1–6) followed by the war with the saints (vv. 7–10) is patterned after Daniel 7. The passage of Dan. 7.20–22 (Theod.) reads as follows:

[v. 20] καὶ περὶ τῶν κεράτων αὐτοῦ τῶν δέκα τῶν ἐν τῇ κεφαλῇ αὐτοῦ καὶ τοῦ ἑτέρου τοῦ ἀναβάντος καὶ ἐκτινάξαντος τῶν προτέρων τρία κέρας ἐκεῖνο ᾧ οἱ ὀφθαλμοὶ καὶ στόμα λαλοῦν μεγάλα καὶ ἡ ὅρασις αὐτοῦ μείζων τῶν λοιπῶν [v. 21] ἐθεώρουν καὶ τὸ κέρας ἐκεῖνο ἐποίει πόλεμον μετὰ τῶν ἁγίων καὶ ἴσχυσεν πρὸς αὐτούς [v. 22] ἕως οὗ ἦλθεν ὁ παλαιὸς τῶν ἡμερῶν καὶ τὸ κρίμα ἔδωκεν ἁγίοις ὑψίστου καὶ ὁ καιρὸς ἔφθασεν καὶ τὴν βασιλείαν κατέσχον οἱ ἅγιοι

---

131. Aune, *Revelation 6–16*, p. 746. We will discuss in a later chapter the identity of the beast (13.1–10), and will argue that the beast rules in the eschatological period of three-and-a-half years (13.5), which coincides with the prophetic testimony of the two witnesses for 1260 days (cf. 11.3) before the kingdom of God comes (11.15; 12.10).

132. This paradox is best summed up by a Johannine Jesus saying: 'Those who love their life lose it, and those who hate their life in this world will keep it for eternal life' (Jn. 12.25). How the saints wage war against the beast will be discussed further in a later chapter.

The clause στόμα λαλοῦν μεγάλα in Rev. 13.5 is exactly identical to the clause found in Dan. 7.20. Similarly, the clause ποιῆσαι πόλεμον μετὰ τῶν ἁγίων in Rev. 13.7 is almost identical to the clause ἐποίει πόλεμον μετὰ τῶν ἁγίων in Dan. 7.21 (Theod.). Structurally, the unit of Rev. 13.1–10 follows Dan. 7.20–22. Making war against the saints comes after the blasphemy motif in Dan. 7.20–21, which order is followed in Rev. 13.1–10, making the dependence of the latter on the former almost certain.[133] Even the period of the beast's activity for forty-two months in Rev. 13.5b is also an allusion to the Danielic period of 'a time, times, and half a time' (Dan. 7.25) which appears in the context of the fourth beast's persecution against the saints in Dan. 7.19–28. It is also apparent that the beast's attack on the saints lasting the pre-determined period of 42 months (Rev. 13.5) will give way to the possession of the kingdom by the saints (Dan. 7.22; cf. Rev. 11.15; 12.10).

The literary unit of 13.1–10 on the beast concludes with a call to whoever has an ear to hear (vv. 9–10):

> [v. 9] Εἴ τις ἔχει οὖς ἀκουσάτω.
> [v. 10] εἴ τις εἰς αἰχμαλωσίαν,
> εἰς αἰχμαλωσίαν ὑπάγει·
> εἴ τις ἐν μαχαίρῃ ἀποκτανθῆναι αὐτὸν
> ἐν μαχαίρῃ ἀποκτανθῆναι.[134]
> ῟Ωδέ ἐστιν ἡ ὑπομονὴ καὶ ἡ πίστις τῶν ἁγίων.

The first 'if' in the beginning of verse 9 introduces the cryptic apocalyptic saying: 'If anyone has an ear, let him hear' stressing the need for added insight and understanding of what follows.[135] The emphasis on τις repeated thrice calls on John's audience to take personal responsibility. The events brought about by the beast's rule will have an effect on *everyone*. None will escape the 'fate' determined for him or her. The apocalyptic feature of pre-determinism appears strong here and is applied by John relentlessly. Those who worship the beast are those whose names are not in the Lamb's book of life (13.8). Conversely, if the person's name (τὸ ὄνομα αὐτου) is in the

---

133. So Beale, *Revelation*, p. 698. See also Beale, 'The Use of Daniel', pp. 129–54.

134. We should note that the couplet εἴ τις ἐν μαχαίρῃ ἀποκτανθῆναι αὐτὸν ἐν μαχαίρῃ ἀποκτανθῆναι adopted by NA27 is attested only by Codex Alexandrinus. For a discussion of variant readings in various Greek manuscripts, see Bruce Metzger, *A Textual Commentary on the Greek New Testament: A Companion Volume to the United Bible Societies' Greek New Testament* (New York: United Bible Societies, 3rd edn, 1971), pp. 749–50; Aune, *Revelation 6–16*, pp. 749–50; Thomas, *Revelation 8–22*, pp. 170–71; Charles, *Revelation Vol. 1*, p. 356; Anne-Marit Enroth, 'The Hearing Formula in the Book of Revelation', *NTS* 36 (1990), pp. 598–608 (606).

135. The hearing formula of 13.9 is found on seven previous occasions in the seven letters to the seven churches (2.7, 11, 17, 29; 3.6, 12, 22). For a discussion on how this hearing formula functions in Revelation, see Enroth, 'The Hearing Formula'.

book of life, his or her destiny is set out in verse 9 – captivity or death. The singular use of 'his name' in 13.8 and τις 'anyone' speaks directly and urgently to each and every individual to side with the Lamb and reject the worship of the beast. The corporate concern gives way to individual choice. To be counted among the community of the saints, each and everyone has to make up his or her own mind. Hence the saying: 'If anyone has an ear, let him hear.' To follow the Lamb and reject idolatry is to be numbered among the saints. Persecution and possible martyrdom await those who dare 'fight against the beast' (13.4). But the war waged by the saints is not by sword but by their endurance and their faith. Thompson says: 'The gist of the admonition [vv. 9–10] seems to be to endure in faith rather than fight with the sword.'[136] The statement: 'Here is endurance and faith of the *saints*' (13.10b) functions as John's concluding exhortation in this part of the text and appropriately closes off the unit of 13.7–10 as a response to verse 7 where the beast is said to make war and conquer the *saints*.

6. *The Career of the Second Beast (Revelation 13.11–18)*

The literary unit of Rev. 13.11–18 is a mirror image of 13.1–10. Similar phraseology begins and ends the pericope. The clause Καὶ εἶδον ἄλλο θηρίον ἀναβαῖνον ἐκ τῆς γῆς in 13.11 parallels that of 13.1: Καὶ εἶδον ἐκ τῆς θαλάσσης θηρίον ἀναβαῖνον. The exhortatory conclusion in 13.10, beginning with the words Ὧδέ ἐστιν are matched by parallel catchphrase with the same expression Ὧδε...ἐστίν in 13.18. Rhetorically, this identical ring composition pattern for both textual units creates parallel panels. The literary technique of narrative parallelism such as we have here, invites the readers to interpret the two panels of texts together probing for connections either by way of similarity or contrast as each panel is allowed to shed light on the other for overall understanding of the whole. Enroth is right when she comments that: 'John has constructed these images [the two beasts] symmetrically so that both resemble each other.'[137]

The phrase ἄλλο θηρίον in 13.11 distinguishes the beast of vv. 11–18 from the beast of 13.1–10. Yet by using a nearly identical form of introduction to the narrative of the second beast, John's readers are invited to interpret the beast from the earth rhetorically in the light (or under the shadow) of the first beast. Before we examine how the narrative of the second beast develops, we will first set out the parallels in a table as follows:

136. Thompson, *Revelation*, p. 140.
137. Enroth, 'The Hearing Formula', p. 305.

The First Beast	The Second Beast
1. Ascends from the sea (v. 1a).	Ascends from the earth (v. 11a).
2. Has ten horns on its heads (v. 1b).	Has two horns like a lamb (v. 11b).
3. The Dragon gives authority to the 1st Beast (v. 2).	The 2nd Beast exercises the 1st Beast's authority (v. 12a).
4. The world is amazed at the 1st Beast whose fatal wound is healed (v. 3).	The 2nd Beast makes the earth worships the 1st Beast whose fatal wound is healed (v. 12b).
5. The 1st Beast speaks arrogant words (v. 5).	The 2nd Beast speaks to deceive (v. 14).
6. The 1st Beast makes war and conquers the saints (v. 7).	The 2nd Beast kills those who refuse to worship the 1st Beast (v. 15).

As shown in the table above, verbal and conceptual parallels abound between the narratives of the two beasts. The second beast also has horns; but only two compared with the ten horns of the first beast. The primary characterization of the second beast is that it *speaks* like a dragon though outwardly its horns are those of a lamb. The reference to a lamb and a dragon cannot be fortuitous. The second beast appears to be like *the Lamb* but its nature takes after *the Dragon*. The duplicity and deceit of the second beast is brought out by John by utilizing two contrasting metaphors 'lamb' and 'dragon' in a paradoxical fashion. Speaking like a dragon implies that the dragon has given ability to the second beast to speak just as the dragon gives his power, throne and great authority to the first beast (13.2). Just as the first beast exercises the authority of the dragon, the second beast exercises the authority of the first beast (13.12b).

Verse 12a, καὶ τὴν ἐξουσίαν τοῦ πρώτου θηρίου πᾶσαν ποιεῖ ἐνώπιον αὐτοῦ, sets out the primary role of the second beast. It is to exercise *all* the authority of the first beast. We have seen that the phrase 'before (ἐνώπιον) him' denotes authorization and service as the two witnesses are said to stand before (ἐνώπιον) the Lord of the earth (cf. 11.4). Thus the second beast is authorized to exercise the authority of his patron and to be at his service. Barr says: 'This beast functions as minister to the first.'[138] The second beast is the lieutenant or executive of the first beast as the former ensures the rule of the latter is made effective worldwide.

A series of ποιέω verbs defines the deeds of the second beast. First, he 'exercises' (ποιεῖ) the authority of the first beast (13.12a). Second, he 'makes' (ποιεῖ) the earth worship the first beast (13.12b). Third, he 'performs' (ποιεῖ) great signs (13.13a) and fourth, he 'makes' (ποιῇ) fire

---

138. Barr, *Tales of the End*, p. 128.

come down from heaven on the earth in the sight of the inhabitants of the earth (13.13b). By using this verb ποιέω, a parallelism is created in verse 12:

A – καὶ τὴν ἐξουσίαν τοῦ πρώτου θηρίου πᾶσαν ποιεῖ ἐνώπιον αὐτοῦ,
A' – καὶ ποιεῖ τὴν γῆν καὶ τοὺς ἐν αὐτῇ κατοικοῦντας ἵνα προσκυνήσουσιν τὸ θηρίον τὸ πρῶτον, οὗ ἐθεραπεύθη ἡ πληγὴ τοῦ θανάτου αὐτοῦ.

The parallelism is carefully crafted stylistically. The mention of the first beast and then the verb ποιεῖ towards the end of line A is reversed by the location of the verb ποιεῖ in the beginning of line A' followed by the mention of the first beast. Bauckham remarks that it is 'typical of John's stylistic habit of varying the precise form of expressions he repeats'.[139] Here John reverses the word order in τοῦ πρώτου θηρίου to τὸ θηρίον τὸ πρῶτον for chiastic effect. Rhetorically, the outcome of the exercise of the authority by the second beast on behalf of the first beast (A) is that the world is made to worship the latter whose plague of death is healed (A').

Verse 13 of Rev. 13 likewise is structured in a parallelism:

A – καὶ ποιεῖ σημεῖα μεγάλα,
A' – ἵνα καὶ πῦρ ποιῇ ἐκ τοῦ οὐρανοῦ καταβαίνειν εἰς τὴν γῆν ἐνώπιον τῶν ἀνθρώπων

The second beast performs great signs (A), the most spectacular of which is to call fire from heaven to earth for public viewing (A'). The parallelism functions rhetorically by beginning with the general and plural (σημεῖα μεγάλα) and shifting to focus on the particular and singular (πῦρ) in A'. Again, John rarely misses an occasion to produce his preference for chiasm. The phrase σημεῖα μεγάλα comes after the verb ποιεῖ in line A but is reversed in the line A'. There πῦρ is emphatic and comes before the verb and such variation in word order, in our view, serves a dual purpose here. First, the fiery sign is given prominence and emphasis by its position in the text. Second, the change in word order produces the chiastic effect when read together with line A. The 'great signs' in line A are specified as supremely manifested in calling down *fire* from heaven.

The second beast is a charismatic figure. He impresses people with marvellous signs. He seeks publicity and uses fame as his *modus operandi*. These signs are *done* to deceive the world populace as the second beast tells them to make an image of the first beast 'who had the plague of sword but lived (ὃς ἔχει τὴν πληγὴν τῆς μαχαίρης καὶ ἔζησεν)' (13.14). Thus verse 14 is a key verse in the unit of 13.11–18 as it functions to sum up the activity of the second beast and acts as a transition to the second part of the second

---

139. Bauckham, *Climax of Prophecy*, p. 394.

beast's activity. In particular the verb λέγων in verse 14 must be given its
due in the characterization of the second beast as one who 'spoke (ἐλάλει)
as a dragon' in the introduction of 13.11. Verse 14 is the only place in
13.11–18 that has the second beast in the act of speaking. He speaks to
deceive as the parallelism in verse 14 shows:

A – καὶ πλανᾷ τοὺς κατοικοῦντας ἐπὶ τῆς γῆς διὰ τὰ σημεῖα ἃ ἐδόθη αὐτῷ
ποιῆσαι ἐνώπιον τοῦ θηρίου,
A' – λέγων τοῖς κατοικοῦσιν ἐπὶ τῆς γῆς ποιῆσαι εἰκόνα τῷ θηρίῳ, ὃς ἔχει τὴν
πληγὴν τῆς μαχαίρης καὶ ἔζησεν.

That the second beast deceives the inhabitants of the earth on account of
the signs which he does (ποιῆσαι) before the beast (A), corresponds to line
A' where the second beast tells the inhabitants of the earth to make an
image for the beast (A').

Not only can the second beast call fire from heaven but he gives 'breath'
(πνεῦμα) to the image of the beast so that the said image speaks and he
causes (ποιήσῃ) all who refuse to worship the image to be killed (v. 15).
'The beast will tolerate no dissent from his self-deification.'[140] The clause
Καὶ ἐδόθη αὐτῷ δοῦναι at the beginning of verse 15 highlights the fact that
the power to give breath to the image is derivative, for the Greek text
translates literally as 'And it was given to it to give'. The implication here
appears to be that the dragon is the source behind the power of the second
beast who is enabled (by the dragon) to activate the lifeless image of the
first beast into a speaking one. It seems that the second beast's hubris
reaches its height. 'The apparent quickening of the image of the beast is the
supreme claim to divine power: the claim to be able to create life as God
himself does.'[141]

The same verb ποιέω in 13.16, used for the eighth and final time in 13.11–
18, introduces the final sub-unit of 13.16–18 where the second beast causes
all to receive a mark on their right hands or on their foreheads. The text of
13.16–17 reads as follows:

[v. 16] Also it causes (ποιεῖ) all, both small and great, both rich and
poor, both free and slave, to be marked on the right hand or the
forehead, [v. 17] so that no one can buy or sell who does not have the
mark, that is, the name of the beast or the number of its name.

'The beast enforces a unity that cuts across all social lines.'[142] Global unity
is founded on economic control and regularization. The mark is described
as the mark of the name of the (first) beast or the number of his name

140. Bauckham, *Theology*, p. 93.
141. Ladd, *Revelation*, p. 184.
142. Keener, *Revelation*, p. 352.

(τὸ χάραγμα τὸ ὄνομα τοῦ θηρίου ἢ τὸν ἀριθμὸν τοῦ ὀνόματος αὐτοῦ) without which none can buy nor sell (v. 17).

Verse 18 as we have seen consists of a paraenesis which is parallel to the exhortation in 13.10. We have noted that vv. 10 and 18 function to close off the narrative on the first and second beasts respectively and divide ch. 13 of Revelation into two halves. The closing call for wisdom in v. 18 summons John's readers to exercise insight and discernment in deciphering (ψηφισάτω) the number of the beast for it is a number of a person (man) and his number is 666. It appears that this call for wisdom is not purely an intellectual exercise out of curiosity in solving a riddle or a cryptic symbol but John's exhortatory directive is intended to be practical, for only those who can figure out the number of the beast can make the choice of rejecting the same.

Read in parallel with 13.1–10, the first beast's activity pales beside that of the second beast. The first beast's only active engagement is his speaking of arrogant words and blasphemies (vv. 5–6) and warring and conquering the saints (13.7). Otherwise he remains a static personality portrayed either as an object of awe (13.3) or worship (13.4). Even his rule over the earth is given in an indirect manner: 'It was given to him to have authority (ἐξουσία ποιῆσαι) for forty-two months' (13.5). Eight times the verb ποιέω is used in reference to the second beast (cf. 13.12 [x2], 13 [x2], 14 [x2], 15, 16] compared to twice in the case of the first beast (cf. 13.5, 7).[143] It appears that the emphasis lies in the second beast's active engagement vis-à-vis the first beast, the world populace, and those who oppose his designs.

In the light of the above, we can draw a number of conclusions. First, the two beasts are given distinct identities and roles, though their careers are seen to intertwine in a remarkable way. They are both agents of the dragon. 'These two agents act in distinctive, but complementary, ways in the dragon's war against the woman's children.'[144] Second, the first beast acts mainly through the agency of the second beast as the latter exercises the authority of the former. More so the second beast actively secures the world's submission to the first beast not only politically but also religiously in that the whole world worships the first beast. Third, the second beast enforces a total monopoly of the global economy in which none can participate unless one receives the mark of the first beast. The picture painted by John in vivid terms is that no area of societal life is untouched

143. Prigent notes: 'the surprising frequency of the verb "to do": not less than 8 instances, of which the second beast is 7 times the subject of the verb. In the eighth case (13.14) the subject is men who make an image of the first beast, but even there it is at his command. We should therefore not be surprised at finding in this paragraph a particular insistence on the concrete nature of an activity that is so clearly highlighted.' Prigent, *Commentary on the Apocalypse*, p. 399.

144. Barr, *Tales of the End*, p. 126.

by the beasts; in fact their dominion is total and absolute over all aspects of life and survival – politics, military, religion, and the economy.

7. *The Concluding Unit (Revelation 14.1–5)*

Barr notes that: 'In this scene of the two beasts John paints an almost pessimistic picture.'[145] But John rarely ends on a pessimistic note. The textual unit which begins at 12.18 does not end at 13.18 but continues on to 14.5. The text of 14.1 reads thus: 'Then I looked, and there was the Lamb, standing on Mount Zion! And with him were one hundred forty-four thousand who had his name and his Father's name written on their foreheads.'

Beasley-Murray writes:

> Every feature of the opening sentence of the first oracle [in Rev. 14] stands in contrast to what is written in ch. 13. The persecuted Christians are no longer at the mercy of their enemies but stand triumphant on Mount Zion, the place of deliverance and divine glory.... They are in the presence of the Lamb instead of being dragged before his caricature, the 'lamb' of the Devil. They bear on their foreheads the name of the Lamb and his Father's name instead of the mark (= the name) of the beast.[146]

The structural pattern for this segment of text proposed by Schüssler Fiorenza is quoted in full as follows:[147]

1. *Vision:* 14.1 describes the 144,000 with the Lamb on Mount Zion.
2. *Audition:* 14.2–3 announce the voice from heaven and the choral song before the throne of God which none could learn except the 144,000 and
3. *Explanation:* 14.4–5 identify the 144,000 with a four-fold characterization: they are virgins, followers of the Lamb, a first fruit, and blameless.

This textual unit which portrays the triumph of the people of God and their characteristics as worthy followers of the Lamb appropriately closes off the segment of text which narrates the suffering and martyrdom of the saints at the hands of the two beasts of Rev. 13.[148] We will examine the

145. Barr, *Tales of the End*, p. 127.
146. Beasley-Murray, *Revelation*, pp. 221–22.
147. Schüssler Fiorenza, *Book of Revelation*, p. 181.
148. Schüssler Fiorenza says: 'The literary context of this segment is also clear: the 144,000 around the Lamb on Mount Zion are the anti-image of the beast and its followers which were depicted in the preceding chapter (Rev. 13).' Schüssler Fiorenza, *Book of Revelation*, p. 181.

meaning of 14.1–5 in detail when we compare this unit with 11.1–2 in the next chapter.

8. *Summary*

We have conducted a literary-structural analysis of Rev. 12.1–14.5 and have demonstrated that Rev. 11 is integrally linked to Rev. 12. In particular, Rev. 11.19 links ch. 11 with ch. 12. Thus D (11.15–19) is linked to 12.1–4 (E). We have demonstrated that Rev. 12 is structured in a chiastic pattern where vv. 1–4 (E) and vv. 5–6 (F) correspond to vv. 15–17 (E') and vv. 13–14 (F') respectively with the pivot at vv. 7–12 (G). We have discussed the meaning and significance of the signs in Rev. 12 and how the chiastic pattern informs the plot of ch. 12. We have also shown that 12.18 functions to conclude 12.1–17 and introduce the literary unit in 13.1–14.5. Thus 12.18 links E' (12.15–17) with D' (13.1–6). The literary unit in 13.1–14.5 is divided into four main units of 13.1–6 (D'), 13.7–10 (C'), 13.11–18 (B'), and 14.1–5 (A'). The task of the next chapter will be to show how Rev. 11 corresponds to Rev. 13.1–14.5 (ABCDD'C'B'A') yielding a macro-chiastic structure for the textual unit of 11.1–14.5 in the form of ABCDEFGF'E'D'C'B'A'. We will also test the validity of the said macro-chiasm using Blomberg's nine criteria.

Chapter 5

THE ABCDD'C'B'A' PARALLELS: TESTING THE MACRO-CHIASM

1. *Introduction*

In the previous chapter, we have shown that the macro-chiasm we propose for Rev. 11.1–14.5 becomes evident in Rev. 12 which is structured in an EFGF'E' pattern. We will demonstrate in this chapter that Rev. 11 corresponds to 13.1–14.5 in the form of an ABCDD'C'B'A' pattern. We will also seek to establish that the AA' pair rings the macro-chiasm of 11.1–14.5 in an *inclusio*. It is our purpose to demonstrate that Rev. 11.1–2 (A) sets the scene for the appearance of the two witnesses and their encounter with the two beasts leading to the establishment of God's kingdom on earth (BB', CC', DD'). In the final section of this chapter we will test the proposed macro chiasm of ABCDEFGF'E'D'C'B'A' using Blomberg's nine criteria.

2. *The AA' Parallels (11.1–2 = 14.1–5):*
The Inclusio of Revelation 11.1–14.5

In this section, we will show that Rev. 11.1–2 corresponds to 14.1–5. We will argue that the lexical terms 'the temple of God' and 'the holy city' in 11.1–2 are intended to parallel the phrase 'Mount Zion' in 14.1. Conceptually, it is our contention that the warfare depicted in 11.2 as the trampling upon the holy city by the nations mirrors the image of warfare waged by the Lamb as he stands on Mount Zion. We will argue that the nations gathered for war in Jerusalem, the holy city (11.2), will be defeated when the Lamb returns to Mount Zion (14.1). Further, both 11.1–2 and 14.1–5 depict worship on earth – the worshippers in the temple precinct and the 144,000 on Mount Zion. Together with the key phrases 'the temple of God' and 'the holy city' in 11.1–2 that correspond to 'Mount Zion' in 14.1, the warfare and worship motifs in 11.1–2 and 14.1–5 serve as *inclusio* for the literary unit of 11.1–14.5.

The Temple of God / The Holy City = Mount Zion
We have seen that repetitions of key words and themes or word-pairs are often used to serve as *inclusios* to envelope literary units. In Rev. 11.1–2 we have the key phrases, 'the temple of God' and 'the holy city', which in our opinion, are repeated in 14.1 with the phrase, 'Mount Zion'.[1] 'Mount Zion' is a unique term in Revelation as it only appears here. Thus, the usage of this rare word 'Mount Zion' in 14.1 is sudden and distinctive and likely intended to mark the structural unit as proposed. As Butterworth observes, 'common words are less likely to be used to mark structure than rare and distinctive words'.[2] Very few modern scholars have recognized this connection, though as early as Henry Alford's *Greek New Testament* the link between 'the temple of God' (11.1) and 'Mount Zion' (14.1) was noted.[3] Thomas comments that: 'The mention of Mount Zion recalls the vision beginning at 11.1, because the temple was on that mount.'[4] It is important to note that the temple is closely associated with Jerusalem, the holy city. Often the Temple and Jerusalem can be used interchangeably.[5] Bratcher remarks that Mount Zion referred to 'the hill (Mount Moriah) on which the temple was built, and also the whole city of Jerusalem'.[6] The main reason that Jerusalem is called the *holy* city is that God's *holy* temple is located there.

---

1. The Temple and the city are often used as a parallel word pair. See Daniel E. Fleming, ' "House"/"City": An Unrecognized Parallel Word Pair', *JBL* 105 (1986), pp. 689–97. Fleming (p. 690) has shown that the word 'house' is often used interchangeably with the word 'temple' as far as the house/temple of God is concerned and that in Ps. 127.1, the word pair 'house'/'city' is actually the 'temple'/'city' pair.

2. Butterworth, *Structure and the Book of Zechariah*, p. 29. While repetition of key words or concepts functions to provide the *leitmotiv* of a literary unit, unique and rare words at the beginning and the end of a said unit are often used to ring the textual unit in an *inclusio*. See our earlier discussion on the nature and function of the *inclusio* in our introductory chapter.

3. H. Alford, *Greek New Testament* Vol. 4 (London: Longmans, 1903), p. 684.

4. Thomas, *Revelation 8–22*, p. 189.

5. In the discussion whether the term, 'house' refers to the temple or the city of Jerusalem in Mt. 23.38, D. Allison and W. Davies argue that though the term 'house' refers immediately to the temple, it includes the city as well. The authors further add that: 'Jewish texts – such as Ezra and 2 Baruch – do not always distinguish between the temple and the capital. Quite often the one implies the other and there are indiscriminate transitions from temple to city or *vice versa*, so that one may often speak of their identification.' D. Allison and W. Davies, *A Critical and Exegetical Commentary on the Gospel According to Matthew* (ICC, 3 vols.; Edinburgh: T & T Clark, 1997), 3:322. Also Warren Carter remarks that the 'house' in Mt. 23.38 probably means both temple and city, 'since the two are closely interconnected (21.1–27) and both were destroyed in 70 CE.' W. Carter, 'Matthew 23.37–39', *Int* 54 (2000), pp. 66–68 (67).

6. Bratcher, *A Translator's Guide to the Revelation to John*, p. 114. B. Gärtner remarks: ' "Mount Zion (ὄρος Σιών)", refers to the rock on which stood Jerusalem, the holy city, the dwelling place of God.' B. Gärtner, *The Temple and Community in Qumran and the New Testament*, p. 90.

The first mention of Jerusalem as Zion is found in 2 Sam. 5.6–7 where the conquest of Jerusalem by David is narrated as follows:[7]

> [v.6] The king and his men marched to *Jerusalem* against the Jebusites, the inhabitants of the land, who said to David, 'You will not come in here, even the blind and the lame will turn you back' – thinking, 'David cannot come in here.' [v.7] Nevertheless David took the stronghold of *Zion*, which is now the city of David.

During David's reign, Jerusalem is known as Zion as shown in the parallelism above. Later in Solomon's rule, Mount Zion became the site for the Temple of God. The Ark of the Covenant was then moved 'from Zion on the south hill of Jerusalem to the "citadel"... to the new city extension to the north. The whole city would now on be referred to as *Zion* (2 Ki. 19.31; Ps. 9.11.).'[8] However, the temple being located on the highest spot in the city, also came to be known as Mount Zion. Mount Zion subsequently became a synonym for Jerusalem. Craigie observed that Mount Zion was 'both the city and the temple'.[9] Likewise, E. W. Heaton remarked that: 'Mount Zion... came to be used as a name for the Temple, which was built on the same ridge (Ps. 74.2), and for the city of Jerusalem (Ps. 51.18; Isa. 10.24).'[10]

In the book of Isaiah, we find the mention of 'Mount Zion and Jerusalem' as a word-pair: 'When the Lord has finished all his work on Mount Zion and on Jerusalem, he will punish the arrogant boasting of the king of Assyria and his haughty pride' (Isa. 10.12). And also in Isa. 24.23, the Lord is said to reign 'on Mount Zion and in Jerusalem': 'Then the moon will be abashed, and the sun ashamed; for the LORD of hosts will reign on Mount Zion and in Jerusalem, and before his elders he will manifest his glory.'[11]

---

7.   Beale writes: 'The fuller name "Mount Zion" in distinction to "Zion" by itself occurs only nineteen times in the OT, at least nine of which allude to a remnant being saved, in connection with either God's name (the remnant being saved for the sake of God's name or by calling on his name) or God's sovereign rule, sometimes both (2 Kgs. 19.31; Isa. 4.2–3; 10.12, 20; 37.30–32; Joel 2.32 [= 3:5]; Obad. 17, 21; Mic. 4.5–8; Pss. 48.2, 10–11; 74.2, 7...).' Beale, *Revelation*, pp. 731–32. We shall see that the idea of 12,000 from every tribe of the sons of Israel is consonant with the idea of the remnant appearing in the texts cited by Beale above.

8.   D. Wiseman, *1 and 2 Kings* (Leicester: Inter-Varsity Press, 1993), p. 209.

9.   Craigie, *Psalms 1–50*, p. 355.

10.   E. W. Heaton, *The Hebrew Kingdoms* (New Clarendon Bible; Old Testament Vol. 3; Oxford: Oxford University Press, 1968), p. 157.

11.   It is interesting to note that at the announcement of the reign of God and his Christ in Rev 11.15 the twenty-four *elders* are said to worship God and affirm the kingship of God, probably an allusion to Isa. 24.23 where the Lord will manifest his glory before his elders and reign on Mount Zion and Jerusalem. For a discussion on the role of elders in Isa. 24.23, see Timothy M. Willis, 'Yahweh's Elders (Isa 24.23): Senior Officials of the Divine Court', *ZAW* 103–104 (1991–2), pp. 375–85.

In both passages above, Mount Zion is probably used as a synonym for Jerusalem. If Mount Zion and Jerusalem are not completely identical terms, then Mount Zion refers specifically to the Temple.

The book of Joel also provides a number of interesting parallels similar to those in the book of Isaiah. First, the lexical terms 'Mount Zion' and 'Jerusalem' appear to be synonymous and are used together in a number of eschatological passages in Joel. Secondly, these passages speak of various events happening on or before the 'great and terrible day of the Lord' or 'in those days', giving these texts a decidedly eschatological bent:

> [v. 30] I will show portents in the heavens and on the earth, blood and fire and columns of smoke. [v. 31] The sun shall be turned to darkness, and the moon to blood, before the great and terrible day of the LORD comes. [v. 32] Then everyone who calls on the name of the LORD shall be saved; for *in Mount Zion and in Jerusalem* there shall be those who escape, as the LORD has said, and among the survivors shall be those whom the LORD calls.
> (Joel 2.30–32; MT – Joel 3.3–5).

> [v. 16] The LORD roars from Zion, and utters his voice from Jerusalem, and the heavens and the earth shake. But the LORD is a refuge for his people, a stronghold for the people of Israel. [v. 17] So you shall know that I, the LORD your God, dwell in Zion, my holy mountain. And Jerusalem shall be holy, and strangers shall never again pass through it.
> (Joel 3.16–17; MT – Joel 4.16–17).

In Joel, the deliverance of the remnant of God's people happens on Mount Zion and in Jerusalem (Joel 2.32). Beale aptly notes that, ' "*Mount Zion*" appears to occur when emphasis is placed on the deliverance of a remnant *and* their protection in the mountain fortress'.[12] Likewise in Rev. 14.1–5, God's victory and deliverance of his people are seen on Mount Zion. The 144,000 described as those redeemed from the earth (14.4) now stand with the Lamb on Mount Zion (14.1).

The book of Daniel gives further support that the holy city is identified with Mount Zion. Here, as in Isaiah, Jerusalem is specifically called the

---

12. Beale, *Revelation*, p. 735 (his emphasis). Cook writes: 'The proto-apocalyptic pericopes of Joel 3 and 4 (Eng: 2.28–3.21) are as strongly rooted in Zion theology as the rest of the book. Joel 3.5 (Eng: 2.32) stresses Mount Zion as the locale where YHWH will provide for survivors of the end-time judgment.' Cook, *Prophecy and Apocalypticism*, p. 192. For a general discussion on the symbolism of Mount Zion, see R. S. Hess and G. J. Wenham (eds.), *Zion, City of our God* (Grand Rapids: Eerdmans, 1999); Ben C. Ollenburger, *Zion the City of the Great King: A Theological Symbol of the Jerusalem Cult* (Sheffield: Sheffield Academic Press, 1987); A. H. Mandey, *Kitab Wahyu: Nubuatan Akhir Zaman* [ET: The book of Revelation: End-time Prophecy] (Jakarta: Mimery Press, 1999), pp. 248–59.

holy city. Daniel 9.16 mentions the city together with the holy mountain, thus identifying them as one entity:

מֵעִירְךָ יְרוּשָׁלַ͏ִם הַר־קָרְשֶׁךָ (MT)
τῆς πόλεώς σου Ἰερουσαλημ ὄρους ἁγίου σου (LXX and Theod.)

This syntactic construction can be translated as 'your city, Jerusalem your holy mountain'. Further in Dan. 9.24 (LXX), the holy city of the MT is translated as τὴν πόλιν Σιων, which identifies the holy city Jerusalem with Mount Zion. Vogel observes that 'your city Jerusalem' in 9.16 is referred to as '"your holy mountain" and is parallel to "your sanctuary" in vs. 17'.[13] All these suggest that 'the holy city' in Rev. 11.2 is also used by John in addition to 'the temple of God' to refer to 'Mount Zion' in 14.1 making these key terms serve as rings around the literary unit of 11.1–14.5.[14]

13.   W. Vogel, *The Cultic Motif in Space and Time*, p. 150. After a detailed study of the various terms used to designate the temple, holy mountain, holy city, Jerusalem and Zion in the book of Daniel, Vogel (p. 154) concludes that: 'The subsequent interchangeableness of designations that are so frequent throughout the OT testifies to the fact that a multifaceted and yet unified theology of a Jerusalem cult tradition had developed. The holy mountain, Zion, the temple, and the city had all the same theological function, namely to evoke the presence of Yahweh and his constant call to worship him. This interchangeableness with other designations, especially with "Zion" and "holy mountain", also strongly suggests that the core element of Jerusalem's significance was the temple and its function as a cultic centre.'

14.   We should note that the word-pair, 'temple-Mount Zion' is used constantly in 1 Maccabees. The mention of 'Mount Zion' together with the 'temple' or 'sanctuary' appears in 1 Macc. 4.36–40 as follows: '[v. 36] Then Judas and his brothers said, 'See, our enemies are crushed; let us go up to cleanse *the sanctuary* and dedicate it.' [v. 37] So all the army assembled and went up to *Mount Zion*. [v. 38] There they saw **the sanctuary** desolate, **the altar** profaned, and the gates burned. In **the courts** they saw bushes sprung up as in a thicket, or as on one of the mountains. They saw also the chambers of the priests in ruins. [v. 39] Then **they tore their clothes and mourned with great lamentation**; they sprinkled themselves with ashes [v. 40] and fell face down on the ground. And when the signal was given with the trumpets, they cried out to Heaven.' In this passage, Mount Zion is clearly linked to the sanctuary and the altar. This strongly suggests that Mount Zion is used here for the Temple Mount. Yaron Z. Eliav has shown that Christians in the second century C.E. still referred to Mount Zion as the Temple Mount. Y. Eliav, '"Interpretive Citation" in the Epistle of *Barnabas* and the Early Christian Attitude towards the Temple Mount', in Craig A. Evans (ed.), *The Interpretation of Scripture in Early Judaism and Christianity: Studies in Language and Tradition* (JSPSup, 33; Sheffield: Sheffield Academic Press, 2000), pp. 353–62. The Maccabean passage quoted above is significant in a number of points. First, the altar is mentioned alongside the temple, a concept which we also find in Rev. 11.1. Moreover, this Maccabean passage narrates the scene of Judas Maccabees and his armies assembling and going up to Mount Zion to cleanse it (1 Macc. 4.36–37). We are not suggesting John of Revelation knew of these Maccabean passages or was influenced by them. Nevertheless, the theme of desolation of Mount Zion by foreign forces and later reclamation by war is akin to the theme we find in Rev. 11.1–2 and 14.1. In 14.1–5, the Lamb and his army of 144,000 standing on Mount Zion could be seen as reclaiming the temple and the city that have been trodden down by the nations (11.2). Other passages in 1 Maccabees treat Mount Zion and the temple interchangeably as 1 Macc. 6.48, 51

In summary, we have seen that throughout various parts of the Bible since the reigns of Kings David and Solomon especially in the Psalms and the Prophets, the temple of God or God's house often appear together with Zion or Mount Zion as a word-pair or in parallel lines. Likewise, the temple is often closely identified with Jerusalem, the holy city.[15] Thus we can conclude that these lexical terms – the temple, the holy city, Jerusalem, Mount Zion are all closely related lexemes, which are often exploited as parallel epithets or word-pairs in parallelism in biblical texts. Hence, a strong case can be made that John could have used the key phrases, 'the temple of God' and 'the holy city' in Rev. 11.1–2 to begin a major section of the book of Revelation which is concluded with the reference to Mount Zion in 14.1.

Measured and Written

We have argued that the measuring of the worshippers in Rev. 11.1 signifies their spiritual protection from forces of evil but not from physical harm. We submit that the worshippers who are *measured* correspond to the 144,000 on whose foreheads are *written* the names of the Lamb and the Lamb's Father (14.1). In the book of Revelation, John uses a number of images to speak of the security of believers. In Rev. 12, we have seen that the protection of the church is symbolized by the male son being caught up to the throne of God (12.5) or the woman being taken into the wilderness (12.6, 14). Prior to Rev. 14, John has depicted the 144,000 as being sealed (7.2–8) before the great tribulation ensues (7.14). The sealing of the 144,000 protects them from the plagues of the seven trumpets (cf. 9.4) but does not appear to protect them physically from the persecution unleashed by the beast during the great tribulation. Schüssler Fiorenza writes:

and 7.33 show: 'The soldiers of the king's army went up to Jerusalem against them, and the king encamped in Judea and at **Mount Zion**.... Then he encamped before **the sanctuary** for many days. He set up siege towers, engines of war to throw fire and stones, machines to shoot arrows, and catapults (1 Macc. 6.48, 51).... After these events Nicanor went up to **Mount Zion**. Some of the priests from **the sanctuary** and some of the elders of the people came out to greet him peaceably and to show him the burnt offering that was being offered for the king (1 Macc. 7.33).' The context of these passages shows conceptual links with Rev. 11.1–2. The armies of nations trample upon the temple and the holy city in Rev. 11.1–2 while in 1 Maccabees, Antiochus Epiphanes' armies waged war against Mount Zion and the sanctuary. In 2 Maccabees, Judas successfully defeated the Antiochus' armies and restored the temple (2 Macc. 10.1–8). In Rev. 14.1, the Lamb stands on Mount Zion and appears victorious over the nations that wage war against Jerusalem (cf. 11.1–2).

15. Similar notions can be deduced from the New Testament as well: 'Then the devil took him [Jesus] to *the holy city* and placed him on the pinnacle of *the temple*' (Mt. 4.5). Also Matthew speaks of the curtain of the temple being torn and the saints being raised from the dead and entering the holy city (Mt. 27.51–53). Hebrews 12.22 mentions Mount Zion, the city of the living God and the heavenly Jerusalem as almost interchangeable terms.

If the figure of the woman in ch. 12 is an image of the messianic community, then like the vision of the sealing of the 144,000 (chap. 7) and the prophetic sign-action of measuring the priestly worshippers (11.1–2), it promises that Christians will be eschatologically protected and saved, although the war waged with the beast might harm and even kill them (12.13–17).[16]

In our analysis of 13.1–14.5, we have seen that the 144,000 in 14.1 is contrasted with those on whose right hands or foreheads are written the mark of the beast (13.16). This suggests that the writing of the name of the Lamb and the Lamb's Father on the foreheads of the 144,000 is designed to protect them from spiritual apostasy, i.e., against accepting the mark or writing of the name of the beast. Again, the imagery signifies spiritual protection for the 144,000 as in the period of beast's persecution many of the saints will suffer martyrdom (13.7–10, 15). Thus we conclude that conceptually the terms 'sealed', 'measured', and 'written on their foreheads' when they are used with respect to believers, have essentially the same meaning. Coupled with the fact that only in 11.1–2 and 14.1–5 is worship portrayed taking place on earth, the depiction of the worshippers in God's temple who are measured (11.1) corresponds to the vision of the 144,000 who have the names of the Lamb and the Lamb's Father written on their foreheads (14.1), making these two scenes function as another literary marker ringing the unit of 11.1–14.5.[17]

The Conceptual Linkage between Revelation 11.1–2 and 14.1–5

We have argued above that John has used synonymous or related key words and phrases in Rev. 11.1–2 and 14.1–5 respectively as markers or boundaries, which envelope the whole literary unit in between. These two sub-units also share similar themes which, if proven, will strengthen our case that 11.1–2 does indeed correspond to 14.1–5. We have noted in some detail that 11.1–2 speaks of a military attack by the nations against the holy city, Jerusalem. If the scene in 11.1–2 depicts warfare, can we say the

---

16. Schüssler Fiorenza, *Revelation: Vision of a Just World*, p. 81. Beale identifies the sealing of the 144,000 in 7.2–8 with the names of God and the Lamb on the foreheads of the 144,000 in 14.1. See Beale, *Revelation*, pp. 410–12. Commenting on 11.1, Beale (pp. 558–59) writes: 'The significance of the measuring means that their salvation is secured, despite physical harm that they suffer. This is a further development of the "sealing" in 7.2–8 and is consistent with *1 Enoch* 61.1–5, where the angelic "measuring" of the righteous elect ensures that their faith will be strengthened and not destroyed, despite the destruction of their bodies.' Speaking of the measuring of worshippers in Rev. 11.1, Charles writes: 'It does not signify preservation from physical destruction, but the spiritual preservation . . .' Charles, *Revelation* Vol. 1, p. 276.

17. Aune writes, 'the worshipers in the temple of God [Rev. 11.1], in my view, are analogous to the 144,000 whom God has sealed [Rev. 7.3–8; cf. 14.1–5]'. Aune, *Revelation 6–16*, p. 598.

same for 14.1–5 as we have suggested in passing? If 14.1–5 does portray warfare, then our contention that 11.1–2 and 14.1–5 are reverse images of each other utilized by John to ring the literary unit in between is further established. The war motif in 14.1–5 will be examined in detail.

a. *The War on Mount Zion (Revelation 14.1–5)*
Bauckham has shown conclusively that the scene depicted in 14.1–5 is best understood as warfare – the 144,000 male virgins consecrated for holy war.[18] Seen in this light, the 144,000 on Mount Zion are the Lamb's standing army. Read in conjunction with the depiction of wars in 17.14 and 19.11ff between the nations under the leadership of the beast and the Lamb and his army, a case can be made that the scene on Mount Zion of the Lamb and his 144,000 companions also depicts warfare.[19] Mount Zion, the earthly Jerusalem according to Bauckham, is 'the place of the messianic

18. Bauckham writes: 'The much misunderstood reference to virginity of the 144,000 (14.4a) belongs to the image of an army. The followers of Christ are symbolized as an army of adult males who, following the ancient requirement of ritual purity for those who fight in holy war (Deut. 23.9–14; 1 Sam. 21.5; 2 Sam 11.9–13; 1 QM 7.3–6).' Bauckham, *Theology*, p. 78. See also Caird, *Revelation*, pp. 178–79. Whether the 144,000 actively fight in the battle here in 14.1 or elsewhere in 17.14 and 19.14 is debatable. Yarbro Collins discusses 17.14 and 14.1–5 and comments: 'Rev. 17.14 hints that the followers of the Lamb might have an active role in the eschatological battle.... If the 144,000 are thought of as fighting alongside the angels in the final battle, the purity regulations relating to the holy war would explain the otherwise rather isolated comment in 14.4 – that they have not defiled themselves with women. These two passages (17.14, 14.4) seem to show that the author was aware of the tradition that the elect would fight in the last battle. But they are just glimpses of such an idea and are not at all emphasized. The dominant conception of the final holy war is similar to that of Daniel, where the people will participate in the new order brought about by the eschatological battle but not in the battle itself.' Yarbro Collins, *Cosmology and Eschatology*, p. 207. John A. Wood comments: 'Christ alone defeats the enemies in the final stage of the eschatological conflict.' J. A. Wood, *Perspectives on War in the Bible* (Macon, GA: Mercer University Press, 1998), p. 75. However, the two passages noted by Yarbro Collins speak of warfare when the Lamb returns from heaven to earth. This does not negate the fact that the elect do not take part in physical warfare during their time on earth, namely during the three-and-a-half years leading to the End. We believe that it is not necessary to draw a sharp distinction whether the 144,000 or the elect take an active role in warfare or are merely participants of the victory of the Lamb in the final eschatological battle depicted in 14.1, 17.14, and 19.14. The mere fact that the elect are seen to be together with the Lamb at the final battle in these passages shows that they are considered as part of the Lamb's army that defeats the enemies and implicitly at least John sees them as taking part in the last battle under the Lamb's leadership. During the three-and-a-half years leading to the End, the elect fight against the enemies with the words of their testimony.

19. For a discussion on the subject of Christ as the Divine Warrior in Rev. 19.11–21, see Thomas B. Slater, 'The Image of the Divine Warrior in Revelation 19.11–21', in *idem*, *Christ and Community: A Social-Historical Study of the Christology of Revelation* (JSNTSup, 178; Sheffield: Sheffield Academic Press, 1999), pp. 209–35; Carrell, *Jesus and the Angels*, pp. 196–219.

king's triumph over the hostile nations (Ps. 2.6)'.[20] Aune remarks that, 'The Lamb, a thinly veiled metaphor for the Davidic Messiah, is depicted as standing in order to suggest that he functions as a warrior prepared to destroy his enemies.'[21]

One difficulty remains with the proposal that 14.1–5 depicts warlike imagery. Is it likely to be a depiction of war on Mount Zion, since the Lamb's entourage is accompanied by singing of a new song with musical chorus as the text of 14.1–5 explicitly states? Old Testament imagery of warfare on Mount Zion is found in number of places. We will examine the texts, which in our opinion probably influenced John in his depiction of holy war on Mount Zion. First, Isa. 31.4–5 reads as follows:

> [v. 4] For thus the LORD said to me, As a lion or a young lion growls over its prey, and when a band of shepherds is called out against it – is not terrified by their shouting or daunted at their noise, so the LORD of hosts will come down to *fight upon Mount Zion* and upon its hill. [v. 5] Like birds hovering overhead, so the LORD of hosts will *protect Jerusalem*; he will protect and deliver it, he will spare and rescue it.

Isaiah 31.4 states that Yahweh will fight upon Mount Zion and in parallel with verse 5, will protect Jerusalem. It is apparent that Yahweh descends on Mount Zion to fight *for* Jerusalem as the parallel, 'protecting Jerusalem' shows.[22] Here we find Mount Zion/Jerusalem parallel in the specific context of Yahweh's warfare on Mount Zion. More interestingly, the warfare of Isa. 31.4–5 is preceded by the description of the Lord's arm

---

20. Bauckham, *Theology*, p. 78. Some commentators (e.g. Mounce, *Revelation*, p. 265) interpret Mount Zion of Rev. 14.1 as the heavenly Mount Zion or New Jerusalem on the ground that Rev. 14.2–5 depicts praise before the throne of God in heaven. Admittedly Rev. 14.2 shifts the scene to heaven as John narrates what he 'heard', namely harpists playing their harps before the throne, but it is not clear whether the 144,000 as distinguished from the harpists are also in heaven. Aune correctly notes that: 'v. 2 introduces an audition of a voice in heaven, clearly distinguishing between Mount Zion and heaven'. Aune, *Revelation 6–16*, p. 803. In our view, concurring with Aune, we take the 144,000 of Rev. 14.1 as standing with the Lamb on earthly Mount Zion. The Lamb and the 144,000 have returned to earth to vanquish the hostile nations and set up God's kingdom on earth.

21. Aune, *Revelation 6–16*, p. 803. On the Lamb's 144,000 associates in 14.1, Beasley-Murray states as follows: 'The persecuted Christians are no longer at the mercy of their enemies but stand triumphant on Mount Zion, the place of deliverance and divine glory (Joel 2.32; cf. Isa. 24.21ff., Mic. 4.6).' Beasley-Murray, *Revelation*, p. 221.

22. R. E. Clements' argument that Yahweh fights *against* Mount Zion is unconvincing given the parallel, 'protecting Jerusalem' which he believed to be a 'Josianic redactor's elaboration'. See R. E. Clements, *Isaiah 1–39* (NCB; Grand Rapids: Eerdmans, 1980), p. 257. J. Oswalt's view that, 'v. 5 which is clearly positive, follows directly on v. 4 with no break and no evidence of any intended contrast' is preferable as in Isa. 31.4–5 the picture is given of one coming to rescue Mount Zion/Jerusalem. J. Oswalt, *Isaiah 1–39* (NICOT; Grand Rapids: Eerdmans, 1986), p. 574.

descending in a flame of consuming fire to strike Assyria with the rod, 'to the sound of *timbrels and lyres*; battling with brandished arm he will fight with him' (Isa. 30.32). While there is some dispute over how Isa. 30.32 is related to the following pericope in Isa. 31.4–5, it is nevertheless clear that we have the juxtaposition of two images of Yahweh in warfare – one accompanied by music (Isa. 30.32) and the other on Mount Zion (Isa. 31.4–5). It is not unreasonable to suggest that John of Revelation could have alluded to Isa. 30.32–31.5 as part of the Old Testament background for depicting warfare on Mount Zion accompanied by the sound of music and song in Rev. 14.1–5.

Similarly in Psalm 149, the people of God are called upon to sing a *new song* (Ps. 149.1; cf. Rev. 14.3) to Yahweh and execute vengeance on the nations by singing the high praises of God with two-edged swords in their hands.[23] The relevant texts read as follows:

> [v. 1] Sing to the LORD a *new song* . . .

> [v. 5] Let them praise his name with dancing, making melody to him with *tambourine and lyre* . . . . Let the *faithful* exult in glory; let them sing for joy on their couches. [v. 6] Let the high praises of God be in their throats and two-edged swords in their hands, [v. 7] to execute vengeance on the nations and punishment on the peoples, [v. 8] to bind their kings with fetters and their nobles with chains of iron, [v. 9] to execute on them the judgment decreed. This is glory for all his *faithful ones*. Praise the LORD!

Psalm 149.6 is structured in a parallelism whereby the phrase 'the high praises' corresponds to 'two-edged sword' and the phrase, 'in their throats' mirrors the phrase 'in their hands'. Prinsloo notes that the parallel structure can be set out as follows:[24]

רוֹמְמוֹת אֵל בִּגְרוֹנָם וְחֶרֶב פִּיפִיּוֹת בְּיָדָם

b   a   b   a

---

23. See Willem S. Prinsloo, 'Psalm 149: Praise Yahweh with Tambourine and Two-edged Sword', *ZAW* 109 (1997), pp. 395–407. Psalm 149 speaks of warfare of the saints against the Lord's enemies accompanied by the praise of Yahweh and singing a new song. Prinsloo (p. 397 n. 10) also lists numerous authors who consider Psalm 149 to be an eschatological hymn. If the Psalm is an eschatological hymn as many have suggested, then it is quite probable that Ps. 149 is alluded to in the eschatological scene of war in Rev. 14.1–5. Longman and Reid remark that: 'Psalm 149 may have also found its original setting in the march toward battle.' Longman and Reid, *God is a Warrior*, p. 39.

24. Prinsloo, 'Psalm 149', p. 405.

He concludes:

> The parallel structure of [vs.] 6 and its hinging function emphasize that
> the praise for Yahweh and the punishment of the nations are actually
> two sides of the same coin.... They [the faithful] present praise to
> Yahweh and they carry out the punishment of the nations (on behalf of
> Yahweh).[25]

The above portion of Psalm 149 shows that singing a new song and making
music with timbrel and lyre are connected with what Prinsloo calls, 'the
punishment by Yahweh...described in a dramatic and hyperbolic manner
using the terminology of the Holy War'.[26] The above scenario enhances
our case for the portrayal of an eschatological war in Rev. 14.1–5. The
144,000 under the leadership of the Lamb engage in warfare accompanied
by music and singing of a new song.[27] Thus a strong case can be made that
Rev. 14.1–5 alludes to both Ps. 149 and Isa. 30.31–31.5 that combine the
motif of singing a new song with fighting on Mount Zion.[28]

Brueggemann has shown how extensively Revelation alludes to the book
of Psalms in general and Psalm 2 in particular.[29] A number of other
scholars also have noted the importance of Psalm 2 in the book of
Revelation. Bauckham remarks that: 'One of John's key Old Testament
texts, allusions to which run throughout Revelation, is Psalm 2.'[30] The
Psalmist in the voice of Yahweh declares that, 'I have set my king on Zion,
my holy hill' (Ps. 2.6). This heavenly pronouncement comes as a result of
nations conspiring and plotting and earthly kings gathering together
against Yahweh and his Anointed for the purpose of war (Ps. 2.1–3). God
from heaven responds in wrath (Ps. 2.5; cf. Rev. 11.18; 6.19; 15.1, 8). The
nations' trampling on the holy city in Rev. 11.2 is not far from the imagery

---

25.   Prinsloo, 'Psalm 149', p. 406.

26.   Prinsloo, 'Psalm 149', p. 406.

27.   Note also that the Lamb's companions in war (17.14) are called *faithful* echoing the
faithful ones in Ps. 149.9. According to Prinsloo, these faithful ones (חֲסִידִים) 'act as Yahweh's
assistants in carrying out punishment'. Prinsloo, 'Psalm 149', p. 405. Apart from Ps. 149, the
singing of a *new song* is often associated with victory in warfare when Yahweh intervenes to
rescue his people from their enemies (cf. Pss. 96.1, 9–13; 98.1–9; 144.9–11). Longman and
Reid remark thus: 'It appears that "new song" is a technical term for victory song. These
songs celebrate the new situation brought about by God's warring activity.' Longman and
Reid, *God is a Warrior*, p. 45.

28.   It is our view that most commentators fail to discern the OT background for Rev.
14.1–5 as they do not take sufficient account of the fact that the passage of 14.1–5 juxtaposes
warfare with worship or more precisely the celebration of the victory of war in worship.

29.   Brueggemann, 'The Use of the Psalter in John's Apocalypse', pp. 23, 70.

30.   Bauckham, *Theology*, p. 69. Also John Court writes: 'Psalm 2 is good example of these
ideas, not least because it is applied by John in ch. 11 and elsewhere (see 2.27; compare Acts
4.25–26).' J. Court, *Revelation* (New Testament Guides; Sheffield: Sheffield Academic Press,
1994), p. 50.

of Ps. 2.1–3 with the end result that the Lamb stands in triumph on Mount Zion (Rev. 14.1). Beasley-Murray's comment is apt: 'It is not impossible that Ps. 2.6 was in John's mind at this point. The heathen have raged. God's king stands on his holy hill victorious.'[31] Ford concludes as follows:

> It is from Zion that God as a warrior roaring from heaven comes to judge (Jer. 25.30) and to Zion he will return (Ezek. 43.1–9). Here he will inaugurate his eschatological reign; Isa. 24.23; 52.7; Obad. 21; Micah 4.7; Zeph. 3.16; Zech. 14.9; Pss. 146.10, 149.2. It is here that the Anointed is established (Ps. 2.6) and receives the sceptre as an investiture of power (Ps. 90.2).... This will be a place of entry for the messianic ruler (Zech. 9.9) and the rallying point of the remnant – the nucleus of the messianic restoration.[32]

The allusions to Ps. 2 in Rev. 11.1–2 and 14.1–5 are hard to dispute. Revelation 11.1–2 and 14.1–5 are set in the context of warfare of the nations against the holy city with the eventual triumph of the Lamb on Mount Zion echoing the conflict of nations' motif and the Lord's decree that his anointed is appointed the rightful king on Zion in Ps. 2. The beast of Rev. 13 leads the world in rebellion against the Lord (13.3–6), and blasphemes God, his dwelling and those who dwell in heaven. This echoes the conspiracy, rebellion and blasphemous speech of the kings of the earth in Ps. 2.1–3 with the Lord reacting in mocking laughter from heaven and threats of punishment of the rebellious kings with his wrath and fury (Ps. 2.4–5). We surmise that Rev. 14.1–5 read in the light of the texts of Isa. 31.4–5 and Ps. 2 provides polyvalent imagery. The Lamb engages in warfare on Mount Zion (Isa. 31) and triumphs over the kings of the earth and rules from Mount Zion (Ps. 2).[33]

---

31. Beasley-Murray, *Revelation*, p. 222. Craigie thought the Psalm reflected 'movement and completeness; beginning with the tumultuous nations, then the poet turns to God before concluding (chiastically) with the nations again, now subdued rather than tumultuous'. Craigie, *Psalms 1–50*, p. 65.

32. Ford, *Revelation*, p. 240.

33. Robert Cole aptly notes that Ps. 2 (v. 10) speaks of the idea that 'all kings of the earth are brought into submission to the chosen king ruling on Mt Zion'. R. Cole, 'An Integrated Reading of Psalms 1 and 2', *JSOT* 98 (2002), pp. 75–88 (76). Other Psalms also speak of God's intervention on Mount Zion. For example, Ps. 76.2–4 speaks of God's abode in Salem (Jerusalem) and his dwelling in Zion where he broke the flashing arrows, the shield, the sword, and the weapons of war (cf. Ps. 48). Mitchell Dahood translates Ps. 76.3 as follows: 'His covert was in Salem, and his lair in Zion.' M. Dahood, *Psalms II* (New York: Doubleday, 1986), p. 217. Dahood (p. 218) notes that the Psalmist conceives of God as the Lion of Judah. Speaking of Ps 76.2, Marvin Tate says: 'The imagery of God in v. 2 is that of a leonine warrior who takes a powerful position in Jerusalem on Mount Zion and defeats all attackers.' M. Tate, *Psalms 51–100* (WBC; Dallas: Word, 1990), p. 261. Ps. 74, on the other hand, laments the desolation of the Mount Zion and prays that God would remember his congregation which he redeemed to be the tribe of his heritage and Mount Zion where he came to dwell (v.

So the nations are allowed to trample on Jerusalem for forty-two months (11.2). At the end of that period, the Lamb returns to reign on Mount Zion (14.1). The aftermath of war on Mount Zion will see the kingdom of the Lord established in Jerusalem. Aune argues that Mount Zion in 14.1 is the earthly Jerusalem and the centre for the eschatological kingdom. He writes:

> The scene in v 1 is set on earth...since v 2 introduces an audition of a voice from heaven, clearly distinguishing between Mount Zion and heaven. In Jewish eschatological expectation, Mount Zion = Jerusalem served as the center of the eschatological kingdom (Joel 2.32; Isa. 24.23; 31.4; Mic. 4.7; Zech. 14.4–5; *Jub.* 1.28; 4 Ezra 13.29–50; *2 Bar.* 41.1–4).[34]

Likewise Suharyo comments, 'Penglihatan ini mulai di bumi, tepatnya di kota suci, kota yang dikasihi (Way 20.9) yaitu Yerusalem dan lebih khusus lagi bukit Sion yang merupakan tempat tinggal Tuhan (*bdk*. Mzm 74.2; 132.15).'[35] [ET: This vision [14.1] begins on earth, exactly in the holy city, the beloved city (Rev. 20.9), namely, Jerusalem and more specifically Mount Zion which is the dwelling place of God (cf. Pss. 74.2; 132.15)].

We have earlier noted that Isa. 24.23 states that the Lord of hosts will reign on Mount Zion. Aune suggests that Rev. 14.1 also alludes to Isa 24.23 and observes that,

> While the MT of Isa. 24.23 expresses the eschatological hope that 'the Lord of hosts will reign on Mount Zion,' *Tg. Isa.* 24.23 (tr. Chilton, *Isaiah Targum*) substitutes the manifestation of God's *kingdom* for the visitation of God himself: 'for the kingdom of the Lord of hosts will be revealed on the Mount of Zion.' Similarly in *Tg. Isa.* 31.4 (tr. Chilton),

---

2). The Psalmist further asked God to direct his steps to the perpetual ruins for the enemy has destroyed everything in the sanctuary (v. 3). Pss. 74 and 76 may provide the background to the images of Rev. 14.1–5 where the Lamb (also called the Lion of the tribe of Judah in 5.5) is said to stand on Mount Zion (God's steps on the sanctuary) and the 144,000 consisting of the twelve tribes of Israel (Rev. 7.2–8) as the tribe of God's heritage and the redeemed of the Lord (Rev. 14.4). For a discussion of the Divine Warrior motif in Pss. 74 and 76, see Harold W. Ballard, *The Divine Warrior Motif in the Psalms* (North Richland Hills, Texas: Bibal Press, 1999), pp. 62–65.

34.   Aune, *Revelation 6–16*, p. 803. 4 Ezra 13.34–40 (cited also by Aune) provides a striking parallel. The relevant verses read as follows: '[v. 34]. and an innumerable multitude shall be gathered together...to fight against him. [v. 35]. But he shall stand on the summit of Mount Zion. [v. 37]. But he, my son, shall reprove the nations...[v. 38]. and shall reproach them to their evil thoughts and with tortures... [v. 39]. and then shall he destroy them without labour of the Law which is compared unto fire. And whereas thou didst see that he summoned and gathered to himself another multitude which was peaceable – [v. 40]. These are the ten tribes.'

35.   Suharyo, *Kitab Wahyu*, p. 101.

'so the kingdom of the Lord of hosts will be revealed to settle upon the Mount of Zion and upon its hill.'[36]

This is what John envisages happening on Mount Zion when at the end of the age, the enemy nations will be destroyed by God's wrath when the Lamb returns to Mount Zion and executes judgment and makes war against the nations that trample on the holy city. Jerusalem will be restored and become the seat of the kingdom of the Lord and his Christ (11.15; cf. 12.10).

In conclusion, we have demonstrated that the term 'Mount Zion' in Rev 14.1 corresponds to the terms 'the Temple' and 'the holy city' in 11.1–2. We have also shown that the term 'Mount Zion' is specifically the site where the Temple was built, although the term 'Mount Zion' is often used as a synonym for the city, Jerusalem. It appears that by depicting the Lamb as standing on Mount Zion in 14.1, John is saying that the desolation of the city *and* the temple (cf. 11.2) is now at an end for the time of the nations' trampling is over (42 months in 11.2).

b. *Worship on Mount Zion*

There is another image, which in our view is equally prominent in Rev. 14.1–5. We have seen that Mount Zion is the site of the Jerusalem temple and is often used interchangeably with the city of Jerusalem. The scene in Rev. 11.1 depicts *worship* before it mentions *warfare* (11.2). The worshippers are measured along with the temple and the altar. Those who worship, τοὺς προσκυνοῦντας being the third object of John's intended measurement alongside the temple of God and the altar has often been marginalized in the discussion of Rev. 11.1–2. In fact, the worshippers may be the climax of John's measuring as the worshippers are mentioned last for emphasis in the list of 'objects' to be measured. The worshippers are said to worship 'in it' or 'in the midst of it' (ἐν αὐτῷ), possibly in the court where the altar of burnt offering is located.[37] The significance of 'worship'

---

36. Aune, *Revelation 6–16*, p. 804. Aune's observation concurs with our view that the picture of the Lamb standing on Mount Zion (14.1) is linked with the revelation of the kingdom of the Lord and his Christ (cf. 11.15; 12.10).

37. Worship is seen take place around or about the altar as seen in the Pss 26.6; 51.19; 84.3; 118.27. Psalm 43.3–4 is especially significant and reads as follows:

[v. 3] O send out your light and your truth;
let them lead me;
let them bring me to your holy hill
and to your dwelling.
[v. 4] Then I will go to the altar of God
to God my exceeding joy;
and I will praise you with the harp
O God, my God.

here must be given its due weight as nowhere else is worship depicted on *earth* except in Rev. 11.1–2 and 14.1–5. J.-P. Ruiz observes thus:

> With its frequent references to worship taking place around God's heavenly throne, and with 'all the inhabitants of the earth' engaged in worship of the Beast and its image, it seems peculiar somewhat that the Apocalypse makes no mention of any worship of God actually taking place on earth, aside from the enigmatic reference in 11.1 to the measurement of the temple and those who worship there.[38]

The worshippers are measured in order to be protected during the three-and-a-half years period. Revelation 14.1–5, however, presents the scene after the expiration of the three-and-a-half years period, when a band of worshippers is depicted as worshipping on Mount Zion. That the scenes of worship in 11.1–2 and 14.1–5 are both set in Jerusalem (11.2)/Mount Zion (14.1) further strengthen our case that the worshippers in 11.1 correspond to the 144,000 companions of the Lamb. The Lamb's followers, who faithfully worship God in the time of the great tribulation, as represented by the worshippers of 11.1, will be privileged to sing the new song as the 144,000 followers of the Lamb when they stand victoriously on Mount Zion.[39]

Jonathan A. Draper notes that the 144,000 'male virgins' of Rev. 14 can also be taken as a reference to priests in temple service.[40] The emphatic 'male' imagery here is due to the fact that only males serve as priests. Their virginal state speaks of ritual purity demanded of the priests on duty in the temple. Not only are soldiers enjoined against sexual intercourse with

---

What is interesting to note in the above Psalm is that a number of phrases and terms like 'holy hill', 'your dwelling', 'the altar of God', and 'the harp' are found also in Rev. 11.1–2 and 14.1–2. More significant is that 'the altar of God' is parallel to 'the harp' in Ps. 43.4 which supports our contention that the worshippers near *the altar* in Rev. 11.1 correspond to the 144,000 that participate in worship where the harpists are said to play their *harps* in Rev. 14.2 (κιθαρῳδῶν κιθαριζόντων ἐν ταῖς κιθάραις αὐτῶν; literally – harpists harping in their harps).

38. J.-P. Ruiz, 'Politics of Praise: A Reading of Revelation 19:1–10', in *SBL Seminar Papers* (Atlanta: Scholars Press, 1997), pp. 374–94 (378). Although, the word 'worship' is not used in Rev. 14.1–5, we will argue that the scene of the 144,000 who participate in the singing of the new song constitutes worship on Mount Zion. Weber states: 'The vocation of God's servants in heaven consists of worship. As the sphere of heaven extends to the earth, worship is the centre of the servants' vocation on earth as well.' Weber, *The Way of the Lamb*, p. 39.

39. For a study of the theme of discipleship in Revelation, see D. E. Aune, 'Following the Lamb: Discipleship in the Apocalypse', in R. N. Longenecker (ed.), *Patterns of Discipleship in the New Testament* (Grand Rapids: Eerdmans, 1996), pp. 269–84 and E. Schüssler Fiorenza, 'The Followers of the Lamb: Visionary Rhetoric and Socio-Political Situation', in F. F. Segiova (ed.), *Discipleship in the New Testament* (Philadelphia: Fortress Press, 1985), pp. 144–65.

40. J. A. Draper, 'The Heavenly Feast of Tabernacles: Revelation 7.1–17', *JSNT* 19 (1983), pp. 133–47 (136–37).

women when embarking on a holy war but priests also are to refrain from sexual activity when they are on active duty in the temple (cf. Lev. 15.18; Deut. 23.9–14; 1 Sam. 21.3).[41] William Milligan also noted that the names of God and of the Lamb marked on the foreheads of the 144,000 (14:1b) were a 'token of their priestly state'.[42] The fact that the 144,000 are companions of the Lamb that was slaughtered provides another clue to its cultic and sacrificial context. The group of 144,000 represents those martyred or slaughtered for the sake of the Word of God and the testimony of Jesus. They have become sacrificial offerings to God and are thus referred to as first fruits (14.4b).[43] Sweet's remark is apt: 'the priests become the offering'.[44]

This picture of the Lamb's associates as priests is not far from John's emphasis that Jesus Christ has made the members of the church into a kingdom and priests serving God the Father (Rev. 1.6; 5.10). The call to worship God and desist from worshipping the beast is a clarion call throughout Revelation especially highlighted in the middle chapters of Revelation. As the worship motif permeates 11.1–14.5,[45] it is not implausible that 14.1–5 portrays scenes of *worship* as well as *warfare* corresponding to worship and warfare motifs in 11.1–2, which dual motifs serve as double *inclusio* to the whole literary unit of 11.1–14.5.

The above discussion on biblical as well as extra biblical texts is focused on those passages which we believe provide the most probable literary sources drawn on by John in constructing the Mount Zion scene of 14.1–5.

---

41.   Sweet comments thus: 'For orthodox Jews (and Christians) marriage and sexual intercourse were good, but the latter was temporarily defiling (Lev. 15.18) and thus a disqualification for priestly or military duty.' Sweet, *Revelation*, p. 222. Sweet combines well the images of the 144,000 as warriors and priests. He (p. 222) comments that the 144,000 'male virgins' represent Christians who see themselves as 'metaphorically on military and priestly service'.

42.   W. Milligan, *Revelation* (The Expositor Bible; New York: Hodder & Stoughton, 1901), p. 242.

43.   Aune argues convincingly that the use of the term 'first fruits' to describe the 144,000 of Rev. 14.1–5 portrays the 144,000 as actual sacrificial offerings to God and to the Lamb. See Aune, 'Following the Lamb', p. 277. According to Aune (p. 277): 'That they are designated in verse 5 as "blameless" (*amōmos*), a term which is often used of flawless sacrificial victims (cf. Exod. 29.1; Lev. 1.3; 4.3; 5.15; 22.21; Ezek. 43.22–23; Philo, *Legum Allegoriae* 1.50; Heb. 9.14; 1 Pet. 1.19), suggests that they are themselves destined to be sacrificial victims – that is, through martyrdom.'

44.   Sweet, *Revelation*, p. 223. The combination of an image as both priest and first fruits should not be seen as contradictory. Though it is the priests' duties to offer up the first fruits, Christians have adapted both images of priests and first fruits as symbols for their status in Christ. Christ himself is both high priest (cf. Heb. 3.1; 5.10) and first fruits (cf. 1 Cor. 15.20, 23).

45.   See our discussion of the worship motif as one of the two key motifs in Rev. 11.1–14.5 in chapter 2.

We have stressed the polyvalent nature of John's imagery in the said passage. Beale has noted thus: 'Sometimes four, five or more different OT references are merged into one picture.'[46] The 144,000 are not explicitly identified as warriors or priests. Yet upon close examination of John's subtle use of literary allusions to the Old Testament passages discussed above, it is found that the images of warriors and priests are the most prominent in Rev. 14.1–5.

In summary, we have already looked at how key lexical units 'the temple of God' and 'the holy city' in 11.1–2 are mirrored by the key term 'Mount Zion' in 14.1. Secondly, the worshippers in the temple (11.1) correspond to the 144,000 male virgins who as warrior-priests participate in the worship of God (14.1–5). The nations that trample (with their feet) the holy city and the outer court of the temple are defeated by the Lamb who stands (on his feet) on Mount Zion. After the suffering and persecution of the final three-and-a-half years narrated in chs 11, 12 and 13 of Revelation, the followers of the Lamb reign triumphantly with the Lamb on Mount Zion (14.1). Revelation 14.1–5 comes as the climax immediately after the narration of events that will unfold within the three and half years begun in 11.1–2 and elaborated by John in the following three chapters of Revelation. The scene of the Lamb standing on Mount Zion with the 144,000 provides the fitting climax to the suffering and persecution of the church depicted in Rev. 11–13 over the final three-and-a-half years. Thus, the unit of Rev. 11.1–14.5 is bound together and marked structurally not only by key words and phrases but also by the two key themes of worship and warfare.

3. *The BB' Pair (11.3–6; 13.11–18):*
The Two Prophets vs. The False Prophet

The nations' trampling over the temple and the holy city coincides with the appearance of the two witnesses who will prophesy during the same temporal period. The parallelism in 11.2–3 suggests that the two witnesses first make their appearance in the holy city Jerusalem at the time when the nations begin to trample upon her. Their prophecy involves speaking out the word of God and the testimony of Jesus, a commission that finds its

---

46. Beale, 'The Use of the Old Testament in Revelation', p. 319. We have to allow for the possibility of other images in Rev. 14.1–5 apart from what we have discussed. Ruben Zimmermann argues that the 144,000 companions of the Lamb called 'virgins' in Rev. 14.4 are described in images of the wedding, 'as an anticipation of the wedding of the lamb'. R. Zimmermann, 'Nuptial Imagery in the Revelation of John', *Bib* 84 (2003), pp. 153–83 (160). While the notion of a marriage in Rev. 14.1–5 cannot be ruled out entirely, it seems that the predominant picture of 14.1–5 is that of chaste Christians ready for war and worship.

paradigm firstly in John's commission in 1.9 and secondly, in John's re-commission to prophesy again in 10.11.[47] Like John, the two witnesses who prophesy are clearly seen as prophets as they are so described in 11.10. Thompson states that: 'In Revelation, only John (10.11) and the two witnesses (11.3) prophesy.'[48] In contrast, the second beast from the earth also speaks but is a false prophet (cf. 16.13; 19.20). Koester notes: 'John understands the second beast to be a false prophet (16.13; 19.20; 20.10), who poses a contrast to the two prophetic witnesses depicted in 11.3–13.'[49] So in the presentation of the two witnesses and the second beast, we have a contest of true and false prophecy.[50]

M. Kiddle and M. K. Ross explain well the contrast between the two witnesses and the second beast. They comment as follows:

> If the Messiah has His chosen and particular 'servants' (that is, prophets) on earth, so also has the Beast. It is they who complete the contrast between the greater actors in the struggle.... We must spare no pain to discern the full force of the contrast... the two witnesses are true prophets, leading men with stern admonition to the true God: the new

47. For a discussion of the important phrase, 'the word of God and the testimony of Jesus', see Trites, *The New Testament Concept of Witness*, pp. 155–64; J. Sweet, 'Maintaining the Testimony of Jesus: The Suffering of Christians in the Revelation of John', in W. Horbury & B. McNeil (eds.), *Suffering and Martyrdom in the New Testament: Studies presented to G M Styler by the Cambridge New Testament Seminar* (Cambridge: Cambridge University Press, 1981), pp. 101–17; B. Dehandschutter, 'The Meaning of Witness in the Apocalypse', in D. Hellholm (ed.), *Apocalypticism in the Mediterranean World and the Near East* (Tübingen: Mohr, 1989), pp. 283–88; G. W. H. Lampe, 'The Testimony of Jesus is the Spirit of Prophecy (Rev. 19.10)', in William C. Weinrich (ed.), *The New Testament Age: Essays in Honor of Bo Reicke* Vol. 1 (Macon, GA: Mercer University Press, 1984), pp. 245–58; Ian G. Wallis, *The Faith of Jesus Christ in early Christian traditions* (SNTSMS, 84; Cambridge: Cambridge University Press 1995), pp. 163–74; Mazzaferri, *Genre*, pp. 306–13.

48. Thompson, *Revelation*, p. 125.

49. Koester, *Revelation*, p. 130.

50. We will discuss in detail the identities of the two witnesses and the two beasts of Rev. 13 in the next chapter. For a discussion on true and false prophecy, see Duff, 'True and False Prophets', in *idem, Who Rides the Beast?*, pp. 113–25; D. Georgi, 'Who is the True Prophet?', *HTR* 79 (1986), pp. 100–26; Barnett, 'Polemical Parallelism', pp. 111–20. Barnett (p. 116) identifies the beast of Rev. 13.11–18 with the false prophet of 19.20. For a study on the true and false prophecy in the OT, see Simon J. DeVries, *Prophet against Prophet* (Grand Rapids: Eerdmans, 1978); James L. Crenshaw, *Prophetic Conflict: Its Effect upon Israelite Religion* (Berlin: de Gruyter, 1971); A. S. van der Woude, 'Micah in Dispute with the Pseudo-Prophets', in *Prophecy in the Hebrew Bible: Selected Studies from Vetus Testamentum* (compiled by David E. Orton; Leiden: Brill, 2000), pp. 24–40; Hans W. Wolff, 'How Can We Recognize False Prophets?', in *idem, Confrontation with Prophets: Discovering the Old Testament's New and Contemporary Significance* (Philadelphia: Fortress Press, 1983), pp. 63–76. For a study on distinguishing true and false prophecy in the *Didache*, an early second century C.E. Christian text, see Aaron Milavec, 'Distinguishing True and False Prophets: The Protective Wisdom of the Didache', *JECS* 2 (1994), pp. 117–36.

Beast is known always elsewhere as 'the false prophet' (xvi. 13, xix. 20, xx. 10), leading men, by marvels and appeal to self-interest, to worship of the false gods, the Beast and the dragon.[51]

The two witnesses-prophets stand before (ἐνώπιον) the Lord of the earth but the second beast exercises his authority and performs signs before (ἐνώπιον) the first beast (13.12, 14) and before the people of the world (ἐνώπιον τῶν ἀνθρώπων).[52] By standing before the Lord of the earth, the two witnesses possess divine authority (ἔχουσιν τὴν ἐξουσίαν) in the execution of their task of prophecy accompanied by signs and wonders but in contrast the second beast exercises the authority of the first beast (τὴν ἐξουσίαν τοῦ πρώτου θηρίου πᾶσαν ποιεῖ) [13.12]. The Lord of the two witnesses is Jesus the crucified one (11.8) or the Lamb that was slaughtered (13.8) but the Master of the second beast is the (first) beast whose mortal wound is healed (13.14). The two prophets speak to promote the worship of God and the Lamb while the false prophet deceives the world into worshipping the dragon and the beast (13.12).[53]

---

51.   M. Kiddle and M. K. Ross, *The Revelation of St. John* (London: Houghton & Stoughton, 1946), pp. 252–53. Keener also notes the contrast between the two witnesses of Rev. 11 and the two beasts of Rev. 13. He writes: 'Finally, the dual nature of the two witnesses provides a literary contrast with the two evil leaders in 13.11–12, one of whom also produces fire (13.13). The anointed king and priest contrast starkly with the wicked ruler and his priest in chapter 13. This portrait reinforces John's contrast between the church and the world system; the latter holds power to kill God's witnesses, but the witnesses will triumph nevertheless, even through their sacrifice.' Keener, *Revelation*, p. 293. See also Hagelberg, *Tafsiran Kitab Wahyu*, p. 257.

52.   An interesting parallel may be found in the clash of Ahab's prophets with Micah the prophet where Ahab's prophets are said to prophesy 'before them' (ἐνώπιον αὐτῶν LXX), namely before Kings Ahab and Jehoshapat so that as Rendtorff suggests, these prophets under the patronage of Ahab can be called '"his" prophets'. Rolf Rendtorff, *The Old Testament: An Introduction* (trans. John Bowker; Philadelphia: Fortress Press, 1986), p. 112. In a similar manner, the second beast can be called the first beast's prophet or mouthpiece as he not only exercises the authority of the first beast 'before him' (ἐνώπιον αὐτου) [Rev. 13.12] but also performs the signs before the beast (ἐνώπιον τοῦ θηρίου) [Rev 13.14]. Kiddle and Ross comment that: 'If this phrase [13.12] is translated, "*before* the Beast," it is then seen to be the same as that used of the two witnesses, who stand "before the Lord of the earth."' Kiddle and Ross, *Revelation*, p. 254. Another parallel in the Micah episode may further illuminate the characteristics of the beast from the earth. Paul E. Dion argues that Zedekiah, Ahab's prophet used a horned mask or horned cap in 1 Kings 22.11. According to Dion, the horned mask was a well known artifact from a known set of prophetical props. See P. E. Dion, 'The Horned Prophet (1 Kings XXII 11)', *VT* 49 (1999), pp. 259–60. If Revelation's beast, depicted as a two-horned lamb, alludes to Zedekiah's wearing of iron horns, it appears that this is another indication that the earth beast is a false prophet in the likes of Zedekiah.

53.   The goal of 'the word of God and the testimony of Jesus' is the worship of God. Thus the angel's response to John's attempt to worship him: 'You must not do that! I am a fellow servant with you and your comrades who hold the testimony of Jesus. Worship God! For the testimony of Jesus is the spirit of prophecy' (19.10b).

The two witnesses are empowered with fearsome signs (11.5–6). Likewise the second beast is said to perform 'great signs' (13.13). When attacked the two witnesses consume their enemies with *fire* but the second beast calls *fire* down from heaven in an impressive display to deceive the nations to worship the beast (13.13).[54] The two witnesses kill only in self defence (11.5) but the second beast (13.15) seeks to kill all who will not worship the image of the beast in pursuance of imperial policy. The two witnesses perform signs of power and strike the earth with plagues to warn the world of the coming day of the wrath of God. The second beast performs signs to bolster the claims of the beast as sovereign of the world (13.13–15).

The verbal and conceptual parallels are tabulated as follows:

The Verbal and Conceptual Parallels in Rev. 11.3–6 and 13.11–18

1. δυσὶν μάρτυσίν (11.3) = κέρατα δύο (13.11)
2. προφητεύσουσιν (11.3) = ἐλάλει (13.11)
3. ἐνώπιον τοῦ κυρίου τῆς γῆς (11.4) = ἐνώπιον αὐτου (13.12)
4. πῦρ (11.5) = πῦρ (13.13)
5. ἀποκτανθῆναι (11.5) = ἀποκτανθῶσιν (13.15)
6. ἔχουσιν τὴν ἐξουσίαν (11.6) = τὴν ἐξουσίαν τοῦ πρώτου θηρίου πᾶσαν ποιεῖ (13.12)

4. *The CC' Pair (11.7–13; 13.7–10): The Making of War and Conquering of the Two Witnesses and the Saints*

After the two witnesses finish their testimony, the beast that ascends from the abyss makes war, conquers and kills them (11.7). Their corpses lie in the street of the great city where their Lord was crucified (11.8). 'For three and a half days members from the peoples and tribes and languages and nations will gaze at their dead bodies and refuse to let them be placed in a tomb' (11.9). This passage of text goes on to describe the scenes of ecstasy where the peoples of the nations rejoice over the death of the two prophets by making merry and sending presents to one another in a self congratulatory mood as 'these two prophets had been a torment to the inhabitants of the earth' (11.10). But after three and a half days, the two witnesses are resurrected and ascend to heaven watched by their enemies

---

54. So Kiddle and Ross, *Revelation*, pp. 253–54. Lying and deceit are major motifs in the letters to the seven churches (cf. 2.2; 14, 20; 3.8). See John Pilch, 'Lying and Deceit in the Letters to the Seven Churches: Perspectives from Cultural Anthropology', *BTB* 39 (1992), pp. 606–24.

(11.11–12). At that hour, a great earthquake hits the city and seven thousand people are said to die as a result (11.13).

We submit that the passage of 11.7–13 (C) corresponds to the passage of 13.7–10 (C'). The statement in 11.7 is nearly identical to 13.7. The parallel texts are set out as follows:

καὶ ὅταν τελέσωσιν τὴν μαρτυρίαν αὐτῶν, τὸ θηρίον τὸ ἀναβαῖνον ἐκ τῆς ἀβύσσου ποιήσει μετ' αὐτῶν πόλεμον καὶ νικήσει αὐτοὺς καὶ ἀποκτενεῖ αὐτούς.	καὶ ἐδόθη αὐτῷ ποιῆσαι πόλεμον μετὰ τῶν ἁγίων καὶ νικῆσαι αὐτούς, καὶ ἐδόθη αὐτῷ ἐξουσία ἐπὶ πᾶσαν φυλὴν καὶ λαὸν καὶ γλῶσσαν καὶ ἔθνος.
(Rev. 11.7).	(Rev. 13.7).

In ch. 11 of Revelation the beast is only mentioned in 11.7, and plays no further role whereas in ch. 13 the beast and his ally (the second beast) dominate the whole chapter. It is often thought that the passing appearance of the beast in Rev. 11 is an interpolation or due to redactional activity by the author or authors of Revelation. Aune comments thus:

> The figure of the beast is introduced here unexpectedly and for the first time in Revelation. Surprisingly, he plays no further role in this pericope.... This actor, however, is introduced a bit too abruptly; his motivation for his actions is not evident, so the phrase 'the beast who ascend from the abyss'...is probably a later redactional addition designed to tie Rev. 11.3–13 more closely to Rev. 13 and 17.[55]

If the larger concentric pattern over 11.1–14.5 is discerned, then the appearance of the beast in 11.7 is not a sudden intrusion but an intentional ploy by John in the narrative of Rev. 11 to anticipate the beast's later activity against the saints in Rev. 13. In short, the two texts of 11.7 and 13.7 are a chiastic parallel pair in the overarching compositional plan of John for Rev. 11.1–14.5. Further, it is John's consistent manner of writing to introduce a character or event in passing only to have it expanded or elaborated upon in subsequent chapters, sometimes after an interruption of several chapters. On occasions, a theme spoken of briefly in one place is later taken up again and expanded.[56] Thus the introduction of the beast in 11.7 whose characterization is further expanded in ch. 13 and also in ch. 17 complies with John's literary technique evident elsewhere. A parallel

---

55. Aune, *Revelation 6–16*, p. 616.

56. Speaking of 11.7, Holwerda comments: 'in a cryptic manner, the warfare between the beast and the church is introduced, anticipating the more extensive description in chapters 13 and 17'. Holwerda, 'The Church and the Little Scroll (Revelation 10, 11)', p. 157.

example is the sounding of the seventh trumpet, which is the third woe, mentioned in passing in 11.15 but only unfolded entirely in Rev. 15–16.[57]

Two significant differences between 11.7 and 13.7 need further explanation. First, the 'two witnesses' of Rev. 11 are substituted by the term 'saints' and secondly, the term 'kill' coming after 'war' and 'conquer' in 11.7 is left out in 13.7. It seems that the church as a whole is called 'saints' in 13.7. The beast not only makes war against the two individual prophets but against the church as a whole.[58] The members of the church are severely persecuted and oppressed and their power shattered (the picture of being conquered) but unlike the two individual prophets, not all the saints are *killed*.[59]

Other verbal and conceptual parallels between 11.7–13 and 13.7–10 further enhance our reading of these two passages as a chiastic parallel pair. Revelation 13.8 mentions 'the Lamb that was slaughtered' corresponding to the clause that 'their Lord was crucified' in 11.8. This conceptual parallel must be given its due consideration given that the clause 'their Lord was crucified' appears only in 11.8. Though the description of the Lamb as 'the Lamb that was slaughtered' is first mentioned in 5.6, its appearance here in 13.8 is timely in the context of Rev. 13. The beast's rule entails much suffering and martyrdom among the saints who are thus enjoined to imitate the example of their crucified Lord as the Lamb that was slain who through death achieved victory.

The formulaic phrase 'peoples and tribes and languages and nations' (τῶν λαῶν καὶ φυλῶν καὶ γλωσσῶν καὶ ἐθνῶν) in 11.9 is repeated in a slightly different form in 13.7: 'every tribe and people and language and nation'

---

57. Other examples include the mention of 'the great tribulation' in Rev. 7.14 which is left unexplained in ch. 7 but later taken up again and expanded in the events of the three-and-a-half-year period of Rev. 11–13. Also the passing announcement that Babylon has fallen in 14.8 is picked up again in detail only in chs 17 and 18. For a discussion on the literary technique to introduce a seemingly passing remark as anticipatory of later events, see Nahum Sarna, 'Anticipatory Use of Information as a Literary Feature of the Genesis Narratives', in *idem, Studies in Biblical Interpretation* (New York: Jewish Publication Society, 2000), pp. 211–21.

58. In the next chapter we will argue that there is oscillation between the portrayal of the two witnesses as two individual prophets and also the corporate church in Rev. 11.3–13. We will see that the emphasis is on the two witnesses as two individuals.

59. Targeting against prominent church leaders is an old and tested method as the best way to destroy the church. The book of Acts narrates many incidents where the leaders of the church were targeted by the authorities for imprisonment and even death (Acts 4.21; 5.17–18; 40; 7.54–58; etc.). The church in general is not immune from persecution as Acts 8.1 indicates: 'That day a severe persecution began against the church in Jerusalem' Before his conversion, Saul is said to ravage the church 'by entering house after house; dragging off both men and women' and committing them to prison (Acts 8.3).

(πᾶσαν φυλὴν καὶ λαὸν καὶ γλῶσσαν καὶ ἔθνος).[60] Closely associated with this aforesaid formula is the phrase 'the inhabitants of the earth' both appearing in 11.10 (οἱ κατοικοῦντες ἐπὶ τῆς γῆς) and 13.8 (οἱ κατοικοῦντες ἐπὶ τῆς γῆς). If these parallel elements are read together, John appears to link the representatives from all the peoples and tribes and languages and nations that gaze upon the carcass of the two witnesses (11.9) with the same group of peoples over which the beast exercises authority in 13.7. Hence the victory of the beast over the two witnesses in 11.7 is welcomed by the masses under the beast's rule (13.7).

By comparing the occurrences of the phrase οἱ κατοικοῦντες ἐπὶ τῆς γῆς in their respective contexts in both 11.10 and 13.8, we can surmise that the inhabitants of the earth rejoice over the deaths of the two witnesses because now their worship of the beast can go on undisturbed. It appears that apart from the plagues which strike the earth and the earth's inhabitants, it is the two prophets' testimony which causes the most consternation among the inhabitants of the earth. The two witnesses' severe reprimand accompanied by signs and plagues against the worship of the beast cannot but cause torment to the inhabitants of the earth who are bent on idolatry. It may be that their rejoicing, making merry and sending presents to one another are all part of the idolatrous activity and glorification of the beast that has conquered and killed the two prophets.

Just as John vividly narrates the circumstances surrounding the death of the two witnesses, he goes on to describe their dramatic resurrection: 'But after the three and a half days, the breath of life from God entered them, and they stood on their feet, and those who saw them were terrified' (11.11). A series of contemporaneous events is said to take place *after* the three and half days. First, the two prophets rise from the dead and immediately ascend to heaven in the cloud (11.12). This is followed by another temporal indicator, 'in that hour' (ἐν ἐκείνῃ τῇ ὥρᾳ) a great earthquake hit the city and felled a tenth part of it killing seven thousand persons in it (11.13a). The rest of the city populace is terrified and give glory to the God of heaven (11.13b).

The passage in 13.7–10 focuses on the suffering and death that will be the lot of the saints in the three-and-a-half years period under the beast's rule. There is no light at the end of the tunnel for the saints except for a call to have endurance and hold on to the faith of Jesus (13.10b). But read chiastically with 11.7–13, the captivity and death of the saints in 13.10a is not the end of the story. The endurance of the saints unto death will lead to their resurrection similar to the resurrection of the two witnesses in 11.11. The spirit of *life* (πνεῦμα ζωῆς) from God that resurrects the two witnesses

---

60. The fourfold formula appears elsewhere in the book of Revelation in 5.9; 7.9; 10.11; 14.6; 17.16. See Bauckham, *Climax of Prophecy*, p. 241.

(11.11) will also raise up the martyred saints whose names are written in the book of *life* (τῷ βιβλίῳ τῆς ζωῆς) of the Lamb that was slain (13.8). The triumph and vindication of the two witnesses serve as the pattern for the rest of the church.

The foregoing numerous verbal, phrasal, clausal, and thematic links between parallel members in CC' point strongly to the fact that John composed these passages as mirror images of one another in the form of a concentric pattern. This method of interpretation which takes the literary structure within the larger chiasm seriously can only add to our understanding of the said passages. The verbal and conceptual parallels are tabulated as follows:

The Verbal and Conceptual Parallels in Rev. 11.7–13 and 13.7–10

1. ποιήσει μετ᾽ αὐτῶν πόλεμον καὶ νικήσει αὐτοὺς καὶ ἀποκτενεῖ αὐτούς (11.7) = ποιῆσαι πόλεμον μετὰ τῶν ἁγίων καὶ νικῆσαι αὐτούς (13.7)
2. ὁ κύριος αὐτῶν ἐσταυρώθη (11.8) = τοῦ ἀρνίου τοῦ ἐσφαγμένου (13.8)
3. τῶν λαῶν καὶ φυλῶν καὶ γλωσσῶν καὶ ἐθνῶν (11.9) = φυλὴν καὶ λαὸν καὶ γλῶσσαν καὶ ἔθνος (13.7)
4. οἱ κατοικοῦντες ἐπὶ τῆς γῆς (11.10) = οἱ κατοικοῦντες ἐπὶ τῆς γῆς (13.8)
5. ἀποκτενεῖ (11.7) = ἀποκτανθῆναι (13.10)
6. πνεῦμα ζωῆς (11.11) = τῷ βιβλίῳ τῆς ζωῆς (13.8)

5. *The DD' Pair (11.15–19; 13.1–6): The Kingdom of the Lord and his Christ and the Throne and Power of the Dragon and the Beast*

We have attempted to show how Rev. 11.15–19 (D) fits into ch. 11 as a whole by paying attention to how John develops his story-line chronologically utilising his favourite temporal indicator of the figure three and a half as the unifying element throughout the narrative in Rev. 11. We will now discuss how 11.15–19 (D) corresponds to its opposing member in the proposed chiasm (D' = 13.1–6). The events of 13.1–6 depict how the beast comes into power and rules over the earth *during the three-and-a-half years* while the passage in 11.15–19 shows how *after the three-and-a-half years* the beast is divested of power and the kingdom of the world (ruled by the beast) comes into the possession of the Lord and his Christ (11.15). Thus the DD' chiastic parallels here speak of God's battle with Satan to overturn the government of the latter which will lead to the establishment of God's government on earth. Thomas Söding comments thus: 'Johannes spricht von der Aufrichtung der Herrschaft Gottes im Kampf mit dem Imperialismus Satans.'[61]

---

61. T. Söding, 'Heilig, heilig, heilig: Zur politischen Theologie der Johannes-Apokalypse', *ZThK* 96 (1999), pp. 49–76 (68).

The beast is said to receive power, great authority and a throne from the dragon (13.2) and rules over the whole earth for a limited period of 42 months (13.5). The kingdom of the world (11.15) is dominated by the beast and the dragon, as it is said that: 'They worshiped the dragon, for he had given his authority to the beast, and they worshiped the beast, saying, "Who is like the beast, and who can fight against it?"' (13.4). The intimacy of the beast and the dragon is brought out by this verse so much so that the beast is seen not just as the dragon's instrument but to a large extent as the dragon's impersonation. It is the dragon *in* the beast, though the latter is not to be strictly identified or equated with the former. Court comments,

> The relation between dragon and beast appears closer and more intricate than the simple relation of chief devil to subordinate demon, and more like the merging of one diabolical image or manifestation into another; this is demonstrated by the close parallelism of their attributes (12.3; 13.1; 17.3).[62]

When the dragon is thrown to earth (12.7–13), he uses the beast as his political tool to set up a world government and this political organization claims not only absolute obedience but also worship from its subjects.[63] Idolatry in Rev. 13 is worship of the state. Thus the beast's hubris is an affront to God's kingdom or government because it usurps the authority, sovereignty, and worship that belong to God alone. Hagelberg writes: 'Kalau pemerintah menuntut disembah, berarti dia menuntut sesuatu yang tidak boleh ia tuntut, sesuatu yang sebenarnya hanya boleh diminta oleh Tuhan Allah. Dia sudah menuntut di luar jangkauan kekuasaannya.'[64] (ET: If the ruler demands worship, this means he demands something which he is not entitled to, something which only the Lord God can rightfully demand. He [the ruler] thus demands something which is beyond the sphere of his authority).

The beast's rule will end at the expiry of the three-and-a-half years period for then ἐγένετο ἡ βασιλεία τοῦ κόσμου τοῦ κυρίου ἡμῶν καὶ τοῦ Χριστοῦ αὐτοῦ, καὶ βασιλεύσει εἰς τοὺς αἰῶνας τῶν αἰώνων (11.15). It is noteworthy that John might have intentionally emphasized that the kingdom belongs to the Lord *and* his Christ in contrast to the worship proffered to the dragon *and* the beast in 13.4. While the beast's kingdom lasts for a short time-span of three-and-a-half years (13.5), God's kingdom

---

62.   Court, *Myth and History*, p. 111.

63.   Söding writes: 'Im Himmel entmachtet (12,7–12), schafft er [der Teufel] sich das effizienteste Instrument, um Herrschaft über "alle Bewohner der Erde" (13,8) zu erringen: eine politische Organisation, die mit dem religiös überhöhten Versprechen von Glück, Erfolg, Reichtum und Macht die Menschen von der Anbetung des "lebendigen Gottes" (7,2) ablenkt.' Söding, 'Heilig, heilig, heilig', p. 69.

64.   Hagelberg, *Tafsiran Kitab Wahyu*, p. 251

reigns forever and ever (11.15). The beast's *throne* given him on earth by the dragon (13.2) mirrors by way of contrast the *thrones* of the twenty-four elders in heaven given to them by God (11.16). While the beast is enthroned and receives worship from the dwellers of the world (13.4), the twenty-four elders *leave their thrones* and fall on their faces and worship God (11.16).

The beast in Rev. 13 is first characterized as having ten horns and seven heads and on its horns are ten diadems and on its heads are blasphemous names (13.1). The beast's hubris seems to lie in its claim to world sovereignty (symbolized by its seven heads and ten horns) and the blasphemous worship proffered to him by the world.[65] The blasphemy motif appears to envelope the section of text from 13.1–6 as vv. 5–6 focus on the beast's uttering of 'haughty and blasphemous words... against God, blaspheming his name and his dwelling, that is those who dwell in heaven'. The inclusion of God's dwelling as an object of the beast's blasphemy in 13.6 is especially of note as the last verse of its corresponding pair in 11.19 narrates that the temple of God is opened in heaven and the ark of his covenant is sighted within the temple. Just as in the beginning of D' the beast's kingdom is contrasted with the kingdom of the Lord at the beginning of D, now at the end of chiastic pair of DD', God's dwelling in heaven in 13.6 mirrors God's temple in heaven in 11.19, a fact which enhances our proposed chiastic pairing of DD'.

Further, the targeted blasphemy against those who dwell in heaven in 13.6 appears to include a reference to the twenty-four elders who sit on their thrones in heaven before God in 11.16.[66] As the objects of the beast's

---

65.   That the beast is seen as Satan's representative is clear as both the dragon and the beast are said to have seven heads and ten horns (12.3; 13.1). The dragon is said to have seven diadems on its seven heads, while the beast has ten diadems on its ten horns. As the word διάδημα (diadem) means a royal crown (BDAG, p. 227), and the number seven stands for completeness, this means the dragon's royal or political power is absolute. Likewise, the ten horns of the beast represent the ten kings who will yield their power and authority to the beast (17.12–13) suggests that the beast rules over the kingdoms of the world (cf. Dan. 7.7). Beale comments: 'As with the dragon's horns and heads, so here [13.1] the number of *seven* heads and *ten* horns emphasizes the completeness of oppressive power and its worldwide effect.... The crowns symbolize the beast's false claims of sovereignty, universal authority in opposition to the true "King of Kings and Lord of Lords," who also wears "many diadems" (19.12, 16).' Beale, *Revelation*, p. 684. The combination of images points to the notion that Satan through the beast exercises worldwide sovereignty. Further, the singular 'kingdom' in the phrase 'the kingdom of the world' (11.15) suggests that the whole world is under the dominion of a single or unified political authority, namely the beast of 11.7 and Rev. 13 (cf. 17.12–13). We will examine in detail the identity of the beast in the next chapter.

66.   The beast's blasphemy against those who dwell in heaven in 13.6 is not likely to be restricted to the twenty-four elders in heaven. However, if 13.6 is read chiastically with 11.16, the group of the twenty-four elders is singled out as taking part in proclaiming God's sovereignty on earth, which in effect signals the end of the kingdom of the beast. Revelation

blasphemy in 13.6 during his rule for 42 months (13.5), the elders are vindicated after the three-and-a-half-year period and accorded the honour of announcing the destruction of the blasphemer–destroyer, the beast and the nations over which he rules (11.16–18). God's *dwelling*, the temple of God opens in heaven with the sight of the ark of God's covenant within the temple accompanied by flashes of lightning, rumblings, peals of thunder, an earthquake, and heavy hail – all portents of judgment on the beast that dares blaspheme the name of God and his *dwelling*.

Compared with other chiastic halves (AA', BB', and CC'), parallels and opposite elements in DD' appear to be more nuanced. The parallels are mostly contrasts in themes, fashioned in both verbal and conceptual parallels. The nuanced and more subtle interplay of contrasts and antithesis between parallel pairs in DD' is further evidence of John's literary artistry. The verbal and conceptual parallels are tabulated as follows:

The Verbal and Conceptual Parallels in Rev. 11.15–19 and 13.1–6

1. τὸν θρόνον αὐτου (13.2) = ἡ βασιλεία τοῦ κόσμου τοῦ κυρίου ἡμῶν καὶ τοῦ Χριστοῦ αὐτου (11.15); τοὺς θρόνους αὐτῶν (11.16)
2. προσεκύνησαν τῷ δράκοντι; προσεκύνησαν τῷ θηρίῳ (13.4) = προσεκύνησαν τῷ θεῷ (11.16)
3. ἐξουσία ποιῆσαι μῆνας τεσσεράκοντα [καὶ] δύο (13.5) = βασιλεύσει εἰς τοὺς αἰῶνας τῶν αἰώνων (11.15)
4. τὴν σκηνὴν αὐτοῦ (13.6) = ὁ ναὸς τοῦ θεοῦ (11.19)
5. τοὺς ἐν τῷ οὐρανῷ σκηνοῦντας (13.6) = οἱ εἴκοσι τέσσαρες πρεσβύτεροι (11.16)

The above parallels are substantial and cumulatively they fit into the chiastic pattern which we have proposed for 11.1–14.5. Conceptually, the corresponding elements are striking in projecting movement in time whereby the reign of the dragon and the beast, who in unison rule the world, will give way to the kingdom of the Lord and his Christ. The rule of the beast for the limited period of forty-two months will be terminated by the in-breaking of God's kingdom that will reign forever and ever. The blasphemy against God's name, his dwelling and those who dwell in heaven will be answered from heaven itself. The ark of his covenant appears within God's opened temple in heaven (11.19): God rises to

---

11.16 probably alludes to Isa. 24.23 where it is said that the Lord's reign will be on Mount Zion and his glory manifested before the elders. Larry Hurtado argues that the twenty-four elders are the heavenly representatives of the elect on earth. See L. Hurtado, 'Revelation 4–5 in the Light of Jewish Apocalyptic Analogies', *JSNT* 25 (1985), pp. 105–24.

vindicate his name and his people. What is declared by the elders (11.16–18) is now ready to be fulfilled. God's kingdom is finally revealed on earth.

6. *Testing the Macro-Chiasm of Revelation 11.1–14.5* *(ABCDEFGF'E'D'C'B'A')*

We have begun the demonstration of our proposed macro-chiasm with a literary-structural analysis of Rev. 11 followed by an analysis of 12.1–14.5. In our literary-structural analysis of 11.1–14.5, we have found that 11.1–2 begins a new literary unit which is only concluded in 14.1–5. We have also established that 11.19 functions as the link between Rev. 11 and Rev. 12 and in like manner 12.18 links Rev. 12 with 13.1–14.5. We have demonstrated that the chiastic pattern begins to emerge clearly in Rev. 12 in the form of an EFGF'E' pattern. In this chapter, we have shown that Rev. 11 corresponds to 13.1–14.5 yielding a macro-chiasm of ABCDEFG-F'E'D'C'B'A' for the literary unit of Rev. 11.1–14.5.

We will now test the proposed macro-chiasm in the form of ABCDEFGF'E'D'C'B'A' using Blomberg's nine criteria. Blomberg's first criterion that the structure of the said passage in question has no better explanation appears to be fulfilled in the light of the lack of agreement on how the literary unit of 11.1–14.5 is structured. We have noted earlier that the majority of scholars following Yarbro Collins have argued or assumed that Rev. 12 begins a new cycle or the second half of the book of Revelation.[67] Most of these writers hold that the book of Revelation can be divided into two halves, Rev. 1–11 and Rev 12–22.[68] Other commentators who do not hold to the view that Revelation is divided into two halves, nevertheless, think that Rev. 12 begins a new section lasting to the end of Rev. 14 or Rev. 15.4.[69] On the other side of the scholarly spectrum, we have Sweet[70], Mazzafferi[71], and recently Svigel[72] and Prigent[73] who have argued that Rev. 11 is integrally linked with Rev. 12–13, but none of these writers demonstrates in any detail how Rev. 11 is connected with Rev. 12–13. Also, Hall has argued that Rev. 10.11–11.1 function as the interlocking verses for the two halves of the book of Revelation. Hall follows Yarbro Collins in seeing Revelation as divided into two halves or two cycles but he differs from Yarbro Collins in arguing that Rev. 11.1 begins the second

---

67. Yarbro Collins, *Combat Myth*, p. 157.
68. Murphy, *Fallen is Babylon*, p. 275.
69. So Beale, *Revelation*, p. 621.
70. Sweet, *Revelation*, p. 46.
71. Mazzaferri, *Genre*, p. 360.
72. Svigel, 'The Apocalypse of John', pp. 55–56.
73. Prigent, *Commentary on the Apocalypse*, p. 367.

half of the book and not Rev. 12 onwards.[74] It is clear that given the disagreement among scholars of how these middle chapters of Revelation are structured, Blomberg's first criterion that other approaches to the literary development of the proposed literary unit must prove problematic, is thus met.

Second, it is submitted that the development of the second half of the macro-chiasm follows a clearly inverse pattern to that of the first half. The AA' pair tells of the temple's outer court and the holy city trampled upon (A) with the state of affairs reversed in A' where the Lamb stands triumphant on Mount Zion (A'). The BB' pair juxtaposes and contrasts the prophetic testimony of the two witnesses with powerful signs against the second beast's deceit through equally impressive signs. The CC' pair sets the fate of the two witnesses and the saints in the hands of the beast. The DD' pair contrasts the worship of Satan and the beast with the worship of God. This chiastic pair narrates how the kingdom of the world is ultimately overthrown and becomes the possession of the Lord and his Christ who will rule forever (D) and is contrasted with the short-lived reign of the beast for three-and-a-half years (D'). The conflict between the woman and her offspring is introduced in 12.1–4 (E) and developed and expanded in 12.15–17 (E'). The escape of the woman who gave birth to her male child in 12.5–6 (F) is repeated in 12.13–14 (F'). At the apex of the macro-chiasm, we have the war in heaven between Michael and the dragon and the announcement of the in-breaking of the kingdom of God and his Christ (G – 12.7–12).

Third, there are clear examples of parallel elements between the halves with many verbal and conceptual parallels that cannot be gainsaid as we hope to have demonstrated in this chapter and Chapter Four. Blomberg's fourth criterion that the verbal parallelism should involve central or dominant imagery or terminology, not peripheral or trivial language is also fulfilled. The repetition of words and phrases like 'worship', 'make war', 'conquer', 'kill or be killed', 'throne', and 'kingdom' occur throughout the chiastic pairs which carry the central meaning of the narrative of 11.1–14.5. Fifth, Blomberg insists that the verbal and conceptual parallelisms should use words and concepts not regularly found elsewhere outside the proposed chiasm. Though the textual unit of Rev. 11.1–14.5 shares similar language with the rest of Revelation, this block of text has its own vocabulary and concepts. God's people are seen to engage in worship *on earth* in the book of Revelation only in 11.1 and 14.1–5. The worship of the dragon/Satan by the inhabitants of the world is only found in this textual unit (13.4). The in-breaking of kingdom of God and his Christ is only depicted here (11.15; 12.10). Warfare in *heaven* is found only in 12.7–9.

74. Hall, 'The Hook Interlocking Structure of Revelation', p. 278.

Fire as a sign of judgment by God's human agents and as a sign of wonder by the second beast is also only recorded within the proposed macro-chiasm (11.5; 13.13). Sixth, we have set out how each chiastic pair in our macro-chiasm exhibits multiple sets of correspondences between each other. And our pattern of ABCDEFGF'E'D'C'B'A' is sufficiently complex beyond the simple ABA' or ABB'A' pattern.

Seventh, the proposed outline divides the text at natural breaks. Blomberg's seventh criterion has been challenged by Porter and Reed and we agree with the latter authors that a chiastic outline may not appear natural in the first instance but upon closer examination of the literary and narrative devices that mark the text, an outline for the whole chiasm is then evident. We have noted that there is considerable dispute on what constitutes natural breaks or sub-units within Rev. 11. Nevertheless, our outline follows what are generally accepted as major divisions of the text not only in Rev. 11 but also in 12.1–14.5. Only two sub-units within our proposed outline require some justification. Instead of dividing 11.7–13 into two sub-units consisting of vv. 7–10 and vv. 11–13 as is often proposed, we have treated vv. 7–13 as a coherent sub-unit on the ground of the chiastic pattern found in vv. 7–13 where the killing of the two witnesses and the non-burial of their corpses in vv. 7–8 is reversed by their resurrection and ascension to heaven and the killing of seven thousand inhabitants of the city by a great earthquake in vv. 12–13. The second sub-unit is 13.1–10 where we have argued for a further division between vv. 1–6 and vv. 7–10 on the ground that the blasphemy motif rings vv. 1–6 in an *inclusio* while the lexical unit 'the saints' and the theme of persecution of the saints serve as the *inclusio* to vv. 7–10. If the chiastic patterns and *inclusio*s as boundary markers are recognized, then our proposed outline as a whole should be viewed as a viable and coherent outline.

Eighth, the centre of the chiasm which forms its climax is a passage worthy of that position in light of its theological or ethical significance. The war in heaven is indeed pivotal to the macro-chiasm, as we have shown that what transpires in heaven directly influences events on earth. The defeat of the dragon and his casting out from heaven to earth results in the period of the great tribulation during which the church is subjected to the most intense persecution, fuelled by the dragon's wrath and carried out by the dragon's allies in the two beasts of Rev. 13 while the word of God is boldly proclaimed by the prophetic testimony of God's two witnesses of Rev. 11. Finally, there is no rupture in the outline in that no member of the chiastic half has to be shifted to fit into an alleged pattern.

In setting up his criteria for testing macro-chiasm Blomberg acknowledges that 'these nine criteria are seldom fulfilled *in toto* even by well-established chiastic structures.... [Conversely] a hypothesis which fulfils most of all of the nine stands a strong chance of reflecting the actual structure of the text in question'.[75] Since the testing of the proposed macro-chiasm for 11.1–14.5 meets all the nine criteria set by Blomberg a strong case can be made for submitting that the said literary unit is indeed structured in a chiastic pattern as proposed.

7. Conclusion

We have attempted to demonstrate that a chiastic reading of Rev. 11.1–14.5 is a way forward to understand the form and content of this literary unit. We have argued that the narrative of the two witnesses of Rev. 11 is purposively composed as a parallel to the narrative of the two beasts of Rev. 13.1–14.5 in an ABCDD'C'B'A' pattern. Together with Rev. 12, the macro-chiasm is structured in an ABCDEFGF'E'D'C'B'A' pattern. This macro-chiasm is seen to be a suitable literary device to structure the narrative of the war between the two witnesses and the two beasts on earth as a reflection of the war in heaven between Michael and the dragon and the conflict between the dragon and the woman in Rev. 12.

It is further shown that the central section or pivot of 12.7–12 (G) is vital for the interpretation of the rest of the macro-chiasm. We have found that the major themes of Rev. 11.1–14.5 are summed up in the pivotal section of 12.7–12. First, the war in heaven between Michael and the dragon which ends with the dragon's defeat and his coming down to earth (12.7–9, 12) results in the war between the dragon and the woman and her offspring (12.1–4; 15–17 [EE']). This heavenly conflict is reflected by the war on earth between the two witnesses of Rev. 11 (BC) and the two beasts of Rev. 13 (B'C'). Secondly, the kingdom of God and the authority of his Christ announced in 12.10 only become reality on earth at the passing away of the kingdom of the world after the termination of the beast's rule for 42 months (11.15–18; 13.5 [DD']).

Thirdly, the dragon's characterization as the deceiver of the whole world (12.9) is seen in the appearance of the second beast that speaks like a dragon and deceives the world into idolatry with supernatural signs and wonders (13.11–18 [B']). In contrast, God sends his two witnesses to prophesy the truth of his word and to warn the world against the idolatrous claims of the beast (11.3–6 [B]). Fourthly, the dragon's constant accusation against the saints in heaven and the declaration that the saints have conquered the dragon by the blood of the Lamb and the words of their testimony (12.10–11) are reflected in the persecution of the beasts against the saints on earth for three-and-a-half years (13.7–10, 15) and prophetic witness of church led by the two witnesses (11.3–7). The saints will ultimately triumph against the beasts and those who die will be resurrected from the dead (11.7–13). As the

75. Blomberg, 'Structure', p. 7.

thematic centre, the pivot of 12.7–12 provides the meaning to each of the several parallel elements that surround it. In Breck's terminology, 'the centre lends content and form to the entire passage'.[76] Thus, we conclude that the pivot of 12.7–12 at the apex of the chiastic structure informs the interpretation of the other chiastic parallels in 11.1–14.5.

---

76. Breck, *The Shape of Biblical Language*, p. 342.

Chapter 6

THE IDENTITY OF THE TWO WITNESSES AND THE TWO BEASTS

1. *Introduction*

We have shown in the previous chapter that Rev. 11.3–6 and vv. 7–13 (BC) corresponded to 13.11–18 and 13.7–10 (B'C') respectively. The BB' pair tells of the contest between true and false prophecy, while the CC' pair depicts the persecution and martyrdom of the two witnesses/saints at the hands of the two beasts. Thus the macro-chiastic structure informs John's readers that the ministry of the two witnesses ought to be read in conjunction with the careers of the two beasts. Further, the time-span of 42 months during which the beast rules the world (13.5) is shown to be the same temporal period when the two witnesses are said to prophesy (11.3).

In this chapter we will seek to identify the two witnesses and the two beasts as the two pairs of eschatological figures locked in combat in the last three and a half years before the dawn of the kingdom of God on earth. From the outset it is vital to note that if the two witnesses are said to appearing before the *eschaton*, i.e., before the in-breaking of the kingdom of God (11.15) as we have shown earlier, then the two beasts depicted as appearing in the same temporal period of three-and-a-half years must also be eschatological figures. The chiastic pair DD' (11.15–19 = 13.1–6) shows that at the end of the beast's rule of 42 months (13.5), the kingdom of this world will have come to the possession of the Lord and of his Christ (11.15–18). Further, the announcement of the kingdom of God and the authority of his Christ at the pivot of the macro-chiasm (12.10) will only be fully consummated on earth when the devil's short time (12.12) of 'a time, times, and half a time' (12.14) finally comes to an end at the expiry of the 42 months (cf. 13.5). The macro-chiastic structure further informs us that the war in heaven (12.7–12) results in the war on earth between the two witnesses of Rev. 11 and the two beasts of Rev. 13. As we have examined the main characters in Rev. 12 in an earlier chapter, it remains for us to look in detail concerning the two pairs of characters that dominate the narratives of Rev. 11 and Rev. 13 respectively.

The origin of the idea of the two witnesses and two beasts is still very much a mystery. W. Bousset's observation more than a century ago still rings true today: 'one point remains unexplained – the origin of the idea of the two witnesses'.[1] No biblical or extra-biblical passage or passages envision the encounter between two prophetic figures and two eschatological opponents at the close of the age. Nevertheless, as we will see, John has creatively conflated and adapted numerous biblical traditions from the Old and New Testaments to depict the two witnesses of Rev. 11 and also the two beasts of Rev. 13. John presents these eschatological figures as the main actors in the final eschatological drama to unfold within the final three and a half years before the End comes. The concept of the End for the purposes of this book is defined as the in-breaking of the kingdom of God into the world which concludes this present age and inaugurates the new age or the age to come (11.15; 12.10; cf. 19.11–21).[2]

2. *The Two Witnesses as Prophets*

Who are the two witnesses? This question is perhaps one of the most vexed in the book of Revelation. Are they two individuals? Are they a symbolic reference to the church? Most commentators would choose either option: the two witnesses are two individuals or that they are symbols for the church. An added difficulty is that there does not appear to be a clear Old Testament reference which we can turn to in the quest for greater precision in identifying the two witnesses. The promise of an eschatological prophet before the great and terrible day of Yahweh speaks of Elijah the prophet returning but not two prophets at the same time (cf. Mal. 3.23; ET – Mal. 4.5). The origin of the idea of the two witnesses is still a much disputed issue and remains unresolved. But we must begin with the text of ch. 11 of Revelation before we search for biblical or extra-biblical precedents for the concept of the two witnesses.

We have demonstrated earlier that the two witnesses appear in the holy city, Jerusalem. Revelation 11.1–2 sets the scene for the appearance of the two witnesses. It is a time when the temple's outer court is desolated by the

---

1. W. Bousset, *The Antichrist Legend: A Chapter in Christian and Jewish Folklore* (trans. A. H. Keane; London: Hutchinson, 1896), p. 210.
2. We should note in the book of Revelation that the dawn of the kingdom of God is seen as inaugurating the millennial kingdom (Rev. 20.1–6). After the 1,000-year kingdom has ended (20.7), another final war takes place at the instigation of Satan at the camp of the saints (20.7–10) before the first heaven and the first earth pass away giving way to a new heaven and a new earth (21.1–2) where God himself is said to dwell among his peoples forever and ever (21.3; cf. 22.5). As our focus is on the events unfolding during the three and a half years before the arrival of the kingdom of God found in Rev. 11.1–14.5, it is not within the purview of this thesis to look at the events narrated in Rev. 20 onwards.

nations who will also trample on the holy city. The two witnesses'
commission to prophesy is set against Jerusalem's darkest hour in that the
city and its temple are defiled by foreign nations which signals the
commencement of the three-and-a-half years before the dawn of the
kingdom of God (11.2–3; cf. 11.15). Since this period is the last period
before the End, the two witnesses are seen as two eschatological prophets
before the dawn of the new age.

The fact that the two witnesses are prophets is not disputed for they are
appointed to prophesy (προφητεύσουσιν) in 11.3 and explicitly called the
two prophets (οἱ δύο προφῆται) in 11.10. Furthermore, their testimony is
equated with their prophecy. The signs that they perform are said to take
place in 'the days of their prophecy' (τὰς ἡμέρας τῆς προφητείας αὐτῶν) in
11.6 and when their ministry is concluded it is said that they finish 'their
testimony' (τὴν μαρτυρίαν αὐτῶν) in 11.7. As we have shown earlier, the role
of the two witnesses as prophets is stressed in 11.3–6 given John's intention
to portray the two witnesses as true prophets in contrast to the second
beast-false prophet of 13.11–18 (BB'). But the content of their prophecy or
testimony is not specified. Their identity is likewise not made explicit.
However, it appears that John has not left his readers without clues.

a. *The Meaning of Sackcloth (Revelation 11.3)*
The only information about the physical appearance of the two witnesses is
that they are clothed with sackcloth (11.3). Often scholars without regard
to the immediate context of the city's and temple's desecration by the
nations in 11.1–2, assume that the mention of the sackcloth points to the
two witnesses as preachers of repentance.[3] It is more likely that the two
witnesses are dressed with sackcloth in *mourning* on account of the

---

3.   Richard Bauckham writes: 'The two witnesses in Rev. 11.3–13 are preachers of
repentance.' R. Bauckham, 'The Martyrdom of Enoch and Elijah: Jewish or Christian?', *JBL*
95 (1976), pp. 447–58 (453). Bauckham did not give any scriptural references or supporting
arguments why the subject of repentance is allegedly preached by the two witnesses. Giblin
remarks that the sackcloth is 'a sign that the two witnesses were to preach a message of
repentance (*metanoia*)'. Giblin, *Revelation*, p. 121. Rodney Petersen is more circumspect: 'The
purpose of the appearance of the two witnesses is to prophesy – but whether this is a call to
repentance or includes the foretelling of future events is left unanswered.' R. Petersen,
*Preaching in the Last Days: The Theme of 'Two Witnesses' in the Sixteenth and Seventeenth
Centuries* (Oxford: Oxford University Press, 1993), p. 7. Thomas attempts to combine the
images of repentance and mourning and comments: 'The sackcloth clothing of the witnesses is
in token of needed repentance and approaching judgment (cf. Isa. 22.12; Jer. 4.8; 6.26; Jon.
3.5, 6, 8; Mt. 11.21). ... It marked their lamentation over the treading down of the holy city
and the prevalence of evil all around them.' Thomas, *Revelation 8–22*, p. 89. Beasley-Murray
cites Jonah 3.5 as scriptural evidence for 'penitence and mourning' but in Jonah 3.5 the people
that wore sackcloth and repented were the people of Nineveh and not the prophet Jonah. See
Beasley-Murray, *Revelation*, p. 183.

desolation which is now the fate of the temple and the holy city. Concerned leading citizens dressed in sackcloth to mourn the impending invasion or fall of Jerusalem and/or the desecration of the temple is a consistent theme in biblical and extra-biblical literature (Jer. 4.7–8, 6.26; Lam. 2.10; Ezek. 7.18; Dan. 9.3; Joel 1.13; Amos 8.10; 1 Macc. 2.12–14; 3.45–47; 2 Macc. 3.19; *Pss. Sol.* 2.19–20).

Daniel the prophet prayed and fasted with sackcloth and ashes on account of Jerusalem's desolation in Dan. 9.3: 'Then I turned to the Lord God, to seek an answer by prayer and supplication with fasting and sackcloth and ashes.' David Satran comments that: 'The combined motif of "fasting and sackcloth and ashes" is a familiar biblical reaction to personal or national calamity (e.g. 1 Kgs. 21.27; Jonah 3.5; Est. 4.3; cf. *m. Ta'anit* 2.1) and is fully consonant with Daniel's despair in the wake of the destruction.'[4] This Danielic imagery of sackcloth and mourning for the ruin of Jerusalem and praying for the city's restoration in Dan. 9 is pertinent to our discussion of the two witnesses as the context of Rev. 11.2 also speaks of the desolation of Jerusalem, the holy city which will be restored after the expiry of three-and-a-half years when the Lamb stands on Mount Zion (14.1).

The prayer of Daniel in sackcloth in Dan. 9 forms the setting for the visions of Dan. 10–12 where Daniel is told that the restoration of the city and the temple will take place after a time of great distress and warfare (cf. Dan. 9.24–27; 10.1; 12.1) which will last for 'a time, times, and half a time' (Dan. 12.6–7), a time-span which is alluded to by John repeatedly in Rev. 11–13 (11.2–3; 12.6, 14; 13.5). Thus we surmise that the witnesses dressed in sackcloth can be better understood not as preachers of repentance but as prophets in mourning for the fate of Jerusalem and God's holy temple in the time of great tribulation lasting for three-and-a-half years until the kingdom of God comes (11.15).

The significance of sackcloth as a sign of mourning is also prominent in the book of 1 Maccabees and the *Psalms of Solomon*. Mattathias and his sons also were said to put on sackcloth to mourn greatly at the desolation of the Jerusalem Temple. The texts of 1 Macc 2.6–8, 12–14 and 1 Macc. 3.45–47 read as follows:

---

4. D. Satran, 'Daniel: Seer, Philosopher, Holy Man', in George W. E. Nickleburg and John J. Collins (eds.), *Ideal Figures in Ancient Judaism* (Septuagint and Cognate Studies, 12; Atlanta: Scholars Press, 1980), pp. 33–48 (35). Vogel thinks that, 'Daniel, mourning for the sins of his people, is hoping that the judgment for his people can be averted and the temple be restored as the place of atonement.' Vogel, 'The Cultic Motif in Space and Time', p. 228.

[2.6] He saw the blasphemies being committed in Judah and Jerusalem,
[v. 7] and said, 'Alas! Why was I born to see this, the ruin of my people,
the ruin of the holy city, and to live there when it was given over to the
enemy, the sanctuary given over to aliens?
[v. 8] Her temple has become like a person without honor;
[v. 12] And see, our holy place, our beauty, and our glory have been laid
waste; the Gentiles have profaned them.
[v. 13] Why should we live any longer?'
[v. 14] Then Mattathias and his sons tore their clothes, <u>put on sackcloth,
and mourned greatly</u>.
3.45 Jerusalem was uninhabited like a wilderness; not one of her
children went in or out. The sanctuary was trampled down, and aliens
held the citadel; it was a lodging place for the Gentiles. Joy was taken
from Jacob; the flute and the harp ceased to play.
[v. 46] Then they gathered together and went to Mizpah, opposite
Jerusalem, because Israel formerly had a place of prayer in Mizpah.
[v. 47] They fasted that day, <u>put on sackcloth</u> and sprinkled ashes on
their heads, and tore their clothes.

The passage in the *Psalms of Solomon* 2.19–21 reads thus:

[v. 19] For the nations reproached Jerusalem, trampling her down, her
beauty was dragged down from the throne of glory.
[v. 20] She <u>clothed herself with sackcloth</u> instead of clothes of beauty, a
rope around her head instead of a crown.
[v. 21] She took off the mitre of glory which God put on her, her beauty
was thrown to the earth in dishonour.
(translation mine).

The passages in 1 Maccabees and the *Psalms of Solomon* clearly speak of
Jerusalem and the temple being trampled as the cause for mourning and
putting on sackcloth by devout Jews. Mattathias and his sons put on
sackcloth and mourned greatly because the Gentiles had profaned the
temple. The author(s) of the *Psalms of Solomon* composed the lament to
depict Jerusalem clothed with sackcloth instead of beautiful clothes on
account of her desecration by the Gentiles.[5]

Another near contemporaneous text with the book of Revelation,
namely the *Ascension of Isaiah* tells of a situation when there was great
iniquity in Jerusalem at the time of King Manasseh:[6]

---

5. It is interesting to note that in *Pss. Sol.* 2.25, the antagonist of Israel is called 'the
dragon' (τοῦ δράκοντος). We have argued that the imagery of the dragon waiting to devour the
child probably derives from Jer. 51.34 (LXX Jer. 28.24) where Nebuchadnezzar is called a
dragon ready to attack Israel.

6. Bauckham argues that the *Ascension of Isaiah* 'most probably dates from the decade
70–80 C.E.' Bauckham, 'The Ascension of Isaiah: Genre, Unity and Date', in *idem, The Fate
of the Dead*, pp. 363–90 (389). Other scholars have proposed a later date for the *Ascension of*

All of them [the prophets] were <u>clothed in sackcloth</u>, and all of them were prophets; they had nothing with them, but were destitute, and they all lamented bitterly over the going astray of Israel.
(*Mart. Isa.* 2.10).

If the mission of the two witnesses in Rev. 11.3 is viewed in the context of the trampling of the holy city in 11.2, then it is not difficult to see that their appearance dressed in sackcloth is a response to what they perceive as the desecration of the holy city and the temple precincts by the nations. The iniquity of Jerusalem must be very great as the great city is spiritually called Sodom and Egypt (11.8).[7] Minear remarks that: 'This mission takes place in the midst of conflict which rages for forty-two months between the trampling nations and the holy city.'[8] There is certainly no suggestion in the text that the sackcloth represents 'the church's prophetic task of calling the world to repentance and perhaps also symbolizes the church's need to repent (11.3)'.[9]

3. *The Two Olive Trees and the Two Lampstands*

The text of Rev. 11.4 attempts to identify the two witnesses as follows:

οὗτοί εἰσιν αἱ δύο ἐλαῖαι καὶ αἱ δύο λυχνίαι αἱ ἐνώπιον τοῦ κυρίου τῆς γῆς ἑστῶτες.

The two witnesses are 'identified' as the two olive trees and the two lampstands that stand before the Lord of the earth.[10] However, the

---

Isaiah within the first decades of second century C.E. So J. M. Knight, 'Ascension of Isaiah', Craig A. Evans & Stanley E. Porter (eds.), *Dictionary of New Testament Background* (Downers Grove: Inter-Varsity Press, 2000), pp. 129–30.

7.   For a discussion of Jerusalem being spiritually called Sodom and Egypt (11.8), see P. Minear, 'Ontology and Ecclesiology in the Apocalypse', *NTS* 13 (1966), pp. 89–105. We agree with Minear (p. 94 n. 1) who notes that the adverb πνευματικῶς in 11.8 is best translated 'as *prophetically* rather than *allegorically* (RSV) for several reasons'. Minear (p. 94 n. 1) reasons that: 'To say allegorically is to stress a conscious literary technique in which a single empirical datum is given a corresponding symbolic equivalent. To say prophetically is to stress the prophet's spiritual gift, a charisma which enables him to see the hidden meanings and the invisible unity of multiple empirical data. Πνευματικῶς suggests the presence of the Spirit and his power, both in John and in the work of the two olive trees. To say *allegorically*, on the other hand, prejudges the kind of thinking and the kind of literature, while to say *prophetically* enables us to avoid this prejudgement.'

8.   Minear, *I Saw a New Earth: An Introduction to the Visions of the Apocalypse* (Washington: Corpus, 1969), p. 98.

9.   Resseguie, *Revelation Unsealed*, p. 42.

10.   For general studies on trees as metaphors in the prophetic literature, see K. Nielsen, *There is Hope for a Tree: The Tree as a Metaphor in Isaiah* (trans. Christine and Frederick Crowley; JSOTSup, 65; Sheffield: Sheffield Academic Press, 1989); B. Oestreich, *Metaphors*

identification of the two witnesses with a double metaphor – the two olive trees and the two lampstands – does not make their identity any clearer unless we know what John meant by the reference to the two olive trees and the two lampstands.[11] It is like solving one mystery with another mystery. Nevertheless, it is clear that John is making an attempt to assist his readers to interpret the two witnesses through the lens of these two metaphors. The allusion to Zech. 4.14 is often cited as the text that lies behind Rev. 11.4. In Zech. 4.14, the vision identifies the two olive trees mentioned in Zech. 4.3, 11–12 as the two sons of oil who stand before the Lord of all the earth.[12] The text of Zech. 4.14 reads thus:

וַיֹּאמֶר אֵלֶּה שְׁנֵי בְנֵי־הַיִּצְהָר הָעֹמְדִים עַל־אֲדוֹן כָּל־הָאָרֶץ

In the vision of Zech. 4, one olive tree stands on the right of the bowl of one lampstand and the other olive tree on its left (Zech. 4.2–3, 11). It appears that the branches of the two olive trees pour out oil through the golden pipes of the lampstand and thus supply it with fresh oil (Zech. 4.13). It is not surprising, therefore, that the two olive trees are then identified as the two sons of fresh oil standing before the Lord of the whole earth (Zech. 4.14). The majority of commentators interpret the olive trees in Zech. 4 as the governor Zerubbabel and the high priest Joshua, the two leaders of the post-exilic community of Israel.[13] This identification is

---

and Similes for Yahweh in Hosea 14.2–9 (1–8). A Study of Hoseanic Pictorial Language (Frankfurt am Main: Peter Lang, 1998), pp. 191–225; B. Green, *Like a Tree Planted: An Exploration of Psalms and Parables Through Metaphor* (Collegeville: The Liturgical Press, 1997). Jacoba Kuikman notes that individuals are often compared to trees. (cf. Deut 20.19). J. Kuikman, 'Christ as Cosmic Tree', *TorJT* 16 (2000), pp. 141–54 (145). Kuikman (p. 145) comments that according to Isa. 11.1: 'The Messiah himself is envisioned as a Tree by Isaiah.' More significantly Kuikman (p. 145) remarks that: 'The messianic future is presaged as "the days of a tree" (Isa. 65.22).' Similarly, the two witnesses identified as trees presage the messianic kingdom to come. For it is said that after the days of their prophecy for 1260 days and their deaths for three-and-a-half days, the kingdom of the world will have come to the possession of the Lord and his Christ (Rev. 11.15). For studies on the lampstand or menorah and its symbolism, see C. Meyers, *The Tabernacle Menorah: A Synthetic Study of a Symbol from the Biblical Cult* (Missoula: Scholars Press, 1976), and L. Yarden, *Tree of Light: A Study of the Menorah, the Seven-Branched Lampstand* (Ithaca, New York: Cornell University Press, 1971).

11.   We disagree with Beasley-Murray that John 'interprets the olive trees as the *two lampstands*'. Beasley-Murray, *Revelation*, p. 184 (his emphasis). It is important to note that both the two olive trees and the two lampstands are articular, a strong indication that John intends *both* metaphors to control what he wants the readers to understand about the two witnesses. Aune writes: 'It is striking that the two witnesses are *both* the two olive trees and the two menorahs.' Aune, *Revelation 6–16*, p. 612 (his emphasis).

12.   While most English versions translate שְׁנֵי בְנֵי־הַיִּצְהָר as 'the two anointed ones', the MT reads literally 'two sons of (fresh) oil'. We will return to this point in a later section.

13.   So D. Petersen, *Haggai & Zechariah 1–8* (OTL; London: SCM, 1984), p. 231; E. Meyers and C. Meyers, *Haggai & Zechariah 1–8* (ABC; New York: Doubleday: 1987), p. 275.

almost certain given that Joshua the high priest is the subject of Zechariah's vision in ch. 3 and Zerubbabel the governor is mentioned thrice (Zech. 4.6, 8, 10) amidst Zechariah's dialogue with an angel about the two olive trees in Zech. 4. God's vision and purpose for the post-exilic community is channeled through the designated leaders to the community, making the imagery of the two olive trees apt in that they pour fresh oil to the post-exilic community symbolized by the golden lampstand. John could have adopted the Zerubbabel and Joshua pairing as best reflecting his conception of the two witnesses and the church corporate as kings and priests (Rev. 1.6; 5.10), since Zerubbabel or *Zemah* (the branch) in the book of Zechariah is a royal figure (cf. Zech. 6.12–14) and Joshua is explicitly called the high priest.[14]

The thrust of Zechariah's message is that the community's well-being and destiny in fulfilling God's purpose lie in the community's recognition and acceptance of the two designated leaders in Zerubbabel and Joshua. If God's appointed agents of restoration are acknowledged, then the post-exilic community comes under the blessing of God in that the temple will be rebuilt and the city of Jerusalem restored to its former glory (Zech. 1.14–17; 2.10–12; 4.6–10; 6.12–15). Zechariah's portrayal of Joshua and Zerubbabel as God's chosen leaders is intended to persuade the community to accept the envisioned future destined for the community under the joint leadership of Zerubbabel and Joshua. Deborah Rooke writes:

> The lampstand episode [Zech. 4] is a reminder after the cleansing episode's [Zech. 3] emphasis on the high priest that there is another significant figure in the community who has Yahweh's favour, and that

See also Holwerda, 'The Church and the Little Scroll (Revelation 10–11)', p. 156; Bernard P. Robinson, 'The Two Persecuted Prophets-Witnesses of Rev. 11', *Scripture Bulletin* 19 (1988), pp. 14–19 (17). As the two sons of oil are not explicitly named, it is understandable that they have also been viewed as eschatological figures. Cook writes: 'Zechariah never viewed his messianic hopes for the diarchy as already realized. Rather, by not naming specific individuals, Zechariah looks forward to the expected high priest and the prince of the coming millennium (Zech. 4.14).' Cook, *Prophecy and Apocalypticism*, pp. 131–32. Howard Clark Kee argues that Zech. 4.14 should be 'regarded as a prediction of the two messiahs, kingly and priestly, who are to appear in Israel on the day of eschatological fulfilment'. H. C. Kee, 'Christology in Mark's Gospel', in Jacob Neusner, William Scott Green, and Ernest S. Frerichs (eds.), *Judaisms and Their Messiahs at the Turn of the Christian Era* (New York: Cambridge University Press, 1987), pp. 187–208 (188).

14. Lund writes: 'The two witnesses in 11.3, 4, are described in symbols which are derived from Zech. 4.2–12, but it would be folly to assume that in the passage in the New Testament we are dealing with Zerubbabel and the high-priest Joshua of the Old Testament passage.' Lund, *Studies in the Book of Revelation*, p. 30. Robinson argues that the notion of the two witnesses represents the Christian community of martyrs exercising 'the twin roles of kingship and priesthood'. See Robinson, 'The Two Persecuted Prophets-Witnesses of Rev. 11', p. 17.

the proper working together of both figures as defined in the cleansing and crowning episodes (and also in the oracular material of 4.6b 10a) is essential for the community's well being.[15]

The focus of Zechariah's vision in ch. 3 is Joshua the high priest through whom God will remove the guilt of the land in a single day (Zech. 3.9). The atonement and cleansing of the land is the prelude to rebuilding the temple in which Zerubbabel would play the major role (Zech. 4.6–10; 6.12–13) with Joshua by his side: 'There shall be a priest by his throne, with peaceful understanding between the two of them' (Zech. 6.13b).

Zerubbabel's and Joshua's roles are distinct but complementary. Zechariah the prophet in the vision of the two olive trees of Zech. 4 appears to depict their leadership as a diarchy. Arguably Joshua is seen as an equal to Zerubbabel in the exercise of the joint leadership over the post-exilic community.[16]

a. *The Influence of Zech. 4 on Revelation 11.1–13*

It is not clear to what extent the context of the book of Zechariah in general and Zech. 4 in particular has influenced John's characterization of the two witnesses. What is clear is that Rev. 11.4 alludes not just to Zech. 4.14 but also to the immediate context of Zech. 4 as the two olive trees are

15.   D. Rooke, *Zadok's Heirs: The Role and Development of the High Priesthood in Ancient Israel* (Oxford: Oxford University Press, 2000), p. 146.

16.   Mark Boda has recently challenged the view that the two olive trees represent Zerubbabel and Joshua. Instead, Boda argues that the two olive trees that stand before the Lord of the whole earth represent the two prophets of the post-exilic community, namely Haggai and Zechariah. See M. Boda, 'Oil, Crowns and Thrones: Prophet, Priest and King in Zechariah 1:7–6:15', *Journal of Hebrew Scriptures* 3 (2001) [e-journal; Accessed 8th August 2002; available from http://www.arts.ualberta.ca/JHS/]. Wolter H. Rose also rejects the identification of the two olive trees with Zerubbabel and Joshua and argues that they are two heavenly beings. See W. H. Rose, *Zemah and Zerubbabel: Messianic Expectations in the Early Postexilic Period* (JSOTSup, 304; Sheffield: Sheffield Academic Press, 2000), pp. 200–2. Rooke has recently argued that Zerubbabel the governor occupies a more prominent position than Joshua the high priest and disputes strongly the notion that they are equal in authority. See Rooke, *Zadok's Heirs*, pp. 146–51. While Rooke's arguments cannot be fully discussed here, we agree that the emphasis on Zerubbabel in Zech. 6 as the temple builder and the one who bears royal authority appears to give Zerubbabel a more prominent role than Joshua the high priest (Zech. 6.11–14). Nevertheless, for our purposes, it is not necessary to decide this point as John of Revelation might have restricted his allusion to the vision of the two olive trees in Zech. 4 where the picture of the two olive trees connotes equality. Speaking of the vision of the two olive trees in Zech. 4.14, S. M. Siahaan comments that, 'Penglihatan ini penting untuk penelitian kita, kerana memastikan kedudukan imam besar dan mengangkat kehormatan Yosua sejajar dengan Zerubabel.' (ET: This vision is important to our discussion because it establishes the position of the high priest and raises Joshua as Zerubbabel equal). S. M. Siahaan, *Pengharapan Mesias dalam Perjanjian Lama* ([ET: *The Messianic Hope in the Old Testament*] Jakarta: BPK Gunung Mulia, 1991), p. 123.

not mentioned in Zech. 4.14 but in the earlier verses of the chapter (4.3, 11–12). Bauckham remarks that: 'John's use of the Old Testament is not a matter of plucking phrases at random out of contexts, but consists in careful and deliberate exegesis of whole passages.'[17] The additional metaphor of the two lampstands after the two olive trees in Rev. 11.4 is probably derived from elsewhere as there is only one lampstand in Zech. 4. Further, the one lampstand in Zech. 4 is not depicted as standing before the Lord of the earth as is the case for the two lampstands in Rev. 11.4. In the text of Rev. 11.4 the phrase '*the* two lampstands' is articular like *the* two olive trees, arguably an indication that for John the two metaphors must be given due consideration as far as the identity of the two witnesses is concerned.

The identification of the two witnesses as the two olive trees read in light of the Zecharianic allusion discussed above indicates that the two witnesses are two individuals. The two olive trees in Zech. 4, whether they represent Zerubbabel and Joshua or Haggai and Zechariah the prophets or future eschatological figures are clearly symbols for two individual leaders of the post-exilic community. Coupled with the fact that the two witnesses are clothed with sackcloth (Rev. 11.3), it is likely that they are two individuals and not some corporate figure or body. Secondly, the image of the two olive trees/two sons of oil as equal partners in supplying fresh oil to the golden lampstand in Zech. 4 is suited for John's representation of the two witnesses as equal in authority and function. Giblin calls the two witnesses 'identical theological twins' for the two witnesses are portrayed as an unbreakable partnership of two.[18] They prophesy, they perform signs and they die, rise again and ascend to heaven as a twosome. They are inseparable in life and in death. All the works are said to be carried out jointly. Minear writes:

> John makes no statement which applies solely to either of the two figures separately. Whatever is done, they do together; whatever is suffered, they suffer together. The time of their prophecy is a single time, beginning and ending simultaneously and having the same duration.[19]

Thus the vision of the two olive trees as the two sons of oil standing before the Lord of the earth explains well the two witnesses' joint service before God.

Thirdly, the imagery of the two olive trees pouring out oil from their branches through the pipes of the lampstand in Zech. 4 speaks of the

17. Bauckham, *Climax of Prophecy*, p. 246.
18. Giblin, *Revelation*, p. 116.
19. Minear, *I Saw a New Earth*, pp. 101–2.

function of the two leaders within the community. Just as the lampstand cannot continue to give its light without a constant supply of oil, the community cannot hope to achieve the purposes of God unless they accept God's appointed leaders and work together in concert and under the leadership of Zerubbabel and Joshua. The prophet Haggai is consistent in depicting the leaders Zerubbabel and Joshua and the community they lead as one entity responding to the voice of the Lord through Haggai (Hag. 1.12–15; 2.2–5). God's word through the prophets is not only directed to the leaders but to all the remnant of the people (Hag. 1.12–15). The promise of the Spirit is made to the leaders and the community (Hag. 2.2–5).

But in Rev. 11.4 the two witnesses are identified as the two olive trees and the two lampstands. Bauckham correctly notes that: '[But] in identifying them [the two witnesses] with the lampstands, he [John] has modified the symbolism of Zechariah's vision.'[20] Now the oil that flows from the olive branches to the one lampstand of Zechariah's vision is a symbol of God's spirit as the oracle to Zerubbabel makes clear: 'This is the word of the Lord to Zerubabbel: "Not by might, nor by power, but by my spirit, says the Lord of hosts"' (Zech. 4.6). Appropriately this oracle is sandwiched between the visions of the two olive trees in Zech. 4.1–5 and 4.11–14.[21] While in Zech. 4 the oil is channeled to the community (symbolized by the lampstand) through the two leaders (symbolized by the two olive trees), there is no suggestion that this Zecharianic notion is carried over to the depiction of two witnesses as the two olive trees and the two lampstands. We agree with Bauckham that: 'If "the two olive trees" have a significance for John more than simply referring to Zechariah's vision, it is probably that the two prophets (cf. [Rev] 11.3, 10), are anointed with the oil of the Spirit.'[22] Since the two witnesses are also the two lampstands which we argue symbolize the church, the Spirit which empowers the two individual prophets is also 'the power of the church's prophetic witness to the world'.[23]

Further, it has been argued that just as the two olive trees in Zech. 4.14 are seen as the two anointed ones or the two Messiahs, the two witnesses of Rev. 11.3–13 are also depicted by John as two messianic figures. According to Howard M. Teeple, consuming their enemies with fire is an attribute of a Messiah and moreover the two witnesses are represented as the two

---

20. Bauckham, *Climax of Prophecy*, p. 165.

21. For a discussion of the imagery of the two olive trees pouring oil into the lampstand in Zech. 4.12, see Wolters, 'Confessional Criticism and the Night Visions of Zechariah', pp. 93–94.

22. Bauckham, *Climax of Prophecy*, p. 165.

23. Bauckham, *Climax of Prophecy*, p. 165.

anointed ones of Zech. 4.14.[24] But in the book of Revelation only Jesus is called the Christ or the Messiah. M. de Jonge states thus: 'In the Apocalypse in its present form there is only one Anointed One: Jesus who died and was exalted to heaven, and who will return in future.'[25] As such it is unlikely that John of Revelation thought of the two witnesses as Messiahs or anointed ones. Therefore, we cannot agree with Teeple's arguments that the two witnesses are to be viewed as Messiahs. We have already seen that the phrase בְנֵי־הַיִּצְהָר in Zech. 4.14 is best translated as 'the two sons of oil', thus a reading that suggests the imagery of the two olive trees as representing two Messiahs or two anointed ones is not entirely defensible.[26]

Rose has argued convincingly, in our view, that the interpretation of the Hebrew phrase בְנֵי־הַיִּצְהָר as 'anointed ones' is flawed. Rose comments that, יצהר is not synonymous with שמן, the usual word for oil, and the word used for anointing oil and oil used to burn a lamp. The phrase בני היצהר should be understood as referring to those who provide oil, that is they are

---

24. Howard M. Teeple, *The Mosaic Eschatological Prophet* (SBL Monographs, 10; Ann Arbor, Michigan: Society of Biblical Literature, 1957), p. 44.

25. M. de Jonge, 'The Use of the Expression ὁ Χριστὸς in the Apocalypse of St. John', p. 268.

26. While it is doubtful whether the text in Zech. 4.14 supports a reading of two Messiahs or anointed ones, some later traditions based on Zech. 4.14 developed in such a way that produced the concept of the two Messiahs found in the Dead Sea Scrolls. Although most scholars agree that Qumran texts like 1 QS 9.10–11 and CD 9b.10, 29; 15.4; 18.7 evince the belief in two Messiahs as eschatological figures, there is no evidence to suggest that John of Revelation is influenced by the notion of the two Messiahs of Qumran in his portrayal of the two witnesses since John is insistent that only Jesus is called the Messiah in the book of Revelation. The monographs and articles on Qumran messianism are too many to list. For a select few examples, see J. J. Collins, *The Scepter and the Star: The Messiahs of the Dead Sea Scrolls and Other Ancient Literature* (New York: Doubleday, 1997); *idem*, 'Messiahs in Context: Method in the Study of Messianism in the Dead Sea Scrolls', in Michael Wise *et al.* (eds.), *Methods of Investigation of the Dead Sea Scrolls and Khirbet Qumran Site: Present Realities and Future Prospects* (New York: Academy of Sciences, 1994), pp. 213–30; *idem*, 'Ideas of Messianism in the Dead Sea Scrolls', in James H. Charlesworth and Walter P. Weaver (eds.), *The Dead Sea Scrolls and the Christian Faith* (Harrisburg, PA: Trinity Press International, 1998), pp. 20–41; Émile Puech, 'Messianism, Resurrection, and Eschatology at Qumran and in the New Testament', in E. Ulrich and J. VanderKam (eds.), *The Community of the Renewed Covenant: The Notre Dame Symposium on the Dead Sea Scrolls* (Notre Dame: University of Notre Dame Press, 1994), pp. 235–56; K. G. Kuhn, 'The Two Messiahs of Aaron and Israel', in K. Stendahl (ed.), *The Scrolls and the New Testament* (New York: Harper, 1957), pp. 54–64; L. D. Hurst, 'Did Qumran Expect Two Messiahs?', *BBR* 9 (1999), pp. 157–80; Joseph A. Fitzmyer, *The Dead Sea Scrolls and Christian Origins* (Grand Rapids: Eerdmans, 2000), ch. 5 'Qumran Messianism', pp. 73–110; James C. VanderKam, 'Messianism in the Scrolls', in E. Ulrich and James C. VanderKam (eds.), *The Community of the Renewed Covenant: The Notre Dame Symposium on the Dead Sea Scrolls* (Notre Dame: University of Notre Dame Press, 1994), pp. 211–34.

oil suppliers.'[27] We can conclude that although the two witnesses are seen as anointed by the Spirit and thus enabled to perform mighty signs (11.5–6), they are not viewed as messianic figures by John.

b. *The Individual and Corporate Dimensions of the Two Witnesses*

By identifying the two witnesses as the two olive trees and the two lampstands, we suggest that John envisions the two witnesses as two individual prophets and also the church corporate. This individual–corporate imagery we envisage for the two witnesses is made clear through the second metaphor in Rev. 11.4. The two witnesses are also the two lampstands. The symbol of a lampstand is used by John to represent a church in 1.20 where it is said that, 'the seven lampstands are the seven churches'. The mention of the lampstand here in 11.4 is probably a symbol for the church as a corporate body as it is in 1.20.

The seven churches addressed by John are the seven churches found in seven cities of Asia Minor, namely Ephesus, Smyrna, Pergamum, Thyatira, Sardis, Philadelphia, and Laodicea (1.11). Yet it has been recognized that the seven churches are not just merely the seven churches addressed by John but that *the number* seven represents the totality of churches in every place or the universal church.[28] John's use of numbers to designate the number of churches in this instance can be at once literal and symbolic. It is literal in that no one disputes that the seven churches are indeed the seven churches named in 1.11 (cf. Rev. 2–3), but also that the seven churches are symbolic of the larger body corporate called the church worldwide and are thus not limited to the churches in the province of Asia Minor. Similarly, we submit that the use of the *two* olive trees is a figure for *two* individual prophets and the reference to the *two* lampstands in 11.4 may be indicative of *two* churches or a portion of the churches.[29] However, it is more likely that the symbolic use of the number two represents the

27. Rose, *Zemah*, p. 195. Although we agree with Rose's arguments that the two sons of oil are not to be interpreted as anointed ones, we disagree with Rose's identification of the two sons of oil in Zech. 4.14 as two heavenly beings (pp. 202–7). Also Edgar W. Conrad writes: 'The word translated "anointed ones" by the NRSV [in Zech. 4.14] is not the word for "anointed one" or "messiah" in Hebrew. In fact, the NRSV translation renders two Hebrew words which can be translated more literally as "sons of oil". The word for "oil" here is not the word used for the oil of anointing. "Sons of oil," then, also has no royal connotations.' E. W. Conrad, *Zechariah* (Readings: A New Biblical Commentary; Sheffield: Sheffield Academic Press, 1999), pp. 108–9.

28. See the earlier discussion in our introductory chapter.

29. We should note that the number two may also denote the proportion of churches worldwide if the number two is viewed literally and as such is part of the seven churches which represent the totality of churches universally. Caird interprets the two lampstands in Rev 11 as 'a proportion of the church in all parts of the world'. Caird, *Revelation*, p. 134. Kiddle and

church in its capacity in giving testimony since the legal requirement for valid testimony is by at least two witnesses. Bauckham comments thus:

> That the two witnesses symbolize the church in its role of witnessing to the world is shown by the identification of them as lampstands (11.4), the symbol of the churches in ch. 1 . . . (1.12, 20). That they are only two does not indicate that they are only a part of the whole church, but corresponds to the well-known biblical requirement that evidence be acceptable only on the testimony of two witnesses (Deut. 19.15). They are therefore the church insofar as it fulfills its role as faithful witness.[30]

Our contention that the two witnesses are two individuals as well as the church corporate in their witness needs further explanation. By stating that the two witnesses are the two olive trees (individuals) and the two lampstands (the churches), John is already hinting to his readers that the two witnesses must be interpreted in both individual and corporate dimensions. Focusing on either the individual or the corporate aspect is not likely to do justice to John's portrayal of the two witnesses. How can the two witnesses be regarded individually and corporately at the same time? We believe Henry Wheeler Robinson's thesis about the 'Hebrew Conception of Corporate Personality' goes some way to explaining the depiction of the two witnesses in Rev. 11.4.[31] In our following discussion, we will only adopt one particular aspect of Robinson's concept of corporate personality, namely that an individual is often seen as representative of his group or conversely the group is often seen viewed through its leading member or representative.[32]

According to Robinson, the Hebrew conception of corporate personality is a fluid concept where individuals within a group and the group as a

---

Ross identify the two witnesses with the portion of the church that will suffer martyrdom. They write: 'The utmost we can say is that the two witnesses stand for that portion of the sevenfold Church which must suffer martyrdom.' Kiddle and Ross, *Revelation*, p. 183.

30. Bauckham, *Theology*, p. 85. See also *idem*, *Climax of Prophecy*, p. 274. So Holwerda, 'The Church and the Little Scroll (Revelation 10–11)', p. 157.

31. H. W. Robinson, *Corporate Personality in Ancient Israel* (Philadelphia: Fortress Press, rev. ed., 1980), pp. 25–44.

32. Different aspects of Robinson's concept of corporate personality have been critiqued by scholars. For example, J. R. Porter has rightly rejected the notion (see Robinson, *Corporate Personality*, pp. 25–26) that legally whatever the individual did in ancient Israel was considered being done by the whole group. J. R. Porter, 'Legal Aspects of Corporate Personality', *VT* 15 (1965), pp. 361–80. See also criticisms of Robinson's concept in J. W. Rogerson, 'The Hebrew Conception of Corporate Personality: A Re-Examination', *JTS* 21 (1970), pp. 1–16; *idem*, *Anthropology and the Old Testament* (Oxford: Basil Blackwell, 1979), pp. 55–57. Rogerson (*Anthropolgy*, p. 56) criticizes Robinson for propounding a theory of Hebrew mentality based on what Rogerson considers, are untenable assumptions. However, Rogerson (p. 56) acknowledges that 'parts of the Old Testament appear to imply what might be called "corporate" sense of an individual figure or speaker'.

corporate body are closely inter-related. Robinson argues that the concept of corporate personality includes 'the fluidity of reference, facilitating rapid and unmarked transitions from one to the many, and many to the one'.[33] Often there is oscillation between the individual and the corporate in Hebrew thought. The individual is at once a member of a group or a representative individual of the group. Conversely the group is related to the individual in that the group is made up of many members and the group is often viewed through an individual or a leading member. For example, the king is the leading member of the nation and its representative individual before God and the people. The nation Israel is often seen as personified in the king. According to G. W. Grogan, 'King and nation can have a common identification (Num. 20.14–21; 22.5)'.[34] Thus David the king is called the lamp of Israel by his soldiers: 'You shall not go out to battle with us any longer, so that you do not quench the lamp of Israel (LXX – τὸν λύχνον Ισραηλ)' (2 Sam. 21.17). If the king is captured or dies, the lamp of Israel is extinguished; the nation of Israel ceases to exist.

Robinson observed that individual personalities attained prominence in the making of Hebrew history and the development of Hebrew religion even when the stress on a communal sense was strong. Robinson acknowledged that this might be paradoxical but stated that: 'Where the corporate sense is strong, the outstanding man will gather to himself the force of the whole group.'[35] Outstanding men like Moses and David gathered to themselves the force of the whole nation. Robinson quotes the comment of S. A. Cook who remarked that: 'Hebrew thought refers with equal facility to a representative individual or to the group he represents.'[36]

Robinson gave a number of examples to support his view that there is considerable fluidity and oscillation between the individual and group in Hebrew thought. First, he cited the example of the prophet's identification with the nation as owing 'not a little to this corporate identity – "for the hurt of the daughter of my people am I hurt" [Jer. 8.21]' where the prophet takes on the persona of the nation and 'temporarily becomes the nation, and makes its needs articulate'.[37] Secondly, the 'I' of the Psalms, according to Robinson often takes on a corporate dimension even if 'the writer of a psalm is indeed an individual and not a syndicate, and that there is a sense in which it may be said that every psalm does represent an individual

33. Robinson, *Corporate Personality*, p. 27.

34. G. W. Grogan, 'The Old Testament Concept of Solidarity in Hebrews', *TynBul* 49 (1998), pp. 159–74 (163).

35. Robinson, *Corporate Personality*, p. 35.

36. S. A. Cook, *Cambridge Ancient History* Vol. 3 (New York: Macmillan, 1925), p. 493. Cited by Robinson, *Corporate Personality*, p. 35.

37. Robinson, *Corporate Personality*, p. 36.

experience and outlook'.[38] Similarly, Esther M. Menn in a recent article writes:

> Features of the Psalms themselves, including their non-specific and highly metaphorical language, their expression of human realities and emotions, and their occasional allusion to original performance within community rites, assure that identification of the psalmic 'I' as historical individuals can never be exhaustive.[39]

Menn concludes that the portrayal of the suffering individual in Psalm 22 'suggests that the fate of the individual is always more tightly linked to the fate of the larger community than might be supposed'.[40]

Thirdly, Robinson proposed that the notion of corporate personality could resolve the much debated identity of 'the Servant of Yahweh' in Deutero-Isaiah. Robinson questioned the need to decide either for a collective or individualistic interpretation in identifying Deutero-Isaiah's Servant of Yahweh.[41] According to Robinson, in the light of the Hebrew conception of corporate personality, 'the Servant can be both the prophet himself as representative of the nation, and the nation whose proper mission is actually being fulfilled only by the prophet and that group of followers who may share his views'.[42] The most debated song is perhaps the

---

38. Robinson, *Corporate Personality*, p. 38.

39. E. M. Menn, 'No Ordinary Lament: Relecture and the Identity of the Distressed in Psalm 22', *HTR* 93.4 (2000), pp. 301–41 (302–3). Menn (p. 303) argues that, 'Psalm 22 includes suggestive indication of a surrounding community presence' and thus cannot be solely viewed as an individual lament.

40. Menn, 'No Ordinary Lament', p. 341. For a general discussion on the identity of the individual in the Psalms, see S. J. L. Croft, *The Identity of the Individual in the Psalms* (Sheffield: JSOT Press, 1986).

41. Much has been written about the Servant or the Servant Songs in Deutero-Isaiah. For a few select examples, see Gordon P. Hugenberger, 'The Servant of the Lord in the "Servant Songs" of Isaiah', in Philip E. Satterthwaite *et al.* (eds.), *The Lord's Anointed: Interpretation of Old Testament Messianic Texts* (Carlisle: Paternoster Press, 1995), pp. 105–39; Rowley, *The Servant of the Lord*, pp. 1–60; Antti Laato, *The Servant of YHWH and Cyrus: A Reinterpretation of the Exilic Messianic Programme in Isaiah 40–55* (Stockholm: Almqvist & Wiksell International, 1992); *idem*, 'The Composition of Isaiah 40–55', *JBL* 109 (1990), pp. 207–28; Millard C. Lind, 'Monotheism, Power, and Justice: A Study in Isaiah 40–55', *CBQ* 46 (1984), pp. 432–46; Hyun Chul Paul Kim, 'An Intertextual Reading of "A Crushed Reed" and "A Dim Wick" in Isaiah 42.3', *JSOT* 83 (1999), pp. 113–24. For an intriguing view that the Servant of Yahweh was an individual named Meshullam found in Isa. 42.19 and 49.7, see Risa Levitt Kohn and William H. C. Propp, 'The Name of "Second Isaiah": The Forgotten Theory of Nehemiah Rabban', in Astrid B. Beck *et al.* (eds.), *Fortunate the Eyes That See: Essays in Honor of David Noel Freedman* (Grand Rapids: Eerdmans, 1995), pp. 223–35.

42. Robinson, *Corporate Personality*, p. 40. See Robinson's discussion on the four Servant songs at pp. 40–42. Kim agrees with Robinson's view on the Servant of Yahweh. Paul Kim writes: 'the servant in the form of a single person can simultaneously carry the nuance of the collective Israel'. Kim, 'An Intertextual Reading', p. 123. We should note that the individual

second Servant song in Isa. 49.1–6. The Servant there is called Israel (v. 3) but yet has a mission to Israel – to bring Jacob back to Yahweh, and that Israel might be gathered to him, and to raise the tribes of Israel and to restore the survivors of Israel (v. 5–6).

In our view, the passage in Isa. 49.1–6 is a classic example of both the individual and corporate dimensions of the Servant being highlighted and brought into stark juxtaposition. The Servant is called Israel because in him *as* Israel, the nation Israel will achieve her destiny as light to the nations and agent of God's salvation to the ends of the earth (v. 6b). The Servant is at once the individual prophet called to restore Israel by raising the tribes of Israel and in the process becomes completely identified with the corporate Israel as God's Servant to the rest of the world. Robinson noted that:

> Hebrew thought is content to bring them [individual and collective] into juxtaposition, because corporate personality could reconcile both.... The double *motif*, i.e., the national mission and the individual vocation, is thus carried through to the end, and it is made possible for Hebrew thought by the reconciling principle of corporate personality.[43]

Burnett sums up the notion of the corporate and the individual in the Old Testament as follows:

> The Hebrew scriptures, then, should not be seen as either to ignore the importance of the individual, or to contain a pattern of progression from corporation to individualism. There is, in fact, a more nuanced theology of individual and community, whereby an individual's actions and relationship to God is important, but only in so far as they are part of a larger narrative framework of the community as a whole.[44]

Following Robinson's observations, a number of interpretive possibilities are open to aid our understanding of the two witnesses who are said to be the two olive trees and two lampstands. The two witnesses are two individual prophets but they are also seen as representatives of a larger group, the church. As outstanding men or leaders within the church, they

and corporate dimensions of the Servant of the Lord are also found in Qumran. F. F. Bruce noted that: 'The priestly Messiah would be a representative of the whole righteous community. And the community itself is viewed as fulfilling the role of the Servant.' F. F. Bruce, *Biblical Exegesis in the Qumran Texts* (Grand Rapids: Eerdmans, 1957), p. 51.

43. Robinson, *Corporate Personality*, pp. 41–42. For a recent discussion on corporate personality, see J. S. Kaminsky, *Corporate Responsibility in the Hebrew Bible* (Sheffield: JSOT Press, 1995). See also Gary W. Burnett, *Paul & the Salvation of the Individual* (Leiden: Brill, 2001), esp. ch. 5 'The Collective and the Individual in Judaism', pp. 68–87, and P. Joyce, 'The Individual and the Community', in J. W. Rogerson (ed.), *Beginning Old Testament Study* (London: SPCK, 1983), pp. 74–89.

44. Burnett, *Paul & the Salvation of the Individual*, p. 77.

gather to themselves the force of the whole church. We can suggest that the church as a corporate body is represented by her leaders and is viewed though the prism of her leading members.[45]

Bruce J. Malina and Jerome H. Neyrey, without reference to Robinson, come to a similar conclusion concerning the nature of ancient personality. Malina and Neyrey comment:

> We submit that what characterized first-century Mediterranean people was not individualistic, but 'dyadic' or group-oriented personality. For people of that time and place, the basic, most elementary unit of social analysis is not the individual person but the dyad, a person in relation with and connected to at least one other social unit, in particular, the family.... They were primarily part of the group in which they found themselves inserted.[46]

What is noted by Malina and Neyrey is especially significant for our understanding of the individual and corporate dimensions of the two witnesses. Though we argue that they are two individual prophets, it is vital that they are understood as very much, in Malina's and Neyrey's terminology, 'part of the group in which they found themselves inserted'. The social unit or group of the prophets in general and of the two witnesses-prophets in particular, is the church. Thus it is perhaps not surprising that John has to use the double imagery of the two olive trees *and* the two lampstands to bring out both the individual and corporate dimensions of the two witnesses.[47]

Having discussed the above, it has to be acknowledged that the passage in Rev. 11.1–13 focuses on the witnesses more as individuals than as the church corporate. We have already mentioned that the fact they are clothed in sackcloth points towards an individual interpretation. Secondly, the confrontation between the two witnesses and their opponents (11.5)

---

45. It is interesting to note that Ignatius in the early second century C.E. wrote to the Trallians: 'that in him [the bishop] I had a vision of your whole congregation' (Ign. *Trall.* 1). To the Ephesians, Ignatius wrote: 'So also have Onesimus and Burrhus; and Euplus and Fronto too; and in their persons I have had a glimpse of you all' (Ign. *Eph.* 1). And to the Magnesians, he wrote: 'It was a privilege to have a glimpse of you in the persons of your saintly bishop Damas and his two clergy, the worthy Bassus and Apollonius, as well as my fellow-servitor Zotion the deacon' (Ign. *Magn.* 2). The translation of Ignatius' writings is taken from *Early Christian Writings: The Apostolic Fathers* (trans. Maxwell Staniforth; Introductions and new editorial material by Andrew Lowth; London: Penguin Books, 1987).

46. Bruce J. Malina and Jerome H. Neyrey, 'First-Century Personality: Dyadic, Not Individual', in Jerome H. Neyrey (ed.), *The Social World of Luke-Acts* (Peabody, MA: Hendrickson, 1991), pp. 67–96 (72–73).

47. Osborne is among the very few commentators that even consider that the two witnesses of Rev. 11 are both individuals and the corporate church. He writes: 'The two lampstands point to a corporate aspect, but the two olive trees point to an individual aspect.' Osborne, *Revelation*, p. 418.

speaks of a confrontation between two prophets and their enemies rather than the whole church against her opponents. This is made evident in that when under attack, the two witnesses kill their enemies with fire that comes out of their mouths (v. 5). It is not likely that John is here envisaging all the members of the church having such extraordinary powers.

Further, many Christians will suffer martyrdom during the span of three-and-a-half years (13.7–10; 17.6; 18.24) while the two witnesses are invincible throughout the whole of the three-and-a-half years period as the textual unit in 11.5–6 makes clear. It is only when they complete their testimony at the end of the three-and-a-half years period that they lose their immunity to harm and they die at the hands of the beast (11.7): 'When they have finished their testimony, the beast that comes up from the bottomless pit will make war on them and conquer them and kill them.'[48] Further, not all Christians are prophets in the manner of the two witnesses (11.10). Bauckham remarks that: 'Revelation clearly distinguishes between prophets and other Christians.'[49] Keener who interprets the two witnesses as a corporate figure for the church as 'the best of available options' acknowledges that the description of the two witnesses as lying in the street for three-and-a-half days can hardly fit the church.[50]

In sum, we submit that viewing the two witnesses as individuals as well as the church corporate is supported by John's identification of the two witnesses as the two olive trees and the two lampstands. As leading individuals within the group, the two witnesses are representatives of the church corporate. This portrayal of the two witnesses as two individuals and also corporate figure is further enhanced if their antagonists, the two beasts are seen to represent two individuals and also the society of the world, as we will argue.

---

48. One argument put forward that the two witnesses must be the church corporate and not two individuals is because it seems strange that two individuals are subject to war. Considene writes: 'Usually no nation or power makes war against two individuals.' Considene, 'The Two Witnesses: Apoc. 11: 3–13', p. 382. We have argued that the two witnesses are not only two individuals but they are also the church corporate. So there is nothing strange about the statement in 11.7. Further, it is not entirely correct to say that one or two individuals cannot be a subject of war. The Psalmist complains that: 'my enemies trample on me all day long, for many fight (LXX – πολεμῶν) against me' (Ps. 56.2). The Psalmist in Ps. 27.3 says: 'Though an army encamp against me, my heart shall not fear; though war (LXX – πόλεμος) rise up against me, yet I will be confident.'

49. Bauckham, *Theology*, p. 119.

50. Keener, *Revelation*, p. 292.

4. *The Signs of the Two Witnesses*

The three signs performed by the two witnesses – the shutting of the skies, the turning of the waters into blood and striking the earth with every kind of plague – are better attributed to two individual prophets and not to the whole church (v. 6). The whole church may be called to witness to the world but there is no suggestion in Revelation that everyone is given power to perform extraordinary miracles like the ones listed in 11.5–6. Revelation 11.6 apart from 11.4 provides another clue to the identity of the two witnesses. The three signs are reminiscent of the signs performed by Elijah and Moses. Bauckham writes: 'In 11.5–6 it is clear that the Old Testament models for the two prophets are Elijah and Moses.'[51] The signs in Rev. 11.5–6 can be illustrated as follows:

11.5 – Consumes enemies with fire   *Elijah* (2 Kings 1.1–14)
11.6a – Authority to shut the heavens   *Elijah* (1 Kings 17.1)
11.6b – Turns the waters into blood   *Moses* (Exod. 7.14–21)
11.6c – Casts every kind of plague   *Moses* (Exod. 9.13–14; 1 Sam 4.8)

Already in 11.5, the power of Elijah is alluded to by the reference to the fire that comes out of the two witnesses' mouths. Elijah the prophet was known as a prophet of fire (Sir. 48.1) because twice he called fire from heaven to consume the prophet's enemies (2 Kgs 1.10–14). Nevertheless, the fire that is the two witnesses' weapon of self defence is said to come out from the mouths of the two witnesses and not from heaven as is the case with Elijah.[52] While Giblin suggests that: 'The witnesses are not said actually to use this power',[53] the statement in 11.5 strongly implies that the power to kill is indeed used against the opponents of the two witnesses. But Elijah was not the only individual to possess this ability to call fire from heaven. It is rarely noticed that Moses in the seventh plague also caused fire to come down from heaven that killed many Egyptians and animals

---

51.   Bauckham, *Climax of Prophecy*, p. 275. Bauckham further (p. 275 n. 57) notes: 'The notion that Moses and Elijah represent the law and the prophets has no basis in the text.' Also Lohmeyer, *Offenbarung*, p. 93.

52.   There is no indication in the text to suggest that fire out of the two witnesses' mouths is to be understood figuratively. Rev. 11.5 is often thought to allude to Jer. 5.14 where Yahweh said: 'I am now making my words in your mouth a fire, and this people wood, and the fire shall devour them.' However, the fire in Jer. 5.14 is a metaphor for Jeremiah's words while in Rev. 11.5, there is no evidence to suggest the words of the two witnesses are likened to fire but rather like Elijah and Moses, the two witnesses kill their enemies with actual fire. Thus we disagree with Lund who remarked that: 'No one need entertain such a fantastic notion that the witnesses of Jesus in time to come shall blow fire out of their mouth to destroy their enemies (II Kings 1.10ff.).' Lund, *Studies in the Book of Revelation*, p. 134.

53.   Giblin, 'Revelation 11.1–13', p. 442.

besides: 'Then Moses stretched out his staff toward heaven, and the Lord sent thunder and hail, and *fire* came down upon the earth' (Exod. 9.23). Apart from Moses and Elijah it appears that no one else in the Bible is recorded to have called down fire to consume their enemies. It is noteworthy that a chiastic reading points to the fire-sign as first of the signs performed by the two witnesses in contrast to the calling of fire from heaven by the land-beast (Rev. 13.13), also the first of a number of signs and wonders performed by the latter on behalf of the sea-beast (13.14–15).

The sign to shut the heaven in order that it might not rain is also an Elijah-like sign. Elijah is said to have told Ahab the king that there would be no rain except at Elijah's word (1 Kgs. 17.1). Biblical traditions have it that Elijah withheld rain from heaven for three and a half years (cf. Lk. 4.25; Jas 5.17). The phraseology in Rev. 11.6 regarding the two witnesses' authority to shut the heaven (κλεῖσαι τὸν οὐρανόν) is verbally similar to the phrase ἐκλείσθη ὁ οὐρανός in the Lukan account (Lk. 4.25). It is not necessary to think that the drought enforced by the two witnesses is world-wide. It is more likely to be local. The term οὐρανός in Rev. 11.6 is not the heaven, the dwelling place of God but the sky.[54] The power of Elijah to stop rain has been compared with Amos 4.7–8 where God selectively gives and withholds rain between one city and another.[55]

Following the sign to shut the heavens, the two witnesses are also authorized to turn waters into blood. This sign is a clear allusion to the power of Moses in his confrontation against Pharaoh where the waters were turned into blood (Exod. 7.14–21). Finally, it is said that the two witnesses have authority to strike the earth with all kinds of plagues as often as they wish.[56] A likely background to this final and all encompassing

---

54. Bambang Mulyono notes that the word, 'heaven' is used 54 times in the book of Revelation. See Bambang Mulyono, *Teologi Ketabahan*, p. 96. According to Bambang Mulyono, the book of Revelation uses the word 'heaven' in five ways. First, it simply means the sky (6.13; 8.13; 9.1). Second, the word 'heaven' appears in the word-pair 'heaven and earth', it points to the idea of heaven being God's creation. Third, 'heaven' is the dwelling place of God (11.13; 12.7–9; 16.11). Fourth, 'heaven' is the dwelling place of angels (10.1). Fifth, the word 'heaven' may have the connotation of the place where the blessing of God originates. For example, Bambang Mulyono (pp. 97–98) suggests the notion of the New Jerusalem coming down from heaven points to the use of the word 'heaven' as the source of blessing. See Bambang Mulyono, *Teologi Ketabahan*, pp. 96–98. It appears that Bambang Mulyono's five categories can be reduced to three: heaven as the dwelling place of God and angels, heaven as the sky, and heaven as God's creation. For a study of the concept 'heaven' and its various connotations and meanings in the New Testament, see Ulrich W. Mauser, '"Heaven" in the World View of the New Testament', *HBT* 9.2 (1987), pp. 31–51.

55. See J. P. Brown, 'The Mediterranean Seer and Shamanism', *ZAW* 93 (1981), pp. 374–400 (385).

56. The NA27 lists 1 Sam. 4.8 (LXX) where it is said by the Philistines that the gods of Israel struck the Egyptians with every kind of plague (ἐν πάσῃ πληγῇ) as a possible background to the phrase ἐν πάσῃ πληγῇ in Rev. 11.6c. Bauckham says: 'The remaining two powers of the

sign may be found in Moses' speech to Pharaoh after the sixth plague in Exod. 9.13–14:

> [v. 13] Then the LORD said to Moses, 'Rise up early in the morning and present yourself before Pharaoh, and say to him, "Thus says the LORD, the God of the Hebrews: Let my people go, so that they may worship me. [v.14] For this time I will send all my plagues upon you yourself, and upon your officials, and upon your people, so that you may know that there is no one like me in all the earth."'

Although it is said in the Exodus narrative that through Moses God would send all the plagues upon the king of Egypt and his people, in Rev. 11.6 the two witnesses are empowered to strike the earth with all kinds of plagues as often as they wish. The authority of the two witnesses exceeds that of Moses in two respects. First, Moses did not have power to execute the plagues unless expressly commanded by God. Each plague performed by Moses and Aaron was done at the command of the Lord (Exod. 7.20; 8.5, 16, 20–21; 9.2). The two witnesses, on the other hand, appear to call down the plagues at their own volition. There is no indication in the text that they have to pray to the Lord or that the Lord must so command them before they perform the signs. Second, the two witnesses are able to do so *as often as they wish*. The nature of the two witnesses' authority far exceeds that of Moses and Elijah put together. This fact alone rules out the contention that the two witnesses are Moses and Elijah *redivivi*.[57] Though the signs the two witnesses perform can be better understood by reference to what Elijah and Moses had performed, the two witnesses stand apart from Elijah and Moses as far as their relative authority and power are concerned.

a. *The Traditions of Moses and Elijah*

As John has portrayed the powers of the two witnesses in the manner of Moses and Elijah, it can be assumed that John intends his readers to read the narrative of the two witnesses in the light of the traditions of Moses and Elijah. The scriptural promise that Elijah the prophet would return before the great and terrible day of the Lord in MT Mal. 3.23 (ET – Mal. 4.5) was very much a live issue in the first century C.E. According to the promise in the book of Malachi, Elijah the prophet will return as the eschatological prophet before the End, i.e., before the great and terrible

---

two witnesses are modelled on those of Moses, who turned the waters into blood (Exod. 7.14–24) and "struck the Egyptians with every sort of plague" (1 Sam. 4.8).' Bauckham, *Climax of Prophecy*, p. 275.

57.   James VanderKam argues that the two witnesses are Moses and Elijah but in our view, VanderKam fails to note sufficiently the striking differences between Moses and Elijah and the two witnesses. See VanderKam, '1 Enoch, Enochic Motifs, and Enoch', p. 90.

day of the Lord. Read in conjunction with the oracle in Mal. 3.1a: 'See, I am sending my messenger to prepare the way before me, and the Lord whom you seek will suddenly come into his temple', Elijah is also thought to come as God's messenger to prepare the way for God, i.e., before God himself makes his appearance in Israel.[58] This expectation was widely held in the first century C.E. as the Gospels' accounts attest.[59]

During Jesus' ministry, a number of his followers and the crowds thought Jesus was Elijah *redivivus* (Mt. 16.14; Mk 6.15; Lk. 9.8). But the synoptic Gospels consistently portray not Jesus but John the Baptist as Elijah. Matthew explicitly identifies John the Baptist as the Elijah who is to come (Mt. 11.14). The Markan account is less explicit but implies that Elijah has come in the person of John the Baptist (Mk 9.13). It is important to note that in both Matthean and Markan accounts, the promise about Elijah's return in Mal. 3.23 appears to be fulfilled when John the Baptist is identified with Elijah. It is clear that Elijah did not return in person and that John the Baptist is *not* Elijah the prophet of old but only that the former is identified as the latter. So according to Matthew and Mark, Elijah has indeed come not in his person (the prophet of eighth century B.C.E.) but in the person of John the Baptist of the first century C.E.[60] This notion is perhaps hard on modern ears but is not novel in the first century, as on several occasions, Jesus himself was thought to be 'John the Baptist risen from the dead, or Jeremiah or one of the prophets of old' (Mt. 16.14; cf. Mk 6.15; Lk. 9.8).

The possibility remains that some other individuals could come in the future and fulfill the expectation of Elijah's return. We should note that Jesus' enigmatic answer in Mk 9.12, 'Elijah is indeed coming first to restore

---

58. See B. V. Malchow, 'The Messenger of the Covenant in Mal 3:1', *JBL* 103 (1984), pp. 252–55. That Elijah is to appear as forerunner of *God* seems clear according to Mal. 3.1, 23. But there is considerable debate whether Elijah was thought of as forerunner of *the Messiah* according to Jewish expectation of the first century C.E. Morris M. Faierstein argues that the concept of Elijah as forerunner of the Messiah is not evident in the first century C.E. M. Faierstein, 'Why Do the Scribes Say That Elijah Must Come First?', *JBL* 100 (1981), pp. 75–86. Faierstein's view is challenged by Dale C. Allison Jr., 'Elijah Must Come First', *JBL* 103 (1984), pp. 256–58. Allison (p. 257) is correct to stress that 'we by no means have certain knowledge of all eschatological expectations held in the variegated Judaism of Jesus' time'.

59. Richard Hiers thinks that it is likely that Jesus connected the coming messenger of Mal. 3.1 with the coming Elijah of Mal. 4.5 (MT – Mal 3:23). See R. Hiers, 'Purification of the Temple: Preparation for the Kingdom of God', *JBL* 90 (1971), pp. 82–90 (88).

60. Beale writes: 'Just as John the Baptist was not a literal reappearance of Elijah, but came "in the spirit and power of Elijah" (Lk 1.17), likewise the two witnesses are not Moses and Elijah reincarnated.' Beale, *Revelation*, p. 573. A. W. Zwiep notes that Malachi's words in Mal. 3.23 'are sometimes taken as to announce the manifestation of an Elijah-like figure, rather than a reappearance of Elijah himself'. A. W. Zwiep, *The Ascension of the Messiah in Lukan Christology* (NovTSup, 87; Leiden: Brill, 1997), p. 61 n. 2.

all things' leaves the possibility open for another future prophet or prophets since John the Baptist could not be said to have restored all things. Thus we disagree with Markus Öhler who suggests: 'That in the person of John Elijah has already come is stated in Mk 9.12, and thus all hope for Elijah's return should be abolished.'[61] Further, the promise of Elijah's return in Mal. 3.23 is said to take place just before the great and terrible day of the Lord. However, the appearance of John the Baptist did not bring about the great and terrible day of the Lord, at least not as traditionally understood. This means that it is not implausible for ancient readers and writers like John of Revelation to anticipate that the promise of Elijah's return awaits a future fulfillment.

Luke is also more equivocal about the identification of John the Baptist with the prophet Elijah as the prophecy on John the Baptist in Lk. 1.16–17 indicates:

> [v. 16] He [John the Baptist] will turn many of the people of Israel to the Lord their God.
> [v. 17] With the spirit and power of Elijah he will go before him, to turn the hearts of parents to their children, and the disobedient to the wisdom of the righteous, to make ready a people prepared for the Lord.[62]

For Luke, unlike Matthew, John the Baptist comes in the spirit and power of Elijah but is not identified with Elijah. The author of John's Gospel, on the other hand, completely rejects any identification of John the Baptist with Elijah the prophet. In a series of questions and answers, John the Baptist denied that he was the Messiah, Elijah or the prophet. We concur with D. L. Bock who suggests that, 'John's [the Baptist] hesitation to accept the Elijah identification may well be a result of his recognizing that Elijah was yet to come'.[63] What is of interest here is that according to the Gospel of John, there are three awaited figures and all three are not to be identified with each other as the passage in Jn 1.19–21 makes clear:

> [v. 19] This is the testimony given by John when the Jews sent priests and Levites from Jerusalem to ask him, 'Who are you?' [v. 20] He confessed and did not deny it, but confessed, 'I am not the Messiah.' [v. 21] And

---

61. M. Öhler, 'The Expectation of Elijah and the Presence of the Kingdom of God', *JBL* 118 (1999), pp. 461–76 (465).

62. Barnabas Lindars writes: 'Elijah's function can be understood in two ways: he is the herald of the coming of the Lord, and he has a social task in preparation for it.' B. Lindars, *The Gospel of John* (NCB; London: Marshall, Morgan & Scott, 1971), pp. 103–4.

63. D. L. Bock, 'Elijah and Elisha', in Joel B. Green, Scot Mcknight and I. Howard Marshall (eds.) *Dictionary of Jesus and the Gospels* (Leicester: Inter-Varsity Press, 1992), pp. 203–6 (205).

they asked him, 'What then? Are you Elijah?' He said, 'I am not.' 'Are you the prophet?' He answered, 'No.'

Elijah the prophet is not to be confused with *the* prophet. The last question in the above passage: 'Are you the prophet?' clearly refers to a prophet like Moses in Deut. 18.15, 18 whom God promised to raise up from among the people of Israel.[64] What is of significance in John's Gospel is that this figure, the prophet like Moses, is understood as a future prophet distinguished from Elijah the prophet who is also seen as an expected figure to come. So in the Johannine account, apart from the Messiah, there are two prophets (Elijah and the prophet like Moses) who will make their appearances in Israel according to the Jewish expectations at the time. Court writes: 'The discussion of the identity of the John the Baptist (Jn 1.20–21) involves three figures, Christ, Elijah and the "prophet like Moses", which may reflect popular expectation.'[65]

John's Gospel is intent on depicting John the Baptist as a witness to Christ (Jn 1.6–7, 32–34). Also in Jn 5.35, John the Baptist is likened to a lamp that burns and shines. Aune says:

> It should be borne in mind that the term λύχνος, 'light,' is also used as a metaphor for witness. Just as the two witnesses are λυχνίαι, 'lights,' so John the Baptist is also spoken of figuratively as ὁ λύχνος ὁ καιόμενος καὶ φαίνων, 'the light which burns and shines' [Jn 5.35].[66]

It appears that the Gospel of John presents John the Baptist as a lampstand that burns and shines *as* a witness for Jesus. We can perhaps draw the parallel here that the two witnesses described as the two lampstands are like John the Baptist called to burn and shine as witnesses for Jesus. Whether or not John of Revelation could have known or been influenced by the traditions that lie behind Jn 1.19–22 is debatable, but it is of immense interest that these traditions speak of two prophetic figures apart from Christ that are thought of as future prophets. Furthermore, John the Baptist is presented as a witness and likened to a lampstand – terminology which is found in Rev. 11.3–4.

b. *The Transfiguration Accounts in the Synoptic Gospels*
A number of scholars have noted that the Synoptic transfiguration accounts where Moses and Elijah appeared together with Jesus could have

---

64. So G. Beasley-Murray, *John* (WBC; Dallas: Word, 1991), p. 24.
65. Court, *Myth and History*, p. 98.
66. Aune, *Revelation 6–16*, p. 612.

served as a model for the two witnesses.[67] In the Old Testament, Moses and Elijah never appear together.[68] But in the New Testament, we have the synoptic accounts of the transfiguration of Jesus where Moses and Elijah or Elijah and Moses (as in Mark's account) are depicted as appearing together with Jesus when Jesus was transfigured before Peter, James, and John (Mt. 17.1–13; Mk 9.2–8; Lk. 9.28–36).[69] In the Lukan account of the Transfiguration, Moses and Elijah are introduced by the emphatic phrase: 'Behold two men!' (ἰδοὺ ἄνδρες δύο). Trites observes: 'This catchphrase appears to be a Lucan device which draws together a number of closely related events, for it appears in Luke's accounts of the Transfiguration, the Resurrection, and the Ascension (Lk. 9.30; 24.4; Acts 1.10; compare 2 Macc. 3.26).'[70] It appears that the twofold motif in Luke's Gospel and Acts accords well with the requirement of at least two witnesses for credible testimony. Further, in Luke's Transfiguration account, the two men, Moses and Elijah are said to have '*stood* with him [Jesus]' (τοὺς δύο ἄνδρας

67. So J. Roloff, *The Revelation of John* (trans. J. E. Alsup; Continental Commentaries; Minneapolis: Fortress Press, 1993), p. 130; Thomas, *Revelation 8–22*, p. 88; Charles, *Revelation Vol. 1*, pp. 280–81.

68. The mention of Moses and Elijah together is found only in Mal. 3.22–23 (ET – Mal. 4.4–5): 'Remember the teaching of my servant Moses, the statutes and ordinances that I commanded him at Horeb for all Israel. Lo, I will send you the prophet Elijah before the great and terrible day of the LORD comes.' This passage speaks only of Elijah's return and makes no reference to Moses' return together with Elijah. Andrew Hill thinks that this passage identifies 'Moses as the first prophet and the greatest of the prophets and Elijah as the last of the prophets'. A. Hill, *Malachi* (WBC; New York: Doubleday, 2000), p. 365. However, the passages in Mal. 3.22–23 and Deut. 18.15, 18 may lie behind the tradition found written in *Deut. Rab.* 3.17: 'He [God] added: Moses, I swear to you, as you devoted your life to their service in this world, so too in the time to come when I bring Elijah, the prophet, unto them, the two of you shall come together.' *Deuteronomy Rabbah* is a later text than the New Testament. What is of interest to us is that the tradition in *Deut. Rab.* could have conflated the accounts in Deut. 18.15, 18 and Mal. 3.22–23, a process of interpretation which we will argue has been adopted by John of Revelation. Also Aune, *Revelation 6–16*, p. 600. For a discussion on the parallels between Elijah and Moses, see J. T. Walsh, *1 Kings* (Berit Olam; Collegeville: Liturgical Press, 1996), pp. 283–87; Dale C. Allison Jr., *The New Moses: A Matthean Typology* (Philadelphia: Fortress Press, 1993), pp. 39–46.

69. See Morna Hooker, '"What Doest Thou Here, Elijah?": A Look at St. Mark's Account of the Transfiguration', in L. D. Hurst and N. T. Wright (eds.), *The GLORY of Christ in the New Testament: Studies in Christology in Memory of George Bradford Caird* (Oxford: Clarendon Press, 1987), pp. 59–70; A. A. Trites, 'The Transfiguration in the Theology of Luke: Some Redactional Links', in L. D. Hurst and N. T. Wright (eds.), *The GLORY of Christ in the New Testament: Studies in Christology in Memory of George Bradford Caird* (Oxford: Clarendon Press, 1987), pp. 71–81. For a discussion of the traditions that may lie behind the Transfiguration of Jesus, see Bruce Chilton, 'The Transfiguration: Dominical Assurance and Apostolic Vision', *NTS* 27 (1980), pp. 115–24. According to Chilton (p. 123), Moses and Elijah were understood to be immortal witnesses to the kingdom coming in force.

70. Trites, 'The Transfiguration in the Theology of Luke', p. 78. See also John Nolland, *Luke 9.21–18.34* (WBC; Dallas: Word, 1993), p. 30.

τοὺς συνεστῶτας αὐτῷ) which may be reflected in the parallel in Rev. 11.4 that the two witnesses *stand* before the Lord of the earth.[71]

Although Moses and Elijah performed extraordinary signs, they were never explicitly described as witnesses for God in the Old Testament. But in the Gospels' transfiguration accounts, Moses and Elijah are portrayed as witnesses of Christ's glory. While Moses and Elijah are not explicitly called witnesses in the transfiguration of Jesus, they are certainly depicted as fulfilling the role of witnesses.[72] Bock writes: 'All three Synoptics depict Elijah as witness at the Transfiguration (Mt. 17; Mk 9; Lk. 9) where he appears with Moses and speaks with Jesus.'[73] Teeple remarked that: 'The reason for selecting Moses and Elijah as the witnesses here must be the fact that both were expected to return as eschatological prophets.'[74]

---

71.   Minear is convinced that the book of Revelation shares many parallel patterns of thought with Luke's Gospel. See Minear, 'Comparable Patterns of Thought in Luke's Gospel', in *idem*, *I Saw a New Earth*, pp. 286–98.

72.   As the reason or reasons for Moses' and Elijah's appearance are not explicitly stated in the transfiguration accounts, scholars have proposed various suggestions to explain their presence. R. T. France lists four possibilities: 1) Moses and Elijah represent the law and the prophets; 2) Moses and Elijah are two out of the three Old Testament men who traditionally did not die (Enoch was the other one; according to Deut. 34 Moses did die, but his burial by God had developed by the first century C.E. into a belief in his 'assumption'; 3) They are the two great leaders who talked with God at Mount Sinai; 4) the two whose 'return' was expected in connection with the Messianic age. He remarks: 'The last seems the most relevant in this context, where their appearance underlines the Messianic role of Jesus, though none of the others is thereby ruled out. It may also be relevant that both Moses and Elijah in their God-given missions experienced rejection and suffering. Jesus is thus indicated as the one in whom the pattern of God's Old Testament servants reaches its ultimate fulfilment.' R. T. France, *Matthew* (TNTC; Leicester: Inter-Varsity Press, 1983), p. 263.

73.   Bock, 'Elijah and Elisha', *DJG*, p. 204. So David M. Hay, 'Moses Through New Testament Spectacles', *Int* 44 (1990), pp. 240–52. Hay (p. 241) writes: 'The primary function of Moses and Elijah here for the three disciples (and the reader) is to attest Jesus' glory (though without addressing the disciples directly). Perhaps one reason for the dual appearance is the Old Testament law about two witnesses (Deut. 19.15, LXX; cf. Mt. 18.16; Mk 15.47).'

74.   Teeple, *The Mosaic Eschatological Prophet*, p. 44. Likewise, Joel Marcus argues that the order Elijah – Moses in the Markan account, 'does not really lessen the Mosaic typology of Mark's transfiguration narrative; instead it ensures that that typology will be interpreted *eschatologically*.... The appearance of "Elijah and Moses", then, indicates that what is pictured in the transfiguration narrative is not a timeless mythic pageant but a vision related to the advent of "the great and terrible day of the Lord" (cf. Mal. 4.5).' J. Marcus, *The Way of the Lord: Christological Exegesis of the Old Testament in the Gospel of Mark* (Louisville: Westminster/John Knox Press, 1992), p. 83 (his emphasis). Charles Edwin Carlston argues that the transfiguration account depicts Elijah and Moses as eschatological prophets and this is taken up by the author of Revelation in Rev. 11.6. See C. E. Carlston, 'Transfiguration and Resurrection', *JBL* 80 (1961), pp. 233–40 (238). Carlston (p. 237) dismisses the idea that Moses and Elijah are portrayed as representatives of the Law and the Prophets and he (p. 239) argues that the focal point of the transfiguration story is the call to obedience and witness. I.

Forerunners of the Kingdom of God

In Mark, the transfiguration of Jesus took place in the context of Jesus' teaching on the coming of the Son of Man and the kingdom of God. The passage in Mark's Gospel before Jesus' transfiguration in Mk 9.2–8 is set out as follows:

> 'Those who are ashamed of me and my words in this adulterous and sinful generation, of them the Son of Man will be also be ashamed when he comes in the glory of his Father and his angels.' And he said to them, 'Truly I tell you, there are some standing here will not taste death until they see the kingdom of God has come with power.'
> (Mk. 8.38–9.1).

When Jesus was transfigured before Peter, James and John, it is said that: 'And there appeared to them Elijah with Moses, who were talking to Jesus' (Mk 9.4; cf. Mt. 17.3). Only Luke adds the comment that the appearances of Moses and Elijah were like Jesus as 'they appeared in glory and were speaking of his departure, which he was about to accomplish at Jerusalem' (Lk. 9.31). What is of interest is that the transfiguration of Jesus is intended to be a preview of the glory of the Son of Man when he returns in glory, an event which coincides with the kingdom of God coming in power.[75] Moses and Elijah are privileged to appear with Jesus at his transfiguration as witnesses to Jesus' impending death (his exodus at Jerusalem) and his future glory in the coming kingdom. According to Teeple, the inclusion of Moses and Elijah may well accord with the Jewish hope that 'Moses and Elijah would come together to usher in the Kingdom of God'.[76]

John the Baptist in his role as the eschatological prophet is also viewed as the forerunner of the kingdom of God. Matthew's Gospel records John the Baptist's inaugural message as 'Repent, for the kingdom of heaven has

---

Howard Marshall thinks the transfiguration account is a 'scene of eschatological anticipation'. I. H. Marshall, *The Gospel of Luke: A Commentary on the Greek Text* (NIGTC; Grand Rapids: Eerdmans, 1979), p. 384.

75. Jewish traditions have it that the advent of the Messiah coincides with the appearance of God's kingdom. For a discussion of these traditions, see Steven Notley, 'The Kingdom of Heaven Forcefully Advances', in Craig A. Evans (ed.), *The Interpretation of Scripture in Early Judaism and Christianity: Studies in Language and Tradition* (JSPSup, 33; Sheffield: Sheffield Academic Press, 2000), pp. 279–311.

76. Teeple, *The Mosaic Eschatological Prophet*, p. 44. Considene thinks that Moses and Elijah function as 'two forerunners of the Messiah' in the transfiguration accounts. Considene, 'The Two Witnesses: Apoc. 11.3–13', p. 385. Outside the synoptic Gospels, the transfiguration account is also discussed in 2 Pet. 1.16–21 as proof that the teaching of the apostles on the parousia (coming) of Jesus is not fictional but based on eyewitness testimony. Jerome H. Neyrey comments that the transfiguration account, among others, is understood as 'a prophecy of the parousia'. J. H. Neyrey, 'The Apologetic Use of the Transfiguration in 2 Peter 1.16–21', *CBQ* 45 (1980), pp. 504–19 (510).

come near' (Mt. 3.2). The passage of Mt. 11.12–14 places John the Baptist as the critical link between the law and the prophets (the old aeon) and the kingdom of God:

> [v. 12] From the days of John the Baptist until now the kingdom of heaven has suffered violence, and the violent take it by force. [v. 13] For all the prophets and the law prophesied until John came; [v. 14] and if you are willing to accept it, he is Elijah who is to come.

Öhler rightly recognizes that: 'John here plays the role of the immediate forerunner of the kingdom of God.'[77] For our purposes, the Gospels portray John the Baptist as forerunner not only of the Messiah but also of the kingdom of God.[78] Both these notions appear to be taken over by John of Revelation in his depiction of the two witnesses.

If the transfiguration account or the tradition that lies behind the transfiguration of Jesus was known to John of Revelation, we can surmise that the pattern of Moses and Elijah as Jesus' witnesses on the Mount of Transfiguration would provide a kind of model for John in his portrayal of the two witnesses. Not only do the pattern of signs and miracles by the two witnesses follow the pattern of Moses and Elijah but more so, the role of the two witnesses *as* witnesses of Jesus also finds its pattern in Moses and Elijah as witnesses of Jesus in the transfiguration account.

Moreover, the two witnesses function as two eschatological prophets in their capacity as witnesses to Jesus' future glory and the coming of the kingdom of God in power. When the two witnesses die at the completion of their testimony at the end of the three-and-a-half years period (Rev. 11.7–8), their resurrection after three-and-a-half days (11.9–10) sets off a chain of events that climax in the kingdom of the world becoming the possession of the Lord and of his Christ (11.15).[79]

The Martyred Prophet

According to Mark, the disciples' vision of Elijah with Jesus on the Mount of Transfiguration apparently led to the disciples' question on the role of Elijah: 'Why do the scribes say Elijah must come first?' (Mk 9.11). Jesus'

---

77. Öhler, 'The Expectation of Elijah', p. 474.

78. Zweip says: 'Beyond the popular, the scribes appear to believe in Elijah's return before the establishment of the messianic kingdom (Mk 9.11–13 // Mt. 17.10–13). Possibly Elijah's appearance on the Mount of Transfiguration (Mk 9.2–10 parr.) also reflects this tradition.' Zweip, *The Ascension of the Messiah*, p. 63.

79. Leivestad comments: 'In my opinion the only plausible solution is that 11.1–13 deals with events which the author expected to take place in the future. The two witnesses, who are to prophesy in word and action of the imminent judgment, are messianic forerunners who have not yet appeared. They are identified with Elijah and Moses, but their appearance is entirely supernatural.' Leivestad, *Christ the Conqueror*, p. 230.

answer provides one of the most enigmatic passages of the New Testament. Jesus said to them:

> [v. 12] Elijah is indeed coming first to restore all things. How then is it written about the Son of Man, that he is to go through many sufferings and be treated with contempt?
>
> [v. 13] But I tell you that Elijah has come, and they did to him whatever they pleased, as it is written about him.

We have already noted that John the Baptist might not have fulfilled Jesus' prophecy that Elijah is indeed coming first to restore all things (Mk 9.12), though the saying in the following verse 13 that 'Elijah has come' appears to refer to John the Baptist. What is of interest to our discussion of the two witnesses is the saying that Elijah must suffer like the Son of Man and more significantly that the suffering of Elijah has scriptural sanction: 'as it is written of him' (Mk 9.13b).[80] However, Joel Marcus comments: 'That expectation is a problem because there is simply no Old Testament passage which prophesies that the Elijah-figure will suffer violence.'[81] According to Marcus, the Gospel of Mark reinterprets the tradition concerning the forerunner of the Messiah in Mk 9.13:

> The Messiah *is* preceded by a forerunner, but he proves himself to be that forerunner, not by accomplishing great triumphs in the public sphere, but precisely by *going before Jesus in the way of suffering and death* [Mk 9.13]. The nature of the forerunner is drastically qualified by the nature of the Messiah he precedes.[82]

The presentation of the two witnesses in Rev. 11 appears to combine both the triumphs and sufferings of the eschatological prophet. John the Baptist did not perform any sign or miracle but the signs of the two witnesses are more powerful than those performed by Moses and Elijah combined.[83] It is explicitly depicted that the two witnesses triumph in the public sphere. They are the untouchables in their days of prophesying. But suffering, death, and humiliation become the lot of the two witnesses when they

---

80. Perhaps by failing to take note of the tradition behind the Markan saying, Bauckham remarks that: 'There is no good evidence of traditions from before the time of Revelation in which returning prophets were expected to suffer martyrdom.' Bauckham, *Climax of Prophecy*, p. 276.

81. J. Marcus, 'Mark 9.11–13: "As It Has Been Written"', *ZNW* 80 (1989), pp. 42–63 (46).

82. Marcus, 'Mark 9.11–13', p. 55 (his emphasis).

83. Though the act of baptizing in water could be construed as a sign performed by John the Baptist, it cannot be listed as a sign in the sense of punitive action or deed like those performed by the two witnesses in shutting the heaven, turning water into blood, and casting every kind of plague as often as they wish.

finish their testimony.[84] We think Craig A. Evans is right when he remarks that: 'Lying behind the slaying of the two witnesses in Rev. 11.7–8 may be a tradition of a martyred Elijah.'[85]

When the two witnesses die, their dead bodies are said to lie on the street of the great city where their Lord was crucified (Rev. 11.8). It is clear that John of Revelation wishes to portray the two witnesses' fate as one suffered by their Lord, Jesus Christ. No individuals in the Bible are said to experience resurrection from the dead and ascension to heaven except Jesus and the two witnesses (Rev. 11.11–12). Black writes: 'The manner of the deaths of the two witnesses is not described, but the parallel with the resurrection and ascension of Christ has suggested that the latter provided the model for the death, resurrection, and the ascension of the witnesses.'[86]

We see that in the transfiguration account Elijah does not only appear as witness to Jesus' glory but after the account he is also said to suffer the same fate as the Son of Man. In the Gospel accounts, Elijah who has come in the person of John the Baptist prepares the way for Jesus the Son of Man in his first appearance on earth. In the same manner, we can draw the parallel that in Revelation the two witnesses like Elijah (and Moses) of the transfiguration account will function as witnesses to Jesus' glory in his coming in power. Just as John the Baptist (in the manner of Elijah) served as forerunner to Christ in his first coming and suffered death as the result, the two witnesses (in the manner of Elijah) will also suffer death in their mission as forerunners for Christ in his second coming in glory.[87] Sweet writes: 'Christian witness is to come to a bloody climax in Jerusalem, crowned by the "end", the coming of the Son of Man.'[88]

---

84. The two witnesses' death in the great city, Jerusalem, where their Lord was crucified may reflect the Lukan saying that, 'it is impossible for a prophet to be killed outside of Jerusalem' (Lk. 13.33b). For a study on the killing of prophets in the OT and early rabbinic traditions, see Betsy Halpern Amaru, 'The Killing of the Prophets: Unraveling a Midrash', *HUCA* 54 (1983), pp. 153–80.

85. Craig A. Evans, *Mark 8.27–16.20* (WBC; Nashville: Thomas Nelson, 2001), p. 44.

86. Black, 'The "Two Witnesses" of Rev. 11.3f.', pp. 235–36. Robinson writes: 'The motif of the three-and-a-half days that elapse between the witnesses' death and their exaltation is clearly based on the tradition of the Resurrection of Jesus after three days.' Robinson, 'The Two Persecuted Prophets-Witnesses of Rev. 11', p. 18. We think that John's use of the three-and-a-half days period instead of the 3 days normally ascribed to Jesus' death is due to John's preference for the figure of three-and-a-half to parallel the three-and-a-half years (1260 days) of the two witnesses' prophetic testimony. Further, it is also possible that the period of three-and-a-half days is intentionally used to differentiate the death and resurrection of the two witnesses from the death and resurrection of Jesus Christ.

87. Margaret Pamment suggests that Moses and Elijah typology was used as showing the pattern of prophets who suffered and were persecuted but were ultimately vindicated by God. See M. Pamment, 'Moses and Elijah in the Story of the Transfiguration', *ExpTim* 92 (1981), pp. 338–39.

88. Sweet, *Revelation*, p. 186.

c. *The Two Witnesses as Executors of God's Judgment*

The two witnesses can also be seen to fulfill the promise contained in Mal. 3.23 as they appear as eschatological prophets *before* the great and terrible day of the Lord, i.e., before the End, a fact which cannot be said of John the Baptist. The emphasis on judgment on the world as the main part of the two witnesses' ministry accords well with the immediate context of the sixth trumpet/second woe where one third of humankind is killed (9.13ff) and various catastrophes and conflicts engulf the world in ever increasing intensity. The end of the two witnesses' testimony leads to the great and terrible day of the Lord when the Lord returns to make war and judges the world (11.17–18; cf. 6.12–17; 17.12–14; 19.11–21).

Akira Satake argues strongly that the two witnesses must be seen as executors of God's judgments and not preachers of repentance.[89] Satake believes that John had no interest in the church bearing witness to the world as in ch. 11 of Revelation the world is the object of God's punishment and not of proclamation from God. Satake writes: 'Die Behauptung, daß sie [church] der Welt die Bekehrung predigen oder daß sie [church] sich mit der Juden- (und Heiden-) mission beschäftigen, findet im Text keinen Anhalt.'[90] According to Satake, the two witnesses are portrayed in a deadly conflict with the world.[91] Beasley-Murray aptly sums up Satake's position: 'Killing opponents who resists the gospel is hardly the conduct of evangelists who are trying to win the world.'[92] Satake takes a corporate view of the two witnesses as the community of the church.[93] According to Satake, the main emphasis of the narrative of the two witnesses is that during the time of the great tribulation the church is protected by God.[94]

We agree with Satake that the two witnesses are portrayed as engaging in a deadly combat with the nations of the world. The power of the two witnesses is awesome. Their enemies who wish to do harm to them are killed with fire (11.5). The ability to kill with supernatural fire is usually reserved to God alone. It is clear in 11.5 that the two witnesses are depicted as precursors of the fiery judgment of God. The *fiery* ministry of the two witnesses under the sixth trumpet/second woe (11.14) is a prelude to the *fiery* destruction of the world through the seven final bowls of wrath in the seventh trumpet/third woe (Rev. 15–16).

---

89. See A. Satake, *Die Gemeindeordnung in der Johannesapokalypse* (Neukirchen-Vluyn: Neukirchener Verlag, 1966), pp. 119–33.
90. Satake, *Die Gemeindeordnung*, p. 125.
91. Satake, *Die Gemeindeordnung*, pp. 122–24.
92. Beasley-Murray, *Revelation*, p. 179.
93. Satake, *Die Gemeindeordnung*, pp. 129, 132.
94. Satake, *Die Gemeindeordnung*, p. 132.

The fire motif associated with God's final judgment on the world is found throughout the Old and the New Testaments.[95] One particular New Testament passage in 2 Pet. 3.7 stands out and reads thus: 'But by the same word the present heavens and earth have been reserved for *fire*, being kept until the day of judgment and destruction of the godless.' Thus a case can be put forward that the two witnesses are viewed as messengers of fire in the like of Elijah, known as a prophet like fire (Sir. 48.1).[96] We also find in Ps. 104.4: 'You make the winds your messengers, fire and flame your ministers.'

In the Gospel of Luke, James and John requested Jesus' permission to call fire from heaven in order to consume the Samaritans who rejected Jesus (Lk. 9.54).[97] From this incident in Luke's Gospel, Michael Oberweis argues that the two witnesses are patterned after James and John, the sons of Zebedee.[98] Oberweis argues that the brothers' request to Jesus that they be seated one on the right and the other on the left of Jesus in the kingdom to come appears to make them the likely candidates for the two witnesses on account of John's allusion to the two olive trees, one standing on the right of the lampstand and the other on the left (Zech. 4.14).[99] Secondly, Oberweis suggests that the two witnesses' ability to pour out fire (Rev.

---

95. For references in the Old Testament, see P. Miller, 'Fire in the Mythology of Canaan and Israel', *CBQ* 27 (1965), pp. 256–61. The prophet Amos in particular was a prophet of fire where all the judgments spoken of were characterized by fire: 'So I will send a fire . . .' (Amos 1.4, 10, 12, 14; 2.2, 5; cf. 5.6; 7.4). See James Limburg, 'Amos 7.4: A Judgment With Fire?', *CBQ* 35 (1973), pp. 346–49. In the New Testament, we find John the Baptist characterizing the Coming One as one who will baptize in the Holy Spirit and fire and burn the chaff with unquenchable fire (Mt. 3.11–12; Lk. 3.16–17). For the view that the earth and the heavens will be destroyed by fire, see 2 Pet. 3.7–12.

96. Fire is often seen as a messenger or agent of God in judgment and warfare. Moshe Weinfeld cites Exod. 14.24–25 and Ps. 97.2–3 and argues that the pillars of fire and cloud function primarily as 'messengers of God who fulfill His mission – in this case [Exod. 14.24–25] the annihilation of the enemy. Emissaries of this type we find in Ps. 97.2–3: "Clouds and mist are around him . . . fire marches before him, burning his foes on every side . . ."' M. Weinfeld, 'Divine Intervention in War in Ancient Israel and in Ancient Near East', in H. Tadmor and M. Weinfeld (eds.), *History, Historiography and Interpretation* (Jerusalem: Magnes Press, 1983), pp. 121–47 (131).

97. James and John, the sons of Zebedee are called 'the sons of thunder' in Mk 3.17. For a discussion on the meaning and legends associated with 'the sons of thunder', see David Parker, 'The Sons of Thunder', in Stanley E. Porter *et al.* (eds.), *Crossing the Boundaries: Essays in Biblical Interpretation in Honour of Michael D. Goulder* (Leiden: E. J. Brill, 1994), pp. 141–47. For a study on the biblical and extra-biblical parallels to Lk. 9.52–56, see Dale C. Allison, Jr., 'Rejecting Violent Judgment: Luke 9.52–56 and its Relatives', *JBL* 121 (2002), pp. 459–78.

98. M. Oberweis, 'Das Martyrium der Zebedaiden in Mk. 10.35–40 (Mt. 20.20–3) und Offb 11.3–13', *NTS* 44 (1998), pp. 74–92.

99. Oberweis, 'Das Martyrium der Zebedaiden', pp. 78–79.

11.5) mirrors James' and John's request to call fire from heaven (Lk. 9.54).[100] Thirdly, Oberweis argues that James and John being present in the Transfiguration of Jesus make them the successors of Moses and Elijah as witnesses to Jesus.[101]

While Oberweis' proposals are not without merits, it is difficult to see how James and John could be seen as a paradigm for Revelation's two witnesses in the way Oberweis suggests. First, sitting on the right and left of Jesus is by no means a certain allusion to Zech 4.14 since in Zech. 4.14 the two olive trees *stand* which is followed by John's depiction of the two witnesses as standing before the Lord of the earth (Rev. 11.4). Secondly, the request by James and John to call fire from heaven remains a request since Jesus rebuffed the brothers' wish (Lk. 9.55). There is no doubt the calling of fire from heaven in Lk. 9.54 alludes to the Elijah incident in 2 Kgs 1.9–11 but the two witnesses are said to pour out fire from their mouths and not call fire from heaven. Thirdly, it is hard to imagine James and John becoming successors to Moses and Elijah as witnesses to Jesus while Peter's role is minimized since Peter also witnessed Jesus' transfiguration. Finally, James and John did not die at the same time as is said of the two witnesses. We are, therefore, not convinced by Oberweis' argument that,

> Der gemeinsame Tod der Zeugen impliziert daher nicht unbedingt Gleichzeitigkeit im Sinne geschichtlicher Chronologie. Gerade wenn sich Offb 11 auf das Martyrium der Zebedaiden bezieht, ist allein schon deren verwandtschaftliches Verhältnis ein hinreichender Grund, beide als Paar in Erscheinung treten zu lassen.[102]

The two witnesses are best seen as messengers of God on earth, and as prophets they herald God's war on the world. God's war in heaven through Michael against the dragon is reflected on earth by God's war against the two beasts by his prophets, the two witnesses. Speaking generally about the role of prophets in the Old Testament, Miller comments: 'The prophets are the heralds and proclaimers of Yahweh's war.'[103] That the two witnesses stand before the Lord of the earth (Rev. 11.4) confirms that they are privy to God's purposes for the world and that they are sent with the full authority of God and his Christ. It is not surprising that in the context of the series of the seven trumpets, the two witnesses will judge those who would do them harm with fire as a kind of final warning to the world within the final eschatological period of three-

---

100. Oberweis, 'Das Martyrium der Zebedaiden', p. 84.
101. Oberweis, 'Das Martyrium der Zebedaiden', p. 85.
102. Oberweis, 'Das Martyrium der Zebedaiden', p. 80.
103. Miller, 'Cosmology and World Order in the Old Testament', pp. 63–64.

and-a-half years before the fiery judgment of the wrath of God (cf. Rev. 15–16).[104]

Furthermore, the witnesses are able to strike the earth with every kind of plague as often as they wish (11.6). No wonder the peoples of the nations rejoice at the death of the two witnesses for the two prophets had tormented them (11.10). Aune remarks thus: 'The miraculous powers wielded by the two witnesses are without exception punitive.'[105] But John puts the blame squarely on the part of the peoples who reject the two witnesses and worship the dragon and the beast (cf. 13.4). Minear's comment is succinct: 'Men's response to God's messengers determined their paternity, their responsibility, their fate.'[106]

Satake's emphasis on the two witnesses as executors of God's judgment in our view is clearly supported by the text of Rev. 11.3–13. Nevertheless, the role of the two witnesses as executors of judgment must be viewed together with their role as witnesses who are to *prophesy* during the three-and-a-half years (11.3). The days that the two witnesses function are called the days of their prophesying (11.6) and are further denoted as their 'testimony' in 11.7.

John, however, does not make explicit the nature and content of their message or prophecy. All we can tentatively suggest is that the two witnesses' prophetic testimony is connected with the mystery of God in 10.7 since Rev. 10 as a whole introduces Rev. 11–13. The frame passages of 10.11 and 14.6–7 that provide the rhetorical context for the macro-chiasm of Rev. 11.1–14.5 may provide a clue to the content of the two witnesses' message. John's call to prophesy again in 10.11 is taken up by the two witnesses' prophesying to the world in general and to many kings in particular (βασιλεῦσιν πολλοῖς – 10.11) as a final warning to them to heed the angel's message in 14.7: 'Fear God and give him glory, for the hour of judgment has come; and worship him who made heaven and earth, the sea and the springs of water.'

Further, this mystery of God announced to God's servants the prophets is apparently proclaimed under the sixth trumpet since when the seventh trumpet sounds, God's mystery is said to come to an end or is fulfilled (10.7). As the two witnesses' prophetic testimony also takes place under the sixth trumpet and their deaths, resurrection, and ascension coincide with the end of the sixth trumpet/second woe (11.14) and lead to the sounding of the seventh trumpet (11.15), one can surmise that the two witnesses as

---

104.   The first three trumpets (possibly the fourth) explicitly list fire as the main instrument of judgment. So also the fourth bowl of the seven last plagues. We find in Sir. 48.10: 'At the appointed time, it is written that you are destined to calm the wrath of God before it breaks out in fury.'

105.   Aune, *Revelation 6–16*, p. 615.

106.   Minear, *I Saw a New Earth*, p. 296.

God's eschatological prophets will play a role in declaring God's mystery to the world.

5. *Summary*

In summary, it is clear that John of Revelation has utilized two main images to describe and identify the two witnesses. First, the images of the two olive trees and the two lampstands (Zech. 4; cf. Rev. 11.4) and secondly, the biblical traditions associated with Moses and Elijah as eschatological prophets (Rev. 11.5–6). The Zecharianic allusion allows John to depict the two witnesses as two individuals leaders of the community (the two olive trees) and also the corporate people of God, the church (the two lampstands). More significantly, the number two symbolizes legally accepted testimony.

It appears that John has conflated the accounts of the promise of Elijah's return as the eschatological prophet (Mal. 3.23) and the tradition about a coming prophet like Moses (Deut. 18.15, 18) as the pattern for the two witnesses being two individual prophets. John the Baptist's role as the eschatological prophet depicted in the Gospels provides a model of how various traditions on Moses and Elijah could have been fused together.[107]

We have seen in the New Testament that Moses and Elijah appeared in the transfiguration of Jesus. The two prophets appeared together as witnesses of Jesus' glory or the kingdom coming in power. In the same manner, John of Revelation could have adopted the various streams of these Old Testament traditions and the traditions that lie behind the transfiguration account concerning the role of Elijah and Moses as eschatological figures. We suggest that John could have fashioned the narrative of the two witnesses in such a way that readers familiar with these traditions will be able to identify the two witnesses as eschatological prophets in the last days before the dawn of the kingdom of God.

The signs that the two witnesses are authorized to execute are also patterned after the miracles performed by Elijah and Moses and this further enhances the importance of the traditions associated with Elijah and Moses. Even the death of the two witnesses probably parallels an Elijah tradition contained in the saying of Jesus that Elijah will suffer a fate similar to that of the Son of Man.[108] We submit that John of

107. Notley comments that: 'Jesus draws upon contemporary expectations for the prophet of the End of Days to signify John [the Baptist]. He fused the hopes for a prophet-like-Moses (Deut. 18.18) and Elijah *redivivus* to indicate his importance.' Notley, 'The Kingdom of Heaven Forcefully Advances', p. 302.

108. Court writes: 'The popular expectations that existed about Elijah and Moses were ripe for reinterpretation, and the Elijah theme had already undergone a Christian

Revelation has freely adapted the traditions of Moses and Elijah in his portrayal of the two witnesses. While it is true that the two witnesses, as Kenneth Strand argues, 'constitute a symbolism drawn from *several prophetic backgrounds* beyond the obvious allusions to Moses and Elijah', it is difficult to deny that the figures of Moses and Elijah as the two greatest prophets become the primary paradigm for the two witnesses-prophets.[109]

We can never be certain to what extent the biblical traditions discussed above influenced John in his portrayal of the two witnesses. Given John's penchant for subtle and nuanced allusions to the biblical text (and possibly to extra-biblical literature) and his style of conflating multiple biblical passages to make a single point, the identity of the two witnesses is not as mysterious as it appears if read in the light of the biblical materials that we have discussed above. We conclude therefore, the two witnesses are best described as the two eschatological prophets (the two olive trees) who together with the church (the two lampstands) witness to the world through mighty signs in the final period of three-and-a-half years before the kingdom of God comes on earth.

6. *The Identity of the (First) Beast*

The first beast is described as having seven diadems and ten horns (Rev. 13.1) in identical fashion to the dragon in 12.3. The beast that rises from the *sea* (13.1) is a clear allusion to Dan. 7.2 where the four great beasts are said to come up from the *sea*. The beast is further described by an allusion to Daniel's fourth beast with ten horns in Dan. 7.7. The beast in Rev. 13.1–2 also takes on the combined characteristics of the first three beasts of the lion, the bear and the leopard in Dan. 7.1–6 but in the reverse order as we noted earlier.[110] 'The combination of four beasts into one highlights the extreme fierceness of this beast [of Rev. 13.1–10].'[111] Yarbro Collins notes: 'In Revelation 13 a single beast rises from the sea which combines salient characteristics of each of the four beasts of Daniel 7.'[112] The fourth beast in Dan. 7 stands for the last king (7.17) or kingdom (7.23) before one like a

---

interpretation in terms of John the Baptist; further reinterpretations were possible within the endeavour to achieve an eschatological understanding of the Christian Church.' Court, *Myth and History*, p. 98.

109.   K. Strand, 'The Two Witnesses of Rev. 11.3–12', *AUSS* 19 (1981), pp. 127–35 (130) (his emphasis).

110.   See Beale, 'The Use of Daniel', pp. 229–40.

111.   Beale, *Revelation*, p. 685. For a study on the symbolism of the beasts in Dan. 7, see Paul A. Porter, *Metaphors and Monsters: A Literary-Critical Study of Daniel 7 and 8* (Toronto, 1985).

112.   Yarbro Collins, *Combat Myth*, p. 162.

son of man (7.13–14) and the holy ones of the Most High (7.18, 22, 27) take possession of the kingdoms under the whole heaven (7.22).

It is significant that the four beasts are said to be four kings that will arise from the earth in Dan. 7.17: 'As for the four beasts, four kings shall arise from the earth.' This means the fourth beast with ten horns of Dan. 7.7 is identified as a king of the earth. In addition, the fourth beast is identified as the fourth kingdom: 'As for the fourth beast, there shall be a fourth kingdom on earth that shall be different from all other kingdoms; it shall devour the whole earth, and trample down, and break into pieces' (7.23). From these two passages of Dan. 7, we are told that the fourth beast is a king *and* a kingdom. In fact, oscillation between the notion of a king and that of a kingdom is found throughout Daniel 7 (cf. 7.17–18, 24–28). G. R. Beasley-Murray states:

> In chap. 7, as elsewhere in Daniel, a fluidity in the concepts of king and kingdom is apparent. In v. 17 the four beasts are said to represent four kings, though they are clearly kingdoms; the description of the first kingdom in v. 4 is dominated by the experience of one king.[113]

We can conclude, therefore, that king and kingdom are interchangeable concepts and often the concept of the king as an individual ruler is identified with the kingdom over which he rules. In other words, the kingdom or the nation is personified in the king, its leading representative. Empire and emperor may be interchangeable, because the empire is vested in the individual emperor. 'The emperor and the empire are more or less identified, as in the Latin mottos *rex pro regno* and *qualis rex, talis grex.*'[114] Hence, it is not necessary to denote the beast as either an individual king or an empire.[115]

---

113. G. R. Beasley-Murray, 'The Interpretation of Daniel 7', *CBQ* 45 (1983), pp. 44–58 (50). Also Collins writes: 'there is a fluid relationship between the king and the kingdom that he represents. . . . The beasts are not mere steno-symbols for corporate entities. They represent kings as well as kingdoms, but in addition they symbolize the chaotic power that these kingdoms embodied.' Collins, *The Apocalyptic Imagination*, p. 103. So also Beale, *Revelation*, p. 868. Michaels says, 'the antichrist in Revelation is both an institution and a person, an empire and an emperor'. Michaels, *Revelation*, pp. 197–98.

114. Hans-Josef Klauck, 'Do They Never Come Back? *Nero Redivivus* and the Apocalypse of John', *CBQ* 63 (2001), pp. 683–98 (688).

115. See Court, *Myth and History*, p. 128. The Latin word, *imperium* is used to signify the authority or rule of Augustus Caesar and his successors. Victor Ehrenberg says: 'Apart from occasional variations, *imperium* now was one of two things, either the dignity and absolute power of the emperor or the empire.' V. Ehrenberg, *Man, State and Deity: Essays in Ancient History* (London: Methuen, 1974), p. 121. We disagree with Aune who comments: 'The beast from the sea in 13.1–10 appears to represent the Roman Empire (not individual), while the beast from the land in 13.11–18, the agent of the first beast, probably represents the *commune Asiae*, i.e., the Koinon of Asia.' Aune, *Revelation 6–16*, p. 729. Gregory Jenks writes: 'It is clear that the writer [John] wanted to characterize the empire generally as satanic, and yet

Thus we deduce that the beast of Rev. 13.1–2 is an individual king as well as a kingdom, following the Danielic understanding of the fourth beast of Dan. 7. In modern terminology, the term 'kingdom' means 'the state' or 'government'. The worship of the beast is the worship of the state (13.8). The rule of the beast which extends to all the inhabitants of the earth is his world empire or world government (13.7b). John has conflated the characteristics of the first three beasts in Dan. 7.1–6 to denote the beast of Rev. 13.1–10. It appears clear that John intends to convey to his readers that the beast of Rev. 13.1–2 is a symbol of a world-kingdom. The beast that rises from the sea to rule the world in the last 42 months represents the apex of all the kingdoms of the world that have arisen in history. The sea, a symbol of chaos and rebellion from where the beast arises, represents the climax of human rebellion against God.[116]

The beast of Rev. 13.1–10, depicted in the manner of the *fourth* beast or the *fourth* kingdom is the *last* kingdom on earth before the kingdom of God takes dominion over all (cf. Dan. 2.40–44). This supports our contention that the beast of Rev 13.1–10 is an eschatological figure. Like the two witnesses of Rev. 11, the beast's rise coincides with the final three and a half years (13.5) before the kingdom of God comes on earth. The beast is a world ruler (13.7), an individual who commands the world's obedience, awe and worship (13.3–4). As a world ruler, he rules over the kings of the earth (cf. 17.12–13; 19.19). As the undisputed king, the kingdom of the world is seen vested in the beast (cf. 11.15). While the beastly figure is often taken to mean the Roman empire or the Roman emperor, we have seen above that John is not particularly interested in any historical identification with Rome but rather shows that this beast takes on all the features of the four beasts of Dan. 7 put together to represent the final world kingdom before the kingdom of God rules over all (cf. Rev.

---

wished to focus on the personification of the empire in the person and activities of the emperor.' G. Jenks, *The Origins and Early Development of the Antichrist Myth* (Berlin: de Gruyter, 1991), p. 245.

116.   Yarbro Collins writes: 'the effect of depicting the four kingdoms as beasts of watery chaos in Daniel 7 is to characterize them as rebellious and as manifestations of chaos rather than order', Yarbro Collins, *Combat Myth*, p. 162. Speaking of the two beasts of Rev. 13, Aune says: 'Their emergence from the realms to which they were appointed, the sea (Rev. 13.1) and the earth (Rev. 13.11), however, is an *eschatological* action that signifies the emergence of chaos from order, i.e., the irruption of chaotic forces as the dying gasp of the old, worn-out creative order just before a period of restoration and renewal.' Aune, *Revelation 6–16*, p. 728 (his emphasis). Provan says, 'the sea...has...symbolic significance in the Old Testament texts. The watery chaos is itself the archetypal enemy of Israel's God, set within its bounds at creation, but always threatening to break out and challenge the divine rule.' Provan, 'Foul Spirits, Fornication and Finance', p. 90. It appears that the beast rises from the sea to challenge God's rule in the world.

11.15; 12.10).[117] Hence, the beast's rule is limited to three-and-a-half years (Rev. 13.5; cf. 11.2–3; 12.6, 14), at the expiry of which, the kingdom of the world would have come into the Lord's possession and of his Christ (cf. 11.15).

Reading the literary units across Rev. 11–13 in an integrated fashion while paying close attention to how the three-and-a-half year temporal period functions to bind the events together is essential to any correct interpretation of Rev. 13 or any unit within 11.1–14.5. The beast's rule comes to an end after the three-and-a-half years when it is defeated by the Lamb and the 144,000 on Mount Zion (14.1). While the Roman empire of the first century C.E. might illuminate some features of Rev. 13, it is our contention that it is unsafe to read specific historical references from the text of Rev. 13 unless there is clear historical proof that this should be done. In fact, most features in Rev. 13 cannot be identified with what is known of Rome or imperial policy of the late first century C.E.

First, there is no historical evidence to suggest there was any *universal* imperial decree for the worship of the Roman emperor at the end of the first century C.E. Thompson writes:

> A criticial examination of the claims made by the standard post-Domitian sources on Domitian's demand to be called *dominus et deus noster* in light of evidence from Domitian's reign suggests that the post-Domitian sources do not reflect accurately political realities from the time of Domitian. Domitian did not encourage divine titles such as *dominus et deus noster*, nor is there evidence that Domitian had become a mad tyrant seeking divinization. The presence of the imperial cult, especially in Asia Minor, is not being questioned; it had been a significant force in the social life of the Asian province from the time of Augustus. There is no indication, however, that Domitian modified the imperial cult by demanding greater divine honors than either his predecessors or successors.[118]

---

117. So Lohmeyer, *Offenbarung*, pp. 107–8. Mounce comments: 'In John's vision the order of the beasts have been rolled into one. Or to put it another way, Daniel's terrible, unidentified fourth beast seems to have 'swallowed' its three predecessors and to have taken on the distinguishing characteristics of each. This should further caution us against identifying John's beast too quickly or exclusively with one specific empire or political system, whether past or future.' Mounce, *Revelation*, p. 158. Pattemore writes: 'Most obvious is the fact that John has combined features of all four of Daniel's beasts into one.... John's mixture of Daniel's beasts allows the image to be applied to all political powers of all time. This decreases the importance of being able to make precise identifications of John's historical-referential meaning.' Pattemore, 'The People of God in the Apocalypse', p. 285. Whether John identifies the beast of Rev. 13 with Rome of the late first century C.E. will be discussed in detail below.

118. Thompson, 'A Sociological Analysis of Tribulation in the Apocalypse of John', pp. 158–59. This is not to deny that in the reign of Domitian, the Emperor cult became more prominent in Ephesus but this does not amount to universal demand for emperor worship as

Friesen concludes that,

> The two periods [Nero's and Domitian's] in which scholars have tried to locate the composition of Revelation have not yet produced much evidence to suggest any great increase in imperial cult activities in Asia. The period of Nero seems to have been rather quiet with regard to imperial worship.... The evidence for imperial cults in Asia from Domitian period also fit (*sic*) within the mainstream alleged for this period. There is no sign of the exaggerated claims alleged for this period.[119]

More devastating to the view that there is universal imperial worship in the late first century C.E. is that there is no mention of Roman cults in all the messages to the seven churches. Friesen notes one possible exception in Rev. 2.13, where the image of Satan's throne has often been taken as a reference to Pergamon as the alleged center of the imperial cults. However, Freisen has shown that Asia had no one center for imperial cults and he argues that, 'the complete absence of other references to imperial cults in the messages to the seven churches makes this interpretation [Pergamon as the center of imperial worship] even more unlikely'.[120] We may conclude that the world (or the Roman world) in the last decade of the first century C.E. did not worship Domitian or any other Roman emperor on a scale demanded by the text of 13.3–4. Revelation 13.3 clearly states the *whole* world or earth (ὅλη ἡ γῆ) follows after the beast and that *all* the inhabitants of the earth (πάντες οἱ κατοικοῦντες ἐπὶ τῆς γῆς) worship the beast (13.8a).

Furthermore, the Roman persecution of Christians either in Nero's reign or Domitian's reign was not widespread as scholars now acknowledge.[121] Revelation 13.7–10 and 13.15 indicate that during the beast's reign

---

demanded by the text in Rev. 13. S. J. Friesen comments that: 'During the reign of Domitian, cultic presence of Rome in Asia Minor became especially prominent with the establishment at Ephesus of a new provincial cult of the Emperors.' S. J. Friesen, *Twice Neokoros: Ephesus, Asia and the Cult of the Flavian Imperial Family* (Leiden: Brill, 1993), p. 27. Thompson's position is affirmed recently by Philip A. Harland, 'Honouring the Emperor or Assailing the Beast: Participation in Civic Life among Associations (Jewish, Christian and Other) in Asia Minor and the Apocalypse of John', *JSNT* 77 (2000), pp. 99–121 (103–4). For a study on idolatry in Asia Minor in general and in Ephesus in particular, see Giancarlo Biguzzi, 'Ephesus, Its Artemision, Its Temple to the Flavian Emperors, and Idolatry in Revelation', *NovT* 40 (1998), pp. 276–90. We disagree with Biguzzi's attempt (p. 290) to identify Domitian with the beast of Rev. 13.1–10.

119.   Friesen, *Imperial Cults*, pp. 148–49.

120.   Friesen, *Imperial Cults*, p. 248 n. 68. For a study of imperial cults in Asia, see Friesen, *Imperial Cults*, pp. 3–131.

121.   See especially L. Thompson, *The Book of Revelation: Apocalypse and Empire* (New York: Oxford University Press, 1990), pp. 95–115. Thompson challenged the prevailing view that there was widespread persecution against Christians in the Roman world in general and in Asia Minor in particular in the last decade of the first century C.E. Thompson's view is now

of terror, it is a government edict to persecute *all* who refuse to submit to the beast or worship its image. Aune comments thus:

> The significance of the imperial cult in the persecution of Christians, however, has frequently been overemphasized. The main concern of the emperors and their representatives was that the people should sacrifice to the cults of the gods, while the deified emperors were often tangential or subordinate to these cults, and distinctions were normally made between the gods and the deified emperors.[122]

But in Rev. 13, worship is offered to the beast, the world ruler and not to the many gods of the Roman cult. While the Emperor cult was menacing and becoming a threat to the Christian faith in the last decade of the first century C.E., and it is not denied that John could have recognized the sinister designs of Rome against the church and used it to paint the picture of what is to come, nevertheless, it must be said that neither Nero nor Domitian fits the picture of the beast presented in Rev. 13.1–10 or Rev. 17. Harland comments: 'To suggest that the author of the Apocalypse was not addressing Christians facing imperial persecution or enforced worship of the emperor does not mean that he was completely distanced from the realities of life in the cities or the churches.'[123]

Secondly, the first beast is said to suffer a deadly wound on one of its heads, and it was healed to the amazement of the world (13.3; cf. vv. 12 and 14). This description regarding the beast has led most commentators

---

accepted by most scholars. So J. M. Ford, 'Persecution and Martyrdom in the Book of Revelation', *The Bible Today* 26 (1990), pp. 141–46. See also Aune, *Revelation 1–5*, pp. lx–lxx. Also Müller writes: 'Der weltweite, umfassende Charakter der Verfolgung schließt aus, daß die auf die Stadt Rom begrenzte Verfolgung unter Nero gemeint ist. Das Tier hat Macht über alle Menschen (Vers 7b).' Müller, *Offenbarung*, p. 251. John Bishop notes: 'Domitian's persecution... was on a very minor scale.... Of widespread persecution of Christians there is little or no evidence...' J. Bishop, *Nero: The Man and the Legend* (London: The Trinity Press, 1964), p. 171. Marriane M. Thompson writes: 'Corroborating evidence for widespread martyrdom of Christians at his [John's] time is missing. But, one might note, neither is it presupposed in the book of Revelation. John himself does not actually state that extensive persecution has begun. The church of Smyrna, for example, has experienced the death of only one martyr (2:13).' M. M. Thompson, 'Worship in the Book of Revelation', *Ex Auditu* 8 (1992), pp. 45–54 (46). The place mentioned in 2.13 is Pergamum and not Smyrna. Thompson (p. 53 n. 6) goes on to note: 'When Polycarp was put to death in Smyrna, about 60 years after the writing of the Revelation, he was the twelfth named in a combined list of martyrs of the cities of Smyrna and Philadelphia (Eusebius, *Eccl. Hist.* IV.15).' While we agree with Witherington that there is some evidence of local oppression, suffering and occasional martyrdom, we are not convinced (as Witherington argues) that there is evidence of systematic and universal persecution of Christians in the late first century C.E. See Witherington, *Revelation*, p. 8.

122. Aune, *Revelation 1–5*, p. lxiv. See also S. R. F. Price, *Rituals and Power: The Roman Imperial Cult in Asia Minor* (Cambridge: Cambridge University Press, 1984), pp. 221–22.

123. Harland, 'Honouring the Emperor', pp. 103–4.

to assume that this is a reference to Nero's suicide and the legend of Nero *redivivus* connected with it.[124] On the other hand, not a few commentators have rejected the identification of the slain head as Nero or any specific emperor. Mounce writes: 'A basic problem with identifying the slain head as Nero (or any specific emperor) is that the text does not say that the *head* was restored. It was the *beast* who recovered from the death stroke upon one of his heads.'[125] Paul Minear argues that most commentators do not give sufficient weight to the fact that the wound though first assigned to one of its heads, is later assigned twice to the beast itself (13.12, 14).[126] Minear argues that the wound or plague (ἡ πληγὴ) spoken of here in Revelation cannot be equated with the wound inflicted by Nero on himself as the empire survived the death of Nero. Minear comments:

> A wound inflicted on a *former* ruler is not a wound inflicted on the empire.... But actually, the wound inflicted by Nero on himself was not an injury to the beast.... It is difficult to maintain that Nero's suicide fulfills such specifications. His death did not jeopardize the power of the empire, because he died as a fugitive and enemy of the state. Imperial authority was not threatened by his death; in fact, his death demonstrated the power of the state over him.[127]

Beale is even more forceful in rejecting the Nero *redivivus* legend as key to the interpretation of Rev 13.3. He writes:

> [But] narrowing the interpretation of v 3 primarily to the fate and legend of Nero brings with it the problem that the legend of Nero's death and resurrection does not fit precisely the descriptions in Revelation 13 and 17. The plague-like sword wound in 13:3, 12, and 14 is inflicted by God or Christ and is not self-inflicted, as the Nero thesis requires. Indeed, it is the beast who recovers from the wound, not merely the head itself. But Nero's death was not a fatal blow to the empire but, to the contrary, demonstrated Rome's power, since he died as an enemy and fugitive of Rome. Furthermore, v 4 says that the beast's revival resulted in universal worship or respect to its authority, but the rumor of Nero's return did not cause all to worship Rome or respect its authority, since the rumor was considered a threat to the empire.[128]

---

124.   On the Nero *redivivus* legend, see Court, *Myth and History*, pp. 131–38 and Yarbro Collins, *Combat Myth*, pp. 174–90. Yarbro Collins (pp. 172–90) argues that the beast from the sea represents Rome and one of the beast's heads that suffers the deadly wound is Nero the emperor. For a recent essay defending the relevance of the Nero *redivivus* myth for the interpretation of the beast, see Klauck, '*Nero Redivivus* and the Apocalypse of John', pp. 683–98.

125.   Mounce, *Revelation*, p. 248 (his emphasis).

126.   P. Minear, 'The Wounded Beast', *JBL* 72 (1953), pp. 93–101.

127.   Minear, 'The Wounded Beast', pp. 96–97.

128.   Beale, *Revelation*, p. 690.

Speaking of the Nero *redivivus* myth, Desmond Ford writes:

> It is possible that John alludes to the current myth, but it is not possible
> that he is here giving it credence. He does not expect a revived Nero. But
> he does expect revived persecution on a world-wide scale, reminiscent of
> what took place in Rome during the days of the mad fiddler.[129]

If Rev. 13.3 speaks of Nero returning to life, this legend is found to be
purely legendary as Nero did not in fact come to life to rule the world as v.
3 explicitly states concerning the beast. There is no concrete evidence to
suggest that the Nero legend even if known to John, has influenced him in
13.3.[130] Furthermore, the myth of Nero's return rarely speaks of Nero
dying and being resurrected to rule the empire again. Klauck writes:

> The most prominent features of the Nero legend so far are: Nero is still
> alive, Nero will return from the East with troops, there are impostors
> who pretend to be Nero, and Nero's name can be given to other persons,
> too. This is not yet the evolved myth we mean when speaking of *Nero*
> *redivivus*. We see some mythical colors already here and there, but
> nowhere does Nero return from the dead or from the underworld.[131]

We submit that hardly any of the features of the Nero *redivivus* legend fit
the characterization of the beast of Rev. 13.3, 12, and 14. According to
John, the death-wound suffered by the beast speaks of the death of the
whole empire and not only of one of its kings. The king and the world-
kingdom/empire (which we have argued to be interchangeable) die but are
miraculously restored. Minear remarks: 'If we are to understand the
wounded head, therefore, we should look not so much for an emperor who
died a violent death, but an event in which the authority of the beast (and
the dragon) was both destroyed and deceptively restored.'[132]

The important question then is how or when the beast is said to be
inflicted with the death-wound. We believe that the answer is found in the

---

129. D. Ford, *The Abomination of Desolation in Biblical Eschatology* (Washington:
University Press of America, 1979), pp. 264–65.

130. So Minear, 'The Wounded Beast', pp. 93–101; Resseguie, *Revelation Unsealed*, pp.
124–27; Mounce, *Revelation*, pp. 247–48.

131. Klauck, '*Nero Redivivus* and the Apocalypse of John', p. 686. Scholars have often
referred to ch. 4 of the *Ascension of Isaiah* as well as to a passage in book 3 of the Jewish
Christian collection of the *Sibylline Oracles* (3.63–74) as providing evidence for Nero *redivivus*
myth, but the dating for these two writings is disputed and these writings could be dated early
to mid second century C.E. The *Ascension of Isaiah* has been dated to the first decades of the
second century C.E. Recently, Jan Willem van Henten has challenged the existence of the
Nero *redivivus* myth in the *Sibylline Oracles*. See J. W. van Henten, '*Nero Redivivus*
Demolished: The Coherence of the Nero Traditions in the *Sibylline Oracles*', *JSP* 21 (2000),
pp. 3–17.

132. Minear, 'The Wounded Beast', p. 97.

defeat of the dragon by Michael (12.7–12). As we have argued extensively earlier, the defeat of the dragon has immense repercussions for those who dwell on earth. While the heavens are told to rejoice, woe is pronounced on the earth when the devil is said to come down to earth (12.12). We have seen earlier that the fall of the dragon is repeatedly emphasized (12.8–11). We have also noted the close-knit relationship between the dragon and the beast. We have argued that the beast is Satan's incarnation on earth (note especially that both the dragon and the beast have seven heads and ten horns [12.3; 13.1]). We submit, therefore, the moment of the beast's death-wound is the moment when the dragon is defeated and rendered powerless (12.8 – οὐκ ἴσχυσεν) and is cast out from heaven and sent to earth (12.12).

In Rev. 13.14, the beast is said to be 'wounded by the *sword* and yet lived'. The sword is an instrument of war and a symbol of warfare.[133] It appears that the beast who dies from the plague of the sword (13.14 – τὴν πληγὴν τῆς μαχαίρης) meets his death as a consequence of warfare. When Satan loses the battle with Michael in heaven, it is as if the sword of warfare slays Satan's representative, the beast on earth.[134] For a moment, the beast dies but is resurrected almost immediately. There is no suggestion that the beast dies for an indeterminate length of time as in all three instances (13.3, 12, 14), the fact of dying and being healed and coming to life again of the beast is mentioned together.

When the dragon is cast down to earth after being defeated in heaven, paradoxically his power does not seem to abate or weaken. In fact in the short time he has on earth, the devil is said to have great wrath! (12.12). When the dragon stands on the seashore on earth (12.18), he calls forth the beast from the sea (13.1). This is the moment, in our view, that the beast lives again as he ascends (ἀναβαῖνον) from the sea (13.1).

In an earlier portrayal of the beast in 11.7, he is said to ascend (ἀναβαῖνον) from the abyss. From the sea or abyss, the beast is resurrected and lives again on earth. When the devil is thrown out of heaven and stands on earth, he resurrects the beast and through the beast, exercises authority over the whole earth (13.3–4). Thus the beast's wound is healed and he is caused to live again by the power of Satan. This integrated reading of Rev. 12–13 will have implications when we come to identify the seventh and the

---

133. Reinier de Blois observes that the word 'sword' in the Old Testament is often used metaphorically of 'violence, aggression, war'. R. de Blois, *Towards a New Dictionary of Biblical Hebrew Based on Semantic Domains* (Amsterdam: Vrije Universiteit, 2000), p. 22. I wish to thank Reinier de Blois for giving me a copy of his published doctoral dissertation.

134. Minear argues that, 'the sword is the symbol of God's wrath; the wound is a God-inflicted plague which simultaneously destroys the authority of head, beast and dragon'. Minear, 'The Wounded Beast' p. 99. But Minear fails to link the slaying by the sword to the heavenly war between Michael and Satan.

eighth king who is said to be also one of the seven kings (17.11) in the next section.

a. *The Seven Mountains of Revelation 17.9*

We will now discuss the meaning of 'the seven mountains' of 17.9 which is generally thought to depict Rome. The Greek text of 17.9–11 reads as follows:

[v. 9] ὧδε ὁ νοῦς ὁ ἔχων σοφίαν. αἱ ἑπτὰ κεφαλαὶ ἑπτὰ ὄρη εἰσίν, ὅπου ἡ γυνὴ κάθηται ἐπ' αὐτῶν. καὶ βασιλεῖς ἑπτά εἰσιν· [v. 10] οἱ πέντε ἔπεσαν, ὁ εἷς ἔστιν, ὁ ἄλλος οὔπω ἦλθεν, καὶ ὅταν ἔλθῃ ὀλίγον αὐτὸν δεῖ μεῖναι. [v. 11] καὶ τὸ θηρίον ὃ ἦν καὶ οὐκ ἔστιν καὶ αὐτὸς ὄγδοός ἐστιν καὶ ἐκ τῶν ἑπτά ἐστιν, καὶ εἰς ἀπώλειαν ὑπάγει.

In this complex passage of highly symbolic material it is best to proceed with caution in identifying any of the kings with a specific Roman emperor. The attempt to identify the beast with any known Roman emperor is simply futile because the beast is the eighth king and clearly from John's perspective, the beast is a future figure. Thus the beast cannot be identified with Nero or Domitian. Even if we identify the 'one who is living now' (the sixth king) with either Nero or Domitian, we are not told who the seventh king is, described cryptically as 'the one who has yet to come but when he comes, he will remain for a short while' (17.10). The beast who is the eighth but is also one of the seven, is also left unidentified.[135]

All we can tentatively propose is that the beast will be the seventh *and* also the eighth king because the depiction of beast as the one that 'was and is not and is about to ascend from the bottomless and go to destruction' (17.8) appears to refer to the beast who reigned as king and died but then rises from the dead as the eighth king, thus making him also one of the seven.[136] As the eighth king, he goes into destruction, namely he becomes the world ruler and persecutor of the saints in the last three-and-a-half years (cf. 13.5–10) but will himself be destroyed when the kingdom of God comes (cf. 11.15–18; cf. 12.10).

Thus the seven kings are not literally seven kings. It is unlikely that the seven mountains represent Rome because it is said that the seven heads are seven mountains on which the woman sits (ὅπου ἡ γυνὴ κάθηται ἐπ' αὐτῶν).

---

135. Beasley-Murray writes: 'The awkward fact is that no arrangement of the line of emperors yields a satisfactory solution to the problem which John unintentionally sets us.' Beasley-Murray, *Revelation*, p. 256.

136. Thompson notes the parallel between Rev. 17.11 and 17.8 and concludes that 'the parallel indicates that the "eighth" king was one of the seven kings who died and is about to ascend from the abyss as an "eighth." In other words, he will rule twice.' Thompson, *Revelation*, p. 162.

The seven mountains constitute an explanation of the seven heads, not the physical landscape of Rome.[137] The seven heads that are seven mountains are further interpreted as seven kings (17.9). Both the dragon and the beast are said to have seven heads (12.3; 13.1). As the seven heads of the dragon and the beast are not to be understood literally, it is unlikely that the seven mountains of 17.9 should be interpreted literally. In this highly symbolic language, it appears unlikely that the seven mountains are seven literal mountains where the city of Rome was founded. Mountains like horns in 12.3 and 13.1 are symbols of strength and power.[138] We do well to note the possible Old Testament background for Rev. 17.9.

In Zech. 6.1, four chariots are seen coming out from between two mountains of bronze. The four chariots are further identified as the four winds of heaven which are said to go out into the world after presenting themselves before the Lord of all the earth (Zech. 6.5). In the book of Zechariah, the symbolism of mountains may stand for heavenly powers which mirror political powers on earth. Zerubbabel is said to face opposition in the figure of a great mountain: 'What are you, O great mountain? Before Zerubbabel you shall become a plain' (Zech. 4.7). The horns of the nations from the four winds of heaven that plunder Zion will on that day join themselves to the Lord and become his people (Zech. 1.18–2.13; MT – Zech. 2.1–17).

It appears that the political powers symbolized by horns in Zech. 1.18 (MT – 2.1) are also symbolized by a great mountain in Zech. 4.7. In both instances, God will break the horns of the nations and make the mountain into a plain, thus granting the people of Judah and Zerubbabel victory over all opposition.

Interestingly, the reference to a woman sitting in a basket being flown to the land of Shinar (LXX – the land of Babylon) in Zech. 5.5–11 is sandwiched between the mention of 'a mountain' and 'mountains' in chs 4 and 6 of the book of Zechariah respectively. Thus, in Zech. 1–6, we have various symbols of horns, winds, mountains, and a woman depicting heavenly and earthly forces in operation, either for or against the restoration programme of the post-exilic community under the leadership of Zerubbabel and Joshua.

The apocalyptic imagery of Zechariah is close to the imagery found in the book of Daniel. In Dan. 2, the stone that is cut from a mountain strikes

---

137. This point will be discussed in detail below.

138. Beale comments that the term 'mountain' in Revelation 'is used figuratively to connote strength.... This usage points beyond a literal reference to Rome's "hills" and to a figurative meaning, "kingdoms," especially in the light of 8.8 and 14.1. Mountains symbolize kingdoms in the OT and Jewish writings, for example, Isa. 2.2; Jer. 51.25; Ezek. 35.3; Dan. 2.35, 45; Zech. 4.7; *I En.* 52; *Tg. Isa.* 41.15.' Beale, *Revelation*, p. 868.

the statue and becomes a great mountain that fills the earth is clearly a symbol for the kingdom of God (cf. Dan. 2.35, 44–45).

In the book of Daniel, the symbol of a mountain is a positive metaphor while in the book of Zechariah, it is both positive (cf. Zech. 6.1) and negative (cf. Zech. 4.7). Since the great mountain in Dan. 2 is a symbol for a political power, the kingdom of God, it is likely that the great mountain that opposes Zerubbabel in Zech. 4.7 is also a symbol for a political power, but in this instance an evil power that opposes the purposes of God. The four winds of heaven in Zech. 6.5 function as a positive symbol as they are said to stand before the Lord of all the earth. But in the book of Daniel, the imagery of the four winds of heaven probably functions as a negative symbol for they stir the great sea from which four beasts arise.[139]

It is often noted that chs 50 and 51 of the book of Jeremiah provide the primary Old Testament background for Rev. 17–18.[140] Jeremiah 50–51 narrates the prophet Jeremiah's vision of the judgment that will befall Babylon. A number of passages in Jer. 51 are alluded to by John in Rev. 17. The woman who holds a golden cup that makes the inhabitants of the earth drunk in Rev. 17.1–5 is an allusion to Jer. 51.7: 'Babylon was a golden cup in the Lord's hand, making all the earth drunken; the nations drank of her wine, and so the nations went mad.' The woman-whore who is seated on many waters in Rev. 17.1 is a clear allusion to Jer. 51.13: 'You will live by mighty waters, rich in treasures.' More significantly for our purposes in Rev. 17.9, the passage in Jer. 51.24 speaks specifically of Babylon as a 'destroying mountain' that will be judged by the Lord and made into a burnt mountain:

> I am against you, O destroying mountain,
> says the Lord,
> that destroys the whole earth;
> I will stretch out my hand against you, and roll you down from the crags,
> and make you a burned-out mountain.

The woman-Babylon of Rev. 17 is pictured as seated on seven mountains that are identified as seven kings in 17.9. Already in 17.3, the woman is said

---

139. There is some ambiguity whether the four winds of heaven in Dan. 7 is a positive or negative symbol. It may not be necessary to decide one way or the other as the four winds of heaven which may denote chaotic forces are nevertheless under the control of God. There is less ambiguity in the reference to the four winds of the earth in Rev. 7.1 which are clearly depicted as under the control of the four angels of God (cf. Rev. 9.15).

140. See A. Yarbro Collins, 'Revelation 18: Taunt-Song or Dirge?', in J. Lambrecht (ed.), *L'Apocalypse johannique et l'Apocalyptique dans le Nouveau Testament* (BETL 53; Leuven: Leuven University Press, 1980), pp. 185–204; Provan, 'Foul Spirits, Fornication and Finance', pp. 81–100.

to be seated on a scarlet beast that has seven heads and ten horns. So the woman in Rev. 17 is depicted by John as one who sits or is seated on:

- Many waters (v. 1).
- A Scarlet beast (v. 3).
- Seven mountains (v. 9).[141]

Since the first two objects, 'many waters' and 'scarlet beast' on which the woman is seated are figures of speech or metaphors, it is likely that the third object, 'seven mountains' is also to be taken metaphorically. The many waters are identified as peoples and multitudes and nations and languages (17.15). The scarlet beast that has seven heads and ten horns is the eighth king who will arise and go into perdition (17.8, 11). With the allusion to Jer. 51.24, it seems clear that the seven mountains are symbols for kingdoms just as the destroying mountain is a symbol for the kingdom of Babylon. Babylon is said to become a burnt-out mountain in Jer. 51.24. The description of the burning of the woman-Babylon in Rev. 17.16 confirms John's allusion to Jer. 51.24. We have already noted that the seven mountains are identified as seven kings in Rev. 17.9. Thus we conclude that the seven mountains symbolize all the kingdoms of the world over which the woman is said to rule (cf. 17.18).[142]

In Rev. 13 and Rev. 17, we also have images of horns, mountains, and a woman. The background of the four winds of heaven stirring the great sea in Dan. 7.2 is implicit in Rev. 13.1 as the beast is said to arise from the sea, making the allusion to Dan. 7.2 almost certain. We have seen that in both Zechariah and Daniel, mountains are symbols for political powers. Babylon is called 'a destroying mountain' in Jer. 51.25. We submit that the seven mountains in Rev. 17.9 must also be interpreted likewise to mean political powers. Thus the seven mountains are not seven literal mountains on which the city of Rome was founded. They are not to be interpreted as seven Roman emperors or succession of seven Roman empires. Rather, they are the totality of political powers or kings ruled by the woman.

In an earlier passage in Rev. 17, the woman is said to be seated on many waters which represent the many peoples of the nations (17.1, 15). It is not implausible that the symbol of the seven mountains on which the woman is seated is another symbol of the woman's rule over the world, which in this particular instance, signifies her rule over the *kings* of the earth (cf. 17.18)

---

141.   Rossing writes: 'Babylon's seat is variously identified as "many waters" (Rev. 17.1; see Jer. 51.13), a beast (Rev. 17.3, 7), and seven hills (Rev. 17.9), a reference to Rome's seven hills.' Rossing, *The Choice between Two Cities*, p. 66. We disagree with Rossing that the seven hills refer to Rome.

142.   We should note that in Isa. 47.5, Babylon is called the queen of kingdoms. *Targum Isaiah* 41.15 translates the MT 'hills as chaff' as 'kingdoms as chaff'. See Ford, *Revelation*, p. 289.

as the seven mountains are explicitly said to be seven kings. But as in Zech. 4.7, these mountains will also become a plain when the great mountain of God's kingdom (cf. Dan. 2.35) overturns the mountain of the kingdom of the world (cf. Rev. 11.15).

As the number seven speaks of totality and completeness, it is more likely that a symbolic import is intended by the reference to seven kings. They represent the totality of kings or empires in history that have ruled the world. Recent scholars have preferred the symbolic interpretation of the number seven in 17.6. Beale comments:

> The number 'seven' is not a literal number designating the quantity of kings in one epoch but is figurative for the quality of fullness or completeness.... As in 12.3 and 13.1–2, fullness of oppressive power is the emphasis here. Therefore, rather than seven particular kings or kingdoms of the first century or any other, the seven mountains and kings represent the oppressive power of world government throughout the ages, which arrogates to itself divine prerogatives and persecutes God's people when they do not submit to the evil state's false claims.[143]

Resseguie is even more forceful and he comments:

> This is one of the most misunderstood passages in Revelation. Commentators frequently take this reference literally, not figuratively, although all other numbers in the book are symbolic. They usually assume that the city with seven mountains is Rome. However, seven – as with all numbers in this book – is symbolic: the city with seven mountains is the archetypal human city, the antichristian city, the city in rebellion from God which follows the beast and is thus the antithesis to the New Jerusalem. Seven mountains represent the whole civilized world – a figurative tower of Babel – striving towards the heavens, to be godlike. Therefore, the city with seven mountains has little to do with ancient Rome except that Rome contributed to humankind's self-deification enterprise.[144]

---

143. Beale, *Revelation*, p. 869.

144. Resseguie, *Revelation Unsealed*, pp. 58–59. We agree with Resseguie's comments on 17.9 except his remark that all numbers in Revelation are symbolic. We have seen that the seven churches (1.4, 11) are in fact seven literal churches although they might represent the whole church. On the seven mountains, Aune likewise comments: 'John is not referring to seven specific kings; rather he is using the number seven as an apocalyptic symbol.... For several reasons, the *symbolic* rather than the *historical* approach to interpreting the seven kings is convincing. (a) Seven, a symbolic number used widely in the ancient world, occurs fifty-three times in Revelation to reflect the divine arrangement and design of history and the cosmos. The enumeration of just *seven* kings, therefore, suggests the propriety of a symbolic rather than a historical interpretation. (b) The *seven* heads of the beast, first interpreted as seven hills and then as seven kings, is based on the archaic mythic tradition of the seven-

The seventh king then is the last king in that series of kings and empires and when he or it dies or passes away, the complete succession of world empires and rulers pass away with him. The eighth, who is also one of the seven, is *the last world ruler* that will come as Satan's representative, hence the description of him as going into perdition or destruction. Satan now thrown down from heaven to earth (12.13, 18) calls forth the beast from the sea (13.1), and in and through the beast, Satan rules the world for the final three-and-a-half years.[145]

We submit that the seventh king and the eighth king are one and the same person or entity (17.8–11). The beast who suffers a death-wound (13.3, 12, 14) is the seventh king and when he is resurrected and lives again, he becomes the eighth king. Thus the eighth king is also one of the seven.

We surmise that the seven kings represent governments or empires throughout history which, despite violence and injustice, rule with a semblance of law and order in contrast to the eighth that goes into perdition. So when the seventh dies or passes away, all law and order pass away with him and the eighth called the beast will arise and go into perdition or lawlessness to deceive the world into perdition and destroy those who refuse to worship him.

b. *Does Babylon Refer to Rome?*

We should note that the lament of the fall of Babylon in Rev. 18 has often been interpreted by commentators as referring to Rome. But the argument that Rev. 18 refers to contemporary Rome has been strongly disputed by Provan.[146] It is beyond the scope of this book to discuss Rev. 18 in detail but the questions and issues which Provan has raised concerning the identification of Babylon with Rome in Rev. 18 are equally applicable in our study of the beast in Rev. 13 and Rev. 17. We agree with Provan that a clear understanding of how the language of the text operates in Rev. 18 is crucial to the interpretation of the chapter. According to Provan, the language in Rev. 18 brought over from other biblical texts already has a supra-historical quality. Provan writes:

headed dragon widely known in the ancient world.... Since the author is working with traditional material, this again suggests that precisely *seven* kings should be interpreted symbolically.' Aune, *Revelation 17–22*, p. 948.

145. Speaking of the relationship between the dragon and the beast in 12.18–13.2, Müller writes thus: 'Ohne daß dies geschildert wird, ist wohl gedacht, daß der Drache das Aufsteigen des Tieres aus dem Meer bewirkt (Vers i). Wie der Drache (12,3) hat das Tier sieben Häupter und entsprechend Dan 7,7 zehn Hörner; es ist somit das irdische Abbild des Drachen, des Satans. Ausdrücklich vermerkt dann Vers 2 b, daß der Drache dem Tier seine Macht und Gewalt zueignet. Es ist die Inkarnation des Teufels.' Müller, *Offenbarung*, p. 249.

146. Provan, 'Foul Spirits, Fornication and Finance', pp. 81–100.

It has already transcended particularity, and moved into the realm of the stereotypical, the hyperbolic, the apocalyptic.... Sennacherib king of Assyria is as much an archetype of the world power opposed to God as Hezekiah king of Judah is an archetype of the faithful ruler of God's people. When the language of enemies is used, therefore, in a text like Revelation 18, so heavily influenced by the Old Testament, great caution has to be exercised in moving from the world of the text to the world of the author, and beyond that to the world outside the author's head.[147]

We can state the same concerning the language used of the beast in Rev. 13.1–10, where the beast is identified and described by the use of Old Testament texts particularly from the book of Daniel. The beast has become an archetype of the world power opposed to God. King Nebuchadnezzar of Babylon in the sixth century B.C.E. or Antiochus Epiphanes IV in the second century B.C.E. have transcended their particularity to become universal stereotypical symbols of kings and kingdoms that oppose God and trample on his people and his holy temple. It is not surprising that Rome is labeled by 1 Pet. 5.13 as another 'Babylon' because like Babylon, Rome has destroyed the temple of God and conquered the holy city in 70 C.E. But the language of Rev. 13 and Rev. 17 transcends the particularity of Rome. Christopher Rowland says of the book of Revelation:

> The visionary experience, while conditioned by life under Roman dominion, is not determined by it. It is the Beast and Babylon, not Rome and Caesar, which are the vehicles of John's message. As such they have a wider appeal than a narrowly focused political analysis rooted in particular historical events.[148]

Provan highlights the danger of restricting the text to the particular and the need to be aware of the universalizing nature of the language. Provan affirms that the particular is often the starting point but equally that 'the particular is only a function of the universal'.[149] He cites with approval Leon Morris' remark that Babylon is not Rome 'though doubtless to men of the first century there is no better illustration of what Babylon means

147. Provan, 'Foul Spirits, Fornication and Finance', p. 96.

148. C. Rowland, *Revelation* (Epworth Commentaries; London: Epworth Press, 1993), p. 24. Ford comments that: 'one must not make the mistake of stopping here as if our author's interest were only or primarily centered on the particular event. A particular event is the point of departure, and so we must start with it and take into consideration the universal application.' Ford, *Revelation*, p. 281.

149. Provan, 'Foul Spirits, Fornication and Finance', p. 98.

than contemporary Rome'.[150] When John's readers considered the beast of Rev. 13, they would no doubt *think* of Rome but for reasons stated above, it is unlikely that they would *identify* the beast with Rome since the text clearly shows that contemporary Rome does not match John's description of the beast.

So we conclude that in Rev. 13 and Rev. 17 (cf. 11.7) John foresees the day when a king or kingdom will arise to rule the whole world (13.3), will demand total submission to its regime (13.7), will command worship of its leader (13.4), will blaspheme God (13.5–6), and through the second beast, will deceive the world with mighty signs and miracles (13.13–14), will control all aspects of the economy (13.16–17), and will kill all who refuse to follow its dictates (13.7–10, 15). If this view is taken, then there is a strong case to say that the events of Rev. 13 as well as those in Rev. 11 and Rev. 17 have not taken place at the time of John's writing but will unfold within the three-and-a-half years repeatedly stated by John as the last eschatological period (11.2–3; 12.6, 14; 13.5) before the coming of the kingdom of God and Christ (11.15; 12.10).

7. *The Identity of the Second Beast*

The identity of the second beast in Rev. 13.11–18 is not difficult to pin down. John identifies the second beast as the false prophet in 16.13, 19.20, and 20.10.[151] As the false prophet, the second beast deceives the world with mighty signs including calling fire from heaven and giving 'spirit' to the image of the beast so that it could speak, all in a show in order that the inhabitants of the world will worship the first beast (13.13–15). The false prophet is not just a magician or sorcerer but also a false religious leader.[152] To John, the second beast who looks like a lamb but speaks like a dragon is

---

150.   L. Morris, *The Revelation of St John* (London: Tyndale Press, 1969), p. 180. Cited by Provan, 'Foul Spirits, Fornication and Finance', p. 99. Laws writes: 'If the beast of the Apocalypse is Rome, he is Rome seen as the climax or consummation of the history of the wickedness of pagan empires.' S. Laws, *In the Light of the Lamb: Image, Parody, and Theology in the Apocalypse of John* (Wilmington, DE: Michael Glazier, 1988), p. 37.

151.   Reddish argues that the second beast is modeled after Behemoth, the land monster while the first beast is an adaptation of the ancient mythological sea monster Leviathan. Reddish, *Revelation*, p. 257. However, what is known of the two creatures Leviathan and Behemoth from 2 Esd. 6, I *En.* 60 and 2 *Bar.* 29 show vast dissimilarity to what is spoken of the two beasts in Rev. 13. Further, the datings of the apocalyptic texts cited are disputed whether they predate Revelation or that they are later interpolations of an earlier text. Hence, it is not altogether certain John has alluded to these legendary monsters in his depiction of the two beasts.

152.   Beale rightly recognizes that: 'The beast [from the earth] has primarily a religious role since it is later repeatedly called 'the false prophet' (16.13; 19.20; 20.10).' Beale, *Revelation*, p. 707.

the deceiver *par excellence*. As the false religious leader or false prophet, it promotes and enforces the worship of a false god, the first beast. As our macro-chiastic structure shows that the narrative of the second beast is composed as a contrast to the two witnesses-prophets of Rev. 11 (BB'), it is submitted that the second beast is also an eschatological figure, which like the sea-beast on whose behalf the second beast exercises authority, functions as an eschatological opponent of the two eschatological prophets.

There is, however, no evidence to suggest that the second beast represents those in the imperial priesthood or provincial bureaucracy that function to promote the Emperor cult in Asia Minor in the late first century C.E.[153] The priests and bureaucrats certainly did not play such a prominent and powerful role as depicted by the authority of the second beast. Aune admits that: 'The identity of the second beast from the earth is problematic.'[154] After reviewing a host of proposals listed by various scholars, Aune concludes: 'Of these various possibilities, the most likely solution is that the beast from the earth represents the imperial priesthood.' but acknowledges that, 'very little is really known about priests in imperial cults, however'.[155] Speaking of the second beast, A. Yarbro Collins writes:

> The vision about the beast from the earth (13.11–18) would have called to mind the leading families of Asia Minor, who had control of both political office and the various priesthoods. These families, as well as the general populace of the region, were very enthusiastic in supporting and even extending the worship of the emperor.[156]

---

153. Barnett thinks that the false prophet is 'the High Priest (*archiereus*) of the Province [of Asia Minor]'. Barnett, 'Polemical Parallelism', p. 116. Commenting on Rev. 13.13–17, de Heer says, 'Dalam ayat-ayat ini digambarkan kegiatan para imam, yang bekerja melayani di kuil-kuil yang didirikan untuk peribadatan bagi kaisar.' (ET: In these verses the activity of the priests is depicted, those who serve in the temples built for the cult of Caesar). de Heer, *Kitab Wahyu*, p. 193. de Heer does not limit the identification of the second beast with the priests of the Caesar cult in the first century C.E. He (p. 193) goes on to state that, 'binatang kedua itu muncul setiap kali dalam bentuk-bentuk baru. Setiap negara totaliter mempunyai 'nabi-nabinya' sendiri, alat-propagandanya sendiri. Alat-alat propaganda itu selalu mendirikan semacam religi tiruan atau pseudo-religi sekitar negara totaliter itu.' (ET: The second beast arises every time in new forms. Every totalitarian state has its own 'prophets', its own tools of propaganda. This propaganda tool always builds up religions of imitation or pseudo-religions to bolster the totalitarian state). Also Beasley-Murray states that: 'There can be no doubt that the second beast is thereby identified with the promoters of the cult of the emperor.' Beasley-Murray, *Revelation*, p. 216. The phrase 'no doubt' used by Beasley-Murray is perhaps overly strong as many details of Rev. 13.11–18 do not match what is known of the priesthood of the Caesar cult.

154. Aune, *Revelation 6–16*, p. 756.

155. Aune, *Revelation 6–16*, p. 756.

156. A. Yarbro Collins, '"What the Spirit Says to the Churches": Preaching the Apocalypse', *Quarterly Review* 4 (1984), pp. 69–84 (82).

Friesen agrees with Yarbro Collins and writes:

> The beast from the Earth was not quite an allegory, but the range of its
> referents is clear: it signified the network of people and overlapping
> institutions in Asia.... The elite families...led sacrifices, underwrote
> festivals, built temples, voted honors, and so forth as part of their full
> range of civic duties. The elite families mobilized the masses in support
> of the emperor and enhanced their own standing in the process.[157]

We dispute that the referent to the second beast is as clear as Friesen
alleges. None of the elite families, whether they were priests or civic office
holders, could be clearly linked to the signs said to be performed by the
beast from the earth like calling fire from heaven to earth and making the
image of the beast speaks (Rev. 13.13–15), as we will now note.

When we consider the passage in 13.11–18, it is also clear that a number
of events spoken of there have no historical precedents. First, there is no
evidence that anyone was able to call fire from heaven for public viewing as
the second beast is said to do (13.13). Secondly, there is no evidence to
show that an image of the emperor could speak and command worship in
the late first century C.E.

We are not convinced by the arguments put forward by Steven J.
Scherrer that the mighty signs in Rev. 13.13–15 can be identified with the
miracles of the Roman imperial priesthood.[158] Scherrer thinks that, 'it is
unlikely that he [John] would invent powerful and impressive miracles and
attribute them to his archrival and opponent were there no evidence
whatsoever for their existence'.[159] This argument is flawed as there is no
reason why John could not have attributed the powerful miracles to the
second beast since, in John's estimation, Satan has come down to earth (cf.
12.13, 18) and through the two beasts in Rev. 13, Satan is bent to deceive
the world by powerful signs. Further, in his portrayal of the second beast,
John is more interested in contrasting the false prophet's power against the
power of the two witnesses rather than pointing to some historical evidence
in support of the second beast's signs.[160] If calling fire from heaven must
have some historical referent, then the same must be true of the fire that
comes out of the two witnesses' mouths (11.5). We believe that John is
more interested in depicting the second beast (and also the two witnesses)
using scriptural references. The second beast by calling fire from heaven
but being called a false prophet is portrayed as an anti-Elijah figure. By the

157. Friesen, *Imperial Cults*, p. 203.

158. See S. J. Scherrer, 'Signs and Wonders in the Imperial Cult: A New Look at a Roman
Religious Institution in the Light of Rev. 13.13–15', *JBL* 103 (1984), pp. 599–610.

159. Scherrer, 'Signs and Wonders in the Imperial Cult', p. 600.

160. See our earlier discussion of the chiastic pairs of Rev. 11.3–6 and 13.11–18.

same token, the two witnesses are patterned after Elijah the prophet. Duff writes:

> The expectation of Elijah's return at the end of time is presupposed in Revelation 13.13. By alluding to the tradition here (and elsewhere in the Apocalypse), John sets up a dualism between Elijah, the eschatological prophet par excellence, and anti-Elijah, the false prophet par excellence.[161]

Scherrer relies on Lucian's account, *Alexander the False Prophet* to support his notion that the image of beast speaking in Rev. 13.15 is historically verifiable.[162] Tales about statues or idols that spoke, which circulated in the late first century C.E., hardly constitute the specificity of John's description of the *image of the beast* speaking. Beasley-Murray cites the tale of a statue of a certain Neryllinus at Troas which was supposed to utter oracles and to heal the sick, and the statue of Alexander and Proteus at Parium that allegedly uttered oracles, but those hardly amount to convincing evidence that the image of the beast that speaks in Rev. 13.15 is thereby historically verified.[163] Price, for example, seeks to identify the statue built for Domitian or Titus[164] in Ephesus (89/90 C.E.) as the image of the beast spoken of in Rev. 13.14–15:

> It is tempting to think that the establishment of the provincial cult of Domitian at Ephesus, with its colossal cult statue, is what lies behind our text [Rev. 13.14–15]. Indeed I have seen no other interpretation which fits the known geographical and temporal context.[165]

However, Biguzzi argues that the Ephesian statue built for the cult of Domitian (or Titus) could not be identified with the image of the beast of Rev 13.14–15 since 'the colossal statue of Ephesus was not a "talking-statue" like that of Rev. 13.15'.[166] We agree with Biguzzi that, 'even though this statue may not be the εἰκών of Rev. 13, its colossal dimensions also help one to understand John's reaction vis-à-vis the emperor's pretence of being super-human and the object of a cult'.[167]

The increasingly widespread imperial worship in Asia Minor would have certainly influenced John in his portrayal of the beasts of Rev. 13, but to

---

161. Duff, *Who Rides the Beast?*, p. 121.

162. Scherrer, 'Signs and Wonders in the Imperial Cult', pp. 601–02.

163. Beasley-Murray, *Revelation*, p. 217 n. 2.

164. Friesen argues that the emperor represented by the Ephesian statue was not Domitian but Titus. See Friesen, *Twice Neokoros*, p. 62.

165. Price, *Rituals and Power*, p. 197.

166. Biguzzi, 'Ephesus, Its Artemision, Its Temple', p. 286.

167. Biguzzi, 'Ephesus, Its Artemision, Its Temple', p. 286.

identify the second beast with the elite families of Asia Minor or any group does not match historical evidence. We submit therefore that what is known of the imperial priesthood in the late first century C.E. does not tally with what is written explicitly concerning the second beast from the earth in 13.11–18 and elsewhere in 16.13, 19.20, and 20.10.

Thirdly, and perhaps the strongest argument against interpreting Rev. 13 as referring to historical events in the first century, is that there is no evidence to the effect that the world population was marked with the mark of the beast to enable them to participate in the economic system. Suggestions that the passage in 13.18 only speaks of Roman coins with the emperor's image fail to convince since the text is explicit about the marking of the number of the beast in one's *right hand* or *forehead*.[168] No such evidence is ever found for such marking on a wide scale in the last decade of the first century C.E. Thompson writes: 'So far as I know, images of the emperor at this time were never rigged up to speak. Nor were there tattoos required for buying and selling. To identify them with images on coins stretches the tattoos beyond recognition.'[169]

Fourthly, various attempts to calculate the number 666 to signify either Nero or Domitian or another Emperor have failed to gain any kind of uniform approval among scholars. Rick van de Water states: 'No one, however, has come up with a convincing match.'[170] By some ingenuity, commentators have calculated the number to represent Nero, Titus, or

---

168.   Yarbro Collins thinks that the mark 'refers to Roman coins and the author is calling for separatism and economic boycott'. Yarbro Collins, 'Persecution and Vengeance in the Book of Revelation', p. 741. In another place, Yarbro Collins suggests that the mark may refer to the imperial stamp on official documents. See Yarbro Collins, *Cosmology and Eschatology*, p. 212. See also E. A. Judge, 'The Mark of the Beast', *TynBul* 42 (1991), pp. 158–60. For a discussion of Roman coinage and their relevance in the NT, see Larry Kreitzer, *Striking New Images: Roman Imperial Coinage and the New Testament World* (JSNTSup, 134; Sheffield: Sheffield Academic Press, 1996); *idem*, 'A Numismatic Clue to Acts 19.23–41: The Ephesian Cistophori of Claudius and Aggrippina', *JSNT* 30 (1987), pp. 59–70; *idem*, 'Apotheosis of the Roman Emperor', *BA* (Dec. 1990), pp. 211–17.

169.   Thompson, *Revelation*, p. 143. Thompson (p. 143) comments: 'In a general way, the beasts disclose religious dimensions of the Roman empire' but acknowledges that one cannot be certain whether the character and activity of the two evil beasts reveal anything more specific about the empire.

170.   R. van de Water, 'Reconsidering the Beast from the Sea', *NTS* 46 (2000), pp. 245–61 (254). Although van de Water argues that the beast of Rev. 13 is not the Roman government and on this point we agree with him, nevertheless, we disagree with van de Water (p. 246) when he proposes that the two beasts represent political messianism in Palestine and diaspora Judaism united in opposition against the followers of Jesus. Van de Water's position is untenable since references to Jerusalem are only found in 11.2, 8, 13 and not once in Rev. 13. To read Rev. 11–13 as supporting the kind of political messianism in Palestine envisaged by van de Water is unwarranted for the sheer lack of reference to political messianism in the text.

Domitian.[171] Again, the number 666 can be seen as both literal and symbolic. At the literal level, the number 666 is the name of a man or person by way of gematria (cf. 13.18), but at the symbolic level, the number 666 represents the grasping at perfection (symbolized by the number 7) and falling short of it. Laws writes,

> The number [666] can be seen to have an immediate symbolic force: conventionally, the complete number or the number of perfection is thought to be the number seven, and we have seen how prominently patterns or cycles of seven feature in the structure of the Apocalypse; the beast, by contrast, is six-six-six, always incomplete, doomed to failure, or as 17.11 puts it, 'to perdition'.[172]

If the beast of Rev. 13.1–10 is an eschatological figure as we argue, there is no need to identify the number 666 with any emperor of the first century C.E. We agree with J. Nelson Kraybill that 'we should not limit symbolism in Revelation to specific entities in John's own day'.[173] Similarly, Jörg Frey writes: 'Die im Modus der Vision vorgeführte Welt der Apokalypse ist kein System von Zeichen, das einfach in die reale Welt der Adressaten übersetzbar wäre.'[174] All the above should caution us against seeing historical referents in the events spoken of in Rev. 13.

Further, the second beast is even said to be empowered to kill anyone who refuses to worship the image of the first beast (13.15). No such authority was held by anybody or any of the elite families of Asia Minor in late first century C.E. The second beast's deeds are not limited to the religious sphere but extend to the control of the economy. Although the provincial elite families possessed wealth and had significant control over economic activity in the region, such control did not extend to total monopoly and exclusion of others from commercial transactions envisaged by John in Rev. 13.16–18. The second beast is said to cause everyone to receive a mark of the first beast without which no one can buy or sell (13.16–17).

Finally, the second beast as the false prophet is listed among the triad (dragon, the beast, the false prophet) in the sixth bowl of 16.13–14, from whose mouths demonic spirits come forth to perform signs, going abroad to gather and assemble the kings of the whole world for battle on the great

---

171. For a discussion of the number 666 and gematria, see Aune, *Revelation 6–16*, pp. 770–73; Bauckham, 'Nero and the Beast', in *idem, Climax of Prophecy*, pp. 384–52; Gideon Bohak, 'Greek-Hebrew Gematrias in *3 Baruch* and in Revelation', *JSP* 7 (1990), pp. 119–21; Yarbro Collins, 'Number Symbolism in Jewish and Early Christian Apocalyptic Literature'; Bovon, 'Names and Numbers in Early Christianity', 267–88; Laws, 'Appendix: The Number of the Beast', in *idem, In the Light of the Lamb*, pp. 47–51.

172. Laws, *In the Light of the Lamb*, p. 48.

173. J. Nelson Kraybill, *Imperial Cult and Commerce in John's Apocalypse* (Sheffield: Sheffield Academic Press, 1996), p. 26 n. 6.

174. Frey, 'Die Bildersprache der Johannesapokalypse', p.183.

day of God the Almighty. In the passage in 16.13–14 the beast and the false prophet are presented as eschatological figures where they take an active part in summoning the kings of the world for war at the *eschaton*, i.e., on the great day of God the Almighty. We have noted earlier that the sounding of the seventh trumpet in 11.15 consists of the outpouring of the seven bowls of plagues of Rev. 16. As the seventh trumpet sounds at the end of the second woe/sixth trumpet (11.14), i.e., after the three-and-a-half years have expired (cf. 11.2–3), it follows that the seven bowls of Rev. 16 come after the said three-and-a-half years. They are poured out just before the coming of the Lamb to war and judge. As the beast and the false prophet are mentioned in the narration of the sixth bowl, so the beast and the false prophet will be present in the eschatological war that will bring this present age to a close and lead to the setting up of the kingdom of God on earth.

In another scene where the rider on the white horse with his armies descend from heaven to war with the beast and his armies (19.11–16), the false prophet together with the beast are said to be captured and thrown alive into the lake of fire that burns with sulfur (19.19–20). Reading the passages in 16.13–14 and 19.19–20 together, we see that the two beasts of Rev. 13 fight against the Lamb and his armies to the very end until their capture and punishment. The beast and the false prophet are thus eschatological figures that will arise in the last days, i.e., the three-and-a-half years before the End comes.

8. *The War Waged by the Two Witnesses against the Two Beasts*

Finally in this chapter, we will discuss the nature of the warfare waged by two witnesses against the nations of the world. It is not clear whether the two witnesses encounter their main antagonists, the two beasts face to face. Although it is stated that the beast that ascends from the bottomless pit will make war, conquer, and kill the two witnesses (11.7), the nature of their encounter prior to the deaths of the two witnesses is left unstated. Neither is it clear that the two witnesses encounter the second beast-false prophet in the period of the three-and-a-half years although our literary analysis shows that John has composed the narrative of the ministry of the two witnesses-prophets (11.3–6) as a mirror image of the career of the false prophet (13.11–18). What is clear is the direct encounter of the two witnesses with the inhabitants of the earth led by the two beasts (11.10).[175]

---

175.   Friesen comments: 'This conflict between the churches and those who worship the Beast dominates the latter half of the book. This is not two equal communities facing off; John portrays it as a small network of faithful witnesses against everyone else.' Friesen, *Imperial Cults*, p. 192.

As the two witnesses are also representatives of the churches, we surmise that the warfare waged by the two witnesses (and the church) is war against the international community led by the beasts. As the beasts of Rev. 13 are also the representatives of the society which they lead, it is clear that the war waged by the two witnesses against the two beasts is also a warfare waged between the church and the society of the world.

How does the church represented by the two witnesses wage war against the society represented by the two beasts? We believe that the life and death of the two witnesses provide a paradigm to understand the nature of the conflict. The two beasts wage war against the church by physical force (13.7, 9–10, 15; cf. 11.7). Many Christians are killed by the two beasts. Since the sea-beast is a king, therefore he has at his disposal the whole state apparatus and machinery to enforce his rule over all. As the saints are said to be killed by the sword (13.10), an instrument of war, it is apparent that the beast uses state terrorism as his *modus operandi*. The church is subjected to the might of the state, and many will fall victim to the terror unleashed by the government of the beast.

But the church does not resort to terror in retaliation. The saints do not wage war against the beast with physical force or violence with the exception that only those who wish to harm the two witnesses are killed (11.5).[176] The rest of the nations are merely tormented by the testimony of the two prophets attested by powerful signs (11.10). As we have argued that the mighty signs described in 11.5–6 are limited to the two individual witnesses-prophets, it appears that the church as a whole wages war by the word of their testimony. It is by the blood of the Lamb and the word of their testimony that the saints are said to conquer their enemies (12.11). 'The blood of the Lamb' is a weapon of warfare because like their Lord who was crucified (11.8) or the Lamb that was slain (5.6, 9, 12; 13.8), the saints conquer not by physical force or violence but by laying down their lives for the truth in the manner of their Lord. Johns writes: '[But] the primary weapon by which this conflict would be engaged was the weapon

---

176.   The book of Revelation following the book of Daniel differs from other apocalyptic texts in that the righteous in Revelation do not engage in physical warfare against the forces of evil. In contrast, the War Scroll of Qumran (1 QM) narrates the eschatological war in which the Sons of Light, who belong to the lot of God, are opposed by the Sons of Darkness, whose leader is Belial. See Aune, 'Qumran and the Book of Revelation', p. 641. Revelation follows closely the model presented by the book of Daniel which rejects violence as a form of resistance but instead chooses to persevere and suffer. For a comparison between different models of resistance found in apocalyptic texts, see Yarbro Collins, 'The Political Perspective to the Revelation to John', pp. 198–217. The only exceptions where the elect partakes of an eschatological battle in Revelation are found in 17.14 and perhaps in 14.1–5 and 19.14.

of faithful witness – a witness that the author fully expected would lead to their martyrdom.'[177] Pattemore explains:

> The victory of the people of God, then, has a double source. It is dependant on the one hand on the victory (through death) of the Lamb.... On the other hand it is achieved in the lives of the people of God by means of their own witness to and faithfulness to Christ, and their identification with him in suffering and death:[178]

We surmise that the saints conquer in the knowledge that Jesus Christ has freed them from sin by his blood and has made them to be a kingdom and priests (1.5–6). Though they may lose their lives as a result, they are promised resurrection and as priests of God and of Christ, they will reign with him for a thousand years (cf. 20.6).

The phrase 'the word of their testimony' in 12.11 is ambiguous. It may mean that the saints confess Christ openly or hold to the testimony of (about) Jesus (cf. 12.17).[179] Even their faithful confession is patterned after the example of Jesus Christ. He is the faithful witness (1.5). As faithful witness, Jesus Christ once stood before Pontius Pilate, the Emperor's Representative and has 'borne his witness, even at the cost of his life (cf. John 18.33–19.16; 1 Tim. 6.13)'.[180] This accepting of death is not fatalistic but realistic. Death constitutes the likely outcome on the account of the word of their testimony. 'Dying is the result; witnessing is the cause.'[181] Those who venture to speak for God and reject violence risk death from those who are anti-God. Mitchell G. Reddish states thus: 'The book of Revelation recognizes that a conflict exists between God and the world, and whoever ventures to be God's spokesperson, God's witness, to the world risks death.'[182]

The conflict of the church against the beasts is a life and death struggle. It seems that the Christians 'lose' the battle as they suffer violence and

---

177. Johns, 'The Lamb in the Rhetorical Program of the Apocalypse of John', p. 784.

178. Pattemore, 'The People of God in the Apocalypse', p. 300. See also Wes Howard-Brook, 'Revelation: Claiming the Victory Jesus Won over Empire', in Wes Howard-Brook and Sharon H. Ringe (eds.), *The New Testament – Introducing the Way of Discipleship* (Maryknoll, New York: Orbis Books, 2002), pp. 188–206.

179. We agree with Leivestad that: 'It is not advisable to try to give a too definite meaning to these phrases; their ambiguity has to be accepted.' Leivestad, *Christ the Conqueror*, p. 225.

180. Boring, *Revelation*, p. 76.

181. B. K. Blount, 'Reading Revelation Today: Witness as Active Resistance', *Int* 54 (2000), pp. 398–412 (410).

182. M. G. Reddish, 'Martyr Christology in the Apocalypse', *JSNT* 33 (1988), pp. 85–95 (92). It is also important to note that not all who witness suffer death. Though those who bear witness must be prepared to lay down their lives, martyrdom is not universal. Ford remarks that: '[Therefore], in Revelation the notion of witness does not necessarily involve the death of the person who testifies.' Ford, 'Persecution and Martyrdom', p. 146.

martyrdom. In fact, the battle can only be carried out to its end by those who love not their lives unto death (12.11c). The war is not for the faint or cowardly. Those who shrink back are counted as faithless and cowards and are condemned to suffer along with fornicators, murderers, sorcerers, idolaters, and all liars in the lake of fire (21.8). It is with utmost seriousness that John calls to 'war' in the last eschatological conflict of the people of God against the forces of evil. Bauckham writes: 'John's message is not, "Do not resist!" It is, "Resist!" – but by witness and martyrdom, not by violence.'[183] It is an all or nothing battle. It is war against the beasts. As Reddish remarks: 'Authentic witnessing involves not only witnessing "to," but witnessing "against." The true witness is the one willing to confront power structures and the power brokers, to challenge the system.'[184] The battle waged by the church is not to initiate violence or retaliate with physical force; it is by the word of their testimony that they will triumph over all adversity, even through death. For the victors are promised the glories of the New Jerusalem; for the losers the everlasting torment of the lake of fire.

After the many images of warfare in Rev. 11–14, John describes those who had conquered the beast and its image and the number of its name, as standing beside the sea of glass with harps of God in their hands. And the conquerors sing the song of Moses, the servant of God, and the song of the Lamb (15.2–3). The saints are said to conquer three things: 1) the beast 2) its image 3) the number of its name. First, the saints are those who refuse to follow the beast like the rest of the world (cf. 13.3). Second, they are worshippers of God and they refuse to worship the image of the beast and instead choose death (13.15). In speaking generally of worship in the early church, Hurtado notes: 'There are basically two main identifying marks of early Christian worship, when considered in its religious context: (1) Christ is reverenced as divine alongside God, and (2) worship of all other gods is rejected.'[185] Barnett has defined worship in Revelation as the mind's conviction and the mouth's confession that reality, truth and goodness are to be found in God and the Lamb and not in any other.[186]

Third, they reject the mark or number of the beast's name which in effect condemns them to economic deprivation (13.16–18). They choose hunger and starvation instead of the delicacies of Babylon. The sufferings of the church are very real indeed: persecution, starvation, and martyrdom are their lot. Yet out of it all, they are said to conquer and triumph. The Greek text of 15.2 reads as follows:

---

183. Bauckham, *Theology*, p. 92.
184. Reddish, *Revelation*, p. 224.
185. Hurtado, *On the Origins of Christian Worship*, p. 39. Hurtado (pp. 65–69) discusses the various Greek words used for 'worship' in the NT.
186. See Barnett, 'Polemical Parallelism', p. 113.

Καὶ εἶδον ὡς θάλασσαν ὑαλίνην μεμιγμένην πυρὶ καὶ τοὺς νικῶντας ἐκ τοῦ
θηρίου καὶ ἐκ τῆς εἰκόνος αὐτοῦ καὶ ἐκ τοῦ ἀριθμοῦ τοῦ ὀνόματος αὐτοῦ
ἑστῶτας ἐπὶ τὴν θάλασσαν τὴν ὑαλίνην ἔχοντας κιθάρας τοῦ θεοῦ.

Translated literally, the saints are said to be those who are conquering 'out of' or 'from' (ἐκ) the beast, out of his image and out of the number of his name (τοὺς νικῶντας ἐκ τοῦ θηρίου καὶ ἐκ τῆς εἰκόνος αὐτοῦ καὶ ἐκ τοῦ ἀριθμοῦ τοῦ ὀνόματος αὐτοῦ). The participle νικῶντας followed by the preposition ἐκ in all three genitival objects is a peculiar construction. But the meaning of the clause is clear as we have explained. The present active participle νικῶντας with the preposition ἐκ emphasizes the continuous activity of conquering the obstacles placed before them. This 'conquering' signifies the constant struggle which is their lot in the last three and a half years *and* from which God will deliver and protect them though they may have to suffer martyrdom.[187]

The church is called to witness actively to the world in this time of great tribulation in the manner of the testimony of the two witnesses. The saints are not called to silence but to war with the confession of their mouths in witness and in worship.[188] It is their worship of God which results in their confessing of God in the words of their testimony. John Sweet remarks, ' "the word of their testimony" (12.11) points sharply to the inseparability of worship and witness'.[189] True worship compels and impels their witness to the world of the truth of their God against all claimants. Filho sums up thus:

> Through the continuous remembrance of the power of God and of Christ in the hymns of the worship service, in direct contradiction to the visible power in the world, John makes of worship a place of learning: the confession of faith in the sovereignty of God and of Christ ought to be heard as a witness to the world, but, at the same time, as a protest against all sovereignty that is opposed to God.[190]

---

187. Thomas puts it thus: 'The combination of the verb νικάω ... and ἐκ ... gives the dual concept of victory over and deliverance from the temptation to worship the beast's image and receive his mark. They prevailed over the coercion to which others acquiesced ... and so will receive the appropriate rewards.' Thomas, *Revelation 8–22*, p. 233. Leivestad comments, 'Generally when applied to Christ and the Christians νικάω implies a paradoxical "martyrological" victory, a triumph through death.' Leivestad, *Christ the Conqueror*, p. 213.

188. For a discussion of John's call to active witness and the nature of witness, see Blount, 'Reading Revelation Today: Witness as Active Resistance', pp. 398–412.

189. J. Sweet, 'Revelation', in John Barclay and John Sweet (eds.), *Early Christian Thought in its Jewish Setting* (Cambridge: Cambridge University Press, 1996), pp. 160–73 (168). For a discussion of the close relationship between worship and witness, see A. W. Missen, 'Witness and Worship in the Apocalypse' (Unpublished M.Theol. thesis; University of Otago, Dunedin, New Zealand, 2001), esp. pp. 99–118.

190. Filho, 'The Apocalypse of John', p. 234.

Confession of one true God excludes all others. 'Christians were, by definition, religiously intolerant.'[191]

Although the message of the two witnesses and the content of Christian proclamation are left unstated in Revelation, it is perhaps indicated in the angel's proclamation of the eternal gospel: 'Fear God and give him glory. For the hour of his judgment has come; and worship him who made the heaven and earth, the sea and the springs of waters' (14.6–7). Like the two witnesses, the saints may suffer death, but like the two witnesses they too will experience the resurrection promised them (11.11–12; cf. Dan. 12.2). Through their deaths, they conquer their enemies (12.11; 15.2–3) and will return triumphant to earth with the Lamb to rule over the nations of the world (14.1).[192]

9. *Conclusion*

We have seen how the chiastic pairs (BB', CC') inform our interpretation of the two witnesses and the two beasts. The prophetic testimony of the two witnesses in B (11.3–6) is contrasted the deceit and false prophecy of the second beast in B' (13.11–18). Likewise, the beast that ascends from the abyss and makes war, conquers, and kills the two witnesses in C (11.7–13) is the same being/entity that makes war and conquers the saints in C' (13.7–10). Though the saints are handed over to captivity and many are put to death by the sword (13.7–10), read in the light of 11.7–13, the saints are promised hope that like the two witnesses, they will also rise from the dead and will be vindicated by God. The macro-chiastic pattern juxtaposes the two witnesses of Rev. 11 and the two beasts of Rev. 13 and thus functions rhetorically to inform John's readers that the narratives of Rev. 11 and Rev. 13 are to be read in conjunction with each other as a coherent textual unit.

We have argued that the two witnesses are two individual prophets as well as the church corporate. Similarly, the two beasts are not only two individuals but they also represent the society of this world. While the two witnesses are two leaders of the church, the two beasts are the leaders of

---

191. Blount, 'Reading Revelation Today: Witness as Active Resistance', p. 403.

192. We should note with Leivestad that: 'The triumph of the martyr includes more than purely moral and spiritual victory of enduring faith and love. It is an indispensable requirement that the triumph must be made manifest through a glorious vindication.... There can be no vindication of the cause of the oppressed unless their oppressors are convicted and punished. It must at last be demonstrated to all the world who were the real victors in the strife: the mighty men of power or the meek martyrs. This demonstration is a central theme in Revelation.' Leivestad, *Christ the Conqueror*, pp. 216–17. We surmise that the depiction of the 144,000 standing on Mount Zion (14.1) is one such picture of public manifestation of their vindication (cf. 11.11–12).

the world. The two witnesses and the two beasts are portrayed as eschatological opponents locked in combat as their appearances coincide in the same eschatological period of three-and-a-half years (11.3 = 13.5). Society in the final three-and-a-half years is divided into two opposing camps: those who worship the beast and those who refuse to worship the beast. Hence the conflict between the nations led by the beasts and the church led by the two witnesses. The beast will make war and conquer the two witnesses and the saints (11.7; 13.7). The beast will kill the two witnesses and many Christians beside (11.7; 13.8–10). But the two witnesses and the church will triumph through death and conquer their enemies (12.11). It is war between church and state. It is war between the saints and the world community. It is in John's perspective, the war between the two witnesses and the two beasts.

Thus in the last three-and-a-half years, a great warfare between the society of the world and the community of the saints will ensue until divine intervention comes in the form of the kingdom of God breaking into the world, vindicating the saints but destroying those who destroy the earth (11.15–18; 14.1). We conclude, therefore, the two witnesses and the two beasts are eschatological figures that will appear in the last three and a half years before the End.

Chapter 7

SUMMARY AND CONCLUSIONS

1. *Summary and Findings*

The main aim of this study was to explore the literary-structure of Rev. 11.1–14.5 and to understand the form and content of the said textual unit. The purpose of the study was to clarify the nature of events found within this literary unit with special reference to how the figure of three and a half years unifies the seemingly unconnected narratives into an integrated and coherent whole. We have sought to demonstrate that the literary unit of 11.1–14.5 is structured in a macro-chiastic and concentric pattern of ABCDEFGF'E'D'C'B'A'. The following is a summary of our findings and conclusions. We will also make some suggestions for further research and study.

The first chapter focused on setting out the method of literary analysis that would be utilized in study of 11.1–14.5. We have argued that form and content always interact and more importantly discerning literary-structural patterns are vital in determining the meaning and significance of various units integrated within a literary whole. To achieve a literary analysis of the said textual unit, we commenced by examining the language and style of Revelation and found that the language and style of Revelation as a whole, and 11.1–14.5 in particular, follow the Hebraic literary conventions akin to the style of the prophetic literature of the Old Testament. In particular, the rhetorical and compositional devices and techniques such as chiasm, parallelism, parataxis, and structural parallelism are especially important in our literary analysis of 11.1–14.5. Though not extensively discussed, we have also argued that Graeco-Roman rhetorical categories are not entirely suitable for the study of a visionary and prophetic-apocalyptic text such as the book of Revelation.

As our study proposes that Rev. 11.1–14.5 is structured as a macro-chiasm, we have discussed extensively the works of scholars in this field such as Nils Lund, John Breck, Ian Thomson, Roland Meynet, and Wayne Brouwer. We have also sought to adopt a rigorous methodology in testing and evaluating the validity of a macro-chiastic structure. After examining the works of Ian Thomson, John Welch, and Wayne Brouwer, we concluded that Craig Blomberg's nine criteria remained the most comprehensive set of criteria in which a chiastic pattern could be tested and evaluated.

In the second chapter, we argued that Rev. 11.1–14.5 is best viewed as a coherent literary unit. We also noted the many different divisions of the said textual unit proposed by various scholars. The majority of writers would divide Rev. 11 from Rev. 12–14 and argue that Rev. 12 began a completely new section or the second half of the book of Revelation. We have also listed the variety of proposals offered by scholars on how Rev. 11 itself is divided and noted that some writers have strongly argued for the division of Rev. 11.1–2 from the rest of the chapter.

In Chapter 2, we set out the key words and key motifs of Rev. 11.1–14.5. By examining these key words and key motifs, we have found that the dual themes of war and worship were often juxtaposed to unify the said literary unit. Images of war were especially striking throughout Rev. 11.1–14.5 forming a kind of thread throughout the textual unit giving it cohesion and unity. A study of this war imagery yielded the finding that the warfare in heaven (Rev. 12) determined the nature of warfare that transpired on earth (Rev. 11 and Rev. 13). We found that this understanding of the heavenly-earthly warfare supported our main thesis that John portrayed the war between the two witnesses of Rev. 11 and the two beasts of Rev. 13 as a result and consequence of a prior war in heaven between Michael and the dragon (Rev. 12.7–12). In other words, the war on earth was a reflection of the war in heaven. In Chapter 2, we also began to set out the macro-chiastic pattern which we believe best captured the flow and development of the narrative beginning from Rev. 11.1 and concluded in 14.5. At the end of Chapter 2, we discussed the functions of Rev. 10.11 and 14.6–7, noting their many similarities and parallels, and concluded that these passages served as frame passages for Rev. 11.1–14.5.

In Chapter 3, we began to delineate the sub-units making up Rev. 11 and it was demonstrated that Rev. 11 was a coherent and unified literary unit. We have highlighted the importance of understanding the genre and setting of Rev. 11 in its immediate and surrounding contexts. The events said to unfold in Rev. 11.1–14.5 were set within particular geographical and temporal settings, both of which were crucial in our exegesis of the whole textual unit. Especially significant were the physical locations of the temple of God and the holy city of Rev. 11.1–2 which we have shown to be the geographical and spatial setting for Rev. 11 as a whole. We have shown that the temple of God and the holy city of 11.1–2 should be interpreted literally to denote the physical temple in the city of Jerusalem. Further, it was noted that the temporal time-span of three-and-a-half years appeared in Rev 11.2 for the first time in the literary unit of 11.1–14.5. We have demonstrated that both these temporal and spatial indicators strongly supported our contention that Rev. 11.1 and not Rev. 12.1 began a new section which included Rev. 12.1–14.5. A close reading of Rev. 11 showed that the chapter was divided into four sub-units consisting of 11.1–2, vv. 3–6, vv. 7–13, vv. 15–19. These four sub-units were labelled as ABCD of our proposed macro-chiasm. We have argued at length that Rev. 11.14 served not only as the concluding remark that the ministry of the two witnesses took place under the sixth trumpet/second woe, but also introduced the third woe/seventh trumpet. Thus it was demonstrated that Rev. 11.14 served as a link verse between 11.1–13 and 11.15–19. We have argued at length that the seventh trumpet (11.15a) should not be seen as announcing the arrival of the kingdom of God (11.15b-18) as was thought by many scholars, but that the seventh trumpet was indeed the third woe announced in 11.14 which was only fully unfolded in Rev. 15–16. We have also shown that the text of Rev. 11.19 was carefully composed to link Rev. 11 with Rev. 12 and as such integrated Rev. 11 with the vision of the two signs in heaven of Rev. 12.

In Chapters 4 and 5 the chiastic pattern envisaged for Rev. 11.1–14.5 became evident through a literary-structural analysis of Rev. 12.1–14.5. We found that Rev. 12.1–17 was divided into five sub-units consisting of 12.1–4, vv. 5–6, vv. 7–12, vv. 13–14, and vv. 15–17. These sub-units were shown to be structured in a remarkable concentric and symmetrical chiasm where vv. 1–4 corresponded to vv. 15–17, and vv. 5–6 paralleled vv. 13–14, with the pivot at the middle section of 12.7–12 (EFGF'E'). The sub-unit of vv. 7–12 was demonstrably worthy of its central place as the crux and pivot of the whole literary unit, not only of Rev. 12 but also of Rev. 11.1–14.5 given the significance of the heavenly war that led to the defeat and casting down of the dragon from heaven to earth.

In Chapter 4, we also discussed in detail the various symbols and imagery used throughout Rev. 12. We argued that the woman and the male child were symbols and as such must be interpreted symbolically and that both symbols represented the corporate people of God in their different dimensions of existence. The woman clothed with the sun and crowned with twelve stars represented the glorious heavenly status of the people of God, while on earth they suffered persecution and martyrdom symbolized by the woman's birthpangs and cry of torment. The male child symbolized the security of the people of God who were destined to stand before the throne of God in heaven and the absolute certainty that God was able to secure their deliverance from the clutches of the enemy. We have also demonstrated that Rev. 12.18 linked Rev. 12 with Rev. 13 and that the dragon having been cast down to earth, stood on the seashore (12.18) and called forth the two beasts of Rev. 13.

Structurally, we have found that Rev. 13.1–10 and vv. 11–18 were parallel episodes, the first section describing the career of the sea-beast and the second section describing the career of the land-beast which took place within the temporal period of three-and-a-half years (13.5). On closer examination, Rev. 13.1–10 was further divided into vv. 1–6 and vv. 7–10 by clear literary and structural markers. The close of the section on the second beast (13.18) did not conclude the textual unit begun in 11.1 as we have found that the following passage (14.1–5) was carefully composed by John to serve two important purposes. First, the Lamb, with the 144,000 on whose foreheads were written the name of the Lamb and the Lamb's Father, contrasted with the beast and the inhabitants of the earth who were marked with the name of the beast in the preceding passage (13.18). Secondly, Rev. 14.1–5 functioned as a kind of climax to the series of events unfolded throughout the three-and-a-half years commenced in Rev. 11.1– 2. The great tribulation and persecution of the three and a half years have ended with the return of the Lamb and his 144,000 followers who stood triumphantly on Mount Zion. The war and worship scenes in the beginning of the literary unit (11.1–2) were repeated at the end of the textual unit (14.1–5) with another scene of war on Mount Zion as we have shown and the worship of the 144,000 who sang a new song that no one else could learn. We have found that a literary-structural analysis of 13.1– 14.5 yielded a division of text into four sub-units consisting of 13.1–6, vv. 7–10, vv. 11–18, and 14.1–5 (D'C'B'A').

In Chapter 5, we continued the demonstration of the macro-chiasm by examining the parallels between Rev. 11 and Rev. 13.1–14.5 (ABCDD'C'B'A') in the manner that Rev. 12.1–17 was found to be structured chiastically in the form of an EFGF'E' pattern. We demonstrated, through a detailed examination of verbal, structural, and thematic parallels, that the *inclusio* of Rev. 11.1–14.5 was found in the passages of 11.1–2 and 14.1–5.

After the introduction of the events centred in Jerusalem in 11.1–2 (A), we found that a major motif throughout Rev. 11.1–14.5 was the contest between true and false prophecy (BB'). This theme was strikingly highlighted by the contrast and comparison made by John between the two witnesses-prophets of Rev. 11 and the second beast-false prophet of Rev. 13. Again, the pivot of the macro-chiasm (12.7–12) where Satan was called the deceiver of the world (12.9) was critical to the understanding of this contest between true and false prophecy on earth. The false prophet became Satan's instrument to deceive the world into the worship of the first beast and Satan himself (13.4). While the true prophets were sent by God and his Christ (11.4) to perform signs of judgment to warn the world of the impending great day of the Lord (cf. 16.14) and the wrath of God and the Lamb (cf. 6.16–17), the false prophet with impressive signs and wonders deceived the inhabitants of the earth into idolatry and turning away from God.

From the contest between prophets, John proceeded to describe the rise of the beast from the abyss who made war, conquered, and killed the two witnesses in C (11.7–13) and the sea-beast who made war and conquered the saints in C' (13.7–10). We found that the flow and development from B to C told the story that bearing witness to the true God would certainly lead to persecution and possible martyrdom. By continuing the narrative of the death of the two witnesses (11.7–10) to describe their resurrection and ascension to heaven (11.11–13), John made the point that sufferings and death were not the final word, but that the triumph and vindication of the saints would assuredly follow. The bleak picture where those destined to die by the sword would indeed die violently (13.7, 9–10) would be somewhat less harsh if read against the promise of resurrection narrated in 11.11–13. Hence, the promise of resurrection enabled John to exhort the saints to patiently endure, even to death. Again, it is the pivot (12.7–12) that provided the rationale behind all the suffering, violent persecution, state terror and death in CC'. Paradoxically, John commended bearing witness with patient endurance even unto death. The Lamb that was slaughtered (11.7–8; 13.8; cf. 5.5–6) but later exalted to God's throne, became the paradigm of victory for the saints.

From the trampling by the nations over the holy city (A), faithful witness (B) to martyrdom and resurrection (C), John proceeded to describe the overturning of the kingdom of the world to the kingdom of God and of his Christ (D). Read in conjunction with D' (13.1–6), the DD' pair told the story that the rule and blasphemy of the beast would last only a short and limited period of 42 months (13.5) compared to the everlasting reign of God and of his Christ (11.15b). Another major motif of worship of Rev. 11.1–14.5 was highlighted in this section where the inhabitants of the world worshipped the dragon and the beast on earth (13.4), but those in heaven, the twenty-four elders, worshipped God (11.16). The kingdom of God and his Christ, announced in heaven in the pivotal unit of Rev. 12.10, was fully realized and consummated on earth after the three and a half years have lapsed in 11.15–18. Further, we believe that the flow and development of the chiastic pairs within the macro-chiasm allowed us to conclude that the bearing witness of the church on earth in faithfulness and endurance unto death was instrumental and fully in accord with God's purpose, to bring about the end of the kingdom of the world and to establish the everlasting reign of God and Christ on earth.

In Chapter 6, we conducted a thematic study of the two witnesses and the two beasts. We concluded that the two witnesses and the two beasts were two pairs of future eschatological figures that would arise in the three and a half years before the End. The notion of the End in this study was equated with the arrival of the kingdom of God on earth. We argued that the two witnesses were best understood as two individual prophets and also the corporate church engaged in bearing witness to the world. Similarly, the two beasts were two individuals, but they also represented the society of the world or the international community in opposition to God and his church. In Chapter 6, we also discussed the nature of warfare waged by the two witnesses/the saints against the beast/world society.

2. *Suggestions for Further Study*

We have attempted to interpret Rev. 11.1–14.5 with special attention to its formal structure. While we believe the general pattern in the form of a macro-chiasm is a valid structure to study the content of the textual unit, smaller chiasms proposed throughout the larger macro-chiasm may not convince all and as such may need further refining and study. If a large block of text such as Rev. 11.1–14.5 is structured chiastically, a possibility remains, as proposed by Lund's *Studies in the Book of Revelation*, that other smaller and larger units across the book of Revelation are also arranged chiastically. With the application of rigorous criteria in the testing and evaluating a chiasm, we believe verifiable results can be obtained in the chiastic reading of the text of Revelation, far exceeding what was offered by Lund.

We believe that if the language and style of Revelation are recognized as following Hebraic rhetorical conventions, devices, and compositional techniques, much insight can be gained by applying such conventions, devices, and techniques in the study of Revelation. Finally, in identifying the two witnesses as two individuals and also the corporate church, further study is needed to trace and enlarge on the relationship between the two eschatological prophets and the larger church body. Likewise, the relationship between the two beasts and the inhabitants of the earth requires further research beyond what we were able to offer in this book.

3. *Final Conclusion*

We conclude, therefore, that only an integrated and chiastic reading of Rev. 11.1–14.5 can help us understand the way John has presented his story said to unfold in the last days before the dawn of the kingdom of God. John has brilliantly utilized the figure of three and a half, of 42 months (11.2; 13.5), 1260 days (11.3; 12.6), the Danielic 'a time, times, and half a time' (12.14), and the three and a half days (11.9, 11) as temporal and structural markers to unify the narratives found in Rev. 11.1–14.5. By way of a concentric pattern with its pivot in Rev. 12.7–12, John was able to portray that the war on earth between the two witnesses and the two beasts happened as a result of the war in heaven between Michael and the dragon. This literary framework of how Rev. 11.1–14.5 can be read accords well with John's apocalyptic worldview that whatever happened on earth was a reflection of heavenly realities.

John also managed to combine the seemingly paradoxical motifs of war and worship to present his powerful theological message. Anyone who worshipped God would be subjected to war by the beasts. Conversely, those who worshipped the beast might enjoy temporary economic privileges (13.16–18), but they would be subjected to the war waged by the Lamb on the great day of the Lord. Those who refused to worship the beast would wage war against the beast. But the saints waged war not by physical violence but by their words of testimony.

This bearing witness in the face of death appeared to spell defeat but paradoxically it constituted the very means through which the saints conquered the beasts and brought about the end of the kingdom of this world and hastened the dawn of the kingdom of God on earth. The short time of the dragon's wrath (12.12) should not be a time for cowardly silence or worse, apostasy, but a time of triumph for the saints called to witness publicly and fearlessly in anticipation of the imminent arrival of the kingdom of God and of his Christ. The war between the church and the rest of the society points to one denouement: rewards and participation in the kingdom of God for the saints (11.15–18; cf. 20.4–6), and judgment and destruction for the beasts and the international community of the world (11.18; cf. 17.12–14; 19.20–21).

BIBLIOGRAPHY

Abir, Peter Antonysamy, *The Cosmic Conflict of the Church: An Exegetico-Theological Study of Revelation 12,7–12* (Frankfurt am Main: Peter Lang, 1995).

Alford, H., *Greek New Testament* Vol. 4 (London: Longmans, 1903).

Allison Jr., Dale C., 'Elijah Must Come First', *JBL* 103 (1984), pp. 256–58.

—*The End of the Ages Has Come* (Philadelphia: Fortress Press, 1985).

—*The New Moses: A Matthean Typology* (Philadelphia: Fortress Press, 1993).

—*Jesus of Nazareth: Millenarian Prophet* (Minneapolis: Fortress Press, 1998).

—'Jesus & the Victory of Apocalyptic', in Carey C. Newman (ed.), *Jesus and the Restoration of Israel: A Critical Assessment of N. T. Wright's Jesus and the Victory of God* (Downers Grove: Inter-Varsity Press, 1999), pp. 126–41.

—'Rejecting Violent Judgment: Luke 9.52–56 and its Relatives', *JBL* 121 (2002), pp. 459–78.

Allison Jr., Dale C., and W. Davies, *A Critical and Exegetical Commentary on the Gospel According to Matthew* (ICC; 3 vols.; Edinburgh: T & T Clark, 1997).

Alter, Robert, *The Art of Biblical Narrative* (New York: Basic Books, 1981).

—*The Art of Biblical Poetry* (New York: Basic Books, 1985).

—'The Characteristics of Ancient Hebrew Poetry', in Robert Alter and Frank Kermode (eds.) *The Literary Guide to the Bible* (Cambridge, MA: Harvard University Press, 1987), pp. 611–24.

—'Sodom as Nexus: The Web of Design in Biblical Narrative', in Regina M. Schwartz (ed.), *The Book and the Text: The Bible and Literary Theory* (Oxford: Basil Blackwell, 1990), pp. 146–60.

—*The Art of Biblical Literature* (New York: Basic Books, 1992).

Amaru, Betsy Halpern, 'The Killing of the Prophets: Unraveling a Midrash', *HUCA* 54 (1983), pp. 153–80.

Andersen, Francis I., *The Sentence in Biblical Hebrew* (The Hague: Mouton, 1974).

Andersen, Francis I. and David Noel Freedman, *Micah* (AB; New York: Doubleday, 2000).

Auerbach, Erich, *Mimesis* (trans. W. R. Trask; Princeton: Princeton University Press, 1974).

Aune, David E., *The Cultic Setting of Realized Eschatology in Early Christianity* (Leiden: E. J. Brill, 1972).

—*Prophecy in Early Christianity and in the Ancient Mediterranean World* (Grand Rapids: Eerdmans, 1983).

—'The Apocalypse of John and the Problem of Genre', *Semeia* 36 (1986), pp. 65–96.

—'The Prophetic Circle of John of Patmos and the Exegesis of Revelation 22:16', *JSNT* 37 (1989), pp. 103–16.

—'Intertextuality and the Genre of the Apocalypse', in *SBL Seminar Papers* (Atlanta: Scholars Press, 1991), pp. 142–60.

—'Following the Lamb: Discipleship in the Apocalypse', in R. N. Longenecker (ed.), *Patterns of Discipleship in the New Testament* (Grand Rapids: Eerdmans, 1996), pp. 269–84.

—*Revelation 1–5* (WBC; Dallas: Word, 1997).

— *Revelation 6–16* (WBC; Nashville: Thomas Nelson, 1998).

—*Revelation 17–22* (WBC; Nashville: Thomas Nelson, 1998).

—'Qumran and the Book of Revelation', in Peter W. Flint and James C. VanderKam (eds.), *The Dead Sea Scrolls* Vol. 2: *A Comprehensive Assessment after Fifty Years* (Leiden: E. J. Brill, 1999), pp. 622–48.

Aus, Roger D., 'The Relevance of Isaiah 66.7 to Revelation 12 and 2 Thessalonians 1', *ZNW* 67 (1976), pp. 252–68.

Bachmann, M., 'Himmlisch: der "Tempel Gottes" von Apk 11.1', *NTS* 40 (1994), pp. 474–80.

Bailey, Kenneth, *Poet and Peasant and Through Peasant Eyes* (Grand Rapids: Eerdmans, 1983).

—'Inverted Parallelisms and Encased Parables in Isaiah and Their Significance for Old and New Testament Translation and Interpretation', in L. J. de Regt *et al.* (eds.), *Literary Structures and Rhetorical Strategies in the Hebrew Bible* (Assen: Van Grocum, 1996), pp. 14–30.

Baldwin, Joyce G., *Haggai, Zechariah, Malachi* (Leicester: Inter-Varsity Press, 1972).

Ballard, Harold Wayne, *The Divine Warrior Motif in the Psalms* (North Richland Hills, Texas: Bibal Press, 1999).

Bar-Erfat, Shimon, 'Some Observations on the Analysis of Structure in Biblical Narrative', *VT* 30 (1980), pp. 154–73.

—*Narrative Art in the Bible* (Sheffield: Sheffield Academic Press, 2000).

Barker, Margaret, *The Older Testament* (London: SPCK, 1987).

—*The Gate of Heaven. The History and Symbolism of the Temple in Jerusalem* (London: SPCK, 1991).

—*The Revelation of Jesus Christ* (Edinburgh: T & T Clark, 2000).

Barnett, Paul, 'Polemical Parallelism: Some Further Reflections on the Apocalypse', *JSNT* 35 (1989), pp. 111–20.

Barr, David L., 'The Apocalypse as a Symbolic Transformation of the World: A Literary Analysis', *Int* 38 (1984), pp. 39–50.

—'The Apocalypse of John as Oral Enactment', *Int* 40 (1986), pp. 243–56.

—*Tales of the End: A Narrative Commentary on the Book of Revelation* (Santa Rosa, California: Polebridge Press, 1998).

Barrios, George A., *Jesus Christ and the Temple* (Crestwood, New York: St. Vladimir's Seminary Press, 1980).

Bauckham, R., 'The Martyrdom of Enoch and Elijah: Jewish or Christian?', *JBL* 95 (1976), pp. 447–58.

—'Nero and the Beast', in R. Bauckham, *The Climax of Prophecy* (Edinburgh: T & T Clark, 1993).

—*The Climax of Prophecy* (Edinburgh: T & T Clark, 1993).

—*The Theology of the Book of Revelation* (Cambridge: Cambridge University Press, 1993).

—'The Apocalypse as a Christian War Scroll', in R. Bauckham, *The Climax of Prophecy* (Edinburgh: T & T Clark, 1993).

—'The Ascension of Isaiah: Genre, Unity and Date', in R. Bauckham, *The Fate of the Dead: Studies on Jewish and Christian Apocalypses* (Leiden: E. J. Brill, 1998).

—*The Fate of the Dead: Studies on Jewish and Christian Apocalypses* (E. J. Leiden: Brill, 1998).

Beagley, A. J., *The 'Sitz im Leben' of the Apocalypse with Particular Reference to the Role of the Church's Enemies* (BZNW, 50; Berlin: de Gruyter, 1987).

Beale, Gregory K., 'The Danielic Background for Revelation 13.18 and 17.9', *TynBul* 31 (1980), pp. 163–70.

—*The Use of Daniel in Jewish and Apocalyptic Literature and in the Revelation of St. John* (Lanham: University Press of America, 1984).

—'The Use of Daniel in the Synoptic Eschatological Discourse and the Book of Revelation', in David Wenham (ed.), *Gospel Perspectives: Jesus Tradition Outside the Gospels* Vol. 5 (Sheffield: JSOT Press, 1985), pp. 129–54.

—'The Use of the Old Testament in Revelation', in D.A. Carson and H.G.M. Williamson (eds.), *It is Written: Scripture Citing Scripture* (Festschrift B. Lindars; Cambridge: Cambridge University Press, 1988), pp. 318–52.

—'Solecisms in the Apocalypse as Signals for the Presence of OT Allusions', in C. A. Evans & J. A. Sanders (eds.), *Early Christian Interpretation of the Scriptures of Israel* (Sheffield: Sheffield Academic Press, 1997), pp. 421–43.

—*John's Use of the Old Testament in Revelation* (Sheffield: Sheffield Academic Press, 1998).

—*The Book of Revelation* (NIGNT; Grand Rapids: Eerdmans, 1999).

Beasley-Murray, G. R., *The Book of Revelation* (NCB; Grand Rapids: Eerdmans, 1974).

—'The Interpretation of Daniel 7', *CBQ* 45 (1983), pp. 44–58.

—*John* (WBC; Dallas: Word, 1991).

Beckwith, I. T., *The Apocalypse of John* (New York: Macmillan, 1919).

Beckwith, Roger T., *Calendar and Chronology, Jewish and Christian* (Leiden: E. J. Brill, 1996).

Berlin, Adele, 'Motif and Creativity in Biblical Poetry', *Prooftexts* 3 (1983), pp. 231–41.

—*The Dynamics of Biblical Parallelism* (Bloomington: University of Indiana Press, 1985).

Biguzzi, Giancarlo, 'Ephesus, Its Artemision, Its Temple to the Flavian Emperors, and Idolatry in Revelation', *NovT* 40 (1998), pp. 276–90.

—'A Figurative and Narrative Language: Grammar of Revelation', *NovT* 45 (2003), pp. 382–402.

Bilde, Per, 'Josephus and Jewish Apocalypticism', in Steven Mason (ed.), *Understanding Josephus: Seven Perspectives* (Sheffield: Sheffield Academic Press, 1998), pp. 35–61.

Bishop, John, *Nero: The Man and the Legend* (London: The Trinity Press, 1964).

Black, C. Clifton, 'An Oration at Olivet: Some Rhetorical Dimensions of Mark 13', in Duane F. Watson (ed.), *Persuasive Artistry: Studies in the New Testament Rhetoric in Honor of George A. Kennedy* (JSNTSup, 50; Sheffield: Sheffield Academic Press, 1991), pp. 66–92.

—'Rhetorical Criticism', in Joel B. Green (ed.), *Hearing the New Testament* (Grand Rapids: Eerdmans, 1995), pp. 256–77.

Black, Matthew, *The Scrolls and Christian Origins: Studies in the Jewish Background of the New Testament* (California: Scholars Press, 1961).

—'The "Two Witnesses" of Rev. 11.3f. in Jewish and Apocalyptic Tradition', in E. Bammel, C. K. Barrett, and W. D. Davies (eds.), *Donum Gentilicium: New Testament Studies in Honour of David Daube* (Oxford: Clarendon Press, 1978), pp. 225–37.

Blessing, Kamila, 'Desolate Jerusalem and Barren Matriarch: The Distinct Figures in the Pseudepigrapha', *JSP* 18 (1998), pp. 47–69.

Bloch-Smith, Elizabeth, ' "Who is the King of Glory?" Solomon's Temple and Its Symbolism', in M. D. Coogan, J. C. Exum and L. E. Stager (eds.), *Scripture and Other Artifacts: Essays on the Bible and Archaeology in Honor of Philip J. King* (Louisville: Westminster/John Knox Press, 1994), pp. 18–31.

Blomberg, Craig, 'The Structure of 2 Corinthians 1–7', *CTR* 4 (1989), pp. 3–20.

Bloomquist, Gregory L., 'Rhetorical Argumentation and the Culture of Apocalyptic: A Socio-Rhetorical Analysis of Luke 21', in Stanley E. Porter and Dennis L. Stamps (eds.), *The Rhetorical Interpretation of Scripture* (JSNTSup, 180; Sheffield: Sheffield Academic Press, 1999), pp. 173–209.

Blount, Brian K., 'Reading Revelation Today: Witness as Active Resistance', *Int* 54 (2000), pp. 398–412.

Boadt, Lawrence, 'Isaiah 41:8–13: Notes on the Poetic Structure and Style', *CBQ* 35 (1973), pp. 20–34.

Bock, D. L., 'Elijah and Elisha', in Joel B. Green, Scot Mcknight and I. Howard Marshall (eds.), *Dictionary of Jesus and the Gospels* (Leicester: Inter-Varsity Press, 1992), pp. 203–6.

Boda, Mark J., 'Chiasmus in Ubiquity: Symmetrical Mirages in Nehemiah 9', *JSOT* 71 (1996), pp. 55–70.

—'Oil, Crowns and Thrones: Prophet, Priest and King in Zechariah 1:7–6:15', *Journal of Hebrew Scriptures* 3 (2001); available from http://www.arts.ualberta.ca/JHS/

Bohak, Gideon, 'Greek-Hebrew Gematrias in *3 Baruch* and in Revelation', *JSP* 7 (1990), pp. 119–21.

Boring, M. E., *Revelation* (Louisville: John Knox Press, 1989).

Bousset, W., *The Antichrist Legend: A Chapter in Christian and Jewish Folklore* (trans. A. H. Keane; London: Hutchinson, 1896).

Bovon, François., 'Names and Numbers in Early Christianity', *NTS* 47 (2001), pp. 267–88.

Boyd, Gregory, *God at War: The Bible and the Spiritual Conflict* (Downers Grove: Inter-Varsity Press, 1997).

Bratcher, Robert G., *A Translator's Guide to the Revelation to John* (New York: United Bible Societies, 1984).

Breck, John, 'Biblical Chiasmus: Exploring Structure for Meaning', *BTB* 17 (1987), pp. 70–74.

—*The Shape of Biblical Language: Chiasmus in the Scriptures and Beyond* (Crestwood, New York: St. Vladimir's Seminary Press, 1994).

Briggs, Robert A., *Jewish Temple Imagery in the Book of Revelation* (Frankfurt am Main: Peter Lang, 1999).

Brouwer, Wayne, *The Literary Development of John 13–17: A Chiastic Reading* (SBLDS, 182; Atlanta: Society of Biblical Literature, 2000).

Brown, J. P., 'The Mediterranean Seer and Shamanism', *ZAW* 93 (1981), pp. 374–400.

Brown, William P. and John T. Carroll, 'The Garden and the Plaza: Biblical Images of the City', *Int* 54 (2000), pp. 3–12.

Brownlee, William H., 'The Priestly Character of the Church in the Apocalypse', *NTS* 5 (1958–59), pp. 224–25.

—*The Meaning of Qumran Scrolls for the Bible with Special Attention to the Book of Isaiah* (New York: Oxford University Press, 1964).

Bruce, F. F., *Biblical Exegesis in the Qumran Texts* (Grand Rapids: Eerdmans, 1957).

—*A Mind for What Matters: Collected Essays* (Grand Rapids: Eerdmans, 1990).

Brueggemann, Dale A., 'The Use of the Psalter in John's Apocalypse' (Unpublished PhD dissertation; Philadelphia: Westminster Theological Seminary, 1995).

Bruehler, Bart B., 'Seeing through the עינים of Zechariah: Understanding Zechariah 4', *CBQ* 63 (2001), pp. 430–43.

Buber, Martin, *Werke. II, Schriften zur Bibel* (Munich: Kösel, 1964).

Burnett, Gary W., *Paul & the Salvation of the Individual* (Leiden: Brill, 2001).

Butterworth, M., *Structure and the Book of Zechariah* (JSOTSup, 130; Sheffield: JSOT Press, 1992).

Caird, G. B., *A Commentary on the Revelation of St. John the Divine* (New York: Harper and Row, 1966).

—*The Language and Imagery of the Bible* (Philadelphia: Westminster Press, 1980).

Callahan, Allen Dwight, 'The Language of Apocalypse', *HTR* 88 (1995), pp. 453–70.

—'Apocalypse as Critique of Political Economy: Some Notes on Revelation 18', *HBT* 21 (1999), pp. 46–65.

Carlston, Charles Edwin, 'Transfiguration and Resurrection', *JBL* 80 (1961), pp. 233–40.

Carnegie, David R., 'Worthy is the Lamb: The Hymns in Revelation', in Harold Rowdon (ed.), *Christ the Lord. Studies in Christology Presented to Donald Guthrie* (Leicester: Inter-Varsity Press, 1982), pp. 243–56.

Carrell, Peter R., *Jesus and the Angels: Angelology and the Christology of the Apocalypse of John* (Cambridge: Cambridge University Press, 1997).

Carter, Warren, 'Matthew 23.37–39', *Int* 54 (2000), pp. 66–68.

Charles, R. H., *A Critical and Exegetical Commentary on the Revelation of St. John* (2 vols; Edinburgh: T & T Clark, 1920).

—*Lectures on the Apocalypse: The Schweich Lectures 1919* (London: Oxford University Press, 1922).

Chilton, Bruce D., 'The Transfiguration: Dominical Assurance and Apostolic Vision', *NTS* 27 (1980), pp. 115–24.

—*The Aramaic: The Isaiah Targum* (Edinbrugh: T & T Clark, 1987).

—*Pure Kingdom: Jesus' Vision of God* (Grand Rapids: Eerdmans, 1996).

Chilton, David, *The Days of Vengeance: An Exposition of the Book of Revelation* (Ft. Worth, Texas: Dominion Press, 1987).

Clark, D. J., 'Criteria for Identifying Chiasm', *Linguistica Biblica* 35 (1975), pp. 63–72.

Clements, R. E., *God and Temple* (Oxford: Basil Blackwell, 1965).

—*Isaiah 1–39* (NCB; Grand Rapids: Eerdmans, 1980).

—'Apocalyptic, Literary and Canonical Tradition', in W. Hulitt Gloer (ed.), *Eschatology and the New Testament: Essays in Honor of George Raymond Beasley-Murray* (Peabody, MA: Hendrikson, 1988), pp. 15–27.

—*Old Testament Prophecy: From Oracles to Canon* (Louisville: Westminster/John Knox Press, 1996).

Clifford, Richard J., *The Cosmic Mountain in Canaan and the Old Testament* (Cambridge, MA.: Harvard University Press, 1972).

—*Fair Spoken and Persuading: An Interpretation of Second Isaiah* (New York: Paulist Press, 1984).

Clines, David J. A., *Ezra, Nehemiah, Esther* (NCB; Grand Rapids: Eerdmans, 1984).

Clines, David J. A. *et al.* (eds.), *Art and Meaning: Rhetoric in Biblical Literature* (JSOTSup, 19; Sheffield: JSOT Press, 1982).

Cohn, Robert, 'The Literary Logic of 1 Kings 17–19', *JBL* 101 (1982), pp. 333–50.

—'Literary Technique in the Jeroboam Narrative', *ZAW* 97 (1985), pp. 23–35.

Cole, Robert, 'An Integrated Reading of Psalms 1 and 2', *JSOT* 98 (2002), pp. 75–88.

Collins, Adela Yarbro, *The Combat Myth in the Book of Revelation* (HDR, 9; Missoula: Scholars Press, 1976).

—'The Political Perspective of the Revelation of John', *JBL* 96 (1977), pp. 241–56.

—*The Apocalypse* (New Testament Message, 22; Wilmington, DE: Michael Glazier, 1979).

—'Revelation 18: Taunt-Song or Dirge?', in J. Lambrecht (ed.), *L'Apocalypse johannique et l'Apocalyptique dans le Nouveau Testament* (BETL, 53; Leuven: Leuven University Press, 1980), pp. 185–204.

—*Crisis & Catharsis: The Power of the Apocalypse* (Philadelphia: The Westminster Press, 1984).

—' "What the Spirit Says to the Churches": Preaching the Apocalypse', *Quarterly Review* 4 (1984), pp. 69–84.

—'Persecution and Vengeance in the Book of Revelation', in David Hellholm (ed.), *Apocalypticism in the Mediterranean World and the Near East* (Tübingen: Mohr, 1989), pp. 729–50.

—'Feminine Symbolism in the Book of Revelation', *BibInt* 1 (1993), pp. 20–33.

—*Cosmology and Eschatology in Jewish and Christian Apocalypticism* (Leiden: E. J. Brill, 1996).

—'Number Symbolism in Jewish and Early Christian Apocalyptic Literature', in A. Yarbro Collins, *Cosmology and Eschatology in Jewish and Christian Apocalypticism* (Leiden: E. J. Brill, 1996) pp. 55–138.

—'The Book of Revelation', in John J. Collins (ed.), *The Encyclopedia of Apocalypticism* Vol. 1: *The Origins of Apocalypticism in Judaism and Christianity* (New York: Continuum, 1998), pp. 384–414.

Collins, John J., 'The Mythology of Holy War in Daniel and the Qumran War Scroll: A Point of Transition in Jewish Apocalyptic', *VT* 25 (1975), pp. 596–612.

—*The Apocalyptic Vision of the Book of Daniel* (Missoula: Scholars Press, 1977).

—'Introduction: Toward the Morphology of a Genre', *Semeia* 14 (1979), pp. 1–20.

—*Daniel* (Augsburg: Fortress Press, 1993).

—'Messiahs in Context: Method in the Study of Messianism in the Dead Sea Scrolls', in Michael Wise *et al.* (eds.), *Methods of Investigation of the Dead Sea Scrolls and Khirbet Qumran Site: Present Realities and Future Prospects* (New York: Academy of Sciences, 1994), pp. 213–30.

—*The Scepter and the Star: The Messiahs of the Dead Sea Scrolls and Other Ancient Literature* (New York: Doubleday, 1997).

—'From Prophecy to Apocalypticism: The Expectation of the End', in John J. Collins (ed.), *The Encyclopedia of Apocalypticism* Vol. 1: *The Origins of Apocalypticism in Judaism and Christianity* (New York: Continuum, 1998), pp. 129–61.

—*The Apocalyptic Imagination: An Introduction to the Jewish Matrix of Christianity* (Grand Rapids: Eerdmans, 2nd edn, 1998).

—'Ideas of Messianism in the Dead Sea Scrolls', in James H. Charlesworth and Walter P. Weaver (eds.), *The Dead Sea Scrolls and the Christian Faith* (Harrisburg, PA: Trinity Press International, 1998), pp. 20–41.

Conrad, Edgar, *Zechariah* (Readings: A New Biblical Commentary; Sheffield: Sheffield Academic Press, 1999).

Considene, Joseph S., 'The Two Witnesses: Apoc. 11: 3–13', *CBQ* 4 (1946), pp. 377–92.

Cook, S. A., *Cambridge Ancient History* Vol. 3 (New York: Macmillan, 1925).

Cook, Stephen L., *Prophecy and Apocalypticism: The Postexilic Social Setting* (Minneapolis: Fortress Press, 1995).

Cothenet, Edouard, 'Earthly Liturgy and Heavenly Liturgy according to the Book of Revelation', in *Roles in the Liturgical Assembly: the Twenty-Third Liturgical Conference Saint Serge* (trans. M. J. O'Donnell; New York: Pueblo, 1981), pp. 115–35.

Court, John M., *Myth and History in the Book of Revelation* (Atlanta: John Knox Press, 1979).

—*Revelation* (New Testament Guides; Sheffield: Sheffield Academic Press, 1994).

Craigie, Peter C., *Psalm 1–50* (WBC; Waco: Word, 1983).

Crenshaw, James L., *Prophetic Conflict: Its Effect upon Israelite Religion* (Berlin: de Gruyter, 1971).

—*The Psalms: An Introduction* (Grand Rapids: Eerdmans, 2001).

Croft, S. J. L., *The Identity of the Individual in the Psalms* (Sheffield: JSOT Press, 1986).

Cross, Frank Moore, 'The Divine Warrior in Israel's Early Cult', in Cyrus Gordon (ed.), *Biblical Motifs* (Cambridge, MA.: Harvard University Press, 1966), pp. 12–30.

—*Canaanite Myth and Hebrew Epic: Essays in the History of the Religion of Israel* (Cambridge, MA.: Harvard University Press, 1973).

Dahood, Mitchell, *Psalms II* (New York: Doubleday, 1986).

Dailey, Frances Flannery, 'Non-Linear Time in Apocalyptic Texts: The Spiral Model', in *SBL Seminar Papers* (Atlanta: Scholars Press, 1999), pp. 231–45.

Davies, W. D. and Dale C. Allison Jr., *A Critical and Exegetical Commentary on the Gospel According to Matthew* (International Critical Commentary, 3 vols.; Edinburgh: T & T Clark, 1997).

Davila, James, 'Melchizedek, Michael and War in Heaven', in *SBL Seminar Papers* (Atlanta: Scholars Press, 1996), pp. 259–73.

Day, John, *God's Conflict with the Dragon and the Sea: Echoes of a Canaanite Myth in the Old Testament* (Cambridge: Cambridge University Press, 1985).

de Blois, Reinier, *Towards a New Dictionary of Biblical Hebrew Based on Semantic Domains* (Amsterdam: Vrije Universiteit, 2000).

de Heer, J. J., *Kitab Wahyu* (Jakarta: BPK Gunung Mulia, 2000).

de Jonge, M., 'The use of the expression ὁ Χριστὸς in the Apocalypse of St. John', in J. Lambrecht (ed.), *L'Apocalypse johannique et l'Apocalyptique dans le Nouveau Testament* (BETL, 53; Leuven: Leuven University Press, 1980), pp. 267–81.

Dehandschutter, B., 'The Meaning of Witness in the Apocalypse', in D. Hellholm (ed.), *Apocalypticism in the Mediterranean World and the Near East* (Tübingen: Mohr, 1989), pp. 283–88.

de Silva, David A., 'The Persuasive Strategy of the Apocalypse: A Socio-Rhetorical Investigation of Revelation 14.6–13', in *SBL Seminar Papers* (Atlanta: Scholars Press, 1998), pp. 785–806.

de Silva, D. *Introducing the Apocrypha: Message, Context, and Significance* (Grand Rapids: Baker Academic, 2002).

DeVries, Simon J., *Prophet against Prophet* (Grand Rapids: Eerdmans, 1978).

Dion, Paul E., 'The Horned Prophet (1 Kings XXII 11)', *VT* 49 (1999), pp. 259–60.

Donegani, Isabelle, *"A cause de la parole de Dieu et du témoignage de Jésus…"*: *Le témoignage selon l'apocalypse de Jean: Son enracinement extra-biblique et biblique: Sa force comme parole de sens* (Ebib n.s. 36; Paris: Gabalda, 1997).

Douglas, Mary, 'The Poetic Structure in Leviticus', in David P. Wright, David Noel Freedman and Avi Hurvitz (eds.), *Pomegranates & Golden Bells: Studies in Biblical, Jewish, and Near Eastern Ritual, Law, and Literature in Honor of Jacob Milgrom* (Winona Lake: Eisenbrauns, 1995), pp. 239–56.

Draper, Jonathan A., 'The Heavenly Feast of the Tabernacles: Revelation 7.1–17', *JSNT* 19 (1983), pp. 133–47.

du Rand, Jan A., ' "Your Kingdom Come on Earth as it is in Heaven": The Theological motif of the Apocalypse of John', *Neot* 31 (1997), pp. 59–75.

Duff, Paul B., 'True and False Prophets', in Paul B. Duff, *Who Rides the Beast? Prophetic Rivalry and the Rhetoric of Crisis in the Churches of the Apocalypse* (Oxford: Oxford University Press, 2001).

—*Who Rides the Beast? Prophetic Rivalry and the Rhetoric of Crisis in the Churches of the Apocalypse* (Oxford: Oxford University Press, 2001).

Dumbrell, William J., *The End of the Beginning: Revelation 21–22 and the Old Testament* (NSW, Australia: Lancer Books, 1985).

Edwards, James, 'Markan Sandwiches: The Significance of Interpolations in Markan Narratives', *NovT* 31 (1989), pp. 193–216.

Ehrenberg, Victor, *Man, State And Deity: Essays in Ancient History* (London: Methuen, 1974).

Eliav, Yaron Z., ' "Interpretive Citation" in the Epistle of *Barnabas* and the Early Christian Attitude towards the Temple Mount', in Craig A. Evans (ed.), *The Interpretation of Scripture in Early Judaism and Christianity: Studies in Language and Tradition* (JSPSup, 33; Sheffield: Sheffield Academic Press, 2000), pp. 353–62.

Enroth, Anne-Marit, 'The Hearing Formula in the Book of Revelation', *NTS* 36 (1990), pp. 598–608.

Eriksson, Anders, Thomas H. Olbright and Walter Übelacker (eds.), *Rhetorical Argumentation in Biblical Texts. Essays from the Lund 2000 Conference* (Emory Studies in Early Christianity; Harrisburg, PA: Trinity Press Interntional, 2002).

Evans, Craig A., *Mark 8:27–16:20* (WBC; Nashville: Thomas Nelson, 2001).

Exum, J. Cheryl, 'Promise and Fulfilment: Narrative Art in Judges 13', *JBL* 99 (1980), pp. 43–59.

Faierstein, Morris M., 'Why Do the Scribes Say That Elijah Must Come First?', *JBL* 100 (1981), pp. 75–86.

Fekkes, J., *Isaiah and the Prophetic Traditions in the Book of Revelation: Visionary Antecedents and Their Development* (Sheffield: JSOT Press, 1994).

Feuillet, André, *The Apocalypse* (trans. Thomas Crane; New York: Alba House, 1964).

—*Johannine Studies* (trans. Thomas Crane; New York: Alba House, 1964).

Filho, José Adriano., 'The Apocalypse of John as an Account of a Visionary Experience: Notes on the Book's Structure', *JSNT* 25 (2002), pp. 213–34.

Fiorenza, Elizabeth Schüssler, 'Apocalyptic and Gnosis in the Book of Revelation', *JBL* 92 (1973), pp. 565–81.

—'Composition and Structure of the Book of Revelation', *CBQ* 39 (1977), pp. 344–66.

—'Apocalypsis and Propheteia: Revelation in the Context of the Early Christian Prophecy', in J. Lambrecht (ed.), *L'Apocalypse johannique et l'Apocalyptique dans le Nouveau Testament* (BETL, 53; Leuven: Leuven University Press, 1980), pp. 105–28.

—'The Followers of the Lamb: Visionary Rhetoric and Social-Political Situation', in F. F. Segiova (ed.), *Discipleship in the New Testament* (Philadelphia: Fortress Press, 1985), pp. 144–65.

—*Revelation: Vision of a Just World* (Minneapolis: Fortress Press, 1991).

—*The Book of Revelation: Justice and Judgment* (Philadelphia: Fortress Press, 2nd edn, 1998).

Fitzmyer, Joseph A., *The Dead Sea Scrolls and Christian Origins* (Grand Rapids: Eerdmans, 2000).

Fleming, Daniel E., '"House"/ "City": An Unrecognized Parallel Word Pair', *JBL* 105 (1986), pp. 689–97.

Flusser, David, *Judaism and the Origins of Christianity* (Jerusalem: The Magnes Press, 1988).

Ford, Desmond, *The Abomination of Desolation in Biblical Eschatology* (Washington: University Press of America, 1979).

Ford, Josephine Massyngberde, *Revelation* (AB; New York: Doubleday, 1975).

—'Persecution and Martyrdom in the Book of Revelation', *The Bible Today* 26 (1990), pp. 141–46.

—'The Christological Function of the Hymns in the Apocalypse of John', *AUSS* 36 (1998), pp. 207–29.

Forsyth, N., *The Old Enemy: Satan and the Combat Myth* (Princeton, N.J.: Princeton University Press, 1987).

France, Richard T., *Matthew* (TNTC; Leicester: Inter-Varsity Press, 1983).

Frankfurter, David, 'Jews or Not? Reconstructing the "Other" in Rev. 2.9 and 3.9', *HTR* 94 (2001), pp. 403–25.

Frechette, Christopher G., 'Chiasm, Reversal and Biblical Reference in 1QH 11.3–18 (= Sukenik Column 3): A Structural Proposal', *JSP* 21 (2000), pp. 71–102.

Frey, Jörg, 'Die Bildersprache der Johannesapokalypse', *ZThK* 98 (2001), pp. 161–85.

Friebel, Kelvin G., *Jeremiah's and Ezekiel's Sign-Acts: Rhetorical Nonverbal Communication* (JSOTSup, 283; Sheffield: Sheffield Academic Press, 1999).

Friesen, Steven J., *Twice Neokoros: Ephesus, Asia and the Cult of the Flavian Imperial Family* (Leiden: E. J. Brill, 1993).

—*The Imperial Cults and the Apocalypse of John: Reading Revelation in the Ruins* (Oxford: Oxford University Press, 2001).

Galambush, Julie, *Jerusalem in the Book of Ezekiel: The City as Yahweh's Wife* (SBLDS, 130; Atlanta: Scholars Press, 1992).

Garrow, Alan J. P., *Revelation* (London: Routledge, 1997).

—'Revelation's Assembly Instructions', in Kent E. Brower and Mark W. Elliot (eds.), *Eschatology in Bible and Theology* (Downers Grove: Inter-Varsity Press, 1999), pp. 187–98.

Gärtner, B., *The Temple and Community in Qumran and the New Testament. A Comparative Study in the Temple Symbolism of the Qumran Texts and the New Testament* (SNTSMS, 1; Cambridge: Cambridge University Press, 1965).

Gaventa, B. R., 'The Maternity of Paul: An Exegetical Study of Galatians 4:19', in R. T. Fortna and B. R. Gaventa (eds.), *The Conversation Continues: Studies in Paul and John in Honor of J. Louis Martyn* (Nashville: Abingdon Press, 1990), pp. 189–201.

—'Our Mother St. Paul: Toward the Recovery of a Neglected Theme', *PSB* 17 (1996), pp. 29–44.

Geller, Stephen A., *Parallelism in Early Hebrew Poetry* (Missoula: Scholars Press, 1979).

Georgi, D., 'Who is the True Prophet?', *HTR* 79 (1986), pp. 100–26.

Giblin, C. H., 'Structural and Thematic Correlations in the Theology of Revelation 16–22', *Bib* 55 (1974), pp. 487–504.

—'Revelation 11.1–13: Its Form, Function, and Contextual Integration', *NTS* 30 (1984), pp. 433–39.

—*The Book of Revelation* (Good News Studies, 34; Collegeville: The Liturgical Press, 1991).

—'Recapitulation and the Literary Coherence of John's Apocalypse', *CBQ* 56 (1994), pp. 81–95.

—'From and Before the Throne: Revelation 4.5–6a Integrating Imagery of Revelation 4–16', *CBQ* 60 (1998), pp. 500–13.

Gibson, J. C. L., *Language and Imagery in the Old Testament* (London: SPCK, 1998).

Giesen, Heinz, *Die Offenbarung des Johannes* (Regensburg: Friedrich Pustet, 1997).

Gillingham, Susan, 'Psalmody and Apocalyptic in the Hebrew Bible: Common Vision, Shared Experience?', in John Barton & David J. Reimer (eds.), *After the Exile: Essays in Honour of Rex Mason* (Macon, GA: Mercer University Press, 1996), pp. 147–69.

—'From Liturgy to Prophecy: The Use of Psalmody in the Second Temple Judaism', *CBQ* 64 (2002), pp. 470–89.

Goldingay, John, *Daniel* (WBC 30; Waco: Word, 1989).

Gordon, Cyrus, 'Leviathan: Symbol of Evil', in Alexander Altmann (ed.), *Biblical Motifs* (Cambridge, MA.: Harvard University Press, 1966), pp. 1–10.

Goulder, Michael D., 'The Apocalypse as an Annual Cycle of Prophecies', *NTS* 27 (1981), pp. 322–41.

Grabbe, Lester L., 'Dan(iel) for All Seasons: For Whom was Daniel Important?', in John J. Collins and Peter W. Flint (eds.), *The Book of Daniel: Composition and Reception* Vol. 1 (Leiden: Brill, 2001), pp. 229–46.

Grassi, Joseph A., 'The Liturgy of Revelation', *The Bible Today* (1986), pp. 30–37.

Green, Barbara, *Like a Tree Planted: An Exploration of Psalms and Parables Through Metaphor* (Collegeville: The Liturgical Press, 1997).

Greenstein, Edward L., 'How Does Paralleism Mean?', in *A Sense of Text: The Art of Language in the Study of Biblical Literature* (Philadelphia: The Dropsie College, 1982), pp. 41–70.

Grogan, G. W., 'The Old Testament Concept of Solidarity in Hebrews', *TynBul* 49 (1998), pp. 159–74.

Hadianto, Jarot, 'Apokaliptisme Menurut Uraian John J. Collins', *Forum Biblika* 12 (2000), pp. 10–16.

Hagelberg, Dave, *Tafsiran Kitab Wahyu dari Bahasa Yunani* (Yogjakarta, Indonesia: Yayasan ANDI, 1997).

Hall, Mark Seaborn, 'The Hook Interlocking Structure of Revelation: The Most Important Verses in the Book and How They May Unify Its Structure', *NovT* 44 (2002), pp. 278–96.

Hanson, Paul, *The Dawn of Apocalyptic: The Historical and Sociological Roots of Jewish Apocalyptic Eschatology* (Philadelphia: Fortress Press, 2nd edn, 1979).

Haran, Menahem, *Temples and Temple Service in Ancient Israel* (Winona Lake: Eisenbrauns, 1985).

Harland, Philip A., 'Honouring the Emperor or Assailing the Beast: Participation in Civic Life among Associations (Jewish, Christian and Other) in Asia Minor and the Apocalypse of John', *JSNT* 77 (2000), pp. 99–121.

Harris, Michael A., 'The Literary Functions of Hymns in the Apocalypse of John' (Unpublished PhD dissertation; Louisville, Kentucky: Southern Baptist Theological Seminary, 1988).

Hartman, Lars F., 'Form and Message: A Preliminary Discussion of "Partial Texts" in Rev. 1–3 and 22, 6ff.', in David Hellholm (ed.), *Apocalypticism in the Mediterranean World and the Near East* (Tübingen: Mohr, 1989), pp. 129–49.

Harvey, John D., *Listening to the Text: Oral Patterning in Paul's Letters* (Grand Rapids: Baker Books, 1998).

—'Orality and Its Implications for Biblical Studies: Recapturing an Ancient Paradigm', *JETS* 45 (March 2002), pp. 99–110.

Hauser, A. J., 'Judges 5: Parataxis in Hebrew Poetry', *JBL* 99 (1980), pp. 23–41.

Hawthorne, Gerald F., 'The Role of the Christian Prophets in the Gospel Tradition', in Gerald F. Hawthorne with Otto Betz (eds.), *Tradition & Interpretation in the New Testament: Essays in Honor of E. Earle Ellis for his 60th birthday* (Grand Rapids: Eerdmans, 1987), pp. 119–33.

Hay, David M., 'Moses Through New Testament Spectacles', *Int* 44 (1990), pp. 240–52.

Hays, Richard, *Echoes of Scriptures in the Letters of Paul* (New Haven: Yale University Press, 1989).

—'Conversion of Imagination', *NTS* 45 (1999), pp. 392–412.

Hayward, C. T. R., *The Jewish Temple: A Non-Biblical Sourcebook* (London: Routledge, 1996).

Heaton, E. W., *The Hebrew Kingdoms* (New Clarendon Bible, Old Testament Vol. 3; Oxford: Oxford University Press, 1968).

Hedrick, William Kimbro, 'The Sources and Use of the Imagery in Apocalypse 12' (Unpublished Th.D. dissertation; Berkeley, California: Graduate Theological Union, 1971).

Heil, John Paul, 'The Fifth Seal (Rev 6.9–11) as a Key to the Book of Revelation', *Bib* 74 (1993), pp. 220–43.

—'The Chiastic Structure and Meaning of Paul's Letter to Philemon', *Bib* 82 (2001), pp. 178–206.

Hellholm, David, 'The Problem of Apocalyptic Genre and the Apocalypse of John', *Semeia* 36 (1986), pp. 13–64.

Hengel, Martin, *Studies in the Gospel of Mark* (trans. J. Bowden; Philadelphia: Fortress Press, 1985).

Hess, R. S. and G. J. Wenham, (eds.), *Zion, City of our God* (Grand Rapids: Eerdmans, 1999).

Hiers, Richard H., 'Purification of the Temple: Preparation for the Kingdom of God', *JBL* 90 (1971), pp. 82–90.

Hill, Andrew, *Malachi* (WBC; New York: Doubleday, 2000).

Hill, David, 'Prophecy and Prophets in the Revelation of St. John', *NTS* 18 (1971–1972), pp. 401–08.

—*New Testament Prophecy* (London: Marshall, Morgan & Scott, 1979).

Holladay, William, *Jeremiah: Spokesman Out of Time* (Philadelphia: United Church Press 1975).

—*The Architecture of Jeremiah 1–20* (Lewisburg, PA.; Bucknell University Press 1976).

Holm-Neilsen, Svend, *Hodayot: Psalms from Qumran* (Aarhus: Universitetsforla-get, 1960).

Holwerda, David E., 'The Church and the Little Scroll (Revelation 10–11)', *CTJ* 34 (1999), pp. 148–61.

Hong, Joseph, 'Chapter and Verse Divisions in the Bible: Their Origins, and Their Use in Today's Common Language Translations', *BT* 48 (1997), pp. 401–10.

Hooker, Morna D., '"What Doest Thou Here, Elijah?": A Look at St. Mark's Account of the Transfiguration', in L. D. Hurst and N. T. Wright (eds.), *The GLORY of Christ in the New Testament: Studies in Christology in Memory of George Bradford Caird* (Oxford: Clarendon Press, 1987), pp. 59–70.

House, Paul R., (ed.), *Form Criticism and Beyond* (Winona Lake: Eisenbrauns, 1992).

Houston, Graham, *Prophecy Now* (with a foreword by I. Howard Marshall; Leicester: Inter-Varsity Press, 1989).

Howard-Brook, Wes, 'Revelation: Claiming the Victory Jesus Won over Empire', in Wes Howard-Brook and Sharon H. Ringe (eds.), *The New Testament – Introducing the Way of Discipleship* (Maryknoll, New York: Orbis Books, 2002), pp. 188–206.

—'John's Gospel's Call to Be Reborn of God', in Wes Howard-Brook and Sharon H. Ringe (eds.), *The New Testament – Introducing the Way of Discipleship* (Maryknoll, New York: Orbis Books, 2002), pp. 80–102.

Hugenburger, Gordon P., 'The Servant of the Lord in the "Servant Songs" of Isaiah', in Philip E. Satterthwaite *et al.* (eds.), *The Lord's Anointed: Interpretation of Old Testament Messianic Texts* (Carlisle: Paternoster Press, 1995), pp. 105–39.

Hughes, Paul E., 'Moses' Birth Story: A Biblical Matrix for Prophetic Messianism', in Craig A. Evans and Peter W. Flint (eds.), *Eschatology, Messianism, and the Dead Sea Scrolls* (Grand Rapids: Eerdmans, 1997), pp. 10–22.

Humphrey, Edith M., 'The Sweet and the Sour: Epics of Wrath and Return in the Apocalypse', in *SBL Seminar Papers* (Atlanta: Scholars Press, 1991), pp. 451–60.

—*The Ladies and the Cities: Transformation and Apocalyptic Identity in Joseph and Aseneth, 4 Ezra, the Apocalypse and the Shepherd of Hermas* (JSPSup, 17; Sheffield: Sheffield Academic Press, 1995).

—'In Search of a Voice: Rhetoric through Sight and Sound in Revelation 11.15–12.17, in Gregory Bloomquist and Greg Carey (eds.), *Vision and Persuasion: Rhetorical Dimensions of Apocalyptic Discourse* (St Louis, MO: Chalice Press, 1999), pp. 141–60.

Hurowitz, V., *I Have Built You an Exalted House: Temple Building in the Bible in the Light of Mesopotamia and Northwest Semitic Writings* (JSOTSup, 115; Sheffield: JSOT Press, 1992).

Hurst, L. D., 'Did Qumran Expect Two Messiahs?', *BBR* 9 (1999), pp. 157–80.

Hurtado, Larry, 'Revelation 4–5 in the Light of Jewish Apocalyptic Analogies', *JSNT* 25 (1985), pp. 105–24.

—*On the Origins of Christian Worship* (London: The Paternoster Press, 1999).

Jauhiainen, M., 'The Measuring of the Temple Reconsidered', *Bib* 83 (2002), pp. 507–26.

Jeffrey, David Lyle, 'How to Read the Hebrew Prophets', in Vincent L. Tollers and John Maier (eds.), *Mappings of the Biblical Terrain: The Bible as Text* (Lewisburg, PA.: Bucknell University Press, 1990), pp. 282–98.

Jenks, Gregory C., *The Origins and Early Development of the Antichrist Myth* (Berlin: de Gruyter, 1991).

Johns, Loren, 'The Lamb in the Rhetorical Program of the Apocalypse of John', in *SBL Seminar Papers* (Atlanta: Scholars Press, 1998), pp. 762–84.

Johnson, Aubrey R., *The One and Many in the Israelite Conception of God* (Cardiff: University of Wales Press, 1961).

—*The Vitality of the Individual in the Thought of Ancient Israel* (Cardiff: University of Wales Press, 1964).

Joyce, P., 'The Individual and the Community', in J. W. Rogerson (ed.), *Beginning Old Testament Study* (London: SPCK, 1983), pp. 74–89.

Judge, E. A., 'The Mark of the Beast', *TynBul* 42 (1991), pp. 158–60.

Kaiser, Barbara Bakke, 'Poet as "Female Impersonator": The Image of Daughter Zion as Speaker in Biblical Poems of Suffering', *JR* 67 (1987), pp. 164–82.

Kaltner, John, 'Is Daniel Also among the Prophets?: The Rhetoric of Daniel 10–12', in Gregory Bloomquist and Greg Carey (eds.), *Vision and Persuasion: Rhetorical Dimensions of Apocalyptic Discourse* (St Loius, MO: Chalice Press, 1999), pp. 41–59.

Kaminsky, J. S., *Corporate Responsibility in the Hebrew Bible* (Sheffield: JSOT Press, 1995).

Kang, S.-M., *Divine War in the Old Testament and the Ancient Near East* (BZAW, 177; Berlin: de Gruyter, 1989).

Kee, Howard Clark, 'Christology in Mark's Gospel', in Jacob Neusner, William Scott Green, and Ernest S. Frerichs (eds.), *Judaisms and Their Messiahs at the Turn of the Christian Era* (New York: Cambridge University Press, 1987), pp. 187–208.

Keener, Craig S., *Revelation* (The NIV Application Commentary; Grand Rapids: Zondervan, 2000).

Keet, Cuthbert C., *A Study of the Psalms of Ascents: A Critical and Exegetical Commentary upon Psalms CXX – CXXXIV* (London: The Mitre Press, 1969).

Kennedy, George A., *New Testament Interpretation Through Rhetorical Criticism* (Chapel Hill, NC: University of North Carolina Press, 1984).

Kessler, Martin, 'A Methodological Setting for Rhetorical Criticism', in David J. A. Clines *et al.* (eds.), *Art and Meaning: Rhetoric in Biblical Literature* (JSOTSup, 19; Sheffield: JSOT Press, 1982), pp. 1–19.

Kiddle, M. and M. K. Ross, *The Revelation of St. John* (London: Houghton & Stoughton, 1946).

Kikawada, Isaac M., 'Some Proposals for the Definition of Rhetorical Criticism', *Semitics* 5 (1977), pp. 67–91.

Kim, Hyun Chul Paul, 'An Intertextual Reading of "A Crushed Reed" and "A Dim Wick" in Isaiah 42.3', *JSOT* 83 (1999), pp. 113–24.

Kirby, J. T., 'The Rhetorical Situations of Revelation 1–3', *NTS* 34 (1988), pp. 197–207.

Kistemaker, Simon J., 'The Temple in the Apocalypse', *JETS* 43 (2000), pp. 433–41.

Klauck, Hans-Josef, 'Do They Never Come Back? *Nero Redivivus* and the Apocalypse of John', *CBQ* 63 (2001), pp. 683–98.

Klaus, Nathan, *Pivot Patterns in the Former Prophets* (JSOTSup, 247; Sheffield: Sheffield Academic Press, 1999).

Klawans, Jonathan, 'Pure Violence: Sacrifice and Defilement in Ancient Israel', *HTR* 94:2 (2001), pp. 133–55.

Kloos, C., *Yhwh's Combat with the Sea: A Canaanite Tradition in the Religion of Ancient Israel* (Leiden: Brill, 1986).

Knibb, Michael, 'Prophecy and the Emergence of the Jewish Apocalypses', in R. J. Coggins *et al.* (eds.), *Israel's Prophetic Traditions* (Cambridge: Cambridge University Press, 1982), pp. 155–80.

—'Eschatology and Messianism in the Dead Sea Scrolls', in Peter W. Flint and James C. VanderKam (eds.), *The Dead Sea Scrolls* Vol. 2: *A Comprehensive Assessment after Fifty Years* (Leiden: Brill, 1999), pp. 379–402.

Knight, Jonathan M., *Revelation* (Sheffield: Sheffield Academic Press, 1999).

—'Ascension of Isaiah', Craig A. Evans & Stanley E. Porter (eds.), *Dictionary of New Testament Background* (Downers Grove: Inter-Varsity Press, 2000), pp. 129–30.

Koester, C. R., *The Dwelling of God: The Tabernacle in the Old Testament, Intertestamental Jewish Literature, and the New Testament* (Washington, D.C.: Catholic Biblical Association of America, 1989).

—*Revelation and the End of All Things* (Grand Rapids: Eerdmans, 2001).

Kohn, Risa Levitt and William H. C. Propp, 'The Name of "Second Isaiah": The Forgotten Theory of Nehemiah Rabban', in Astrid B. Beck *et al.* (eds.), *Fortunate the Eyes That See: Essays in Honor of David Noel Freedman* (Grand Rapids: Eerdmans, 1995), pp. 223–35.

Korpel, M. C. A. and J. C. de Moor, 'Fundamentals of Ugaritic and Hebrew Poetry', in W. van der Meer and J. C. de Moor (eds.), *The Structural Analysis of Biblical and Canaanite Poetry* (JSOTSup, 74; Sheffield: JSOT Press, 1988), pp. 1–61.

Kraft, Heinrich, *Die Offenbarung des Johannes* (Tübingen: Mohr, 1974).

Kraybill, J. Nelson, *Imperial Cult and Commerce in John's Apocalypse* (Sheffield: Sheffield Academic Press, 1996).

Kreitzer, Larry J., 'A Numismatic Clue to Acts 19.23–41: The Ephesian Cistophori of Claudius and Aggrippina', *JSNT* 30 (1987), pp. 59–70.

—'Apotheosis of the Roman Emperor', *BA* (Dec. 1990), pp. 211–17.

—*Striking New Images: Roman Imperial Coinage and the New Testament World* (JSNTSup, 134; Sheffield: Sheffield Academic Press, 1996).

Kugel, James, *The Idea of Biblical Poetry: Parallelism and Its History* (New Haven: Yale University Press, 1981).

Kuhn, K. G., 'The Two Messiahs of Aaron and Israel', in K. Stendahl (ed.), *The Scrolls and the New Testament* (New York: Harper, 1957), pp. 54–64.

Kuikman, Jacoba, 'Christ as Cosmic Tree', *TorJT* 16 (2000), pp. 141–54.

Laato, Antti, *The Servant of YHWH and Cyrus: A Reinterpretation of the Exilic Messianic Programme in Isaiah 40–55* (Stockholm: Almqvist & Wiksell International, 1992).

—'The Composition of Isaiah 40–55', *JBL* 109 (1990), pp. 207–28.

Ladd, George Eldon, *A Commentary on the Revelation of John* (Grand Rapids: Eerdmans, 1972).

Lambrecht, J., 'A Structuration of Revelation 4,1–22,5', in J. Lambrecht (ed.), *L'Apocalypse johannique et l'Apocalyptique dans le Nouveau Testament* (BETL, 53; Leuven: Leuven University Press, 1980), pp. 77–104.

—'The Opening of the Seals (Rev 6,1–8,6)', *Bib* 79 (1998) 198–221.

Lampe, G. W. H., 'The Testimony of Jesus is the Spirit of Prophecy (Rev. 19.10)', in William C. Weinrich (ed.), *The New Testament Age: Essays in Honor of Bo Reicke* Vol. 1 (Macon, GA: Mercer University Press, 1984), pp. 245–58.

Laws, Sophie, *In the Light of the Lamb: Image, Parody, and Theology in the Apocalypse of John* (Wilmington, DE: Michael Glazier, 1988).

Le Grys, A., 'Conflict and Vengeance in the Book of Revelation', *ExpTim* 104 (1992), pp. 76–80.

Lee, Michelle V., 'A Call to Martyrdom: Function as Method and Message in Revelation', *NovT* 40 (1998), pp. 164–94.

Leivestad, R., *Christ the Conqueror: The Idea of Conflict and Victory in the New Testament* (London: SPCK, 1954).

Lenglet, A., 'La Structure Littéraire de Daniel 2–7', *Bib* 53 (1972), pp. 169–90.

Lim, Johnson Teng Kok, *The Sin of Moses and the Staff of God* (Assen: Van Gorcum, 1997).

Limburg, James, 'Amos 7:4: A Judgment With Fire?', *CBQ* 35 (1973), pp. 346–49.

Lind, Millard C., 'Monotheism, Power, and Justice: A Study in Isaiah 40–55', *CBQ* 46 (1984), pp. 432–46.

Lindars, Barnabas, *The Gospel of John* (NCB; London: Marshall, Morgan & Scott, 1971).

Linton, George, 'Reading the Apocalypse as an Apocalypse', in *SBL Seminar Papers* (Atlanta: Scholars Press, 1991), pp. 161–86.

Lohse, Eduard, *Die Offenbarung des Johannes* (Göttingen: Vandenhoeck & Ruprecht, 1976).

Lohmeyer, E., *Die Offenbarung des Johannes* (Tübingen: Mohr, 2nd edn, 1953).

Longenecker, Bruce W., 'Linked Like a Chain: Rev 22.6–9 in Light of an Ancient Transition Technique', *NTS* 47 (2001), pp. 105–17.

Longman III, J. Tremper, 'The Divine Warrior: The New Testament Use of an Old Testament Motif', *WTJ* 44 (1982), pp. 290–307.

Longman III, J. Tremper and Daniel G. Reid, *God is a Warrior* (Studies in the Old Testament Biblical Theology; Grand Rapids: Zondervan, 1995).

Lund, Nils, *Studies in the Book of Revelation* (Chicago: Covenant Press, 1955).

—*Chiasmus in the New Testament: A Study in Formgeschichte* (Peabody, MA: Hendrickson, repr., 1992).

Lundbom, Jack R., *Jeremiah: A Study in Ancient Hebrew Rhetoric* (Winona Lake: Eisenbrauns, 2nd edn, 1997).

—'Parataxis, Rhetorical Structure, and the Dialogue over Sodom in Genesis 18', in Philip R. Davies and David J. A. Clines (eds.), *The World of Genesis: Persons, Places, Perspectives* (JSOTSup, 257; Sheffield: Sheffield Academic Press, 1998), pp. 136–45.

—*Jeremiah 1–20* (AB; New York: Doubleday, 1999).

Lust, Johan, 'Cult and Sacrifice in Daniel: The Tamid and the Abomination of Desolation', J. Quaegebeur (ed.), *Ritual and Sacrifice in the Ancient Near East* (Leuven: Peeters, 1993), pp. 285–99.

Mackay, T. W., 'Early Christian Exegesis of the Apocalypse', in E. A. Livingstone (ed.), *Studia Biblica 1978* (JSNTSup, 3; Sheffield: JSOT Press, 1980), pp. 257–63.

Macky, P. M., 'More about Metaphors', in A. Orden (ed.), *Metaphor and Thought* (Cambridge: Cambridge University Press, 1979), pp. 19–43.

—*The Centrality of Metaphors to Biblical Thought: A Method for Interpreting the Bible* (Studies in the Bible and Early Christianity; Lewiston: Edwin Mellen Press, 1990).

Malchow, B. V., 'The Messenger of the Covenant in Mal. 3.1', *JBL* 103 (1984), pp. 252–55.

Malina, Bruce J., *The New Jerusalem in the Revelation of John: The City as Symbol of Life with God* (Collegeville: The Liturgical Press, 2000).

—*Social-Science Commentary on the Book of Revelation* (Minneapolis: Fortress Press, 2000).

Malina, Bruce J. and Jerome H. Neyrey, 'First-Century Personality: Dyadic, Not Individual', in Jerome H. Neyrey (ed.), *The Social World of Luke-Acts* (Peabody, MA: Hendrickson, 1991), pp. 67–96.

Mandey, A. H., *Kitab Wahyu: Nubuatan Akhir Zaman* (Jakarta: Mimery Press, 1999).

Marcus, Joel, 'Mark 4:10–12 and Marcan Epistemology', *JBL* 103 (1984), pp. 557–74.

—'Mark 9, 11–13: "As It Has Been Written"', *ZNW* 80 (1989), pp. 42–63.

—*The Way of the Lord: Christological Exegesis of the Old Testament in the Gospel of Mark* (Louisville: Westminster/John Knox Press, 1992).

Marshall, I. Howard, *The Gospel of Luke: A Commentary on the Greek Text* (NIGTC; Grand Rapids: Eerdmans, 1979).

—*Acts* (TNTC; Leicester: Inter-Varsity Press, 1980).

Marshall, John W., *Parables of War: Reading John's Jewish Apocalypse* (Ontario: Wilfrid Laurier University Press, 2001).

Martens, Elmer A., 'Narrative Parallelism and Message in Jeremiah 34–38', in Craig A. Evans & William F. Stinespring (eds.), *Early Jewish and Christian Exegesis: Studies in the Memory of William Hugh Brownlee* (Atlanta: Scholars Press, 1987), pp. 33–49.

Martinez, F. Garcia, *The Dead Sea Scrolls Translated: The Qumran Texts in English* (trans. Wilfred G. E. Watson; Leiden: E. J. Brill, 1994).

Mauser, Ulrich W., ' "Heaven" in the World View of the New Testament', *HBT* 9.2 (1987), pp. 31–51.

Mazzaferri, Frederick, *The Genre of the Book of Revelation From a Source-Critical Perspective* (Berlin: de Gruyter, 1989).

McIlraith, D. A., ' "For the Fine Linen is the Righteous Deeds of the Saints": Works and Wife in Revelation 19:8', *CBQ* 61 (1999), pp. 513–29.

McKelvey, R. J., *The New Temple* (Oxford: Oxford University Press, 1969).

McKnight, Scott, 'Jesus and the Twelve', *BBR* 11 (2001), pp. 203–31.

McNamara, Martin, 'Symbolic Animals', *The Way* 41 (2001), pp. 211–23.

McNicol, Allan J., 'Revelation 11.1–14 and the Structure of the Apocalypse', *ResQ* 22 (1979), pp. 193–202.

McVann, Mark, 'Rituals of Status Transformation in Luke-Acts', in Jerome H. Neyrey (ed.), *The Social World of Luke-Acts* (Peabody, MA: Hendrickson, 1991), pp. 333–60.

Meadowcroft, T., 'Who are the Princes of Persia and Greece (Daniel 10)? Pointers Towards the Danielic Vision of Earth and Heaven', *JSOT* 29 (2004), pp. 99–113.

Mealy, J. Webb, *After the Thousand Years: Resurrection and Judgement in Revelation 20* (JSNTSup, 70; Sheffield: JSOT Press, 1992).

Meeks, Theophile J., 'Old Testament Translation Principles', *JBL* 81 (1962), pp. 143–54.

Meeks, Wayne A., *The First Urban Christians: The Social World of the Apostle Paul* (New Haven: Yale University Press, 1983).

Melugin, Roy F., 'Muilenburg, Form Criticism, and Theological Exegesis', in Martin J. Buss (ed.), *Encounter with the Text* (Missoula: Scholars Press, 1979), pp. 91–99.

Menn, Esther M., 'No Ordinary Lament: Relecture and the Identity of the Distressed in Psalm 22', *HTR* 93.4 (2000), pp. 301–41.

Metzger, Bruce, *A Textual Commentary on the Greek New Testament: A Companion Volume to the United Bible Societies' Greek New Testament* (New York: United Bible Societies, 3rd edn, 1971).

Meyers, Carol L., *The Tabernacle Menorah: A Synthetic Study of a Symbol from the Biblical Cult* (Missoula: Scholars Press, 1976).

—'David as Temple Builder', in Patrick D. Miller Jr., Paul D. Hanson and S. Dean McBride (eds.), *Ancient Israelite Religion: Essays in Honor of Frank Moore Cross* (Philadelphia: Fortress Press, 1987), pp. 357–76.

—'Realms of Sanctity: The Case of "Misplaced" Incense Altar in the Tabernacle Texts of Exodus', in Michael Fox *et al.* (eds.), *Texts, Temples and Tradition: A Tribute to Menahem Haran* (Winona Lake: Eisenbrauns, 1996), pp. 33–46.

Meyers, Eleanor Scott, 'The Church in the City: Past, Present and Future', *Int* 54 (2000), pp. 23–35.

Meyers, Eric and Carol Meyers, *Haggai & Zechariah 1–8* (AB; New York: Doubleday: 1987).

Meynet, Roland, *Rhetorical Analysis: An Introduction to Biblical Rhetoric* (JSOTSup, 256; Sheffield: Sheffield Academic Press, 1998).

Michaels, J. Ramsey, *Interpreting the Book of Revelation* (Grand Rapids: Baker Book House, 1992).

—*Revelation* (The IVP New Testament Series; Downers Grove: Inter-Varsity Press, 1997).

Milavec, Aaron, 'Distinguishing True and False Prophets: The Protective Wisdom of the Didache', *JECS* 2 (1994), pp. 117–36.

Milgrom, Jacob, *Numbers* (JPS Torah Commentary; Philadelphia: Jewish Publication Society, 1990).

Miller, Patrick D., Jr., 'Fire in the Mythology of Canaan and Israel', *CBQ* 27 (1965), pp. 256–61.

—*The Divine Warrior in Early Israel* (Cambridge, MA.: Harvard University Press, 1973).

—'Cosmology and World Order in the Old Testament: The Divine Council as Cosmic-Political Symbol', *HBT* 9.2 (1987), pp. 53–78.

—*Israelite Religion and Biblical Theology: Collected Essays* (JSOTSup, 267; Sheffield: Sheffield Academic Press, 2000).

Milligan, W., *The Book of Revelation* (New York: Armstrong, 1901).

Mills, Mary E., *Human Agents of Cosmic Power* (Sheffield: JSOT Press, 1990).

Minear, Paul S., 'Comparable Patterns of Thought in Luke's Gospel', in Paul S. Minear, *I Saw a New Earth: An Introduction to the Visions of the Apocalypse* (Washington: Corpus, 1969).

—'The Wounded Beast', *JBL* 72 (1953), pp. 93–101.

—'Ontology and Ecclesiology in the Apocalypse', *NTS* 13 (1966), pp. 89–105.

—*I Saw a New Earth: An Introduction to the Visions of the Apocalypse* (Washington: Corpus, 1969).

—'Far as the Curse Is Found: The Point of Rev. 12.15–16', *NovT* 33 (1991), pp. 71–77.

Miscall, Peter D., 'Isaiah: The Labyrinth of Images', *Semeia* 54 (1991), pp. 103–21.

Missen, A. W., 'Witness and Worship in the Apocalypse' (Unpublished M.Theol. thesis; University of Otago, Dunedin, New Zealand, 2001).

Mitchell, D. C., *The Message of the Psalter: An Eschatological Programme in the Book of Psalms* (JSOTSup, 252; Sheffield: Sheffield Academic Press, 1997).

Morris, Leon, *The Revelation of St John* (London: Tyndale Press, 1969).

Moyise, Steve, *The Old Testament in the Book of Revelation* (JSNTSup, 115; Sheffield: Sheffield Academic Press, 1995).

—'The Language of the Old Testament in the Apocalypse', *JSNT* 76 (1999), pp. 97–113.

—*The Old Testament in the New* (Continuum: London and New York, 2001).

—'Does the Author of Revelation Misappropriate the Scriptures?', *AUSS* 40 (2002), pp. 3–21.

Moyise, Steve, (ed.), *The Old Testament in the New Testament. Essays in honour of J. L. North* (Sheffield: Sheffield Academic Press, 2000).

Muilenburg, James, 'A Study in Hebrew Rhetoric: Repetition and Style', in G. W. Anderson *et al.* (eds.), *Congress Volume* (Leiden: E. J. Brill, 1953), pp. 97–111.

—'Form Criticism and Beyond', *JBL* 88 (1969), pp. 1–18.

Müller, U. B., *Die Offenbarung des Johannes* (Gütersloh: Gütersloher Verlagshaus Mohn, 1984).

Mulyono, Y. Bambang, *Teologi Ketabahan: Ulasan Atas Kitab Wahyu Yohanes* (Jakarta: BPK Gunung Mulia, 1996).

Murphy, Frederick J., *Fallen is Babylon: the Revelation to John* (Harrisburg, PA: Trinity Press International, 1998).

Mussies, G., *The Morphology of Koine Greek as Used in the Apocalypse of John: A Study in Bilingualism* (NovTSup, 27; Leiden: E. J. Brill, 1971).

—'The Greek of the Book of Revelation', in D. Hellholm (ed.), *Apocalypticism in the Mediterranean World and the Near East* (Tübingen: Mohr, 1989).

Nakhro, Mazie, 'The Meaning of Worship according to the Book of Revelation', *BSac* 158 (2001), pp. 75–85.
—'The Manner of Worship according to the Book of Revelation', *BSac* 158 (2001), pp. 165–80.
Neufeld, Tom Yoder, *Put on the Armour of God: The Divine Warrior from Isaiah to Ephesians* (JSNTSup, 140; Sheffield: Sheffield Academic Press, 1997).
Neyrey, Jerome H., 'The Apologetic Use of the Transfiguration in 2 Peter 1.16–21', *CBQ* 45 (1980), pp. 504–19.
Niehaus, Jeffrey J., *God at Sinai: Covenant & Theophany in the Bible and Ancient Near East* (Grand Rapids: Zondervan, 1995).
Nielsen, Kirsten, *There is Hope for a Tree: The Tree as a Metaphor in Isaiah* (trans. Christine and Frederick Crowley; JSOTSup, 65; Sheffield: Sheffield Academic Press, 1989).
Nolland, John, *Luke 9.21–18.34* (WBC; Dallas: Word, 1993).
Notley, R. Steven, 'The Kingdom of Heaven Forcefully Advances', in Craig A. Evans (ed.), *The Interpretation of Scripture in Early Judaism and Christianity: Studies in Language and Tradition* (JSPSup, 33; Sheffield: Sheffield Academic Press, 2000), pp. 279–311.
O'Rourke, John J., 'The Hymns of the Apocalypse', *CBQ* 30 (1968), pp. 399–409.
Oberweis, Michael, 'Das Martyrium der Zebedaiden in Mk. 10.35–40 (Mt 20.20–3) und Offb 11.3–13', *NTS* 44 (1998), pp. 74–92.
Oestreich, Bernhard, *Metaphors and Similes for Yahweh in Hosea 14.2–9 (1–8). A Study of Hoseanic Pictorial Language* (Frankfurt am Main: Peter Lang, 1998).
Öhler, Markus, 'The Expectation of Elijah and the Presence of the Kingdom of God', *JBL* 118 (1999), pp. 461–76.
Olbricht, Thomas H., 'The Flowering of Rhetorical Criticism in America', in Stanley E. Porter and Thomas H. Olbricht (eds.), *The Rhetorical Analysis of Scripture: Essays from the London Conference* (Sheffield: Sheffield Academic Press, 1997), pp. 79–102.
Ollenburger, Ben C., *Zion the City of the Great King: A Theological Symbol of the Jerusalem Cult* (Sheffield: Sheffield Academic Press, 1987).
Oropeza, B. J., 'Apostasy in the Wilderness: The Eschatological Warning of Paul to the Corinthian Congregation' (Unpublished Ph.D. dissertation; University of Durham, 1998).
—'Apostasy in the Wilderness: Paul's Message to the Corinthians in a State of Eschatological Liminality', *JSNT* 75 (1999), pp. 49–68.
Osborne, Grant R., *Revelation* (Baker Exegetical Commentary on the New Testament; Grand Rapids: Baker Academic, 2002).
Oswalt, John, *Isaiah 1–39* (NICOT; Grand Rapids: Eerdmans, 1986).
Overholt, Thomas W., *The Threat of Falsehood: A Study in the Theology of the Book of Jeremiah* (London: SCM Press, 1970).
Pamment, Margaret, 'Moses and Elijah in the Story of the Transfiguration', *ExpTim* 92 (1981), pp. 338–39.
Parker, David, 'The Sons of Thunder', in Stanley E. Porter *et al.* (eds.), *Crossing the Boundaries: Essays in Biblical Interpretation in Honour of Michael D. Goulder* (Leiden: E. J. Brill, 1994), pp. 141–47.

Pattemore, Stephen W., 'The People of God in the Apocalypse: A Relevance-Theoretic Study' (Unpublished PhD dissertation; University of Otago, Dunedin, New Zealand, 2000).

Paulien, Jon, *Decoding Revelation's Trumpets* (Andrews University Seminary Doctoral Dissertation Series, 21; Berrien Springs: America University Press, 1988).

—'Elusive Allusions: The Problematic Use of the Old Testament in Revelation', *BR* 33 (1988), pp. 37–53.

Peerbolte, L. J. L., *The Antecedents of Antichrist: A Traditio-Historical Study of the Earliest Christian Views on Eschatological Opponents* (Leiden: Brill, 1995).

Percer, Leo, 'The War in Heaven: Messiah and Michael in Revelation 12' (Unpublished PhD dissertation; Texas: Baylor University, 1999).

Petersen, David L., *Haggai & Zechariah 1–8* (OTL; London: SCM, 1984).

Petersen, Rodney L., *Preaching in the Last Days: The Theme of 'Two Witnesses' in the Sixteenth and Seventeenth Centuries* (Oxford: Oxford University Press, 1993).

Phillips, Elaine A., 'Serpent Intertexts: Tantalizing Twists in the Tales', *BBR* 10.2 (2000), pp. 233–45.

Pilch, John, 'Lying and Deceit in the Letters to the Seven Churches: Perspectives from Cultural Anthropology', *BTB* 39 (1992), pp. 606–24.

Porter, J. R., 'Legal Aspects of Corporate Personality', *VT* 15 (1965), pp. 361–80

Porter, Paul A., *Metaphors and Monsters: A Literary-Critical Study of Daniel 7 and 8* (Toronto, 1985).

Porter, Stanley E., 'The Language of the Apocalypse in Recent Discussion', *NTS* 35 (1989), pp. 582–603.

—'Theoretical Justification for the Application of Rhetorical Categories to Pauline Epistolary Literature', in Stanley E. Porter and Thomas H. Olbricht (eds.), *Rhetoric and the New Testament: Essays from the 1992 Heidelberg Conference* (JSNTSup, 90; Sheffield: JSOT Press, 1993), pp. 100–22.

—'Ancient Rhetorical Analysis and Discourse Analysis of the Pauline Epistles', in Stanley E. Porter and Thomas H. Olbricht (eds.), *The Rhetorical Analysis of Scripture: Essays from the London Conference* (Sheffield: Sheffield Academic Press, 1997), pp. 249–74.

Porter, Stanley E. and J. T. Reed, 'Philippians as a Macro-Chiasm and Its Exegetical Significance', *NTS* 44 (1998), pp. 213–31.

Prévost, Jean-Pierre, *How to Read the Apocalypse* (trans. John Bowden and Margaret Lydamore; London: SCM, 1993).

Price, S. R. F., *Rituals and Power: The Roman Imperial Cult in Asia Minor* (Cambridge: Cambridge University Press, 1984).

Prigent, Pierre, *L'Apocalpyse de Saint Jean* (Lausanne: Delachaux et Niestlé, 1981).

—*Commentary on the Apocalypse of St. John* (trans. Wendy Pradels; Tübingen: Mohr, 2001).

Prinsloo, Willem S., 'Psalm 149: Praise Yahweh with Tambourine and Two-edged Sword', *ZAW* 109 (1997), pp. 395–407.

Provan, Iain, 'Foul Spirits, Fornication and Finance: Revelation 18 from an Old Testament Perspective', *JSNT* 64 (1996), pp. 81–100.

Puech, Émile, 'Messianism, Resurrection, and Eschatology at Qumran and in the New Testament', in E. Ulrich and J. VanderKam (eds.), *The Community of the Renewed Covenant: The Notre Dame Symposium on the Dead Sea Scrolls* (Notre Dame: University of Notre Dame Press, 1994), pp. 235–56.

Quispel, G., *The Secret Book of Revelation* (New York: McGraw-Hill, 1979).

Reddish, Mitchell G., 'Martyr Christology in the Apocalypse', *JSNT* 33 (1988), pp. 85–95.

—*Revelation* (Macon, GA; Smith and Helwys, 2001).

Rendsberg, Gary R., 'Redactional Structuring in the Joseph Story: Genesis 37–50', in Vincent L. Tollers and John Maier (eds.) *Mappings of the Biblical Terrain: The Bible as Text* (Lewisburg, PA: Bucknell University Press, 1990).

Rendtorff, Rolf, *The Old Testament: An Introduction* (trans. John Bowker; Philadelphia: Fortress Press, 1986).

Resseguie, James L., *Revelation Unsealed* (Leiden: E. J. Brill, 1998).

Rissi, Mathias, *Time and History: A Study on the Revelation* (Virginia: John Knox Press, 1965).

Robbins, Vernon K., 'The Present and Future of Rhetorical Analysis', in Stanley E. Porter and Thomas H. Olbricht (eds.), *The Rhetorical Analysis of Scripture: Essays from the London Conference* (Sheffield: Sheffield Academic Press, 1997), pp. 24–52.

—'Rhetorical Ritual: Apocalyptic Discourse in Mark 13', in Gregory Bloomquist and Greg Carey (eds.), *Vision and Persuasion: Rhetorical Dimensions of Apocalyptic Discourse* (St Louis, MO: Chalice Press, 1999), pp. 95–121.

Roberts, J. J. M., 'Isaiah and his Children', in Ann Kort and Scott Morschauser (eds.), *Biblical and Related Studies Presented to Samuel Iwry* (Winona Lake: Eisenbrauns, 1985), pp. 193–203.

Robinson, Bernard P., 'The Two Persecuted Prophets-Witnesses of Rev. 11', *Scripture Bulletin* 19 (1988), pp. 14–19.

Robinson, H. W., *Corporate Personality in Ancient Israel* (rev. ed.; Philadelphia: Fortress Press, 1980).

Robinson, John, *Redating the New Testament* (Philadelphia: The Westminster Press, 1976).

Rofé, Alexander, *Introduction to the Prophetic Literature* (Sheffield: Sheffield Academic Press, 1997).

Rogerson, J. W., 'The Hebrew Conception of Corporate Personality: A Re-Examination', *JTS* 21 (1970), pp. 1–16.

—*Anthropology and the Old Testament* (Oxford: Basil Blackwell, 1979).

Roloff, J., *The Revelation of John* (trans. J. E. Alsup; Continental Commentaries; Minneapolis: Fortress Press, 1993).

Rooke, Deborah W., *Zadok's Heirs: The Role and Development of the High Priesthood in Ancient Israel* (Oxford: Oxford University Press, 2000).

Rose, Wolter H., *Zemah and Zerubbabel: Messianic Expectations in the Early Postexilic Period* (JSOTSup, 304; Sheffield: Sheffield Academic Press, 2000).

Rossing, Barbara, *The Choice Between Two Cities: Whore, Bride, and Empire in the Apocalypse* (Harrisburg, PA: Trinity Press International, 1999).

Rowland, Christopher, *Revelation* (Epworth Commentaries; London: Epworth Press, 1993).

—'The Book of Revelation', in *New Interpreter's Bible* (12 Vols; Nashville: Abingdon Press, 1998).

Rowley, H. H., *The Servant of the Lord* (Oxford: Basil Blackwell, rev. 2nd edn, 1964).

Royalty, R. M., Jr., 'The Rhetoric of Revelation', in *SBL Seminar Papers* (Atlanta: Scholars Press, 1997), pp. 596–617.

—*The Streets of Heaven: The Ideology of Wealth in the Apocalyse of John* (Macon, GA; Mercer University Press, 1998).

Ruiz, Jean-Pierre, *Ezekiel in the Apocalypse: The Transformation of Prophetic Language in Revelation 16,17–19,10* (Frankfurt am Main: Peter Lang, 1993).

—'Revelation 4.8–11; 5.9–14: Hymn of the Heavenly Liturgy', in *SBL Seminar Papers* (Atlanta: Scholars Press, 1995), pp. 216–20.

—'Politics of Praise: A Reading of Revelation 19.1–10', in *SBL Seminar Papers* (Atlanta: Scholars Press, 1997), pp. 374–94.

Russell, David Syme, *The Method and Message of Jewish Apocalyptic* (London: SCM Press, 1964).

—*Prophecy and the Apocalyptic Dream: Protest and Promise* (Peabody, MA: Hendrickson, 1994).

Ryken, Leland, *et al.* (eds.), *Dictionary of Biblical Imagery* (Downers Grove: Inter-Varsity Press, 1998).

Sabin, Marie, 'Reading Mark 4 as Midrash', *JSNT* 45 (1992), pp. 3–26.

Sarna, Nahum, 'Anticipatory Use of Information as a Literary Feature of the Genesis Narratives', in Nahum Sarna, *Studies in Biblical Interpretation* (New York: Jewish Publication Society, 2000).

—*Studies in Biblical Interpretation* (New York: Jewish Publication Society, 2000).

Satake, Akira, *Die Gemeindeordnung in der Johannesapokalypse* (Neukirchen-Vluyn: Neukirchener Verlag, 1966).

Satran, David, 'Daniel: Seer, Philosopher, Holy Man', in George W. E. Nickleburg and John J. Collins (eds.), *Ideal Figures in Ancient Judaism* (Septuagint and Cognate Studies, 12; Atlanta: Scholars Press, 1980), pp. 33–48.

Scherrer, Steven J., 'Signs and Wonders in the Imperial Cult: A New Look at a Roman Religious Institution in the Light of Rev. 13.13–15', *JBL* 103 (1984), pp. 599–610.

Scheunemann, D., *Berita Kitab Wahyu* (Malang, Indonesia: Yayasan Penerbit Gandum Mas, 1997).

Schmitt, John J., 'The Motherhood of God and Zion as Mother', *RB* 92 (1985), pp. 557–69.

Schnelle, Udo, *The History and Theology of the New Testament Writings* (trans. M. E. Boring; London: SCM, 1998).

Schowalter, D. N., *The Emperor and the Gods* (HDR, 28.; Minneapolis: Fortress Press, 1993).

Schroer, Silvia, ' "Under the Shadow of Your Wings" : The Metaphor of God's Wings in the Psalms, Exodus 19.4, Deuteronomy 32.11 and Malachi 3.20, as Seen through the Perspectives of Feminism and History of Religion', in Athalya Brenner & Carole R. Fontaine (eds.), *Wisdom and Psalms* (The Feminist Companion to the Bible [Second Series]; Sheffield: Sheffield Academic Press, 1998), pp. 264–82.

Schwemer, Anna Maria, 'Prophet, Zeuge und Märtyrer: Zur Entstehung des Märtyrerbegriffs im frühesten Christentum', *ZThK* 96 (1999), pp. 320–50.

Seng, Helmut, 'Apk 11,1–14 im Zusammenhang der Johannesapokalypse: Aufschluss aus Lactantius und Hippolytos', *Vetera Christianorum* 27 (1990), pp. 111–21.

Shea, William, 'Chiasm in Theme and by Form in Revelation 18', *AUSS* 20 (1982), pp. 249–56.

Shepherd, Tom, 'The Narrative Function of Markan Intercalation', *NTS* 41 (1995), pp. 522–40.

Siahaan, S. M., *Pengharapan Mesias dalam Perjanjian Lama* (Jakarta: BPK Gunung Mulia, 1991).

Sims, J. H., *A Comparative Literary Study of Daniel and Revelation* (Lewiston: Edwin Mellen Press, 1994).

Slater, Thomas B., *Christ and Community: A Socio-Historical Study of the Christology of Revelation* (JSNTSup, 178; Sheffield: Sheffield Academic Press, 1999).

—'The Image of the Divine Warrior in Revelation 19.11–21', in Thomas B. Slater, *Christ and Community: A Social-Historical Study of the Christology of Revelation* (JSNTSup, 178; Sheffield: Sheffield Academic Press, 1999).

Smelik, W. F., 'On Mystical Transformation of the Righteous into Light in Judaism', *JSJ* 26 (1995), pp. 122–44.

Smith, Ian, 'A Rational Choice Model of the Book of Revelation', *JSNT* 85 (2002), pp. 97–116.

Smith, Mark S. (with contributions by Elizabeth M. Bloch-Smith), *The Pilgrimage Pattern in Exodus* (JSOTSup, 239; Sheffield: Sheffield Academic Press, 1997).

Smith, Robert H., ' "Worthy is the Lamb" and Other Songs of Revelation', *Current Theology of Mission* 25 (1998), pp. 500–06.

Snyder, Barbara W., 'Combat Myth in the Apocalypse: The Liturgy of the Day of the Lord and the Dedication of the Heavenly Temple' (Unpublished PhD dissertation; Graduate Theological Union and University of California, Berkeley, 1991).

—'Triple-Form and Space/Time Transition: Literary Structuring Devices in the Apocalypse', in *SBL Seminar Papers* (Atlanta: Scholars Press, 1991), pp. 440–50.

Söding, Thomas, 'Heilig, heilig, heilig: Zur politischen Theologie der Johannes-Apokalypse', *ZThK* 96 (1999), pp. 49–76.

Soskice, Janet, *Metaphor and Religious Language* (Oxford: Clarendon Press, 1985).

—*Speaking in Parables* (repr., London: SCM, 2002).

Spatafora, Andrea, *From the 'Temple of God' to God as the Temple: A Biblical Theological Study of the Temple in the Book of Revelation* (Tesi Gregoriana Serie Teologia, 27; Rome: Gregorian University Press, 1997).

Steinmann, A. E., 'The Tripartite Structure of the Sixth Seal, the Sixth Trumpet, and the Sixth Bowl of John's Apocalypse (Rev. 6.12–7.17; 9.13–11.14; 16.12–16)', *JETS* 35 (1992), pp. 69–79.

Sternberg, Meir, *The Poetics of Biblical Narrative: Ideological Literature and the Drama of Reading* (Bloomington: Indiana University Press, 1985).

—'Time and Space in Biblical (Hi)story Telling: The Grand Chronology', in Regina M. Schwartz (ed.), *The Book and the Text: The Bible and Literary Theory* (Oxford: Basil Blackwell, 1990), pp. 81–145.

Stevens, David E., 'Daniel 10 and the Notion of Territorial Spirits', *BSac* 157 (2000), pp. 410–31.

Stevenson, Gregory Matthew, *Power and Place: Temple and Identity in the Book of Revelation* (Berlin: de Gruyter, 2001).

Stienstra, Nelly, *Yahweh is the Husband of his People* (Kampen: Kok Pharos, 1993).

Strand, Kenneth A., 'Chiastic Structure and Some Motifs in the Book of Revelation', *AUSS* 16 (1978), pp. 401–08.

—'The Two Witnesses of Rev. 11.3–12', *AUSS* 19 (1981), pp. 127–35.

—'The "Spotlight-on-Last-Events" Sections in the Book of Revelation', *AUSS* 27 (1989), pp. 201–21.

Sturm, Richard, 'Defining the Word "Apocalyptic": A Problem in Biblical Criticism', in Joel Marcus and Marion L. Soards (eds.), *Apocalyptic and the New Testament: Essays in honour of J. Louis Martyn* (Sheffield: Sheffield Academic Press, 1989), pp. 17–48.

Suharyo, I., *Kitab Wahyu: Paham dan Maknanya bagi Hidup Kristen* (Lembaga Biblika Indonesia; Yogjakarta, Indonesia: Kanisius, 1993).

Svigel, Michael J., 'The Apocalypse of John and the Rapture of the Church: A Reevaluation', *TrinJ* 22 (2001), pp. 23–74.

Sweet, J. P. M., *Revelation* (London: SCM, 1979).

—'Maintaining the Testimony of Jesus: The Suffering of Christians in the Revelation of John', in W. Horbury & B. McNeil (eds.), *Suffering and Martyrdom in the New Testament: Studies presented to G M Styler by the Cambridge New Testament Seminar* (Cambridge: Cambridge University Press, 1981), pp. 101–17.

—'Revelation', in John Barclay and John Sweet (eds.), *Early Christian Thought in its Jewish Setting* (Cambridge: Cambridge University Press, 1996), pp. 160–73.

Swete, H. B., *The Apocalypse of John* (London: Macmillan, 3rd edn, 1908).

Talbert, Charles H., *The Apocalypse* (Louisville: Westminster/John Knox Press, 1994).

Talmon, Shermaryahu, 'The "Desert Motif" in the Bible and in Qumran Literature', in A. Altmann (ed.), *Biblical Motifs* (Cambridge, Mass.: Harvard University Press, 1966), pp. 32–63.

Tan, Kim Huat, *The Zion Traditions and the Aims of Jesus* (Cambridge: Cambridge University Press, 1997).

Tan, Paul, *In Power and Glory* (Singapore, 1987).

Tate, Marvin, *Psalms 51–100* (WBC; Dallas: Word, 1990).

Teeple, Howard M., *The Mosaic Eschatological Prophet* (SBL Monographs, 10; Ann Arbor, Michigan: Society of Biblical Literature, 1957).

Thomas, Robert L., *Revelation 8–22* (An Exegetical Commentary; Chicago: Moody Press, 1995).

Thompson, Leonard L., 'Cult and Eschatology in the Apocalypse of John', *JR* 49 (1969), pp. 330–50.

—'A Sociological Analysis of Tribulation in the Apocalypse of John', *Semeia* 36 (1986), pp. 147–74.

—*The Book of Revelation: Apocalypse and Empire* (New York: Oxford University Press, 1990).

—'The Literary Unity of the Book of Revelation', in Vincent L. Tollers and John Maier (eds.), *Mappings of the Biblical Terrain: The Bible as Text* (Lewisburg, Penn.: Bucknell University Press, 1990), pp. 347–63.

—*Revelation* (ANTC; Nashville: Abingdon Press, 1998).

Thompson, Marriane Meye, 'Worship in the Book of Revelation', *Ex Auditu* 8 (1992), pp. 45–54.

Thompson, S., *The Apocalypse and Semitic Syntax* (SNTSMS, 52; Cambridge: Cambridge University Press, 1985).

Thomson, Ian H., *Chiasmus in the Pauline Letters* (JSNTSup, 111; Sheffield: Sheffield Academic Press, 1995).

Trever, John C., 'The Qumran Teacher- Another Candidate?', in Craig A. Evans & William F. Stinespring (eds.), *Early Jewish and Christian Exegesis: Studies in the Memory of William Hugh Brownlee* (Atlanta: Scholars Press, 1987), pp. 101–22.

Trible, Phyllis, *Rhetorical Criticism: Context, Method and the Book of Jonah* (Minneapolis: Fortress Press, 1995).

Trites, Allison A., *The New Testament Concept of Witness* (SNTSMS, 31; Cambridge: Cambridge University Press, 1977).

—'The Transfiguration in the Theology of Luke: Some Redactional Links', in L. D. Hurst and N. T. Wright (eds.), *The GLORY of Christ in the New Testament: Studies in Christology in Memory of George Bradford Caird* (Oxford: Clarendon Press, 1987), pp. 71–83.

Turner, Nigel, 'The Style of the Book of Revelation', in *A Grammar of New Testament Greek by J. H. Moulton, Vol. 4 Style* (Edinburgh: T & T Clark, 1976).

—*Christian Words* (Edinburgh: T & T Clark, 1980).

VanderKam, James C., 'Messianism in the Scrolls', in E. Ulrich and James C. VanderKam (eds.), *The Community of the Renewed Covenant: The Notre Dame Symposium on the Dead Sea Scrolls* (Notre Dame: University of Notre Dame Press, 1994), pp. 211–34.

—'1 Enoch, Enochic Motifs, and Enoch', in James C. VanderKam and William Adler (eds.), *The Jewish Apocalyptic Heritage in Early Christianity* (Assen: Van Gorcum, 1996), pp. 33–101.

van de Water, Rick, 'Reconsidering the Beast from the Sea', *NTS* 46 (2000), pp. 245–61.

van der Woude, Adam S., 'Zion as Primeval Stone in Zechariah 3 and 4', in W. Claassen (ed.), *Text and Context: Old Testament and Semitic Studies for F. C. Fensham* (Sheffield: JSOT Press, 1988), pp. 237–48.

—'Micah in Dispute with the Pseudo-Prophets', in *Prophecy in the Hebrew Bible: Selected Studies from Vetus Testamentum* (compiled by David E. Orton; Leiden: Brill, 2000), pp. 24–40.

van Henten, Jan Willem, 'Dragon Myth and Imperial Ideology in Revelation 12–13', in *SBL Seminar Papers* (Atlanta: Scholars Press, 1994), pp. 496–515.

—'*Nero Redivivus* Demolished: The Coherence of the Nero Traditions in the *Sybylline Oracles*', *JSP* 21 (2000), pp. 3–17.

van Leeuwen, Raymond C., 'What Comes out of God's Mouth: Theological Wordplay in Deuteronomy 8', *CBQ* 47 (1985), pp. 55–57.

van Oyen, Geert, 'Intercalation and Irony in the Gospel of Mark', in F. Van Segbroeck *et al.* (eds.), *The Four Gospels 1992* (Festschrift Frans Neirynck; Leuven: Leuven University Press, 1992), pp. 949–74.

van Schaik, A.P., ''Αλλος ἄγγελος in Apk 14', in D. Hellholm (ed.), *Apocalypticism in the Mediterranean World and the Near East* (Tübingen: Mohr, 1989), pp. 217–28.

Vanni, U., 'Liturgical Dialogue as a Literary Form in the Book of Revelation', *NTS* 37 (1991), pp. 348–72.

Vermes, Geza, *An Introduction to the Complete Dead Sea Scrolls* (London: SCM, 1999).

Viviano, Benedict T., 'The Structure of the Prologue of John (1:1–18): A Note', *RB* 105 (1998), pp. 176–84.

Vogel, Winfried, 'The Cultic Motif in Space and Time in the Book of Daniel' (Unpublished D.Theol. dissertation; Andrews University, 1999).

Vos, L. A., *The Synoptic Traditions in the Apocalypse* (Kampen: Kok, 1965).

Wakeman, Mary, 'The Biblical Earth Monster in the Cosmogonic Combat Myth', *JBL* 88 (1969), pp. 313–20.

—*God's Battle with the Monster: A Study in Biblical Imagery* (Leiden: E. J. Brill, 1973).

Walker, P. *Jesus and the Holy City: New Testament Perspectives on Jerusalem* (Grand Rapids: Eerdmans, 1996).

Wallace, Daniel B., *Greek Grammar Beyond the Basics: An Exegetical Syntax of the New Testament* (Grand Rapids: Zondervan, 1996).

Wallis, Ian G., *The Faith of Jesus Christ in early Christian traditions* (SNTSMS, 84; Cambridge: Cambridge University Press 1995).

Walsh, J. T., *1 Kings* (Berit Olam; Collegeville: Liturgical Press, 1996).

Watson, Duane F., (ed.), *Persuasive Artistry: Studies in the New Testament Rhetoric in Honor of George A. Kennedy* (Sheffield: Sheffield Academic Press, 1991).

—'Rhetorical Criticism of Hebrews and the Catholic Epistles Since 1978', *CurBS* 5 (1997), pp. 175–207.

Watson, Wilfred G. E., 'Chiastic Patterns in Biblical Hebrew Poetry', in John W. Welch (ed.), *Chiasmus in Antiquity: Structure, Analyses, Exegesis* (Hildesheim: Gerstenberg Verlag, 1981), pp. 118–68.

—*Classical Hebrew Poetry: A Guide to its Techniques* (JSOTSup, 26; Sheffield: JSOT Press, 1984).

—'Problems and Solutions in Hebrew Verse: A Survey of Recent Work', *VT* 93 (1993), pp. 372–84.

Weber, Hans-Ruedi, *The Way of the Lamb: Christ in the Apocalypse* (Geneva: WCC Publications, 1988).

Weinfeld, M., 'Divine Intervention in War in Ancient Israel and in Ancient Near East', in H. Tadmor and M. Weinfeld (eds.), *History, Historiography and Interpretation* (Jerusalem: Magnes Press, 1983), pp. 121–47.

—'Expectations of the Divine Kingdom in Biblical and Postbiblical Literature', in Henning Graf Reventlow (ed.), *Eschatology in the Bible and in the Jewish and*

Christian Tradition (JSOTSup, 243; Sheffield: Sheffield Academic Press, 1997), pp. 218–32.

Weingreen, J., *A Practical Grammar for Classical Hebrew* (Oxford: Clarendon Press, 2nd edn, 1959).

Welch, John W., (ed.), *Chiasmus in Antiquity: Structure, Analyses, Exegesis* (Hildesheim: Gerstenberg Verlag, 1981).

Wengst, Klaus, 'Babylon the Great and the New Jerusalem: The Visionary View of Political Reality in the Revelation of John', in Henning Graf Reventlow, Yair Hoffman and Benjamin Uffenheimer (eds.), *Politics and Theopolitics in the Bible and Postbiblical Literature* (JSOTSup, 171; Sheffield: Sheffield Academic Press, 1994), pp. 189–202.

Whybray, R. H., *Isaiah 40–66* (Grand Rapids: Eerdmans, 1981).

Wilcox, P. and D. Paton-Williams, 'The Servant Songs in Deutero-Isaiah', *JSOT* 42 (1988), pp. 79–102.

Willis, Timothy M., 'Yahweh's Elders (Isa 24,23): Senior Officials of the Divine Court', *ZAW* 103–104 (1991–2), pp. 375–85.

Wilson, Mark, 'Revelation', in Clinton E. Arnold (ed.), *Zondervan Illustrated Bible Backgrounds Commentary* Vol. 4 (Grand Rapids: Zondervan, 2002), pp. 244–383.

Wise, Michael O. and James Tabor, 'The Messiah at Qumran', *BAR* (Nov/Dec. 1992), pp. 60–65.

Witherington III, B., *Revelation* (Cambridge: Cambridge University Press, 2003).

Wolff, Hans Walter, *Confrontation with Prophets: Discovering the Old Testament's New and Contemporary Significance* (Philadelphia: Fortress Press, 1983).

—'How Can We Recognize False Prophets?', in Hans W. Wolff, *Confrontation with Prophets: Discovering the Old Testament's New Testament Contemporary Significance* (Philadelphia: Fortress Press, 1983).

Wolters, Al, 'Confessional Criticism and the Night Visions of Zechariah', in Craig Bartholomew *et al.* (eds.), *Renewing Biblical Interpretation* (Grand Rapids: Paternoster Press, 2000), pp. 90–117.

Wongso, Peter, *Kitab Wahyu* (Malang, Indonesia: Seminari Alkitab Asia Tenggara, 1996).

Wood, John A., *Perspectives on War in the Bible* (Macòn, GA: Mercer University Press, 1998).

Wright, N. T., *The New Testament and the People of God* (Minneapolis: Fortress Press, 1992).

Wueller, Wilhelm, 'Where is Rhetorical Criticism Taking Us?', *CBQ* 49 (1987), pp. 448–63.

Yarden, L., *Tree of Light: A Study of the Menorah, the Seven-Branched Lampstand* (Ithaca, New York: Cornell University Press, 1971).

Zimmermann, R., 'Nuptial Imagery in the Revelation of John', *Bib* 84 (2003), pp. 153–183.

Zweip, A., *The Ascension of the Messiah in Lukan Christology* (NovTSup, 87; Leiden: Brill, 1997).

INDEX OF REFERENCES

OLD TESTAMENT
Genesis
3   138, 139,
            156
3.13   138
3.13 (LXX) 139
3.24   139
18–19   57
37   156
37.9   130, 150

Exodus
1–15   61
1.16   157
2.2   157
2.2 (LXX)   157
2.3   157
7.14–21   234
7.20   235
8.5   235
8.16   235
8.20–21   235
9.2   235
9.13–14   235
9.13   235
9.14   235
9.23   234
14.24–25   246

Leviticus
15.18   197

Numbers
16.2 (LXX) 147
16.32   147

Deuteronomy
18.15   238, 239,
            249

18.18   238, 239,
            249
19.15 (LXX)
            240
20.19   220
23.9–14   197
34   240

Joshua
7.19   111
10.10–12   166

1 Samuel
4.8 (LXX)   234
21.3   197

2 Samuel
5.6–7   184
5.6   184
5.7   184
21.17   228

1-Kings
11.26–14.20 76
17–19   59
17.1   234
21.27   217

2 Kings
1.9–11   247
1.10–14   233
19.31   184

1 Chronicles
9.25   134

Nehemiah
8.8   9
9.3   10

Esther
4.3   217

Psalms
2   21, 192, 193
2.1–3   192, 193
2.4–5   193
2.5   192
2.6   192
2.9   161
2.10   193
7.2   146
9.11   184
22   229
22.13   146
25.14   134
26.6   195
27.3   232
36.25   146
43.3–4   195
43.3   195
43.4   195, 196
48   193
51.18   184
51.19   195
54.2   146
56.2   232
57.4   146
66.12   146
74   193, 194
74.2   184, 194
74.3   194
76   194
76.3   193
84.3   195
87   150
96.1   192
96.9–13   192
97.2–3   246

98.1–9	192
104.4	246
118.27	195
124	146, 147
124.1–2	146
124.1	146
124.2	146
124.3	146
124.4	146
124.5	146
124.6	146
124.7	146, 147
124.8	146
144.9–11	192
149	21, 191, 192
149.1	191
149.5	191
149.6	191
149.7	191
149.8	191
149.9	191, 192

Ecclesiastes
| 3.15 | 134 |

Isaiah
8.7–8	147
8.8	72
9.11	146
10.12	184
10.24	184
24–27	19
24.23	184, 194, 208
26	155, 156
26.16–18	154, 155
26.16	155
26.17	154, 155
26.17 (LXX)	154
26.18	155
26.20	155
27	155
27.1	155
30.31–31.5	192
30.32–31.5	191
30.32	191
31	193
31.4–5	190, 191, 193
31.4	190

31.5	190
43.1–2	146
47.5	262
49.1–6	230
49.3	230
49.5–6	230
49.6	230
56–66	19
66	156
66.6–8	152
66.6	152, 153
66.7	152, 153
66.7 (LXX)	153
66.7–14	150
66.7–8	153–55
66.8	152, 153

Jeremiah
4.3	151
4.5	151
4.7–8	217
4.11	151
4.19–26	163
4.19	155
4.27	151
4.30	155
4.31	72, 150
5.14	233
6.26	217
13.16	111
27–29	60
27–28	60
28 (LXX)	156
28.24 (LXX)	218
28.34 (LXX)	72, 156
29	60
34–38	60
34	60
34.1–7	60
34.15	60
35	60
38.14–23	60
50–51	261
50	261
51	261
51.7	261
51.13	261, 262
51.24	261, 262
51.25	262

| 51.34 | 146, 156, 218 |
| 51.34 (MT) | 72, 156 |

Lamentations
2.1	103
2.10	217
2.15	102

Ezekiel
2.8–3.4	15
7.18	217
8–10	101, 102
29.3	157
29.6 (LXX)	98
32.2	157
38–39	19
40	98
40.2–42.20	98

Daniel
1.12	151
2–7	21
2	120, 260
2.10	19
2.19	19
2.22–23	192.28–29
	19
2.35	261, 263
2.40–44	252
2.44–45	261
2.47	19
7–12	19, 120
7	120, 171, 173, 250–52, 261
7.1–6	171, 250, 252
7.2	250, 262
7.7	146, 250, 251
7.13–14	251
7.17–18	251
7.17	250, 251
7.18	251
7.19–28	174
7.20	174
7.20 (Theod.)	173
7.20–22 (Theod.)	173

7.21   138
7.21 (Theod.)
                137, 138,
                173, 174
7.22   174, 251
7.22 (Theod.)
                173
7.23   250, 251
7.24–28   251
7.25   6, 103, 151,
                174
7.27   251
8–12   120
8   156
8.1–12   154
8.9–14   102, 103,
                154, 156
8.9   102
8.10–11   135
8.10   103, 154
8.13   103
8.14   103
8.22–25   154
9   217
9.3   217
9.16   151, 186
9.17   186
9.19   151
9.24–27   217
9.24   151
9.24 (LXX)   186
10–12   78, 137
10   15, 78
10.1   217
10.12–14   78
10.12   217
10.13–21   165
10.13   131, 137
10.20   138
10.20 (Theod.)
                134
10.21   134, 137
11   78
11.32   17
12.1   131, 137,
                167, 217
12.1 (LXX)   131
12.1 (MT)   131
12.1 (Theod.)
                131, 167
12.2   277

12.3   154
12.6–7   217
12.7   6, 103, 151,
                165
12.10   17
12.11   103
12.12   103
21.11–12   165

Hosea
9.13   134

Joel
1.13   217
2.30–32   185
2.30   185
2.31   185
2.32   185
3–4   19
3.3–5 (MT)   185
3.16–17   185
3.16   185
3.17   185
4.16–17 (MT)
                185

Amos
1.4   246
1.10   246
1.12   246
1.14   246
2.2   246
2.5   246
4.7–8   234
5.6   246
7.4   246
8.10   217

Jonah
3.5   216, 217

Micah
3.12–4.2   150
4.9–11   72
4.9–10   150, 155

Habakkuk
3   19

Haggai
1.12–15   224

2.2–5   224

Zechariah
1–6   19, 21, 260
1.14–17   221
1.18–2.13   260
1.18   260
2   99, 100
2.1 (MT)   260
2.1–17 (MT)
                260
2.1–5   99, 100
2.1–4 (MT)   99
2.2ff   100
2.4   98
2.5–9 (MT)   99
2.5   99
2.10–12   221
3–4   100
3   221, 222
3.9   222
4   220–23, 260
4.1–5   224
4.2–3   220
4.2   98
4.3   220, 223
4.6–10   221, 222
4.6   221, 224
4.7   260, 261,
                263
4.8   221
4.10   221
4.11–14   224
4.11–12   220, 223
4.11   220
4.12   224
4.13   220
4.14   100, 107,
                109, 220,
                222, 223,
                225, 226,
                246, 247
5.5–11   260
6   222, 260
6.1   261
6.5   260
6.11–14   222
6.12–15   221
6.12–14   221
6.12–13   222
6.13   222

8.2–3	150	*2 Maccabees*		*Luke*	
9–14	19	3.19	217	1.16–17	237
12.3	99	3.26	239	1.16	237
12.3 (LXX)	99, 100	10.1–8	187	1.17	236, 237
				2.25	94
Malachi				2.38	94
3.1	236	New Testament		3.15–17	246
3.22–23	239	*Matthew*		4.25	234
3.23	215, 236,	3.2	242	9	240
	237, 245,	3.11–12	246	9.8	236
	249	4.5	97, 187	9.28–36	239
3.23 (MT)	235, 236	11.12–14	242	9.30	239
4.4–5 (ET)	239	11.12	242	9.31	241
4.5	236	11.13	242	9.52–56	246
4.5 (ET)	215, 235	11.14	236, 242	9.54	246, 247
		16.14	236	9.55	247
APOCRYPHA		17	240	11.20–22	137
2 Esdras		17.1–13	239	11.20	137
1–2	151	17.3	241	11.21	137
6	266	18.16	240	11.22	137
9–10	152	20.20–23	246	13.33	244
9.38–10.59	152	23.37	150	13.34	150
10.7	152	23.38	183	21.20	94
10.27	152	24.8	165	21.24	94
10.44	152	24.15–21	165	24.4	239
10.48	152	24.15	17		
10.50	152	27.51–53	187	*John*	
16.37–39	165	27.53	97	1–4	72
				1.1–18	77, 127
Ecclesiasticus				1.1–5	127
48.1	233, 246	*Mark*		1.6–8	127
48.10	248	3.17	246	1.6–7	238
		3.20–35	46	1.6	127
1 Maccabees		5.21–43	46	1.7	72
2.6–8	217	6.7–32	46	1.8	72
2.6	218	6.15	236	1.9–11	127
2.7	218	8.38–9.21	241	1.12–13	127
2.8	218	9	240	1.14	127
2.12–14	217	9.2–8	239, 241	1.15	127
2.12	218	9.4	241	1.16–18	127
2.13	218	9.11	242	1.19–22	238
2.14	218	9.12	236, 237,	1.19–21	237
3.45–47	217		243	1.19	237
3.45	218	9.13	236, 243	1.20–21	238
3.46	218	10.35–40	246	1.20	237
3.47	218	11.12–25	46	1.21	237
4.36–40	186	13.8	165	1.32–34	238
4.36–37	186	13.14–19	165	3.11	72
6.48	186	14.1–11	46	3.32	72
6.51	186	14.53–72	46	4.39	72
7.33	187	15.47	240	5.35	238

12.25 173
13–17 52
18.33–19.16 274

Acts
1.6 94
1.7 94
1.10 239
4.21 203
5.17–18 203
5.40 203
7.54–58 203
8.1 203
8.3 203

1 Corinthians
3.6 25
15.20 197
15.23 197

2 Corinthians
11.26 87

Galatians
4.19 163

1 Timothy
6.13 274

Hebrews
3.1 197
5.10 197
12.22 187

James
5.17 234

1 Peter
5.13 265

2 Peter
1.16–21 241
3.7–12 246
3.7 246

Jude
9 165

Revelation
1–11 209
1–3 27

1.1–8 41
1.1 1, 17, 18, 104, 123, 124
1.2 16
1.3 9, 16, 17, 104
1.4 27, 263
1.5–6 140, 274
1.5 274
1.6 197, 221
1.9 199
1.11 226, 263
1.12 26, 27
1.16 26
1.19–3.22 151
1.20–2.1 166
1.20 3, 26, 27, 226
2–3 27, 56, 70, 124, 226
2.2 201
2.5 157
2.7 174
2.11 174
2.13 139, 254
2.14 201
2.16 70
2.17 174
2.18 171
2.20 201
2.26–28 161
2.26–27 160, 161
2.29 174
3.1 166
3.4 172
3.6 174
3.8 201
3.9 139
3.12 174
3.22 174
4–22 75
4–5 61, 62, 74
4 61–63
4.1 104
4.3–6 62
4.5 62, 121
4.8–11 62
4.11 63
5 61–63
5.1 62, 63

5.5–6 283
5.5 70, 166, 194
5.6 62, 169, 203, 273
5.7 62, 63
5.8–10 62
5.9 82, 204, 273
5.10 140, 197, 221
5.11–14 166
5.12 63, 273
6–16 26
6 115
6.2 70, 115
6.3–4 148
6.5 115
6.8 115
6.11 24
6.12–17 245
6.13 234
6.16–17 282
6.19 192
7 2, 203
7.1 261
7.2–8 130, 187, 194
7.2 81
7.9–17 24
7.9 24, 82, 204
7.13–14 24
7.14 78, 187, 203
8–14 78
8.1–9.21 116
8.1–5 115
8.1 115
8.2 166
8.3 81
8.5 121
8.7–12 109
8.13 114, 116, 145
8.13 234
8.15 121
9 2
9.1–15.8 78
9.1–11 109
9.1 145, 234
9.4 187
9.7 70
9.9 70
9.11 145

9.12–13	118
9.12	2, 89, 115, 118
9.13–21	109, 116, 118, 145
9.13	67, 114, 118
9.13ff	245
9.15	261
9.18–19	145
9.18	146
9.19	145
10–14	31, 67
10–13	137
10	15, 16, 68, 79, 81, 82, 86, 90, 93, 94, 137, 248
10.1–11.14	67, 116
10.1–11.13	67, 114
10.1–11.4	45
10.1–11	47, 80
10.1	2, 81, 234
10.2	86, 87
10.6–7	114
10.7	2, 79, 81, 82, 117, 124, 248
10.8–11.2	69
10.8–11	15, 94
10.8–10	82
10.11–11.3	35
10.11–11.1	90, 209
10.11	39, 47, 79, 80, 82, 83, 90, 104, 199, 204, 248, 280
11–14	275
11–13	2, 4–6, 68, 78, 79, 82, 90, 116, 158, 169, 198, 203, 217, 248, 253, 270
11–12	31, 34, 68, 165
11	3–6, 14, 26, 30, 31, 34, 44–46, 48, 57–61, 64, 65, 67–69, 71–73, 78, 83–88, 90, 92- 94, 97, 100–104, 109, 119, 120, 122, 123, 128, 129, 135, 148, 169, 181, 182, 198, 200, 202, 203, 209, 211, 212, 214, 215, 226, 231, 243, 245, 252, 266, 267, 277, 280–82
11.1–14.5	2–4, 6, 8, 10, 12, 13, 21, 22, 25–27, 30, 32, 33, 35, 37–39, 41, 43, 45– 49, 53, 58, 59, 63–67, 69, 70–76, 79–84, 86, 87, 95, 100, 116, 123, 126, 140, 149, 181, 182, 186, 188, 197, 198, 202, 208–10, 212, 213, 215, 248, 253, 279–84
11.1–13.18	145
11.1–15	120
11.1–14	69, 89
11.1–13	33, 69, 84–87, 95, 110, 114, 116, 122, 231, 242, 281
11.1–3	107
11.1–2	7, 27, 32, 33, 47, 65, 69, 70, 74, 76, 77, 84–88, 90–99, 100–107, 109, 110, 120, 122, 123, 135, 152, 154, 156, 157, 181–183, 187–89, 193, 195–98, 209, 215, 216, 280–82
11.1	5, 27, 32, 47, 48, 69, 80, 90, 92, 93, 95, 96, 98, 100, 102, 107, 183, 186–88, 195, 196, 198, 205, 209, 280–82
11.1ff	98
11.2–3	2, 5, 27, 35, 92, 94, 105, 107, 198, 216, 217, 253, 266, 272
11.2	2, 5, 35, 58, 79, 87, 88, 90, 92, 94, 97, 99–101, 103, 105– 107, 169, 182, 186, 192, 194–96, 217, 219, 270, 280, 284
11.3–14	69, 88, 106, 109
11.3–13	2, 69, 84–86, 88, 105, 199, 203, 224, 248
11.3–7	79, 89, 166, 212

11.3–6	7, 65, 76, 87, 109, 110, 122, 212, 214, 216, 268, 272, 277, 281	11.7–8	88, 110, 111, 211, 242, 244, 283		105, 111, 114, 122, 202, 204, 234, 270
11.3–4	86, 109, 238	11.7	70–72, 78, 88, 97, 102, 110, 120, 145, 156, 169, 201– 205, 207, 216, 232, 248, 258, 266, 272, 273, 278	11.14–14.5	85
11.3	2, 5, 33, 35, 57, 58, 85, 87, 88, 90, 103, 105– 108, 110, 169, 173, 201, 214, 216, 219, 223, 224, 248, 278, 284			11.14–15	116
				11.14	2, 67, 69, 84, 88, 89, 109, 113–16, 122, 245, 248, 272, 281
		11.7ff	119	11.15–14.20	67
		11.8–9	111	11.15–19	7, 45, 65, 76, 84, 114–16, 118, 120–22, 140, 181, 205, 214, 281
		11.8	33, 57, 86, 87, 92, 93, 169, 200, 201, 203, 205, 219, 244, 270, 273		
11.4	3, 25, 26, 57, 85, 100, 107, 109, 169, 176, 201, 219, 220, 222–24, 226, 227, 233, 240, 249, 282			11.15–18	116, 118, 122, 214, 259, 278, 281, 283, 285
		11.9–12.5	152		
		11.9–10	72, 88, 97, 110, 112, 242	11.15	2, 21, 34, 61, 84, 89, 94, 96, 114–22, 124, 140, 159, 164, 167–69, 173, 174, 184, 195, 203, 205, 206– 208, 210, 214–17, 220, 242, 248, 252, 253, 263, 266, 272, 281, 283
11.4ff	35	11.9	82, 88, 113, 169, 201, 203–205, 284		
11.5–6	61, 107–109, 201, 226, 232, 233, 249, 273				
		11.10	57, 107, 109, 111, 112, 201, 204, 205, 216, 224, 232, 248, 272, 273		
11.5	25, 61, 108, 109, 120, 201, 211, 231–33, 245, 247, 268, 273				
		11.11–13	110, 211, 283		
11.6	88, 108, 112, 201, 216, 233, 234, 248	11.11–12	87, 88, 112, 202, 244, 277	11.16–19	2
				11.16–18	84, 116, 118, 121, 208, 209
		11.11	61, 89, 110, 112–14, 119, 169, 204, 205, 284	11.16	72, 118, 207, 208, 283
11.7–13	7, 65, 76, 110, 112, 122, 202– 204, 211, 212, 214, 277, 281, 283				
		11.12–13	110, 111, 114, 211	11.17–18	245
		11.12	111–13, 204	11.17	118, 120
11.7–10	68, 87, 110, 211, 283	11.13	3, 33, 72, 74, 86–88, 97,	11.18	100, 119, 121, 192, 285
				11.19–21.17	116

11.19–15.4	90	12.1–4	7, 76, 125, 126, 132,		253, 266, 284
11.19–12.1	128		143–47, 149,	12.7–13	206
11.19	32, 68, 84, 86, 93, 95, 121, 122, 128, 148, 152, 181, 207–209, 281		156, 167, 168, 181, 210, 212, 281	12.7–12	7, 44, 65, 67, 71, 72, 75– 78, 83, 124, 126, 136, 139, 149, 165–68, 181,
		12.1–3	93, 124, 125		
12–22	209	12.1–2	150		210, 212–14,
12–14	2, 45, 68, 280	12.1	67, 82, 117, 123, 128, 129, 132, 134, 151–54, 281		258, 280–84
12–13	5, 166, 209, 258			12.7–9	48, 125, 126, 133, 136, 137, 139, 164, 210, 212, 234
12	3–6, 14, 24, 31, 34, 44– 46, 59, 64, 65, 67–71, 73, 75, 77, 85, 86, 93, 102, 103, 120, 123–29, 131–33, 135, 137, 140, 141, 143–45, 147–49, 151, 155, 156, 158–60, 163, 165, 167, 168, 181, 182, 187, 198, 209, 210, 212, 214, 280, 281	12.2	72, 129, 154, 157, 165	12.7–8	78, 138, 143
		12.3	73, 117, 123, 127–29, 132, 134, 138, 207, 250, 258, 260	12.7	70, 72, 73, 75, 125, 127, 132–36, 138, 145, 165, 167
		12.4–6	125	12.8–12	141
		12.4	73, 103, 125–29, 131, 132, 135, 147, 148, 154, 156, 157	12.8–11	135, 136, 138, 139, 142, 258
				12.8–10	137
				12.8–9	125, 126
		12.5–6	7, 76, 126, 132, 143, 144, 147, 149, 160, 167, 168, 181, 210, 281	12.8	135–38, 142, 155, 166
				12.9	73, 78, 135, 136, 138, 139, 141, 143, 149, 158, 167, 212, 282
12.1–22.5	68				
12.1–21.8	68	12.5	126, 132, 143, 150, 153, 157, 158, 160–62, 187	12.10–12	48, 125, 126, 133, 136, 141
12.1–19.21	120				
12.1–14.5	5, 89, 123, 181, 209, 211, 281			12.10–11	125, 212
				12.10	6, 21, 34, 73, 89, 119, 121, 127, 135, 136, 139–42, 159, 164, 167–69, 173, 174, 195, 210, 212, 214, 215, 253, 259, 266
12.1–14.2	68	12.6	2, 5, 6, 86, 90, 103, 126–28, 132, 133, 143, 144, 147–50, 153, 156, 159, 162, 164, 165, 167, 169, 187, 217,		
12.1–17	65, 128, 148, 164, 168, 281, 282				
12.1–6	124–26, 132, 133, 143, 155, 156				
12.1–5	152, 155, 157, 162, 164				

12.11	70, 71, 135–38, 141, 142, 166, 170, 273–78	12.17–18	143, 171
		12.17	70, 72, 73, 82, 125, 127, 128, 148, 151, 153, 160, 164, 274
12.12	6, 74, 78, 125, 126, 136, 140–42, 145, 155, 212, 214, 258, 285	12.18–14.5	82, 171
		12.18–13.18	116
12.13–18	125	12.18–13.4	171
12.13–17	124–26, 147, 148	12.18–13.2	264
		12.18–13.1	145
12.13–14	7, 76, 126, 143, 144, 149, 160, 167, 168, 181, 210, 281	12.18	5, 148, 168, 169, 180, 209, 258, 264, 268, 281
		12ff	68
12.13	72, 73, 125–27, 132, 135, 136, 143, 148, 157, 264, 268	13	3, 5, 6, 25, 44, 48, 59–61, 64, 65, 68–71, 73, 78, 82, 83, 85, 90, 94, 102, 103, 123, 145, 148, 149, 153, 168, 169, 171, 172, 179, 180, 193, 198–200, 202, 203, 206, 207, 211, 212, 214, 215, 252–55, 262, 264–66, 268–73, 277, 280–82
12.14–18	123		
12.14–17	86, 147, 150, 156		
12.14–16	125		
12.14	2, 5, 6, 25, 90, 94, 103, 126–28, 133, 143, 144, 147, 149, 153, 159, 164, 165, 167, 169, 187, 214, 217, 253, 266, 284		
12.15–18	212		
12.15–17	7, 76, 126, 145–47, 149, 154, 167, 168, 181, 210, 212, 281	13.1–14.5	45, 46, 58, 64, 65, 72, 73, 77, 165, 181, 182, 188, 209, 212, 282
12.15–16	25, 157	13.1–18	73
12.15	73, 127, 145, 147, 156	13.1–10	73, 168–70, 173–75, 179, 211, 252, 255, 265,
12.16	73, 74, 147, 157		

	271, 281, 282
13.1–6	7, 65, 76, 121, 140, 170, 172, 173, 181, 205, 207, 211, 214, 282, 283
13.1–4	130
13.1–2	85, 170, 171, 250, 252
13.1	5, 35, 85, 86, 148, 149, 168, 170, 175, 176, 207, 250, 258, 260, 262, 264
13.2	73, 170–72, 176, 206–208
13.3–18	85
13.3–6	193
13.3–4	252, 254, 258
13.3	170, 176, 179, 254–58, 264, 266, 275
13.4	70, 72–74, 140, 170, 171, 175, 179, 206–208, 210, 248, 266, 282, 283
13.5–10	259
13.5–6	170, 171, 179, 207, 266
13.5	2, 5, 85, 90, 103, 156, 169, 173, 174, 176, 179, 206, 208, 212, 214, 217, 252, 253, 266, 278, 282–84

13.6   170, 207,
            208
13.7–14.1   82
13.7–10   7, 65, 76,
            110, 166,
            170, 172,
            173, 175,
            181, 188,
            202–204,
            211, 212,
            214, 232,
            254, 266,
            277, 282,
            283
13.7   70–72, 82,
            120, 137,
            138, 156,
            169, 170,
            172–76, 179,
            202–205,
            252, 266,
            273, 278,
            283
13.8–10   278
13.8   73, 172–75,
            200, 203–
            205, 252,
            254, 273,
            283
13.9–10   174, 175,
            273, 283
13.9   174, 175
13.10   170, 172,
            174, 175,
            179, 204,
            205, 273
13.11–18   7, 64, 65, 76,
            139, 168,
            169, 175,
            178, 181,
            199, 212,
            214, 216,
            266–68, 270,
            272, 277,
            281, 282
13.11   35, 73, 85,
            86, 168, 171,
            175, 176,
            178, 201
13.12   73, 172, 176,
            177, 179,

13.13–17   200, 201,
            255–58, 264
            267
13.13–15   201, 266,
            268
13.13–14   266
13.13   176, 177,
            179, 201,
            211, 234,
            268
13.14–15   234, 269
13.14   172, 176–79,
            200, 255–58,
            264
13.15   73, 169, 171,
            176, 178,
            179, 188,
            201, 212,
            254, 266,
            269, 271,
            273, 275
13.16–18   82, 169, 271,
            275, 285
13.16–17   178, 266,
            271
13.16   169, 178,
            179, 188
13.17   160, 178,
            179
13.18   5, 124, 169,
            179, 180,
            270, 271,
            282
14   2, 67, 70,
            187, 196,
            209
14.1–20   117
14.1–5   5, 7, 32, 47,
            65, 70, 74,
            76, 77, 80–
            82, 100, 102,
            123, 169,
            181, 182,
            185, 186,
            188–98, 209,
            273, 282
14.1–2   196
14.1   28, 30, 32,
            35, 47, 48,
            85, 169, 171,
            180, 182,

            183, 185–90,
            193–98, 217,
            253, 277,
            278
14.2–5   48, 73, 190
14.2–3   180
14.2   190, 196
14.3   191
14.4–5   63
14.4–5   180
14.4   185, 194,
            197, 198
14.5   70, 180, 280
14.6–20   81
14.6–12   80
14.6–7   39, 47, 49,
            79, 81–83,
            248, 277,
            280
14.6   80–82, 204
14.7   111, 248
14.8   78, 80, 203
14.9   80
15–16   114, 116,
            118, 120,
            122, 203,
            245, 248
15   117
15.1   2, 117, 124,
            166, 192
15.2–4   74
15.2–3   275, 277
15.2   70, 275
15.4   209
15.5–16.21 90
15.5   90, 121
15.8   192
16   117
16   272
16.1   90
16.9   111
16.11   234
16.13–14   271, 272
16.13   64, 73, 199,
            266, 270
16.14   70, 282
16.17–21   121
16.17   90
16.18–21   121
17–18   90, 120,
            261

17	78, 203, 255, 261, 262, 264–66	20.2	73	**QUMRAN**	
		20.4–6	285	*1QH*	
		20.6	274	11	163
17.1–22.7	90, 91	20.7–10	215	11.3–18	21, 72, 162, 163
17.1–7	151	20.7	215		
17.1–5	261	20.8	70	11.6–9	162
17.1	261, 262	20.10	64, 199, 270	11.6	162
17.3	261, 262	21	91	11.7	162
17.6	120, 232, 263	21.1–17	181	11.8	162, 163
		21.1–2	215	11.9	163
17.7	262	21.1ff	98	11.10	162
17.8–11	264	21.3	151, 215		
17.8	259, 262	21.7	166	*1QS*	
17.9–11	259	21.8	63, 275	9.10–11	225
17.9	259–63	21.9–10	152		
17.10	259	21.12	130	*CD*	
17.11	259, 262	21.15	98	15.4	225
17.12–14	245, 285	21.22–22.6	74	18.7	225
17.12–13	207, 252	22.3	91	9b.10	225
17.14	70, 189, 192, 273	22.5	215	9b.29	225
		22.6–21	41	20.22b–23	97
17.15	82, 262	22.7	17		
17.16	204, 262	22.9	16, 91	*4QFlor*	17
17.18	152, 262	22.9	104		
18–19	104	22.10	17	**TARGUMS**	
18	22, 78, 203, 264	22.18–19	17	*Targum of Isaiah*	
		22.18	16	41.15	262
18.4	151	22.19	16		
18.24	232			**MISHNAH**	
19	91, 120	**OTHER ANCIENT**		*Ta'anit*	
19.1–10	74	**REFERENCES**		2.1	217
19.1	140				
19.5–7	140			**MIDRASH**	
19.7–8	152	**PSEUDEPIGRAPHA**		*Deuteronomy Rabbah*	
19.8	152	*Psalms of Solomon*		3.17	239
19.10	166, 200	2.19–21	218		
19.11–21	121	2.19–20	217	**JOSEPHUS**	
19.11–21	189, 215, 245	2.19	218	*Antiquities of the Jews*	
		2.20	218	2.9.6	157
19.11–16	272	2.21	218	10.257–68	17
19.11	70	2.25	218		
19.11ff	189			**HOMER**	
19.14	189, 273	*1 (Ethiopic) Enoch*		*Iliad*	
19.15	160	60	266	2.308	130
19.19–20	272				
19.19	70, 252	*2 (Syriac) Baruch*		**IGNATIUS**	
19.20–21	285	29	266	*Ephesians*	
19.20	64, 199, 266, 270			1	231
		4 Ezra			
20	215	13.34–40	194	*Magnesians*	
20.1–6	91, 215			2	231
20.1–3	167	*Martyrdom of Isaiah*		*Trallians*	
		2.10	219	1	231

INDEX OF AUTHORS

Abir, P.A. 76, 77, 125, 126
Alford, H. 183
Allison Jr., D.C. 23, 27, 183, 236, 239, 246
Alter, R. 34, 36, 37, 57, 71, 72
Amaru, B.H. 244
Andersen, F.I. 42, 151
Auerbach, E. 57
Aune, D.E. 1, 2, 5–10, 16, 17, 19, 20, 26, 39, 46, 57, 68, 75, 80, 85, 89, 93–95, 98–101, 105, 107, 108, 110, 112, 116, 117, 119, 120, 124, 127, 128, 130, 132, 136, 139, 141, 143, 152, 158, 171–74, 188, 190, 194–97, 202, 220, 238, 239, 248, 251, 252, 255, 264, 267, 271, 273
Aus, R.D. 150

Bachmann, M. 92, 93, 96
Bailey, K. 54
Baldwin, J.G. 21
Ballard, H.W. 194
Bar-Erfat, S. 8, 88
Barker, M. 7
Barnett, P. 63, 64, 199, 267, 275
Barr, D.L. 8, 9, 70, 176, 179, 180
Barritos, G.A. 91
Bauckham, R. 7–10, 20, 68, 70, 75, 79, 82, 84, 90–92, 96, 97, 99, 101, 103, 106, 121, 122, 144, 166, 177, 178, 189, 190, 192, 204, 216, 218, 223, 224, 227, 232–35, 243, 271, 275
Beagley, A.J. 94
Beale, G.K. 5, 9, 11–14, 19, 20, 23, 39, 68, 82, 89, 96, 98, 109, 114, 115, 133, 134, 138, 148, 152–54, 162, 172, 174, 184, 185, 188, 198, 207, 209, 236, 250, 251, 256, 260, 263, 266
Beasley-Murray, G.R. 18, 68, 81, 103, 111, 115, 130, 180, 190, 193, 216, 220, 238, 245, 251, 259, 267, 269
Beckwith, I.T. 103, 162
Berlin, A. 37
Biguzzi, G. 1, 5, 65, 254, 269
Bilde, P. 17
Bishop, J. 255

Black, C.C. 31, 54, 56
Black, M. 69, 164, 244
Blessing, K. 151
Bloch-Smith, E. 91
Blomberg, C. 51, 52, 212, 280
Bloomquist, G.L. 31, 56
Blount, B.K. 274, 276, 277
Boadt, L. 21
Bock, D.L. 237, 240
Boda, M. 222
Bohak, G. 271
Boring, M.E. 8, 63, 68
Bousset, W. 215
Bovon, F. 27, 271
Boyd, G. 75
Bratcher, R.G. 100, 183
Breck, J. 32, 40–43, 77, 80, 133, 213, 279
Briggs, R.A. 20, 91, 92, 94, 96
Brouwer, W. 38, 50, 53, 80, 279, 280
Brown, J.P. 234
Brown, W.P. 87
Brownlee, W. 36, 163
Bruce, F.F. 230
Brueggemann, D.A. 80, 192
Bruehler, B.B. 21
Buber, M. 71
Burnett, G.W. 230
Butterworth, M. 21, 183

Caird, G.B. 8, 23, 70, 92, 95, 96, 111, 189, 226
Carlston, C.E. 240
Carnegie, D. 136
Carrell, P.R. 166, 189
Carroll, J.T. 87
Carter, W. 183
Charles, R.H. 10, 11, 15, 37, 69, 103, 104, 108, 112, 134, 174, 188, 239
Chilton, B. 153, 239
Clark, D.J. 52
Clements, R.E. 9, 91, 190
Clifford, R.J. 61, 91
Clines, D.J.A. 44
Cohn, R. 59, 76
Cole, R. 193
Collins, J.J. 18, 19, 78, 102, 225
Conrad, E.W. 226

Considene, J.S. 69, 232
Cook, S.A. 228, 229
Cook, S.L. 19, 185, 221
Cothenet, E. 136
Court, J. 92, 105, 107, 135, 139, 144,
    150, 154, 155, 172, 192, 206, 238,
    249–51, 256
Craigie, P. 21, 184, 193
Crenshaw, J. 21
Crenshaw, J.L. 199
Croft, S.J.L. 229
Cross, F.M. 75

Dahood, M. 193
Dailey, F.F. 168
Danker, F. 92
Davies, W. 183
Davila, J. 151, 164
Day, J. 75, 155
de Blois, R. 258
Dehandschutter, B. 199
de Heer, J.J. 22, 93, 104, 106, 149
de Jonge, M. 68, 225
deSilva, D.A. 56, 80, 151, 152
DeVries, S.J. 199
Dion, P.E. 200
Donegani, I. 15
Douglas, M. 34, 40, 80
Draper, J.A. 196
Duff, P.B. 139, 199, 269
Dumbrell, W.J. 75
du Rand, J.A. 75

Edwards, J. 46
Ehrenberg, V. 251
Eliav, Y.Z. 186
Enroth, A.-M. 174, 175
Eriksson, A. 30
Evans, C.A. 244
Exum, C.J. 29

Faierstein, M.M. 236
Fekkes, J. 13, 19
Feuillet, A. 11, 68, 92, 149, 154
Filho, J.A. 65, 276
Fiorenza, E. Schüssler 8, 17–19, 28, 45,
    46, 66, 82, 111, 124, 149, 180, 188,
    196
Fitzmyer, J.A. 225
Fleming, D.E. 183
Flusser, D. 103

Ford, D. 257
Ford, J.M. 93, 136, 150, 159, 193, 255,
    262, 265, 274
Forsyth, N. 75
France, R.T. 240
Frankfurter, D. 165
Frechette, C.G. 21, 163
Freedman, D.N. 151
Frey, J. 12, 156, 271
Friebel, K.G. 127
Friesen, S.J. 74, 254, 268, 269, 272

Galambush, J. 150
Garrow, A. 10, 79, 92
Gärtner, B. 91, 183
Gaventa, B.R. 155, 163
Georgi, D. 199
Giblin, C.H. 8, 45, 55, 69, 75, 78, 92, 93,
    107, 110, 223, 233
Gibson, J.C.L. 23
Giesen, H. 104, 106
Gillingham, S. 21, 80
Goldingay, J. 21, 102
Goulder, M. 78
Grabbe, L.L. 17
Grassi, J.A. 136
Green, B. 220
Greenstein, E.L. 35
Grogan, G.W. 228

Hadianto, J. 18
Hagelberg, D. 115, 134, 150, 206
Hall, M.S. 90, 91, 210
Hanson, P.D. 19
Haran, M. 91
Harland, P.A. 254, 255
Harris, M.A. 136
Hartman, L. 90
Harvey, J.D. 9, 37, 38, 40
Hauser, A. 58
Hawthorne, G.F. 16
Hay, D.M. 240
Hays, R. 56
Hayward, C.T.R. 92
Heaton, E.W. 184
Hedrick, W.K. 129
Heil, J. 80
Hengel, M. 46
Hess, R.S. 185
Hiers, R. 236
Hill, A. 239

Hill, D. 16, 20
Holladay, W. 8, 29, 35
Holm-Nielsen, S. 163
Holwerda, D.E. 16, 202, 221, 227
Hong, J. 117
Hooker, M. 239
House, P.R. 29
Houston, G. 16
Howard-Brook, W. 127, 274
Hugenberger, G.P. 229
Hughes, P.E. 157
Humphrey, E.M. 55, 79, 125
Hurst, L.D. 225
Hurtado, L. 140, 208, 275

Jauhiainen, M. 102
Jeffrey, D.L. 14
Jenks, G. 251, 252
Johns, L. 56, 274
Joyce, P. 230
Judge, E.A. 270

Kaiser, B.B. 155, 163
Kaltner, J. 15
Kaminsky, J.S. 230
Kang, S.-M. 75
Kee, H.C. 221
Keener, C. 7, 70, 82, 112, 150, 178, 200, 232
Keet, C.C. 146
Kennedy, G. 29, 31, 38, 39, 48, 54, 69
Kessler, M. 30
Kiddle, M. 199–201, 226
Kikawada, I. 29
Kim, H.C.P. 229
Kirby, J.T. 55
Kistemaker, S.J. 92
Klauck, H.-J. 251, 256, 257
Klaus, N. 44, 152
Klawans, J. 102
Kloos, C. 75
Knibb, M. 19
Knight, J.M. 70, 219
Koester, C. 7, 156, 199
Kohn, R.L. 229
Korpel, M.C.A. 44
Kraft, K. 15, 69, 98
Kraybill, N.J. 271
Kreitzner, L. 270
Kugel, J. 36, 37

Kuhn, K.G. 225
Kuikman, J. 220

Laato, A. 229
Ladd, G.E. 8, 19, 178
Lambrecht, J. 26, 114, 115
Lampe, G.W.H. 199
Laws, S. 266, 271
Lee, M.V. 45
Leivestad, R. 70, 104, 242, 274, 276, 277
Lenglet, A. 21
Lim, J.T.K. 98
Limburg, J. 246
Lind, M.C. 229
Lindars, B. 237
Linton, G. 17, 18
Lohmeyer, E. 69, 233, 253
Lohse, E. 103
Longenecker, B. 16
Longman III, J.T. 74, 75, 192
Lund, N. 22, 24, 25, 38–40, 45, 55, 80, 88, 168, 221, 233, 279, 284
Lundbom, J.R. 28, 57
Lust, J. 102

Mackay, T.W. 95
Macky, P.M. 25
Malchow, B.V. 236
Malina, B.J. 7, 88, 231
Mandey, A.H. 185
Marcus, J. 240, 243
Marshall, I.H. 94, 95, 241
Marshall, J.W. 92, 100
Martens, E.A. 36, 60
Martinez, F.G. 163
Mauser, U.W. 234
Mazzaferri, F. 20, 68, 199, 209
McIlraith, D.A. 152
McKelvey, R.J. 91
McKnight, S. 130
McNamara, M. 85, 169
McNicol, A. 19, 69, 86, 98, 151
McVann, M. 159
Meadowcroft, T. 78
Meeks, T. 57
Meeks, W.A. 87
Menn, E.M. 229
Metzger, B. 174
Meyers, C.L. 21, 91, 220
Meyers, E. 21, 220
Meyers, E.S. 87

Meynet, R. 44, 53, 54, 56, 57, 80, 279
Michaels, J.R. 68, 251
Milavec, A. 199
Milgrom, J. 8, 38
Miller Jr., P.D. 75, 166, 246, 247
Milligan, W. 197
Mills, M.E. 78
Minear, P. 156, 219, 223, 240, 248,
    256–58
Miscall, P.D. 146
Missen, A.W. 276
Mitchell, D.C. 21
Moor, J.C. de 44
Morris, L. 266
Mounce, R. 8, 130, 131, 134, 253, 256,
    257
Moyise, S. 12, 14, 19, 80
Muilenberg, J. 28–31, 33, 53
Müller, U.B. 103, 110, 255, 264
Mulyono, Y.B. 140, 234
Murphy, F. 68, 111, 209
Mussies, G. 11, 14

Neufeld, T.Y. 75
Neyrey, J.H. 231, 241
Niehaus, J.J. 101
Nielsen, K. 219
Nolland, J. 239
Notley, S. 241, 249

O'Rourke, J.J. 136
Oberweis, M. 246, 247
Öhler, M. 237, 242
Olbright, T.H. 30, 55
Ollenberger, B.C. 185
Oropeza, B.J. 159
Osborne, G.R. 7, 89, 169, 231
Oswalt, J. 190
Overholt, T.W. 60

Pamment, M. 244
Parker, D. 246
Pattemore, S.W. 68, 253, 274
Paulien, J. 13
Peerbolte, L.J.L. 6
Percer, L. 68, 134, 141, 165
Petersen, D.L. 220
Petersen, R.L. 216
Phillips, E.A. 139, 165
Pilch, J. 201
Porter, J.R. 227

Porter, P.A. 250
Porter, S.E. 11, 31, 52, 54, 55
Price, S.R.F. 255, 269
Prigent, P. 7, 14, 69, 138, 141, 179, 209
Prinsloo, W.S. 191, 192
Propp, W.H.C. 229
Provan, I. 22, 252, 261, 264–66
Puech, E. 225

Quispel, G. 105

Reddish, M.G. 7, 105, 266, 274, 275
Reed, J.T. 52
Reid, D.G. 74, 75, 191, 192
Rendsburg, G.R. 66
Rendtorff, R. 200
Resseguie, J. 27, 77, 86, 130, 158, 219,
    257, 263
Rissi, M. 151, 158
Robbins, V.K. 30, 56
Roberts, J.J.M. 147
Robinson, B.P. 221, 244
Robinson, H.W. 227, 228, 230
Robinson, J. 92
Rofé, A. 117
Rogerson, J.W. 227
Roloff, J. 239
Rooke, D. 222
Rose, W.H. 222, 226
Ross, M.K. 199–201, 227
Rossing, B. 87, 262
Rowland, C. 78, 119, 265
Rowley, H.H. 120, 229
Royalty Jr., R.M. 55, 56
Ruiz, J.-P. 19, 196
Russell, D. 17
Ryken, L. 24

Sabin, M. 57
Sarna, N. 203
Satake, A. 245
Satran, D. 217
Scherrer, S.J. 268, 269
Scheunemann, D. 159
Schmitt, J.J. 151
Schroer, S. 147
Schwemer, A.M. 158
Seng, H. 69
Shea, W. 45
Shepherd, T. 46
Siahaan, S.M. 222

Sims, J.H. 45
Slater, T.B. 189
Smilek, W.F. 154
Smith, I. 56
Smith, M.S. 91
Snyder, B.W. 18, 45
Söding, T. 205, 206
Soskice, J. 25
Spatafora, A. 91, 92, 96, 97, 106
Steinmann, A.E. 114
Sternberg, M. 35, 57
Stevens, D.E. 131
Stienstra, N. 150
Strand, K.A. 45, 86, 250
Sturm, R. 1, 2
Suharyo, I. 13, 19, 194
Svigel, M.J. 6, 144, 151, 152, 160–62, 209
Sweet, J. 9, 11, 68, 105, 112, 114, 169, 197, 199, 209, 244, 276
Swete, H.B. 13, 116, 169

Talbert, C. 8, 45, 55, 75, 124
Talmon, S. 159
Tan, K.H. 97, 150
Tan, P. 159
Tate, M. 193
Teeple, H.M. 225, 240, 241
Thomas, R.L. 81, 111, 115, 116, 150, 174, 183, 216, 239, 276
Thompson, L.L. 3, 16, 24, 45, 58, 79, 104, 105, 112, 115, 130, 141, 172, 175, 199, 253, 254, 259, 270
Thompson, M.M. 255
Thompson, S. 11, 14
Thomson, I.H. 40, 41, 47–50, 80, 279, 280
Trever, J.C. 17
Trible, P. 72
Trites, A.A. 27, 199, 239
Turner, N. 11, 14, 96

Übelacker, W. 30

van de Water, R. 270

van der Woude, A.S. 199
VanderKam, J.C. 86, 225, 235
van Henten, J.W. 149, 257
van Leeuwen, R.C. 42
Vanni, U. 10, 27
van Oyen, G. 46
van Shaik, A.P. 81
Vermes, G. 163
Viviano, B.T. 77, 127
Vogel, W. 186, 217
Vos, L.A. 94

Wakeman, M. 75
Walker, P. 92, 95
Wallace, D.B. 10, 46
Wallis, I.G. 199
Walsh, J.T. 239
Watson, D.F. 54
Watson, W.G.E. 37
Webb Mealy, J. 9
Weber, H.-R. 9, 196
Weinfeld, M. 246
Weingreen, J. 119
Welch, J. 38, 49, 50, 80, 280
Wengst, K. 87
Wenham, G.J. 185
Whybray, R.H. 153
Willis, T.M. 184
Wilson, M. 76
Wiseman, D. 184
Witherington III, B. 7, 55, 255
Wolff, H.W. 199
Wolters, A. 21, 224
Wongso, P. 13, 15, 67, 73, 80, 166, 168
Wood, J.A. 189
Wright, N.T. 23
Wueller, W. 30

Yarbro Collins, A. 27, 29, 68, 69, 127, 130, 133, 135, 146, 149, 150, 152, 160, 189, 209, 250, 252, 256, 261, 267, 270, 273

Zimmermann, R. 198
Zweip, A.W. 236, 242